FOR REFERENCE
Do Not Take From This Room

DEMCO

D0812212

State Estimates of the Gross National Product 1947, 1958, 1963

Volume I of
Multiregional Input-Output Analysis

Edited by
Karen R. Polenske

This is the first volume in a series entitled *Multiregional Input-Output Analysis,* edited by Karen R. Polenske. Other volumes in the series will contain a presentation of the complete multiregional input-output model and additional descriptions of the data assembly, as well as state estimates of output, employment, and payrolls for 1947, 1958, and 1963, state estimates of technology and regional estimates of interregional trade flows for 1963, and 1970 and 1980 projections of final demands, outputs, and interregional trade.

State Estimates of the Gross National Product 1947, 1958, 1963

Karen R. Polenske and
Carolyn W. Anderson
Richard Berner
William R. Buechner
Bo Carlsson
Orani Dixon
Peter Dixon
W. Norton Grubb
Frans J. Kok
Mary M. Shirley
James F. Smith
Isabelle B. Whiston

Lexington Books
D.C. Heath and Company
Lexington, Massachusetts
Toronto   London

330.973
P76s

The data contained in this book are the result of federally supported research. They may be freely used with the customary crediting of the source.

Copyright © 1972 by D.C. Heath and Company.

All rights reserved. No part of this publication may be reproduced or transmitted in any form or by any means, electronic or mechanical, including photocopy, recording, or any information storage or retrieval system, without permission in writing from the publisher.

Published simultaneously in Canada.

Printed in the United States of America.

International Standard Book Number: 0–669–62539–6

Library of Congress Catalog Card Number: 79–145900

Table of Contents

JAN 9 '73

HUNT LIBRARY
CARNEGIE-MELLON UNIVERSITY

List of Figures

List of Tables

Preface

The state final demand estimates described in this volume were compiled for use in the multiregional input-output model that has been formulated and implemented at the Harvard Economic Research Project for the Economic Development Administration, U.S. Department of Commerce. Tabulations of the state estimates for 1947, 1958, and 1963, which are contained in the statistical appendix, have been reconciled with the final demands given in the national input-output tables for the three respective years. Although the research was begun in 1966, revisions to the state final demands could be completed only after the 1963 table was published in November 1969. Four additional sets of data were required for the implementation of the multiregional model: outputs, employment, and payrolls; interindustry flows; interregional trade flows; and projected final demands. In subsequent volumes of this series, the methodology of constructing these estimates and the theoretical structure of the overall multiregional model will be described.

A considerable amount of reliance was placed throughout this study on the data and documentation from the 450-order 1947 input-output study that was prepared by the Bureau of Labor Statistics in the early 1950s. Because these data are extremely detailed, the composition of purchases of an 80-order industry was often easy to discern by inspecting the subindustry figures in the 1947 table. The data and methodology used to construct the 1947 table are well documented both in a Technical Supplement published with the table and in individual worksheets that were available for reference at the Harvard Economic Research Project. The extensive use made of the 1947 documentation during the multiregional input-output research project, in fact, provided the main impetus for the present series of publications. Since this is the first time that United States data have been assembled for such a comprehensive, large-scale multiregional model, it seemed important to explain the exact procedures used to estimate the state data, thus providing a basis for analyzing, evaluating, and adjusting the figures. All published and unpublished sources used are cited, unless permission to do so was specifically withheld by the agency from which the information was obtained. To make the reading of this technical writing less tedious, only a brief reference to the source is given in the text, followed by a number or numbers in square brackets. The numbers refer to the complete bibliography listing provided at the end of the text.

When two or more names appear as authors of a chapter, the last person named is the one who was responsible for the revisions made during 1970 to the initial estimates. The original research reports to the Economic Development Administration upon which the six chapters in this volume are based are listed below:

Report Number	Title	Author(s)	Date
5	Alignment of 1960 BLS Consumer Expenditure Categories with the 80-Order OBE Input-Output Industrial Classification	Karen R. Polenske and James F. Smith	February 1968
7	Personal Consumption Expenditures, 1947, 1958, 1963	Karen R. Polenske and Isabelle B. Whiston	August 1968
9	State Estimates of Exports from the United States, 1947, 1958, 1963	William R. Buechner	August 1968
11	State Estimates of Gross Private Domestic Investment, 1947, 1958, 1963	Carolyn W. Anderson and Douglas W. McMillan	August 1968
12	State Estimates of Net Purchases of Goods and Services by State and Local Governments, 1947, 1958, 1963	Richard B. Berner	August 1968
13	State Estimates of Federal Government Purchases, 1947, 1958, 1963	Bo Carlsson and Norton Grubb	August 1968
14	State Estimates of Personal Consumption Expenditures, 1947, 1958, 1963, Scheme II	Karen R. Polenske and Isabelle B. Whiston	August 1968

The final methodologies used for the estimates were sometimes altered from those described in the reports listed here. Also, after the 1963 table became available in 1969, adjustments were made to the state estimates to improve the comparability of the sets of data for the three years. A summary of the major alterations made to the final demands since the original reports were written was given in "A Multiregional Input-Output Model for the United States," submitted as Report No. 21 to the Economic Development Administration (EDA) in December 1970. The tabulations presented in the statistical appendix to the present volume are consistent with the data tapes submitted to the EDA and were calculated using the methodologies described in full detail in the text.

Since the overall multiregional research project was officially begun, in March 1967, a major portion of the work has been done at the Harvard Economic Research Project (HERP) by a research and programming staff of approximately ten people, three full-time and seven part-time. A substantial amount of the data assembly, however, was completed by the staff members of Jack Faucett Associates under subcontracts with HERP or, as in two cases, under separate contracts, one with the Office of Business Economics for the interregional trade flows and one with the Office of Civil Defense for the initial estimates of 1963 outputs.

The major portion of the funds for the final demand estimates was provided under contract #7-35212 with the Office of Economic Research, Economic Development Administration, Department of Commerce. For the last year of the contract, additional government agencies that had become interested in the overall multiregional project supplied part of the funds to complete the research and to revise and update the material that had been presented in the reports to the Economic Development Administration. The agencies were the Office of Economics and Systems Analysis, Department of Transportation; the Bureau of Labor Statistics, Department of Labor; the Office of Emergency Preparedness, Executive Office of the President; the Office of Civil Defense, Department of Defense; and the Bureau of Mines, Department of the Interior. In addition, funds for essential overhead expenditures, such as library and other research facilities, were provided from a general grant to the Harvard Economic Research Project from the National Science Foundation.

As far as possible, all material in this volume has been checked for accuracy. Some of the chapters, however, were written by staff members of the Harvard Economic Research Project who were no longer available to assist with the final revisions either to the data or to the descriptions presented. I therefore take full responsibility for any errors that may have escaped detection.

Karen R. Polenske

Acknowledgments

Any large-scale research project requires the cooperation and assistance of many people. I extend sincere thanks to all who assisted directly or indirectly with the research reported in this volume.

In addition to writing one of the chapters in the volume, Carolyn W. Anderson also made an important contribution by organizing the final sets of data, keeping them updated, and documenting the sets of state estimates that have been prepared. Her assistance helped to insure that the estimates presented in the series of studies have been, at least initially, cross-checked for accuracy.

Jack G. Faucett, of Jack Faucett Associates, Inc., who has an extremely thorough understanding of the methodology of assembling sets of national input-output data, was of special assistance throughout the study in discussions of how national methodology could be applied at a regional level.

The project has also benefited greatly from the intellectual stimulus received from present or former staff members at the Harvard Economic Research Project, especially Anne P. Carter, André Danière, Wassily Leontief, and Frances K. Mesher.

Irene S. Raught edited and typed the original reports as well as this manuscript and made substantial improvements to the writing and presentation of the material in this volume.

Staff members of the Office of Business Economics provided considerable advice and supplied many sets of unpublished data concerning the national input-output table. Especially valuable was the assistance received from Claiborne Ball, Joseph Cangialosi, Jean R. Frazier, Martin L. Marimont, Janet B. Riddle, Eugene P. Roberts, Nancy W. Simon, Irving Stern, Beatrice N. Vaccara, and Albert J. Walderhaug.

Material that was used in calculating the state estimates was also contributed by numerous people in other government agencies, including H. Albert Green and Frederick J. Nelson, Department of Agriculture; Aaron S. Sabghir, Department of Commerce; Kung-Lee Wang, Bureau of Mines, Department of the Interior; George Dodson and Delores Corcoran, General Services Administration; Francis M. Twiss, Bureau of the Census; Jack Alterman, Joseph A. Clorety, Jr., Donald P. Eldridge, Ronald E. Kutscher, and Richard P. Oliver, Bureau of Labor Statistics, Department of Labor; and Roger Riefler, Office of the Secretary of Defense, and Samuel C. Zark, Statistical Services, Comptroller's Office, The Pentagon. Catherine E. Martini, National Association of Real Estate Boards, also furnished useful information.

Many research and programming staff members of the Harvard Economic Research Project participated in the research reported in this volume. Alison Morgan provided valuable assistance on the estimation of the personal consumption expenditures before the project was officially begun. The ways in which the others helped with this study were so numerous that rather than risk making an incomplete or inaccurate acknowledgment, I am only listing their names: Donald R. Boulanger, Nancy Bromberger, Lal Chugh, Charles Conrod, Pamela M. King, Douglas W. McMillan, Paul Munyon, Peter A. Petri, Mark Schaefer, Sanford K. Smith, Peter W. Solenberger, Michael M. Tansey, George Timson, Gordon Tucker, John V. Wells, Ann Wyman, and Warren Vest.

Finally, none of this writing could have been completed without the use of unpublished data, computer programs, and other material available at the Harvard Economic Research Project. During the past year, I have also benefited from the facilities so kindly made available to me at the University of Cambridge, both within the Faculty of Economics and at King's College. The year's stay in England has enabled me to complete the editing of this volume and to write a draft of the final volume of the series.

List of Abbreviations

AEC   Atomic Energy Commission
BLS   Bureau of Labor Statistics
CCC   Commodity Credit Corporation
Census   Bureau of the Census
CES   Consumer Expenditures Survey
CP   Census of Population
DOD   Department of Defense
DPA   Defense Purchases Act
EDA   Economic Development Administration
FG   Federal Government
GNP   Gross National Product
GPCF   Gross Private Capital Formation
GSA   General Services Administration
HERP   Harvard Economic Research Project
IO   Input-Output
IOPCE   Input-Output Personal Consumption Expenditures
MRIO   Multiregional Input-Output
NAREB   National Association of Real Estate Boards
NASA   National Aeronautics and Space Administration
NBER   National Bureau of Economic Research
NEXP   Net Foreign Exports
NICB   National Industrial Conference Board
NICBY   National Industrial Conference Board Income Distribution
NINV   Net Inventory Change
NIPA   National Income and Product Accounts
NIPCE   National Income Personal Consumption Expenditures
OBE   Office of Business Economics
PCE   Personal Consumption Expenditures
R&D   Research and Development
SIC   Standard Industrial Classification
SLG   State and Local Government

**State Estimates
of the Gross
National Product
1947, 1958, 1963**

1 A General Framework for the Construction of Regional Product Accounts

Karen R. Polenske

In this volume, the methodologies of estimating state final demands are described, and industry-by-state tabulations of the data are presented. The purpose of the study was to assemble sets of state final demands that can be used within a multiregional input-output framework and to make those estimates as consistent as possible with the national economic accounts. The components of final demand, or what is generally referred to at the national level as the gross national product (GNP), are personal consumption expenditures, gross private capital formation, net inventory change, net foreign exports, state and local government purchases of goods and services, and federal government purchases. For each of these six major components, data were assembled for 87 industries in each of 51 regions (50 states and the District of Columbia) for 1947, 1958, and 1963, the three years for which comparable national input-output tables are presently available from the Office of Business Economics.

Although the final demands were compiled for use in the multiregional input-output model that has been formulated and implemented at the Harvard Economic Research Project, they are also useful for economic analyses in general. These data are only one part of five major sets of multiregional input-output data that have been compiled for each region. The other four sets are: base-year outputs, employment, and payrolls; 1963 interindustry flows; 1963 interregional flows; and 1970 and 1980 projected final demands, all of which will be described in succeeding volumes of this series. A consistent set of multiregional input-output tables has been assembled for each state for 1963. The 1947 and 1958 state final demands provide historical supplements to these tables. For each of the three years, the state estimates are consistent at the aggregate level with the respective Office of Business Economics national input-output tables. The six components of final demand have also been projected to 1970 and 1980 and have been made consistent with the national 1970 and 1980 projections published by the Bureau of Labor Statistics, thus providing comparable state final demand data for five years in all.[1] Given the base-year technology and interregional trade data and the projected set of final demands, 1970 and

---

1. The methodology for making the state projections is described in the third volume of this series of studies, *1970 and 1980 State Projections of the Gross National Product* [73].

1980 regional outputs and interregional trade flows have been generated simultaneously using a multiregional input-output model.

This volume contains the explanations and actual estimates for the product side of the state economic accounts. In the second volume of this series of studies, *State Estimates of Outputs, Employment, and Payrolls* [70], estimates are given for the employee component of the income side of the accounts, both in monetary and physical units. No estimates have been made for the rest of the labor nor for the capital component of the regional income accounts, but the framework of the accounting system used is flexible, and these extensions can be easily incorporated into the accounts when additional information becomes available.

National and Regional Economic Accounts

National economic accounts were first officially published in the United States in 1934 [160], while state income estimates were officially released in 1939 [61]. Since that time, the national accounts have been greatly expanded, and they are now published on a routine basis with considerable detail to stress the various industrial, institutional, and other organizational structures of the economy. The total amount of income received in the economy must, by definition, equal the total expenditures made within a given year. At the national level, statistics are published for both the income and the product accounts, but state estimates have usually been calculated only for the income, rather than the product, accounts. Prior to the present study, in fact, no consistent set of regional product accounts, detailed by industry and state, has been available for the United States. An excellent and comprehensive survey of the historical development of national accounts in the United States and other countries is available in two volumes written by Studenski [75]; consequently, only the highlight of this development as it pertains to the present set of estimates is discussed in this section.

National Economic Accounts

Present users of the national accounts are often frustrated because the details of the methodology used to assemble the statistics are not described in any single document. The only extensive documentation of the accounts presently available is in *National Income, 1954* [166], published sixteen years ago. To obtain a current description of the composition of the data, users of the national economic accounts must refer to several other sources, including three additional publications of the Department of Commerce: (1) *U.S. Income and*

Output [177]; (2) "The National Income and Product Accounts of the United States; Revised Estimates, 1929-1964" [167, pp. 6-56]; and (3) *The National Income and Product Accounts of the United States, 1929-1965* [168]. Ambiguities exist in the descriptions presented in these publications, some methodology has changed, and the information is incomplete. When the revised national figures were published in 1965, however, they had been made consistent with the concepts of final demand used in the input-output tables.

The first national input-output table published by the government was the one for 1947 prepared by the Bureau of Labor Statistics (BLS) [194]. Since 1950, two additional national tables have been published—the 1958 table in 1965 [176] and the 1963 table in 1969 [164], these by the Office of Business Economics (OBE). A 1947 table that has an industrial classification comparable with that of the 1958 and 1963 tables is also available in unpublished form from the OBE [169]. The data and the basic input-output conventions used to assemble the 450-order input-output table for 1947 by the BLS are extremely well documented both in the 1947 Technical Supplement, published by the National Bureau of Economic Research (NBER) [62], and in the individual mimeographed worksheets that provide industry-by-industry descriptions [197]. It was evidently the intention of the organizers of the 1947 study to publish a complete documentation of it after the industry reports had been edited "for consistency, clearness, and data disclosures" [12, p. 99], but the official work on input-output was abruptly discontinued for several years by the federal government beginning in 1952, and these plans could not be carried out. Some of the procedures developed for the 1947 input-output study have changed for the 1958 study and again for the 1963 study; but, as of the summer of 1971, no complete documentation of either of the latter two studies had been published. During this study, the inadequate documentation of the national figures naturally complicated the effort to assemble regional data on a basis consistent with the national aggregates.

Regional Economic Accounts

Numerous articles have been written about the feasibility of extending the national economic accounting concepts to a regional level and about some of the conceptual problems in constructing any set of regional accounts. For example, in the volume *Design of Regional Accounts,* which contains articles on various aspects of regional accounting, Ruggles and Ruggles specifically addressed the question of

... whether regional breakdowns of the national economic accounts are desirable and, if desirable, whether they are feasible either independently or as a derivative in the process of obtaining the national estimates. [71, p. 121]

In an earlier publication, Werner Hochwald discussed some of the conceptual difficulties of extending the income side of the regional economic accounts [51]. Actual estimations of detailed regional economic accounts are, however, extremely rare. A very early attempt to estimate regional income data by state and to establish a methodology to do this on a systematic basis was reported in a study by Maurice Leven, published in 1925 by the NBER [58]. As already mentioned, the first official publication of state estimates was in 1939 [61]. Discussions of regional accounts have centered on the issues of how the economic accounts should be defined, what regional classification should be used, how the computational difficulties of compiling such vast arrays of data should be handled, and whether the accounts should be assembled by separate regional units or by a central agency.

One of the basic difficulties with establishing regional accounts has stemmed from differences in where income is earned versus where it is received and where a product is bought versus where the buyer lives. Personal income and product accounts can be specified by where the income recipients work, or where they live, or where they spend their money; and variations therefore occur in the way in which the data are collected and published. There is also a problem in determining the regional location of consumption for an industrial firm or a government body, since the region where the good or service is used may not coincide with the region where it is recorded as a purchase. The central office of a firm, for example, may record a capital purchase that then appears under the gross private capital formation sector of final demand for the specific region where the office is located, but this capital good may be used by a plant situated in any one of a number of regions in which the firm operates. Similarly with the public sector, the purchase of a good or service may be recorded in the accounts of a federal government agency in Washington, D.C., whereas the actual consumption may occur in one of the regions or even overseas. Because the desired income or product account concept will undoubtedly change from one economic analysis to another, regional data should preferably be provided for each type of basic concept.

The choice of an appropriate regional economic unit is another pervasive problem in establishing regional accounts. Some data are published by counties, others by urban areas, watershed districts, political wards, census regions, and so on. Although considerable effort has been made by some analysts to show that an economic spatial unit other than the state would be more appropriate for regional economic analyses,[2] the fact remains that most data are available for states, not for other regional classifications. Also, state data can be easily aggregated into some of the more common regional groupings, such as census regions; or disaggregated; or split into other regional units required for particular regional

---

2. Karl A. Fox, for example, designates his spatial classifications as functional economic areas [36].

studies. The desired spatial unit will obviously vary depending upon the economic analysis that is to be made. Data must sometimes be assembled, for example, by watershed districts for the study of water uses and requirements within a community, by Standard Metropolitan Statistical Areas (which may cut across county, state, and other regional boundaries) for urban studies, etc. For a sizable number of regional policy decisions, however, the state political body is responsible for implementing the policies; and data compiled by states may be the most appropriate for studies of the economic impact of these policies.

A few of the past reservations about the feasibility of compiling regional economic accounts have undoubtedly occurred because the statistical system requires the handling of millions of figures. Early computer techniques and capacities were extremely limited, and massive sets of data, such as those required for a comprehensive set of regional economic accounts, could not be effectively and efficiently collected and maintained on a routine basis. Because rapid advances are being made in the use of computers, the problems of data collection, storage, and retrieval do not presently seem to be insurmountable. In fact, a completely new approach to national and regional economic accounts may now be feasible, given the recent developments in computer technology.

Although supplemental regional statistics required for a particular analysis can often be collected only by the regional group concerned, there are several reasons for giving a central agency the basic task of constructing or, at least, of coordinating the assembly of a general set of regional accounts. First, this would eliminate a tremendous duplication of research effort and would therefore reduce the total expenditure of time and funds presently allocated to assembling general sets of regional data. More than twenty state input-output tables have been assembled by different research groups in the United States during the past fifteen years. The basic methodology of compiling each set of accounts took time to learn, and additional time was required to make all the estimates internally consistent. If the data had already been available, the analysts could have used their time more profitably to investigate the specific policy issues of their state or to improve and expand these data with supplemental statistics that may be peculiar to their state.

Second, a central agency can give consideration to longer-term issues that may arise or to the benefit of maintaining consistency with other accounting systems and of providing data that can be used for multipurposes. For short-term projects which are to provide answers to specific policy questions, the expenditure of the time and money required to assemble consistent sets of regional data may seem unwarranted. Even if data were accurately and consistently compiled from state to state, integrating statistics from one state with those from another would be difficult because of the different years covered by each study. It may even be that if regional accounts were compiled in each region with no central coordination, the summation of these accounts would provide an estimate of total GNP that would vary widely from the observed national aggregate.

Although compilation of the accounts on a routine basis by a central agency does not insure that the figures are correct, major inconsistencies can be easily determined and rectified because the national data can be used to provide a reasonable control over the regional estimates.

Third, because most regional economic research units probably encounter opposition to the allocation of adequate funds for data assembly, the statistics are often hastily compiled, almost no consideration is given to maintaining consistency with other classification systems (industrial, regional, etc.), and the methodology used is seldom documented. Outsiders not only have no way of ascertaining how the estimates were calculated and therefore cannot change or improve them, but they also have no basis for determining how accurately the data have been estimated and therefore how reliable the conclusions are. If the basic set of regional accounts were to be routinely assembled by one central group, only a small fraction of the total cost of compiling a reliable set of accounts for each region would be incurred, and it should be easier to insure that the accounts are consistent and that the methodology is documented.

From the preceding discussion, it is evident that the compilation of regional economic accounts requires consideration of special problems not encountered in constructing national accounts; that detailed regional data are not as readily accessible as national data for establishing a set of accounts; and that, consequently, the expansion of regional accounts within a general and comprehensive framework has been a great deal slower than for the national accounts. Some type of systematic, unified regional accounting system should, however, be established and routinely maintained, in view of the present proliferation of regional studies. Anyone who has worked extensively with regional economic data knows that vast quantities of statistics are published each year, but even so, great gaps exist in the data base. If sufficient industrial and regional detail is maintained when the regional accounts are compiled and if the components are available on different accounting bases (for example, both by where the purchaser lives and by where the purchase is made), many of the conceptual and other difficulties in assembling and using a set of regional accounts can be eliminated, or, at least, considerably lessened. Then the data can be expanded, improved, aggregated, disaggregated, or recombined in numerous ways by individual economic research units to suit their particular purposes and needs, using the centrally assembled accounts as control totals in each case.

In the next section of this chapter, a description is given of a multiregional accounting system that can be utilized for many different regional studies.

The Multiregional Input-Output Accounting System

In order to clarify the basic framework within which the state final demands were assembled, a brief description of the regional input-output tables of the multiregional accounting system is presented here. An important contribution of this system is that it discloses gaps and inconsistencies in the series of available statistics because of the framework used and because of the need to maintain data consistency in three ways: within each region, from region to region, and, finally, among all regions and the national aggregates.

Figure 1-1 shows how the purchases by industries and final consumers within each of the 51 regions of the economy are organized. In the figure, each large rectangular block represents a regional input-output table for a particular region. All of the interindustry and final current account purchases made by industries and by public and private consumers located within that particular region are represented by the block. Each row of a specific regional table shows the total distribution of a commodity to the intermediate and final users within that region. The rows specify the producing industries but do not designate the region in which the goods were produced. Each column of the table shows the total purchases of goods, services, and value added by the particular intermediate or final user located in that region. It should be noted that these columns provide a detailed specification of all purchases by the region in which they are consumed, regardless of their region of origin or of the region where the consumer, say an individual, lives. To obtain the region of production for each item and to complete the multiregional accounting system, the accounts must be expanded to include trade among the regions. This expansion will not be explained in the present volume, because it does not directly relate to the estimation of the regional final demands.

The large block within each regional table represents the interindustry sales and purchases, with the rows specifying the producing industry and the columns specifying the purchasing industry. For the present study, the number of producing industries exactly equals the number of purchasing industries; therefore, the block is square. (A rectangular block of data will occur if, as in some studies, the number of purchasing industries exceeds the number of producing industries.) The rectangle along the bottom of each regional table represents the payments to factors of production: wages and salaries, rent, depreciation, taxes, etc. All of these are usually lumped in the national input-output tables and are referred to as value added.

The rectangle at the right of each regional table represents the purchases by final consumers (public and private) in the region. These normally include the six major components listed at the beginning of this chapter and explained, component by component, below. The small rectangle in the lower right-hand corner of each regional table represents essentially the wage and salary payments to domestic household employees and government employees. In addition, some balancing items for the foreign sector are included here. For the state estimates, data were compiled for the six basic components of final demand, and, wherever possible, estimates were made for these value added components of the final demand columns as well.

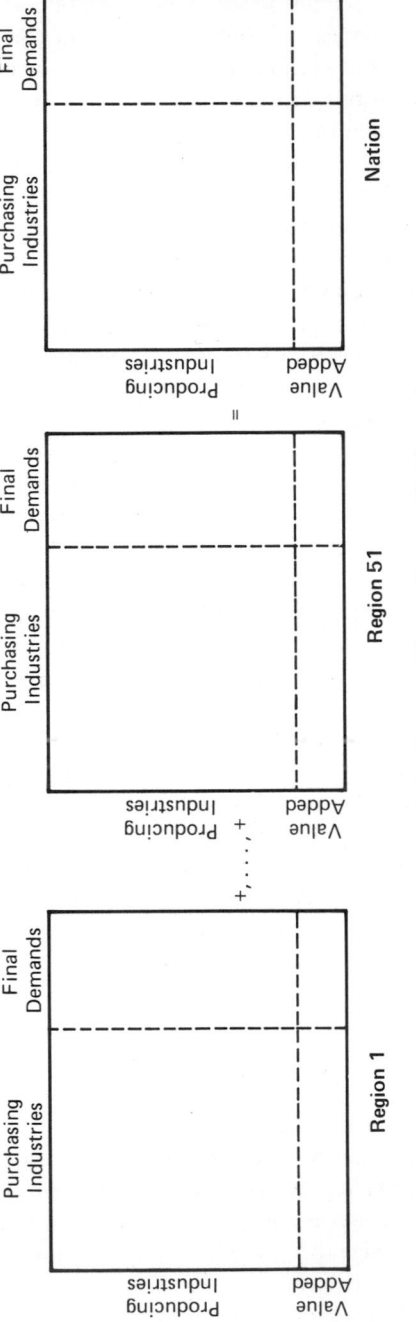

Figure 1-1. Regional Input-Output Tables.

The user of national input-output tables is accustomed to working with a balanced table where the sums of corresponding rows and columns of the table must be equal, since the total consumption of output must equal the total production for each industry in a given year. For a particular regional input-output table, the sum of all elements in each row of the table gives the total consumption only by users within the region, while the sum of all elements in each column gives the total input requirements of each industry within the region, that is, the total value of production. If none of the good or service produced by the industry in a given region is traded, these corresponding row and column sums will therefore also be identical. (This occurs, for example, for many of the service industries.) The sums of corresponding rows and columns in a regional table, however, will not be equal for most industries, with the differences being attributable to interregional trade.

Although only the final demand sectors of the multiregional input-output table are described later in the book, the entire regional table has been explained here so that the reader will understand how the final demands can be integrated into the complete accounting system. The state final demand estimates were not deflated because of the problems involved in trying to assemble regional price deflators, but the national price deflators can be used as a first approximation. In later chapters, very detailed definitions and explanations of the individual components of the final demand sector of the accounts will be given; but a few general comments about each of the components are included here to supplement that discussion.

Regional Final Demands

At the national level, personal consumption expenditures have averaged approximately 65 percent of total GNP during the last decade. Federal government purchases and state and local government purchases of goods and services have each comprised about 10 percent. The remaining 15 percent has been distributed among the other three items of final demand—gross private capital formation, net inventory change, and net foreign exports—all of which are extremely variable from year to year. Of the three, gross private capital formation is generally the largest component. Net inventory change and net foreign exports can be positive or negative, depending upon the economic conditions within the economy. At the regional level, say for states, personal consumption expenditures still outweigh all the other items of final demand in the aggregate, but the distribution among the six basic components may naturally vary from the national proportions.

Personal Consumption Expenditures.   All purchases of durable and non-durable goods by private consumers are included in this final demand component regardless of the length of life of the consumer goods. Thus, products that if purchased by an industry would appear in the capital accounts are recorded as a current account transaction and are combined with those products that are definitely bought and used by private consumers in a given year. The only major exception is that houses purchased by consumers are included as part of the new construction component of gross private capital formation. Within each element in this final demand column, the purchases by foreigners and by nonprofit institutions are combined with those of private residents of the United States. For many regional economic studies, separate accounts should be provided for each of these categories of purchases; but it was not feasible to attempt such detailed estimates for the present study.

For the personal consumption calculations, the only comprehensive regional data available were for 1960, and they were separated into only four regions. These data therefore had to be used to obtain the 1947, 1958, and 1963 estimates by state. Two major adjustments were made to the initial state estimates calculated from these regional data. First, imputations were made. At the national level, over 10 percent of the total are imputed items, that is, goods or services for which no actual monetary transaction is recorded but for which a value is calculated and added to the total purchases of the particular product. (An example is rent of owner-occupied houses.) Although in the aggregate the percentage is rather small, for IO-70, Finance & insurance, over 30 percent and for IO-71, Real estate & rental, over 70 percent of the personal consumption expenditures are attributable to imputations. The methods used to estimate the imputations for these and other industries at the state level are explained in Chapter 2. Second, special estimates were made for some of the goods and services that were purchased outside the home state of the consumer. This adjustment was required because of the nature of the regional consumption data used and because all data had to be specified by the state where the goods were actually purchased.

Gross Private Capital Formation.   All of the private purchases shown in the final demand sector of the regional input-output tables are current account transactions except for the column of gross private capital formation figures. This column includes depreciation because it is gross, and it includes purchases of both plant and equipment, but it excludes any sale of capital to the government sectors because they are outside the private sector and also because all sales to the public sectors are considered to occur on current account. Since all of the private sector capital sales by each industry are grouped together as a single entry in this column of final demand, the private purchaser of the capital good is not explicitly discernible. The detailed accounting that can be made of these capital purchases at the national and regional level is explained in Chapter 3.

When the state estimates were made for this study, a detailed, officially published national capital flow table, specifying the purchaser and producer of the capital plant and equipment, was available only for 1958. The state estimates for the other two years were calculated using capital data from three privately constructed tables: 1947 tables of capital stocks and flows and a 1963 table of capital flows. For the state estimates, column coefficients were calculated for each of these national matrices and were weighted by state estimates of capital expenditures.

Net Inventory Change. When the term "gross private domestic investment" is used, this refers to gross private capital formation plus net inventory change. Net inventory change was treated as a separate component for the present study. It represents a netting of the inventory additions minus the inventory depletions in the private sector of the economy for a given year. Thus, each element can be either positive or negative, depending upon the magnitude of the additions relative to the depletions. In the column, an element called "inventory valuation adjustment" is included to adjust the total for the differences in the value of the goods when they are placed in inventory compared with their value when they are withdrawn from inventory. This adjustment can be positive or negative depending upon whether prices have decreased or increased, respectively, over the given time period. (State estimates were not made for this element.) For some studies, inventory depletions are separated from inventory additions and are transferred from being a column of negative figures to being a row of positive figures in the input-output table. The row totals of the national matrix then sum to the gross supply of goods produced in any year, rather than to the more customary gross supply of goods produced in the given year. For the implementation of the multiregional model, this latter procedure was used.

Although the state inventory data presented in the accompanying statistical appendix for the two agricultural industries, IO-1, Livestock & livestock products, and IO-2, Other agricultural products, are reliable because they were obtained directly from unpublished data at the Department of Agriculture, the state estimates for the other industries had to be only roughly approximated, as explained in Chapter 3, because of the extreme paucity of available data.

Foreign Exports and Imports. With two exceptions, each element in the net foreign export column represents gross exports from the United States of a given good or service. The two exceptions are in the import rows where negative entries appear. These elements, which are the totals of all imports into the United States, can be obtained by summing the two import rows of the national input-output table.[3] When the entire column of exports is totalled, the

---

3. Although some input-output tables contain only one import row, the discussion in this section will pertain to the methodology used for the 1958 and 1963 national tables, which contain two import rows. These two negative entries, however, are combined as one element in the accompanying set of state product accounts.

sum becomes net exports and can be negative if total imports exceed total exports in a given year.

The imports are separated into two categories, directly allocated imports and transferred imports. In earlier input-output studies, these were referred to as noncompetitive and competitive imports, respectively, although there are some slight definitional differences in the new terms. In general, an import is classified as directly allocated or noncompetitive if a final user purchases the import in a substantially unaltered form, or if there is no domestic production of the good or service or, at least, no close substitute.

Substitutability was determined on a judgmental basis using the following guide: the import should be interchangeable with a domestically produced item without any change in the technology of the consuming industry or the resultant product. [164, p. 25]

In the input-output accounts, directly allocated imports are always handled as a row, that is, they are recorded as inputs purchased by given industries, and the value of their output is distributed to other industries in the same manner as any other direct purchase as part of the total cost of materials of the industry.

Imports are classified as transferred or competitive if the product is produced domestically and if the import is not directly consumed by a final user. In the accounts, these imports can be treated either as a positive row or a negative column of figures. The transferred imports are assumed to have been recorded as a row of inputs in the first part of the following discussion. As the initial input-output table is constructed, the value of these imports is added to the value of output of the domestic industry, and the total value is distributed along the respective industry row to the various intermediate and final purchasers. The sum of the elements in each row then represents the total domestic plus foreign supply of the given good or service, which explains why an input-output table with all imports recorded as a row is sometimes referred to as a total supply base table. If the transferred imports are treated as a negative column of final demand, this has the effect of subtracting from the total supply of the industry the amount that is supplied from foreign sources, leaving only the gross domestic production of the industry. A table constructed in this way is sometimes referred to as a gross domestic output base table. The (negative) transferred import figures are frequently combined, element by element, with the gross export figures, in which case any individual element in the combined column can be either negative or positive depending upon the value of the imports relative to the value of the exports for the industry. Because import data were extremely difficult to obtain by state of final consumption, estimates for the multiregional input-output system could be made only at a regional, rather than the state, level and only for total imports rather than industry by industry. The foreign trade data presented in the accompanying statistical appendix therefore are for net exports, but the total import figure for the United States is given rather than state estimates.

The state export estimates were assembled using two separate methodologies, explained in detail in Chapter 4, because the location of final consumption can be interpreted in two ways—by place of production or by port of exit. The particular set of export data used for an analysis will depend upon the type of regional study that is being undertaken and, if a multiregional study is made, upon the nature of the model and the way in which the other data components, especially the interregional trade flows, have been specified. It is possible, for example, that a research group would assemble transportation data to include only transportation of goods produced and consumed domestically and that goods produced domestically but destined for foreign consumption would not be included in these transport statistics. In this case, foreign exports should be estimated separately and specified by place of production only.

Export data were first compiled for 1947, 1958, and 1963 by place of production, because when this study was begun, these were the only data that could be obtained on a comparable basis for the three years. Additional export data were published in 1967 and 1968, and this has made it possible to assemble a set of export statistics by state (port) of exit for 1963. Because some regional studies may require exports by place of production, both sets of estimates have been included in the present volume. The exports by port of exit, however, are used in the multiregional input-output model developed at the Harvard Economic Research Project. Although it was impossible to assemble comparable sets of port-of-exit data for 1947 and 1958, detailed export statistics are now being collected by the Bureau of the Census on a routine basis, so fairly accurate sets of state data could be assembled if sufficient funds were allocated to processing the computer tapes.

Government Sectors. The purchases of general government agencies are treated differently from those of government enterprises in the national and regional economic accounts. For the general government agencies, both capital and current account purchases of goods and services are included in the final demand sector of the national income accounts. Public agencies are classified as government enterprises if they sell sufficient goods and services to the general public to cover over half of their current operating costs. For the government enterprises, the capital and current account purchases are separated, with the current account purchases being treated as intermediate purchases (comparable with those of private industry) and the capital account purchases being combined with the government final purchases. The final demand purchases by the public sectors of the economy, as defined above, are usually separated into two major

HUNT LIBRARY
CARNEGIE-MELLON UNIVERSITY

components, state and local and federal government purchases of goods and services.

State and Local Government.   The estimation of the state and local govern-ment purchases was relatively straightforward, as explained in Chapter 5. A considerable quantity of accurate state data is available on total state and local general government purchases by function, and these data were used to weight national purchases that were detailed by industry and by function. For the final estimates, state data could be compiled for most of the capital account purchases of the state and local government enterprises, and these data were added to the general government state estimates.

Federal Government.   In contrast to the state and local government data, no comprehensive set of state statistics giving details on industrial purchases is published for the federal government. The special estimates that were required for research and development, the Commodity Credit Corporation, and other elements of this final demand column are explained in Chapter 6. Two major factors may affect the accuracy of the state estimates that were made for this study. First, state-by-state figures for the capital purchases of federal government enterprises could not be assembled. In the Budget of the United States, the capital account purchases by the federal government enterprises are frequently not even recorded separately at the national level.

Second, it was often impossible to determine exactly where the good or service purchased by a federal agency was actually consumed. Goods that are transported by special means, such as the military, should be estimated separately and recorded as being purchased in the state where the production occurs; otherwise, the demand for nongovernment transport of the good to the final place of consumption will be mis-specified. No information was available, however, to separate federal government purchases into these two transport categories. Although not even the percentage of total purchases shipped on government transport could be ascertained for the three years, it is assumed that having to treat both categories of government purchases identically did not create significant inaccuracies in the estimates. Another problem in determining the location of final consumption was that many federal government purchases are only recorded on a main account in a central office in Washington, D.C., whereas the good might actually be consumed in some other region of the country. Sometimes a particular method of recording the statistics has been adopted for security reasons (for example, exports of military goods are often combined as one item in the export statistics). But frequently no uniform method of recording purchases so that they can be employed in regional studies has been used by the federal agencies and enterprises. In a few cases, regional data are collected, and worksheets could be obtained directly from the government agency.

Construction of State Estimates

Although various methodologies and many different data sources were used to assemble the figures, the basic procedure was to determine the national definition for the particular component of final demand, to obtain a specific definition for the industrial component, to find any available state data that could be used to make consistent sets of state estimates, and then, if possible, to establish a general methodology for assembly of the data. Detailed explanations of the estimation procedures and specific data source references are given in later chapters. All data were assembled by state, for 87 industries, by place of final consumption, and for the three years 1947, 1958, and 1963. Special procedures for constructing the state estimates were developed for each component of final demand.

Regional Classification

The state was chosen as the regional unit for this study because it was the most detailed spatial unit for which a consistent set of reliable regional data could be assembled, given the time and budget constraints. Although considerable differences of opinion exist as to how an "ideal" regional economic classification should be defined, it is hoped that the present set of state economic accounts and the explanations of how they were constructed may at least be used as a prototype for future studies. As discussed earlier in the chapter, the spatial classification desired will undoubtedly vary from one analysis to another.

Industrial Classification

All figures were assembled using the 87-industry input-output classification published by the OBE with the 1958 table (included as Table A-1 in the appendix to this volume) except that IO-74, Research & development (R&D), was eliminated and treated as it is in the 1963 table. Since this adjustment affected only the federal government data, it is explained in detail in Chapter 6.

The definitions of a few input-output industries differ in the 1958 and 1963 input-output tables. The changes known at this time and the value of total output affected are summarized in Table 1-1. Because it was impossible in most cases to adjust the final demand figures for 1947 and 1958 to the new 1963

Table 1-1
Changes in Input-Output Industry Classification from 1958 to 1963

Input-Output Industry		SIC Industry[a]		
Number	1963 Output ($ million)	Number	1963 Output ($ million)	Percent[b]
(1)	(2)	(3)	(4)	(5)
4[c]	1,772	073	+ 80	+4.5
70	33,700	66	− 860	−2.6
71	83,887	66	+ 860	
		6541	+ 137	
			+ 997	+1.2
73	35,945	6541	− 137	
		7361	+ 145	
		7391	+ 1,193	
			+ 1,201	+3.3
74	0	7391	− 1,193	−
77	33,160	7361	− 145	−0.4

[a] A plus sign indicates that the SIC industry was included in and a negative sign
that it was excluded from the 1963 industry as compared with the 1958 industry.
[b] (Column 4 ÷ column 2) x 100.
[c] SIC 073 was not included in any input-output industry in 1958 as no data were
available for it.

definitions, only the R&D adjustment was made. The changes in definitions for
the other industries were so slight, as seen in Table 1-1, that the comparability
of the state data for the three years should not be greatly impaired.

Location of Final Consumption

The regional accounts were constructed to show the state in which the good
or service was actually "consumed,"[4] regardless of where it was produced or
where the consumer lived. The accurate specification of the place of final consumption was especially important for the multiregional input-output research
project because when the final demands are combined with the other state data
for the implementation of the model, they partially determine the shipments of
goods between regions. Thus, misestimates of where goods were actually consumed could have serious repercussions on the accuracy of the transportation
flow estimates and also on the estimates of regional production.

_____

4. This term is somewhat ambiguous since, for example, foreign exports are sometimes
considered to be "consumed" at their place of production and at other times at their port of
exit; but in either case, they are further "consumed" when they reach their foreign destination. The meaning, however, is felt to be clear in the context of each description.

Selection of Years

The three years 1947, 1958, and 1963 were initially selected for the assembly of the base-year state data because national input-output data were available for those years. The reason for selecting both 1958 and 1963 was simple. Since many of the 1963 census data had not yet been published when this study was begun in 1966 and no fixed date had been set for the publication of the 1963 input-output table, state estimates were assembled for both 1958 and 1963. This provided a set of state estimates for 1958 that could have been used for the multiregional model if the 1963 table had not been available in time. As the state estimates for these two years were being constructed, most of the research time was required to determine the composition of the industrial purchases, to discover the sources from which the state data could be obtained, and to establish the procedures used to calculate the estimates. Only a small amount of additional time was required to transcribe numbers for two years rather than one, because the data for these two years could usually be obtained from the same source or type of source.

The decision to assemble data for 1947 as well was less straightforward. At the time the study was begun, it was anticipated that complete sets of data for the three years could be compiled for all components of the regional economic accounts, thus providing valuable historical information that could be used to analyze the economic changes that have been occurring in regions of the United States. Final demands were therefore assembled for the three years. During the first year, it became evident, however, that the construction of comparable inter-industry and interregional trade data by state for the three years would be too difficult and overly expensive. Those data were finally assembled for 1963 only. Another factor in the initial decision to assemble data for 1947 was that the 1947 documentation had been referred to continually for previous research at the Harvard Economic Research Project and that no description of the 1963 study existed because it was not yet prepared, while almost no information had been released with the 1958 study. Although the 1947 material would have been referred to in any case, many of the subtleties of the data or meanings of the descriptions could be discovered only as the various 1947 state estimates were actually being made. The documentation of the 1947 table is still far superior to that presently available for the 1958 and 1963 tables.

State Estimation Procedures

In estimating final demands by state, there were no previous methodologies to follow except where data were available from the same sources as are used for the national economic accounts. A tremendous amount of experimentation was therefore required to develop reasonable techniques for constructing the state estimates. If state data were available from the same source for all components of a given final demand, this source was generally used. Data obtained from numerous sources were less desirable for two reasons. First, time and budget limitations restricted the number of data that could be compiled item by item. Judgments about a particular set of data being better than another usually had to be intuitive, of course, as there was no absolute set of data against which the various estimates could be checked. Second, and related to the first reason, statistics from different sources were, in general, not comparable in terms of data composition, extent of coverage, etc. These noncomparabilities were difficult to determine because of lack of documentation. To improve their comparability, extensive adjustments would have been needed if the data were to be used.

For each final demand component, several alternative techniques of assembling the data were considered before the methods described in the succeeding chapters were chosen. A presentation of the alternative methods and the reasons for rejecting them might have been as valuable to some readers as the descriptions of the methods actually chosen, but the inclusion of these in the text would perhaps have created confusion in an already unwieldy set of explanations. The members of the research staff who constructed the present set of estimates were generally confronted with several sets of data, and they had to determine which should be used. The three possibilities described below illustrate the types of decisions that were made.

1. Two sets of data were available, one a reasonably accurate distribution series but for a year other than the one desired, and the second a less accurate set of data but for the actual year. A decision had to be made as to how reasonable it was to assume that the state distributions did not vary between the two years and that the first set of data therefore could be used as allocation factors for the national data of the actual year.

2. Data were available only for aggregate regions or for the nation rather than for states. A decision had to be made whether an accurate set of state estimates could be provided by weighting the regional or national data by a series of aggregate state figures or whether some proxy should be employed to make the state allocations.

3. Only very sparse regional data or none at all were available. A decision had to be made as to an appropriate distribution series that could be used to allocate the national figures to the states. Employment, payroll, or production data were often used as the allocation factors.

In constructing the state figures for the three years, comparability among the three sets of numbers was maintained for each component, wherever possible, so that the data could also be used for historical analyses. Although the state figures should be generally comparable from year to year, a few discrepancies were noticed even in the national tables, and these affected the respective state estimates. The ones that were easily recognizable were cases where an entry was zero in one year but positive in another; where an entry changed from a positive to a negative figure or vice versa; or, as in a few instances, where the change between two years was so large as to raise doubts as to the comparability of the figures. Some of these were actual changes, but others occurred from alterations in the procedures or definitions used for the national tables. The discrepancies are usually noted in the following chapters, but no adjustments were made either to the national or state figures because of complications that might have occurred from altering only specific elements within the published sets of consistent national accounts.

Certain particular characteristics of the data and data sources had to be continually considered throughout this study—among them, the recent revisions made to the 1947 input-output table and to the national input-output accounts in general, the lack of documentation of the 1958 and 1963 input-output tables, and the variations that occurred in the sources of data for the three years (which necessitated altering the methodology used for each of the three calculations). In addition, time and budget limitations were a constant restraint. All of these created six major problems. First, particular adjustments could not always be made to the data for all three years. When splits were applied to the personal consumption expenditures data, for example, they were determined from the 1958 data, and the same splits had to be applied to the 1947 and 1963 data. Because the composition of purchases for some items changed significantly between 1958 and the other two years, the use of the same splits for each year may have caused inaccuracies in the 1947 and 1963 estimates. Second, the detailed 450-order 1947 table sometimes had to be referred to when determining the composition of an industry for the 1958 and 1963 estimates. A large change in the industry mix, however, had occasionally taken place between 1947 and 1958 or 1963. Because it was not always possible to ascertain the exact changes that had occurred, the 1958 and 1963 state estimates may contain some inaccuracies for industries where rapid changes in the industry mix could be expected. Third, sometimes even the 1947 documentation did not provide sufficient information for the 1958 and 1963 estimates. In these instances, if the national industrial purchase was small, no allocation was generally made to the state; if it was large, a guess as to the contents and the state allocation of the purchases was made. Fourth, in the national final demands, some 1947 final demand figures are present where there should be none since industrial conversion splits were applied to all components of an industry when the 1947 input-output table was recently revised. These values are usually small, and consequently no effort was made to correct for the discrepancies. Fifth, all data in the national economic accounts were altered when revisions were made in the early 1960s. As a result, some revised 1947 national final demands are not directly traceable to the worksheets without a considerable amount of effort; this prevented the members of the research staff from obtaining complete information about the relevant components. Sixth, except in one or two instances, fewer state data were available for 1947 than for 1958 and 1963; and because of the time and budget limitations less effort was devoted to assembling the 1947 figures. The assembly of final demands for 1947 was well worthwhile, however, since it provided information that improved the comparability between all the state estimates and the national tables. For all these reasons, caution should be used when the 1947, 1958, and 1963 state data are compared.

By compiling accounts for all three years simultaneously, the estimates for this study were significantly improved by the cross-checks that could be made among the three data sets. Complete industry-by-state tabulations of the three data sets for each of the six final demand components are given in the accompanying statistical appendix. Each set of state estimates sums to the respective GNP figures for the United States.

Conclusion

From the preceding discussion, it is evident that all the data assembled should be considered as initial estimates and that many improvements can be made to the data and in the methods used to assemble them. To be usable, data should be completely documented as to the sources from which they were obtained; the adjustments made; the components of each figure; and, if a viable alternative exists, the reason for using one set of data rather than an alternative series. Unfortunately, very few data have such complete documentation. The rationale of the present volume is to provide as complete a description as possible of the methods used to assemble the final demands by state. Economists who have worked with the national economic accounts realize that vast amounts of time can be spent just in determining the various sources used to make the estimates unless a comprehensive set of references is given. The assembly of data obviously takes time. A rather long lag always occurs between the moment the need for particular data is realized and the time the data become available to the general user. For the final demand estimates, the entire research took approximately two years to complete, but it was spread over more than four years. The initial set of estimates was prepared in about a year and a half; then, other aspects of the multiregional research project were completed, with revisions being made to the final demands during the last year of the project, after the 1963 input-output table had been published.

In all cases, the statistics actually used in the study had already been collected and were therefore assembled from secondary sources, such as statistical publications of the government, unpublished worksheets, or data tapes. The organization of special surveys to collect supplemental data was not feasible. From the results of the final demand study, however, it is obvious that certain state estimates could have been substantially improved if additional data had been obtained from special surveys (designed to extend the regional and industrial coverage of present surveys) or if revisions could have been made to the methods of recording regional statistics that are available in published and unpublished form.

2 Personal Consumption Expenditures

Karen R. Polenske,
Isabelle B. Whiston, and
Frans J. Kok

The largest component of the United States gross national product (GNP) is personal consumption expenditures. During the last 30 years, this component as a percent of total GNP (constant $1958) varied between a low of 47.4 percent in 1944 to a high of 66.8 percent in 1947. The percentage has hovered between 64 and 65 for the past decade. The aggregate includes all actual expenditures for goods and services by private individuals plus the services rendered to individuals by nonprofit institutions. If the activities of a nonprofit organization, however, closely parallel those of an enterprise, they are excluded from the personal consumption expenditures. The houses purchased by private consumers are also excluded from the expenditures figures (the value appears as part of gross private capital formation), but all other purchases of durable goods by private consumers, such as cars, refrigerators, stoves, and television sets, are included as current purchases although they may be used by the consumer for more than one year. In addition, imputations are made for the rental value of owner-occupied housing, for food, clothing, and lodging received in kind by employees, and so on. Because of the statistical difficulties in separating the expenditures made by foreign visitors from those made by private U.S. residents, each individual entry contains both expenditures. The total, however, has been adjusted through a single negative entry in IO-85, Rest of the world industry, of the personal consumption expenditures column to exclude the expenditures by foreigners.

This chapter contains a description of the procedures used to make the state estimates of personal consumption expenditures. For each of the three years under study, 1947, 1958, and 1963, the state consumption expenditures obtained sum to national consumption figures that are consistent with the input-output personal consumption expenditures data. The set of figures for each state represents the total purchases of the specified consumer goods and services in that state, regardless of the area of production. For example, the figures for Massachusetts give the consumer purchases made in stores located in that state, although the goods may have been produced anywhere within the United States, and the people making the purchases may live anywhere in the United States.

21

State estimates for personal consumption expenditures were obtained for the three years by combining information from:

1.   1950 and 1960 censuses of population (*CP*), taken by the Bureau of the Census [142].
2.   1950 and 1960 consumer expenditures surveys (CES), taken by the Bureau of Labor Statistics (BLS) [198; 199].[1]
3.   1947, 1958, and 1963 input-output personal consumption expenditures (IOPCE) prepared by the Office of Business Economics (OBE) [169; 176; 164].

The CES average consumption expenditures for each of four regions were converted to input-output categories and were then weighted by the appropriate state population figures to obtain the state vectors of final demand.

Detailed Description of the Data

Several adjustments had to be made to the population data and the consumption expenditures data before the state estimates could be calculated.

Population Estimates

Since the CES population data were given only for regions of the United States, the state estimates of the number of families[2] within given income distribution classes were calculated from CP data for 1950 and 1960. The essential differences in the coverage of the population data from the CES and the CP are shown in Table 2-1. It should be understood, of course, that additional information is given in each source on the number of families distributed by sex, age of head of household, etc., but the only comparable sets of state population data for 1950 and 1960, disaggregated by type of family and place of residence,

---

1. The 1950 CES data were used only for an adjustment of the population figures by income groups (see pp. 23–28). Originally, average consumption expenditures for 1947 were to be estimated using the 1950 data, but this was not feasible because of the lack of comparability between the 1950 and 1960 studies. Two main difficulties with the 1950 study were: (1) It excluded rural areas, and if rural data (such as Department of Agriculture survey information [157]) from another study were used, a complete coverage of the population could not be easily assured. (2) The 1950 and 1960 CES commodity classifications are not directly comparable, and no time was available to make another complete alignment, using the 1950 data. Consequently, the 1960 average consumption expenditures data were used throughout the calculations for all three years.

2. Wherever the word "families" is used, it should be interpreted as covering both families and unrelated individuals.

were found in Table 66 of each state volume of the *U.S. Census of Population, 1960* [142]. The descriptions in Table 2-1, accordingly, refer only to data specifically used in the calculations.

A very detailed discussion of the disparities between the CES and CP in the number of families within income distribution groups has been presented by Helen Lamale [57] and in a Bureau of the Budget Statistical Evaluation Report [82]. Since the CES and CP figures were collected for different purposes and by different methods, the data cannot be expected to be exactly comparable. From the 1950 and 1960 CP data, state estimates for 1947, 1958, and 1963 were calculated for the number of consumer units within eight income distribution classes by state for two types of family units (unrelated individuals and families of two or more persons) and for two places of residence (urban and rural).

Four basic adjustments were made to the population data used in this study:

Adjustment from a Before-Tax to an After-Tax Income Base. The major difference between the CES and the CP data which affected their use in this study was that the data in the CES are classified by after-tax income groups, while before-tax income groups are used for the CP data. To make the two sets of data compatible, the CP data were adjusted from a before-tax to an after-tax income base using 1950 and 1960 CES population data to determine the relationship between the two classifications. The 1950 CES population data were obtained from the publication *Study of Consumer Expenditures, Incomes and Savings* [198], while the 1960 CES data were obtained from the publication *Survey of Consumer Expenditures, 1960-61* [199]. This is the only place in the calculations where the 1950 CES data were used.

Both the CES and CP data were regrouped to comparable places of residence (rural and urban) and to the income group classifications shown in Table 2-2 before the adjustments were made. Since the CES data were available only by region, the state CP figures for population within each income group in a particular region were adjusted to an after-tax income base by using the average for the respective region. The 1960 CES rural data had to be used for the adjustments to the 1950 rural population figures because the 1950 survey did not cover rural families. Although adjustments of the CP data to the after-tax base could have been made in several ways, the following procedure was chosen in order to use the CES population data, which give an average after-tax income and an average before-tax income for each income group.

Step 1. Both the 1950 and 1960 CES data had to be adjusted for compatibility with the CP groupings of rural and urban.
  a.   1950 CES data: For each of the three regions in the 1950 survey [198, Vol. I, tt. 3, 17], the figures from the three places of residence (large

Table 2-1
Summary Description of Population Statistics

	1960 Consumer Expenditures Survey	1950 and 1960 Census of Population
Purpose of study	Detailed measure of family expenditures	A demographic survey
Income definition	Includes wages and salaries (including commissions, bonuses, and tips) before payroll deductions, net income from self-employment in business or profession, income other than earnings (rent, interest, dividends, social security, pensions, disability insurance, trust funds, public or private assistance or other governmental payments, regular contributions from persons outside the family), and food and housing received as pay. Excludes other money receipts (inheritances, lump-sum settlements, gifts), receipts from the sale of assets (house, car), withdrawal of bank deposits or money borrowed, and occupational expenses (tools, union dues).	Same as the CES, except food and housing received as pay are not included and occupational expenses (tools, union dues) are not excluded.

Income distribution groups	Reported in after-tax income groups.
	
	Ten after-tax income groups:
	  Under $ 1,000
	$ 1,000–$ 1,999
	$ 2,000–$ 2,999
	$ 3,000–$ 3,999
	$ 4,000–$ 4,999
	$ 5,000–$ 5,999
	$ 6,000–$ 7,499
	$ 7,500–$ 9,999
	$10,000–$14,999
	$15,000 and over
		Reported in before-tax income groups.
		
		Nine before-tax income groups:
		  Under $ 1,000
		$ 1,000–$ 1,999
		$ 2,000–$ 2,999
		$ 3,000–$ 3,999
		$ 4,000–$ 4,999
		$ 5,000–$ 5,999
		$ 6,000–$ 6,999
		$ 7,000–$ 9,999
		$10,000 and over
		(In 1950 there was an undistributed group.)

Family types:	Groups consumer units by individuals and families.	Groups consumer units by individuals and families.

Definition of family unit	An "economic" family, usually related and usually living together who pool their income and draw from common funds for their major items of expense. (Includes children away at school.)	A "social" family – persons living together and related by blood, marriage, or adoption.
Definition of individuals	Persons living alone or with others with whom they do not pool income and expenditures.	Persons living alone or with someone to whom they are not related. (Includes children living away from home at school.)
Geographical divisions	Four regions: Northeast, North Central, South, West (includes Alaska and Hawaii).	Forty-eight states for 1950 and fifty states for 1960, plus the District of Columbia for both years.
Residence	Groups consumer units by those living in urban, rural nonfarm, and rural farm communities.	Groups consumer units by those living in urban and rural communities.
Population:		
Civilian	Excludes institutional population.	Excludes inmates of institutions.
Military	Includes military personnel living off post.	Includes military personnel living in barracks on post as well as off post.
Time period:		
Family	Family as it existed throughout the calendar year preceding the date of interview (that is, 1960 or 1961) – records an average size family for year.	Family as a point in time, March or April, of census year.
Income	Records all income from the preceding calendar year of the above family members which they received while they were family members, i.e., 1960 or 1961.	Records the income of the family above as of the preceding year, 1949 or 1959.
Coverage	Sample of 13,728 consumer units, that is, a 0.25 percent sample.	Every fourth household and unrelated individuals enumerated in the 1960 Census, that is, a 25 percent sample.

Table 2–2

Income Groups: 1950 and 1960 Census of Population and 1960 Consumer Expenditures Survey

1950 and 1960 Census of Population[a] *(before-tax income groups)*	*1960 Consumer Expenditures Survey (after-tax income groups)*
Under $1,000	Under $ 1,000
$ 1,000–$1,999	$ 1,000–$ 1,999
$ 2,000–$2,999	$ 2,000–$ 2,999
$ 3,000–$3,999	$ 3,000–$ 3,999
$ 4,000–$4,999	$ 4,000–$ 4,999
$ 5,000–$5,999	$ 5,000–$ 5,999
$ 6,000–$6,999 } *b*	{ $ 6,000–$ 7,499
$ 7,000–$9,999 }	{ $ 7,500–$ 9,999
$10,000 and over	{ $10,000–$14,999
	{ $15,000 and over

[a]For the 1950 CP data, the "unreported" families were distributed over the remaining income groups.

[b]Brackets indicate income groups which were combined to form comparable coverage between the two sets of data. The census of population figures were adjusted from a before-tax to an after-tax base.

cities, small cities, suburbs) were aggregated to form a total urban category. An average after-tax income and an average before-tax income were calculated for each of the nine income distribution groups (refer to description of 1950 data in Table 2–5, page 33. Because data were available only for urban consumers in 1950, rural figures from the 1960 CES were used.

b. 1960 CES data: Urban, rural farm, and rural nonfarm data were available. The two latter categories were aggregated to form a single rural category to be compatible with the rural classification in the CP data. An average after-tax income and an average before-tax income were calculated for each of the new rural income groups.

c. 1950 and 1960 CES data: A graph was constructed for each population classification by plotting the CES before-tax income on the horizontal axis and the CES after-tax income on the vertical axis. A prototype graph is shown in Figure 2–1.

(1) The average after-tax income was plotted against the average before-tax income for each income interval using the CES data.

(2) A curve was fitted to the points plotted.

(3) The before-tax income corresponding to an after-tax income used as an interval was read from the graph, that is, the before-tax income corresponding to an after-tax income of $1000, $2000, etc. For an after-tax income of $5000, for example, the graph shows a before-tax income of $5700.

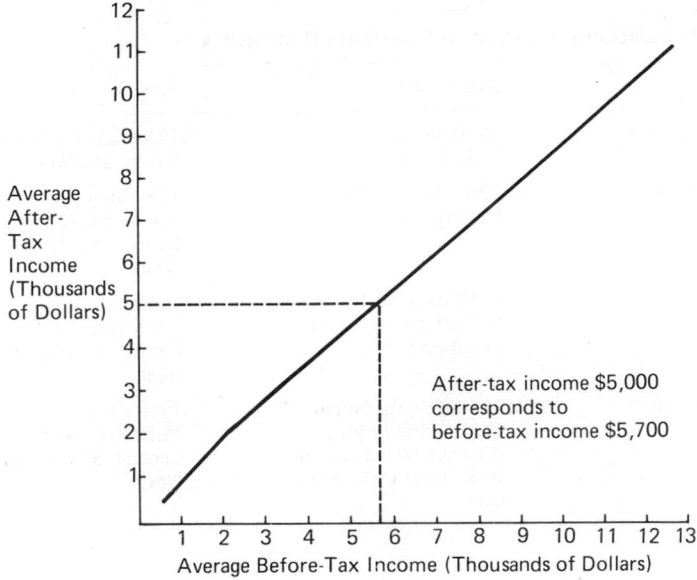

Figure 2–1. Average After-Tax Income Plotted Against Average Before-Tax Income for Each CES Income Group.

Step 2. The 1950 and 1960 CP data were adjusted to an after-tax income base. Before the adjustment could be made, both the CES and the CP data had to be aggregated to the eight income distribution groups given earlier in Table 2–2. The undistributed number of families in the 1950 CP state data was allocated to the eight income groups in proportion to the number of families already in each group. For the 1950 urban and the 1960 urban and rural calculations, the histograms described below were drawn using the CP state data aggregated to the three regions of the 1950 CES and the four regions of the 1960 CES. Since the 1950 survey data covered only the urban population, the 1950 CP rural data by state were aggregated to four regions, and the 1960 CES rural data were used for those histograms. The histogram for the total United States for a particular consumer category was used in place of a regional histogram in cases where the CES sample for a region was too small to be meaningful. The exact data used for each category are specified in Table 2–3.

The regional CP data were redistributed in terms of the new income intervals corresponding to the after-tax income intervals of the CES data (obtained from the graphs described above).

    a.   A histogram was constructed for each CP consumer type in each region, using the original before-tax intervals on the *x*-axis and the number of families on the *y*-axis. On the prototype histogram drawn in Figure 2–2, this is shown by the solid vertical lines.

Table 2–3
CES Population Data Used to Construct Histograms

	Individuals	*Families*
1950 Urban	1950 data for total United States.	1950 data for North, South, and West.
1950 Rural	1960 data for total United States.	1960 data for Northeast, North Central, South, and West.
1960 Urban	1960 data for Northeast, North Central, South, and West.	1960 data for Northeast, North Central, South, and West.
1960 Rural	1960 data for North Central and South. (For the Northeast and West, total United States data.)	1960 data for Northeast, North Central, South, and West.

b. A curve was fitted to the histogram.

c. The new income intervals which correspond to the after-tax income intervals of the CES data obtained from the graphs described in Step 1 were plotted along the x-axis (see dotted lines).

d. The number of families in the new income intervals was estimated from the histograms. For example,

income group $1 = C_1$
income group $2 = C_2 + S_2$
income group $3 = C_3 - S_2 + S_3$
etc.

e. The regional total number of families for each income group was used as a control for redistributing the number of families in each state within a before-tax income group corresponding to an after-tax income group of the CES data.

Step 3. The new state CP figures by after-tax income groups for 1950 and 1960 were used to interpolate and extrapolate, using a procedure described later (pp. 47–49), to obtain the 1947, 1958, and 1963 state population figures.

Undistributed Population. For the CP data in 1950, a residual number of families was not counted in any of the income distribution classes. This residual figure for each state and each family type was allocated to the established income classes in proportion to the number of families originally enumerated in the respective income classes.

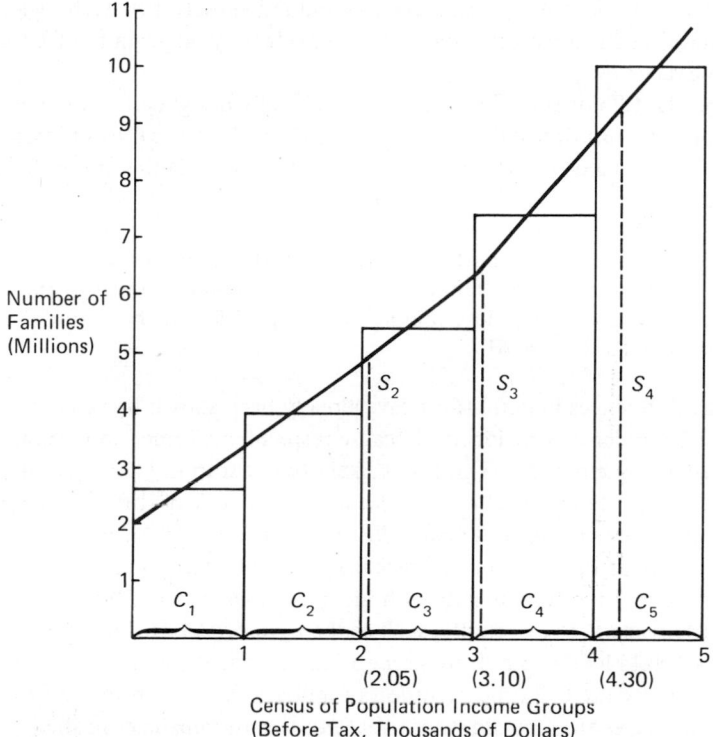

Figure 2–2. Redistribution of Census of Population Data to After-Tax Income Groups.

Alaska and Hawaii. Population figures for these two states were required only for the 1963 calculations. The 1960 CP data for the two states were adjusted from the before-tax to the after-tax income groups by using the proportions developed for the Western region. The overall rate of growth of population between 1960 and 1963 in each respective state was calculated from state figures given in the *U.S. Census of Population, 1960* [142] and from a *Current Population Reports* for 1963 [120]. The state rate of growth of population between 1960 and 1963 was used to augment the 1960 CP figures for all income groups in the respective state since separate figures for 1963 by income distribution group were not available.

Inconsistencies in the CES and CP Definitions of Population. Even after the adjustment of the CP data to an after-tax income base, differences still existed in the CES and CP number of families reported for each income class. The percentage distribution of families by income group from the two sources of data is shown in Table 2–4 for urban families and individuals. For each region, the percentage for the lowest income class is considerably larger in the CP than in the CES data.

Neither the CP nor the CES study was specifically designed to assemble family income distribution statistics. According to the Statistical Evaluation Report of the Bureau of the Budget, the differences in the figures are probably attributable to

... variations in (1) income reporting accuracy; (2) the definition of "income" used; (3) the definition of the "family," i.e., the income-receiving unit; and (4) the time reference used in determining the composition of the "family" and the income reported. [82, p. 6]

Some of the differences in definitions have already been shown in Table 2–1. In general, the CP under-reports income because respondents forget about non-regular, small income receipts. This is less likely to occur in the CES because some internal consistency checks are made, such as a check of the income receipts against the expenditures made. For this reason, the CES tends to account for more of the total income receipts of the population and shows a lower percentage of the respondents with incomes of less than $3000. Other differences between the two studies, such as the time period of the study, the inclusion of a child living away from home as an individual by the CP but as a part of a family by the CES, the exclusion of military families from the CES population universe, etc., certainly contribute to the discrepancies in the percentage distribution; but, according to the report by the Bureau of the Budget, " ... it is not possible to quantify precisely the contribution of each factor separately" [82, p. 6]. Adjustments to the state data to account for the differences were not made in the present study because of time and data limitations.

Consumption Estimates

For this study, the regional data from the 1960 consumer expenditures survey were weighted by the state estimates of population to calculate state personal consumption expenditures. Adjustments had to be made to the consumption data because of differences in the coverages of the consumer expenditures survey and the input-output personal consumption expenditures with which the CES data were to be linked. A comparison of the coverage of the two data sets is given in Table 2–5. The variations in the coverage occur because of the different purposes for which the two sets of data were assembled. For the consumer expenditures study, a cross-section survey is conducted on an average of once a decade and is used to revise the benchmark for the consumer price

Table 2-4

Comparison of 1960 Urban Population Data from the Consumer
Expenditures Survey and the Census of Population

		Individuals		Families	
	Income Group	CES	CP	CES	CP
			(Percent)[a]		
Region 1					
Northeast	Under $1,000	10.0	33.3	0.3	2.9
	$ 1,000–$1,999	28.6	20.3	2.9	4.7
	$ 2,000–$2,999	18.7	16.3	6.1	6.3
	$ 3,000–$3,999	16.8	13.0	9.3	10.4
	$ 4,000–$4,999	13.1	7.4	14.0	14.7
	$ 5,000–$5,999	3.9	3.1	15.1	15.1
	$ 6,000–$9,999	7.6	5.0	38.3	32.2
	$10,000 and over	1.3	1.6	14.0	13.7
		100.0	100.0	100.0	100.0
Region 2					
North Central	Under $1,000	12.6	38.2	0.4	3.3
	$ 1,000–$1,999	27.9	18.6	3.6	4.9
	$ 2,000–$2,999	22.1	14.1	6.7	6.5
	$ 3,000–$3,999	14.8	11.9	9.9	8.9
	$ 4,000–$4,999	11.0	8.3	13.9	14.2
	$ 5,000–$5,999	5.7	4.5	16.2	14.8
	$ 6,000–$9,999	5.2	3.8	38.2	37.3
	$10,000 and over	0.7	0.6	11.1	10.1
		100.0	100.0	100.0	100.0
Region 3					
South	Under $1,000	17.6	42.4	0.9	7.0
	$ 1,000–$1,999	32.5	21.8	8.3	7.9
	$ 2,000–$2,999	20.7	13.2	12.6	10.8
	$ 3,000–$3,999	12.0	9.6	14.4	12.9
	$ 4,000–$4,999	8.3	5.8	14.1	13.8
	$ 5,000–$5,999	4.9	2.9	12.6	12.7
	$ 6,000–$9,999	2.9	3.3	29.2	25.8
	$10,000 and over	1.1	1.0	7.9	9.1
		100.0	100.0	100.0	100.0
Region 4					
West	Under $1,000	7.6	26.7	0.2	3.1
	$ 1,000–$1,999	26.2	25.3	3.7	5.0
	$ 2,000–$2,999	14.7	13.8	6.1	6.4
	$ 3,000–$3,999	19.1	13.4	7.8	8.7
	$ 4,000–$4,999	13.6	8.8	11.4	11.9
	$ 5,000–$5,999	6.3	4.3	14.6	13.7
	$ 6,000–$9,999	11.4	7.5	40.6	36.8
	$10,000 and over	1.1	0.2	15.6	14.4
		100.0	100.0	100.0	100.0

[a]The CP percentages were calculated after the adjustments mentioned on pages 23–28 had been made.

Table 2-5
Summary Description of Consumer Expenditures Statistics

Item	1950 Consumer Expenditures Survey	1960 Consumer Expenditures Survey	Input-Output
Source of data	Sample survey of private consumers, taken in 1950. An extensive survey is taken about every 10 years.	Sample survey of private consumers, taken in 1960–1961. An extensive survey is taken about every 10 years.	Annual publications of various federal government statistical units. Over four-fifths of the personal consumption expenditures data are assembled using commodity flows.
Purpose of assembling data	Used to establish a benchmark for the consumer price index.	Used to establish a benchmark for the consumer price index.	Published by the Office of Business Economics as part of the regular statistical series for the national income accounts.
Coverage of data:	All private consumers, excluding individuals in institutions and military personnel living on base.	All private consumers, excluding individuals in institutions and military personnel living on base.	All consumers in the U.S.: private, military, individuals in institutions.
Regions	Three regions: North, South, West.	Four regions: Northeast, North Central, South, West.	No consistent set of regional figures is collected by the federal government at the present time.
Residence	Covers people living in the United States, but excludes consumer expenditures of foreigners visiting the United States. Groups consumer units by those living in large cities, small cities, and suburbs. Farm consumer units were excluded from the survey.	Covers people living in the United States, but excludes consumer expenditures of foreigners visiting the United States. Groups consumer units by those living in urban, rural nonfarm, and rural farm communities.	Covers people living anywhere in the United States and includes consumer expenditures of foreigners visiting the United States.

Family types	Groups consumer units by individuals and families.	Groups consumer units by individuals and families.	Data are not published by family type.
Income distribution groups[a]	Nine after-tax income groups: Under $ 1,000 $ 1,000–$ 2,000 $ 2,000–$ 3,000 $ 3,000–$ 4,000 $ 4,000–$ 5,000 $ 5,000–$ 6,000 $ 6,000–$ 7,500 $ 7,500–$10,000 $10,000 and over	Ten after-tax income groups: Under $ 1,000 $ 1,000–$ 1,999 $ 2,000–$ 2,999 $ 3,000–$ 3,999 $ 4,000–$ 4,999 $ 5,000–$ 5,999 $ 6,000–$ 7,499 $ 7,500–$ 9,999 $10,000–$14,999 $15,000 and over	Data are not published by income distribution groups.
Consumption categories	Over 40 items; an aggregate set of 13 expenditure categories was also published.	Over 300 items; an aggregate set of 21 expenditure categories was also published.	Eighty-seven industrial sectors for the 1947 and 1958 tables; 367 industrial categories for the 1963 tables.
Prices	Purchaser prices in current dollars.	Purchaser prices in current dollars.	Producer prices in current and in constant 1958 dollars.

[a]The 1950 CP has nine before-tax income groups plus an "unreported" classification, and the 1960 CP has nine before-tax income groups with the "unreported" already distributed within the nine groups. (For the specific income groups, refer to Table 2–2.)

index. No special emphasis is placed in the sampling process upon obtaining accuracy at the regional level.

For the present study, this was the only comprehensive set of regional data available to use for time-series estimates of state personal consumption expenditures. The CES data are available for four geographic regions of the United States (Northeast, North Central, South, and West), two types of consumer units (unrelated individuals and families of two or more persons), three places of residence (urban, rural farm, and rural nonfarm), and ten income groups. Table A-3 in the appendix lists the states within each of the four regions. The CES data are also given by size of family; however, comparable 1950 and 1960 population data could not be easily assembled for this classification. A prototype showing the layout of the CES data is included here as Table 2-6.

From the 1960 CES data, average consumption figures for each of 126 categories were used. In the alignment in Appendix B of this book, a number has been assigned to each of the 379 consumption items listed in the *Survey of Consumer Expenditures, 1960-61* [199]. Not all of the 379 items were used in the computations since many represent subclassifications of a specific expenditures category. Only 126 of them were used. These represent a full coverage of the expenditures included in the survey. Because the consumption data were not as complete as desired, a number of adjustments had to be made to the data during the course of the calculations. Specific problems that were considered included: imported goods; expenditures made by foreigners; out-of-home-city expenditures; incomplete consumer expenditures survey data; transportation, trade, and insurance margins; and imputations.

Imported Goods.   In the national input-output tables, imports of consumer goods are treated in two ways. Some major imports, such as cars and rugs, are included in the purchase figure from the respective industry.[3] Most imports, however, are grouped together, and a single figure is shown for the purchases by consumers from IO-80, Imports. In 1958, the latter sum was $3855 million, or 1.3 percent of the total personal consumption expenditures. No distinction is made in the CES between consumption items that are domestically produced and those that are imported. The procedure, therefore, for the present study was to treat all imports as part of IO-80. The amount of each CES item imported was determined by applying the percentages given in Appendix B of this book to each CES item. Because the percentages were assumed to remain constant from region

---

3.Refer to footnote 6 on page 9 of Nancy Simon's article in the *Survey of Current Business* [74] for the reason car imports were treated in this manner in 1958. Nineteen of the imports, representing $732.7 million of the $6064 million directly allocated imports, that had been transferred to the domestic industry in 1958 (such as passenger cars) were directly allocated in 1963 because of changes in import codes. Since information about this change was not received from the OBE until after the state estimates had been calculated, no adjustments for this could be made.

Table 2-6

Prototype of Consumer Expenditures Data for One Region

Consumer Expenditures Survey Commodity Classification*	Urban		Rural Non-Farm		Rural Farm	
	Individuals	Families	Individuals	Families	Individuals	Families
	10 Income Distribution Groups	10 Income Distribution Groups	10 Income Distribution Groups	10 Income Distribution Groups	10 Income Distribution Groups	10 Income Distribution Groups
1. Food, total							
10. Out of home city, total food							
12. Alcoholic beverages							
13. Tobacco							
16. Rented dwelling, total							
20. Owned dwelling, total							
.							
.							
120. Clothing, clothing materials, & services, total							
137. Footwear, total							
145. Jewelry & watches							
.							
.							
292. Automobile purchase							
293. Automobile operation, total							
294. Gasoline							
295. Motor oil							
301. Insurance							
.							
.							
375. To organizations, total gifts							
379. Value of home-produced food							

*Some of the 379 items, representing either aggregates or subcategories of other CES items, were not used in the calculations. The inclusion or exclusion of an item in the calculation and the sequential number assigned to each CES category are specified in Appendix B.

to region, the state allocation of imports may be fairly unrealistic. No significant distortion should occur for the commodities from which the imported amounts were subtracted, however, as the imported goods represented only a small fraction of total consumer purchases of the items.

Expenditures Made by Foreigners. Figures for IO-85, Rest of the world industry, were calculated separately for each year and added to the final producer price matrix. These figures represent expenditures made by foreigners visiting the United States. Some specific information about the amount and location of expenditures made by Canadians and Mexicans, which represent over 50 percent of total foreign expenditures, is available in publications of the federal government [60; 72; 139]. The expenditures were distributed mainly to states bordering the two countries. Since no information was available as to where other foreigners spend money, the expenditures made by them were distributed to the states in proportion to figures for total receipts of hotels, eating places, car rentals, and amusements. The data were obtained from various census publications (for 1947, [83; 85]; for 1958, [87; 90]; for 1963, [91; 93]).

Out-of-Home-City Expenditures. In a national input-output table, no distinction is required to determine where a consumer lives versus where he spends his money, except for expenditures made abroad, which are a very small proportion of the national total. For a state input-output table, expenditures made by the resident of a given state outside of the home state can be large, and all these expenditures must be allocated to the state where the money is assumed to be actually spent. Five items in the CES are specifically classified as out-of-home-city expenditures and required particular consideration:[4]

    CES   10.00 Food out of home city, total
    CES   32.00 Lodging out of home city, total
    CES 305.00 Public transportation out of home city, total
    CES 346.00 Recreation out of home city
    CES 359.00 All-expense tours

Public transportation out of home city, CES 305.00, was assumed to be purchased in the home city; consequently, the expenditures were allocated in the same way as other consumer expenditures for a given region. The definition of these expenditures given in the CES is: "Out of home city includes fares on trains, intercity buses, planes, and ships, as well as local transportation when away from the home city" [199, p. 160]. Because most of the train, bus, plane, and ship tickets were probably purchased in the home city where a consumer

---

4. It is obvious that a resident of, say, New York State may buy clothing and other items while on a winter vacation in Florida, but no specific information was available from the CES or other sources to adjust for expenditures other than the five listed here.

lived, the direct use of the CES data with no adjustment seemed justified for these items. The expenditures in the portion of the total that includes taxis, city buses, and so on, were certainly incurred out of the home city, but no information was available to separate these expenditures from the others. In any case, the percentage of total out-of-home-city expenditures spent for taxis, etc., was probably quite small.

For all-expense tours, CES 359.00, it was assumed that the expenditures were split among food, lodging, transportation, and entertainment in the same proportion as the national expenditures on the four out-of-home-city items. A direct allocation of 24 percent was made on this basis to IO-65, Transportation & warehousing. The remaining 76 percent of all-expense tours was distributed to input-output industries along with the other out-of-home-city expenditures as shown in Table 2-7.

For the three remaining out-of-home-city expenditures, the total national figure was distributed to states according to Census of Business data by using each state's proportion of the national total of receipts from eating places for CES 10.00, from hotels for CES 32.00, and from amusements for CES 346.00, respectively [83; 85; 87; 90; 91; 93]. Some of these out-of-home-city expenditures may represent money spent abroad, but no special adjustment was made for this because no state data were available.

Incomplete Consumer Expenditures Survey Data. For rural farm individuals in Region 1, Northeast, and Region 4, West, no CES data were available. The average consumption figures for rural farm individuals in the total United States were used, therefore, in the calculations for these regions.

For several income groups in the remaining data, no consumers were included in the consumer expenditures survey. The Census of Population figures, however, do have family units recorded for these income groups. In each instance, the average national vector of consumption expenditures was inserted into the column in the state purchaser price consumption matrices before proceeding with the final calculations. Without this adjustment, the omissions listed in Table 2-8 would have occurred for the rural individuals.

The limited coverage of the sample also created unrealistic estimates in certain cases. For some items of consumption, the regional average consumption expenditure was obtained from a sample of only one consumer unit. Many distortions will then occur. A consumption expenditure, for example, will be recorded either for rented dwellings or owned dwellings, but not for both, and all consumer units within a particular income class are thus assumed to rent (own) their homes, although this would certainly not be true. Also, the average expenditures of the one consumer unit selected in the sample may not be representative of other consumer units in that income group. A few specific examples of some of the larger distortions in consumer expenditures that occurred in the 1960 survey are provided in Table 2-9.

Table 2-7
Distribution of All-Expense Tours

				Input-Output Industry No.	Percent
CES	10.00 plus	32 percent of CES	359.00	1	3.00
				2	4.90
				3	0.80
				10	0.01
				14	87.79
				65	0.20
				69	0.50
				80	2.80
CES	32.00 plus	38 percent of CES	359.00	72	94.50
				77	5.50
CES	346.00 plus	6 percent of CES	359.00	76	100.00

Table 2-8
Omissions from Consumer Expenditures Survey Data for Rural
Individuals

Region	Number of Consumers	Income Group
Northeast	16,971	$ 5,000–$5,999
South	6,822	$10,000 and over
West	17,255	$ 5,000–$5,999
West	5,956	$10,000 and over
Total	47,004	

Table 2-9
Examples of Distortions in Consumer Expenditures Survey Data

Region	Consumer Unit Classification	Income Group	Average Consumption Expenditures
North Central	Single, rural farm	$10,000–$14,999	Contributions and gifts: $8,500
North Central	Single, rural farm	$ 6,000–$ 7,499	Automobile purchase: $2,499
South[a]	Single, rural farm	$ 5,000–$ 5,999	Domestic service: $2,400
West	Family, urban	Under $1,000	Food, total: $1,074

[a]In this case, since there was no other consumer unit in this group for the total United States, the figure for the South distorted the group for the Northeast and West, as well, because the total figure for the United States was used in these regions.

Transportation, Trade, and Insurance Margins.   The transportation, trade, and insurance margins were calculated from the data in the national input-output tables by dividing each margin figure by the purchaser value figure for the respective personal consumption expenditure. The margin values for 1947, 1958, and 1963 are given in Table 2-10. (Refer to the table note for insurance margins.) The data for 1947 were calculated from detailed computer listings of the 450-order 1947 input-output table. In transferring the 450-order 1947 data into an 80-order classification, comparable with the 1958 and 1963 input-output tables, the values of purchases from certain industries had to be split among input-output industries. The splits were applied to all entries for an industry in the row of the input-output table, although, in certain cases, this split resulted in an arbitrary assignment of a value to a 1947 personal consumption expenditures category when a purchase actually did not occur. Thus, in the 1947 personal consumption expenditures data, some purchaser price values and margins were obtained although no value was shown in 1958 or 1963. Since the state figures were to tie in with the published national input-output tables, and since the same splits had been used for the OBE 1947 national table, no adjustments were made for these obvious inconsistencies in the data.

As the personal consumption expenditures figures were transformed from purchaser to producer prices, the problem of allocating the margin figures by region occurred. For this study, the relative margin markup was assumed to be the same in each region; in addition, the purchase of transportation and trade was assumed to occur in the region where the good was bought by the consumer. Both assumptions may be somewhat unrealistic, but a different method of distributing the transportation and trade margins would have required information that was not readily available. For transportation, the regional allocation was not as biased by the procedure used as appears at first glance since over one-third of the total purchase of transportation by consumers was for travel, which had been allocated on a regional basis.

Imputations.   Imputations are made for certain consumer expenditures items in the national income accounts. Table 2-11 provides an idea of the importance of these imputations; it relates the input-output industry affected, the amount of the imputations in 1958, and the percentage the imputation is of the total personal consumption purchases from that input-output industry.

Since for the CES only the actual expenditures of the consumer are obtained, no exact correspondence exists between an imputed item in the national income figures and the expenditures that are recorded in the CES. Special calculations were required to allocate the imputations to the states. A detailed list of the value of the imputations in 1947, 1958, and 1963 is provided in Table 2-12.

Table 2-10
1947, 1958, and 1963 Transportation and Trade Margins

Industry Number	Industry Title	Transportation			Wholesale and Retail Trade		
		1947	1958	1963	1947	1958	1963
1	Livestock & livestock prdts.	.0112	.0205	.0328	.2064	.2193	.2147
2	Other agricultural prdts.	.0906	.1320	.0899	.3030	.3415	.4539
3	Forestry & fishery prdts.	.0088	.0376	.0753	.3006	.5443	.3050
.							
7	Coal mining	.3059	.2140	.2077	.2260	.3331	.3562
8	Crude petro., natural gas	.1306	—	—	.2716	—	—
9	Stone & clay mining	.0765	.3486	.0516	.2866	.1191	—
.							
13	Ordnance & accessories	.0703	.0019	.0046	.3018	.5146	.4462
14	Food & kindred prdts.	.0287	.0266	.0146	.2494	.2837	.3346
15	Tobacco manufactures	.0076	.0151	.0058	.6091	.2735	.3339
16	Fabrics	.0097	.0070	.0065	.2820	.5306	.5308
17	Textile prdts.	.0156	.0142	.0155	.4396	.5022	.4423
18	Apparel	.0089	.0167	.0049	.3374	.3748	.3669
19	Misc. textile prdts.	.0093	.0109	.0091	.3768	.4418	.4169
20	Lumber & wood prdts.	.0856	.0687	.0374	.2451	.3056	.3030
21	Wooden containers	.0674	—	—	.4981	—	—
22	Household furniture	.0274	.0196	.0190	.3842	.4068	.3913
23	Other furniture	.0294	.0134	.0591	.1652	.4802	.4732
24	Paper & allied prdts.	.0263	.0406	.0189	.4034	.3800	.3376
25	Paperboard containers	.0290	.0318	.0129	.3889	.1118	.3533
26	Printing & publishing	.0120	.0366	.0117	.2218	.3042	.3092
27	Chemicals, selected prdts.	.0488	.0559	.0506	.3326	.2404	.3572
28	Plastics & synthetics	.0126	.0282	.0286	.3740	.2356	.2274
29	Drugs & cosmetics	.0264	.0221	.0205	.3366	.4068	.4183
30	Paint & allied prdts.	.0203	.0178	.0190	.2758	.5018	.4447
31	Petroleum, related inds.	.0655	.0352	.0420	.4802	.4612	.4792
32	Rubber, misc. plastics	.0159	.0168	.0163	.3657	.4188	.3729
33	Leather tanning & prdts.	.0085	—	.0076	.4821	—	—
34	Footwear, leather prdts.	.0095	.0143	.0173	.3333	.4141	.3988
35	Glass & glass prdts.	.0333	.0286	.0341	.4285	.5217	.3964
36	Stone & clay prdts.	.0309	.0406	.0403	.4250	.4194	.3802
37	Primary iron, steel mfr.	.0434	.0256	.0362	.2563	.4246	.3362
38	Primary nonferrous mfr.	.0165	.0184	.0111	.4037	.4003	.3128

39	Metal containers	.0282	—	—	.3643	—	—
40	Fabricated metal prdts.	.0190	.0169	.0305	.4152	.2737	.1744
41	Screw mach. prdts., etc.	.0133	.0190	.0121	.4722	.2963	.4205
42	Other fab. metal prdts.	.0093	.0150	.0153	.4286	.4447	.3801
43	Engines & turbines	.0180	.0112	.0210	.3555	.3030	.1337
44	Farm mach. & equip.	.0315	.0238	.0223	.3069	.2304	.2572
45	Construction mach. & equip.	.0227	—	—	.3612	—	—
.							
47	Metalworking mach. & equip.	.0217	.0136	.0057	.3075	.3606	.2074
48	Special mach. & equip.	.0178	.0109	.0052	.3595	.3465	.3550
49	General mach. & equip.	.0145	—	—	.4688	—	—
50	Machine shop prdts.	.0145	.0141	.0212	.4690	—	.5160
51	Office, computing machines	.0118	.0229	.0061	.4017	.4723	.4644
52	Service industry machines	.0205	.0211	.0149	.4714	.4268	.3219
53	Elect. transmission equip.	.0112	.0184	.0146	.5222	.2437	.2022
54	Household appliances	.0203	.0187	.0215	.4143	.3764	.3720
55	Electric lighting equip.	.0142	.0122	.0151	.4435	.2855	.3582
56	Radio, TV, etc. equip.	.0118	.0131	.0195	.4488	.4045	.3206
57	Electronic components	.0131	.0148	.0042	.4305	.4501	.3457
58	Misc. electrical mach.	.0138	.0204	.0122	.4236	.2946	.3915
59	Motor vehicles, equip.	.0200	.0096	.0196	.3138	.1758	.1795
60	Aircraft & parts	.0096[a]	.0098	.0001	.3553	.2790	.0703
61	Other transport. equip.	.0155	.0174	.0220	.3139	.3015	.2327
62	Professional, scien. instru.	.0078	.0125	.0044	.4999	.4375	.4885
63	Medical, photo. equip.	.0066	.0175	.0031	.5676	.6230	.6094
64	Misc. manufacturing	.0104		.0102	.4545	.4200	.4361
.							
80	Imports	.0002	.0312	.0330	.0103	.2765	.3258
.							
83	Scrap & used goods	—	—	—	1.0000[b]	1.0088	1.1171

NOTE: The ratios were calculated by dividing the margin figure by the value of the personal consumption expenditures figure in *purchaser* prices. An insurance margin existed only for IO–80. Since the ratio for 1958 was .0033, the same ratio was used for 1947 because no data existed for 1947. For 1963, the ratio was .0012.

[a]The 1958 transportation margin ratio was used for 1947 because precise information was lacking in the 1947 study.

[b]Since no producer value figure existed for IO–83, the entire purchaser price value was assigned to the wholesale and retail trade margin.

SOURCES: The 1947 margins were calculated from the detailed 450-order 1947 computer listings [194]. The 1958 and 1963 margins were obtained from OBE unpublished data that supplement the published 1958 and 1963 input-output tables.

Table 2-11
1958 Imputations for Consumer Expenditures

Input-Output Industry No.	Imputations	1958 Value (billions)	Percent of Total PCE Purchase
1, 2, 3, 14, 16, 18, 34, 71	Value of food, clothing, and housing furnished in kind to government (including military) and business employees	$ 2.0	–
1, 2, 14, 20	Food and fuel produced and consumed on farms	1.5	–
70	Services rendered to individuals and nonprofit institutions by financial intermediaries (except insurance companies) without explicit charge	4.1	34.5
71	Space rental value of owner-occupied housing (including farms) and institutional buildings	29.0	72.6

Services Furnished Without Payment by Financial Intermediaries. These services consist of the handling, storage, and protection of money by banks and other financial institutions for their customers. Although the services are provided free (in return for use of a client's money), an imputation for the productive service is made in the national income accounts and appears as part of the purchase by consumers from IO-70, Finance & insurance. In 1958, the imputation represented more than one-third (34.5 percent) of the total purchases by consumers from this industry, and commercial banks comprised almost three-quarters of the total financial intermediary imputation. Personal income was chosen as a proxy to distribute the national total to the states for each of the three years.

Food Consumed on Farms. The national imputation was distributed using state data estimated from CES 379.00, Value of home-produced food, for each of the three years (see Appendix B).

Rental Value of Owner-Occupied Dwellings. The national imputation was distributed using state data estimated from CES 20.00, Owned dwelling, total, and CES 26.00, Owned vacation home, cabin, etc., total. These totals consisted of the interest, taxes, and property insurance paid by home owners and were assumed to be at least partially representative of the rental value of the owner-occupied housing (see Appendix B).

Food, Clothing, and Housing in Kind. For certain workers, employers furnish food, clothing, and housing. These payment-in-kind arrangements are particularly common for the military, restaurant, hotel, hospital, private school,

Table 2–12

Value of Imputed Personal Consumption Expenditures (millions of dollars)

Imputation	1947	1958	1963
Space rental value, total	$9,700	$29,000	$39,900
Owner-occupied nonfarm dwellings	8,400	26,800	37,100
Institutional buildings	200	700	1,100
Owner-occupied farm dwellings	1,100	1,500	1,700
Food and fuel consumed on farms, total	$2,800	$ 1,500	$ 1,000
Food	2,560	1,410	952
Fuel	240	90	48
Services furnished without payment by financial intermediaries, total	$1,474	$ 4,075	$ 6,229
Commercial banks	1,149	2,991	4,414
Savings and loan	120	576	1,117
Mutual savings	150	274	361
Credit unions	14	120	206
Finance, n.e.c.	41	114	131
Food, clothing, and housing in kind, total	$1,653	$ 1,946	$ 2,050
Food furnished employees			
Domestic help	305	512	499
Military	413	509	464
Services	205	292	388
Eating and drinking places	288	286	334
Prisons and government hospitals	72	157	164
Water transportation	45	0	0
Standard clothing issued military personnel	229	58	64
Employees' lodging	96	132	137

SOURCE: U.S. Department of Commerce, *The National Income and Product Accounts of the United States, 1929–1965* [168, p. 153] and unpublished data from the Office of Business Economics.

and domestic help employees. The food imputation was assigned to four input-output industries, IO-1, IO-2, IO-3, and IO-14; the clothing imputation to three, IO-16, IO-18, and IO-34; and the lodging imputation to one, IO-71.

Food. This imputation was divided into six subcategories: (1) Military food was distributed to states on the basis of military payrolls by state for 1958 and 1963, using the 1959 data for both 1947 and 1958. (2) For domestic help, personal income data were used for the state distributions. (3) The payrolls for eating places were used to distribute the imputed food expenditures for those employees on the assumption that eating places comprised the largest share of the eating- and drinking-place imputation. (4) For hospitals, data on the number of government hospital beds were used for 1947, while for 1958 and

1963, the costs of administration and other benefits of the Veterans Administration were used, as it appeared that a sizable amount of the total was for medical expenses. Since no breakdown was available at the national level between hospitals and prisons, the latter component was ignored. (5) The national imputed value for water transportation was only $45 million and was given only for 1947; consequently, the figure was added on to the hotel portion of the services figure. (6) The services value was separated at the national level into hotels, private hospitals, and private schools on the basis of employment data [192] ; and the figures for these three components were distributed to the states using payrolls for hotels, number of hospital beds for private hospitals, and the payrolls of institution staff for the private school portion, respectively.

Clothing. The total amount was for clothing of military personnel and was distributed according to the military payroll figures.

Lodging. The national figure was distributed to the states using the same procedure as described above for the services portion of the food imputation.

The allocation factor and specific source used for each of the individual imputations discussed above are listed in Table 2–13.

Data Requirements and Computation Procedures

The basic assumption in using the CES data for the present study was that the average consumption expenditures of a particular type of family unit for specific consumer goods do not vary over time nor among states within a given region. Variations in the estimates of consumer expenditures from year to year or from state to state within a region were assumed to occur from changes in the number of families within the separate income groups.

The transformation of the 126 CES categories to the 80-order input-output classification was accomplished by using the alignment given in Appendix B. Because of time limitations when the alignment was made, the same ratios, calculated from the 1958 data, were used to convert the CES categories to input-output industries for all three years. The total expenditures for each commodity by consumers within a state was calculated by multiplying the average consumption expenditures of each income group within a *region* by the estimated number of consumer units in the respective groups in the *state*. The state estimates were obtained both for urban and rural consumer units (rural includes the CES rural farm and rural nonfarm groups).

The total estimated consumption expenditures for each state were then adjusted from purchaser to producer prices. Finally, the discrepancy between the estimated total consumption expenditures for a particular commodity and the actual figure shown in the input-output table was distributed to the states by adjusting the original estimated producer price figure for each state by a uniform percentage factor. The assumption was that if the total consumption expendi-

Table 2-13
Allocation Factors and Specific Sources Used to Allocate Imputed Values

Imputation	Allocation Factor	Source		
		1947	1958	1963
Rental value of owner-occupied dwellings	CES 20.00 and CES 26.00		a	a
Food consumed on farms	CES 379.00		a	a
Services furnished without payment by financial intermediaries	Personal income	[129, t. 322, p. 284]	[132, t. 408, p. 312]	[136, t. 457, p. 332]
Food furnished employees				
Military	Military payroll	[133, t. 319, p. 258]	[133, t. 319, p. 258]	[135, t. 344, p. 259]
Domestic help	Personal income	[129, t. 322, p. 284]	[132, t. 408, p. 312]	[136, t. 457, p. 332]
Eating and drinking places	Payrolls in eating places	[84]	[88]	[92]
Hospitals	Costs of administration and other benefits of the Veterans Administration			
	Number of government hospital beds (added to services)	[129, t. 94, p. 83]	[132, t. 330, p. 253]	[136, t. 375, p. 273]
Water transportation		—	—	—
Services				
Hotels	Payrolls	[86]	[90]	[94[b]]
Private hospitals	Number of hospital beds	[127, t. 94, p. 83]	[132, t. 92, p. 77]	[136, t. 92, p. 75]
Private schools	Payrolls of instructional staff	[130, t. 143, p. 121]	[134, t. 164, p. 128]	[135, t. 168, p. 127]
	(Number of teachers in private schools multiplied by Salary of public school teachers)	[130, t. 140, p. 119]	[134, t. 162, p. 127]	[135, t. 166, p. 126]

[a] See Appendix B of this book.
[b] Payrolls of motels were included for 1963.

tures was underestimated (overestimated), the bias occurred in the same relative magnitude in all states. For example, in 1958 the estimated national total for tobacco expenditures was 32 percent less than the figure shown in the 1958 input-output table. Since consumers are known to underestimate their tobacco expenditures, a uniform 32 percent increase was made to each state figure for those expenditures. Thus, the final state estimates were forced to be consistent with the figures in the national input-output table. The procedure was necessarily an arbitrary one, since more precise information on regional differences in such discrepancies was not available. A thorough discussion of the variations that occur at the national level between the consumer survey and the national income figures is presented by Helen H. Lamale [57, pp. 136-149].

The basic steps used to transform the regional data published in the CES to the final input-output state consumption estimates are simple, but the actual computations became complicated because both the population and the consumption data required the adjustments discussed earlier in this chapter before they formed a relatively comparable coverage. Some, but not all, of the discrepancies in the figures arise from inaccurate information provided by consumers and recorded in the survey. Also, because the various government agencies collect the data for different purposes and use dissimilar methods of obtaining the data, the results are not always directly compatible. For this reason, problems always arise in attempting to integrate cross-section and time-series consumption expenditures data. Some of these problems are discussed in a paper written by Lester D. Taylor [77]. The last part of this section describes in explicit detail the nature of the data and the procedures used to estimate the state consumption expenditures for 1947, 1958, and 1963.

Data Requirements

The data are listed in this section according to different matrices used in the computations.

$^{CES}_{60}C$ rectangular matrix, 126 x 60, for each of 4 regions. Each element gives the 1960 CES average consumption expenditures for one of the 126 consumption categories in one of the 60 income distribution groups.

$^{CES}_{60}\hat{F}$ diagonal matrix, 60 x 60, for each of 4 regions giving the number of 1960 CES consumer units in each of the 60 income distribution groups.

$^{CES}_{60}E$ rectangular matrix, 126 x 60, for each of 4 regions. The matrix is calculated by multiplying each element in a specific column of the average consumption expenditures matrix, $^{CES}_{60}C$, by the respective number of consumer units from the matrix $^{CES}_{60}\hat{F}$.

λ rectangular matrix, 86 x 126, containing a complete alignment of each of the 126 CES items to the respective input-output industry. In some cases, the CES item is split among several industries. The alignment and the percentage splits are listed in Appendix B of this book.

$_t\gamma$ rectangular matrices, 86 x 3, of transportation, trade, and insurance margins, one for each year t calculated from the 1947, 1958, and 1963 personal consumption expenditures data in the respective input-output tables. The margins are given in Table 2-10.

$^{CP}_{tj}F$ rectangular matrices, 32 x 49 for 1947 and 1958 and 32 x 51 for 1963, one for each of the j states and for each of the t years, containing the number of families in each of 32 income classes: 8 income distribution classes for each of 2 places of residence (urban, rural) and 2 family types (unrelated individuals and families of 2 or more persons), adjusted to an after-tax base. The 49 columns represent the 48 states plus the District of Columbia; the 51 columns include Alaska and Hawaii.

$MEDY_t$ a scalar, giving the median income in year t for one of the four major categories of families (urban and rural cross-classified by families and individuals).

Specific Procedures Used for the Calculations

The transformation of the CES average consumption expenditures figures for each region into state personal consumption expenditures data for the 80-order input-output classification proceeded in seven basic steps. The step-by-step procedure is outlined below:

Step 1. The number of family units was estimated by state for each of the eight income distribution groups within each of the four population categories (families and individuals cross-classified by urban and rural). For the calculations, the 1950 and 1960 population data published in the *U.S. Census of Population, 1960* [142] were used after the adjustments mentioned earlier in this chapter had been made. A modified version of a technique being developed at the U.S. Bureau of the Census by Mitsuo Ono was employed [66]. For each of the four population categories within each state, the basic assumption was made that the relative distribution of income around the median income remains stable over time. The same step-by-step procedure described below was used for each population group during the calculations, with the population separated into the eight income distribution groups given in Table 2-2.

    a.   Calculate the annual rate of growth, r, of median income, $MEDY$, over the period t to $t + n$.

$$\log r = \frac{\log MEDY_{t+n} - \log MEDY_t}{(t+n) - t} \tag{2.1}$$

    b.   Apply the rate of growth of median income to an original set of income intervals to obtain the income intervals for which the relative distribution holds in the future year.

    c.   Calculate the relative distribution of family units for the original set of income intervals.

    d.   Multiply the percentages obtained in (c) above by the total number of consumer units for the respective family type in a state to obtain for that state the total population in the given year in each of the eight separate income distribution groups.

Over the given time period, all incomes were assumed to grow by the rate r, or, in other words, the relative distribution of income was assumed to be the same in the two time periods, although the actual income intervals, in general, expanded when a projection was made to a future year or contracted when the calculations were made for a year in the past. The procedure can be illustrated by a simple example, as given in Table 2-14.

For the example, the rate of growth of median income is assumed to have been calculated as 50 percent. The base-year relative income distribution is shown in the first column of the table. By applying the rate of growth, 50, to the incomes bordering the intervals (10, 20, and 30), these incomes were calculated to be 50 percent higher (15, 30, and 45, respectively) in the projected year. For example, 20 percent of the family units were in the interval 0–15 in the projected year whereas the same relative number were in the 0–10 income interval in the base year. The next step was to calculate the percent in each original income interval. Those percentages are given in the third column. In the last step, these final percentages were multiplied by the projected number of total units in that family type, in this case, 1000, to obtain the fourth column of figures.

The accuracy of this method was checked by taking 1949 income distribution data for selected states and making projections to 1959; then, the 1959 projected figures were compared with actual 1959 income distribution data. An example of this check for the state of Illinois is given in Table 2-15. The projection is the least accurate for the highest income group. Some research was being undertaken in the summer of 1970 at the Bureau of the Census in cooperation with the Regional Economics Division of the OBE to improve the

Table 2-14
Distribution of Number of Families by Income Intervals

Original		Projected	
Percentage Distribution	Income Intervals	Percentage Distribution	Number of Families
20	0–10	13	130
35	10–20	19	190
25	20–30	23	230
20	30 and over	45	450
100		100	1000

Table 2-15
Test Results: Cumulative Income Distribution of Urban Families in Illinois (percent)

Income (less than)	1949 CP	1959 Estimate	1959 CP
$ 1,000	8.4	3.4	3.3
2,000	16.0	10.5	7.7
3,000	32.2	14.7	13.4
4,000	58.4	21.9	21.3
5,000	74.4	32.3	33.8
6,000	83.8	43.3	47.5
10,000	96.6	78.6	87.2

accuracy for the highest income groups, but time limitations prevented incorporating any new, untested techniques into the present set of calculations. The accuracy of the estimates depends, of course, upon the stability of the relative distribution of income around the median income. (In the Ono study, mean income was used in place of median income, but these data were not available for all states and all population categories.) For the method to be appropriate, the income intervals should be kept small. The intervals, however, expand as projections are made further and further into the future; accordingly, the projection method begins to break down for long-term projections. In the present study, however, the 1950 distributions were extrapolated to 1947, and the 1960 distributions were extrapolated to 1958 and to 1963; therefore, a relatively small time period was involved for each of the three sets of estimates, and the population estimates were assumed to be reasonably accurate.

Step 2. The CES average consumption figures were aggregated into income distribution groups and family classes that were comparable with the CP data.

a. The CES average consumption expenditures data within each of the 60
    income distribution categories, shown in Table 2–6, were multiplied
    by the CES number of consumer units within the respective income
    distribution group to obtain CES total expenditures data which could
    then be aggregated to the desired income distribution and residence
    groupings:

$$\underset{60}{CES}E \;=\; \underset{60}{CES}C \;*\; \underset{60}{CES}\hat{F}$$

$\quad$ (126 x 60) $\quad$ (126 x 60) $\quad$ (60 x 60) $\hfill$ (2.2)

b. For comparability with the CP data, the total expenditures, $\underset{60}{CES}E$, and
    the consumer unit, $\underset{60}{CES}\hat{F}$, matrices were aggregated to eight income
    groups and two places of residence, urban and rural. The latter residence
    was a combination of the CES rural farm and rural nonfarm groups. The
    two matrices for each region now were dimensioned (126 x 32) and
    (32 x 32), respectively.

c. Each element in a specific column of the aggregated CES consumption
    expenditures matrix was divided by the CES number of consumer units
    for the respective income group to obtain again the CES average
    consumption expenditures figure, now representing 32 rather than 60
    groups of consumers. (To simplify notations, the matrix $\underset{60}{CES}F$ will be
    used to represent a matrix with the number of consumer units for the
    particular income group entered in each cell in a column, and the $\div$ will
    be used to represent a term-by-term division of one matrix by another.)
    The equation is:

$$\underset{60}{CES}C \;=\; \underset{60}{CES}E \;\div\; \underset{60}{CES}F$$

$\quad$ (126 x 32) $\quad$ (126 x 32) $\quad$ (126 x 32) $\hfill$ (2.2a)

Step 3. The CES average consumption figures were transformed to the
IOPCE classification for each of the three years:

$$\underset{t}{IO}C \;=\; \lambda \;*\; \underset{60}{CES}C \qquad t = 1947, 1958, 1963$$

$\quad$ (86 x 32) $\quad$ (86 x 126) (126 x 32) $\hfill$ (2.3)

Steps 2 and 3 were repeated for each of the four regions.

Step 4. The input-output average consumption expenditures figures
obtained for each of the four regions were multiplied by the population figures
for the states in that region to obtain a matrix for each state of total consump-

tion expenditures.[5] (The CP number of families for each year is obtained using the method described under Step 1 above.) The equation is:

$$\underset{tj}{^{IO}}E \;\; = \;\; \underset{t}{^{IO}}C \;\; * \;\; \underset{tj}{^{CP}}\hat{F} \qquad t = 1947, 1958, 1963$$
$$\text{(86 x 32)} \qquad \text{(86 x 32)} \quad \text{(32 x 32)} \quad j = 1, \ldots, 49 \qquad\qquad (2.4)$$

Step 5. The figures in each row of the individual state consumption expenditures matrices were summed to provide the total consumption expenditures by state on each item for the particular year. The row totals from each state were used to form the columns in a new matrix S', which contained the estimated consumption expenditures by state:

$$\underset{t}{^{IO}}S' \;\; = \;\; \sum_{k=1}^{32} \underset{tj}{^{IO}}E_k \qquad\qquad t = 1947, 1958, 1963$$
$$\qquad\qquad j = 1, \ldots, 49$$
$$\text{(86 x 49)} \qquad\quad \text{(86 x 32)} \qquad\qquad\qquad\qquad (2.5)$$

Step 6. The transportation, trade, and insurance margin operator matrix, γ, for each year was used to convert the matrix of state consumption expenditures from purchaser (pu) to producer (pr) prices:[6]

$$\underset{t}{^{IO}}S' \;(\$pr) \;= \;\; \underset{t}{\gamma} \quad * \quad \underset{t}{^{IO}}S' \;(\$pu) \qquad t = 1947, 1958, 1963$$
$$\text{(86 x 49)} \quad\;\; \text{(86 x 86)} \qquad \text{(86 x 49)} \qquad\qquad\qquad (2.6)$$

Step 7. Each row of the estimated state expenditures matrix was adjusted by a factor, given in the matrix ϕ. The result was matrix S, where the row sum was consistent with the personal consumption expenditures figures in the national input-output table for the respective year.

$$\underset{t}{^{IO}}S(\$pr) \;\; = \;\; \underset{t}{\phi} \quad * \quad \underset{t}{^{IO}}S'(\$pr) \qquad t = 1947, 1958, 1963$$
$$\text{(86 x 49)} \qquad \text{(86 x 86)} \qquad \text{(86 x 49)} \qquad\qquad\qquad (2.7)$$

---

5. In each year, the District of Columbia was counted as a state. For 1963, Alaska and Hawaii were included in the calculations, but, to avoid confusing notations in the equations, the number 49 is used throughout this part of the chapter to represent the number of states.

6. The actual transportation and trade margin figures in matrix γ, described under Data Requirements and shown in Table 2–10, were manipulated from the matrix dimensioned (86 x 3) to a matrix dimensioned (86 x 86) in order to calculate the producer price data correctly. Essentially, the latter matrix was designed to reduce each purchaser price figure to producer prices and at the same time to augment the figure in the transportation and trade rows to include the margins. For personal consumption expenditures, each column sum of the purchaser price matrix must exactly equal the corresponding column sum of the producer price matrix.

The final result was a set of state consumption estimates in producer prices for each of the three years. These data are listed in the accompanying statistical appendix.

For eight industries in the 1947 state allocations, no distribution was made in the initial set of calculations just described because the CES/IO alignment was based on the 1958 input-output figures, and no consumption entries occurred for these industries in the table. The 1947 national figures for the industries were therefore allocated to the states using the percentage distribution either of the 1947 state output figures [70] or of the estimated state personal consumption expenditures for a related industry. The data for two industries were allocated according to outputs: IO-8, Crude petroleum & natural gas (this figure represents sales by a few companies directly to final consumers) and IO-67, Radio & TV broadcasting (this figure represents studio fees, parking fees, and miscellaneous outputs of the industry which were allocated to households in the 1947 table).

For the remaining six industries, the state allocation was made according to the distribution of the estimated state personal consumption expenditures for a related industry. The probable reason for the 1947 entry is given under the comments in Table 2–16. If no explanation can be given for the entry, the word "None" appears; if, when the 1947 input-output table was recently revised, the entry was created by the application of industrial conversion splits to all components of an industry, the comment "Created by revisions to the 1947 table" appears.

Conclusion

The personal consumption expenditures by state could obviously have been estimated using data and procedures different from those described in this chapter. One alternative approach would have been to assemble state data for each expenditure item from statistics published in various sources, a method that was required for some of the other final demand components. At first glance, individual allocations of each item appear to be an easier, and perhaps even a more accurate means of obtaining the state personal consumption estimates. Experience with the data assembly for other final demand components, however, indicates that the approach requires considerable perusal of the litera-ture for the "best" allocation series, diligent investigation of each data source to ascertain the actual composition of the statistics, and numerous adjustments of the data to make them comparable definitionally with the national income accounts. For these reasons, the compilation of state data using this approach would probably have required as much time as the method actually used, without providing a more accurate set of estimates. But alternative methods and data sources should certainly continue to be considered, especially in view of

Table 2-16
Special Distributions Used for 1947 State Allocations

Input-Output Industry Data to Be Allocated	Input-Output Industry Distribution Used for Allocation	Comments
21 Wooden containers	20 Lumber & wood products, except containers	None
33 Leather tanning & industrial leather products	34 Footwear & other leather products	None
39 Metal containers	42 Other fabricated metal products	None
45 Construction, mining, oil field machinery & equipment	44 Farm machinery & equipment	Created by revisions to the 1947 table
49 General industrial machinery & equipment	54 Household appliances	Created by revisions to the 1947 table but could also represent purchases of appliance parts
50 Machine shop products	75 Automobile repair & services	Represents car-owner purchases of repair parts

the limitations of the approach used in this study. It should be noted, however, that H. Albert Green advocated this same methodology to estimate personal consumption expenditures by county [48].

The noncomparabilities in coverage of the population, the CES, and the input-output data have been cited throughout the chapter. Wherever possible, given the data and time limitations, adjustments were made to the three sets of statistics to improve their comparability. The most important problems are now reviewed. For the state population data, two problems exist. First, the necessary adjustment of the data from a before-tax to an after-tax income base had to be made using regional, rather than state, controls. Second, the adjusted 1950 and 1960 state population data were employed as a base distribution to provide 1947, 1958, and 1963 estimates; but the calculation procedure used probably does not obtain very accurate estimates for the highest income class. For the present study, the inaccuracies may be lessened because the distributions had to be extrapolated for, at most, three years. An improved method should be found to estimate the number of families in the highest income class.

The consumption estimates for all three years could be improved if the appropriate data can be found. For each consumption item, expenditures by foreigners should be excluded from the IOPCE data and allocated separately to the states. Special adjustments should also be made for expenditures by private organizations. Both of these are included in the IOPCE figures but are not accounted for in the CES data. In addition, consideration should be given to a means of adjusting the regional average expenditures for those items where considerable variations may occur among the states within a given region. For the 1947 set of consumption estimates, two additional factors may contribute to any inaccuracies. First, the consumption alignment between the CES and the IOPCE data was constructed using 1958 information. The percentage splits for 1947 may vary significantly. Second, the average consumption expenditures were for 1960, but even within a given income class, these expenditures certainly changed between 1947 and 1960. Additional study is required to ascertain whether or not either of these two factors is important in terms of the present set of estimates.

During this study, two major attempts were made to determine the accuracy of the state estimates.[7] The first was a review of the entire estimation procedure, but, in particular, of the assumption that significant variations in average personal consumption expenditures occur among income classes and from region to region. If the assumption does not hold, the amount of detail could be reduced for future studies. Statistical tests on the CES data, however, were not completed because of time limitations. The second was an effort to compare for

---

7. The first was undertaken by Paul G. Munyon during the summer of 1969 before a completely revised set of state estimates was available. The second was undertaken by Frans J. Kok during the summer of 1970 with the revised set of estimates.

each state the total of the personal consumption expenditures estimates with disposable income, the only set of official state data presently available as a measure of consumption. When the estimate was less than disposable income, the difference was assumed to be personal saving. The consumption estimates, however, cannot be directly compared with disposable income because the first measures total expenditures for personal consumption in the state, regardless of where the consumer lives, whereas the disposable income figures are for income accruing to residents of a state. For a few states, therefore, the personal consumption expenditures exceeded the disposable income figures. This occurred, for example, in Florida, but it seemed reasonable, because the tremendous number of visitors would certainly augment the personal consumption expenditures in the state. For other states, the comparisons were less conclusive and indicated the need to adjust the two sets of data to a compatible residential measure.

Because personal consumption expenditures comprise such a large percentage of the total GNP, additional investigations should be conducted to determine whether or not the state estimates are accurate, and if not, to establish an improved method of estimating the state data. The state estimates that have been assembled for each of the three years are contained in the accompanying statistical appendix.

3

Gross Private Domestic Investment

Carolyn W. Anderson

Gross private domestic investment is usually separated into two major components: gross private capital formation and net change in inventory. In the national income accounts, the gross private capital formation component is defined to include private purchases of durable capital goods (machinery and equipment with life spans greater than one year) and of new construction. Net purchases of used plant and equipment, as well as miscellaneous overhead and installation charges, are also included. Because these figures are gross measures of capital formation, there is no deduction for depreciation. Capital formation by the public sector is included in the government final demand components and is not considered in this chapter.

The net inventory change component of gross private domestic investment represents the overall, or net, change in the physical volume of inventories for the years under study. Again, changes in government stockpiles of goods are not estimated, as they are included in the government sector of final demand.

In this chapter, the methods used to estimate the two components of gross private domestic investment by state for the years 1947, 1958, and 1963 are described. The chapter is divided into two sections corresponding to the two components, and each of the two sections can be read as a separate entity. For each of the three years, the estimated state final demand figures are listed separately for gross private capital formation and for net change in inventories in the accompanying statistical appendix.

Gross Private Capital Formation

Vectors of gross private capital formation (GPCF) show how much capital was produced and sold by each industry, that is, they show the types of capital goods consumed in a given year. For obtaining state GPCF vectors, the ideal data would provide the capital technology of each industry, that is, the types of capital purchased by each producing industry in the state. These industry vectors would then be summed to obtain total gross private capital formation in the state. Rather than giving detail on the kinds of plant and equipment required to produce the output of each particular industry, however, available state data on capital formation are limited to figures on total expenditures by industry on plant and equipment.

57

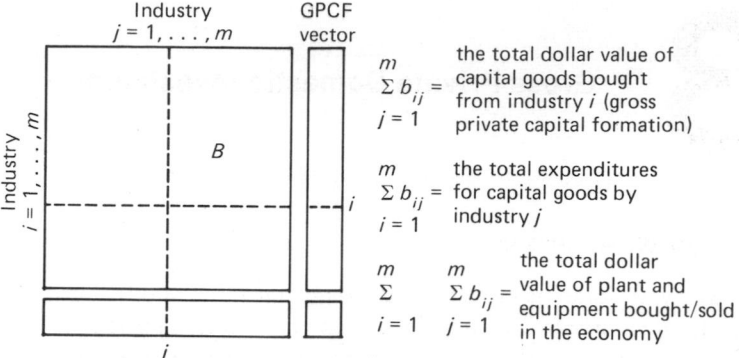

Figure 3-1. National Capital Flow Matrix.

A General Outline of Procedure

The method used to estimate state gross private capital formation was based on the assumption that the capital technology for each state is the same as the capital technology shown in the national capital flow matrix. In the first part of this section, national and state capital flow matrices are defined and a general description is given of the methodology used to construct state capital flow matrices employing state capital expenditures figures together with the national capital flow matrix. The second part gives a detailed account of the data sources and methodology used to construct state estimates of gross private capital formation for each of the three years.

The National Capital Flow Matrix. A national capital flow matrix is an input-output matrix dealing exclusively with plant and equipment sold on capital account. A given industry produces a certain amount of capital, keeping some for its own use and selling the rest to other industries. At the same time, this industry also buys capital goods from other industries. The national capital flow matrix, *B,* shown in Figure 3-1, is an industry-by-industry matrix. Because the same industries are listed for the rows and the columns, it is a square matrix. Each element, b_{ij}, of the matrix shows the dollar value of capital produced by industry i and bought on capital account by industry j in a given year.[1] The sales on capital account by a particular industry are shown along a given row of the national capital flow matrix, while the corresponding column of the matrix represents purchases of different types of capital goods by that industry. In a national capital flow matrix, the row sums form a column vector indicating how much of the total amount of capital produced in the nation is bought *from* each

---

1. Capital flow matrices can also be given in physical units. In this study, all capital flows referred to are in dollar values.

industry in a given year. This vector shows total national gross private capital formation. In contrast, the column sums of the national capital flow matrix show how much of the total amount of capital produced in the economy is bought *by* each industry on capital account.

State Capital Flow Matrices.   A capital flow matrix for a state is analogous to the national capital flow matrix, with an important qualification. Although the columns of the state capital flow matrix give figures for the purchases of capital by each industry in the state, the rows represent the industry which produces this capital regardless of the state in which it is produced. Thus, the state matrix provides information on the state in which purchases of capital goods are made, but not on the state(s) in which these capital goods are produced. The rows of a state capital flow matrix, then, sum to a column vector of state gross private capital formation, showing how much of the total national final demand for capital goods originates in that state. If these state final demands are added together, the total is the national gross private capital formation vector. Figure 3-2 shows the relationship between the state and national capital flow matrices.

As shown in Figure 3-2, the data sources used in this study provide information on the *total* amount of capital purchased by a particular industry in a given state. Preferably, the total capital purchases for each industry would be separated into expenditures for each particular type of plant, machinery, or equipment, thus giving the industries from which the various capital goods were purchased; but the available state data generally only separate total expenditures for new machinery and equipment from total expenditures for new plant.

General Methodology for Constructing State Capital Flow Matrices.   For each of the three years, 1947, 1958, and 1963, the overall method used to construct capital flow matrices for the states was the same. The total of new plant purchased by industries in each state could be obtained as separate information. This total is a lump sum, that is, the plant figure is not separated according to type of plant purchased, nor are the purchasing industries given by state. Since new plant is sold by only one industry, IO-11,[2] New construction, the estimated state total for plant purchased was inserted into the respective state vector of estimated gross private capital formation. In the national capital flow matrix, row 11 represents the new construction industry; therefore, when row 11 is removed, the column sums of the matrix show purchases of equipment only. All references to capital flow matrices in the remaining pages of this part will be to the adjusted matrices (with row 11 removed) and may be thought of as matrices with elements of "equipment flows."

Because no consistent sets of information were available on how industries

---

2. IO-11 refers to the 80-order input–output classification of the Office of Business Economics, given in Appendix A, Table A-1.

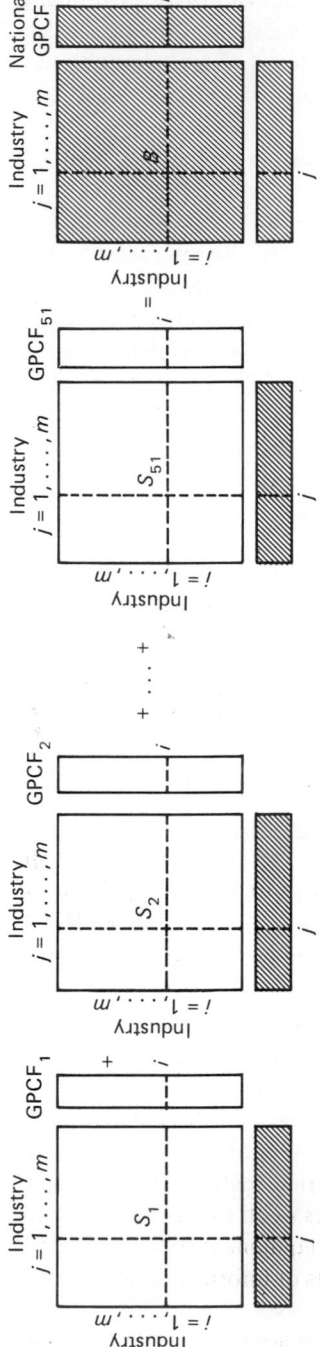

Figure 3-2. Basic Relationship Between State and National Capital Flow Matrices. (Available data are represented by the cross-hatched areas. There are 51 state capital flow matrices, representing the 50 states and Washington, D.C.)

in each state apportion their purchases of various types of capital equipment, the assumption was made that each industry follows the purchasing pattern for that industry shown in the national capital flow matrix. In other words, the capital technology for each industry (that is, the types of capital equipment required to produce output) was assumed to be constant for all states. Capital equipment coefficients[3] were calculated from the national capital flow matrix by dividing the elements of each column by the respective column sum, resulting in a vector each cell of which expressed for a particular industry the expenditures for a given type of equipment as a percent of the total value of capital equipment purchased by that industry. The capital equipment coefficients of a given industry in each state were assumed to be the same as the national capital equipment coefficients calculated for that industry. Symbolically,

$$\frac{b_{ij}^{national}}{\sum_{i=1}^{m} b_{ij}^{national}} \equiv \frac{b_{ij}^{state}}{\sum_{i=1}^{m} b_{ij}^{state}}$$

where B is the adjusted national capital equipment flow matrix.

For each state, data on the total value of capital equipment purchased by each industry were multiplied by the capital coefficients of the respective industries to obtain state capital equipment flow matrices. When this operation had been completed for all states, the rows of each state capital equipment flow matrix were summed, giving GPCF vectors (equipment only) for each state. This relationship is shown diagrammatically in Figure 3-2. The expenditure for new plant was estimated separately and included in the final GPCF vector for each state.

Data Requirements and Computation Methodology

In the construction of state vectors of gross private capital formation for 1947, 1958, and 1963, the data represented by the cross-hatched areas in Figure 3-2 were used. These data are: (1) The national vector of final demand for capital, which gives the amount of capital produced by each industry in the economy; (2) the national capital flow matrix, which contains interindustry transactions in goods purchased on capital account; and (3) state row vectors of capital equipment expenditures, which give the amount of new machinery and

---

3. These capital coefficients differ from the ones normally referred to in economic literature. This is the ratio of the element in a column to a column sum (total capital purchased by the industry), whereas normally capital coefficients refer to the ratio of capital purchased to total capacity in the industry.

equipment purchased by each industry in the state. The three sets of data were used to estimate state final demand for machinery and equipment only. To estimate state final demand for each new plant, a fourth set of data, the value of total private construction by state, was used.

The national GPCF vectors were obtained from the 1947 [169], 1958 [176], and 1963 [164] input-output tables of the Office of Business Economics (OBE).

National Capital Flow Matrices.   Because no national capital flow matrix has been published for 1947, the national capital flows for 1947 had to be estimated. National capital flow matrices were published by the Bureau of Labor Statistics (BLS) for 1958 [189] and by Jack Faucett Associates for 1963 [14].[4]

1947 National Capital Flow Matrix.   The 1947 national capital flow matrix was constructed for this study in the following way. First, the 1947 GPCF figures were assigned to purchasing industries in the same proportions as those shown in the 1958 capital flow matrix. For 17 of the input-output industries for which 1947 GPCF figures are given, no capital flows are shown in the 1958 capital flow table. These industries are listed in Table 3-1. For the first 13 of the industries shown in the table, capital flows were estimated by distributing the 1947 GPCF total for each industry in proportion to the entries in the corresponding rows of an unpublished coefficient matrix of 1947 capital stocks estimated by staff members of the Harvard Economic Research Project [49]. These capital stock figures for 1947 could have been used as allocation factors for all industries rather than the 1958 capital flow figures. Since capital flow figures represent purchases of machinery and equipment for expansion as well as for replacement of the present capital stock that has depreciated, the 1958 capital flows were considered to be better for estimating 1947 capital flows than the 1947 capital stocks. Finally, for the last four industries shown in the table, no 1947 capital stock information exists, although there is a figure for gross private capital formation. The lack of capital stock data for three of the industries represents, as far as can be ascertained, noncomparabilities between the 1947 and 1958 GPCF vectors due to changes in the definition of capital. Because no data were available for use in estimating which industries purchased the capital produced by these four industries in 1947, the GPCF figure for each industry was allocated to the states on the basis of an appropriate percentage distribution (described below) and inserted into each state final demand vector after its construction.

IO-1, Livestock & livestock products.   According to "The 1947 Inter-industry Relations Study" published by the BLS [196], the capital flow for this industry consists entirely of horses and mules. Thus, the final demand for capital from IO-1 was allocated to the states on the basis of the number of horses

---

4.The OBE plans to publish a 1963 national capital flow matrix in 1971.

Table 3–1

Industries for Which There Are Gross Private Capital Formation Figures in 1947 But Not in 1958 (thousands of dollars)

Industry Number	Industry Title	1947 GPCF	Percent of Total GPCF
16	Broad & narrow fabrics, yarn & thread mills	$ 3,120	.009
19	Miscellaneous fabricated textile products	17	.000
21	Wooden containers	12,416	.036
24	Paper & allied products, except containers & boxes	1,807	.005
26	Printing & publishing	216	.000
27	Chemicals & selected chemical products	109	.000
35	Glass & glass products	20,884	.060
36	Stone & clay products	4	.000
38	Primary nonferrous metals manufacturing	835	.002
41	Screw machine products, bolts, nuts, etc., & metal stampings	2,441	.007
50	Machine shop products	7	.000
73	Business services	2	.000
77	Medical, educational services, & nonprofit organizations	10,134	.031
1	Livestock & livestock products	21,116	.061
13	Ordnance & accessories	906	.003
31	Petroleum refining & related industries	401	.001
83	Scrap, used & second hand goods	986,000	2.845

and mules in each state in 1949 [129] — 1949 being the closest year to 1947 for which state data were available.

IO-13, Ordnance & accessories. The BLS source [196] defines the capital produced by this industry as consisting mainly of pistols and revolvers. The final demand for capital from IO-13 was distributed to the states according to the number of persons employed in each state in 1947 by the small-arms industry [104, p. 828 n.].

IO-31, Petroleum refining & related industries. The BLS source [196] defines the capital produced by this industry as consisting of gasoline, lubricating oils, and grease. The total demand for capital from IO-31 was allocated to the states in proportion to the 1947 percentage of total petroleum production in each state [129].

IO-83, Scrap, used & secondhand goods. Since no state information on purchases of capital goods from this industry was available, the national figure

was distributed to the state GPCF vectors after their construction using each
state's percentage of national gross private capital formation as an allocation
factor. The assumption here was that the amount of scrap and used equipment
purchased in a given state is roughly proportional to the total of new capital
goods purchased in that state.

In summary the following procedures were used to construct a 1947 capital
flow matrix for use in this study: (1) Where 1958 capital flows existed for
corresponding 1947 GPCF figures, the 1958 purchasing pattern was assumed to
be true for 1947; (2) where no capital flow figures were available, 1947 GPCF
figures were allocated to purchasing industries in proportion to the capital
stocks of those industries in 1947; (3) in cases where neither 1958 capital flow
figures nor 1947 capital stock figures were available as allocation factors, the
1947 GPCF figures were allocated to the states on the basis of an appropriate
percentage distribution and inserted into each state final demand vector after
its construction.

1958 National Capital Flow Matrix.   The national capital flow matrix used
for 1958 was published by the BLS [189]. Except for the allocation to
purchasing industries of capital equipment sold by IO-83, Scrap, used & secondhand goods, employing the method explained above for 1947, no adjustments
had to be made to the BLS 1958 national capital flow matrix.

1963 National Capital Flow Matrix.   Several adjustments were made to
the 1963 capital flow matrix published by Jack Faucett Associates [14] before it was used in this study. For the industries shown in Table 3–2, no data
appear in the rows of the 1963 capital flow matrix, whereas figures do appear
in the published GPCF vector for 1963 [164]. Capital flow estimates for 1963
were made separately for these four industries.

IO-38, Primary nonferrous metals manufacturing.   For this industry, the
assumption was made that purchases of capital goods were in proportion to
1958 capital stocks of the industry, that is, that the IO-38 figures for gross
private capital formation represented replacement investment only. The 1958
capital stock matrix [50] provided the most recent (closest to 1963) capital
stock figures readily available.

IO-50, Machine shop products.   Since there were no 1958 capital stock
figures for this industry, the 1963 national GPCF figure for IO-50 was allocated
to row 50 of each state GPCF vector, after its construction, in proportion to the
total estimated gross private capital formation in each state.

IO-80, Gross imports of goods & services.   The capital equipment sold in
1963 by this industry was allocated to the purchasing industries in proportion to
purchases of capital from IO-80 shown in the 1958 capital flow matrix [189].

IO-83, Scrap, used & secondhand goods.   The total amount of capital
purchased by industries in each state from this industry was estimated in the

Table 3-2

Industries in the 1963 GPCF Vector for Which the 1963 Capital Flow Matrix Has No Figures

Industry Number	Industry Title	1963 GPCF	Percent of Total GPCF
		($000)	
38	Primary nonferrous metals manufacturing	$ 22,115	.027
50	Machine shop products	6,414	.008
80	Gross imports of goods & services	165,700	.206
83	Scrap, used & secondhand goods	− 971,600	1.207

Table 3-3

Industries for Which 1963 Capital Flow Figures Are Combined

Industry Number	Industry Title	1963 GPCF	Percent of Total GPCF
		($000)	
65	Transportation & warehousing	$ 574,379	.713
66	Communications, except radio & TV broadcasting	485,078	.602
69	Wholesale & retail trade	4,857,520	6.033
71	Real estate & rental	1,224,000	1.520

same manner as for 1947 and 1958. The allocation factors are the state percentages of total national gross private capital formation in 1963.

In addition to making estimates of 1963 national capital flows for the four industries discussed above, one further adjustment was made to the 1963 capital flow matrix. The figures for purchases of capital from several of the service industries, shown in Table 3-3, are lumped together in the 1963 table. These lump-sum figures were separated into flows from the four industries as explained below.

IO-65, Transportation & warehousing; and IO-69, Wholesale & retail trade. The 1963 capital flow matrix was originally constructed by Jack Faucett Associates using 1958 transportation and trade margin data. The margins on the 1963 capital flows were recalculated for this study using transportation and trade margins for the 1963 national GPCF vector, obtained from an OBE computer tape which furnished figures for total transportation margins and total trade margins paid by each industry on its purchases of capital goods in 1963. These calculated figures were then placed in rows 65 and 69, respectively, in the 1963 national capital flow matrix.

IO-66, Communications, except radio & TV broadcasting. The capital produced by this industry was allocated to purchasing industries in 1963 in proportion to purchases from IO-66 shown in the 1958 capital flow matrix [189].

IO-71, Real estate & rental. In a footnote to the BLS 1958 capital flow matrix [189, p. 52, n. 2], the capital produced and sold by this industry is stated as consisting of commissions on real estate transactions. In the same source [189, p. 51], the total amount of capital sold by IO-71 is allocated to IO-70, Finance & insurance. For this reason, the total 1963 GPCF figure for IO-71 was inserted into column 70 of row 71 in the 1963 capital flow matrix.

In summary, before the 1963 national capital flow matrix was used in this study, the following adjustments were done to make it compatible with the published 1963 vector of national gross private capital formation: (1) Flows were estimated for four industries that appeared in the national GPCF vector but for which no estimates were given in the capital flow matrix. (2) Separate estimates were made for four of the service industries which had been lumped together. This operation included recalculating the transportation and trade margins on capital purchases using 1963 data.

State Capital Expenditures Data. The main information used to construct state vectors of gross private capital formation was data on purchases of capital equipment by each industry in each state. As shown in Figure 3–2, state row vectors of total capital equipment purchases by industry, referred to as capital expenditures data, were used, together with column coefficients of the national capital flow matrix, to construct state column vectors of gross private capital formation.

The state capital expenditures data were constructed in the form of a state-by-industry matrix of capital expenditures. The relationship between this state-by-industry capital expenditures matrix and the industry-by-industry national capital flow matrix is shown in Figure 3–3.

Most of the state data on capital expenditures were taken from various publications of the Bureau of the Census and are classified by Standard Industrial Classification (SIC) codes. All data given by SIC codes had to be reclassified into the corresponding input-output classification. For 1958 and 1963, an IO/SIC correspondence table was published by the Office of Business Economics [176, p. 33]. An alignment of the 1947 SIC numbers to the 1958 input-output classification was obtained from the Harvard Economic Research Project [76].

Whenever state capital expenditures data were not available for a given industry, an allocation factor was used to distribute the national capital equipment expenditures figure for that industry to the states. In most cases, the allocation factors used in this study were data from the percentage-of-gross-output matrices for 1947, 1958, and 1963. These gross output figures by input-output industry and by state were obtained from Jack Faucett Associates

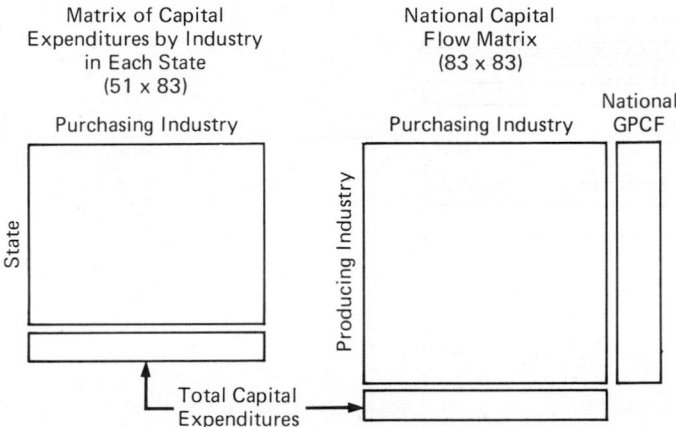

Figure 3-3. Relationship Between the Matrix of Capital Expenditures (State-by-Industry) and the National Capital Flow Matrix.

for each year [70] ; these matrices will be referred to without further source references in the remaining pages of this chapter.

The particular procedure used to develop state estimates of capital expenditures for a given industry was determined by the nature of the available data. In Figure 3-4, the capital equipment expenditures data available for constructing a state-by-industry matrix for the years 1958 and 1963 are shown. The available data are indicated by the x's. The same data are available for 1947 with the exception of internal data for the mining and manufacturing industries. As shown in the figure, state data on expenditures for capital were given in one of several forms: (1) for a sector rather than for individual industries, say for the agricultural sector rather than for each separate agricultural industry; (2) for individual industries, but only in selected states; or (3) for individual industries at the national level only. Corresponding to the three levels of detail in the available state capital equipment expenditures data, three general methods were used to construct the final state-by-industry capital equipment expenditures matrix. Table 3-4 shows the specific industries for which each procedure was used in each of the three years and lists the sources of state capital expenditures data for each year.

Estimation Procedure 1. In many cases, state data were available for groups of industries but not for the individual industries within the group. For example, Figure 3-5 shows available state data on capital purchases by agriculture. These data were for the agricultural sector rather than for the agricultural input-output industries, IO-1, Livestock & livestock products, and IO-2, Other agricultural products. The figure also shows that these state capital equipment expenditures

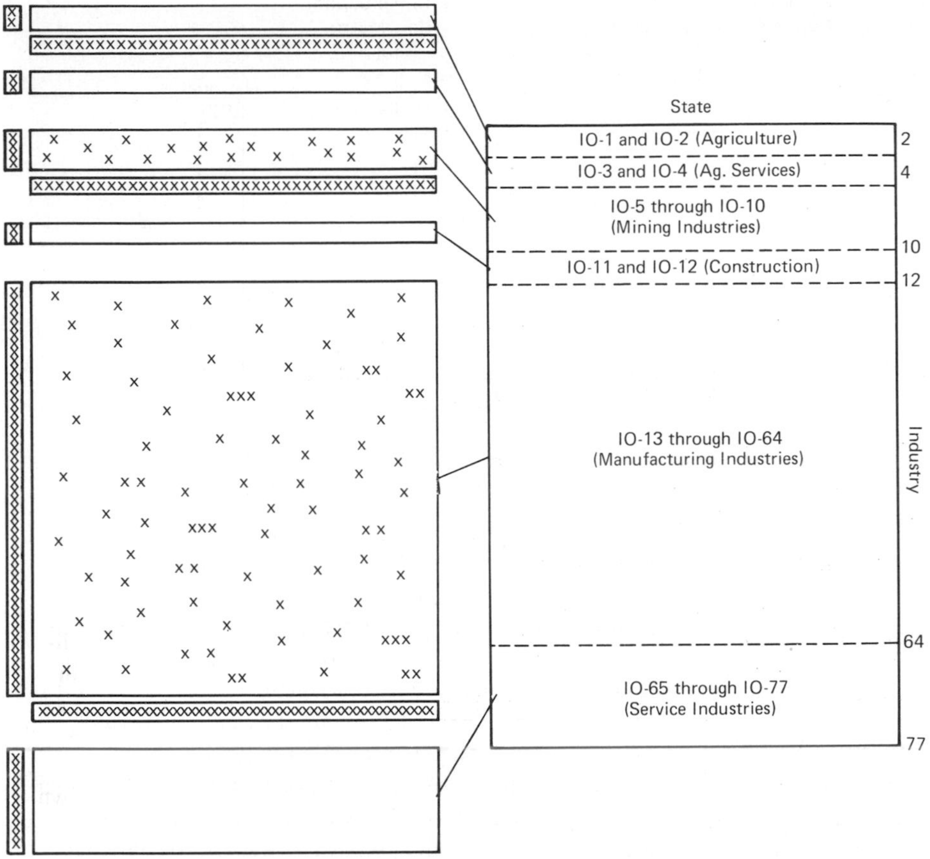

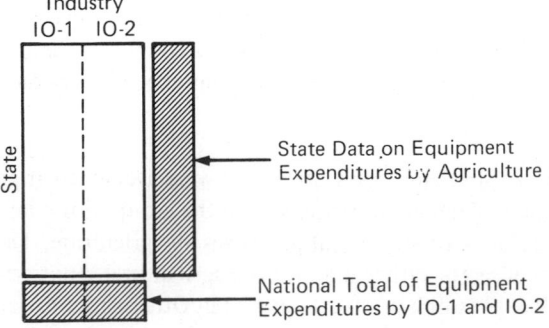

State

IO-1 and IO-2 (Agriculture)   2
IO-3 and IO-4 (Ag. Services)   4
IO-5 through IO-10
(Mining Industries)
                                                          10
IO-11 and IO-12 (Construction)
                                                          12

IO-13 through IO-64
(Manufacturing Industries)

Industry

                                                          64
IO-65 through IO-77
(Service Industries)

                                                          77

Figure 3–4. State Data Available on Capital Expenditures by Industry
for 1958 and 1963.

Industry
IO-1   IO-2

State

State Data on Equipment
Expenditures by Agriculture

National Total of Equipment
Expenditures by IO-1 and IO-2

Figure 3–5. State Data Available for the Agricultural Sector. (Available
data are indicated by cross-hatched areas.)

Table 3–4
Procedures and Data Sources Used to Estimate Industry-by-State Capital Expenditures for 1947, 1958, and 1963

Sector	Industry	1947			1958			1963		
		Procedure	Percent[a]	Source[b]	Procedure	Percent[a]	Source[b]	Procedure	Percent[a]	Source[b]
Agriculture	{ IO-1 and IO-2	1[c]	8.9	[158, t. 10]	1	11.1	[158, t. 10]	1	10.7	[158, t. 10]
	{ IO-3 and IO-4	3	0.7	–	3	0.7	–	3	0.4	–
Mining	IO-5 through IO-10	3	4.8	–	2	4.8	[113, t. 2A]	2	2.6	[114, t. 2A]
Construction	IO-11 and IO-12	3	3.5	–	3	3.6	–	3	5.3	–
Manufacturing	IO-13 through IO-64	1	26.6	[103, t. 2; 104, t. 4]	2	24.4	[106, t. 3; 108, t. 4]	2	24.2	[109, t. 3; 111, t. 5]
Services	IO-65 through IO-77	3	55.5	–	3	55.1	–	3	56.8	–

[a]Percent of total capital expenditures represented by each sector.
[b]Sources of state capital expenditures data are given for Procedures 1 and 2 only. Procedure 3 was used when no state data were available.
[c]1949 figures were used for 1947 since these are the earliest available state data.

statistics for the agricultural sector, together with the national statistics for capital equipment purchased by each individual agricultural industry, form control totals of would-be row and column sums of an industry-by-state matrix of capital equipment expenditures. An industry-by-state matrix of gross output was used as an allocation series to distribute the control vectors of capital equipment expenditures to each cell within the industry-by-state matrix, employing an iterative method developed to force a matrix to add to given row and column sums. As shown in Table 3-4, this procedure was used to estimate capital equipment expenditures for IO-1, Livestock & livestock products, and IO-2, Other agricultural products, in 1947, 1958, and 1963; and for the manufacturing sector, IO-13 through IO-64, in 1947.

Estimation Procedure 2. For the mining and manufacturing sectors in 1958 and 1963, capital expenditures were given for individual industries in each state. These data comprised the bulk of industrial capital equipment expenditures in the two years. As shown in Table 3-4, about 5 percent of total capital purchases were by industries in the mining sector, while almost 25 percent were by industries in the manufacturing sector. These capital purchases formed the industry-by-state matrices of capital equipment expenditures for the two years. However, in cases where only one firm operates in a state, disclosure of information about that industry in that state would, in effect, reveal balance-sheet statistics on that firm. Since such disclosure is illegal, gaps appear in the capital equipment expenditures for the mining and manufacturing sectors in 1958 and 1963, as shown in Figure 3-4. Here, a more elaborate version of Procedure 1 (described above) was used. Control totals of capital expenditures of the two sectors were given for each state, as well as total equipment expenditures by the individual industries within each sector at the national level. Percentage-of-gross-output figures were used to construct state capital expenditures estimates for those industries for which data were not disclosed, while the industry-by-state data already available were preserved.

Estimation Procedure 3. When no state capital expenditures data were available for a particular industry, the total national value of capital expenditures by that industry was taken from the column sums of the national capital flow matrix for the given year and allocated to the states in proportion to the gross output of that industry in each state. The assumption underlying this procedure was that the state distribution of new machinery and equipment expenditures by a given industry is proportional to the values of its production in each state. For the service industries, this assumption does not hold, since gross output is not related to capital equipment expenditures for the service sector. More suitable allocation series were available for the service industries listed in Table 3-5. The allocation factors used for these industries are discussed below. For all other service industries, data and time limitations forced the use of percentage-of-gross-output figures as allocation series.

Table 3–5
Service Industries for Which Selective State Allocation Factors Were Used

Industry Number	Industry Title	Year(s)
65	Transportation & warehousing	1958, 1963
66	Communications, except radio & TV broadcasting	1947, 1958, 1963
67	Radio & TV broadcasting	1947
68	Electric, gas, water, & sanitary services	1947, 1958, 1963

IO-65, 1958. Capital expenditures for IO-65 in 1958 were estimated by dividing the industry into five subindustries: (1) railroads, (2) water carriers, (3) pipeline carriers, (4) motor carriers, and (5) air transport. For each subindustry of the transportation industry, the total of capital stock plus depreciation reserve for 1958 was subtracted from the same total for 1959 [9; 52]. These estimates of capital expenditures were used as weights to distribute the actual capital expenditures figures from the 1958 capital flow matrix to the transportation subindustries. The subtotals were allocated to the states in the following manner:

For railroads and pipelines, the allocation of capital expenditures to the states was based upon the miles of rail and pipeline in each state [52]. For motor carriers, the number of commercial vehicles registered in each state [132] was used to allocate the national capital expenditures figure. Similarly, aircraft expenditures were distributed by the number of aircraft at general airports [18]. For water transport, a crude index based on the tonnage shipped through various ports was used. Data for tonnage shipped on rivers and canals [132] were divided in half, attributing half to each state at the two ends of the river section involved. These allocation factors were used to distribute the capital expenditures in each subindustry to the states. Once this had been done, the capital expenditures for each subindustry in a state were added to give a total capital expenditures figure for IO-65 in that state.

IO-65, 1963. For IO-65 in 1963, national equipment expenditures totals for six subindustries were given in the 1963 capital flow matrix [14]: (1) IO-6501, Railroad transportation, (2) IO-6502, Air transportation, (3) IO-6503, Trucks & warehousing & stockyards, (4) IO-6504, Water transportation, (5) IO-6505, Pipelines, and (6) IO-6506, Other transportation. Expenditures for each subindustry were allocated individually to the states and then aggregated to obtain state capital expenditures figures for IO-65 as a whole.

For IO-6501, Railroad transportation, the change in number of carloads of freight shipped from each state between 1962 and 1964 [53; 54] was used to distribute the national total for railroad transportation capital equipment expenditures to the states. The allocation factor used for IO-6502, Air transportation, was the total number of aircraft registered in each state at the end of 1963 [19].

Since 93 percent of the capital equipment expenditures of IO-6503, Trucks & warehousing & stockyards, consisted of trucks and other motor vehicles, the distribution was made on the basis of trucks. Data were available on the increase in registrations of all trucks during 1963 [161, t. MV-9, p. 16] and also on the number of trucks registered in 1963 which were used "for hire," that is, which were rented for transport of goods, rather than used by firms for local utility work [136, t. 805, p. 575]. Of the categories listed, "for hire" seemed to be closest to the sorts of trucks represented in IO-6503. Because these data were available only on a one-time basis, and not for the change during 1963, they had to be combined with the data on all trucks to obtain an approximation of the growth of trucking activities in different states as well as the presence of this particular kind of trucking activity in different states. This was estimated by taking the figure on the increase in truck registrations for all trucks during 1963 and dividing it into the total number of trucks at the beginning of 1963, thus obtaining a percentage growth figure for total trucking activities for each state. By multiplying the percentage growth figure by the number of trucks registered as "for hire" in each state, an estimated increase in the number of trucks "for hire" in each state during 1963 was calculated. These data were used as the allocation factors for IO-6503.

For IO-6504, Water transportation, the best information available was data on the amount of cargo shipped out of U.S. ports in 1963 [136, tt. 815, 817, pp. 602-603] and 1964 [137, tt. 849, 851, pp. 600-601]. The change in tonnage shipped out of ports in each state between 1963 and 1964 was used to distribute the national capital expenditures figure for this subindustry to the others. In many cases, data were listed for a port that had harbors in more than one state (the Port of New York, for example, has harbors in both New York and New Jersey) or for a river that bordered on more than one state. These data therefore had to be allocated to the states along the river or forming part of the port, and there was no basis for the allocations except for the judgment of the researcher.

Because capital equipment purchases by the pipeline subindustry, IO-6505, were scattered among a number of different sellers, it was impossible to distribute them on the basis of purchases of a particular product, as had been done for some of the other transportation subindustries. The distribution was made with data on the construction of petroleum pipelines by state for 1964. The data are based on estimated oil pipeline construction costs from a confidential study by the Association of Oil Pipelines [5].

For the sixth transportation subindustry, IO-6506, Other transportation, a procedure similar to that followed for IO-6503 was used, as 90 percent of all capital expenditures by this subindustry were for trucks and other motor vehicles.

IO-66, 1947 and 1958. For this industry, the 1946, 1947, 1957, and 1958 figures for telephone plant in service for Class A telephone carriers were recorded from the balance sheet of each company [28; 29; 25; 26]. The difference between the figures for 1946 and 1947 and 1957 and 1958 was obtained, giving investment figures for 1947 and 1958 for each Class A telephone company. IO-66 included both the telephone and telegraph industries. Because most Class A telephone companies deal in both telephone and telegraph services, the estimates constructed were considered adequate. This gross investment figure was then multiplied by the national ratio of equipment expenditures to gross investment for that year [28; 29; 25; 26], resulting in a figure for investment in new equipment for each company. These equipment expenditures were then allocated to the state in which each company has its headquarters.

IO-66, 1963. For distributing the national equipment expenditures figure for IO-66, Communications, except radio & TV broadcasting, to the states, the change in value of plant during 1963 was used, since equipment made up 71 percent of what was called total new capital plant in 1963. The change in capital plant equipment for the Bell System was calculated by subtracting the value at the beginning of 1963 [20; 22] from the value at the end of the year [21; 23]. Because Bell companies are concentrated in urban areas, these data alone do not make an adequate allocation series. Figures for the change in number of telephones in each state in 1963 were obtained for all companies and just for the Bell companies by subtracting the number of telephones at the beginning of the year [135, t. 703, p. 515] from the corresponding figure at the end of the year [136, t. 718, p. 517]. The ratio of change in number of telephones to change in value of total capital plant for the Bell companies was used as an index to derive the change in plant (equipment) for all companies in each state in 1963.

IO-67, 1947. Capital expenditures of IO-67, Radio & TV broadcasting, were distributed using AM radio station data on capital expenditures by state [24]. For 1947 the television industry, as well as the FM radio industry, was quite small; thus, the use of AM radio data alone seemed justified.

IO-68, 1947 and 1958. IO-68 comprises electric, gas, water, and sanitary services. Since in 1958 electric and gas utilities spent about $4.7 billion on plant and equipment together out of the industry total of $5.8 billion, the capital expenditures of these two subindustries in 1947 and 1958 were considered adequate for use as an allocation factor. The total capital expenditures figure for IO-68 in 1947 and 1958 was distributed to the states in proportion to the capital expenditures by electric and gas utilities in those years. Figures for "increase over the previous year in electric utility plant in service" were taken from balance sheets of all Class A and Class B electric utility companies by state [31; 32]. To obtain total capital expenditures figures for electric utilities by state, these figures were then totaled. Because no information separating plant from equipment expenditures on a regional or a state level was available, total capital expenditures figures were used as an allocation factor.

Although some of the details were different due to variations in presentation of the data, the same basic procedure was used for gas utilities. Balance-
sheet statistics of each company were given for its entire operation, rather than
by state, and the states in which each company operates were listed separately
[35]. Since no data were available to divide the capital expenditures of each gas
utility by state, the total for each company was given to every state in which it
operated. This meant that the total of the state figures was considerably greater
than the national total, but, since these figures were used only as allocation
factors, the final expenditures figures did add to the national total.

The data for capital expenditures by electric and gas utilities in each state in
1947 and 1958 were summed and then used to allocate the national capital
expenditures total for IO-68 in 1947 and 1958 to the states.

IO-68, 1963. The national capital flow matrix for 1963 [14] gives capital
expenditures figures for three subindustries of IO-68: (1) IO-6801, Electric
companies & systems, (2) IO-6802, Gas companies & systems, and (3) IO-6803,
Water, sanitary, etc., services. State distributions were estimated for each of the
three subindustries and then aggregated to form a capital expenditures figure by
state for the entire industry.

The distribution for IO-6801, Electric companies, was made on the basis of
the difference between total value of plant and equipment of electric utilities in
1962 [33, pp. 500–528A] and that in 1963 [34, pp. 500–528A]. For IO-6802,
Gas companies & systems, the total value (in physical units) of four kinds of gas
utility plant in each state for 1963 [1, t. 50, pp. 59–60] was subtracted from
that for 1964 [2, t. 50, pp. 59–60]. The one-year lag was used to allow for the
lag between the time the construction is put in place and the time the new
capacity appears in the account books. The difference was taken for each kind of
plant in each state, and the differences for each kind of plant were weighted by
the national construction output total for each kind of plant in 1963 [1, t. 186,
p. 212]. After the weighted differences had been aggregated, the total was used
as the final distributive series. IO-6803, Water, sanitary, etc. services, includes
privately supplied water and sewage systems as well as irrigation and steam
generation services. For this subindustry, the most reasonable allocation factor
seemed to be the increase in overall water use by state. The data were calculated
by subtracting the total use in 1960 [181, p. 198] from the total use in 1965
[187, t. 26, pp. 46–47].

Once the three procedures had been used to construct a state-by-industry
matrix of capital equipment expenditures for 1947, 1958, and 1963, each state
vector of total equipment purchased by each industry was multiplied by the
column coefficients of the national capital equipment flow matrix for that year
to obtain a capital equipment flow matrix for each state. The row sums of each
state capital equipment flow matrix show the final demand for capital equipment
originating in that state.

Total Private Construction by State. After state vectors of final demand for new machinery and equipment were constructed, they were adjusted to represent flows of both plant and equipment. State figures for new construction were calculated as follows: For the various components of private construction in 1947, 1958, and 1963, figures from unpublished worksheets of Jack Faucett Associates [13] were summed for each year to obtain the value of total private construction by state. The final demands for new machinery and equipment were estimated for each state, as described above, and then these private construction figures were inserted into row 11 of the respective state final demand vectors to yield total GPCF figures by state. When this adjustment had been made, the state vectors of final demand for gross private capital formation were complete.

Net Change in Inventories

The object of the research done for this portion of the study was to construct state vectors of net change in inventories for the years 1947, 1958, and 1963. National figures for net change in inventories were obtained from the final demand sector of the input-output tables for 1947 [169], for 1958 [176], and for 1963 [164].

Since reliable inventory data on the state level are almost nonexistent, some means had to be found to allocate the national figures to the states. Although inventory change is related to business conditions, sales, and interest rates, these factors are difficult to quantify at the state level and thus were not used. Percentage-of-gross-output figures were chosen as allocation factors to approximate the percentage distribution of net change in inventories among the states. Because net change in inventories is such a small part of gross national product (0.2 percent in 1947, 0.3 percent in 1958, and 1.0 percent in 1963) relative to the other components of final demand, only a small proportion of the total research effort was devoted to the assembly of these state estimates.

Actual net inventory change figures by state for the agricultural sector, IO-1 and IO-2, were available for all three years from the U.S. Department of Agriculture [156]. No state allocations were made for IO-80, Imports; IO-83, Scrap, used, & secondhand goods; and IO-87, Inventory valuation adjustment, because no state information existed. For the remaining input-output industries, the national figures for net inventory change for all three years were allocated to the states according to the percentage distribution of the Faucett percentage-of-gross-output matrices for each respective year [70].

Conclusion

The purpose of this chapter has been to describe the methods used to estimate the two components of gross private domestic investment in each state for the years 1947, 1958, and 1963.

For state gross private capital formation, the information needed is data on types of capital purchased by each industry in a given state. The available state data do not lend themselves to this purpose since they detail total capital expenditures by each industry in the state, but these totals are not separated according to types of capital purchased. For this reason, a method was established to estimate state gross private capital formation indirectly, using the available state data on total capital expenditures by industry together with national capital flow data to construct state capital flow matrices. In this manner it was possible to ascertain how much of total national gross private capital formation would take place in each state if the national "capital technology" is assumed to be constant for each state.

This national capital technology is represented by the capital flow matrix for each year. The 1963 capital flow data were revised slightly to be consistent with the gross private capital formation figures in the input-output table for 1963. The 1958 capital flows required no adjustments. The capital flow matrix for 1947 had to be constructed by approximation and is less representative of the capital technology in 1947 than are the capital flow tables for 1958 and 1963.

The methodology used to construct state estimates of final demand for capital seems to be a justifiable means of approximation under present data limitations. The state data on capital expenditures used to estimate state capital flows determine the reliability of the resultant state final demand vectors. Of the state capital expenditures figures used, the most valid are the estimates for the manufacturing sector in 1958 and in 1963. These are cases where both row *and* column sums are available for controls as well as where a considerable amount of the data was already complete. As noted earlier, the missing data were estimated under the assumption that the figures actually used approximate the percentage distribution of capital purchases. Whenever possible, output figures were used since it was assumed that there is a fairly close correlation between capital expenditures and gross output. Percentage-of-gross-output figures were considered adequate allocation factors for most industries except the service, import, government, and special industry sectors.

Future work in this area would be valuable if directed toward investigation of differing capital technologies among states as well as toward further collection of data on capital purchases by industry and by state.

The state estimates of net change in inventories in 1947, 1958, and 1963 obtained in this study are necessarily rough, because no data source could be located that contained even relatively consistent sets of state net inventory data. Improvement of these estimates would have required a considerable amount of research which did not seem justified at the present time given that inventory change is such a small percentage of aggregate final demand.

4 Exports from the United States

William R. Buechner and
Peter Dixon

One of the significant characteristics of modern industrial economies is the high level of interdependence between economic regions. Whether due to differences in the supplies of factors of production, different technologies, or different consumer preferences, the result is a constant flow of commodities across regional boundaries. With the division of the world into sovereign countries, and these further divided into states and commonwealths, soviet republics, provinces, counties, etc., two types of trade flows can take place. On the one hand, goods can be shipped from producers in one country to consumers in foreign countries, with the exports crossing national frontiers. On the other hand, the economic regions within a country, following economic principles similar to those that give rise to international trade, can trade goods and services with one another.

For an economic region, both sources of trade give rise to production and employment within the region. The two types of exports, however, are treated differently within the framework of the multiregional input-output model. Exports from one country to another are viewed as an exogenous part of final demand. Trade among regions is an integral part of the multiregional model and a determinant of the division among the various regions of the total output generated by the final demand. The focus of this chapter is on U.S. international—rather than intranational—exports of goods and services, and thus the terms "foreign trade" and "exports" will refer to trade with and exports to foreign countries.

Foreign exports can be incorporated into a multiregional model in two ways. The first method is to allocate all exports to the states from which they were shipped to their ultimate foreign destination. While allocation by port of exit will attribute exports to only a few states or regions, all states will eventually share in the production of goods for export through the intranational trade flows in the multiregional model. This is the treatment of foreign trade that is most

---

The research reported in the first part of this chapter was completed by William R. Buechner in the summer of 1968, while the research reported in the second part was performed by Peter Dixon in the summer of 1970. KRP

consistent with the scope and intent of the multiregional model. In the last part of this chapter, Peter Dixon describes this treatment, which was used to assemble a set of vectors for 1963. A second procedure for handling foreign exports is to determine the states where the exports had been produced. This is the procedure that was followed to assemble consistent sets of export vectors for 1947, 1958, and 1963. While it was recognized at the outset that these foreign trade data would not be consistent with the other final demand vectors, which give the demand at place of final consumption, insufficient information as to whether or not the transportation data to be assembled would include the shipments of imported and exported goods dictated this treatment of foreign trade. Because it was impossible to know when the study was begun how the interregional trade data would be assembled, and because the only export data readily available at that time for the three base years were by place of production, the sets of estimates of foreign exports were assembled according to the region where the exports were produced rather than the region where the port of exit was located.

Foreign Exports by Place of Production

The total U.S. foreign trade vector in the final demand portion of the input-output matrices for 1947, 1958, and 1963 was divided into 51 separate regional vectors, one for each state plus the District of Columbia. The remainder of this section of the chapter documents the development of these sets of vectors. Depending on the nature of the data available, the allocation of foreign exports to the states followed either of two estimation procedures. Following one procedure, exports of goods produced by industries in the agricultural, mining, and service sectors of the economy, as well as exports of manufactured goods for 1947, were allocated among the states in proportion to each state's production of the relevant industry's output. Because it had to be assumed that all states exported the same proportion of their output for any industry, the resulting vectors do not necessarily identify the states that actually produced the exported goods. For the other estimating procedure, the availability of two Bureau of the Census studies giving the place where exports of manufactured goods were produced in 1960 [140] and 1963 [141] made it possible to allocate manufacturing exports for 1958 and 1963 to the producing states. These portions of the export vectors therefore come closest to achieving the goals of this study.

To facilitate the documentation, the input-output industries have been combined into five sectors: agricultural, mineral, construction, manufacturing, and service industries. The estimation procedures employed to allocate the exports of agricultural goods to the states are explained first, with the documentation of the remaining sectors following in order.

Agricultural Sector

The agricultural sector consists of the first four industries in the 80-order Office of Business Economics (OBE) input-output classification. Due to the nature of the available data, the allocation processes used to determine the locus of production of the exports of two of the component industries of this sector— IO-1, Livestock & livestock products, and IO-2, Other agricultural products— differ from the allocation processes used for the other two—IO-3, Forestry & fishery products, and IO-4, Agricultural, forestry, & fishery services.

Allocation of IO-1 and IO-2 Exports. The allocation of the exports of these two industries among the states for the years 1947, 1958, and 1963 was based on two reports, published by the U.S. Department of Agriculture, analyzing the production by state of exports of agricultural commodities.[1] These reports include not only the value of agricultural exports attributed to each state for fiscal years 1954, 1960, and 1964, but also, for the last year, a breakdown by state of the total exports into separate figures for 19 different commodity groups (18 specific commodity groups plus a 19th residual—"other"— group). This latter breakdown was the foundation of the allocation process for all three years.

For fiscal year 1964, Tontz and Angelidis distributed the exports of each commodity group among the states in proportion to the output in each state of those products comprising the commodity group.[2] For each commodity group, export shares by state were calculated by Tontz and Angelidis according to the formula:

$$x = a\left(\frac{b}{c}\right)$$

where

   x = value of export share of the commodity for the given state

   a = total value of exports of the commodity from the United States in fiscal 1964

   b = quantity of the commodity produced or value of commodity sold in the given state in fiscal 1964

   c = quantity of the commodity produced or value of the commodity sold in the nation in fiscal 1964

---

1. The source of commodity data used for 1963 is a report by Robert L. Tontz and Alex P. Angelidis [78, t. 2, pp. 21–25]. Supplementary data used for 1947 and 1958 are contained in another report by Tontz and Isaac E. Lemon [79, t. 2, p. 20].

2. A full explanation of the process is contained in Tontz and Angelidis [78, pp. 15–16].

Certain commodity groups were handled slightly differently, but in each case some variant of this simple formula was used. Having developed figures for all 18 commodity groups for each state, Tontz and Angelidis then aggregated the figures to obtain a single estimate of agricultural exports from each state. This set of figures accounted for approximately 90 percent of the total value of exports of agricultural products from the United States in fiscal 1964. The residual, reported as commodity group No. 19 in the report, was allocated by Tontz and Angelidis among the states in proportion to these subtotals to obtain a state distribution of agricultural exports for all 19 commodity groups. These 19 commodity figures were aggregated in the present study into figures for the two input-output industries by (1) assigning each of the 18 identified commodity groups to one of the two input-output industries; (2) summing the specific figures to obtain a subtotal for each state for the two input-output industries; and (3) allocating exports for the 19th, "other," commodity group among the input-output industries in proportion to the two subtotals for each state. The commodity groups were aggregated into input-output industries as follows:

IO-1   (1)   Dairy products
       (2)   Meat & products, excl. poultry
       (3)   Hides & skins
       (4)   Poultry products
       (5)   Lard & tallow
      (19)   Part "other"

IO-2   (6)   Wheat
       (7)   Wheat flour
       (8)   Rice, excl. paddy
       (9)   Total feed grain
      (10)   Cotton, excl. linters
      (11)   Soybean
      (12)   Flax seed
      (13)   Soybean oil
      (14)   Cottonseed oil
      (15)   Protein meal
      (16)   Tobacco, unmanufactured
      (17)   Fruits, nuts, & preparations
      (18)   Vegetables & preparations
      (19)   Part "other"

The allocations for 1947 and 1958 were based on the 1963 figures plus additional data from the report by Tontz and Lemon cited above. In this source [79, p. 20], an estimate of the total value of agricultural exports was given by state for the fiscal years 1954 and 1960. These state export totals were not broken down by Tontz and Lemon into commodity groups as the fiscal 1964 figures had been. The disaggregation of the state exports for fiscal 1954 and 1960 into two figures for the input-output industries was based upon two simplifying assumptions:

1. First, it was assumed that the fiscal 1960 state export totals could be used as an approximation of the estimates that would have been obtained for 1958 (or fiscal 1959) and, similarly, that the fiscal 1954 figures could be used as a proxy for 1947. Underlying this procedure is the assumption that such factors as climate, technology, transportation costs, etc., do not change significantly over a short period of time, or, more generally, that the pattern of agricultural production is relatively stable for short periods.

2. As a corollary, it was assumed that the commodity composition of agricultural production for each state also held constant over time. The value of agricultural exports from each state, as reported by Tontz and Lemon for fiscal 1954 and 1960, was divided between the two input-output industries for those years in the same proportion as held in 1963. Thus, if in 1963, 80 percent of the exports from a state were from IO-1, Livestock & livestock products, and 20 percent were from IO-2, Other agricultural products, then the same ratio was assumed to hold in 1947 and 1958.

One problem encountered in the allocation process concerned the treatment of agricultural exports under government-financed programs, such as the Food for Peace program and its predecessors. The figures reported in this study do include exports under government programs. Excluding government-financed exports from state totals would have significantly altered the allocation pattern. The inclusion of government-financed exports is based on the procedure used in the 1947 input-output study [62, ch. 3, pp. 29–31]; the 1958 and 1963 input-output study procedures are consistent in this case with the 1947 procedures. Concerning unilateral transactions in kind, the procedure used in the 1947 study was as follows:

For the industry or industries producing the commodity or commodities in question, the values of the gifts were recorded as exports from the concerned industries. . . . This procedure was followed notwithstanding the fact that the domestic industries concerned may have actually sold their particular output to the government rather than to foreign trade. [62, ch. 3, pp. 30–31]

Thus, in this study the agricultural commodity exports include government-financed as well as commercial exports.

Allocation of IO-3 Exports. The process used for assembling export figures for IO-3, Forestry & fishery products, followed a procedure conceptually identical to that employed for the 1963 exports of IO-1 and IO-2. For 1947, 1958, and 1963, the reported U.S. value-of-exports figure for IO-3 was disaggregated into component subindustries; the figure for each subindustry was then allocated among the various states in proportion to an allocation factor. For each state the estimates for the subindustries were then summed to obtain a single value of IO-3 exports. Disaggregation of IO-3 into subindustries for 1947 was based on information from the 1947 input-output study [62]; three of the 450 industries from the 1947 industry classification comprise IO-3, Forestry & fishery products. For 1958 and 1963, the industry could be separated into four component subindustries.

The component subindustries, plus the value-of-export figures used as weights, are given in Table 4-1. For 1947, the subindustries are identified by their 450-order input-output numbers; for 1958 and 1963, they are identified by the Standard Industrial Classification (SIC) numbers given in the sources used. Because no sources or studies could be found that explicitly allocated the exports of the forestry and fishery subindustries among the various exporting states, production by state was employed as an allocation proxy. The proxy used for each subindustry and the source of the data are summarized in Table 4-1.

Allocation of IO-4 Exports. No exports of agricultural services were indicated for 1947 and therefore no allocation was developed for that year. For 1958 and 1963, the total U.S. value of exports of IO-4, Agricultural, forestry, & fishery services, was allocated to the states in proportion to a single proxy, since no breakdown into subindustries could be established. For 1958, first quarter 1962 taxable payrolls for SIC 07, Agricultural services, were used as the allocation proxy [118, t. 1], due to the scarcity of earlier information. The same proxy for the first quarter of 1964 was used to effect the 1963 distribution [119, t. 1A].

Mining Sector

There are six input-output industries primarily engaged in mining: IO-5 through IO-10. The estimation of the value of exports by state for these six industries followed the procedure employed in the estimates of agricultural exports. For each of the six industries, the total U.S. value of exports was first disaggregated into component subindustries—either by 450-order input-output classification, as for 1947, or by SIC number, as for 1958 and 1963. The correspondence between the 80-order and the 450-order input-output industries is given in Table 4-2 for 1947, along with the value of exports for the 450-order industries. The correspondence between the input-output industries and the SIC subindustries for 1958 and 1963, along with the weights assigned to each subindustry, is given in Table 4-3. The extent of the disaggregation for the two latter years was determined by the level at which allocation factors and export figures could be obtained.

The total U.S. export figures for each subindustry was allocated to the various states according to a production proxy. The proxies used for 1947 are given in Table 4–2. For 1958 and 1963, the allocation factor was total value of shipments for the relevant mineral subindustry from each state. The source of factors for these two years was the *Census of Mineral Industries, 1958* [113] and *1963* [114].

One minor problem arose in this allocation. For some states, the Bureau of the Census withheld the state value-of-shipments figures in order not to divulge figures for individual companies. Regional information, however, was available in these cases; thus, whenever the value-of-shipments figure had been withheld for a state or group of states, a residual for the relevant region was computed by subtracting the sum of the reported state figures from the regional figure. This residual was distributed among those states for which the value of shipments was lacking, in proportion to the number of employees reported in the mineral subindustry. The exports of the subindustries were then allocated among the states in proportion to these value-of-shipments proxies and finally aggregated to the respective 80-order input-output industrial classification.

Construction Sector

All exports of IO-11, New construction, for 1958 and 1963 appeared to be involved with the construction of foreign embassies in this country. The total export figure was therefore allocated to the District of Columbia for both years. No exports of this industry were indicated for 1947.

No exports of IO-12, Maintenance & repair construction, were indicated for any of the three years, so no allocation was performed.

Manufacturing Sector

The industries comprising the manufacturing sector are IO-13 through IO-64. The first part of this section documents the assembly of the manufacturing portion of the state export vectors for 1947. Because of the similarities in the data available for 1958 and 1963, the development of exports of manufactures from the various states is combined for these two years in the second part.

1947 Allocation of Manufactures. The procedure for allocating manufacturing exports to the states for 1947 was the same as that used for allocating the agricultural and mineral exports. The basic source of export figures for 1947 was the export final demand vector of the 1947 detailed computer listing [194]. About 300 of the 450-order input-output industries were included in the manufacturing sector and were thus component subindustries of IO-13 through

Table 4-1
Value of Exports and Allocation Factors by Subindustries of IO-3, Forestry and Fishery Products

Year	Number	Title	Exports Value[b]	Exports Percent	Allocation Factor	Source of Data
			(millions)			
1947	IO-16	Forestry products	$ 7.8	31	Total value of saw timber by states for 1947	[129, t. 809, p. 732]
	IO-19	Fisheries	.4	2	Total value of catch, all types of fish, by states	[188, Section Summaries]
	IO-20	Hunting & trapping	16.4 / 24.6	67 / 100	Total forest land area by states[c]	[129, t. 808, p. 731]
1958	SIC 08	Forestry products	3.5	36	Taxable payroll for SIC 08 for first quarter, 1962[d]	[118, t. 1, for all states]
	SIC 09	Fishery products SIC 09120, Finfish	1.6	16	Value of catch of finfish for 1958 by states, all types of waters	[182, Section Summaries]
		SIC 09130, Shellfish	2.5	25	Value of catch of shellfish for 1958 by states, all types of waters	[182, Section Summaries]
	SIC 1900	Miscellaneous marine products	2.3 / 9.9	23 / 100	Total value of manufactured fishery products for 1958 by states[g]	[182, Section Summaries]
1963	SIC 08	Forestry products	6.1	25	Taxable payroll for SIC 08 for first quarter, 1964[d]	[119, t. 1A, for all states]
	SIC 09	Fishery products SIC 09120, Finfish	4.5	19	Value of catch of finfish for 1963 by states, all types of waters	[183, Section Summaries]

SIC 09130, Shellfish	9.1	38	Value of catch of shellfish for 1963 by states, all types of waters	[183, Section Summaries]
SIC 1900 Miscellaneous marine products	$\dfrac{4.3}{24.0}$	$\dfrac{18}{100}$	Total value of manufactured fishery products for 1963 by states[e]	[183, Section Summaries]

[a] For 1947, the subindustries are identified by their 450-order input-output numbers; for 1958 and 1963, they are identified by the SIC numbers given in the sources used.

[b] The source of the 1958 national value figures was: *U.S. Commodity Exports as Related to Output, 1958* [143, t. A, p. 8]. According to the 1958 input-output study [176, p. 39], United States exports of IO-3 were $30 million – roughly three times the amount reported in the cited source. To accommodate this discrepancy, all the figures used as weights were approximately tripled; the weighting, however, remained the same. The 1963 source was: *U.S. Commodity Exports and Imports as Related to Output, 1963 and 1962* [146, t. 1A, p. 14]. Again, the total figure from this source will not necessarily correspond to the figure published in the 1963 study.

[c] Although value of catch or value of skins and furs would probably have been a better proxy, no figures were available. On the assumption that hunting and trapping output is related to the "wild" land in a state, total forest land area was chosen as the best available proxy with which to allocate exports.

[d] The earliest payroll data for SIC 08, Forestry products, comparable to those used for 1963, were for the first quarter of 1962. Rather than use arbitrarily constructed data for 1958, the 1962 data were used to allocate the 1958 exports.

[e] The exact nature of exports of SIC 1900, Miscellaneous marine products, was impossible to identify from the export-output studies (cited above as sources). Since the two other subindustries include all possible types of live catch, the value of manufactured fishery products was employed to distribute exports of miscellaneous marine products among the various producing states.

Table 4-2
Exports of Mineral Industries, 1947 (millions of dollars)

1958 80-order IO	1947 450-order IO	Description	Exports Value[a]	Exports Percent	Allocation Factor	Source of Data
5	1011	Iron ores	9,169	82.3	Total production of all iron ores, in tons, 1947	[184, p. 602]
	1040	Miscellaneous metal ores	1,966	17.7	Total value of shipments of manganese & tungsten ores, 1954	[112, Section 10-I, pp. 4–6]
			11,135	100.0		
6	1021	Copper ores	32	0.5	Output of copper ores in tons, 1947	[184, p. 454]
	1030	Lead & zinc ores	201	3.4	Output of zinc ores, 1947[b]	[184, pp. 687, 1247]
	1040	Miscellaneous metal ores	3,740	63.8	Production of gold, and of silver, in oz., 1947[c]	[184, p. 567]
	1051	Bauxite mining	1,892	32.3	Production – all distributed to Arkansas	[184, p. 174]
			5,865	100.0		
7	1110	Anthracite mining	61,012	16.6	Production – all distributed to Pennsylvania	[184, pp. 337–378]
	1210	Bituminous coal & lignite	306,133	83.4	Production of bituminous coal & lignite in thousands of tons	[184, p. 264]
			367,145	100.0		
8	1310	Crude petroleum & natural gas	104,244	100.0	Value at wells of production of crude petroleum & natural gas for 1946[d]	[184, pp. 807, 915]
9	1450	Clay, ceramics, & refractory materials	3,287	46.0	Value of clays sold by producer, 1947[e]	[184, pp. 241, 243–244, 248, 253–254]

	1462	Natural abrasives	1,046	14.7	Value of production of abrasive stones, 1947	[184, pp. 97–113]
	1490	Miscellaneous nonmetallic mining	2,806 / 7,139	39.3 / 100.0	Value of production of gypsum, mica, asphalt & talc, 1947[f]	[184, pp. 591, 790, 158, 1144, 581, 781, 1140, 153]
10	1472	Chemical & mineral fertilizer mining	2,489	7.1	Value of production of component minerals, 1947[g]	[184, pp. 22–24, 747, 743–745, 137–141, 1133, 164, 1009]
	1473	Fluorspar	257	0.7	Value of shipments from mines, 1947	[184, p. 500]
	1475	Phosphate rock	9,165	26.2	Value at mines of output sold or used by producers, 1947	[184, p. 978]
	1477	Sulfur	23,101 / 35,012	66.0 / 100.0	Production, 1947	[184, p. 1124]

[a]The values were calculated from the export final demand column in the 1947 detailed computer listing [194].

[b]The table on p. 687 indicated that there were no lead ore exports in 1947. Thus, output of zinc ores alone was used.

[c]The combined export figure was first separated into gold and silver components. Each of these was then allocated by production, and the two figures were added for each state to arrive at a single industry figure.

[d]The total export figure was split into the two indicated components, and each was allocated separately.

[e]The export figure for the industry was disaggregated into exports of (1) kaolin clay, (2) fire clay, and (3) other clays. The three parts were allocated separately and the figures added together.

[f]The total value of exports was split into the four indicated parts and each allocated separately.

[g]The industry was split into five parts – barite, potash salts, sodium salts, boron minerals, and pyrites – and each part was allocated separately. State totals for 1472 were obtained by adding the subtotals.

Table 4-3
Exports of Mineral Industries by SIC Subindustries, 1958 and 1963 (millions of dollars)

1958 IO	SIC	Description	Exports			
			1958		1963	
			Value	Percent	Value	Percent
5	1011	Iron ores	34.4	68.5	76.4	65.1
	1062	Manganese ores	0.7	1.4	0.9	0.8
	1064	Tungsten ore	–	–	} 40.0	} 34.1
	1069	Ferroalloy ores, excluding vanadium	15.1	30.1		
			50.2	100.0	117.3	100.0
6	1051	Bauxite & aluminum ores	1.0	50.0	1.0	50.0
	109	Miscellaneous metal mining	1.0	50.0	1.0	50.0
			2.0	100.0	2.0	100.0
7	11	Anthracite mining	35.8	6.8	43.7	9.2
	12	Bituminous coal & lignite mining	489.9	93.2	429.9	90.8
			525.7	100.0	473.6	100.0
8	13111	Crude petroleum	14.7	50.0	4.6	50.5
	13112	Natural gas	14.7	50.0	4.4	48.4
	1321	Natural gas liquids	–	–	0.1	1.1
			29.4	100.0	9.1	100.0
9	141	Dimension stone	1.7	4.2	–	–
	142	Crushed & broken stone	5.1	12.5	3.8	6.4
	144	Sand & gravel	3.5	8.6	4.3	7.2
	145	Clay, ceramic & refractory materials	12.1	29.6	22.4	37.7
	149	Miscellaneous nonmetallic minerals	2.8	6.9	19.2	32.3
	1400	Other, n.e.c.	15.6	38.2	9.7	16.3
			40.8	100.0	59.4	100.0
10	1473	Fluorspar	0.2	0.3	0.2	0.3
	1475	Phosphate rock	25.2	38.9	40.7	53.4
	1477	Sulfur	39.3	60.7	35.3	46.3
			64.7	100.0	76.2	100.0

SOURCE: U.S. Bureau of the Census, *U.S. Commodity Exports as Related to Output, 1958* [144] and *U.S. Commodity Exports and Imports as Related to Output, 1963 and 1962* [146].

IO-64. The proxy used to allocate the value of exports for the subindustries to the states was payrolls by states, taken from the *Census of Manufactures, 1947* [104, t. 2].[3]

In most cases, a 450-order input-output industry corresponded to a single 1947 census industry and no interpretation or mapping was required. In many cases, however, a single 1947 input-output industry was composed of more than one 1947 census industry. To handle these cases, the payroll figures for the component census industries were added for each state and the sum used as the allocation factor.[4] After the U.S. export figures for all of the 450 industries were allocated among the various states, the vectors were aggregated to the 80-order input-output classification.

1958 and 1963 Allocation of Manufactures. The data used for determining state exports of manufactured goods for these two years are unique in that they almost ideally satisfy the goal of this study. The information available for 1958 and 1963 made it possible to determine, within certain limits, the states wherein the goods exported had actually been manufactured. The basic data sources used for the allocation were Bureau of the Census (Census) surveys on the production location of manufactured goods exported to foreign countries for the years 1960 and 1963 [140; 141].[5]

Because the procedures used in this study to allocate manufactured exports among the states rested heavily on these Census surveys, the survey methodology will be briefly outlined in order to expedite the explanation of the allocation process.[6]

The manufacturers who were surveyed by the Census were asked how much of their output they exported directly or knew would be exported by wholesalers without further modification. The Census reports covered SIC product groups 19 through 39, with data being collected and published at the three-digit SIC level. For each of the 50 states and for the District of Columbia, two types of export data were reported: (1) the actual value of exports from the United States of manufactured products, by two-digit SIC product groups; and (2) the value of those exports reported by the manufacturers who were included in the survey, both by two- and three-digit SIC product groups.

The survey obviously accounted, in total, for zero to 100 percent of the known value of exports of each SIC product group. The results of the survey,

---

3. Value of shipments could also have been used as a proxy. Because this figure was missing for some of the industries, payrolls was used as the proxy. (The state output estimates were not available at the time this allocation was made.)

4. The correspondence of 1947 input-output and 1947 census industries was obtained from a Bureau of Labor Statistics manual [195, pp. 1–20].

5. The 1960 Census data were used for the 1958 allocation, as no comparable figures were available for any year prior to 1960.

6. For a complete explanation of the survey methodology, see *Census of Manufactures, 1963* [141] and *Current Industrial Reports* [140].

therefore, had to be adjusted for each product group to conform to the known national export totals. The method used by the Census to adjust the survey figures depended on the proportion of the known U.S. total value of exports for each SIC product group accounted for in the survey.

1. If the survey data accounted for over two-thirds of the actual U.S. exports for a two-digit SIC product group, the residual was divided among the states in proportion to the reported state figures. This allocation of the unreported residual was made at the three-digit SIC level.
2. If the reported exports for a two-digit SIC product group exceeded one-third but were less than two-thirds of the known U.S. total, the residual was split, again by three-digit SIC groups, according to a formula designed to include information on both the reported export figure and production for each state.
3. If the survey data accounted for less than one-third of the total known exports for a product group, the unreported residual was divided among the states in proportion to production, again at the three-digit SIC level.

Table 4–4 gives, for each of the two-digit SIC product groups covered in the Census report, the total U.S. value of exports, f.o.b., the amount reported in the survey, and the latter as a percent of the former, for 1963. The percentages indicate how the unreported export residuals were allocated among the states in the Census report (according to one of the three methods described above). The percentages also determined how each industry was treated in this study.

The major task of this phase of the project, then, was to transform the total U.S. export figures for the two-digit SIC product groups, for the 50 states and the District of Columbia, into input-output industry figures. In all but five cases, the two-digit SIC product groups include more than one input-output industry;[7] for example, product group SIC 34 incorporates ten input-output industries. The correspondence between two- and three-digit SIC product groups and input-output industries is given later in Tables 4–5 and 4–7.

Two different estimation procedures were employed in this study, depending on the proportion of the total U.S. exports of an SIC product group accounted for in the 1963 Census survey.[8]

---

7. The five SIC product groups corresponding to single input-output industries, along with the correspondence, are:

SIC	IO
20	14
21	15
27	26
29	31
30	32

8. Regardless of the proportions that existed in the 1960 survey, each two-digit product group was treated in 1960 the way it had been treated in 1963.

Table 4–4

Total Actual and Reported Exports from the United States, 1963
(millions of dollars)

			Total Value of U.S. Exports	
SIC	Product Group Description	Actual	Reported by Manufacturers	Column 2 As Percent of Column 1
		(1)	(2)	(3)
20	Food & kindred products	$ 1,710.2	$ 700.6	41.0
21	Tobacco products	498.7	308.1	61.8
22	Textile mill products	266.2	32.1	12.1
23	Apparel & related products	119.5	<10.0	<10.0
24	Lumber & wood products	192.9	<25.0	<10.0
25	Furniture & fixtures	26.4	–	–
26	Paper & allied products	452.0	318.1	70.4
27	Printing & publishing	168.5	94.5	56.1
28	Chemicals & allied products	1,869.5	1,354.4	72.4
29	Petroleum & coal products	428.5	428.5	100.0
30	Rubber & plastic products, n.e.c.	240.1	164.8	68.6
31	Leather & leather products	60.8	17.9	29.4
32	Stone, clay & glass products	197.7	153.1	77.4
33	Primary metal industries	852.1	700.0	82.2
34	Fabricated metal products	546.6	389.7	71.3
35	Machinery, excl. electrical	3,473.3	2,647.6	76.2
36	Electrical machinery	1,206.8	990.8	82.1
37	Transportation equipment	2,590.6	2,097.1	81.0
38	Instruments & related products	697.2	416.3	59.7
39,19	Miscellaneous manufacturing	679.8	174.0	25.6
		$16,277.4	$11,003.7	67.6

SOURCE: U.S. Bureau of the Census, "Survey of the Origin of Exports of Manufactured Products," in *Census of Manufactures, 1963* [141, tt. 1–2].

Method 1. If the survey accounted for less than two-thirds of the value of
exports of a given two-digit SIC product group, based on the 1963 survey, and
the SIC product group included more than one input-output industry, the
allocation of the published two-digit SIC state exports figures to the corresponding input-output industries for each state was effected solely through the use of
production proxies. SIC product group 38 in 1963 was an exception. Because
the survey data were fairly complete, and because SIC 38 mapped onto only two
input-output industries, Method 2 was used for 1963, although Method 1 was
used for 1958. The production proxy employed for the allocation was payrolls
by state, as given in the relevant industry table in the *Census of Manufactures,
1958* [107, t. 2] and *1963* [110, tt. 2 and 2A]. (At the time these allocations
were made, the 1958 and 1963 state output estimates were not available.)

The technique of allocation in Method 1 is fairly straightforward. If the published total export figure for an SIC product group for a given state had to be broken into input-output industry figures, the SIC figure was divided in proportion to payrolls for the corresponding input-output industries for that state. An illustration might be helpful at this point. Assume that the Census reported that for 1963 the value of exports for SIC product group X from Missouri was one hundred million dollars: the question to be asked is how much of this $100 million should be allocated to input-output industry Y and how much to industry Z. The payroll figures for Missouri from the relevant tables in the *Census of Manufactures, 1963* were the key. If, say, the payroll figures for input-output industry Y turned out to be $200 million and the comparable figure for industry Z was $300 million, then 40 percent of the exports from Missouri of SIC product group X would be allocated to IO-Y and 60 percent to IO-Z. The allocation of SIC X exports from any other state among the two input-output industries would depend on the payroll data for that state, as would the allocation of other SIC product groups. Identification of the SIC product groups allocated in this way and the source of the payroll figures used are indicated in Table 4–5.[9]

Method 2.   This method made considerably greater use of the material reported in the two Census surveys. As stated above, when the survey accounted for two-thirds or more of the total value of exports of a product group, the survey figures were used in the Census report to allocate the unreported portion among the states; thus, for this study as well, the survey figures alone were deemed sufficient to determine the state allocation of exports of the input-output industries.

The type of information included in the Census report, along with the symbols to be used in the mathematical description of Method 2, are easily described. For any state, k, the following information is given in the 1963 Census report [141]:

E_i^k =   the value of exports from state k for two-digit SIC product group i, as reported in the survey.

e_j^k =   the reported value of exports from state k of three-digit SIC subgroup j.

a_j^k =   a symbol designating that state k reported exports of three-digit SIC subgroup j, which the Census could not report without disclosing figures for individual companies. (The Census did, however, disclose a range of values within which the withheld figure fell.)

---

9. Whenever payroll figures for various states were withheld to avoid disclosing information for individual enterprises, payroll estimates were made on the basis of employment figures.

Table 4-5
Industries Allocated by Method 1, 1958 and 1963

| SIC | Input-Output Industry | | Sections in Sources | |
	Number	Title	Census of Manufactures, 1958 [107, t. 2]	Census of Manufactures, 1963 [110, tt. 2 and 2A]
22				
221,2,3,4,6,8	16	Fabrics	22	22
227,9	17	Textile prdts.		
225	18	Apparel		
23				
all exc. 239	18	Apparel	23	23
239	19	Misc. textile prdts.		
24				
all exc. 244	20	Lumber & wood prdts.	24	24
244	21	Wooden containers		
25				
all exc. 251	23	Other furniture	25	25
251	22	Household furniture		
26				
all exc. 265	24	Paper & allied prdts.	26	26
265	25	Paperboard containers		
31				
all exc. 311 and	34	Footwear, leather prdts.	31	31
312	33	Leather tanning & prdts.		
311,312				
38				
381,2,4,7	62	Professional, scien. instru.	38	
383,5,6	63	Medical, photo. equip.		
39,19				
39	64	Misc. manufacturing	39	39
19	13	Ordnance & accessories		

For all three-digit SIC subgroups j included in two-digit SIC product group i, for any state k, the following holds:

$$E^k_i = \sum_j e^k_j + \sum_j a^k_j \tag{4.1}$$

In the Census report, the United States is divided into nine regions, and the survey figures are reported for each region as well as for each state. Regions are composed of from three to nine states. For any region r, E^r_j = exports for three-digit SIC product grouping j reported from region r. Thus, for each region:

$$E^r_j = \sum_k e^k_j + \sum_k a^k_j \tag{4.2}$$

The above yields information for each region resembling that in Table 4–6 from which it was possible to estimate the undisclosed export figures with reasonable accuracy. The crucial factor is that a range of values was given for each undisclosed figure, thus creating upper and lower bounds for each export figure a^k_j. In estimating these figures, three constraints were taken into account:

1.   The reported upper and lower bound for each a^k_j.
2.   The regional total for the unknown sum of the a^k_j's for each three-digit SIC subgroup j.
3.   A total for the unknown $\sum_j a^k_j$ for each state k.

The second constraint is obtained by rewriting equation (4.2):

$$\sum_k a^k_j = E^r_j - \sum_j e^k_j \tag{4.3}$$

for each SIC subgroup j.

The third constraint is obtained by rewriting equation (4.1):

$$\sum_j a^k_j = E^r_j - \sum_j e^k_j \tag{4.4}$$

for each state k.

The elements in Table 4–6 can be rearranged in terms of a matrix with only the unknown a^k_j's, although this will not be presented here. Each row would embody one equation, such as equation (4.3) above, and each column would represent one equation (4.4). Within the framework of this revised regional matrix, the unknown a^k_j's were estimated, with the estimated figures falling within the upper and lower bounds as reported in the Census surveys. Again, payrolls was used as the basic allocating factor, although whenever this factor yielded numbers outside of the reported boundary figures, a number close to the effective boundary was arbitrarily chosen and the estimation process continued.

Table 4–6
Sample Export Equations for Region r

3-Digit SIC Product Group	State					Region r
	1	2		k	m	
1	e_1^1 +	a_1^2	+...+	0	+...+ a_1^m	= E_1^r
2	e_2^1 +	e_2^2	+...+	e_2^k	+...+ e_2^m	= E_2^r
$\vdots$	$\vdots$	$\vdots$		$\vdots$	$\vdots$	$\vdots$
j	a_j^1 +	a_j^2	+...+	e_j^k	+...+ e_j^m	= E_j^r
$\vdots$	$\vdots$	$\vdots$		$\vdots$	$\vdots$	$\vdots$
n	a_n^1 +	e_n^2	+...+	e_n^k	+...+ a_n^m	= E_n^r
2-Digit State Totals	E_i^1 +	E_i^2	+...+	E_i^k	+...+ E_i^m	= E_i^r

The process was repeated for each region and each two-digit SIC product group until estimates were calculated for all of the undisclosed value of export figures.

Another step was taken before the export figures were aggregated to the 80-order input-output classification. Let

X_i^k = the actual value of the exports for the two-digit SIC product group i for state k as reported by the Census.

Each of the given and newly calculated e_j^k's was multiplied by the factor X_i^k/E_i^k for the relevant two-digit product group i, so that all exports allocated by the Census to each state were assigned. These last figures were aggregated from the three-digit SIC order to the 80-order input-output classification. The industries treated by Method 2 are identified in Table 4–7.

The figures resulting from the mathematics described above are as close to actual value of foreign export production figures for each state as could be obtained. Two factors should be considered, however, as the data are used:

1. In some cases, the state total for a two-digit SIC product group—E_i^k, or the regional total for a three-digit grouping—E_j^r, would be withheld for the purpose of preventing disclosures for individual companies. These had to be estimated by a process similar to that described above before the unknown state figures could be derived.

2. The existence of undisclosed state export figures—indicated by the symbol a in the above explanation— was revealed only in the 1963 report. The 1960 study [140], which was used as the basis for the 1958 allocation of

Table 4–7
Industries Allocated by Method 2, 1958 and 1963

	Input-Output Industry	
SIC	Number	Title
28		
281,6,7,9	27	Chemicals, selected prdts.
282	28	Plastics & synthetics
283,4	29	Drugs & cosmetics
285	30	Paint & allied prdts.
32		
321,2,3	35	Glass & glass prdts.
324–9	36	Stone & clay prdts.
33		
331,2,9	37	Primary iron, steel mfr.
333,4,5,6	38	Primary nonferrous mfr.
34		
341	39	Metal containers
343,4	40	Fabricated metal prdts.
345,6	41	Screw mach. prdts., etc.
342,7,8,9	42	Other fab. metal prdts.
35		
351	43	Engines & turbines
352	44	Farm mach. & equip.
353[a]	{ 45	Construction mach. & equip.
	{ 46	Materials hand. mach. & equip.
354	47	Metalworking mach. & equip.
355	48	Special mach. & equip.
356	49	General mach. & equip.
357	51	Office, computing machines
358	52	Service industry machines
359	50	Machine shop prdts.
36		
361,2	53	Elect. transmission equip.
363	54	Household appliances
364	55	Electric lighting equip.
365,6	56	Radio, TV, etc. equip.
367	57	Electronic components
369	58	Misc. electrical mach.
37		
371	59	Motor vehicles, equip.
372	60	Aircraft & parts
373,4,5,7	61	Other transport. equip.
38[b]		
381,2,4,7	62	Professional, scien. instru.
383,5,6	63	Medical, photo. equip.

NOTE: The source of payroll data was the relevant sections of Volume II of the *Census of Manufactures, 1958* [107] and *1963* [110].

[a]The data for SIC product group 353 were used to allocate exports for IO–45 and IO–46 because more disaggregated data were unavailable.

[b]For 1963 only.

manufacturing exports, omitted any indication of where the undisclosed exports should appear. When the revealed data for the states in a region did not add to the regional totals, it was initially assumed that the undisclosed exporting states in 1960 were the same as in 1963. Thus, if a state exported some of a three-digit SIC industry in 1963, and the cell was empty in 1960 (with some undisclosed exports existing in the latter year), a portion of the 1960 residual was allocated to that state. The allocation of the residual among the states was generally made in the same proportions as in 1963. Occasionally, however, it was impossible to use the 1963 proportions and still have the 1960 rows and columns add to the relevant totals. In these cases, the 1960 constraints dictated the allocation.

Service Sector

This final economic sector is comprised of the 22 industries from IO-65 through IO-86. In an interesting turnabout, the information available for the 1947 allocation appears to be superior to that available for 1958 and 1963. Not only is it easier to disaggregate the input-output industries into components in 1947, but the 1947 interindustry study [62, ch. 3, pp. 60-61] also identifies the exact nature of the service exports. The identification is much more difficult in 1958 and 1963. For this reason, much of the 1958 and 1963 allocation process rests on information derived from the 1947 interindustry study, and the 1947 allocation is considered first. Sources used for the allocation factors are given in Table 4-8 for 1947.

1947 Allocation of Service Industries. For 1947, the service industries can be divided into two general categories according to the manner in which the exports of a given industry were purchased by foreign consumers. The first group consists of those industries whose services were exported as margins or markups in conjunction with the exports of manufacturing, mining, or agricultural goods. The total value of exports for 1947 of IO-69, Wholesale & retail trade, and part of the value of exports of IO-65, Transportation & warehousing, were purchased as margins. The remaining group was comprised of service industries whose exports were directly purchased by foreign consumers, such as marine insurance underwritten by American companies for foreign interests, electricity sold to Canada and Mexico, and ocean transportation supplied by American shipping companies.

Margin Service Exports. For the two input-output industries whose exports were purchased as margins on the exports of other industries, the 1947 value of these margin exports, as well as the allocation of the transportation margins among the various kinds of transportation services provided to foreign purchasers, is given in Table 4-9.

Table 4–8
Allocation Factors of Service Industries, 1947

1958 80-order IO	1947 450-order IO	Allocation Factor	Source
65	6167	Miles of track in states near Canada	[129, t. 589]
	6170	Volume of exports from ocean ports	[129, t. 636]
	6171	Tonnage shipped from Great Lakes ports	[129, t. 627]
	6173	Value of exports by air from gateway airports	[137, t. 867]
	61692	Same as 6170	[129, t. 636]
66	6191	Number of toll calls by state	[30, t. 6, p. 10]
	6192	Revenues of cable and wireless companies	[30, pp. 161, 168]
68	4911	Production of electrical energy	[129, t. 559]
70	61971	Fire and marine insurance premiums	[129, t. 508]
71		Value added by manufacture, 1947, of all goods	[109, pp. 86–94]
73	6203	Receipts of advertising agencies	[86, t. IQ, p. 0.46]
76	62083	1958 allocation factor	Table 4–10 below
78		Postal employees	[128, t. 225]
83	50931,2	Total estimated exports by state of IO–13 through IO–64	Statistical appendix to this study

Table 4–9
Exports of Margin Industries, 1947 (thousands of dollars)

1958 80-order IO	1947 450-order IO	Description	1947 Value[a]
65	6167	Railroads	$ 625,160
	6168	Trucking	143,163
	6171	Other water transportation	50,561
	6173	Air transportation	1,222
	6174	Pipeline transportation	9,187
	61691	Warehousing & storage	13,470
69	61751	Wholesale trade	1,039,239

[a]This identification was made from the final demand export vector of the 1947 detailed computer listing [194].

For each of the seven subindustries whose exports were treated as margins, the exporting industries which used the transportation and/or trade service, and the amounts which each purchased, could be determined from the 1947 input-output study. The result for each of these seven subindustries was a 450-order column vector identifying the amount of each service purchased as margin markups on the exports of other industries. These seven individual vectors were then grouped into two vectors, one for total transportation and one for wholesale trade. These vectors were, however, given only for the United States as a whole. The problem was to break each of these two national vectors into separate vectors for the states.

To simplify the process of allocating the two margin vectors among the states, one major assumption was made: that for each of the 450-order input-output industries, the margin markup was the same for all states. Factors such as distance from exporting port or other variations in transportation and trade costs among states could not be explicitly considered.

Each element of these two service export vectors was allocated among the states in the same proportion as the distribution of exports of the input-output industry using the service. Thus, if a state accounted for 10 percent of the value of the exports of an industry, it was allocated 10 percent of the wholesale trade and/or transportation exports used by that industry as a margin. The resulting pair of 450-order vectors for each of the states indicated the industry distribution of the trade and transportation exports, purchased as margins on the export of goods, from the state. The total value of exports of wholesale trade and the value of transportation exported as a margin for each state was obtained by summing the elements in the two vectors for the state.

Direct Service Exports.   All of the exports of IO-69, Wholesale & retail trade, and almost half of the total exports of IO-65, Transportation & warehousing, are in the form of margin markups on the goods exported. The rest of the value of exports of IO-65, as well as the exports of all other service industries, are directly purchased by foreigners and do not enter into the f.o.b. prices of other goods being shipped from this country. The exports of each of these service industries had to be distributed among the states in proportion to proxies because exact state data were unavailable.

Each of the service industries whose exports were directly purchased is identified below, by both the two-digit 1958 and the four-digit 1947 input-output classification, along with a discussion of the allocation methods used for each. For the directly allocated parts of IO-65, the value-of-export figures used as weights are also included.

IO-65, Transportation & warehousing.

· IO-6167, Railroads ($40,000,000).   The $40 million of directly purchased railroad services exported included transportation revenues earned in Canada and payments to U.S. railroads for hauling Canadian in-transit traffic in the United

States [62, ch. 3, p. 60] . Assuming that these revenues accrued to those states closest to Canada, miles of track located in those states close to or contiguous with Canada was used as the allocation factor. Included were all states in the New England, Middle Atlantic, East North Central, and Pacific regions plus the northernmost states in the Mountain and West North Central regions.

• IO-6170, Ocean transportation ($1,340,335,000). The exports of ocean transportation were not considered a margin service because the purchaser prices of export goods are determined f.o.b.; therefore, ocean transportation services are directly purchased. The main types of services provided are the physical shipping of exports on U.S. flagships, rental of harbor facilities and stevedoring for foreign boats, and miscellaneous minor services [196, Report N170, p. 73] . Because all of these services can be provided only at coastal port facilities, exports of ocean transportation services were allocated in proportion to each state's physical volume of exports from its ocean port. As a result, exports of ocean transportation services were allocated only to coastal states.

• IO-6171, Other water transportation ($4,681,000). The directly allocated portion of exports of other water transportation represents earnings of U.S. vessels carrying U.S. exports to Canada via the Great Lakes [62, ch. 3, p. 60] . Those Great Lakes ports engaged in lake shipping were allocated exports of this service industry, using total tonnage shipped from the ports of each Great Lakes state as the allocation factor.

• IO-6173, Air transportation ($81,590,000). Exports of air transportation consist of revenues earned in carrying United States exports abroad, foreign passengers on U.S. airlines, and foreign air mail [196, Report N173, p. 54] . This traffic had to pass through the five "gateway" customs districts; thus, the value of exports by air from these gateway districts, for the year 1965, was used as an allocation factor.[10]

• IO-61692, Forwarding & arranging transportation ($11,704,000). The 1947 Technical Supplement states that "this figure represents an estimate of agency and brokerage fees and commissions for United States exports shipped on foreign vessels" [62, ch. 3, p. 60] , that is, a payment by foreign shippers to domestic brokers for arranging the shipment of U.S. exports on foreign vessels. Because the nature of the services appears to be similar to domestic ocean transportation, IO-6170, in that only states with ocean ports would provide them, the same allocation factor was used.

The state figures for directly exported transportation services was added to the value of transportation purchased as a margin on the export of goods to obtain a total value for each state for transportation export. These combined figures are the published totals for IO-65, Transportation & warehousing.

----

10. 1965, the earliest year for which this statistic was readily available, was used for 1947, as well as for 1958 and 1963, the assumption being made that the proportion exported by each district did not change significantly over time. Only four states were involved: New York, Illinois, Florida, and California.

IO-66, Communications, except radio & TV broadcasting.

• IO-6191, Telephones ($3,138,000). Although these exports were generally identified as telephone receipts from abroad, there was no specific identification of the types of services rendered [196, Report N191; 62, ch. 3, p. 61]. The number of toll calls originating from each state was used as the allocation factor, under the assumption that each state provides foreign users with the same proportion of services as it supplies domestic users.

• IO-6192, Telegraph ($34,793,000). The major part of this figure is receipts for inbound cable service [62, ch. 3, p. 61]. Total transmission revenues for the various cable and wireless companies involved was used as an allocation factor, with the figures being allocated to the home-office state of each firm. Only four states are involved: New York,[11] California,[12] Massachusetts,[13] and Ohio.[14]

The telephone and telegraph figures for each state were added to obtain state totals for IO-66.

IO-68, Electric, gas, water, & sanitary services. The exports of electric power (IO-4911) went to Mexico and Canada [196, Report 4911, p. 3] in the following proportions:

Canada	$ 160,000
Mexico	1,025,000

Each of these component figures was allocated among the states directly bordering the country in question—four states for Mexico and ten for Canada—in proportion to the production of electrical energy in millions of kilowatt hours.

IO-70, Finance & insurance. As with ocean transportation, non-life insurance (IO-61971) is a purchased service directly related to exports and imports and consists primarily of fire and marine insurance on the exported and imported goods [196, Report N197.1, pp. 49, 61]. The allocation factor used was fire and marine insurance premiums, by state, in 1947.

IO-71, Real estate & rental. Most export receipts are royalty payments by foreign subsidiaries and firms to U.S. firms. For an explanation of the allocation factors used, see IO-71 for 1958 and 1963 (page 106).

IO-73, Business services. This export represents receipts for advertising services (IO-6203) by U.S. companies to foreign users [62, ch. 3, p. 61]. Because the type of advertising services provided could not be determined, the total receipts for each state of all types of advertising agencies was used as the allocation factor.

---

11. All America Cable and Radio, Commercial Cable Co., Mackay Radio and Telegraph, Press Wireless, R.C.A. Communication, Western Union, Radiomarine Corp. of America, Commercial Pacific Cable Co., Mexican Telegraph Co.

12. Globe Wireless Ltd.

13. Tropical Radio Telegraph Co.

14. U.S. Liberia Radio Corp.

IO-76, Amusements.   These motion picture distribution exports (IO-62083) represent receipts from abroad for sales and rentals of American films [62, ch. 3, p. 61]. Because no 1947 figures specifically related to this activity, the 1958 allocation factor was used.

IO-78, Federal government enterprises.   In 1958, the export receipts of federal government enterprises included postal services rendered to foreigners and receipts from the Panama Canal. The allocation for 1947 was based only on the number of post office employees by state, because it appeared that the Panama Canal receipts were not included in the total for the industry.

IO-83, Scrap, used & secondhand goods.   The figure for waste materials (IO-50931 and IO-50932) was divided among the states in proportion to their total exports of the manufacturing industries, IO-13 through IO-64, as no other reasonable allocation factor was available.

1958 and 1963 Allocation of Service Industries.   The information on exports of services for 1958 and 1963 was not as detailed as the 1947 information; much of the 1958 and 1963 allocation of service exports among the states, therefore, had to draw heavily on 1947 information and allocation procedures. The specific sources used for 1958 and 1963 are summarized in Table 4–10. Wherever it was advantageous, the composition of exports for each industry in 1958 and 1963 was assumed to resemble that which existed in 1947. Thus, if, in 1947, the entire export of a service industry appeared to be of one specific type of service or good (or went to one specific country), then it was assumed that the same good also comprised the total amount of exports for the industry in 1958 and 1963 (or went to the same country). Each industry was treated individually, as in 1947, to take full advantage of the different types of allocation factors available.

IO-65, Transportation & warehousing.   As in 1947, a portion of the exports of this service industry was treated as a margin on exports of other goods, while the remainder was directly allocated. For 1958, the transportation industry was separated into nine subindustries, with the total export of each subindustry further divided into margin purchases and direct purchases. The breakdown is given in Table 4–11.

No figures comparable to those in the table were available for 1963 at the time this study was made. For 1963, it was assumed that the total value of transportation exports for that year was divided among the nine subindustries in the same proportion as in 1958, and that for each subindustry, the division between margin and direct purchases was also the same as for 1958. The same basic distribution of transportation and warehousing between margin and direct sales and among the different modes was thus used for both years. Separate allocation factors, however, were employed for the two years to distribute the export figures in Table 4–11 among the states. The allocation process for both 1958 and 1963 involved the following basic pattern.

Table 4-10

Allocation Factors of Service Industries, 1958 and 1963

1958 80-order IO	SIC	Allocation Factor	Source 1958	Source 1963
6501[a]		Miles of railroad in states near Canada	[132, t. 752]	[136, t. 812]
6502[a]		Exports from costal ports, in tons	[132, t. 791]	[136, t. 849]
6503[a]		Shipments from Great Lakes ports	[132, t. 792]	[136, t. 851]
6505[a]		Exports from major gateway customs districts, 1965	[137, t. 865]	[136, t. 865]
66	(Telephone) (Telegraph)	Number of toll calls by state Transmission revenue by company	[26, pp. 16–17] [26, pp. 151, 159]	[27, pp. 16–17] [27, pp. 173, 181]
67		Number of commercial radio & TV broadcast stations	[132, t. 675]	[135, t. 710]
68		Production of electric power	[132, t. 691]	[135, t. 730]
69		Wholesale sales, 1958, 1963	[137, t. 1216]	[137, t. 1216]
70		Fire and casualty insurance premiums	[132, t. 619]	[137, t. 677]
71		Value added by manufacture	[109, pp. 86–94]	[109, pp. 86–94]
72	70, 72, 76	Total receipts for all three SIC product groups	[89, sec. 1, pp. 40, 41, 53]	[93, sec. 2, t. 4]
73	731	Total receipts for advertising	[89, sec. 1, p. 46]	[93, sec. 2, t. 4]
75	75	Receipts of auto repair and service establishments	[89, sec. 1, p. 50]	[93, sec. 2, t. 4]
76	781, 782	Total receipts for motion picture prod. & dist. est.	[89, sec. 1, p. 55]	[93, sec. 8, t. 1]
77		Expenditures of foundations	[136, p. 319]	[138, p. 448]
78		Number of postal employees	[131, t. 497]	[135, t. 545]
79		Generating capacity of publicly owned companies	[131, p. 583]	[136, p. 534]

[a]These are subcategories of IO-65 used by Jack Faucett Associates, *Input-Output Transactions by Transportation Mode, 1947 and 1958* [15].

Table 4-11
Exports of Transportation and Warehousing, by Type, 1958 (thousands of dollars)

Transportation Category	Description	Total	Exports	
			Margin	Directly Purchased
6501	Railroads	$ 513,142	$466,142	$ 47,000
6502	Overseas water trans.	618,700	–	618,700
6503	Domestic water trans.	528,844	49,424	479,420
6504	Trucking & warehousing	317,413	317,413	–
6505	Airlines & aviation serv.	194,510	5,981	188,529
6506	Pipelines	38,236	9,236	29,000
6507	Intercity bus	539	539	–
6508	Trans. serv., n.e.c.	79,980	17,410	62,570
6509	Trans. excise taxes	10,713	10,713	–
		$2,302,077	$876,858	$1,425,219

SOURCE: Jack Faucett Associates, *Input-Output Transactions by Transportation Mode, 1947 and 1958* [15, pp. 80, 90, 90, row 95].

1. As in the 1947 input-output study, a set of eight vectors identifying the margin exports of the transportation subindustries by purchasing input-output industries was obtained from tapes of the 1958 input-output table. These eight vectors were summed to obtain a single 80-order vector representing the total transportation margin exported, by using industry.

2. The total transportation margin figure for each input-output industry was allocated among the various states in the same proportion as their exports of that industry. Thus, if a given state accounted for 10 percent of the exports of a given industry, it was allocated 10 percent of the transportation margin associated with the industry.[15]

3. A single figure representing the value of the transportation margin for each state was obtained by adding the 65 figures obtained for each state in step 2.

4. The directly purchased transportation services were allocated among the states in proportion to separate allocation factors and summed.[16]

5. The two numbers for each state were added to obtain a final allocation, including both the margin exports and the directly allocated exports.

IO-66, Communications, except radio & TV broadcasting. The total export figures for this industry for each year were first separated into telephone and telegraph components, in the same proportion as existed in 1947, and each component was allocated separately to the various states.[17] The two sets of figures were added to obtain the final distribution.

IO-67, Radio & TV broadcasting. Because there were no exports of this industry indicated for 1947, the exact type of services exported cannot be identified. The total number of commercial radio and TV broadcast stations in each state was used as the allocation factor.

IO-68, Electric, gas, water, & sanitary services. On the basis of the information available for 1947, it was assumed that all exports of this industry consisted of electric power sales to Mexico and Canada, and that the states contiguous to these two countries were the sole suppliers. It was further assumed that the same proportions of the total exports of electric power were sold to each country in the two years as were sold in 1947. The allocation factor used was production of electric power in the relevant states.

IO-69, Wholesale & retail trade. In 1947, exports of IO-69 consisted entirely of wholesale trade margins, and it was assumed that for 1958 and 1963

---

15. The allocation factors were exports of IO-1 through IO-64 and IO-83, all of which had been previously determined. Since different export matrices exist for 1958 and 1963, the resulting allocations were different for the two years.

16. Because of lack of information for IO-6506 and IO-6508, this was done only for IO-6501, IO-6502, IO-6503, and IO-6505. In 1958, IO-6506 and IO-6508 were ignored altogether and, in 1963, they were allocated in proportion to the total allocation of the first four. Thus, the margin allocation of steps 1 to 3 is weighted slightly more heavily in the 1958 state totals than in the 1963 state totals.

17. The same type of allocation factor was used for both years, as in 1947.

the same held true. The method of allocation, however, changed. Since no figures were available to separate the total U.S. exports of this service among IO-1 through IO-64, the exports for the industry could not be allocated as they were in 1947. Instead, an allocation factor—total wholesale sales in each state—was used.

IO-70, Finance & insurance. Again, the 1947 information proved useful. In that year, exports of this service industry consisted entirely of fire and marine insurance, and under the assumption that the same held true in 1958 and 1963, fire and casualty insurance premiums for each year were used as the allocation factor.

IO-71, Real estate & rental. Export receipts for this service industry consist primarily of royalty payments by foreign subsidiaries and foreign firms to domestic firms. The best allocation factor would have been corporate assets by state, but data of this type do not exist. Instead, total value of manufactures of all goods by state was used.

IO-72, Hotels & lodging places; personal & repair services, except automobile repair. In 1947, there were no exports by this industry; thus, no clear basis existed for the 1958 or 1963 allocation. The total export figure was allocated among the states in proportion to the sum of receipts by state for SIC 70, 72, and 76.

IO-73, Business services. In 1947, this industry exported only advertising services. Thus, for 1958 and 1963, the factor used was total advertising receipts by state (SIC 731).

IO-75, Automobile repair & services. There were no exports of IO-75 in 1947, and for 1958 and 1963, the indicated amount is very small. Since the export of motor vehicles (IO-59) affects many states, automobile repair services were allocated in proportion to total receipts for automobile repair and service establishments in each state (SIC 75).

IO-76, Amusements. In 1947, exports comprised receipts from foreign film rentals, and the same was assumed for 1958 and 1963. No allocation factor was found that specifically related to this industry, so total receipts of motion picture production, distribution, and service establishments was used (SIC 781 and 782).

IO-77, Medical, educational services, & nonprofit organizations. Since the exact nature of the exports of this industry could not be determined, expenditures of foundations by states was used as the allocation factor.

IO-78, Federal government enterprises. Exports of federal government enterprises in 1958 consist mainly of receipts from Panama Canal tolls [136, p. 603] and exports of postal services. Exports of this industry for 1963 were assumed to consist of the same two components. The division between the two components for both years follows:

Component	1958	1963
	(millions of dollars)	
Total	$61.0	$90.4
Panama Canal	41.8	56.4
Postal Services	19.2	34.0

Since the Panama Canal tolls do not give rise to domestic production, only the postal service exports, which were calculated as a residual, are allocated among the states. The number of post office employees in each state was used as the allocation factor. For 1947, Panama Canal tolls were $17.6 million, which was larger than the total for the industry of $8.4 million; consequently, it was assumed that the Panama Canal values were not included in the 1947 data.

IO-79, State & local government enterprises. The figure for this industry consists primarily of exports of electric power to Canada and Mexico by publicly owned power companies. All exports were allocated to the states contiguous to the two countries in proportion to the generating capacity of these companies.

IO-83, Scrap, used & secondhand goods. Scrap exports were allocated among the states in proportion to total exports of IO-13 through IO-64.

IO-85, Rest of the world industry. Export earnings of IO-85 consist primarily of interest receipts and repatriated profits from American investment abroad. No allocation among the states was performed.

IO-86, Household industry. Earnings of IO-86 consist primarily of income earned abroad by the United States nationals, and no allocation was made to the states.

Foreign Exports by Port of Exit.

In this section of the chapter, the methodology used to estimate exports by state of exit is explained. These export data could be assembled only for the year 1963 because of data and time limitations. For the multiregional input-output model which has been implemented at the Harvard Economic Research Project to calculate the flows of commodities among states, it is necessary to take account of the exports leaving the United States from each port. For example, the shipment of automobiles from Michigan to New York depends not only on final demands by New York consumers, but also on the export volume of auto-mobiles from New York's ports.

Very detailed data on exports by port of exit are available for 1963 in *Export Tabulations* [121]. This publication lists exports by detailed Schedule B commodity classification (the statistical classification of commodities exported from the United States used by the Department of Commerce) and customs districts of exportation. But the data are far too detailed for use in this study, and the conversion of the product classification from Schedule B to the input-output classification was impossible with limited research funds. Therefore, the estimates were made from less detailed data.

Estimates for Agriculture, Mining, Manufacturing, and Scrap Industries

The Bureau of the Census publication, *Highlights of U.S. Exports and Imports* [123], shows, in Table E-5, selected Schedule B commodity groupings and customs regions of export. The earliest year for which this table is available is 1967. For the convenience of the reader, part of the 1967 table is reproduced in Table 4-12. Three major steps were necessary to transform the data in the table into estimates suitable for the multiregional input-output study: (1) conversion of the product classification to the 80-order input-output classification; (2) conversion of the customs regions into states; and (3) adjustment from 1967 to 1963 estimates.

The product reclassification was performed as follows. First, the Schedule B numbers corresponding to each line of Table E-5 were found. In most cases, it was not difficult, using detailed Schedule B export information,[18] to find the Schedule B or group of Schedule B commodities having total exports equal to the figure shown in the "total, all regions" column of the table. Part of the Schedule B assignment is shown in Table 4-13. Next, in order to obtain the maximum possible information from Table E-5, many row subtractions were carried out. For example, by subtracting the data in rows 12, 13, and 14 from those in row 11, the regions of export can be found for the Schedule B group 043 (excluding 043.0), 044 (excluding 044.0), and 045 (excluding 045.9020, 045.9010) which equals 045.1000, 045.2000. When all the row subtractions were made, no row of the resulting table included the exports of any commodity included in another row. Rows which were merely subtotals of other rows (e.g., row 8) were eliminated.

The modified E-5 table, that is, the table remaining after row subtractions and elimination of subtotal rows, contained 126 rows. Table 2 of *U.S. Exports* (FT610) [148] was used to convert the Schedule B classifications of the rows of the modified E-5 table to Standard Industrial Classification export product codes. Then the rows were allocated to input-output categories by using the alignment between four-digit SIC industries and input-output industries given in the 1963 input-output table [164, pp. 26–28]. In most cases the rows of the modified E-5 table contained several four-digit SIC codes and not all of these SIC codes belonged to the same input-output industry. For example, Table 4-13

---

18. For example, *U.S. Exports* (FT410) [147].

Table 4-12

Domestic Merchandise: Selected Schedule B Commodity Groupings and Commodities by U.S. Customs Regions, 1967 (millions of dollars)

Line No.	Commodity Description	Total All Regions	Atlantic Districts (1)	Great Lakes Districts (2)		Special Category (11)	Other (12)	Schedule B Code
1.	Grand total	$31,147.2	$454.2	$2,229.6	...	$1,108.2	$410.8	
2.	Agricultural commodities	6,383.3	36.4	92.3	...	–	0.5	01
3.	Nonagricultural commodities	24,763.9	417.7	2,137.3	...	1,108.2	410.3	02
4.	Food & live animals	4,064.1	26.9	74.3	...	–	–	0
5.	Meat & meat preparations, incl. poultry	151.3	7.9	7.6	...	–	–	01
6.	Dairy products & eggs	116.9	2.2	4.0	...	–	–	02
7.	Grains & cereal preparations	2,681.4	5.4	5.0	...	–	–	04
8.	Wheat & wheat flour	1,207.2	4.3	1.3	...	–	–	041,046
9.	Wheat – unmilled	1,120.2	4.3		...	–	–	041
10.	Wheat flour	87.0	–	1.3	...	–	–	046
11.	Barley, corn, grain sorghums, rye & oats – unmilled	1,060.2	0.5	0.6	...	–	–	043,044,045 (excl. 045.9020)
12.	Barley – unmilled	46.6	–	–	...	–	–	043.0
13.	Corn – unmilled	704.0	0.5	0.7	...	–	–	044.0
14.	Grain sorghums	298.8	–	39.1	...	–	–	045.9010
	· · ·	·	·	·	...	·	·	·
22.	Crude materials, except fur skins – undressed	3,280.1	68.9	82.5	...	–	6.6	2
	· · ·	·	·	·	...	·	·	·

NOTE: This is part of Table E-5 in *U.S. Exports* (FT-410) [147].

Table 4–13
Dairy Products and Eggs

SIC Export Code 1967	SIC Product Code 1963	Schedule B Code	Value of Exports for 1967 (thousands)	Input-Output Industry Number
2023	2023	022.1010–022.2050		
2026	2026	022.3000,024.0030		
2021	2021	023.0010–023.0040		
2022	2022	024.0010–024.0020 024.0040–024.0050		14
2015	2015	025.0030–025.0040	$104,497	
0134	part of 0133	025.0010	3,039	1
0723	0723	025.0020	9,327	4
Total			$116,863	

SOURCES: 1. *U.S. Exports* (FT 610) [148] contains in Table 2 an allocation of Schedule B codes to SIC export product codes and shows in Table 3 the principal differences between SIC product codes and export codes.

2. *U.S. Exports* (FT 410) [147] gives the value of exports for 1967 for each of the Schedule B codes. The "value of exports for 1967" column was obtained by appropriate additions.

3. The 1963 input-output table [165] gives the correspondence between SIC product codes and input-output industries.

4. The *Standard Industrial Classification Manual, 1967,* Appendix C [81] shows changes between 1963 and 1967 SIC product codes.

was constructed for row 6, "Dairy Products and Eggs." Then row 6 was allocated to IO-1, Livestock & livestock products; IO-4, Agricultural, forestry, & fishery services; and IO-14, Food & kindred products, in the ratios 3,039 : 9,327 : 104,497. Similar calculations were performed for each of the rows of the modified E–5 table. When the allocation of rows to input-output industries was completed, the resulting matrix had 65 rows, each referring to one of the input-output industries in the agricultural, mining, or manufacturing sector.[19]

Next, data in the columns of Table E–5 were reclassified from customs regions to states. First, data in columns 11 and 12, "special transactions, all regions," (see Table 4–12) were allocated proportionally to the figures in the other 10 columns. For example, the $6.6 million appearing in the "other" column of row 22 of Table E–5 was allocated to Atlantic districts, Great Lakes districts, New York, etc., in the ratio 68.9 : 82.5 : . . . , etc. For a few rows, the "special transactions, all regions" contained a large proportion (nearly 100 percent) of the total value of exports given for the row. In such cases, the row contained almost no information and was not used. The elimination of these

19. No service exports or exports for construction (IO-11 and IO-12) were given in Table E–5. Services and construction were handled separately, as described later.

Table 4–14
Export Volume of Customs Districts

U.S. Customs Regions and Districts	Volume of Exports by All Methods of Transportation for 1967 (millions)
Atlantic Districts	$ 464.9
Portland, Maine	61.9
St. Albans, Vermont	179.4
Boston, Massachusetts	210.2
Providence, Rhode Island	4.5
Bridgeport, Connecticut	8.9
Great Lakes Districts	$2,296.9
.	.
.	.
.	.

NOTE: This is part of Table E–4 from *Highlights of U.S. Exports and Imports* [123].

rows seriously reduced the allocation of exports only for IO-13, Ordnance & accessories. An alternative method was necessary for estimating the exports from each state for this input-output industry, as described later. After the data in columns 11 and 12 had been allocated, the data in the remaining 10 columns were reclassified into states as follows. For each customs region, Table E–4 in *Highlights of U.S. Exports and Imports* [123] shows the included customs districts and their export volume. Part of the table is reproduced in Table 4–14.

On the basis of this table, data in column 1 of the modified E–5 table were allocated to Maine, Vermont, Massachusetts, Rhode Island, and Connecticut in the ratio 61.9 : 179.4 : 210.2 : 4.5 : 8.9. In a few cases, the procedure produced unsatisfactory results. For example, Hawaii and Alaska are in the same customs region, but it is unreasonable to assume that the export mix from these two states is the same. Estimates of exports by state of production, described in the preceding section of this chapter, were used for these two states. There were other similar cases. Initial calculations showed a substantial export of IO-60, Aircraft & parts, from Montana. This figure merely reflects the fact that Montana belongs to the same customs region as Northern California and Washington. Hence, Montana's apparent exports of IO-60 were reallocated to California and Washington. Only 35 of the 51 regions (50 states plus the District of Columbia) had ports from which nonservice exports left the United States; therefore, with the completion of the column allocation and product reclassification, estimates of exports for 1967 for 65 input-output industries from 35 states had been generated. Finally, 1963 estimates were obtained by assuming that the 1967 export distribution by states was the same as that for 1963, that is, it was assumed that the fraction of the exports of each input-output industry leaving from each state was the same in 1967 as in 1963. These fractions were then applied to the 1963 national input-output export figures [164, p. 32] to obtain estimates of state exports.

Estimates for Construction and
Service Industries

For many of the construction and service industries, the state of exit can be considered to be identical with the state of production. The reader is therefore referred to the earlier section of this chapter where the estimates by state of production for 1963 are explained. Although the state estimates for the two sets of export figures will be identical for most of the construction and service industries, special estimates had to be made by port of exit for the following three industries.

IO-13, Ordnance & accessories. It was assumed that all IO-13 exports left from ocean ports and that exports produced in states with ocean ports left from these ports, e.g., all the estimated California production of IO-13 exports (more than 50 percent of the total) was assumed to leave from California. Production of exports in states without ocean ports (about 22.5 percent of the total) was distributed to states having ocean ports in proportion to their estimated export production.

IO-65, Transportation & warehousing. The directly purchased portion of this industry was allocated using the same data as by place of production. For the margin exports, however, a new set of estimates was required. The 1963 transportation margins, obtained from an OBE computer tape, were applied to the export estimates by state of exit. These margin estimates were then added to the directly purchased estimates to obtain a state distribution of total transportation.

IO-69, Wholesale & retail trade. It was assumed that the exports of this industry consist entirely of wholesale trade margins. The total value of non-service exports leaving each state in 1963 was used as an allocating factor.

Conclusion

Foreign exports can be estimated either by state of production or by state of exit for use in multiregional economic analyses. For each individual study, the set of estimates required will depend upon the nature of the model to be used and the methods employed to assemble the other data components. In the accompanying statistical appendix, foreign exports are given by state of production for 1947, 1958, and 1963 but by state of exit for 1963 only. The present chapter has explained the methodology that can be used to estimate both sets of exports. Because the Census is collecting a considerable amount of regional data on gross foreign exports, state estimates for current years can be more accurately estimated than the figures calculated for this study provided that sufficient funds are obtained for processing the computer tapes.

HUNT LIBRARY
CARNEGIE-MELLON UNIVERSITY

5

Net Purchases of Goods and Services by State and Local Governments

Richard Berner and
Orani Dixon

The estimation of state and local government final demands for each state for 1947, 1958, and 1963 is based upon the governmental net purchases figures. Because the Bureau of the Census data on state and local government expenditures had to be used in making the estimates, a distinction should be made between expenditures and net purchases. Expenditures by the government include grants-in-aid, transfer payments, net interest, and the surplus or deficit of government enterprises, whereas net purchases include only the direct purchases of goods and services. The state final demand estimates therefore comprise the governmental purchases on current and capital account for the general governmental activities, plus the purchases on capital account of state and local government enterprises. Since current account purchases of the enterprises are financed by the sales of goods and services, they are included in IO-79, State & local government enterprises. State and local government agencies are classified in IO-79 if they "cover over half of their current operating costs by the sale of goods and services to the general public" [163, p. 24].

Expenditures by state and local governments (SLG) are usually classified either by character and object or by function. The classification by character and object includes current operation, capital outlay (for construction, equipment, land, and existing structures), assistance and subsidies, interest on debt, and insurance trust. For a more detailed explanation of the character and object classification, the reader is referred to the *Census of Governments, 1962* [100, p. 5]. The SLG net purchases estimated by state for this study were compiled to be consistent with the National Income and Product Accounts (NIPA) [168], in which the SLG net purchases are presented by function. Therefore, the functional classification was used to obtain the state estimates.

For the 1963 national input-output table [165], four major functional categories have been established by the Office of Business Economics (OBE). They are education, public health and welfare, public safety, and "other." These four functions are outlined in more detail in Table 5–1 to show their correspondences with the unpublished 15-function categories used by the OBE for the 1958 input-output study [175].

The SLG expenditures data by state and by function obtained from the *Census of Governments, 1957* [99, t. 31] and *1962* [101, t. 35] were used in

Table 5-1

Major Functional Categories of State and Local Government Purchases 15-Function Classification[a]

1. Elementary, secondary, and other education
2. Institutions of higher education
3. Libraries
4. Hospitals
5. Public health and welfare (including veterans' services)
6. Sanitation (not including sewers and sewerage)
7. Police
8. Fire
9. Correction
10. General government
    (a) Social security administration
    (b) General control
11. Regular highways
12. Local passenger transportation – public parking
13. Nonhighway – airports, water transport, and terminal facilities[b]
14. State toll highways[b]
15. Other
    (a) Sewers and sewerage[b]
    (b) Parks and recreation
    (c) Natural resources
    (d) Housing and community development
    (e) Public facilities
    (f) Other and unallocable
    (g) Liquor stores[b]
    (h) Utilities: gas, electric, and water[b]

[a]The 15 functions are given in unpublished OBE worksheets for 1958. The correspondences between the 4-, 6-, and 15-function classification referred to in this chapter are as follows:

4-function	6-function	15-function
1	1	1,2,3
2	2	4,5,6
3	3	7,8,9
4	{ 4	10
	5	11,12,13,14
	6	15

[b]Only capital outlay expenditures are included.

the estimation of SLG net purchases for 1958 and 1963, respectively. The data have the advantage of being disaggregated, consistent in their functional classification, and well documented. Between 1942 and 1957, however, the publication of these statistics was suspended. Only state government data are available for the year 1947; therefore, a special estimate, explained later, had to be made for the 1947 local government expenditures in order to obtain the total SLG net purchases for 1947.

From the two data sources for 1958 and 1963, the SLG net purchases could be allocated among fifteen functions; however, for 1947, the data could be allocated among only six functions. Therefore, all three-year comparisons of SLG final demands are made for only six functions in this chapter. Also, Alaska

and Hawaii, which are included in the input-output and national income accounts
for 1963, are excluded from the 1963 data when comparisons are made with the
1947 and 1958 data.

General Methodology and Estimation Procedures

In the national input-output accounts, only the SLG governmental expenditures that contribute to the net purchases of goods and services are included.
The input-output data are compiled to be consistent with the NIPA figures;
therefore, the statistics for calendar years are derived as strict arithmetic averages
from the straddling fiscal years.[1] Table 5-2 outlines the way in which the gross
national product figures for state and local governments are calculated by the
staff of the OBE. As shown by the table, a character and object classification,
rather than a functional one, is used in constructing the national total of SLG net
purchases. Total SLG expenditures, as defined by the Bureau of the Census
(Census) and shown in the table as item (1), include the expenditures made on
current and capital accounts by all general governmental units and by state and
local government enterprises and public utilities. Included in this total are
expenditures on assistance and subsidies, insurance trust, interest on debt, and
current account expenditures of state and local government enterprises, none of
which contributes to the NIPA total of SLG net purchases. These expenditures
items appear, however, under the "character and object" classification of the
governmental finances reported by the Census. To obtain a net purchase total
from these expenditures data, all items not contributing to the gross national
product must be subtracted.

Estimation Procedures for Census State Data

After the detailed components of the national data had been determined,
the SLG net purchases were estimated by function for each state using statistics
compiled from the Census publications. This section contains a discussion of the
available Census state data and the adjustments made to those data before they
were used to calculate SLG net purchases by state.

Special Adjustments to Census State Expenditures Data. Wherever the
availability of data made it possible, the Census state data on direct expenditures
were adjusted to adhere to the national income definitions. Some special comments on the adjustments made for assistance and subsidies, insurance trust,
interest on debt, and government enterprises are required at this stage.

---

1. According to the OBE, the national income accounts data for local governments
were fiscal rather than calendar year figures through the calendar year 1962.

Table 5-2

Conversion of State and Local Government Direct General Expenditures to Purchases of Goods and Services (Office of Business Economics Procedure Current in 1970)

	(1)	Total state and local government expenditures (direct general expenditures plus utilities, liquor stores, and insurance trust)
minus:	(2)	Insurance benefits
	(3)	Interest on debt
	(4)	Assistance and subsidies plus payments for foster children in private homes and aid to higher education in schools run by local authorities
	(5)	Purchases of land and existing structures
	(6)	Current operations of government enterprises
	(7)	New construction
	(8)	Personal services to general government (wages plus salaries)
	(9)	Wage supplement (income other than wages and salaries) other than payments to self-administered retirement funds
plus:	(10)	General government force account compensation
equals:	(11)	Other gross purchases
minus:	(12)	Sales other than structures
equals:	(13)	Other purchases
plus:	(14)	Compensation of general government (employees)
	(15)	Structures (including new construction less force account compensation)
	(16)	Purchases less sales of existing structures
equals:	(17)	Net purchases of goods and services
plus:	(18)	Sales of goods and services
equals:	(19)	Gross purchases of goods and services

Assistance and Subsidies, Insurance Trust.   Assistance and subsidies and insurance trust are mainly intergovernmental transfer items which should be eliminated from the expenditures totals of the appropriate functions to obtain the SLG net purchases. These items are included in the current expenditures accounts published by the Census, and no detailed functional data are available. For the state estimates, adjustments to exclude these items were possible for only two functions—education and public health and welfare. For 1958, the total for cash assistance and subsidies is $3,159 million out of a total direct expenditures of $53,712 million (5.9 percent); for 1963, the amount is $3,771 million out of a total of $75,760 million (5.0 percent); for 1947, the amount is unobtainable but presumably small. As a percentage of total direct expenditures at the national level, therefore, the item of assistance and subsidies is not large enough to lead to any serious distortion in the SLG net purchases estimates.

Interest on Debt.   In the Census data, interest on debt is already separated from other expenditures by functions, and total amounts are recorded by states. Therefore, these expenditures could be eliminated from all functions in the estimation of the SLG net purchases.

Government Enterprises.   Government enterprises are treated in a manner analogous to the treatment of private industries. The expenditures for current operations of the state and local government enterprises, given as item (6) of Table 5-2, were therefore excluded from the SLG net purchases of goods and services, leaving only the capital outlays of the enterprises to be estimated for the SLG final demand. For capital outlays, estimates were made for state toll highways, nonhighway transportation (airports, water transportation, and terminal facilities), public parking facilities, and utilities (gas, electricity, water supplies, sewers, and sewage disposals). The capital expenditures amounts are available by state for most, but not all, of these functions.

Because no capital outlay expenditures are reported for the local passenger transportation in any of the three years, nor for liquor stores, nonhighway transportation, and public utilities in 1947, the data for each of these functions were assembled in a special manner.

Local passenger transportation.   This was the only government enterprise for which no capital outlay data were available. Direct expenditures of public parking facilities were, therefore, used as a substitute for capital outlays to obtain the state figures in the three years.

Liquor stores.   For 1947, no data were available from which capital outlay for liquor stores could be estimated, and the amount, which was probably less than 5 percent of total 1947 SLG direct expenditures, had to be excluded. For 1958 and 1963, capital outlay figures were available for state-operated liquor stores of sixteen states. The capital outlay data for locally operated liquor stores by state were estimated for the two years by subtracting the current operating expenses from direct expenditures of local liquor stores. The estimation was made for two states in 1958 and for three states in 1963.

Nonhighway transportation.   Capital outlay expenditures by state in 1958 and 1963 were estimated by applying the national ratios of capital outlay to direct general expenditures for nonhighway transportation, obtained for 1957 and 1962, respectively, to the direct government expenditures for the function in each state. Since no data were directly available for 1947, the amount of 1947 local government capital outlay for nonhighway transport was linearly inter-polated from 1942 and 1957 figures.

Public utilities.   The gas, electricity, and water public utilities are mainly operated by local governments; consequently, only the local capital outlay figures by state for 1957 and 1962 were used to estimate the SLG net purchases of the functions for 1958 and 1963. The 1947 capital outlays had to be estimated by linearly interpolating from the 1942 and 1958 local government capital outlay expenditures for utilities. The 1942 capital outlay figures were obtained from *City Finances, 1942* [95].

1947 Census State Expenditures Data.   As mentioned earlier, the Census data on governmental finances, reported by state and function, exist only for state governments in 1947. Several ways of estimating the 1947 local government data for the various functions were tried. The estimation method chosen for the study was the linear interpolation of the relevant local government expenditures in 1942 and 1957. The proportions among states and functions, and between the two levels of government, were preserved as much as possible by leaving the 1947 state government expenditures data intact and adding to these state data the 1947 interpolated local government expenditures. For each function, the ratio of the SLG estimate for each state to the national total of the function was used to distribute the 1947 NIPA total of SLG net purchases. This method seemed to provide a reasonable approximation, although no information was available to use as a check on the accuracy of the individual estimates. The assumption was that the local government net purchases between 1942 and 1957 were a linear function of time, that is, that the local government net purchases increased by a constant amount each year.

1957 and 1962 Census State Expenditures Data.   The 1957 and 1962 fiscal-year Census data, which were fairly detailed by function and by state, were used to obtain 1958 and 1963 calendar-year figures. The functional classifications in both years are consistent with the exception of regular highway expenditures. While state toll highway data were given separately in 1957, in 1962 the function was included with the regular highway expenditures under a single category entitled "highway." Therefore, in assembling the 1962 data at the 15-function level, state toll highway direct expenditures were subtracted from the total SLG highway expenditures, yielding an estimate of the SLG regular highway expenditures. Then, state toll highway with its capital outlay, obtained from *Compendium of State Government Finances in 1962* [117, t. 18], was entered into the SLG net purchases estimation as a separate function.

Conversion of Expenditures to Net Purchases.   After the SLG expenditures by state and by function had been compiled from the Census publications for the years 1947, 1958, and 1963, the data were adjusted to fit the NIPA totals of net purchases. The columns of the state-by-function matrix for each year were summed to obtain an aggregate amount for each function. For each year, these expenditures totals were then forced to sum to the NIPA total of net purchases, and the new column totals were distributed to each column in proportion to the original entries.

A summary of national totals estimated in this study from the Census data is presented in Table 5–3. These figures can be compared with the NIPA totals of

Table 5–3

Summary of State and Local Government Expenditures and Net
Purchases of Goods and Services (millions of current dollars)

Year	State & Local Government Expenditures (Estimated)	State Government Expenditures (Estimated)	Local Government Expenditures (Estimated)	State & Local Government Net Purchases (NIPA)
1942	$ 8,008	$ 2,494	$ 5,514	$ 7,717
1947[a]	12,560	4,110	8,450	12,560
1947	16,301	4,110	12,191[b]	12,562
1957[c]	37,390	11,848	25,542	36,585
1962[d]	55,358	24,129	31,229	53,731

[a]The 1947 national total for unadjusted SLG expenditures was $16,301 million, shown in the next line. The data used in the estimation of the final demands, however, are those adjusted to the NIPA totals. State government expenditures are estimated from the Compendium of State Government Finances in 1947 [115], which is for fiscal years.

[b]This estimate was obtained by interpolating from the 1942 and 1957 local government figures.

[c]The total of SLG net purchases is adjusted to the NIPA figure for 1958 of $40,563 million [176] when used in the final demand estimation.

[d]The totals are shown for 51 states in 1962 and are later adjusted to the NIPA total of SLG net purchases in 1963 of $58,240 million [164] when used in the final demand estimation.

SOURCES: 1942 data: Census of Governments, 1942 [95; 96; 97; 98] and Governmental Finances in the United States, 1942 [122].

1947 data: Compendium of State Government Finances in 1947 [115] and Revised Summary of State Government Finances, 1942–1950 [124].

1957 data: Census of Governments, 1957 [99] and Compendium of State Government Finances in 1957 [116].

1962 data: Census of Governments, 1962 [101] and Compendium of State Government Finances in 1962 [117].

NIPA data: The National Income and Product Accounts of the United States, 1929–65 [168].

SLG net purchases of goods and services shown in the last column of the table. For 1947, the local government expenditures data do not exist by state, and the estimated amount was obtained from the Census total of state government direct expenditures and the interpolated total of local government direct expenditures. The figures in Table 5–3 show that the estimate of 1947 SLG expenditures provides only a fair approximation of the NIPA total of SLG net purchases in 1947. For 1957 and 1962, however, the Census and the NIPA totals differ by less than 2.2 and 3.0 percent, respectively. The adjustments made to the 1957 and 1962 Census data should, therefore, provide a reasonable approximation of the NIPA total of SLG net purchases in the two years.

Estimation Procedures for State Net Purchases Data

Once the Census state-by-function expenditures matrices for each year had been adjusted to be consistent with the NIPA total of net purchases, the data in each matrix were used for the state calculations of net purchases, classified by input-output industries. The input-output data and the estimation procedures used for this final set of calculations are explained in this section of the chapter.

Total SLG Final Demand. National SLG final demands are available from the OBE for 1947, 1958, and 1963. When these data are compared on an industrial basis, as shown in Table 5–4, some inconsistencies become apparent, especially with respect to the 1947 data compared with the 1958 and 1963 data. Most of the inconsistencies are due to the unavailability of adequate information when the input-output tables were originally compiled. Since 1952, reliable data have become increasingly available for SLG expenditures.

The noncomparability of the data appears in two forms: (1) a change from having a zero entry in 1947 to having some large entries in 1958 and 1963, or vice versa; or (2) a change from having a positive entry to a negative entry, or vice versa. A few examples will illustrate possible explanations of the inconsistencies.

IO-21, Wooden containers. Data are compiled from samples of projects in the state and local government jurisdictions. The amount of purchases is usually low because the samples are weak. The zero entry in 1963 resulted when no record appeared in the sample, and the OBE did not make an independent estimate for the entry.

IO-43, Engines & turbines. These purchases are made mainly by construction projects, most of them private projects. The figures, therefore, should be in IO-11, New construction, and not in the SLG final demand. When the 1947 and 1958 input-output tables were constructed, this fact was not clear; consequently, an entry appears in both years under the SLG final demand. But in the 1963 input-output study, the purchases are entered in IO-11, New construction, and the SLG final demand for IO-43 is zero.

IO-9, Stone & clay mining & quarrying. The Census data on "Charges and Miscellaneous Revenues" include gravel sold by the highway department to private persons; therefore, the entries in 1958 and 1963 are negative. Because the highway project information was not analyzed in detail for the 1947 table, the figure was entered as a positive number.

IO-42, Other fabricated metal products. A possible explanation of the switch from a negative entry to positive entries for this industry is that the sale of products may have come from the "prison" industry, which sells the products to both government and nongovernment purchasers. For the 1958 and 1963 studies, better data must have shown more purchases than sales of these products, leading to the positive entries.

Table 5–4

Industries with Noncomparable Entries for State and Local Government Net Purchases (thousands of dollars)

Industry Number	Industry Title	Amount of SLG Net Purchases		
		1947	1958	1963
10	Chem. & fert. mineral mining	$ –	$ 11,917	$ 23,897
15	Tobacco manufactures	–	367	1,002
21	Wooden containers	324	491	–
28	Plastics & synthetics	–	–	139
35	Glass & glass prdts.	4,304	–	33,061
38	Primary nonferrous mfr.	1,255	–	76
39	Metal containers	272	–	25
40	Fabricated metal prdts.	4,950	–	238
43	Engines & turbines	2,680	2,953	–
67	Radio & TV broadcasting	–	–	16,639
79	State & local gov't enterp.	–	6,039	21,083
82	Office supplies	–	132,080	242,941
9	Stone & clay mining	268	–11,973	–30,000
42	Other fab. metal prdts.	–1,001	46,426	8,145
76	Amusements	3,652	–44,183	–53,338

National SLG Input-Output Data by Function. For 1958, unpublished worksheets of the OBE provide data on the industrial composition of SLG net purchases [175]. The data are available for the 15 functions listed in Table 5–1 and are classified according to the 80-order industrial classification given in the appendix, Table A-1. For 1963, the detailed 370-order input-output table published by the OBE [165] provided the industrial composition of SLG net purchases for four functions. No breakdown of 1947 SLG net purchases by function exists for the 1947 national input-output table, and, as far as is known, no assembly of such data is planned. The 1958 functional distribution, therefore, was used for both 1947 and 1958.

State Estimation of State and Local Government Net Purchases. To obtain the state estimates, an assumption had to be made that the national composition of industrial purchases for a particular function remained constant from state to state, although the functional mix was allowed to vary among states and over time. The functional mix varies even though the same national coefficients are used because the total net purchases for each year are available by function and by state and were used to weight the national coefficients for the respective functions. For each function, the national coefficients of SLG net purchases obtained from the 1958 or 1963 functional distributions were multiplied by the adjusted total net purchases figures for each state to obtain SLG net purchases classified by industry and state. The step-by-step procedure was as follows.

Step 1. Column percentages were calculated from the 1958 and 1963 national industry-by-function matrices of SLG net purchases.

Step 2. The appropriate industry-by-function national matrix was multiplied by the 1947, 1958, or 1963 total net purchases function-by-state matrix to obtain a total SLG net purchases industry-by-state matrix for each of the three years. The sums of the rows of the industry-by-state matrices, however, did not exactly correspond with the total SLG final demands for the respective years.

Step 3. Each row of the industry-by-state matrices was adjusted to add to the OBE final demand for total SLG net purchases for that industry by distributing the national final demand figures in proportion to the original entries in the row.

The results of the calculations described above were the industry-by-state matrices of SLG net purchases for 1947, 1958, and 1963 presented in the statistical appendix.

Summary of National Changes in State and Local Government Net Purchases

In the previous section, the basic adjustments and the estimation procedures used to obtain the state estimates were described; in this section, some of the data examined during the course of the study are summarized, and three-year comparisons of the national data are presented. This information on the composition of the statistics is helpful when the detailed industry-by-state estimates are used, as it throws some light on the reasons for the changes that are occurring in the distribution of SLG purchases among states.

Percentage Distribution of National
SLG Purchases

The actual values and percentage distribution of SLG net purchases among the six functions are shown in Table 5-5 for each year under study. Most proportions at this aggregated 6-function level remained relatively stable over time at the national level; in fact, the shifts in the allocation of purchases over the years appeared to be too insignificant to change the order of importance of the functions in the three years. The last two columns of the table show the compound growth rates for each function during the periods 1947-1958 and 1958-1963.

For 1958 and 1963, data were available for 15 functions, while for 1947

Table 5-5
State and Local Government Net Purchases and Compound Growth Rates by Function

Function	State and Local Government Net Purchases (millions of current dollars)			Percentage Distribution			Compound Growth Rates[a] (percent per annum)	
	1947	1958	1963	1947	1958	1963	1947-1958	1958-1963
1. Education	$ 4,625	$15,550	$23,596	36.8	38.3	40.8	6.6	6.0
2. Public health & welfare	1,555	4,809	6,916	12.4	11.9	12.0	5.8	4.9
3. Public safety	1,132	2,975	4,235	9.1	7.3	7.3	4.4	4.7
4. General government	882	2,125	2,854	7.0	5.3	4.9	3.5	3.5
5. Transportation	2,640	8,812	11,257	21.0	21.7	19.5	6.6	2.4
6. Other	1,726	6,292	8,968	13.7	15.5	15.5	7.4	4.7
Total	$12,560[b]	$40,563[b]	$57,826[b]	100.0	100.0	100.0	6.3	4.7

[a]Compound growth rates were calculated from SLG net purchases in constant 1958 dollars, obtained by adjusting all current dollar amounts according to implicit price deflators for total SLG purchases (1947 = 60.4, 1958 = 100.0, 1963 = 113.2).

[b]The actual values for each function have been adjusted to give the NIPA total for each of the three years and exclude data for Alaska and Hawaii.

SOURCES: The 1947, 1958, and 1963 SLG national net purchases are NIPA totals [168]. The functional data for each year were obtained from *Census of Governments, 1942* [95; 96; 97; 98], *1957* [99], and *1962* [101]; *Compendium of State Government Finances in 1947* [115], *1957* [116], and *1962* [117]; *Governmental Finances in the United States, 1942* [122]; and *Revised Summary of State Government Finances, 1942–1950* [124]. Deflators are from the *Economic Report of the President, 1966* [10, p. 215].

Table 5-6

**Percentage Distribution of State and Local Government Net Purchases
15-Function, 1958 and 1963 Data**

Function	1958	1963
1. Education: elementary, secondary, other	32.7	32.9
2. Higher education	5.2	7.3
3. Libraries	0.5	0.6
4. Hospitals	7.1	6.7
5. Public health & welfare	3.3	4.1
6. Sanitation	1.4	1.2
7. Police	3.9	3.9
8. Fire	2.2	2.0
9. Prisons	1.2	1.4
10. General government	5.2	4.9
11. Regular highways	18.7	18.3
12. Local passenger transport	0.2	0.1
13. Nonhighway transport	0.7	0.8
14. Toll facilities	2.2	0.3
15. Other	15.5	15.5
Total	100.0	100.0

SOURCES: 1. National totals of state and local government net purchases are the
NIPA totals [168].

2. Coefficients for the functional distribution of the national totals were calculated
from data in *Census of Governments, 1957* [99] and *1962* [100; 101] and from
the *Compendium of State Government Finances in 1957* [116] and *1962* [117].

comparable data could be assembled for only six functions. The percentage
distribution of SLG net purchases among the 15 functions is given in Table 5-6.

Of the six functions, the state and local governments spent the most on
education in all three years. The net purchases of the function increased from
36.8 percent of total SLG purchases in 1947 to 38.3 percent in 1958 and to
40.8 percent in 1963. As shown by Table 5-6, the increase for the period from
1958 to 1963 came mainly from the growth in the net purchases of higher
education relative to those of elementary and secondary education and to the
net purchases of libraries.

Transportation was the second largest net purchase item of the six functions,
with the percent of total SLG net purchases increasing from 21.0 in 1947 to
21.7 in 1958, but dropping to 19.5 in 1963. An increase, however, occurred in
the dollar purchases in all three years. As shown by Table 5-6, 18.3 of the 19.5
percent in 1963 was net purchases for highway construction. Interstate highway
investment was attractive to state and local governments because the state pays
only 10 percent of the cost, while the federal government pays the rest.
However, once the initial transportation investment had been made between
1947 and 1958, the major expenditures item in the subsequent period was for
maintenance of that highway construction; consequently, the state governments

could shift expenditures to other priorities, as the decline in the 1963 percentage shows they did. The shift is shown dramatically when the compound growth rates for the two periods are compared. From 1947-1958, the percent rate of growth per annum in transportation net purchases was 6.6, while from 1958-1963, it was only 2.4, the lowest of the six functions. A decline occurred between 1958 and 1963 in the percentages of all components of transportation, except for a very small increase in the percentage of nonhighway transportation. As increasing emphasis was being given to interstate freeways, a sizable cutback occurred in the allocation of net purchases to state toll highways, as indicated by Table 5-6.

The SLG net purchases of "other" are comprised of the following diverse subfunctions: conservation of natural resources, housing and urban renewal and development, general public buildings, local parks and recreation, public utilities, liquor stores, and other unallocable purchases.[2] The function "other" was the third largest in the SLG net purchases for all three years. Although the percent of total SLG net purchases increased from 13.7 in 1947 to 15.5 in 1958, it then levelled off at 15.5 in 1963. Between 1947 and 1958, the per annum rate of growth was the highest of the six functions, 7.4 percent. The percentages for all the subfunctions except housing and urban renewal and other unallocable purchases actually declined between 1958 and 1963. However, the increases of the housing and urban renewal percent from 1.4 to 2.1 and of the other unallocable purchases percent from 3.4 to 4.0 during the same period were sufficient to keep the distribution of SLG net purchases of the total "other" virtually unchanged.

The public health and welfare function, which contains the net purchases of hospitals, public health and welfare, and sanitation, was the fourth largest SLG net purchases item in all three years. As shown in Table 5-5, the function as a percent of total SLG net purchases shifted only slightly from 12 percent during the three years. The percentage figure for the public health and welfare subfunction, however, increased while the percentage figures for the hospital and sanitation subfunctions decreased between 1958 and 1963.

The net purchases of public safety include the purchases for police and fire protection and for correction. The function was the fifth largest net purchase item of the state and local governments in each of the three years. Although the distribution of the net purchases represented 9.1 percent of the total in 1947, it had dropped to 7.3 percent by 1958 and remained at 7.3 percent in 1963. This constancy between 1958 and 1963 in the aggregate percentage figure was accounted for by the percentage figure for police protection remaining unchanged, while a decrease in the distribution of net purchases for fire protection from 2.2 to 2.0 percent was exactly offset by an increase in the distribution of net purchases for prisons from 1.2 to 1.4 percent.

---

2. Only the capital outlays of state and local government enterprises, such as utilities and liquor stores, are included.

The general government function is separated into two subfunctions: general control and social security administration. Of total SLG net purchases, the percentage allocated to this function was the smallest in all three years and declined from 7.0 percent in 1947 to 5.3 percent in 1958 and to 4.9 percent in 1963.

From the discussion above, it is evident that stability of the percentage distribution at the aggregated six-function level sometimes disguises significant variations that are occurring among particular subcomponents of the SLG net purchases. The distribution of the net purchases at a more disaggregated level shows considerably more variation than appears at the less aggregated one. The movement in the subcomponents often has a cancelling effect, leaving the distribution of net purchases of the aggregated function unchanged. Examples of this are apparent for the SLG net purchases of "other" and public safety over the period from 1958 to 1963.

Largest Industrial Suppliers to
State and Local Governments

For each individual function at the national level, IO-11, New construction, and IO-84, Government industry (compensation of employees), account for the bulk of the purchases. The only exception to this is that IO-84 is not represented among the major suppliers to the transportation function. The net purchases from these two industries accounted for 76.7 percent of total SLG net purchases in 1947, 78.1 percent in 1958, and 77.6 percent in 1963. In Table 5-7, the five largest suppliers to each of the six functions in 1958 are shown. Out of the total purchases of each function, the five major suppliers represented a low of 82.5 percent of total purchases for the public health and welfare function and a high of 96.4 percent of total purchases for the transportation function.

Although not shown in the table, small negative figures occur for three of the functions representing sales by state and local governments to industries. For the civilian safety function, these occurred for IO-42, Other fabricated metal products, and IO-83, Scrap, used & secondhand goods. Used vehicles and license plates made in prison are two examples of sales to those industries. Sales of transportation by the state and local governments were made to IO-9, Stone & clay mining & quarrying, and IO-73, Business services, but the largest sales are shown under the "other" function, where sales were made to IO-4, Agricultural, forestry & fishery services, and IO-68, Electricity, gas, water, & sanitation services. The considerable concentration of purchases among such a few industries and the identification of the negative components of the net purchases figures should be useful in future studies when analyses of the state estimates are made.

Table 5-7

Five Largest Industrial Suppliers in 1958 to State and Local Governments (millions of dollars)

Industry Number	Industry Title	Function					
		Education	Public Health & Welfare	Public Safety	General Government	Transportation	Other
11	New construction	$ 3,201	$ 394	$ 133	$ 95	$5,786	$4,007
12	Maint. & repair construction	465	—	—	117	2,311	418
14	Food & kindred prdts.	—	163	—	—	—	—
27	Chemicals, selected prdts.	—	—	—	—	—	172
31	Petroleum, related indus.	—	—	134	—	60	—
59	Motor vehicles, equip.	—	—	109	—	100	—
65	Transportation & warehousing	248	—	—	—	—	—
68	Elec., gas, water & san. serv.	458	—	—	—	—	—
69	Wholesale & retail trade	—	—	70	—	—	—
71	Real estate & rental	—	—	—	72	—	—
73	Business services	—	194	—	68	—	—
77	Med., ed. serv., nonprof. org.	—	314	—	—	—	—
83	Scrap & used goods	—	—	—	—	238	146
84	Government industry	10,329	2,903	2,032	1,448	—	970
	Remainder	849	841	497	325	317	579
	Total	$15,550	$4,809	$2,975	$2,125	$8,812	$6,292
	Purchases of five largest industries as percent of total	94.5%	82.5%	83.3%	84.7%	96.4%	90.8%

SOURCE: U.S. Department of Commerce, "State and Local General Government Net Purchases by Function and Industrial Origin" [175].

Conclusion

The estimates of state and local government net purchases for 1947, 1958, and 1963 at the state level are presented in the statistical appendix. They are based upon the assumption that the state and local government purchase "technology" for an individual function does not change from state to state. Because the national coefficients for each function were weighted by the actual total purchases for that function in each state and then aggregated, the allocations among industries obtained in the final state estimates do vary from state to state. The estimates were based upon data for six functions in 1947, for fifteen functions in 1958, and for four functions in 1963.

6 Federal Government Purchases

**Bo Carlsson,
W. Norton Grubb, and
Mary M. Shirley**

Federal government purchases of goods and services include the current and capital account purchases made for general operations by government agencies plus the capital account purchases of federal government enterprises. Thus, for any given year, all expenditures in that year by the federal government for construction and equipment are treated as purchases, and the government accounts show no charges for depreciation. Both military and nonmilitary purchases are included. The purpose of this chapter is to explain the methodology of allocating federal government purchases to the states. In the first section, the general estimation procedure and sources of data for the nonmanufacturing industries are discussed and an extensive explanation of the military data is given. In the second section, the particular sources and specific methods used for the allocation of federal purchases are enumerated industry by industry.

General Estimation Procedures and
Nature of the Data

The general methodology used was to take the federal government purchases by industry from the national input-output tables for 1947 [169], 1958 [176], and 1963 [164; 165] and to distribute these purchases to the states. Data that could be used to distribute these government purchases to the states proved to be scarce or, in many cases, nonexistent. This scarcity of applicable data was most serious for the nonmanufacturing industries, especially the service industries. Finding complete and accurate information for the state distributions was also a problem in the manufacturing sector, though to a lesser extent. While there were large quantities of information on federal purchases in general, there were relatively few published data available that dealt with purchases on a state-by-state basis. Even when primary statistics on federal purchases were available, they were frequently incomplete or used definitions of purchasing categories that were different from those of the input-output tables published by the Office of Business Economics (OBE). In addition, many of the data were for fiscal rather than calendar years; did not cover the years of the input-output tables; or contained only regional, not state, figures. In many cases, the figures were either too aggregated or too detailed. In other cases, they had been assembled for purposes other than those required for the present study, thus often necessitating special adjustments to make them applicable. When no information was available for a regional distribution, proxies had to be used. When data were given for fiscal rather than calendar years, an average of two fiscal years was taken. Thus, the average of fiscal year 1947 and fiscal year 1948 was assumed to be equivalent to calendar year 1947.

In general, there were fewer regional statistics for 1947 than for 1963, as could be expected. For example, exact state data were available for only three industries in 1947, whereas for 1963 relevant data were published for most manufacturing and several nonmanufacturing industries. For 1958, data were available on a state-by-state basis for seven nonmanufacturing industries; for all other industries, proxies had to be used.

For 1958 and 1963, government purchases were divided into military and nonmilitary purchases. The military category included the Department of Defense (DOD), the National Aeronautics and Space Agency (NASA), and the Atomic Energy Commission (AEC), while the nonmilitary category included all other federal agencies except the current account purchases of federal government enterprises. For 1947, an accurate breakdown between military and nonmilitary purchases was not available; therefore, state distributions were made only for total federal government purchases. The national military figures for 1958 were taken from unpublished worksheets of the OBE [162] and for 1963 from the detailed 1963 input-output table [165]. The 1958 and 1963 state allocations of federal purchases were made separately for military and nonmilitary purchases and then added for each state in order to obtain total federal purchases from each industry in the state.

Because of data limitations, it was not always possible to adhere strictly to this division between military and nonmilitary purchases when calculating the regional distributions. For example, in some cases the figures include NASA, AEC, and government enterprises as part of the "civilian" branch of the federal government. Since NASA and AEC comprise only a small portion of military purchases, very little time was devoted to the enormous task of separating these agencies from the civilian branch and placing them in the military sector. Furthermore, for a few input-output industries (e.g., IO-71, Real estate & rental), separate allocations for military and nonmilitary purchases could not be estimated from the available information, and only a total allocation vector could be used. However, whenever possible, military and nonmilitary purchases were allocated separately. For the manufacturing industries in general, the available state data were much more complete and detailed for military than for nonmilitary purchases. Nonmilitary purchases usually had to be allocated according to some proxy, such as federal civilian employment and industry-by-state matrices of outputs for 1947, 1958, and 1963 assembled by Jack Faucett Associates, henceforth referred to as the Faucett state output data.[1]

Special Adjustments

Two special adjustments were made to the federal government final demand to account for research and development and the Commodity Credit Corporation.

Research and Development. The federal government purchases 97 percent of all research and development, while 90 percent of total research and development is not produced by the research and development industry (SIC 7391, Research, development, & testing laboratories) but is a secondary product of other industries. The explanation for this is that when the federal government purchases an end product from an industry, it specifies part of the contract price to be used to defer the costs of research and development (R&D). In the 1963 input-output table, IO-74, Research & development, was eliminated, and all federal government purchases of R&D were combined with the individual industry purchases. The 1947 and 1958 federal government final demand vectors had to be adjusted for consistency with the 1963 OBE methodology before the purchases could be distributed by state. For the state allocation of federal government purchases, the R&D data were distributed separately from the other industrial purchases. Separate R&D figures were contained in column 74 of the 1947 and 1958 secondary flows in the OBE input-output matrices, and for 1963 the OBE provided unpublished worksheets [171; 172]. For each industry, the R&D component was distributed according to the Faucett state output figures. The exception to this was IO-77, Medical, educational services, & nonprofit organizations, which was not distributed according to output, since R&D makes up most federal government purchases from this industry. Instead, detailed National Science Foundation data [65] were used to distribute these R&D figures.

Commodity Credit Corporation. In the 1963 input-output table, Commodity Credit Corporation (CCC) inventory changes and donations are included under federal government final demand, while the current account CCC expenses

---

1. These data have since been revised and are being published in the second volume of this series, *State Estimates of Outputs, Employment, and Payrolls* [70]. It should also be noted that the major portion of the state allocations had to be made prior to the publication of the 1963 input-output table. Some unpublished defense purchase data for 1962 obtained from the Bureau of Labor Statistics [193], therefore, were used as a guide for the 1963 military distributions.

or gains are included in IO-78, Federal government enterprises. The inventory changes are purchases and sales of commodities which are stockpiled by the CCC, while the inventory donations are gifts, such as the CCC school lunch program. The expenses part of the CCC current account includes the cost of warehousing and transportation, plus any other administrative costs, as well as any losses that were incurred in the disposal of commodities. The gains represent any gains that occurred when the commodities were disposed of. (Commodities may be disposed of through nonrecourse loans, domestic sales, or overseas donations and sales.) For the multiregional model, the figures on the CCC expenses and gains must be subtracted from IO-78 and added to the CCC portion of federal government final demand, as explained below, which will place the data on CCC purchases, sales, and donations in current market prices (see page 218).

The industries affected by the CCC adjustment are IO-2, Other agricultural products; IO-14, Food & kindred products; some of the mining industries (IO-5, IO-6, IO-9, and IO-10); IO-16, Broad & narrow fabrics, yarn & thread mills; IO-27, Chemicals & selected chemical products; IO-36, Stone & clay products; IO-38, Primary nonferrous metals manufacturing; and IO-64, Miscellaneous manufacturing. For most of these industries, CCC purchases, sales, or donations were separated into SIC industry classifications and the corresponding expense or gain was added to each industry. The resulting figure was then allocated according to output by state for each SIC category. Thus, for IO-2, the 1963 CCC inventory change for cotton (SIC 0112) of $419.2 million, plus the cotton inventory donation of $13 thousand, was added to the CCC current account figure for SIC 0112 of $268.1 million, and the sum was distributed to the states according to their production of cotton. These separate distributions were then added (in the example of IO-2, there was a distribution for cotton, SIC 0112; grains, SIC 0113; tobacco, SIC 0114; vegetables, SIC 0123; and oil crops, SIC 0142) to obtain a total distribution for the CCC portion of each industry. This procedure was not used for those input-output categories which had very small CCC purchases or sales (IO-16, IO-36, IO-38, and IO-64). In these cases, the CCC portion of federal government purchases was allocated according to Faucett state output figures [70] for the entire industry. There are also 1963 CCC defense purchases from IO-14, Food & kindred products. According to the OBE, these inventory donations of butter, cheese, and milk amounting to $43 million represent items donated to veterans' hospitals and the like, and they are therefore categorized as federal government defense purchases. Like the nondefense purchases, these CCC inventory donations were allocated according to production of the individual commodities.

There was no information on a breakdown of CCC purchases in 1947 or 1958. For IO-2, the CCC portion of the industry was assumed to correspond to CCC crop loans for those years, and that portion was distributed according to output figures for the entire industry. No attempt was made to separate the CCC portion of the other industries.

General Description of Allocation Procedure

In general, the quality of data varied considerably for military and non-military purchases, the manufacturing and the nonmanufacturing industries, and the recent and more distant years. The best statistics were found for 1963 military purchases from manufacturing industries. There was not as much information on 1963 nondefense purchases, and even less information on both nondefense and defense purchases from the nonmanufacturing industries in 1963, while there was an overall decline in the quality of figures available from 1963 to 1947. The following descriptions of the methodology used to allocate military and nonmilitary purchases from the manufacturing and nonmanufacturing industries for the three years indicate some of the problems encountered in trying to assemble the data.

Nonmanufacturing Industries. The nonmanufacturing industries comprise IO-1 through IO-12 (agriculture, forestry, fishing, mining, and construction) and IO-65 through IO-79 (the service industries and government enterprises). With the exception of statistical publications containing agricultural and mining figures and information available in various volumes of the *Statistical Abstract of the United States,* there were virtually no data for a state distribution of federal purchases from these industries. Since differences in the quality of the data for 1947, 1958, and 1963 were small in the nonmanufacturing industries, approximately the same methods were used for all three years.

For a number of nonmanufacturing industries no applicable data were available to allocate federal purchases by state. In these cases, the state distribution of federal employees was used as a proxy. The assumption was made that federal purchases from a state would be positively correlated with the size of its presence in that state, as indicated by the number of employees it maintains there. For 1947, accurate information was available only for nonmilitary employment; consequently, federal government payroll by state had to be used instead of employment. The nonmanufacturing industries allocated by employment or payroll proxies for all three years are listed in Table 6-1.

Manufacturing Industries. The state data available for the manufacturing industries, IO-13 through IO-64, are somewhat better than the data for the nonmanufacturing industries. In particular, there is detailed state information on military purchases for 1958 and 1963, which will be described in the next section. However, sufficiently detailed statistics on nonmilitary purchases for these two years and on both military and nonmilitary purchases for 1947 proved to be nonexistent.

Because no suitable regional distribution of purchases of the federal government was available for 1947, federal government payroll figures by state had to be used as a proxy. Federal civilian and federal military payrolls from

Table 6-1
Nonmanufacturing Industries Distributed by Federal Government
Employment or Payrolls

Industry Number	Industry Title
4	Agricultural, forestry, & fishery services
12	Maintenance & repair construction
65	Transportation & warehousing (in part)
66	Communications, except radio & TV broadcasting
68	Electric, gas, water, & sanitary services
72	Hotels & lodging places; personal & repair services, except automobile repair
73	Business services
76	Amusements
78	Federal government enterprises
79	State & local government enterprises

NOTE: Proxies were used to allocate the data for some manufacturing industries, as well.

Personal Income by States Since 1929 [174, tt. 4-61, pp. 146-203] were added for each state, and state percentages of total government payroll were obtained by dividing each figure by the national total. Each percentage vector was then multiplied by the total federal purchases from the respective industry. This proxy is preferable to applying the 1963 distribution to 1947, since that method would assume that state shares of federal government purchases have remained unchanged. Despite the distortions inherent in employing such a rough proxy to allocate government purchases, payroll data do give a plausible indication of the size of the federal government's presence (demand) in a state.

Allocation of 1958 and 1963 Military Purchases. For 1963, state-by-state data were available on federal military purchases. For 1958, however, no sources of information on the state-by-state federal military purchases could be found, and the 1963 data had to be used for 1958 after being adjusted wherever possible to reflect the 1958 distribution. Three principal sources of data were used to obtain state estimates for the 1958 and 1963 military purchases. The first was *Shipments of Defense-Oriented Industries, 1965 (Final)* [126] and the 1963 version contained as a special report in the *Census of Manufactures, 1963* [125]. These will be referred to as *Shipments, 1963* or *Shipments, 1965* or, when the reference is general, just *Shipments.* The 1963 publication is the earliest version available. The second source used for estimating state military purchases was *Military Prime Contract Awards by Region and State, Fiscal Years 1962-1966* [179]. This will be referred to as *Prime Contracts.* Although these data go back no further than 1961, state data were published for each fiscal year beginning with 1961. The third source was *Unclassified Defense and Space Contracts: Awards by County, State, and Metropolitan Area, United States, Fiscal Year 1964* [55]. This will be referred to simply as *Unclassified Contracts.* In this case, the earliest data are for 1960.

Subcontracting was not estimated in the military allocation since, for the purposes of the multiregional input-output accounts, subcontracted items can be regarded as inputs used by the prime contracting industry. In other words, the subcontracted item produced in another area is shipped to the prime contracting industry and used by the prime contractor as an input when assembling the final product. If the subcontracted item was produced in a state other than the one in which the final product was assembled and shipped to the prime contractor, it would appear in the Faucett interregional trade data [17] and the production would be allocated to the correct state when the multiregional model is implemented. The federal government purchases of goods produced under prime contract awards were therefore allocated to the state where the final product was assembled by the prime contractor.

State Allocations Using Shipments, 1963 *and* Shipments, 1965.   Six major industry groups having large shipments to the federal government are covered by *Shipments, 1963.*[2] Because *Shipments, 1965* covers these six, as well as nine other groups [126, app. A, p. 67], it was more useful than the 1963 version. In the 1963 publication, the state distribution of shipments by industry is for *total* shipments, not just those made to the federal government. However, regional totals are given for shipments to the government, including both military and nonmilitary purchases. Since government shipments are usually only a fraction of the total shipments for an industry and since they often have a distinct geographical distribution, the regional totals were used, rather than the state distribution of total shipments, to allocate federal government purchases. The regional totals were then distributed to the states using the Faucett output figures for 1963 [70]. Because no similar data were available for 1958, the 1963 regional totals from *Shipments* were used wherever they were used in the 1963 allocation and then distributed to the states by the 1958 Faucett output figures [70].

One difficulty with using this source for the state allocations was that the industry categories do not completely cover the corresponding OBE industries. For example, the communication equipment industry category in *Shipments, 1965* encompasses only SIC 3661 and SIC 3662 [126, app. A, p. 67], while the

---

2. The six groups include: turbines, construction machinery, machine tools, and computers and related products; communication equipment; electronic components and accessories; aerodynamic industries; shipbuilding and repairing and ordnance; and scientific instruments, mechanical measuring devices, optical instruments, and photographic equipment.

corresponding input-output industry, IO-56 (Radio, TV, & communication equipment), also contains SIC 3651 and SIC 3652 [176, p. 33]. However, when the figures in *Shipments* were compared with 1958 and 1963 total purchases by the federal government, the items left out of *Shipments* were usually an insignificant part of total government purchases from the industry. Thus the allocation of federal purchases to the regions by the *Shipments* data was not greatly affected by these omissions, while the allocation of the regional totals to the states by the Faucett output data was entirely unbiased by the categories omitted from the regional totals, since the output figures contained the omitted items.

A second problem with using this source was that some of the industry categories contain several OBE industries. In these cases, the *Shipments* data were used only if no other data were available and if the aggregated industries had a similar geographical distribution. In all cases where these aggregated data were used, care was taken that none of the industries had a clearly predominant share of government purchases since such dominance would bias the distributions for the other aggregated industries.

The *Shipments* data presented a third problem in that some of the regional figures were given as ranges, rather than exact figures, because of prohibitions against full disclosure. In these cases, a region was assigned an amount within its range that was consistent with the total national output of that industry and a regional percentage was then computed. If this percentage, when multiplied by the national total, gave a figure within the range in *Shipments,* that figure was accepted as the regional total. If it fell outside the range, the regions were assigned new figures, starting with the region with the smallest range, until the percentages produced figures within the range. The results were then distributed by the Faucett state output data for 1958 and 1963 [70]. An example of the procedure used with *Shipments* follows.

In *Shipments, 1965,* IO-40, Heating, plumbing & fabricated structural metal products; IO-41, Screw machine products, bolts, nuts, etc., & metal stampings; and IO-42, Other fabricated metal products, are lumped together as fabricated metal products, while *Shipments, 1963* contains no data on these industries. For IO-40, the coverage in *Unclassified Contracts* was sufficiently extensive to be used for a state distribution of federal purchases, but for IO-41 and IO-42, the coverage was inadequate. For the two latter industries, *Shipments, 1965* proved to be a better source even though the three industries were aggregated into one group and the coverage was only partial. Distortions due to the aggregation were insignificant, since the Faucett output data indicated that the state distribution of production was similar in the three industries and since the value of total output was fairly evenly divided among the three industries. Partial coverage also appeared to be a minor problem as the 1963 total for all three industries was $126 million [164] compared with the 1965 figure of $395 million in *Shipments, 1965.* Furthermore, for IO-41 and IO-42, the regional totals in *Shipments, 1965* [126, pp. 14–

Table 6-2

Examples of Allocation Using *Shipments* Data

State	Faucett Output Percentages		Percentage of Regional Output		Final Allocation of Regional Total ($ millions)	
	IO-41 (1)	IO-42 (2)	IO-41 (3)	IO-42 (4)	IO-41 (5)	IO-42 (6)
Connecticut	4.54	5.11	51.95	44.40	14.5	12.4
Maine	0.01	0.69	0.11	0.69	0.1	0.2
Massachusetts	3.29	5.32	37.64	46.22	10.5	13.0
New Hampshire	0.13	0.17	1.49	1.48	0.4	0.4
Rhode Island	0.76	0.78	8.70	6.78	2.4	1.9
Vermont	0.01	0.05	0.11	0.43	0.1	0.1
Total	8.74	11.51	100.00	100.00	28.0	28.0

17] seemed representative for both industries since their relative shares of the census regions were the same.

An example of the method of allocating regional totals from *Shipments* is given in Table 6-2. In columns (1) and (2) are given the industry percentages of national total output for the New England states (obtained from the Faucett state output data). The New England region produces 8.74 percent of the total IO-41 output and 11.51 percent of the total IO-42 output. The percentage distributions of regional output among the states are shown in columns (3) and (4). These percentages are multiplied by total government purchases from IO-41 and IO-42 in New England ($28 million, according to *Shipments, 1965*) to obtain each state's share of government purchases from the industries. The resulting allocation is shown in columns (5) and (6).

Only ranges are given in *Shipments, 1965* for four of the regions: West North Central, South Atlantic, West South Central, and Mountain. As described above, these regions were assigned specific amounts that were consistent with the national total of $395.4 million. Then the regional percentage of total national output in the industry was computed and multiplied by the national total to give a figure in the proper range for the West North Central region.[3] Each of the other regions was assigned a figure in the lower part of the range, starting with the region with the smallest range and ending with the region with the largest range. Once a proper regional total was obtained, it was distributed to the states within the region according to their shares of each industry's total output, calculated from the 1958 and 1963 Faucett state output data.

Since the Faucett percentages are not the same for both IO-41 and IO-42, the regional totals for the areas lacking exact information differ slightly. For

---

3. In the West North Central region, the Faucett regional output percentage is 2.96, which gives $11.7 million when multiplied by $395.4 million. This figure, $11.7 million, is within the given range of $10.0–$19.9 million.

Table 6–3
Industries Allocated According to *Shipments*

Industry Number	*Industry Title*
27	Chemicals & selected chemical products
32	Rubber & miscellaneous plastics products
37	Primary iron & steel manufacturing
38	Primary nonferrous metals manufacturing
41	Screw machine products, bolts, nuts, etc., & metal stampings
42	Other fabricated metal products
49	General industrial machinery & equipment
53	Electric transmission & distribution equipment & electrical industrial apparatus
55	Electric lighting & wiring equipment
56	Radio, TV, & communication equipment
57	Electronic components & accessories
58	Miscellaneous electrical machinery, equipment & supplies
62	Professional, scientific, & controlling instruments & supplies

example, the Faucett regional output percentage for the West North Central region is 4.54 for IO-42 (compared with 2.96 for IO-41), and the regional total, derived by multiplying 4.54 by the national total, is $18.0 million for IO-42 compared with $11.7 million for IO-41.

The industries in Table 6–3 were allocated according to *Shipments, 1965* and the method described above. In the last section of this chapter, the allocation for each industry is discussed in detail.

State Allocations Using Prime Contracts.   The second main source of data, *Prime Contracts* [179], covers 25 categories (called procurement programs) of military procurement, with associated data by state for each fiscal year beginning with 1961. Typically, the procurement programs are very loosely defined. The definitions are based primarily on the use of supplies or work purchased and include such things as packaging materials, maintenance and repair, related training equipment, and research and development. The closest definitions available are in the Claimant Program Code. However, since the latter source is used for classification of military appropriations, its definitions are given in the form of examples of items included and excluded in the various procurement programs. According to the Statistical Services Department of the Comptroller's Office in the Pentagon, no one-to-one correspondence exists between the Claimant Program Code and either the Federal Supply Classification or the Standard Industrial Classification. Nevertheless, the Claimant Program Code is sufficiently specific to allow some "educated guessing" as to which SIC codes should be assigned to the procurement programs. Furthermore, definitions for some of the largest procurement programs (aircraft, weapons, and petroleum) are very close to those used by the OBE. In most cases, therefore, *Prime Contracts* was used as the primary source of data only when the definition of the industries included within the procurement programs closely paralleled the OBE industry definition.

Even in cases where the definitions are fairly clear, as in the ships, combat vehicles, and noncombat vehicles procurement programs, application of the data was complicated by the fact that maintenance and repair are included in the definition. The assumption was made that maintenance and repair of an item are distributed geographically in relation to the production of that item in a region.

Other problems associated with using *Prime Contracts* were (1) incomplete coverage; (2) data for fiscal, not calendar, years; and (3) time lags between the time when a prime contract is awarded and the delivery date. The source is incomplete because it covers only contracts exceeding $10,000 and excludes any contracts "which for security reasons could not be assigned to a state" [179, p. ii]. For fiscal 1963 and 1964, these omissions amounted to $2.0 and $3.1 billion, respectively, compared with overall totals of $25.8 and $24.4 billion for federal prime contracts (excluding classified locations) [179, pp. ii and 5]. The second problem, data available for fiscal years only, meant that the figures for fiscal 1963 and 1964 had to be averaged in order to obtain an estimate for calendar 1963. The third problem, time lags, was important in certain industries operating under long-term contracts, although the averaging of fiscal years lessened the impact of this distortion considerably.

The 1963 *Prime Contracts* distributions were applied to 1958 after being adjusted for changes in total contracts for 1958 to 1963. For each state, the total amount of contracts in 1958 was estimated by averaging the totals for fiscal year 1958 and fiscal year 1959 contained in *Five-Year Trends in Defense Procurement, 1958–1962* [178]. The difference between these net contracts figures and the 1963 totals (the average of fiscal year 1962 and fiscal year 1963 from the same source) was used to adjust the *Prime Contracts* data for each state. Thus, if a state had a total of $50 million in net prime contracts in 1958 and $100 million in 1963, the 1963 contracts were adjusted downward by 50 percent to obtain the 1958 distribution. This adjustment was used to estimate 1958 data for every industry which had been allocated according to *Prime Contracts* in 1963. The industries are listed in Table 6-4.

State Allocations Using Unclassified Contracts.   Defense and space contracts are listed in *Unclassified Contracts* by county and 4-digit SIC code, so state totals were obtained for a particular input-output industry by finding data for the proper SIC code and by adding the amounts for each county in the state. Thus, the assignment of a contract to an industry category using this source was more likely to be accurate than that obtained using data from the two sources discussed previously.

Table 6–4
Industries Allocated According to *Prime Contracts*

Industry Number	Industry Title
13	Ordnance & accessories
31	Petroleum refining & related industries
45	Construction, mining, oil field machinery & equipment
46	Materials handling machinery & equipment
47	Metalworking machinery & equipment
48	Special industry machinery & equipment
50	Machine shop products
59	Motor vehicles & equipment
60	Aircraft & parts
61	Other transportation equipment
63	Optical, ophthalmic, & photographic equipment & supplies
64	Miscellaneous manufacturing

Unfortunately, the exclusion of classified contracts, which represent 49 percent of total contracts, causes incomplete coverage. The problem is made more serious by the further exclusion from this source of any contracts that are for less than $25,000 [55, p. 2]. To determine if the military contracts of an industry were adequately covered by *Unclassified Contracts,* the nature and size of contracts for an industry were evaluated. When deliveries of an industry were likely to be classified or to be too small to be fully covered by this source, an attempt was made to use a more satisfactory source. In addition, the national total for an industry in *Unclassified Contracts* was compared with total government military purchases from that industry to further evaluate whether or not the coverage was sufficient to form the basis of a state distribution. In most cases, the coverage was close to or even higher than the 1963 figures. If other data were available, they were ordinarily used, although *Unclassified Contracts* was consulted for extent of coverage if there was doubt about the industry definition in the other sources.

As in *Prime Contracts,* no adjustment is made in *Unclassified Contracts* for lags between letting the contract and making a purchase. When either source was used, therefore, these lags were ignored. Calendar year 1963 data were not available in *Unclassified Contracts,* and since fiscal year 1964 was the closest year for which information was given, the time discrepancy had to be ignored.

Despite these shortcomings, this was a useful source, especially as a complement to the other sources, in supplying data for industries of relatively minor military importance. It was not used for industries with large military purchases. For those industries listed in Table 6–5 where it was used, the value of defense and space procurement of the relevant 4-digit SIC codes was summed for each state. Then, the DOD and NASA procurement figures were added for each state.

Table 6-5

Industries Allocated According to *Unclassified Contracts*

Industry Number	Industry Title
14	Food & kindred products
16	Broad & narrow fabrics, yarn & thread mills
17	Miscellaneous textile goods & floor coverings
18	Apparel
19	Miscellaneous fabricated textile products
21	Wooden containers
28	Plastics & synthetic materials
29	Drugs, cleaning, & toilet preparations
34	Footwear & other leather products
35	Glass & glass products
36	Stone & clay products
39	Metal containers
40	Heating, plumbing & fabricated structural metal products
43	Engines & turbines
51	Office, computing & accounting machines
52	Service industry machines
54	Household appliances

State Allocations Using Proxies.   The three sources of data discussed above cover the majority of military purchases. For nine industries, however, no military data by state were available; for these, therefore, military purchases were allocated by proxy. The proxy used was Department of Defense military and civilian employment located in the state [150, t. 4, p. 7]. This procedure assumes that federal government consumption by the military will be reflected by the number of military employees it has in a state, thus giving an indication of the size of federal installations in the state; the number of consumers for whom it must purchase office supplies, food, and so on; and a general approximation of the magnitude of the federal military purchasing presence in the state. In the absence of better data, this rough approximation gave the best indication of the federal government as a consumer within a state. Furthermore, the industries treated in this manner were of minor importance in relation to total federal purchases: $222 million compared with a total of $53,594 million in 1958.

Table 6-6 lists those industries that were allocated by proxy.

Military purchases from manufacturing industries were determined using *Shipments* (13 industries), *Prime Contracts* (12 industries), *Unclassified Contracts* (17 industries) and proxy (9 industries). The specific source used for each industry is summarized in Table 6-7.

Allocation of 1958 and 1963 Nonmilitary Purchases.   For 1958 and 1963, the sources of data and methods of allocation described up to this point are for

Table 6–6
Industries Allocated by Proxy

Industry Number	Industry Title
20	Lumber & wood products, except containers
22	Household furniture
23	Other furniture & fixtures
24	Paper & allied products, except containers & boxes
25	Paperboard containers & boxes
26	Printing & publishing
30	Paints & allied products
33	Leather tanning & industrial leather products
44	Farm machinery & equipment

Table 6–7
Manufacturing Industries, 1958 and 1963 Methods of Allocation of Military Purchases

Industry Number	Industry Title	Method
13	Ordnance & accessories	Prime contracts
14	Food & kindred products	Unclassified contracts
15	Tobacco manufactures	(No government purchases)
16	Broad & narrow fabrics, yarn & thread mills	Unclassified contracts
17	Miscellaneous textile goods & floor coverings	Unclassified contracts
18	Apparel	Unclassified contracts
19	Miscellaneous fabricated textile products	Unclassified contracts
20	Lumber & wood products, except containers	Industry No. 3 – proxy
21	Wooden containers	Unclassified contracts
22	Household furniture	Proxy
23	Other furniture & fixtures	Proxy
24	Paper & allied products, except containers & boxes	Proxy
25	Paperboard containers & boxes	Proxy
26	Printing & publishing	Proxy
27	Chemicals & selected chemical products	Shipments
28	Plastics & synthetic materials	Unclassified contracts
29	Drugs, cleaning, & toilet preparations	Unclassified contracts
30	Paints & allied products	Proxy
31	Petroleum refining & related industries	Prime contracts
32	Rubber & miscellaneous plastics products	Shipments
33	Leather tanning & industrial leather products	Proxy

Table 6–7, cont.

Industry Number	Industry Title	Method
34	Footwear & other leather products	Unclassified contracts
35	Glass & glass products	Unclassified contracts
36	Stone & clay products	Unclassified contracts
37	Primary iron & steel manufacturing	Shipments
38	Primary nonferrous metals manufacturing	Shipments
39	Metal containers	Unclassified contracts
40	Heating, plumbing & fabricated structural metal products	Unclassified contracts
41	Screw machine products, bolts, nuts, etc., & metal stampings	Shipments
42	Other fabricated metal products	Shipments
43	Engines & turbines	Unclassified contracts
44	Farm machinery & equipment	Proxy
45	Construction, mining, oil field machinery & equipment	Prime contracts
46	Materials handling machinery & equipment	Prime contracts
47	Metalworking machinery & equipment	Prime contracts
48	Special industry machinery & equipment	Prime contracts
49	General industrial machinery & equipment	Shipments
50	Machine shop products	Prime contracts
51	Office, computing & accounting machines	Unclassified contracts
52	Service industry machines	Unclassified contracts
53	Electric transmission & distribution equipment, & electrical industrial apparatus	Shipments
54	Household appliances	Unclassified contracts
55	Electric lighting & wiring equipment	Shipments
56	Radio, TV, & communication equipment	Shipments
57	Electronic components & accessories	Shipments
58	Miscellaneous electrical machinery, equipment & supplies	Shipments
59	Motor vehicles & equipment	Prime contracts
60	Aircraft & parts	Prime contracts
61	Other transportation equipment	Prime contracts
62	Professional, scientific, & controlling instruments & supplies	Shipments
63	Optical, ophthalmic, & photographic equipment & supplies	Prime contracts
64	Miscellaneous manufacturing	Prime contracts

federal government military expenditures only. For nonmilitary federal government purchases in 1958 and 1963, virtually no data were available on a state-by-state basis.

Once again, employment was assumed to indicate the general size of federal government purchases in a state. For 1958 and 1963, DOD civilian employment was subtracted from total civilian employment. The remaining federal civilian employment vector by states was converted to coefficients and used to distribute those purchases for which no better data exist.

Description of Industry Allocations

This section gives a detailed account of the sources of data and the methods used for each industry. For the manufacturing industries, the descriptions refer only to 1958 and 1963, since the same procedure was used for all of the 1947 manufacturing allocations (see pages 135–136). For the nonmanufacturing industries, however, the 1947 allocations are included.

For a number of industries, specific state allocations of federal government purchases could not be found. The state distribution of total federal purchases or of the separate military and nonmilitary purchase figures were then assumed to correspond to the state distribution of federal payrolls or employment. For 1947, the state distribution of total federal government payroll [174, tt. 4–61, pp. 146–203] was used as a proxy. For 1958 and 1963, separate allocations were made for military [149, t. 9, p. 24, and 150, t. 4, p. 7] and nonmilitary [131, t. 497, p. 394; 135, t. 545, p. 409] employees. The specific sources for these distributions will not be cited again in the remainder of the text. Data for the following industries were distributed by these allocation vectors: IO-4, IO-12, IO-22 through 26, IO-30, IO-44, IO-66, IO-68, IO-72, IO-73, IO-78 through 80, IO-82 through 85, and parts of IO-1 through 3 and IO-65.

The federal government purchases figures that are quoted in the remainder of this chapter were taken from the input-output tables for 1947 [169] and 1958 [176] and from the detailed 370-order table for 1963 [165]. The military figures for 1958 were obtained from unpublished worksheets furnished by the OBE [162]. To eliminate needless repetition, the bibliography reference numbers for these tables are given here, rather than throughout the text. For the same reason, seven other references that are frequently mentioned in the text are specifically cited only here. These are:

1.   1947 Faucett state output data [70]
2.   1958 Faucett state output data [70]
3.   1963 Faucett state output data [70]
4.   *Prime Contracts* [179]

5.   *Shipments, 1963* [125]
6.   *Shipments, 1965* [126]
7.   *Unclassified Contracts* [55]

When just the word *Shipments* is used, the reference is to both the 1963 and 1965 publications (items 5 and 6 above).

IO-1, Livestock & Livestock Products.   Nonmilitary government purchases from this industry were negative in 1947 and 1958, which indicates that the federal government sold more to this industry than it bought. For 1947, the receipts represent the sale of grazing rights on federal land and sales of surplus wool by the Commodity Credit Corporation. Nine percent of the $28 million in receipts for 1947 comes from grazing. These receipts were allocated directly to the appropriate states [129, t. 823, p. 739; 130, t. 823, p. 739]. The residual, 91 percent, was attributed to wool sales and allocated according to the state distribution of wool production [129, t. 804, p. 727]. All nonmilitary purchases from this industry in 1958 were allocated according to the sale of grazing rights [151, t. 761, p. 559; 152, t. 789, p. 571].

Nonmilitary purchases from IO-1 were positive in 1963, indicating purchases, rather than sales. These figures were assumed to represent direct purchases from local farmers for consumption in federal cafeterias and were allocated according to federal civilian employment minus the civilian employees of the Department of Defense.

For 1958 military purchases, the small entry of about $1 million may represent a purchase of animals for experiment stations. In the absence of other information, this figure was allocated by the state distribution of livestock production (including cattle, calves, hogs, sheep, lambs, horses [155, pp. 7–13] and chickens [131, pp. 686–687]).

In 1963 there was a military purchase of $1.7 million from this industry, $1.4 million for poultry and eggs, $0.3 million for meat animals. As in 1958, the meat animals were assumed to be for experiment stations and were allocated according to the 1963 Faucett state output figures. The poultry and egg portion was assumed to be purchases from local producers for consumption on nearby military installations and was allocated according to the Department of Defense military and civilian employees.

IO-2, Other Agricultural Products.   For 1947 and 1958, a breakdown of CCC purchases was not available, so CCC crop loans [159] were used to determine the CCC purchases from this industry. The CCC portion was distributed according to the Faucett state output data for both years, while the remainder was distributed according to military payroll for 1947 and military employment for 1958.

For 1963, unpublished OBE worksheets [171; 172] provided exact data on CCC purchases from this industry. These CCC figures were added to the CCC part of IO-78, Federal government enterprises (see pages 133–134), then the total was distributed according to state production of the individual commodity [153; 154]. The remaining purchases were distributed according to civilian employment. There was also a small military purchase from this industry in 1963, which was assumed to be food for consumption on military installations and was distributed according to military employment.

IO-3, Forestry & Fishery Products
IO-20, Lumber & Wood Products, Except Containers.
For 1947 and 1958, total purchases are negative for both industries. For 1963, the nondefense portion of IO-3 is also negative. These negative figures represent receipts from the sale of timber on federal lands and were allocated according to the Faucett state output data for the respective years. There was also a small, positive military figure in 1963, which was allocated according to military employment.

The data for IO-20 were allocated according to the same methods as IO-3 (but using Faucett state output data for IO-20) on the assumption that the state distribution of federal government purchases is similar because the products of the two industries are related. Thus, the negative purchases from IO-20 in 1947 and 1958 were allocated according to Faucett state output data for IO-20. The positive figures in 1963 were allocated according to employment.

IO-4, Agricultural, Forestry, & Fishery Services.
The purchases from this industry are composed of landscaping services for federal buildings. Since neither landscaping service statistics nor data on the state distribution of federal buildings exist, the state distribution of government employees or payroll for the respective year was used as a proxy for the military and nonmilitary purchases. The distribution data for military purchases include Department of Defense civilian as well as military employees, which were subtracted from the nonmilitary distribution data.

For 1947, the state distribution of total federal government payroll was used. For 1958 and 1963, separate allocations were made for military and non-military purchases.

IO-5, Iron & Ferroalloy Ores Mining
IO-6, Nonferrous Metal Ores Mining
IO-9, Stone & Clay Mining & Quarrying
IO-10, Chemical & Fertilizer Mineral Mining.
These four industries were treated identically since purchases from each were for stockpiling purposes. In general, the procedure was first to determine the amount of specific minerals purchased for stockpiling. Second, the geographic distribution of the production of each of these minerals was found, because state distributions of government

contracts for stockpiling were generally unavailable. Third, each distribution was weighted according to the share of total purchases from the industry for the mineral, and the distributions were summed. Unfortunately, foreign and domestic purchases of minerals were sometimes combined or were incomplete, and production data could not always be obtained because of the nondisclosure rules of the Bureau of the Census. In some cases, therefore, rough estimates had to be made.

For IO-6, 1947 state figures for net purchases were from unpublished data from the General Services Administration (GSA) [41]. This information showed that four minerals (manganese, tantalite, bauxite, and vanadium) were purchased. For IO-9, state figures on 1947 stockpiles of surplus graphite and talc were obtained from another set of unpublished GSA data [47]. These surplus materials were those transferred from other government agencies—especially from the Reconstruction Finance Corporation—and thus do not represent current purchases. According to *Minerals Yearbook, 1947* [184], only fluorspar was purchased from IO-10. There were no federal purchases from IO-5 in 1947. For each industry, physical amounts were converted to dollar values by means of prices taken from the yearbook. State distributions for the production of these seven minerals were taken from the 1947 commodity reviews in *Minerals Yearbook, 1947*. When exact figures were unavailable, any residual was distributed according to the rankings of states known to produce that mineral [184, pp. 29–32].

In 1958, most of the purchases for the supplemental stockpile and the CCC were from foreign sources. The GSA furnished worksheets containing the relevant information on purchases (including obligations to purchase) for the national stockpile [42] and inventory change figures for minerals purchased under the Defense Purchases Act (DPA) [43; 44]. The method used for the 1947 distribution was also used for 1958, with *Minerals Yearbook, 1958* [185] the source of state production information. There were no federal purchases from IO-5 in 1958.

Information on the amounts of minerals purchased for 1963 came from two GSA publications: *Statistical Supplement to the Stockpile Report to the Congress, July–December, 1962* [45] and *1963* [46]. These two reports will be referred to collectively as *Statistical Supplements*. In addition, some unpublished figures were used for IO-6 (specifically for copper, lead, zinc, and aluminum) and for IO-9 (stone and clay). Figures from the *Statistical Supplements* were used for bismuth, cadmium, magnesium, manganese, molybdenum, and nickel for IO-6; to divide total figures between asbestos and graphite for IO-9; and to determine the minerals purchased for IO-5 and IO-10. For IO-6, domestic purchases were separated from foreign purchases by taking the change in inventory of the national stockpile and the DPA stockpile from December 1962 to December 1963 and applying the ratio of domestic to total obligations to purchase minerals for the national stockpile.

There were also small nonmilitary purchases from all four industries in 1963, which proved to be CCC purchases, and were listed as purchases from IO-78, Federal government enterprises, in the 1963 input-output table. These data were adjusted in the manner described earlier (pages 133–134). CCC inventory change figures from the *Statistical Supplements* were used to determine the specific minerals purchased. Finally, in the manner already outlined, data from the commodity reviews of the *Minerals Yearbook, 1963* [186] were used to distribute 1963 defense and nondefense purchases by state for each of the four industries.

IO-7, Coal Mining. Coal is still used by the military to heat certain buildings; therefore, the 1947 distribution was derived from the state allocation of coal production [129, t. 872, p. 782]. For 1963, the allocation was made on the basis of state data supplied by the OBE. The small nondefense purchase in 1963 was assumed to be coal used to heat federal government civilian buildings and the same distribution was used. Since no entry appears in the 1958 input-output table, no state allocation was made for 1958.

IO-8, Crude Petroleum & Natural Gas. Since there were no federal purchases from this industry in 1947, 1958, or 1963, no state allocations were made.

IO-9, Stone & Clay Mining & Quarrying. (See IO-6.)

IO-10, Chemical & Fertilizer Mineral Mining. (See IO-6.)

IO-11, New Construction. For 1947, "value of contracts awarded" data [190, t. 19, p. 25] were used to make the state allocations. Revised figures [191, t. 5, p. 11] were used for the first and fourth quarters.

For 1958, the state distribution of total federal construction was taken from unpublished worksheets of Jack Faucett Associates [16]. Separate distributions were made for military and nonmilitary construction using figures from a study by the Legislative Reference Service [56, t. X, p. 29]. This study gave a state distribution for military construction which was subtracted from the Faucett total to get a distribution for nonmilitary construction.

For 1963, detailed figures on federal construction were compiled by Orani Dixon and Jack V. Wells and are described in EDA Report No. 20, "State New Construction Technologies, 1963" [11].

IO-12, Maintenance & Repair Construction. Since almost no data are published on maintenance and repair construction, the assumption had to be made that federal purchases from this industry occur in proportion to existing buildings, and the state distribution of federal government employees was used as a proxy.

IO-13, Ordnance & Accessories. *Prime Contracts* was used for this industry because ordnance was grouped with ship-building and repairing in both of the *Shipments* publications. As the Claimant Program Code indicates that the combat vehicles, weapons, and ammunition procurement programs correspond approximately to the components of IO-13, the data from these programs were added. The 1963 *Prime Contracts* totals were adjusted for changes in net state prime contracts from 1958 to 1963, and the adjusted distribution for this industry was used for 1958.

IO-14, Food & Kindred Products. Since data for this industry are not included in either of the *Shipments* publications, the state distribution was obtained from *Unclassified Contracts.* This source gave a 1964 total of $266 million worth of federal purchases, whereas the OBE figures were $167 million for 1963 federal military purchases; and, for total federal purchases, $317 million in 1963 and $53 million in 1958. Therefore, the bulk of federal military purchases could be assumed to be covered by *Unclassified Contracts.*

IO-15, Tobacco Manufactures. Since there were no federal purchases from this industry in 1947, 1958, or 1963, no state allocations were made.

IO-16, Broad & Narrow Fabrics, Yarn & Thread Mills.
IO-17, Miscellaneous Textile Goods & Floor Coverings.
IO-18, Apparel.
IO-19, Miscellaneous Fabricated Textile Products.
IO-21, Wooden Containers.
IO-28, Plastics & Synthetic Materials.
IO-34, Footwear & Other Leather Products.
IO-35, Glass & Glass Products.
IO-36, Stone & Clay Products. The state distributions for these industries were taken from *Unclassified Contracts* since it gave the broadest coverage.[4]

---

4. The following figures (in millions of dollars) express the extent of coverage:

Industry Number	Unclassified Contracts Coverage	1958		1963	
		Military	Total	Military	Total
16	$ 38.2	$50	$ 50	$32	$33
17	5.9	4	4	9	12
18	144.7	36	40	45	69
19	65.8	99	103	63	69
21	3.3	2	2	4	4
28	3.7	5	5	42	42
34	38.2	2	69	3	4
35	4.7	2	2	8	12
36	5.4	4	5	27	23

IO-20, Lumber & Wood Products, Except Containers. As stated earlier, the same method of allocation used for IO-3 (Forestry & fishery products) was used for IO-20 since it is similar in nature to IO-3 and since no other data were available. The national total for IO-20, therefore, was allocated according to the Faucett state output figures for the respective year.

IO-21, Wooden Containers. (See IO-16.)

IO-22, Household Furniture.
IO-23, Other Furniture & Fixtures.
IO-24, Paper & Allied Products, Except Containers & Boxes.
IO-25, Paperboard Containers & Boxes.
IO-26, Printing & Publishing.
IO-30, Paints & Allied Products.
IO-44, Farm Machinery & Equipment. No data were available for an allocation of military purchases from these industries, so both defense and nondefense purchases were allocated by proxy. The state distribution of federal government civilian employment was used for the nonmilitary allocation and defense employment for the military distribution.

IO-27, Chemicals & Selected Chemical Products. Although the chemical industry is only partially covered, *Shipments, 1965* proved to be the best data source.[5] The omitted parts of SIC codes 281, 286, 287, and 289 summed to $24 million out of a total military purchase of $965 million from this industry in 1963. The coverage in *Shipments, 1965* of SIC codes 2813, 2819, and 2892 totals $765.5 million [126, p. 14].

Specific amounts are given for the Middle Atlantic, South Atlantic, and Pacific regions. These amounts were distributed to the states within each region using the 1963 Faucett state output data according to the general method described earlier (see pages 137-140). The estimates of regional totals for the East North Central and West North Central regions fell within the proper range and were accepted as final. For the East South Central, West South Central, and Mountain regions, the estimated regional totals had to be modified to obtain figures within the proper range. The West South Central estimated regional total was reduced, and the Mountain estimated regional total was increased. The remaining $241 million was allocated to the East South Central region, the region with the largest range ($200.0-$499.9 million). The final estimates were then distributed to the states using the 1963 Faucett state output data. To obtain the state allocations for 1958, the regional totals used for 1963 were distributed to the states according to the 1958 Faucett state output data.

---

5. Neither *Prime Contracts* nor *Shipments, 1963* covers the chemical industry on a state-by-state basis. *Unclassified Contracts* covers about 25 percent of total federal purchases.

IO-28, Plastics & Synthetic Materials. (See IO-16.)

IO-29, Drugs, Cleaning, & Toilet Preparations. *Unclassified Contracts* was used for the allocation of military expenditures for IO-29 since it is not covered in either of the *Shipments* publications and is included only in a highly aggregated category in *Prime Contracts.* The coverage is $37 million in 1964 compared with $38 million federal military purchases in 1963 and $112 million in 1958, and $73 million total federal purchases in 1963 and $133 million in 1958.

IO-30, Paints & Allied Products. (See IO-22.)

IO-31, Petroleum Refining & Related Industries. *Shipments, 1965* has a distribution for this industry, but no state distribution is given for government purchases, and in several cases, regional totals are given as a range rather than as specific amounts. Because *Prime Contracts* gives a state distribution for IO-31 and the coverage is adequate ($805 million total compared with $606 million federal military purchases in 1963 and $719 million in 1958), it was used to allocate purchases from this industry. The 1958 distribution was adjusted in the usual way according to changes in net state prime contracts.

IO-32, Rubber & Miscellaneous Plastics Products. Since this industry was not covered in *Shipments, 1963,* the source used was *Shipments, 1965.* The latter covers only SIC 3069. Total shipments to the government for that category were $163 million compared with total federal purchases of $171 million in 1963 and $118 million in 1958; therefore, the coverage seemed adequate.

The state distribution was made in the usual manner. The percentage for the Middle Atlantic region gave that area a figure which fell within the proper range for the 1963 distributions. The percentages estimated for the South Atlantic and East South Central regions produced totals that were too small and too large, respectively. The East South Central region was assigned a figure of $4.7 million, and the remaining $20.8 million became the South Atlantic region total. Both figures then fell within the proper range for each region.

IO-33, Leather Tanning & Industrial Leather Products. Since there were no federal purchases from this industry in 1947, 1958, or 1963, no state allocations were made.

IO-34, Footwear & Other Leather Products.
IO-35, Glass & Glass Products.
IO-36, Stone & Clay Products. These three industries were allocated according to data from *Unclassified Contracts.* See IO-16.

IO-37, Primary Iron & Steel Manufacturing.
IO-38, Primary Nonferrous Metals Manufacturing. *Shipments, 1963* contains no information on these two industries, while they are combined in

Shipments, 1965. Since no disaggregated data exist, the 1965 regional totals were used for both industries but were distributed to the states according to 1963 Faucett state output data for each industry. The 1958 Faucett state output data were used to distribute the 1965 regional totals for the 1958 allocation.

IO-39, Metal Containers.   This industry is covered incompletely in *Prime Contracts* and not at all in either of the *Shipments* publications. *Unclassified Contracts* gives state data for SIC codes 3411 and 3491. The sum of total purchases from these two categories in 1964 is $15 million, compared with 1963 federal purchases of $7 million and 1958 purchases of $17 million.

IO-40, Heating, Plumbing & Fabricated Structural Metal Products.   According to *Unclassified Contracts,* the United States total for 1964 for SIC codes 343 and 344 is $47 million as compared with $52 million federal military purchases in 1963 and $2 million in 1958, and $58 million total federal purchases in 1963 and $2 million in 1958. Thus, the coverage was sufficient to represent the state distribution of federal prime contracts in the industry.

IO-41, Screw Machine Products, Bolts, Nuts, etc., & Metal Stampings.
IO-42, Other Fabricated Metal Products.   These two industries were thoroughly discussed on pages 138–140 as an example of the methodology used when the two *Shipments* publications were data sources. Both industries were allocated according to *Shipments, 1965,* which lumps them together. Thus, the same regional totals were distributed twice for 1963, once using the 1963 Faucett state output data for IO-41 and once using the Faucett state output data for IO-42. Then the same 1963 regional totals were distributed in the same way for 1958, using the 1958 Faucett state output data for IO-41 and IO-42.

IO-43, Engines & Turbines.   *Unclassified Contracts* is the data source for this industry since *Prime Contracts* does not cover the industry, while in both of the *Shipments* publications it is divided into two groups and each group is aggregated with several different industries. The value of prime contracts in SIC 351 was added for each state. The total for the United States in 1964 is $175 million as compared with 1963 military purchases of $157 million and 1958 purchases of $235 million and 1963 total federal purchases of $179 million and 1958 purchases of $239 million, which seemed adequate coverage for a state distribution.

IO-44, Farm Machinery & Equipment. (See IO-22.)

IO-45, Construction, Mining, Oil Field Machinery & Equipment.   Since this industry is lumped with three others in *Shipments, 1965,* the best source was

Prime Contracts. The construction equipment procurement program definition seemed to correspond closely to the OBE industry definition. The regional figures exclude mining and oil field equipment, probably an unimportant omission as far as federal purchases are concerned. The average for fiscal years 1963 and 1964 from this source is $101 million as compared with the 1963 military purchases of $99 million and 1958 purchases of $78 million as well as the 1963 total federal purchases of $105 million and 1958 purchases of $80 million. As before, the data were adjusted according to differences in net military contracts by state from 1958 to 1963 and the adjusted distribution used for 1958.

IO-46, Materials Handling Machinery & Equipment. The only available source of data for this industry was *Prime Contracts.* The materials handling equipment procurement program corresponds to the OBE definition for this industry except that SIC 3534, Elevators & moving staircases, is excluded from this procurement program by the OBE and included in IO-11, New construction. The usual adjustment was made before using this distribution for 1958.

IO-47, Metalworking Machinery & Equipment.
IO-48, Special Industry Machinery & Equipment.
IO-50, Machine Shop Products. The production equipment procurement program in *Prime Contracts* was the only data source for IO-47, since this industry is not in either of the *Shipments* publications, while the coverage in *Unclassified Contracts* for fiscal 1964 is only about 12 percent of the military purchases in 1958. However, two other industries are included in this procurement program—IO-48, Special industry machinery & equipment, and IO-50, Machine shop products. Therefore, all three of these industries were allocated in the same manner.

IO-49, General Industrial Machinery & Equipment. IO-49 is not included in *Shipments, 1963,* while in *Shipments, 1965* it is combined with IO-43, IO-46, and IO-58 in "other machinery." The industry comprises only $342.7 million out of $1,342.1 million total shipments for the whole category. However, since all industries in the category are smiliar, it was assumed that the state distribution of shipments was similar, and the national data were allocated according to this distribution.

IO-50, Machine Shop Products. (See IO-47 and IO-48.)

IO-51, Office, Computing & Accounting Machines. In *Unclassified Contracts,* the data for SIC 357 in 1964 cover $206 million federal purchases, compared with 1963 military purchases of $330 million and 1958 military purchases of $71 million and total federal purchases of $448 million in 1963 and

$75 million in 1958. Since the two *Shipments* publications and *Prime Contracts* do not cover the entire industry and aggregate data from several other industries, *Unclassified Contracts* had to be used.

IO-52, Service Industry Machines. In *Unclassified Contracts,* the 1964 contracts of IO-52 total $18 million, compared with $44 million military purchases in 1963 and $62 million in 1958 and total federal purchases of $47 million in 1963 and $64 million in 1958. Although the coverage was not completely satisfactory, the only alternative would have been to obtain the data from *Prime Contracts* for the "all other supplies and equipment" procurement program, which is an aggregation of a large number of different items (the industry is not included in either of the *Shipments* publications). Therefore, the *Unclassified Contracts* distribution had to suffice.

IO-53, Electric Transmission & Distribution Equipment & Electrical Industrial Apparatus.
IO-55, Electric Lighting & Wiring Equipment.
IO-58, Miscellaneous Electrical Machinery, Equipment & Supplies. The only disaggregated data for the individual industries are in a partial coverage in *Unclassified Contracts.* However, IO-53 and IO-55 are covered in part and IO-58 in full by the electric transmission and industrial apparatus; wiring devices; and miscellaneous electrical equipment categories in *Shipments, 1963.* (Although the 1963 regional distribution was used for all three industries for both years, the state distributions were based on the 1958 and 1963 Faucett state output data, which list each industry separately.) For the East South Central, West South Central, and Mountain regions, only ranges are given. For IO-53, the ranges were sufficiently close to regional estimates obtained using the Faucett state output data to be accepted, except that the regional figures for the East South Central and West South Central regions were modified to obtain figures in the proper range, and the Mountain region was allocated the residual amount.

A similar procedure was used for IO-55 and IO-58. According to the Faucett state output data, the output of both industries in the Mountain region was 10 to 20 times smaller than the range given in *Shipments, 1963,* while the output amounts for the East South Central and West South Central regions were larger than the range, a discrepancy probably due to the aggregation of the three industries in this source. Therefore, the amounts finally allocated to the East South Central and South Central regions were slightly larger than the given range, and the amount allocated to the Mountain region, as a residual, was about half of the given range.[6]

---

6. It was possible to adjust the figures to fall within the proper range, but they were then so different from the Faucett state output data that the results seemed unreasonable. For example, the Faucett state output percentage of 17 allocated $1.4 million shipments to the Mountain region, while the range given in *Shipments, 1963* is $20.0–$49.9 million. The final allocation was a compromise of $9.1 million.

IO-54, Household Appliances. Because the industry is aggregated with many others under the "all other supplies and equipment" category in *Prime Contracts,* the state distribution in *Unclassified Contracts* was used even though the coverage is $4 million in 1964 compared with $8 million military purchases in 1963 and $20 million in 1958 as well as total federal purchases of $10 million in 1963 and $21 million in 1958.

IO-55, Electric Lighting & Wiring Equipment. (See IO-53.)

IO-56, Radio, TV, & Communication Equipment. Since IO-56 and IO-57 are aggregated as one industry in *Prime Contracts,* the best source of data was *Shipments, 1963.* However, the latter source gives information only for SIC 366. This omission is not serious since federal purchases from the other part of IO-56, SIC 365, were only $39 million in 1963, compared with $4251 million for SIC 366 [165]. Since *Shipments, 1963* gives federal purchases from SIC 366 (codes 3661 and 3662) as $5913 million, while total federal military purchases from IO-56 are $4290 million, the coverage seemed adequate. In *Shipments, 1963,* totals are given for the Northeast, South, North Central, and West sections of the country and for three of the nine regions: New England, Middle Atlantic, and South Atlantic. To determine the total for the other nine regions, the sectional totals were distributed to the regions using the 1963 Faucett state output data. This was done by first making a trial allocation. If the estimated regional totals fell within the range given in *Shipments, 1963,* as in the Mountain and Pacific regions, this allocation was considered final, and the totals were distributed in the usual manner to the states. If the regional total fell outside the given range, as in the East North Central, West North Central, East South Central, and West South Central regions, the regional totals were altered to fit the range.

IO-57, Electronic Components & Accessories. The method used to allocate federal purchases from IO-57 to the states was similar to that used for IO-56. *Shipments, 1963* was again the source since its definition of the electronic components and accessories category is the same as the OBE definition for IO-57, while in *Prime Contracts* IO-56 and IO-57 are aggregated.

IO-58, Miscellaneous Electrical Machinery, Equipment & Supplies. (See IO-53.)

IO-59, Motor Vehicles & Equipment. IO-59 is more comprehensively covered in *Prime Contracts* than in either of the *Shipments* publications. For fiscal years 1963 and 1964, an average of the noncombat vehicles procurement program figures was taken for each state.

IO-60, Aircraft & Parts. Both *Shipments, 1963* and *Prime Contracts* provide information on this industry. However, in the former source the relevant industry group contains an extraneous category (SIC 1925, Complete guided missiles, a part of IO-13), and the total for the category is considerably larger than the value of military purchases from IO-60 in 1963. For these reasons, *Prime Contracts* is a better source. The airframes and related assemblies and spares; aircraft engines and related spares; and other aircraft equipment and supplies procurement programs were added, and an average was taken for fiscal years 1963 and 1964 for each state. In this source, the national total of prime contracts from IO-60 is $5824 million, compared with $6773 million federal military purchases in 1963 and $6509 million purchases in 1958 as well as total federal purchases of $7532 million in 1963 and $6499 million in 1958. The usual adjustment was made to the 1963 regional data before calculating the 1958 distribution.

IO-61, Other Transportation Equipment.   The data in *Prime Contracts* for two procurement program categories, ships and transportation equipment, were added for fiscal 1963 and 1964. The $1639 million total prime contracts is considerably larger than the $985 million figure for military purchases in 1963 probably because military prime contract awards to the industry include maintenance and repair, as well as certain items, such as ordnance and navigation instruments, that the OBE classifies under the producing industry rather than under IO-61, Other transportation equipment. The OBE total was allocated using the data in *Prime Contracts,* although this procedure probably caused some distortion by allocating too much of the total to states with Navy maintenance and repair shipyards.

IO-62, Professional, Scientific, & Controlling Instruments & Supplies. This industry is only partly covered in *Prime Contracts,* and the part that is covered, medical and dental supplies and equipment, is a small portion of the whole industry.[7] *Shipments, 1963* also covers only a portion of the industry. Therefore, data from *Shipments, 1965* were used. This source, however, aggregates IO-62 and IO-63 into two industry groups that do not correspond to the OBE industry definitions.[8] The federal purchases from IO-63 are small relative to those from IO-62 ($99 million military purchases and $147 million total federal purchases from IO-63 compared with $316 million military and $405 million total federal

---

7. Total federal military purchases from the portion of the industry covered, SIC 3842 and 3843, were $23.4 million in 1963, as compared with $292.7 million from the other industry categories (SIC 3311, 3321, 3822, 3841, and 387).

8. The *Shipments* category called "scientific instruments, mechanical measuring devices, optical instruments, and photographic equipment" is made up of SIC 3811 and 3821 from IO-62 and of SIC 3831 and 3861 from IO-63. Similarly, "surgical and dental equipment, ophthalmic goods and watches and watchcases" is made up of SIC 3842, 3843 3871, and 3872 from IO-62 and of SIC 3851 from IO-63.

purchases from IO-62 in 1963); therefore, its inclusion was ignored. The data for the scientific instruments, etc., category and the surgical and dental equipment, etc., category were added for each region and then distributed by state according to the 1963 Faucett state output data for 1963 and the 1958 Faucett state output data for 1958. Since the regional totals for IO-62 and IO-63 were distributed according to the state output percentages for IO-62 alone, the amount of distortion caused by including IO-63 was reduced. The regional totals for surgical and dental equipment, etc., summed to a figure that was larger than the national total. For this reason, exact regional figures were used when available, but when ranges were given, a value close to the lower bound was chosen.

IO-63, Optical, Ophthalmic, & Photographic Equipment & Supplies. In both of the *Shipments* publications, the data for this industry are split between two categories, each containing data for other industries. *Prime Contracts* covers photographic equipment and supplies (SIC 3861), not optical and ophthalmic goods (SIC 3831 and 3851). Because 1963 federal purchases from SIC 3861 were $89 million compared with $10 million for the other two categories and total military purchases of $99 million, it was assumed that optical and ophthalmic prime contracts are unimportant and that the state distribution in *Prime Contracts* could be used. The usual adjustment was made to obtain the 1958 distribution.

IO-64, Miscellaneous Manufacturing. *Prime Contracts* and *Unclassified Contracts* both contain data for this industry. The latter covers $4.6 million of contracts, compared with $10 million military purchases and $8 million total federal purchases in 1963 and $33 million military purchases and $36 million total federal purchases in 1958. In addition, only 13 states are listed as selling SIC 39 goods to the federal government, which seems unlikely, since this is not a highly specialized industry. *Prime Contracts* is the better source, even though the relevant procurement program, all other supplies and equipment, includes industries in addition to IO-64. Because of the general nature of the industry, the distortion caused by the aggregation was probably not very significant. The data were adjusted as usual for the 1958 distribution.

IO-65, Transportation & Warehousing. This industry was divided into two parts to calculate the state allocation. The first is directly allocated transportation and warehousing, which includes the transportation and warehousing of CCC stocks (including the CCC adjustment taken from government industry IO-78, as described on pages 133–134) and the transportation of government employees. This portion of IO-65 was allocated according to the state distribution of federal government employees.

The remainder of the industry is the transportation margins on purchases made by the federal government. The margins were taken from the 1963 80-order input-output table and applied to all government purchases. The result was summed for each state, and the distribution was used for this portion of IO-65. The two parts of this industry were then added.

The same method was applied to 1958 purchases using margins calculated from the 80-order flows in the 1958 input-output table. Similar margins were unavailable for 1947, so the 1958 margins were applied to federal government purchases in 1947.

IO-66, Communications, Except Radio & TV Broadcasting. Purchases from this industry consist primarily of telephone and telegraph services. This is one of a number of service industries for which there were no exact data and which were distributed to the states according to the number of federal employees in each state, since purchases of these services would probably be proportional to personnel.

IO-67, Radio & TV Broadcasting. Since there were no federal purchases from this industry in 1947, 1958, or 1963, no state allocations were made.

IO-68, Electric, Gas, Water, & Sanitary Services. As with IO-66, purchases of these services were distributed to the states according to the number of federal employees.

IO-69, Wholesale & Retail Trade. The purchases from this industry consist of trade margins on all purchases made by the federal government. These margins were taken from the 1958 and 1963 OBE 80-order input-output tables, using the 1958 margins for 1947 as well.

IO-70, Finance & Insurance. The OBE indicated that figures for this industry represent miscellaneous financial charges on federal government transactions. Therefore, these "purchases" were allocated according to the regional distribution of all federal government expenditures after state distributions for both nonmanufacturing and manufacturing industries had been completed.

IO-71, Real Estate & Rental. Transactions with this industry involve the leasing of property by the federal government. Although exact figures for the regional distribution of such leases were available for 1958 [39] and 1963 [40], the data were not collected prior to 1953 and were not separated into military and nonmilitary leasing. Therefore, the 1947 distribution had to be derived by straight-line extrapolation of the 1958 and 1963 state data. As the differences between these two years were small, the resulting 1947 distribution seemed quite accurate, with the exception of Rhode Island, Oklahoma, Colorado, and Nevada, which had negative percentages. To correct this, the percentages were set at one-half of the 1958 value, and the other percentages were adjusted by a multiplicative factor.

IO-72, Hotels & Lodging Places; Personal & Repair Services, Except Automobile Repair. Since no data were available for the federal government purchases of hotel services, which make up the bulk of this industry, the state distribution of government employees was used for the allocation. For the portion spent for hotels, the assumption was that government officials travel to see other government officials and installations, so that the hotels they use were distributed according to the distribution of federal employees.

IO-73, Business Services. The OBE indicated that the amounts for this industry are obtained as a residual. The federal purchases from this industry include a wide variety of services such as inspection, drafting, photography, mapping, etc. Presumably, all the services are used by the government for its day-to-day operations; therefore, the state distribution of federal government employees was used for the allocation.

IO-74, Research & Development. IO-74 was eliminated as a separate industry in the 1963 national input-output table. The 1947 and 1958 state estimates were adjusted for consistency with the 1963 treatment of the industry (see page 133).

IO-75, Automobile Repair & Services. Purchases from this industry were assumed to correspond to the distribution of government-owned vehicles. The GSA publishes these data back to 1951, and a straight-line extrapolation was made from the 1951 [37] and 1958 [38] military plus nonmilitary data for the 1947 allocation. The 1947 figures for Rhode Island and Delaware were too small and were inflated to their 1951 values.

IO-76, Amusements. Information received from the OBE indicated that purchases from this industry represent training and educational films bought from the movie industry. Therefore, federal purchases were allocated according to the Faucett state output data for the industry.

IO-77, Medical, Educational Services, & Nonprofit Organizations. Purchases from this industry represent payments to civilian institutions for educational and medical services for the military and for research and development. Under Public Law 346, the Veteran's Administration supports the education of certain veterans by making direct payments to educational institutions. Of the 1947 purchases, 99 percent was spent for the education and training of veterans under that law. The remaining 1 percent, $6.2 million, was spent at civilian institutions for the education of military personnel [180, t. 76, p. 128]. No state allocation was available for 1947; however, there was an allocation of these purchases for 1953–1954 [180, t. 77, p. 129].[9] The latter was used on the assumption that the distribution did not change appreciably from 1947 to 1953.

In 1958 and 1963 the majority of federal government purchases from IO-77 represented R&D purchases from civilian institutions, such as research centers and educational institutions. The National Science Foundation published detailed information on these federal government purchases for 1958 [63] and 1963 [64], and these data were used for the state allocations.

IO-78, Federal Government Enterprises. Purchases from the Post Office comprise most of the federal government's transactions with this industry. In the absence of any state-by-state data, the allocations were made according to federal government employment.

IO-79, State & Local Government Enterprises. As indicated by the OBE, federal purchases from this industry consist mainly of payments to public sewerage facilities and tolls paid on state highways. Again, the allocations had to be made according to federal government employment.

IO-80, Imports. The OBE indicated that these imports are essentially purchases overseas by United States defense installations and federal purchases of imported items. The first category probably makes up the bulk of the purchases and consists of NATO construction expenditures, equipment purchased abroad, salaries to foreigners, on-shore procurement by the Navy, special-duty imports for defense purposes, and interest paid to foreign countries. In the absence of more detailed information on the composition of these purchases, however, they were allocated according to federal employment.

IO-81, Business Travel, Entertainment, & Gifts. As there were no federal purchases from this industry in 1947, 1958, or 1963, no state allocations were made.

IO-82, Office Supplies.
IO-83, Scrap, Used & Secondhand Goods.
IO-84, Government Industry. These industries were allocated according to federal employment. For IO-84, the values of $1556 million for 1947, $3030 million for 1958, and $2456 million for 1963 were not allocated to states because they represent wage and salary payments to military employees overseas.

IO-85, Rest of the World Industry. According to the OBE, the negative figures for this industry represent interest receipts by government agencies. A

---

9. The 1953–1954 figures include, by state, the amounts for tuition, equipment, and supplies under Public Law 346.

large part of these receipts is collected by the export-import bank, the Treasury, and the State Department. The figures for this industry had to be allocated by federal employment.

IO-86, Household Industry.

IO-87, Inventory Valuation Adjustment. As there were no federal purchases from this industry in 1947, 1958, and 1963, no state allocations were made.

Conclusion

It was frequently mentioned in the preceding description that data were available only on a regional, rather than a state, basis. At least two of the sources used in this study, however, have breakdowns by units smaller than states. *Shipments* gives information for some Standard Metropolitan Statistical Areas, but the data are not separated by industry and industry group. *Unclassified Contracts,* on the other hand, does give information by four-digit SIC code and by county; however, the lack of comprehensive coverage seriously limits the usefulness of the data for small-area studies.

In general, consistent sets of federal government data are not available on a regional level, or are obtainable only from unpublished sources. For the data that are published, greater uniformity in the industrial classifications used for the various publications of federal government data would facilitate the calculation of accurate state estimates. Data in *Prime Contracts,* for example, should be classified in categories consistent with *Shipments* and the OBE industrial classifications. More complete breakdowns by SIC codes would also improve the quality of the estimates. If data similar to *Prime Contracts* were available for nonmilitary purchases, or if *Shipments* data were separated into private industry, military, and nonmilitary government shipments, the nonmilitary manufacturing industry estimates could be improved. In the present study, only output or employment data by industry and by state could be used to estimate the state shares of nonmilitary purchases. For industries such as IO-80, Imports, and IO-85, Rest of the world industry, more specific information on the composition of government purchases would allow a higher degree of accuracy in determining how they should be allocated to the states.

The state estimates described in the previous sections reflect the data, the time, and the resources available. The problems encountered in this study should serve as an indication of the additional federal government data that are required to improve the estimates of federal government purchases by state. The state estimates for 1947, 1958, and 1963 are given in the accompanying statistical appendix.

Appendix A:
Classification Tables

Table A-1
Input-Output Industry Numbers, Titles, and Related SIC Codes

Industry Number	Industry Title	Related SIC Codes (1957 edition)[a]
1	Livestock & livestock products	013, pt. 014, 0193, pt. 02, pt. 0729
2	Other agricultural products	011, 012, pt. 014, 0192, 0199, pt. 02
3	Forestry & fishery products	074, 081, 082, 084, 086, 091
4	Agricultural, forestry, & fishery services	071, 0723, pt. 0729, 085, 098
5	Iron & ferroalloy ores mining	1011, 106
6	Nonferrous metal ores mining	102, 103, 104, 105, 108, 109
7	Coal mining	11, 12
8	Crude petroleum & natural gas	1311, 1321
9	Stone & clay mining & quarrying	141, 142, 144, 145, 148, 149
10	Chemical & fertilizer mineral mining	147
11	New construction	138, pt. 15, pt. 16, pt. 17, pt. 6561
12	Maintenance & repair construction	pt. 15, pt. 16, pt. 17
13	Ordnance & accessories	19
14	Food & kindred products	20
15	Tobacco manufactures	21
16	Broad & narrow fabrics, yarn & thread mills	221, 222, 223, 224, 226, 228
17	Miscellaneous textile goods & floor coverings	227, 229
18	Apparel	225, 23 (excluding 239), 3992
19	Miscellaneous fabricated textile products	239
20	Lumber & wood products, except containers	24 (excluding 244)
21	Wooden containers	244
22	Household furniture	251
23	Other furniture & fixtures	25 (excluding 251)
24	Paper & allied products, except containers & boxes	26 (excluding 265)
25	Paperboard containers & boxes	265

26	Printing & publishing	27
27	Chemicals & selected chemical products	281 (excluding alumina pt. of 2819), 286, 287, 289
28	Plastics & synthetic materials	282
29	Drugs, cleaning, & toilet preparations	283, 284
30	Paints & allied products	285
31	Petroleum refining & related industries	29
32	Rubber & miscellaneous plastics products	30
33	Leather tanning & industrial leather products	311, 312
34	Footwear & other leather products	31 (excluding 311, 312)
35	Glass & glass products	321, 322, 323
36	Stone & clay products	324, 325, 326, 327, 328, 329
37	Primary iron & steel manufacturing	331, 332, 3391, 3399
38	Primary nonferrous metals manufacturing	2819 (alumina only), 333, 334, 335, 336, 3392
39	Metal containers	3411, 3491
40	Heating, plumbing, & fabricated structural metal products	343, 344
41	Screw machine products, bolts, nuts, etc., & metal stampings	345, 346
42	Other fabricated metal products	342, 347, 348, 349 (excluding 3491)
43	Engines & turbines	351
44	Farm machinery & equipment	352
45	Construction, mining, oil field machinery & equipment	3531, 3532, 3533
46	Materials handling machinery & equipment	3534, 3535, 3536, 3537
47	Metalworking machinery & equipment	354
48	Special industry machinery & equipment	355
49	General industrial machinery & equipment	356
50	Machine shop products	359
51	Office, computing, & accounting machines	357
52	Service industry machines	358
53	Electric transmission & distribution equipment & electrical industrial apparatus	361, 362
54	Household appliances	363
55	Electric lighting & wiring equipment	364
56	Radio, TV, & communication equipment	365, 366

Table A-1, cont.

Industry Number	Industry Title	Related SIC Codes (1957 edition)[a]
57	Electronic components & accessories	367
58	Miscellaneous electrical machinery, equipment, & supplies	369
59	Motor vehicles & equipment	371
60	Aircraft & parts	372
61	Other transportation equipment	373, 374, 375, 379
62	Professional, scientific, & controlling instruments & supplies	381, 382, 384, 387
63	Optical, ophthalmic, & photographic equipment & supplies	383, 385, 386
64	Miscellaneous manufacturing	39 (excluding 3992)
65	Transportation & warehousing	40, 41, 42, 44, 45, 46, 47
66	Communications, except radio & TV broadcasting	481, 482, 489
67	Radio & TV broadcasting	483
68	Electric, gas, water, & sanitary services	49
69	Wholesale & retail trade	50 (excluding manufacturers sales offices), 52, 53, 54, 55, 56, 57, 58, 59, pt. 7399
70	Finance & insurance	60, 61, 62, 63, 64, 66, 67
71	Real estate & rental	65 (excluding 6541 and pt. 6561)
72	Hotels & lodging places; personal & repair services, except automobile repair	70, 72, 76 (excluding 7694 and 7699)
73	Business services	6541, 73 (excluding 7361, 7391, and pt. 7399), 7694, 7699, 81, 89 (excluding 8921)
74	Research & development	(eliminated in 1963 study)
75	Automobile repair & services	75
76	Amusements	78, 79
77	Medical, educational services, & nonprofit organizations	0722, 7361, 80, 82, 84, 86, 8921

78	Federal government enterprises	. . . .
79	State & local government enterprises	. . . .
80a	Directly allocated imports of goods & services	. . . .
80b	Transferred imports of goods & services	. . . .
81	Business travel, entertainment, & gifts	. . . .
82	Office supplies	. . . .
83	Scrap, used, & secondhand goods	. . . .
84	Government industry	. . . .
85	Rest of the world industry	. . . .
86	Household industry	. . . .
87	Inventory valuation adjustment	. . . .
88	Personal consumption expenditures	
89	Gross private fixed capital formation	
90	Net inventory change	
91	Net exports	
92	Federal government purchases	
93	State & local government net purchases	

[a]These are the SIC codes assigned to industries in the 1958 input-output study. They differ slightly from those assigned in the 1963 study.

Table A-2
States Listed by Sequential Order Used for MRIO Study

State[a]		State	
Number	Name	Number	Name
1	Alabama	27	Nevada
2	Arizona	28	New Hampshire
3	Arkansas	29	New Jersey
4	California	30	New Mexico
5	Colorado	31	New York
6	Connecticut	32	North Carolina
7	Delaware	33	North Dakota
8	District of Columbia	34	Ohio
9	Florida	35	Oklahoma
10	Georgia	36	Oregon
11	Idaho	37	Pennsylvania
12	Illinois	38	Rhode Island
13	Indiana	39	South Carolina
14	Iowa	40	South Dakota
15	Kansas	41	Tennessee
16	Kentucky	42	Texas
17	Louisiana	43	Utah
18	Maine	44	Vermont
19	Maryland	45	Virginia
20	Massachusetts	46	Washington
21	Michigan	47	West Virginia
22	Minnesota	48	Wisconsin
23	Mississippi	49	Wyoming
24	Missouri	50	Alaska
25	Montana	51	Hawaii
26	Nebraska		

[a] All tables published for the multiregional input-output (MRIO) study have the states arranged in this sequential order.

Table A-3
States Listed by Four Consumer Expenditures Survey Regions

Region 1 – Northeast	Region 2 – North Central	Region 3 – South	Region 4 – West
1. Connecticut	10. Illinois	22. Alabama	39. Arizona
2. Maine	11. Indiana	23. Arkansas	40. California
3. Massachusetts	12. Iowa	24. Delaware	41. Colorado
4. New Hampshire	13. Kansas	25. District of Columbia	42. Idaho
5. New Jersey	14. Michigan	26. Florida	43. Montana
6. New York	15. Minnesota	27. Georgia	44. Nevada
7. Pennsylvania	16. Missouri	28. Kentucky	45. New Mexico
8. Rhode Island	17. Nebraska	29. Louisiana	46. Oregon
9. Vermont	18. North Dakota	30. Maryland	47. Utah
	19. Ohio	31. Mississippi	48. Washington
	20. South Dakota	32. North Carolina	49. Wyoming
	21. Wisconsin	33. Oklahoma	50. Alaska
		34. South Carolina	51. Hawaii
		35. Tennessee	
		36. Texas	
		37. Virginia	
		38. West Virginia	

Appendix B:
Alignment of 1960 Consumer Expenditures Survey Categories with the 80-Order Input-Output Industrial Classification

**Karen R. Polenske and
James F. Smith**

This appendix contains an alignment between the 379 consumer expenditures categories published in the 1960 Bureau of Labor Statistics consumer expenditures survey (CES) and the 80-order Office of Business Economics input-output industrial classification. The alignment is required to make state estimates of personal consumption expenditures, discussed in Chapter 2, consistent with the published national input-output personal consumption figures.

Each CES category was assigned to input-output (IO) industries by determining the specific commodities included within the CES item, assigning Standard Industrial Classification (SIC) numbers to the commodities, and, finally, calculating the CES/IO percentage distribution or directly aligning the CES category to an input-output industry.

Procedure

Determination of Specific Commodities Within Each CES Category. A verbal description of the items included in or excluded from some of the consumer expenditures categories is given in a definition and explanation section in most of the 1960 CES volumes [199]. The National Industrial Conference Board (NICB) has published a summary of data from the original CES computer tapes entitled *Expenditure Patterns of the American Family* [59]. In some cases, the breakdown by commodity is more detailed in the NICB volume than in the CES volume, and the NICB statistics could be used to determine the commodity composition of a specific CES category. Also, the definitions given in the back of the NICB volume are sometimes more detailed than in the CES volume. Both sources had to be used to obtain a complete definition of the CES categories.

Assignment of SIC Numbers to the CES Category. After the composition of a particular CES category was determined, an assignment was made of the respective SIC number(s) to the CES category. The 1957 SIC manual [80] was used to determine the number(s). If an even more detailed description of the

173

components of a particular SIC number was required, the 1958 *Numerical List of Manufactured Products* [105], which contains SIC codes broken down to the seven-digit level, was consulted.

Calculation of the CES/IO Percentage Distribution of a Direct Alignment of the CES Category to an Input-Output Industry. The next step was to determine the input-output industry or industries to which the CES item should be assigned. In many instances all SIC numbers for a particular CES item could be directly aligned with only one input-output industry. SIC numbers are listed with their respective input-output industry in the 1958 input-output table [176, p. 33]. Although a few minor variations (mainly for the service industries) in this listing appear with the 1963 input-output table [164, pp. 26–29], the latter was not available when this alignment was completed; therefore, the 1958 classification was used. If a CES item contained commodities produced by more than one input-output industry, the percentage contributed by each industry was determined using one of three sources.

Unless otherwise specified, percentage distributions shown on the alignment were calculated using figures contained in the October 1965 *Survey of Current Business* article by Nancy W. Simon [74]. The article contains an alignment between the national income personal consumption expenditures (NIPCE) categories and the input-output industries.

Of considerable value in developing the alignment was an unpublished detailed listing of consumer items included within the national income categories, referred to hereafter as the *1958 Detailed NIPCE Listing* [170]. The information in this listing was assembled by the staff of the National Economics Division of the Office of Business Economics (OBE) for use as a bridge between the NIPCE figures and the 1958 input-output study. Additional work in developing the purchaser value figures was done by the staff of the National Income Division of the OBE. Since the data in the listing were preliminary figures used by Nancy W. Simon, the values from which the percentage distributions were calculated are not included in the comments unless the values coincided with the figures published in her article. In the comments, a reference is always given to the *1958 Detailed NIPCE Listing* if it was used; consequently, the omission of the percentage distribution values can be readily noted.

For a few commodities the extra consumer detail required was available only in the NICB volume [59]. The NICB volume was used to provide percentage breakdowns by income distribution groups since that volume contained more detail than the CES for certain consumption items.[1] The percentages calculated

---

1. For these specific CES items, percentages were calculated from the NICB volume both by income distribution group and by region. In each case the percentages varied more for different income groups than for different regions; consequently, only the first percentage distribution was used.

from the NICB volume are recorded in the comments at the end of the following alignment.

One additional reference was used in developing the alignment. For the rented dwelling category, contract rent was distributed between rent, utilities, and fuel using regional data provided by the National Association of Real Estate Boards (NAREB) [4]. At first, data from the U.S. Bureau of the Census, Census of Housing were tried since the data were available by states. The percentage of total contract rent which should be allocated to the utility and fuel industries, however, could not be estimated from the information contained in that publication.

In the cases where a CES item was directly aligned with only one input-output industry, no percentage distribution was required. In the alignment between the consumer expenditures survey and the input-output industry classification which follows, detailed information on the reasons for some of the alignments and an explanation of the method of constructing the various percentage distributions are given in the accompanying comments.

Description

Column 1: (to left of decimal) CES Number. For this study, a serial number was assigned to each line of the 1960 consumer expenditures survey classification. For example, 35.00 is the thirty-fifth line of consumer expenditures in the CES volumes and bears the label "coal and coke." Numbers were assigned to 379 different lines. The numbering of the lines began with the consumption expenditure for "total food" and continued sequentially through the item entitled "contributions to educational, medical, political, and other organizations." The category "value of home-produced food," which is listed later in the survey classification, was included as the last element of the alignment.

Column 1: (to right of decimal) CES Number. For this study, the number .00 was assigned if the consumer expenditures item listed to the left of the decimal could be directly aligned with one specific input-output industry. If the consumer expenditures category listed to the left of the decimal was allocated to more than one input-output industry, a series of sequential numbers, .01, .02, .03, and so on, was assigned to the components of each CES item.

Column 2: Title of Consumer Expenditures Survey Item. If the serial number ends in 00, the exact title given that consumer expenditures item in the 1960 CES volumes [199] is used. If the serial number ends in a number other than 00, the title represents an attempt to describe the particular consumption component. An asterisk preceding the title indicates that a special comment concerning this expenditures item is included in the documentation following the alignment table. The comments also contain the value figures whenever a percentage distribution is shown in the alignment unless the value figures could not be published. The values listed are always for 1958 because those were the only ones available at the time this alignment was constructed.

Column 3: SIC Number.   The Standard Industrial Classification number(s) assigned to the product consumed. (Numbers are left-adjusted.) SIC numbers are not available for IO-80, Imports, or IO-83, Scrap, used & secondhand goods. Also, SIC numbers are not given in the alignment in cases where it was impossible to specify the exact SIC number which would pertain to that consumer expenditures item.

Column 4: Input-Output Industry Number.   The number of the input-output industry to which the consumer expenditures item was assigned.

Column 5: Percentage of Distribution.   If a consumer expenditures survey item had to be split among several input-output industries, the percentage that was allocated to the respective input-output industry listed in the fourth column is recorded here. In cases where separate percentage distributions for different income groups were computed from the National Industrial Conference Board publication [59], the letters NICBY appear in the column, and the percentages by income distribution groups are listed in the comments that follow the alignment. The letters NAREB refer to percentage distributions calculated by region from data published by the National Association of Real Estate Boards [4].

A number in parentheses refers to a particular CES serial number and has one of two interpretations.

1. If no asterisk precedes the title in Column 2, the consumption expenditure under consideration is a component of a total consumer expenditures category given by the number in parentheses and did not need to be allocated separately to an input-output industry. For example, CES 59.00, 60.00, and 61.00 were all allocated to IO-66, Communications, except radio & TV broadcasting. Since they are the components of CES 58.00, telephone and telegraph, total, the number 58 appears in parentheses under the percentage column to indicate that the total was used, not the components.

2. If an asterisk precedes the title in Column 2, the consumption expenditure under consideration had to be added to or subtracted from the consumption expenditure associated with the CES serial number listed in parentheses. In this case, a comment, included at the end of the alignment, states whether an addition or a subtraction had to be made.

If there is no entry in Columns 4, 5, or 6, that individual consumer expenditures item was not allocated to an input-output industry. This indicates one of two possibilities.

1. If no asterisk precedes the title in Column 2, the item was allocated from a more detailed listing of the data. For example, CES 14.00, housing, total, was not allocated to an input-output industry, but the basic components of CES 14.00, namely, 16.00, 20.00, 26.00, and 32.00, were allocated to input-output industries.

2. If an asterisk precedes the title in Column 2, the item was not allocated to any input-output industry. In such a case, the documentation accompanying this alignment explains why no allocation was made.

Column 6: NIPCE Number. The numbers listed in this column indicate the NIPCE categories that are included within a particular consumer expenditures category. These NIPCE category classifications aided in aligning the consumer expenditures items to the input-output industries. In cases where a consumption expenditure was split between two or more input-output industries, the values listed in Nancy W. Simon's article [74] were used to calculate the percentage breakdown if sufficient detail was not available in the NICB publication [59]. In certain cases, an a, b, or c is attached to an NIPCE number, but these sub-classifications are designated only on the unpublished *1958 Detailed NIPCE Listing* [170]. The letters are retained in case the alignment is ever reworked.

Table B.1

ALIGNMENT OF 1960 CONSUMER EXPENDITURES SURVEY CATEGORIES
WITH THE 80-ORDER INPUT-OUTPUT INDUSTRIAL CLASSIFICATION

CES NO.	TITLE OF CES CONSUMPTION ITEM	SIC NO.	IO NO.	PER-CENT	NIPCE NO.
1.00	*FOOD,TOTAL				I.1-I.3
1.01	FOOD (LIVESTOCK AND LIVESTOCK PROD.)		1	3.0	
1.02	FOOD (OTHER AGRICULTURAL PRODUCTS)		2	4.9	
1.03	FOOD (FISHERY PRODUCTS)		3	0.8	
1.04	FOOD (ROCK SALT)		10	0.0	
1.05	FOOD (FOOD AND KINDRED PRODUCTS)		14	87.8	
1.06	FOOD (CHEM. AND SELECTED CHEM. PROD.)		27	0.0	
1.07	FOOD (TRANSPORTATION AND WAREHOUSING)		65	0.2	
1.08	FOOD (WHOLESALE AND RETAIL TRADE)		69	0.5	
1.09	FOOD (IMPORTS)		80	2.8	
2.00	FOOD PREPARED AT HOME		(1)		
3.00	FOOD AWAY FROM HOME		(1)		
4.00	IN HOME CITY, TOTAL FOOD		(1)		
5.00	BOARD		(1)		
6.00	MEALS AT WORK		(1)		
7.00	MEALS AT SCHOOL		(1)		
8.00	OTHER MEALS AND BEVERAGES		(1)		
9.00	SNACKS		(1)		
10.00	*OUT OF HOME CITY, TOTAL FOOD		(1)		
11.00	MEALS AS PAY		(1)		
12.00	*ALCOHOLIC BEVERAGES		(1)		I.1-I.2
13.00	*TOBACCO				I.5
13.01	TOBACCO	21	15	98.6	
13.02	PIPES AND LIGHTERS	3999	64	1.3	
13.03	TOBACCO (IMPORTS)	80	0.1		
14.00	HOUSING, TOTAL				
15.00	SHELTER, TOTAL				IV.1-.4
16.00	*RENTED DWELLING, TOTAL				
16.01	COAL MINING	11,12	7	NAREB	
16.02	WOOD,ETC.	241,242	20	NAREB	
16.03	FUEL OIL	2911	31	NAREB	
16.04	COKE	3312	37	NAREB	
16.05	ELECTRICITY,GAS,WATER,SANITARY SERV.	49	68	NAREB	
16.06	* RENTED DWELLING	651	71	NAREB	
17.00	RENT		(16)		
18.00	REPAIRS		(16)		
19.00	SPECIAL FEES, ETC.		(16)		
20.00	*OWNED DWELLING, TOTAL	65	71		
21.00	INTEREST ON MORTGAGES		(20)		
22.00	TAXES DUE IN SURVEY YEAR		(20)		
23.00	PROPERTY INSURANCE		(20)		
24.00	*REPAIRS AND REPLACEMENTS		30	(20)	
25.00	OTHER EXPENSES		(20)		

ALIGNMENT(CONT'D)

CES NO.	TITLE OF CES CONSUMPTION ITEM	SIC NO.	IO NO.	PER-CENT	NIPCE NO.
26.00	*OWNED VACATION HOME, CABIN, ETC. TOTAL	65	71		
27.00	INTEREST ON MORTGAGES			(26)	
28.00	TAXES DUE IN SURVEY YEAR			(26)	
29.00	PROPERTY INSURANCE			(26)	
30.00	*REPAIRS AND REPLACEMENTS		30	(26)	
31.00	OTHER EXPENSES			(26)	
32.00	*LODGING OUT OF HOME CITY				
32.01	HOTELS AND LODGING PLACES	70	72	94.5	IV.2,4
32.02	STUDENT LODGING	82	77	5.5	IV.2
33.00	*OTHER REAL ESTATE	65	71		
34.00	FUEL, LIGHT, REFRIG. AND WATER, TOTAL				
35.00	*COAL AND COKE				V.8D
35.01	COAL MINING	11,12	7	98.1	
35.02	COKE	3312	37	1.9	
36.00	WOOD, SAWDUST, PRESSED WOOD, LOGS, ETC.	241,242	20		V.8D
37.00	KEROSENE	2911	31		V.8D
38.00	FUEL OIL	2911	31		V.8D
39.00	OTHER SOLID AND PETROLEUM FUELS	2911,2999	31		V.8D
40.00	GAS	492	68		V.8B
41.00	ELECTRICITY	491	68		V.8A
42.00	GAS AND ELECTRICITY (COMBINED BILLS)	4931,4932	68		V.8A,B
43.00	*WATER	494	68		V.8C
43.01	WATER, SANITARY SERV., PRIVATE		68	93.5	V.8C
43.02	WATER,SANITARY SERV., ST. + LOC. GOVT.		79	6.5	V.8C
44.00	SEWAGE				V.8C
44.01	PRIVATE	4952	68	(43)	
44.02	STATE AND LOCAL GOVERNMENT		79	(43)	
45.00	GARBAGE AND TRASH COLLECTION				V.8C
45.01	PRIVATE	4953	68	(43)	
45.02	STATE AND LOCAL GOVERNMENT		79	(43)	
46.00	WATER, SEWAGE, GARBAGE (COMBINED BILLS)				V.8C
46.01	PRIVATE	4939	68	(43)	
46.02	STATE AND LOCAL GOVERNMENT		79	(43)	
47.00	WATER SOFTENING SERVICE	7399	73		V.11
48.00	ICE	2097	14		V.8D
49.00	FOOD FREEZER RENTALS	4223	65		V.11
50.00	*OTHER EXPENSES				
51.00	HOUSEHOLD OPERATIONS, TOTAL				
52.00	*LAUNDRY SUPPLIES				V.6B
52.01	STARCH	2046	14		NICBY
52.02	BLEACHES	2899	27		NICBY
52.03	OTHER LAUNDRY SUPPLIES	284	29		NICBY
53.00	*CLEANING SUPPLIES				V.6B
53.01	SYNTHETIC SCOURING PADS, SPONGES	282	28		NICBY
53.02	DEODORIZERS,POLISHES,AMMONIA,DETERG.	2841,2842	29		NICBY
53.03	SCOURING PADS WITH SOAP	3291453	36		NICBY

ALIGNMENT(CONT'D)

CES NO.	TITLE OF CES CONSUMPTION ITEM	SIC NO.	IO NO.	PER-CENT	NIPCE NO.
54.00	*HOUSEHOLD PAPER SUPPLIES				V.6C
54.01	NAPKINS, TOWELS, TOILET PAPER	2649,2621	24	NICBY	
54.02	CUPS AND PLATES	2654	25	NICBY	
54.03	ALUMINUM FOIL	3352	38	NICBY	
55.00	*LAUNDRY AND CLEANING, SENT OUT	721	72		II.5,6V.11
56.00	DOMESTIC SERVICE	8811	86		V.10
57.00	*DAY NURSERY CARE	8211	77		X.2
58.00	TELEPHONE AND TELEGRAPH, TOTAL	4811,4821	66		V.9
59.00	LOCAL TELEPHONE			(58)	
60.00	LONG DISTANCE TELEPHONE			(58)	
61.00	TELEGRAMS AND CABLEGRAMS			(58)	
62.00	OTHER HOUSEHOLD EXPENSES, TOTAL				
63.00	*REPAIRS OF FURNITURE AND EQUIPMENT				V.11
63.01	ELECTRICAL AND FURNITURE REPAIR	7621,7641	72	92.2	
63.02	OTHER REPAIR	7699	73	7.8	
64.00	MOVING, FREIGHT, EXPRESS, AND STORAGE	421,4721	65		V.11
65.00	*POSTAGE AND WRITING MATERIAL				V.4C,7,11
65.01	STATIONERY AND PAPER SUPPLIES	2649	24	19.3	V.7
65.02	GREETING CARDS,ALBUMS,ENGRAVING	2771,275,	26	35.9	V.7
65.02		274			
65.03	INK	2899372	27	0.2	V.7
65.04	TACKS AND STAPLES	33152	37	0.6	V.7
65.05	FOUNTAIN PENS	3951	64	3.6	V.4C
65.06	POSTAGE		78	40.4	V.11
66.00	*OTHER EXPENSES				
66.01	NURSERY PRODUCTS		2	73.1	IX.7
66.02	CHRISTMAS TREES		3	4.8	IX.3
66.03	PEAT	1498	9	2.8	V.6B
66.04	FLAGS	2399041	19	0.8	V.5
66.05	FERTILIZERS AND PESTICIDES	287	27	2.4	V.6B
66.06	CHRISTMAS TREE LAMPS	3641055	55	1.9	IX.3
66.07	CHRISTMAS TREE LIGHTING OUTFITS	3699271	58	4.3	IX.3
66.08	MATCHES AND CANDLES	3983,3984	64	9.9	V.6A
67.00	HOUSE FURNISHINGS AND EQUIPMENT, TOTAL				
68.00	*HOUSEHOLD TEXTILES, TOTAL				V.4,V.5
68.01	WOVEN HOUSEHOLD PRODUCTS	22	16	30.9	
68.02	LACE AND LINEN GOODS AND BATH MATS	229,2272	17	1.2	
68.03	KNITTED HOUSEHOLD GOODS	2259	18	0.7	
68.04	MISC. FABRICATED TEXTILE PRODUCTS	239	19	64.0	
68.05	SPONGE + FOAM RUBBER PILLOWS,SHEETING	3069	32	1.1	
68.06	ELECTRIC BLANKETS	3634385	54	2.1	
68.07 *	SERVICES		86	0.0	
69.00	SHEETS				V.5
69.01	WOVEN SHEETS	2211	16	(68)	
69.02	OTHER SHEETS	2392	19	(68)	
69.03	HOSPITAL,CRIB SHEETING,RUBBER COATED	3069815	32	(68)	
70.00	PILLOWCASES .				V.5
70.01	WOVEN PILLOWCASES	2211	16	(68)	
70.02	OTHER PILLOWCASES	2392	19	(68)	

ALIGNMENT(CONT'D)

CES NO.	TITLE OF CES CONSUMPTION ITEM	SIC NO.	IO NO.	PER-CENT	NIPCE NO.
71.00	PILLOWS				V.4
71.01	PILLOWS	2392	19	(68)	
71.02	SPONGE + FOAM RUBBER PILLOWS	3069345	32	(68)	
72.00	BLANKETS,COMFORTERS,QUILTS,BEDSPREADS				V.4
72.01	SYNTHETIC,SILK,WOOL,COTTON BEDCOVERS	2221,2231,	16	(68)	
72.01		2211			
72.02	LACE GOODS	2292	17	(68)	
72.03	KNITTED BEDSPREADS	2259	18	(68)	
72.04	OTHER BEDCOVERINGS	2392	19	(68)	
72.05	ELECTRIC BLANKETS	3634385	54	(68)	
73.00	CURTAINS				V.5
73.01	LACE CURTAINS	2292	17	(68)	
73.02	KNITTED CURTAINS	2259	18	(68)	
73.03	NON-WOVEN CURTAINS	2391,2392	19	(68)	
74.00	DRAPERIES				V.5
74.01	WOVEN DRAPERIES	2211,2221	16	(68)	
74.02	NON-WOVEN DRAPERIES	2391	19	(68)	
75.00	TABLECLOTHS,PLACEMATS,NAPKINS	2392	19	(68)	V.5
76.00	SLIPCOVERS	2392	19	(68)	V.5
77.00	TOWELS				V.5
77.01	WOVEN TOWELS(COTTON)	2211	16	(68)	
77.02	LINEN TOWELS	2299	17	(68)	
77.03	KNITTED TOWELS	2259	18	(68)	
77.04	OTHER TOWELS	2392	19	(68)	
78.00	OTHER READY-MADE ITEMS				V.5
78.01	BATH MATS,TUFTED	2272	17	(68)	
78.02	OTHER HOUSEFURNISHINGS	2392	19	(68)	
78.03	RUBBER PADS	3069	32	(68)	
79.00	MATERIALS AND SERVICES				V.5
79.01	FABRICS, THREAD, ETC.	22	16	(68)	
79.02 *	SERVICES		86	(68)	
80.00	*FURNITURE, TOTAL				V.1,2
80.01	HOUSEHOLD FURNITURE	251	22	96.3	
80.02	LOCKERS, METAL PARTITIONS, ETC.	254	23	0.6	
80.03	IMPORTS		80	1.4	
80.04	USED FURNITURE		83	1.7	
81.00	LIVING ROOM FURNITURE			(80)	
82.00	DINING ROOM FURNITURE			(80)	
83.00	BEDROOM FURNITURE			(80)	
84.00	KITCHEN FURNITURE			(80)	
85.00	PORCH AND GARDEN FURNITURE			(80)	
86.00	OTHER FURNITURE			(80)	
87.00	FLOOR COVERINGS, TOTAL				V.4
88.00	*SOFT SURFACE FLOOR COVERINGS	227	17		
89.00	WALL-TO-WALL FLOOR COVERINGS			(88)	
90.00	ROOM SIZE FLOOR COVERINGS			(88)	
91.00	OTHER SOFT SURFACE FLOOR COVERINGS			(88)	

ALIGNMENT(CONT'D)

CES NO.	TITLE OF CES CONSUMPTION ITEM	SIC NO.	IO NO.	PER-CENT	NIPCE NO.
92.00	*HARD SURFACE FLOOR COVERINGS				
92.01	TILE	3253,3292	36	NICBY	
92.02	OTHER HARD SURFACE	3982	64	NICBY	
93.00	OTHER FLOOR COVERINGS, INCL. RUG PADS	2291	17		
94.00	MAJOR APPLIANCES, TOTAL				
95.00	*REFRIGERATORS				V.2
95.01	REFRIGERATORS	3632	54	99.1	
95.02	IMPORTS		80	0.1	
95.03	USED REFRIGERATORS		83	0.8	
96.00	*HOME FREEZERS				V.2
96.01	HOME FREEZERS	3632	54	99.1	
96.02	IMPORTS		80	0.1	
96.03	USED FREEZERS		83	0.8	
97.00	*DISHWASHERS				V.2
97.01	DISHWASHERS	3639	54	99.2	
97.02	IMPORTS		80	0.0	
97.03	USED DISHWASHERS		83	0.8	
98.00	*COOKING STOVES				V.2
98.01	HEATING STOVES	3433	40	13.6	
98.02	COOKING STOVES	3631	54	85.5	
98.03	IMPORTS		80	0.1	
98.04	USED COOKING STOVES		83	0.8	
99.00	*WAXERS, ELECTRIC				V.2
99.01	WAXERS, ELECTRIC	3639	54	99.2	
99.02	IMPORTS		80	0.0	
99.03	USED WAXERS, ELECTRIC		83	0.8	
100.00	*GARBAGE DISPOSAL UNITS				V.2
100.01	GARBAGE DISPOSAL UNITS	3639	54	99.2	
100.02	IMPORTS		80	0.0	
100.03	USED GARBAGE DISPOSAL UNITS		83	0.8	
101.00	*VACUUM CLEANERS				V.2
101.01	VACUUM CLEANERS	3635	54	99.0	
101.02	IMPORTS		80	0.2	
101.03	USED VACUUM CLEANERS		83	0.8	
102.00	*WASHING MACHINES				V.2
102.01	WASHING MACHINES	3633	54	99.2	
102.02	IMPORTS		80	0.0	
102.03	USED WASHING MACHINES		83	0.8	
103.00	*CLOTHES DRYERS				V.2
103.01	CLOTHES DRYERS	3633	54	99.2	
103.02	IMPORTS		80	0.0	
103.03	USED CLOTHES DRYERS		83	0.8	
104.00	*WASHER-DRYER COMBINATIONS				V.2
104.01	WASHER-DRYER COMBINATIONS	3633	54	99.2	
104.02	IMPORTS		80	0.0	
104.03	USED WASHER-DRYER COMBINATIONS		83	0.8	

ALIGNMENT(CONT'D)

CES NO.	TITLE OF CES CONSUMPTION ITEM	SIC NO.	IO NO.	PER-CENT	NIPCE NO.
105.00	*AIR CONDITIONERS(DEMOUNTABLE)				V.2
105.01	AIR CONDITIONERS(DEMOUNTABLE)	3585	52	99.2	
105.02	IMPORTS		80	0.0	
105.03	USED AIR CONDITIONERS		83	0.8	
106.00	*DEHUMIDIFIERS				V.2
106.01	DEHUMIDIFIERS	3585	52	99.2	
106.02	IMPORTS		80	0.0	
106.03	USED DEHUMIDIFIERS		83	0.8	
107.00	*SEWING MACHINES				V.2
107.01	SEWING MACHINES	3636	54	73.2	
107.02	IMPORTS		80	26.0	
107.03	USED SEWING MACHINES		83	0.8	
108.00	*IRONING MACHINES				V.2
108.01	IRONING MACHINES	3633	54	99.2	
108.02	IMPORTS		80	0.0	
108.03	USED IRONING MACHINES		83	0.8	
109.00	*SMALL APPLIANCES				V.2
109.01	SMALL APPLIANCES	363	54	99.1	
109.02	IMPORTS		80	0.1	
109.03	USED SMALL APPLIANCES		83	0.8	
110.00	*HOUSEWARES,TOTAL				V.3
110.01	WOODEN KITCHENWARE	2499	20	0.9	
110.02	RUBBER AND PLASTIC KITCHENWARE	3069,3079	32	17.4	
110.03	GLASS KITCHENWARE	3221,3229	35	13.0	
110.04	STONE AND CLAY KITCHENWARE	326	36	12.3	
110.05	NON-FERROUS METAL KITCHENWARE	3361	38	0.4	
110.06	NON-ALUMINUM KITCHENWARE	3461	41	18.7	
110.07	OTHER CUTLERY AND CAN OPENERS	342,348	42	9.7	
110.08	SILVERWARE	3914	64	19.5	
110.09	IMPORTS		80	8.1	
111.00	CHINA AND GLASSWARE				V.3
111.01	PLASTIC	3079	32	(110)	
111.02	GLASSWARE	3229	35	(110)	
111.03	CHINA	3262,3263	36	(110)	
112.00	KNIVES,FORKS,SPOONS,ETC.				V.3
112.01	OTHER CUTLERY	3421	42	(110)	
112.02	SILVERWARE	3914	64	(110)	
113.00	COOKING UTENSILS(NON-ELECTRIC)				V.3
113.01	COOKING UTENSILS,GLASS	3229	35	(110)	
113.02	ALUMINUM COOKING UTENSILS	3361	38	(110)	
113.03	NON-ALUMINUM COOKING UTENSILS	3461	41	(110)	
114.00	KITCHENWARE				V.3
114.01	WOODEN KITCHENWARE	2499	20	(110)	
114.02	RUBBER AND PLASTIC KITCHENWARE	3069,3079	32	(110)	
114.03	GLASS KITCHENWARE	3221	35	(110)	
114.04	EARTHENWARE	3269	36	(110)	
114.05	ALUMINUM KITCHENWARE	3361	38	(110)	
114.06	OTHER METAL KITCHENWARE	3461	41	(110)	
114.07	CAN OPENERS AND WIRE KITCHENWARE	3423,3481	42	(110)	

ALIGNMENT(CONT'D)

CES NO.	TITLE OF CES CONSUMPTION ITEM	SIC NO.	IO NO.	PER-CENT	NIPCE NO.
115.00	*CLEANING EQUIPMENT				V.3-V.5
115.01	MOPS (DRY, WET, SPONGE)	2392	19	35.5	V.5
115.02	PAILS,ASH CANS,ETC.	3461	41	17.8	V.3
115.03	CARPET SWEEPERS	3589261	52	5.0	V.4
115.04	BROOMS AND BRUSHES	3981	64	41.7	V.5
116.00	*LAUNDRY EQUIPMENT				
116.01	CLOTHESLINES	22981	17	0.0	
116.02	LAUNDRY BAGS	2392081	19	63.4	V.5
116.03	BASKETS, CLOTHESPINS	2499561	20	36.6	V.3
116.04	LAUNDRY TRAYS	3272,3261	36	0.0	
116.05	LAUNDRY TUBS	3431	40	0.0	
117.00	MISC. ITEMS (HOUSE FURNISHINGS), TOTAL				
118.00	INSURANCE ON FURNISHINGS, EQUIP, APPAREL	633	70		V.11
119.00	*OTHER MISC. HOUSE FURNISHINGS				
119.01	MIRROR + PICTURE FRAMES, STEP LADDERS	2499	20	NICBY	V.4B
119.02	CURTAIN RODS, BLINDS AND SHADES	2591	23	NICBY	V.4B
119.03	HAND LUGGAGE	3161	34	NICBY	II.3C
119.04	MIRRORS (HOUSEHOLD) AND GLASS VASES	3229,3231	35	NICBY	V.4B,V.5
119.05	STATUARY,CONCRETE AND ART GOODS	3269,3299	36	NICBY	V.4B
119.05		3272			
119.06	TOOLS(HAND,GARDEN),VACUUM BOTTLES,ETC.	342	42	NICBY	V.3,4B,D
119.07	LAWN MOWERS	3522	44	NICBY	V.4D
119.08	MACH. + POWER TOOLS	354	47	NICBY	V.4D
119.09	WOODWORKING TOOLS	355	48	NICBY	V.4D
119.10	TYPEWRITERS AND SCALES	3572,3576	51	NICBY	V.4B,C
119.11	FRACTIONAL HORSEPOWER MOTORS	36211	53	NICBY	V.4D
119.12	HOUSEHOLD SERVICE MACHINES,NEC	3639381	54	NICBY	V.4B
119.13	ELECTRIC LIGHT BULBS AND LAMPS	3641,3642	55	NICBY	V.4B,V.6
119.14	HANDCARTS AND WHEELBARROWS	37992	61	NICBY	V.4D
119.15	CLOCKS, TIMING MECHANISMS	3871	62	NICBY	V.4B
119.16	BABY CARRIAGES + PAINT BRUSHES, ETC.	3943,3981	64	NICBY	V.5,IX.4
120.00	*CLOTHING, CLOTHING MAT. AND SERV. TOTAL				
120.01	CLOTHING		16	0.0	II.3A,B
120.02	CLOTHING		17	0.2	II.3A,B
120.03	CLOTHING		18	93.7	II.3A,B
120.04	CLOTHING		19	0.4	II.3A,B
120.05	CLOTHING		24	0.4	II.3A,B
120.06	CLOTHING		32	0.1	II.3A,B
120.07	CLOTHING		34	2.9	II.3A,B
120.08	CLOTHING		64	0.5	II.3A,B
120.09	CLOTHING (IMPORTS)		80	1.9	II.3A,B
120.10	USED CLOTHING		83	-0.1	II.3A,B
121.00	CLOTHING, MEN AND BOYS, 18 YR, + OVER,TOT.		(120)		II.3B
122.00	OUTERWEAR, TOTAL		(120)		II.3B
123.00	OVERCOATS		(120)		II.3B
124.00	TOPCOATS		(120)		II.3B
125.00	JACKETS, HEAVY		(120)		II.3B
126.00	JACKETS, LIGHTWEIGHT		(120)		II.3B

ALIGNMENT (CONT'D)

CES NO.	TITLE OF CES CONSUMPTION ITEM	SIC NO.	IO NO.	PER-CENT	NIPCE NO.
127.00	SWEATERS		(120)		II.3B
128.00	RAINCOATS		(120)		II.3B
129.00	SUITS, SPORT COATS, AND TROUSERS		(120)		II.3B
130.00	WORK TROUSERS, OVERALLS, DUNGAREES		(120)		II.3B
131.00	SHIRTS, DRESS		(120)		II.3B
132.00	SHIRTS, OTHER		(120)		II.3B
133.00	OTHER OUTERWEAR		(120)		II.3B
134.00	UNDERWEAR		(120)		II.3B
135.00	NIGHTWEAR		(120)		II.3B
136.00	HOSIERY		(120)		II.3B
137.00	*FOOTWEAR, TOTAL				II.1
137.01	RUBBERS	32		10.1	
137.02	SHOES	34		87.7	
137.03	IMPORTS	80		2.2	
138.00	SHOES (STREET, WORK, CASUAL)		(137)		II.1
139.00	SPECIAL SPORT SHOES (GOLF, BOWLING, ETC.)		(137)		II.1
140.00	OTHER FOOTWEAR		(137)		II.1
141.00	HATS, GLOVES, AND ACCESSORIES, TOTAL		(120)		II.3B
142.00	HATS AND CAPS		(120)		II.3B
143.00	GLOVES		(120)		II.3B
144.00	ACCESSORIES		(120)		II.3B
145.00	*JEWELRY AND WATCHES				II.7
145.01	JEWELRY CASES	34		2.9	
145.02	WATCHES	62		14.3	
145.03	MISC. JEWELRY	64		79.1	
145.04	JEWELRY IMPORTS	80		2.2	
145.05	SECOND-HAND JEWELRY	83		1.5	
146.00	OTHER (HATS,GLOVES,ETC.) ACCESSORIES		(120)		II.3B
147.00	EXPENDITURES NOT ALLOCATED		(120)		II.3B
148.00	CLOTHING, BOYS, 16+ 17 YR, TOTAL		(120)		II.3B
149.00	OUTERWEAR, TOTAL		(120)		II.3B
150.00	OVERCOATS		(120)		II.3B
151.00	TOPCOATS		(120)		II.3B
152.00	JACKETS, HEAVY		(120)		II.3B
153.00	JACKETS, LIGHTWEIGHT		(120)		II.3B
154.00	SWEATERS		(120)		II.3B
155.00	RAINCOATS		(120)		II.3B
156.00	SUITS, SPORT COATS, AND TROUSERS		(120)		II.3B
157.00	WORK TROUSERS, OVERALLS, DUNGAREES		(120)		II.3B
158.00	SHIRTS, DRESS		(120)		II.3B
159.00	SHIRTS, OTHER		(120)		II.3B
160.00	OTHER OUTERWEAR		(120)		II.3B
161.00	UNDERWEAR		(120)		II.3B
162.00	NIGHTWEAR		(120)		II.3B
163.00	HOSIERY		(120)		II.3B
164.00	FOOTWEAR, TOTAL		(137)		II.1
165.00	SHOES (STREET, WORK, CASUAL)		(137)		II.1
166.00	SPECIAL SPORT SHOES (GOLF, BOWLING, ETC.)		(137)		II.1

ALIGNMENT(CONT'D)

CES NO.	TITLE OF CES CONSUMPTION ITEM	SIC NO.	IO NO.	PER-CENT	NIPCE NO.
167.00	OTHER FOOTWEAR		(137)		II.1
168.00	HATS, GLOVES, AND ACCESSORIES, TOTAL		(120)		II.3B
169.00	HATS AND CAPS		(120)		II.3B
170.00	GLOVES		(120)		II.3B
171.00	ACCESSORIES		(120)		II.3B
172.00	JEWELRY AND WATCHES		(145)		II.7
173.00	OTHER (HATS,GLOVES,ETC.) ACCESSORIES		(120)		II.3B
174.00	EXPENDITURES NOT ALLOCATED		(120)		II.3B
175.00	CLOTHING, BOYS, 2 THRU 15 YRS, TOTAL		(120)		II.3B
176.00	OUTERWEAR, TOTAL		(120)		II.3B
177.00	OVERCOATS AND COAT SETS		(120)		II.3B
178.00	JACKETS, HEAVY		(120)		II.3B
179.00	JACKETS, LIGHTWEIGHT		(120)		II.3B
180.00	SWEATERS		(120)		II.3B
181.00	RAINCOATS		(120)		II.3B
182.00	SNOWSUITS, SKI SUITS, ETC.		(120)		II.3B
183.00	SUITS, SPORT COATS, AND TROUSERS		(120)		II.3B
184.00	PLAY CLOTHES		(120)		II.3B
185.00	SHIRTS		(120)		II.3B
186.00	OTHER OUTERWEAR		(120)		II.3B
187.00	UNDERWEAR		(120)		II.3B
188.00	NIGHTWEAR		(120)		II.3B
189.00	HOSIERY		(120)		II.3B
190.00	FOOTWEAR, TOTAL		(137)		II.1
191.00	SHOES		(137)		II.1
192.00	SPECIAL SPORT SHOES (GOLF, BOWLING, ETC)		(137)		II.1
193.00	OTHER FOOTWEAR		(137)		II.1
194.00	HATS, GLOVES, AND ACCESSORIES		(120)		II.3B
195.00	JEWELRY AND WATCHES		(145)		II.7
196.00	EXPENDIT(CLOTHING,BOYS 2-15)NOT ALLOCATED		(120)		II.3B
197.00	CLOTHING, FEMALE, 18 YRS AND OVER, TOTAL		(120)		II.3A
198.00	OUTERWEAR, TOTAL		(120)		II.3A
199.00	WINTER COATS, CLOTH		(120)		II.3A
200.00	LIGHTWEIGHT COATS, TOPPERS		(120)		II.3A
201.00	FUR COATS, STOLES, ETC.		(120)		II.3A
202.00	RAINCOATS		(120)		II.3A
203.00	JACKETS		(120)		II.3A
204.00	SWEATERS		(120)		II.3A
205.00	SUITS		(120)		II.3A
206.00	DRESSES		(120)		II.3A
207.00	SKIRTS, JUMPERS, ETC.		(120)		II.3A
208.00	BLOUSES, SHIRTS		(120)		II.3A
209.00	SLACKS, DUNGAREES, SHORTS, ETC.		(120)		II.3A
210.00	OTHER OUTERWEAR		(120)		II.3A
211.00	UNDERWEAR		(120)		II.3A
212.00	NIGHTWEAR		(120)		II.3A
213.00	HOSIERY		(120)		II.3A

ALIGNMENT(CONT'D)

CES NO.	TITLE OF CES CONSUMPTION ITEM	SIC NO.	IO NO.	PER-CENT	NIPCE NO.
214.00	FOOTWEAR, TOTAL		(137)	II.1	
215.00	SHOES (STREET, DRESS, CASUAL)		(137)	II.1	
216.00	SPECIAL SPORT SHOES (GOLF, BOWLING, ETC)		(137)	II.1	
217.00	OTHER FOOTWEAR		(137)	II.1	
218.00	HATS, GLOVES, AND ACCESSORIES, TOTAL		(120)	II.3A	
219.00	HATS		(120)	II.3A	
220.00	GLOVES		(120)	II.3A	
221.00	HANDBAGS, PURSES		(120)	II.3A	
222.00	JEWELRY AND WATCHES		(145)	II.7	
223.00	OTHER (HATS,GLOVES,ETC.) ACCESSORIES		(120)	II.3A	
224.00	EXPENDITURES NOT ALLOCATED		(120)	II.3A	
225.00	CLOTHING, GIRLS, 16+ 17 YRS., TOTAL		(120)	II.3A	
226.00	OUTERWEAR, TOTAL		(120)	II.3A	
227.00	WINTER COATS, CLOTH		(120)	II.3A	
228.00	LIGHTWEIGHT COATS, TOPPERS		(120)	II.3A	
229.00	FUR COATS, STOLES, ETC.		(120)	II.3A	
230.00	RAINCOATS		(120)	II.3A	
231.00	JACKETS		(120)	II.3A	
232.00	SWEATERS		(120)	II.3A	
233.00	SUITS		(120)	II.3A	
234.00	DRESSES		(120)	II.3A	
235.00	SKIRTS, JUMPERS, ETC.		(120)	II.3A	
236.00	BLOUSES, SHIRTS, ETC.		(120)	II.3A	
237.00	SLACKS, DUNGAREES, SHORTS, ETC.		(120)	II.3A	
238.00	OTHER OUTERWEAR		(120)	II.3A	
239.00	UNDERWEAR		(120)	II.3A	
240.00	NIGHTWEAR		(120)	II.3A	
241.00	HOSIERY		(120)	II.3A	
242.00	FOOTWEAR, TOTAL		(137)	II.1	
243.00	SHOES, (STREET, DRESS, CASUAL)		(137)	II.1	
244.00	SPECIAL SPORT SHOES (GOLF, BOWLING, ETC.)		(137)	II.1	
245.00	OTHER FOOTWEAR		(137)	II.1	
246.00	HATS, GLOVES, AND ACCESSORIES, TOTAL		(120)	II.3A	
247.00	HATS		(120)	II.3A	
248.00	GLOVES		(120)	II.3A	
249.00	HANDBAGS, PURSES		(120)	II.3A	
250.00	JEWELRY AND WATCHES		(145)	II.7	
251.00	OTHER (HATS,GLOVES,ETC.) ACCESSORIES		(120)	II.3A	
252.00	EXPENDITURES NOT ALLOCATED		(120)	II.3A	
253.00	CLOTHING, GIRLS, 2 THRU 15 YRS, TOTAL		(120)	II.3A	
254.00	OUTERWEAR, TOTAL		(120)	II.3A	
255.00	WINTER COATS AND COAT SETS		(120)	II.3A	
256.00	SNOWSUITS, SKI SUITS, ETC.		(120)	II.3A	
257.00	LIGHTWEIGHT COATS, TOPPERS		(120)	II.3A	
258.00	RAINCOATS		(120)	II.3A	
259.00	JACKETS, HEAVY		(120)	II.3A	
260.00	JACKETS, LIGHTWEIGHT		(120)	II.3A	
261.00	SWEATERS		(120)	II.3A	
262.00	SUITS		(120)	II.3A	

ALIGNMENT(CONT'D)

CES NO.	TITLE OF CES CONSUMPTION ITEM	SIC NO.	IO NO.	PER-CENT	NIPCE NO.
263.00	DRESSES			(120)	II.3A
264.00	SKIRTS AND JUMPERS			(120)	II.3A
265.00	BLOUSES AND SHIRTS			(120)	II.3A
266.00	SLACKS, DUNGAREES, SHORTS, ETC.			(120)	II.3A
267.00	OTHER OUTERWEAR			(120)	II.3A
268.00	UNDERWEAR			(120)	II.3A
269.00	NIGHTWEAR			(120)	II.3A
270.00	HOSIERY			(120)	II.3A
271.00	FOOTWEAR, TOTAL			(137)	II.1
272.00	SHOES			(137)	II.1
273.00	SPECIAL SPORT SHOES (GOLF, BOWLING, ETC.)			(137)	II.1
274.00	OTHER FOOTWEAR			(137)	II.1
275.00	HATS, GLOVES, AND ACCESSORIES			(120)	II.3A
276.00	JEWELRY AND WATCHES			(145)	II.7
277.00	EXPENDIT(CLOTHING,GIRLS 2-15)NOT ALLOCATED			(120)	II.3A
278.00	CLOTHING, CHILD. UNDER 2 YRS, TOTAL			(120)	II.3A
279.00	COATS, BUNTINGS, SNOWSUITS, SWEATERS,ETC.			(120)	II.3A
280.00	DRESSES, SUITS, ETC.			(120)	II.3A
281.00	UNDERWEAR, DIAPERS, AND SLEEPING GARMENTS			(120)	II.3A
282.00	STOCKINGS, SOCKS			(120)	II.3A
283.00	BOOTIES, SHOES			(137)	II.1
284.00	LAYETTES AND OTHER			(120)	II.3A
285.00	EXPENDITURES NOT ALLOCATED			(120)	II.3A
286.00	*CLOTHING MAT. (YARD GOODS, NOTIONS) TOT.		16		II.3A
287.00	*CLOTHING UPKEEP, TOTAL		72		II.2,5,8
288.00	DRY CLEANING AND PRESSING	727,7216	72	(287)	II.5
289.00	SHOE REPAIRS AND SERVICES	7251	72	(287)	II.2
290.00	OTHER CLOTHING SERVICES	7631,7271	72	(287)	II.5,8
290.00		7299,7693			
291.00	TRANSPORTATION, TOTAL				
292.00	*AUTOMOBILE PURCHASE				VIII.1A,B
292.01	AUTO AIR CONDITIONERS	3585793	52	0.3	VIII.1B
292.02	AUTO RADIOS	3651110	56	0.4	VIII.1B
292.03	PASSENGER CARS	3717	59	88.5	VIII.1A
292.04	USED CARS		83	10.8	VIII.1A
293.00	*AUTOMOBILE OPERATION, TOTAL				
293.01	AUTO SEAT COVERS	239901	19	1.1	VIII.1B
293.02	AUTO CHEMICAL PRODUCTS	28993	27	1.1	VIII.1B
293.03	AUTO POLISH AND CLEANERS	2842411	29	0.6	VIII.1B
293.04	TIRES,TUBES,RUBBER HOSES,ETC.	3011,3069	32	20.6	VIII.1B
293.05	TIRE CHAINS	3481941	42	0.3	VIII.1B
293.06	AUTO LIGHTS	3641,3642	55	0.4	VIII.1B
293.07	AUTO BATTERIES + ELECTRICAL EQUIPMENT	3691,3694	58	3.7	VIII.1B
293.08	MOTOR VEHICLE PARTS	3717	59	2.2	VIII.1B
293.09	TRANSPORTATION FACILITIES, NEC	4784	65	0.1	VIII.1E
293.10	AUTO STORAGE,REPAIR,SERVICES	752,753,	75	65.8	VIII.1C
293.10		7541			
293.11	REGISTRATION,LICENSES,TOLLS	92	79	3.7	VIII.1E
293.12	USED AUTO EQUIPMENT		83	0.4	VIII.1B

ALIGNMENT(CONT'D)

CES NO.	TITLE OF CES CONSUMPTION ITEM	SIC NO.	IO NO.	PER-CENT	NIPCE NO.
294.00	GASOLINE	2911131	31		VIII.1D
295.00	MOTOR OIL	29116	31		VIII.1D
296.00	LUBRICATION,WASHING,ETC.				VIII.1B,C
296.01	AUTO POLISHES AND CLEANERS	2842411	29	(293)	VIII.1B
296.02	AUTO SERVICES	7541	75	(293)	VIII.1C
297.00	TIRES AND TUBES	3011	32	(293)	VIII.1B
298.00	BATTERIES AND OTHER EQUIPMENT				VIII.1B
298.01	CHEMICALS,CHEMICAL PRODUCTS	28993	27	(293)	
298.02	LIGHTING FIXTURES	3641,3642	55	(293)	
298.03	AUTO BATTERIES	3691	58	(293)	
299.00	OPERATING EXPENSES NOT ALLOCATED				VIII.1B
299.01	AUTO SEAT COVERS	239901	19	(293)	
299.02	AUTO RUBBER MATS	3069423	32	(293)	
299.03	TIRE CHAINS	3481941	42	(293)	
299.04	ELECT. EQUIP. FOR INTERNAL COMBUST. ENG.	3694	58	(293)	
299.05	MOTOR VEHICLE PARTS	3717	59	(293)	
300.00	REPAIRS AND PARTS				VIII.1B,C
300.01	AUTO V-BELTS, RADIATOR HOSES	3069	32	(293)	VIII.1B
300.02	MOTOR VEHICLE EQUIPMENT	3717	59	(293)	VIII.1B
300.03	AUTO REPAIR	753	75	(293)	VIII.1C
300.04	USED AUTO EQUIPMENT		83	(293)	VIII.1B
301.00	INSURANCE	633	70		VIII.1F
302.00	REGISTRATION AND OTHER EXPENSES				VIII.1C,E
302.01	TRANSPORTATION FACILITIES, NEC	4784	65	(293)	VIII.1E
302.02	AUTO STORAGE, ETC.	752	75	(293)	VIII.1C
302.03	REGISTRATION LICENSES, FEES, ETC.	92	79	(293)	VIII.1E
303.00	PUBLIC TRANSPORTATION IN HOME CITY	4111,4121	65		VIII.2
304.00	*CAR POOL				
305.00	PUBLIC TRANSPORTATION OUT OF HOME CITY	40,41,44,	65		VIII.3
305.00		45			
306.00	*OTHER TRANSPORTATION				
306.01	SAILS AND OTHER PRODUCTS	2394098	19	1.0	IX.4
306.02	BOAT + AVIATION GAS + BOAT LUB. OIL	2911	31	7.7	VIII.1D
306.03	TIRES,TUBES,LIFE RAFTS,ETC.	3011,3069	32	1.7	IX.4
306.04	MARINE HARDWARE	3429111	42	0.0	IX.4
306.05	INTERNAL COMBUSTION ENGINES	3519	43	12.9	IX.4
306.06	CIVILIAN AIRCRAFT,ETC.	3721	60	2.7	IX.4
306.07	BOATS,BICYCLES,TRAILERS,ETC.	373,375,	61	73.4	VIII.1A,
306.07		379			IX.4
306.08	BICYCLE REPAIR	7692	72	0.6	IX.4
307.00	MEDICAL CARE, TOTAL				VI.1-7
308.00	*PREPAID CARE				VI.7
308.01	ACCIDENT AND HEALTH INSURANCE	632	70	11.4	
308.02	MEDICAL AND OTHER PREPAID HEALTH SERV.	80	77	88.6	
309.00	DIRECT EXPENSES, TOTAL				
310.00	FOR HOSPITALIZED ILLNESS	80	77		VI.6
311.00	PHYSICIANS SERVICES OUTSIDE HOSPITAL	8011	77		VI.3
312.00	DENTAL SERVICES	8021,8072	77		VI.4

ALIGNMENT(CONT'D)

CES NO.	TITLE OF CES CONSUMPTION ITEM	SIC NO.	IO NO.	PER-CENT	NIPCE NO.
313.00	*EYE CARE, INCLUDING GLASSES	3851	63		VI.2
314.00	OTHER PRACTITIONERS	803,804	77		VI.5
315.00	*DRUGS AND MEDICINES				VI.1
315.01	CHEMICALS	281	27	0.0	
315.02	DRUGS AND MEDICINE	283	29	100.0	
316.00	*MEDICAL APPLIANCES AND SUPPLIES				VI.1,2
316.01	MISC. RUBBER AND PLASTICS PRODUCTS	3069,3079	32	26.6	VI.1
316.02	HEARING AID BATTERIES	369204	58	0.6	VI.2
316.03	MEDICAL APPLIANCES AND SUPPLIES	384	62	72.8	VI.1,2
317.00	OTHER MEDICAL CARE	807,809	77		VI.5
318.00	PERSONAL CARE, TOTAL				III.1,2
319.00	HAIRCUTS, MEN AND BOYS	7241	72		III.2
320.00	HAIRCUTS, WOMEN AND GIRLS	7231	72		III.2
321.00	SHAVES	7241	72		III.2
322.00	WAVES, SHAMPOOS, TINTING, ETC.	723,724	72		III.2
323.00	OTHER PERSONAL CARE SERVICES	7299	72		III.2
324.00	*PERSONAL CARE SUPPLIES, TOTAL				III.1,V.6,
324.00					VI.1
324.01	CLEANSING TISSUE AND SANITARY SUPPLIES	2649	24	13.8	V.6,VI.1
324.02	PERFUMES, COSMETICS, MISC. TOILETRIES	284	29	73.1	III.1
324.03	HAIRCURLERS AND HAIRPINS, RUBBER	3069	32	0.2	III.1
324.04	MANICURE SETS AND RAZORS	3421	42	5.3	III.1
324.05	DRY ELECTRIC SHAVERS	36342	54	3.1	III.1
324.06	BRUSHES,CURLERS,WIGS,ETC.	39	64	3.9	III.1
324.07	IMPORTS		80	0.6	III.1
325.00	TOILET SOAP	28413	29	(324)	III.1
326.00	DENTAL SUPPLIES(TOOTHBRUSHES,PASTE,ETC.)				
326.01	TOOTHPASTE,MOUTHWASHES,ETC.	28444	29	(324)	III.1
326.02	TOOTHBRUSHES	3981321	64	(324)	III.1
327.00	SHAVING EQUIPMENT AND PREPARATIONS				
327.01	SHAVING PREPARATIONS	28441	29	(324)	III.1
327.02	RAZORS, RAZOR BLADES	34212	42	(324)	III.1
327.03	DRY ELECTRIC SHAVERS	36342	54	(324)	III.1
328.00	CLEANSING TISSUES	2649311	24	(324)	V.6
329.00	FACE POWDER,CREAMS,OTHER COSMETICS,ETC.	2844	29	(324)	III.1
330.00	HAIR EQUIPMENT AND PREPARATIONS				
330.01	SHAMPOO AND HAIR DRESSINGS	2844	29	(324)	III.1
330.02	HAIR CURLERS,PINS,COMBS,RUBBER	3069	32	(324)	III.1
330.03	BRUSHES,CURLERS,WIGS,ETC.	3981,3964,	64	(324)	III.1
330.03		3999			
331.00	OTHER PERSONAL CARE SUPPLIES				
331.01	SANITARY SUPPLIES	2649	24	(324)	VI.1
331.02	OTHER COSMETICS	2844	29	(324)	III.1
331.03	MANICURE SETS, PEDICURE SCISSORS, ETC.	3421161	42	(324)	III.1
331.04	IMPORTS		80	(324)	III.1

ALIGNMENT (CONT'D)

CES NO.	TITLE OF CES CONSUMPTION ITEM	SIC NO.	IO NO.	PER-CENT	NIPCE NO.
332.00	*RECREATION, TOTAL				IX.5,6
332.01	MUSICAL INSTRUMENT CASES	3161081	34	0.2	IX.5
332.02	TV,RADIO,PHONO.RECEIVING SETS + EQUIP.	365,3662	56	64.9	IX.5
332.03	ELECTRONIC ACCESSORIES	367	57	7.9	IX.5
332.04	MISC. ELECTRICAL EQUIPMENT	369	58	0.7	IX.5
332.05	MUSICAL INSTRUMENTS AND PARTS	3931	64	6.0	IX.5
332.06 *	REPAIRS	7621	72	19.3	IX.6
332.07 *	RENTAL OF MUSICAL INSTRUM.,PIANO,ETC.	7399	73		
332.08	USED RADIO,TV,MUSICAL INSTRUMENTS		83	1.0	IX.5
333.00	TELEVISION				IX.5,6
333.01	TV RECEIVING SETS + EQUIPMENT	3651,3662	56	(332)	IX.5
333.02	TV ELECTRONIC ACCESSORIES	3672	57	(332)	IX.5
333.03	MISC. ELECTRICAL TV EQUIPMENT	369	58	(332)	IX.5
333.04	TV REPAIRS	7621	72	(332)	IX.6
333.05	USED TV SETS, ETC.		83	(332)	IX.5
334.00	RADIO				IX.5,6
334.01	RADIO RECEIVING SET AND EQUIPMENT	3651,3662	56	(332)	IX.5
334.02	RADIO ELECTRONIC ACCESSORIES	3671	57	(332)	IX.5
334.03	MISC. ELECTRICAL EQUIPMENT	369	58	(332)	IX.5
334.04	RADIO REPAIRS	7621	72	(332)	IX.6
334.05	USED RADIO SETS, ETC.		83	(332)	IX.5
335.00	PHONOGRAPHS, TAPE RECORDERS, ETC.				IX.5
335.01	PHONOGRAPHS, TAPE RECORDERS, ETC.	3651,3652	56	(332)	
335.02	ELECTRONIC ACCESSORIES	367	57	(332)	
335.03	MISC. ELECTRICAL EQUIPMENT	369	58	(332)	
335.04 *	REPAIRS	7621	72	(332)	
335.05	USED PHONOGRAPHS,TAPE RECORDERS,ETC.		83	(332)	
336.00	MUSICAL INSTRUMENTS				IX.5
336.01	MUSICAL INSTRUMENT CASES	3161081	34	(332)	
336.02	MUSICAL INSTRUMENTS AND PARTS	3931	64	(332)	
336.03 *	REPAIRS	7696	72	(332)	
336.04 *	RENTAL,PIANO,ETC.	7399	73	(332)	
337.00	SPECTATOR ADMISSIONS, TOTAL				IX.8
338.00	MOVIES	7831	76		IX.8A
339.00	*SPORTS EVENTS				IX.8C
339.01	ENGRAVING	2753	26	1.6	
339.02	MISC. AMUSEMENT SERVICES	794	76	98.4	
340.00	CONCERTS, PLAYS, ETC.	7921	76		IX.8B

ALIGNMENT(CONT'D)

CES NO.	TITLE OF CES CONSUMPTION ITEM	SIC NO.	IO NO.	PER- CENT	NIPCE NO.
341.00	*PARTICIPANT SPORTS(FEES,EQUIP.,ETC.)				
341.01	ANIMAL FARMS	0193	1	1.4	IX.12
341.02	SMALL ARMS AND AMMUNITION	1951,1961	13	6.5	IX.3,4
341.03	FISHING NYLON	22982	17	0.4	IX.3
341.04	TENTS,SLEEPIGN BAGS,ETC.	239	19	0.9	IX.4
341.05	OTHER NOVELTIES,GAMES,ETC.	2649547	24	0.2	IX.3
341.06	PLAYING CARDS	2751,2752	26	1.0	IX.3
341.07	FIREWORKS	2899329	27	0.3	IX.3
341.08	RUBBER + PLASTIC BALLS,BALLOONS,TOYS	3069,3079	32	0.9	IX.3
341.09	LEATHER GOODS	3199	34	0.6	IX.4
341.10	POCKET AND FOLDING KNIVES	3421141	42	0.5	IX.4
341.11	SPECIALTY TRANSFORMERS, EXCL. PARTS	36121	53	0.0	IX.3
341.12	PHOTO LIGHTING, PROJECTION LAMPS	3641	55	1.1	IX.3
341.13	CAMERAS,PHOTO EQUIP,FIELD GLASSES,ETC.	383,386	63	14.3	V.4,IX.3,4
341.14	DOLLS,TOYS,ART,SPORT,+ ATHLETIC GOODS	39	64	34.5	V.7,IX.3,4
341.15	AMUSEMENTS,SPORTS,COUNTRY CLUB DUES	78,79	76	19.6	IX.10,12
341.16	ANIMAL HOSPITALS,SOCIAL CLUB DUES	0722,86	77	16.0	IX.9,12
341.17	IMPORTS		80	1.6	IX.3,4,12
341.18	USED EQUIPMENT		83	0.2	IX.4
342.00	CLUB DUES AND MEMBERSHIPS				IX.9,10
342.01	GOLF AND COUNTRY CLUBS	7947	76	(341)	
342.02	SOC.,FRATERNAL,CIVIC SERVICE CLUBS	86	77	(341)	
343.00	HOBBIES				
343.01	OTHER NOVELTIES,GAMES,ETC.	2649547	24	(341)	IX.3
343.02	LEATHER GOODS	3199	34	(341)	IX.4
343.03	PHOTOGRAPHIC LIGHTING,PROJECTION LAMPS	3641	55	(341)	IX.3
343.04	CAMERAS,PHOTOGRAPHIC EQUIP,MICROSCOPES	383,386	63	(341)	V.4,IX.3,4
343.05	ARTISTS MATERIALS, ETC.	3952,3981	64	(341)	V.7
343.06	USED CAMERAS AND PHOTO EQUIPMENT		83	(341)	IX.4
344.00	PETS(PURCHASE AND CARE)				
344.01	ANIMAL FARMS	0193	1	(341)	IX.12
344.02	* PET FOOD	2042	14	NICRY	
344.03	LEATHER GOODS(LEASHES,ETC.)	3199	34	(341)	IX.4
344.04	ANIMAL HOSPITALS AND VETERINARIAN OFF.	0722	77	(341)	IX.12
345.00	TOYS AND PLAY EQUIPMENT				
345.01	OTHER NOVELTIES,GAMES,ETC.	2649547	24	(341)	IX.3
345.02	RUBBER AND PLASTIC BALLS,BALLOONS,TOYS	3069,3079	32	(341)	IX.3
345.03	SPECIALTY TRANSFORMERS, EXCL. PARTS	36121	53	(341)	IX.3
345.04	GAMES,TOYS,DOLLS,AND ATHLETIC GOODS	394	64	(341)	IX.3,4
346.00	RECREATION OUT OF HOME CITY				
346.02	AMUSEMENTS	78,79	76	(341)	IX.10,12
347.00	OTHER RECREATION				
347.01	TENTS,SLEEPING BAGS,ETC.	239	19	(341)	IX.4
347.02	PLAYING CARDS	2751,2752	26	(341)	IX.3
347.03	FIREWORKS	2899329	27	(341)	IX.3
347.04	AMUSEMENTS	78,79	76	(341)	IX.12

ALIGNMENT(CONT'D)

CES NO.	TITLE OF CES CONSUMPTION ITEM	SIC NO.	IO NO.	PER-CENT	NIPCE NO.
348.00	READING, TOTAL				
349.00	*NEWSPAPERS				IX.2
349.01	PRINTING AND PUBLISHING	2711	26	101.4	
349.02	WASTEPAPER		83	-1.4	
350.00	MAGAZINES				IX.2
350.01	PRINTING AND PUBLISHING	27	26	(349)	
350.02	WASTEPAPER		83	(349)	
351.00	*BOOKS BOUGHT(NOT SCHOOL OR TECHNICAL)				IX.1
351.01	PRINTING AND PUBLISHING	2731,2732	26	99.4	
351.02	* USED BOOKS		83	0.6	
352.00	OTHER READING	8231	77		
353.00	EDUCATION, TOTAL				
354.00	TUITION AND FEES	82	77		X.1,2,3
355.00	*BOOKS,SUPPLIES, AND EQUIPMENT				
355.01	TECHNICAL AND ED.BOOKS AND MAGAZINES,	272,273,	26	66.3	V.7,IX.1,2
355.01	LOOSE-LEAF BINDERS	2782231			
355.02	GLUE	2891	27	2.5	V.7
355.03	RUBBER CEMENT, MISC. SUPPLIES	3069	32	1.7	V.7
355.04	* PENCILS,BALL-PT.PENS,CRAYONS,ETC.	395	64	29.0	V.4,7
355.05	* USED BOOKS		83	0.5	IX.1
356.00	MUSIC AND OTHER SPECIAL LESSONS	829	77		X.3
357.00	*OTHER EDUCATION	824,829	77		X.3
358.00	MISCELLANEOUS,TOTAL				
359.00	*ALL-EXPENSE TOURS,ETC.				IX.12
359.01	FOOD		14		
359.02	TRANSPORTATION		65		
359.03	LODGING		72		
359.04	AMUSEMENTS		76		
360.00	*OTHER MISCELLANEOUS				
360.01	STONE MINING(FUNERAL EXPENSES)	1411	9	NICBY	VII.6
360.02	TOMBSTONES	3272,3281	36	NICBY	VII.6
360.03	INTEREST AND BANK SERVICE CHARGES	60	70	NICBY	VII.1,2
360.04	* CEMETERY UPKEEP AND MANAGEMENT	6531,6551	71	NICBY	VII.6
360.05	FUNERAL DIRECTORS	7261	72	NICBY	VII.6
360.06	LEGAL SERVICES	8111	73	NICBY	VII.5
361.00	*PERSONAL INSURANCE,TOTAL				VII.4
361.01	INSURANCE	63	70	99.0	
361.02	IMPORTS		80	1.0	
362.00	LIFE,ENDOWMENT,ANNUITY,ETC.			(361)	
363.00	*VETERANS				
364.00	GROUP(DEDUCTED FROM PAY)			(361)	
365.00	OTHER LIFE ETC. INSURANCE			(361)	
366.00	MUTUAL AID			(361)	
367.00	DISABILITY INCOME			(361)	
368.00	OTHER PERSONAL INSURANCE			(361)	
369.00	*SOC.SEC.,RR AND GOVT.RETIREMENT				
370.00	PRIVATE RETIREMENT			(361)	
371.00	GIFTS AND CONTRIBUTIONS, TOTAL				
372.00	TO PERSONS NOT IN FAMILY, TOTAL GIFTS				

ALIGNMENT(CONT'D)

CES NO.	TITLE OF CES CONSUMPTION ITEM	SIC NO.	IO NO.	PER-CENT	NIPCE NO.
373.00	*CASH				
374.00	*GOODS AND SERVICES				
374.01	FRUIT,VEGETABLES,FLOWERS,ETC.	01	2	3.4	
374.02	FOOD AND KINDRED PRODUCTS	20	14	63.7	
374.03	APPAREL	225	18	15.5	
374.04	BOOKS	27	26	3.4	
374.05	COSMETICS	283,284	29	5.2	
374.06	SMALL APPLIANCES	363	54	3.4	
374.07	RADIO AND TELEVISION	365	56	1.9	
374.08	MUSICAL + SPORTS EQUIPMENT	39	64	3.5	
375.00	TO ORGANIZATIONS, TOTAL GIFTS	82,84,86	77		X,XI
376.00	COMMUNITY CHEST, RED CROSS, ETC.	86	77 (375)		XI
377.00	CHURCH AND OTHER RELIGIOUS ORGANIZATIONS	86	77 (375)		XI
378.00	ED., MEDICAL, POLITICAL AND OTHER GIFTS	82,84,86	77 (375)		X,XI
379.00	*VALUE OF HOME-PRODUCED FOOD				I.4
379.01	LIVESTOCK AND LIVESTOCK PRODUCTS	01	1	30.5	
379.02	OTHER AGRICULTURAL PRODUCTS	01	2	28.2	
379.03	FOOD AND KINDRED PRODUCTS	20	14	41.3	

Alignment Comments

In this section, additional detail is given for those CES items that have an asterisk after the number in the alignment table. The comments, which are given for each item that has an asterisk, can be located by finding the appropriate boldface CES number on the left.

1.00 The percentage distribution for total food expenditures, CES 1.01–1.09, was calculated from all the input-output industry values listed for NIPCE I-1 through I-3.

CES No.	Input-Output Industry No.	NIPCE Value ($ millions)	Percent
1.01	1	2,278	3.0
1.02	2	3,670	4.9
1.03	3	635	0.8
1.04	10	1	0.0
1.05	14	65,772	87.8
1.06	27	30	0.0
1.07	65	120	0.2
1.08	69	377	0.5
1.09	80	2,087	2.8
Total		74,970	100.0

As shown, the value of the purchase of rock salt, CES 1.04, is only $1 million. This is the only consumption item included in IO-10, Chemical & fertilizer mineral mining, in the personal consumption expenditures final demand.

10.00 The value for food bought out of the home city, CES 10.00, was subtracted from the value of total food expenditures, CES 1.00, and was allocated to states in a separate calculation described in Chapter 2.

12.00 The expenditures on alcohol, CES 12.00, were added to the total food expenditures, CES 1.00, before distribution.

13.00 The percentage distribution for tobacco, CES 13.01–13.03, was calculated from the values contained in the *Census of Manufactures, 1963* [109, pp. 21A-13, 39D-24] and *U.S. Commodity Exports and Imports as Related to Output, 1962 and 1961* [145, p. 57]. Imports of smoking pipes, etc., that would be assigned to IO-64, Miscellaneous manufacturing, were ignored because detailed information was unavailable.

CES No.	Input-Output Industry No.	Census of Manufactures and Import Value ($ millions)	Percent
13.01	15	3,139	98.6
13.02	64	43	1.3
13.03	80	3	0.1
Total		3,185	100.0

16.00 Gas, water, and electricity (a portion of IO-68) and heating fuel (portions of IO-7, IO-20, IO-31, and IO-37) were removed from total rented dwelling CES 16.00, using percentages calculated from an article by the National Association of Real Estate Boards (NAREB) entitled "Apartment Building Experience Exchange of Rental Income and Operating Expense Data" [4]. The 1964 edition was used because the 1959 edition does not separate the items of expenditure into a usable form. The percentage for fuel, CES 16.03 and 16.04, was distributed in the proportions found in NIPCE V-8d.

CES No.	Input-Output Industry No.	Percent of Total Rent		
		North	South	West
16.01	7	0.7 ⎫	0.7 ⎫	0.8 ⎫
16.02	20	0.1 ⎬ 5.2	0.1 ⎬ 5.3	0.1 ⎬ 5.5
16.03	31	4.4 ⎭	4.5 ⎭	4.6 ⎭
16.04	37	0.0	0.0	0.0
16.05	68	4.9	6.8	6.1
16.06	71	89.9	87.9	88.4
Total		100.0	100.0	100.0

16.06 The rental dwelling proportion, CES 16.06, of the total rented dwelling expenditures was used to distribute the paid rental portion of the national total of IO-71, Real estate & rental.

20.00⎫ The total for interest, taxes, insurance, and maintenance, CES 20.00 plus
26.00⎭ CES 26.00, was used as a proxy to distribute the imputed rent of the owner-occupied dwelling portion of the national total of IO-71, Real estate & rental.

24.00⎫ The total for repairs and replacements, CES 24.00 plus CES 30.00, was
30.00⎭ used as a proxy for IO-30, Paints & allied products.

32.00 The percentage distribution for lodging out of home city, CES 32.01–32.02, was calculated from the values of IO-72 and IO-77 listed in NIPCE IV-2 and IV-4. The values were allocated to states in a separate calculation described in Chapter 2.

CES No.	Input-Output Industry No.	NIPCE Value ($ millions)	Percent
32.01	72	1,327	94.5
32.02	77	77	5.5
Total		1,404	100.0

33.00 Other real estate, CES 33.00, was ignored because it is only 1 percent of the shelter total, CES 15.00, and no separate information was available for this as a part of IO-71, Real estate & rental.

35.00 The percentage distribution for coal and coke, CES 35.01–35.02, was calculated from the values of IO-7 and IO-37 listed in NIPCE V-8d.

CES No.	Input-Output Industry No.	NIPCE Value ($ millions)	Percent
35.01	7	576	98.1
35.02	37	11	1.9
Total		587	100.0

43.00 The percentage distribution shown under water, CES 43.01–43.02, is a breakdown of the combined water and sewage expenditures (CES 43.00, 44.00, 45.00, 46.00). It was calculated from the values of IO-68 and IO-79 listed in NIPCE V-8c; the expenditure on septic tank cleaning (SIC 7699), which is not listed separately in the CES, was ignored.

CES No.	Input-Output Industry No.	NIPCE Value ($ millions)	Percent
43.01	68	980	93.5
43.02	79	68	6.5
Total		1,048	100.0

50.00 The expenditure on other fuel, utility, etc., expenses, CES 50.00, is small and was ignored.

52.00 The percentage distributions by income class for laundry supplies, CES 52.01–52.03, were calculated from values listed in the NICB volume [59, p. 64]. The following correspondences hold:

NICB Item	CES Category	Input-Output Industry No.
58 (starch)	52.01	14
57 (bleaches, disinfectants)	52.02	27
54, 55, 56 (liquid laundry detergents, soap, dry synthetic detergents)	52.03	29

The expenditure on bluing, NICB item 59, was omitted since it was insignificant.

Income Distribution Group	NICB Value (dollars)				Distribution (percent)			
	52.01	52.02	52.03	Total	52.01	52.02	52.03	Total
Under $3,000	.01	.04	.20	.25	4.0	16.0	80.0	100.0
$3,000–$5,000	.03	.08	.38	.49	6.1	16.3	77.6	100.0
$5,000–$7,500	.03	.09	.49	.61	4.9	14.8	80.3	100.0
$7,500–$10,000	.04	.10	.57	.71	5.6	14.1	80.3	100.0
$10,000–$15,000	.03	.11	.61	.75	4.0	14.7	81.3	100.0
$15,000 and over	.03	.10	.51	.64	4.7	15.6	79.7	100.0
National Average	.03	.08	.43	.54	5.6	14.8	79.6	100.0

53.00 The percentage distributions by income class for cleaning supplies, CES
53.01–53.03, were calculated from values listed in the NICB volume [59,
p. 64]. The following correspondences hold:

NICB Item	CES Category	Input-Output Industry No.
62* (sponges, SIC 282125, and synthetic scouring pads)	53.01	28
60, 61, 63, 64, 65, 66 (liquid household detergents, scouring powder, floor waxes, other household polishes, insect sprays, powders, air fresheners, deodorizers)	53.02	29
62* (nonsynthetic scouring pads)	53.03	36

*One-half is allocated to IO-28 and one-half to IO-36.

Income Distribution Group	NICB Value (dollars)				Distribution (percent)			
	53.01	53.02	53.03	Total	53.01	53.02	53.03	Total
Under $3,000	.005	.090	.005	.100	5.0	90.0	5.0	100.0
$3,000–$5,000	.010	.170	.010	.190	5.3	89.4	5.3	100.0
$5,000–$7,500	.015	.230	.015	.260	5.8	88.4	5.8	100.0
$7,500–$10,000	.025	.240	.025	.290	8.6	82.8	8.6	100.0
$10,000–$15,000	.020	.270	.020	.310	6.5	87.0	6.5	100.0
$15,000 and over	.025	.410	.025	.460	5.4	89.2	5.4	100.0
National Average	.015	.190	.015	.220	6.8	86.4	6.8	100.0

54.00 The percentage distributions by income class for household paper
supplies, CES 54.01–54.03, were calculated from values listed in the NICB
volume [59, p. 64]. The following correspondences hold:

NICB Item	CES Category	Input-Output Industry No.
68, 69, 70, 71 (wax paper, toilet tissue, paper napkins, and paper towels)	54.01	24
72 (paper plates, cups)	54.02	25
67 (aluminum foil)	54.03	38

NICB item 73 is not included in the percentage breakdown since no
clarifying details were available.

Income	NICB Value (dollars)				Distribution (percent)			
Distribution Group	54.01	54.02	54.03	Total	54.01	54.02	54.03	Total
Under $3,000	.13	*	.01	.14	92.9	0.0	7.1	100.0
$3,000–$5,000	.23	.01	.03	.27	85.2	3.7	11.1	100.0
$5,000–$7,500	.29	.02	.05	.36	80.6	5.6	13.8	100.0
$7,500–$10,000	.37	.03	.06	.46	80.4	6.5	13.1	100.0
$10,000–$15,000	.39	.03	.07	.49	79.6	6.1	14.3	100.0
$15,000 and over	.42	.02	.10	.54	77.8	3.7	18.5	100.0
National Average	.28	.02	.04	.34	82.4	5.9	11.7	100.0

*Less than one-half cent.

55.00 No allocation of laundry and cleaning sent out, CES 55.00, was made to IO-77, Medical, educational services, & nonprofit organizations, because the CES does not include institutional population.

57.00 Day nursery care was allocated only to IO-77 since it is part of the education industry. Child care in private homes was ignored.

63.00 The percentage distribution for repairs of furniture and equipment, CES 63.01–63.02, was calculated from the values of IO-72 and IO-73 listed in NIPCE V-11. Part of IO-72 in NIPCE V-11 is laundry and cleaning of house furnishings, but no information was available to separate this amount from CES 63.00; therefore, the entire purchaser's value of IO-72 listed in NIPCE V-11, was used in the distribution of furniture repair.

CES No.	Input-Output Industry No.	NIPCE Value ($ millions)	Percent
63.01	72	733	92.2
63.02	73	62	7.8
Total		795	100.0

65.00 The percentage distribution for postage and writing materials, CES 65.01–65.06, was calculated from the values of IO-24, IO-26, IO-27, and IO-37 listed in NIPCE V-7, for IO-78 listed in NIPCE V-11, and for IO-64 listed in NIPCE V-4c, and values listed in the *1958 Detailed NIPCE Listing.* Because this last reference had to be used, the values cannot be given here.

66.00 The percentage distribution for other household operation expenses, CES 66.01–66.08, was calculated from the values of IO-24, IO-26, and IO-27 listed in NIPCE V-5, V-6a, V-6b, IX-3, and IX-7, with some figures from the *1958 Detailed NIPCE Listing.* Because this last reference had to be used, the values cannot be given here.

68.00 The percentage distribution for total household textiles, CES 68.01–68.07, was calculated from the values of IO-16, IO-17, IO-18, and IO-19 listed in NIPCE V-4 and V-5 and from the values for IO-19, IO-32, and IO-54 obtained from the *1958 Detailed NIPCE Listing.* Because this last reference had to be used, the values cannot be given here.

68.07⎫ Because no consumer expenditures information was available, the amount
79.02⎭ of total household textiles, CES 68.07, and materials and services, CES
79.02, that should have been allocated to IO-86, Household industry, for
household help was ignored.

80.00   The percentage distribution for total furniture, CES 80.01–80.04, was
calculated from the values for IO-22, IO-23, IO-80, and IO-83 listed in
NIPCE V-1. The percentage for IO-22 includes the value of sewing machine
cabinets (NIPCE V-2) obtained from the *1958 Detailed NIPCE Listing*.
Because the latter reference had to be used, the values cannot be listed
here.

88.00   According to Nancy W. Simon, no rug imports are included in the IO-80,
Imports, figures given in her article [74, p. 8] for NIPCE V-4. In the input-
output tables, all rug imports are transferred to the domestic rug industry
and are allocated from the domestic industry since separate details on the
import of rugs cannot be confirmed.

92.00   The percentage distributions by income class for hard surface floor
coverings, CES 92.01–92.02, were calculated from values listed in the NICB
volume [59, p. 72] . The following correspondences hold:

NICB Item	CES Category	Input-Output Industry No.
38 (tile)	92.01	36
39 (other hard surface floor coverings)	92.02	64

No allocation could be made to IO-36 (SIC 32725), precast terrazzo floor
tile, nor to IO-41 (SIC 3461), stamped metal floor tile, since no detailed
consumer expenditure information was available.

Income Distribution Group	NICB Value (dollars)			Distribution (percent)		
	92.01	92.02	Total	92.01	92.02	Total
Under $3,000	0.15	2.31	2.46	6.1	93.9	100.0
$3,000–$5,000	0.25	3.32	3.57	7.0	93.0	100.0
$5,000–$7,500	1.38	3.59	4.97	27.8	72.2	100.0
$7,500–$10,000	2.16	3.79	5.95	36.3	63.7	100.0
$10,000–$15,000	1.77	4.41	6.18	28.6	71.4	100.0
$15,000 and over	1.60	8.11	9.71	16.5	83.5	100.0
National Average	1.04	3.53	4.57	22.8	77.2	100.0

 95.00– The percentage distributions for major and small appliances, CES 95.00
109.00   through 109.00, were calculated from the values for IO-52, IO-54, and
IO-83 listed in NIPCE V-2. The percentage allocated to IO-83 for used
appliances is considered to remain unchanged for each type of appliance
because no information was available to vary the ratio.

CES No.	Input-Output Industry No.	NIPCE Value ($ millions)	Percent	Percent
.01	52	375 ⎫	8.9 ⎫	99.2
	54	3,790 ⎭	90.3 ⎭	
.03	83	34	0.8	0.8
Total		4,199	100.0	100.0

No distribution could be calculated for the flexible-cord set portion of IO-38, Primary nonferrous metals manufacturing, nor for the other electric products portion of IO-58, Miscellaneous electrical machinery, equipment & supplies, although both of these are included in NIPCE V-2.

The value for calculating the percentage assigned to IO-80, Imports, for sewing machines, CES 107.00, was taken from *U.S. Commodity Exports and Imports as Related to Output, 1958* [144]. In all other cases, since the percentage of IO-80 was less than 0.5 and not given in this source, the percentages were calculated from unpublished information received from the OBE and from the *1958 Detailed NIPCE Listing.*

No percentage was assigned to IO-80 for air conditioners, CES 105.00, and dehumidifiers, CES 106.00, because no figure was given in the import information for SIC 3585 (refrigerators, etc.).

110.00   The percentage distribution for total housewares, CES 110.01–110.09, was calculated from the values of IO-20, IO-32, IO-35, IO-36, IO-38, IO-41, IO-42, IO-64, and IO-80, listed in NIPCE V-3, with two exceptions: clothes-pins (SIC 2499561) were excluded from the value listed for IO-20 and pails (SIC 3461) were excluded from the value listed for IO-41. These data were obtained from the *1958 Detailed NIPCE Listing;* therefore, the values cannot be given here. The values for CES 110.00 through CES 114.00 were aggregated and distributed according to NIPCE V-3. The values for CES 115.00 and CES 116.00 were distributed separately.

115.00   The percentage distribution for cleaning equipment, CES 115.01–115.04, was calculated from the *1958 Detailed NIPCE Listing;* therefore, the values cannot be given here. The value for this consumption item was excluded from the distribution percentages listed under total housewares, CES 110.00.

116.00   The percentage distribution for laundry equipment, CES 116.01–116.05, was calculated only for IO-19 and IO-20 since the values for clothes-lines (IO-17), laundry trays (IO-36), and laundry tubs (IO-40) were not available; in any case, the consumption expenditures on these latter items are very small. Because the values were obtained from the *1958 Detailed NIPCE Listing,* they cannot be given here. The value for laundry equipment, CES 116.00, was excluded from the percentage distribution listed under total housewares, CES 110.00.

119.00   The percentage distributions for other miscellaneous house furnishings, CES 119.01–119.16, were calculated from the NICB volume [59, p. 78], NICB items 81 through 90. The figures for NICB items 84, 88, 89, and 90 were additionally divided into input-output industries with the use of national averages calculated from the *1958 Detailed NIPCE Listing*.

NICB Item	Input-Output Industry No.
81 (baby carriages, strollers)	64
82 (electric light bulbs)	55
83 (typewriters)	51
84 (clocks, pictures, vases, etc.)	20, 35, 36, 62
85 (lamps)	55
86 (hand luggage)	34
87 (lawn mowers)	44
88 (tools: hand, power, garden)	42, 47, 48
89 (general household hardware)	36, 64
90 (other items)	20, 23, 35, 42, 51, 53, 54, 61, 62, 64

CES No.	IO No.	Income Distribution Group						
		Under $3,000	$3,000– $5,000	$5,000– $7,500	$7,500– $10,000	$10,000– $15,000	$15,000 and over	National Average
		(Percent)						
119.01	20	3.5	3.5	4.2	4.2	4.2	8.1	4.5
119.02	23	6.7	6.9	6.8	6.8	6.2	5.5	6.5
119.03	34	5.1	3.4	4.7	4.9	7.9	8.1	5.7
119.04	35	1.8	1.8	1.9	1.9	1.8	2.0	1.8
119.05	36	5.2	5.6	5.9	6.1	5.8	7.9	6.1
119.06	42	10.1	10.9	13.2	13.6	12.0	9.7	12.2
119.07	44	22.8	20.6	17.5	17.5	15.1	14.0	17.4
119.08	47	2.0	2.2	2.9	3.1	2.6	2.1	2.6
119.09	48	1.3	1.4	2.0	2.1	1.8	1.4	1.8
119.10	51	5.0	6.7	6.3	6.2	8.3	4.5	6.5
119.11	53	0.3	0.3	0.3	0.3	0.3	0.3	0.3
119.12	54	1.1	1.1	1.1	1.1	1.0	0.9	1.0
119.13	55	24.1	23.0	20.3	20.2	21.6	21.9	21.3
119.14	61	0.2	0.2	0.2	0.2	0.2	0.1	0.2
119.15	62	3.8	3.7	4.5	4.6	4.7	8.8	4.9
119.16	64	7.0	8.7	8.2	7.2	6.5	4.7	7.2
Total		100.0	100.0	100.0	100.0	100.0	100.0	100.0

120.00   The average expenditures on total footwear (CES 137.00, 164.00, 190.00, 214.00, 242.00, 271.00, and 283.00), jewelry and watches (CES 145.00, 172.00, 195.00, 222.00, 250.00, and 276.00), clothing material (CES 286.00), and clothing upkeep (CES 287.00) were subtracted from the average expenditures on total clothing, clothing material, and services (CES 120.00), and the remainder was distributed according to the percentage distribution listed.

The percentage distribution was calculated from the values for IO-16,

IO-17, IO-18, IO-19, IO-24, IO-32, IO-34, IO-64, IO-80, and IO-83 listed in NIPCE II-3a and the values for IO-16, IO-18, IO-19, IO-32, IO-34, IO-80, and IO-83 listed in NIPCE II-3b. The value of the hand luggage component of leather products, obtained from the *1958 Detailed NIPCE Listing,* was excluded from the expenditures for IO-34. The expenditures for IO-16, Broad & narrow fabrics, yarn & thread mills, include only shoelaces. The clothing material component, CES 286.00, was distributed directly to IO-16.

CES No.	Input-Output Industry No.	NIPCE Value ($ millions)			
		II-3a	II-3b	Total	Percent
120.01	16	–	8	8	0.0
120.02	17	30	–	30	0.2
120.03	18	11,596	6,715	18,311	93.7
120.04	19	78	6	84	0.4
120.05	24	70	–	70	0.4
120.06	32	17	1	18	0.1
120.07	34	417	156	573	2.9
120.08	64	101	–	101	0.5
120.09	80	260	118	378	1.9
120.10	83	–36	17	–19	–0.1
Total		12,533	7,021	19,554	100.0

137.00   The average expenditures for total footwear (CES 137.00, 164.00, 190.00, 214.00, 242.00, 271.00, and 283.00) were subtracted from the average expenditures for total clothing (CES 120.00). The average expenditures for total footwear were distributed according to the percentages given under CES 137.00. The percentages were calculated from the values for IO-32, IO-34, and IO-80 listed in NIPCE II-1.

CES No.	Input-Output Industry No.	NIPCE Value ($ millions)	Percent
137.01	32	412	10.1
137.02	34	3,571	87.7
137.03	80	91	2.2
Total		4,074	100.0

145.00   The average expenditures for jewelry and watches (CES 145.00, 172.00, 195.00, 222.00, 250.00, and 276.00) were subtracted from the average expenditures for total clothing (CES 120.00). The average expenditures for jewelry and watches were distributed according to the percentages given under CES 145.00. The percentages were calculated from the values for IO-34, IO-62, IO-64, IO-80, and IO-83 listed in NIPCE II-7.

CES No.	Input-Output Industry No.	NIPCE Value ($ millions)	Percent
145.01	34	54	2.9
145.02	62	264	14.3
145.03	64	1,464	79.1
145.04	80	41	2.2
145.05	83	27	1.5
Total		1,850	100.0

286.00   The average expenditures on clothing material, CES 286.00, were subtracted from the total clothing expenditures figures, CES 120.00, and allocated directly to IO-16.

287.00   The average expenditures on clothing upkeep, CES 287.00, were subtracted from the total clothing expenditures figures, CES 120.00, and allocated directly to IO-72.

292.00   The percentage distribution for automobile purchases, CES 292.01–292.04, was calculated from the values for IO-59 and IO-83 listed in NIPCE VIII-1a and the values for IO-52 and IO-56 listed in NIPCE VIII-1b.

CES No.	Input-Output Industry No.	NIPCE Value ($ millions)	Percent
292.01	52	35	0.3
292.02	56	55	0.4
292.03	59	11,302	88.5
292.04	83	1,379	10.8
Total		12,771	100.0

Automotive finance charges (SIC 6146, IO-70) could not be separated from automobile purchases because the amount of the finance charges could not be determined.

   According to the article by Nancy W. Simon [74, p. 19, n. 7], the imports of cars were not treated as part of IO-80 but were included in IO-59, Motor vehicles & equipment. Parts bought with cars were also included in IO-59.

293.00   The percentage distribution for total automobile operation, CES 293.01–293.12, was calculated from the values for IO-19, IO-27, IO-29, IO-32, IO-42, IO-55, IO-58, IO-59, and IO-83 listed in NIPCE VIII-1b; for IO-75 listed in NIPCE VIII-1c; and for IO-65 and IO-79 listed in NIPCE VIII-1e.

CES No.	Input-Output Industry No.	NIPCE Value ($ millions)	Percent
293.01	19	75	1.1
293.02	27	76	1.1
293.03	29	38	0.6
293.04	32	1,372	20.6
293.05	42	20	0.3
293.06	55	30	0.4
293.07	58	248	3.7
293.08	59	145	2.2
293.09	65	6	0.1
293.10	75	4,387	65.8
293.11	79	244	3.7
293.12	83	26	0.4
Total		6,667	100.0

The values listed for CES 296.00, 297.00, 298.00, 299.00, 300.00, and 302.00 were aggregated and distributed according to the percentage distribution of CES 293.00.

304.00 The expenditures for car pool, CES 304.00, were not assigned to any input-output industry because they are not included in the NIPCE.

306.00 The percentage distribution for other transportation, CES 306.01–306.08, was calculated from the values for IO-61 listed in NIPCE VIII-1a; IO-31 in NIPCE VIII-1d; and IO-19, IO-32, IO-42, IO-43, IO-60, IO-61, and IO-72 in NIPCE IX-4; and the *1958 Detailed NIPCE Listing.* Because this last reference had to be used, the values cannot be listed here. No allocation was made for motorcycle repair (SIC 7699). Internal combustion engines (IO-43, SIC 3519) are listed in NIPCE IX-4; therefore, they were included under CES 306.00. Although some automotive engines are also included in SIC 3519, they could not be separated.

308.00 In the NIPCE, health insurance covers premiums minus claims, while prepaid care, CES 308.00, covers total premiums. A percentage distribution was therefore calculated by adding the values for IO-70 and IO-77 listed in NIPCE VI-3, VI-6, and VI-7.

CES No.	Input-Output Industry No.	NIPCE Value ($ millions)				Percent
		VI-3	VI-6	VI-7	Total	
308.01	70	–	–	1,128	1,128	11.4
308.02	77	4,574	4,202	1	8,777	88.6
Total		4,574	4,202	1,129	9,905	100.0

313.00 According to Nancy W. Simon, the services of optometrists are part of the retail trade margin for IO-63, Optical, ophthalmic, & photographic equipment & supplies, in NIPCE VI-2; therefore, all of CES 313.00 was assigned to IO-63.

315.00 The percentage distribution for drugs and medicines, CES 315.01–315.02, was calculated from the values for IO-27 and IO-29 listed in NIPCE VI-1.

CES No.	Input-Output Industry No.	NIPCE Value ($ millions)	Percent
315.01	27	1	0.0
315.02	29	2,687	100.0
Total		2,688	100.0

316.00 The percentage distribution for medical appliances and supplies, CES 316.01–316.03, was calculated from the values for IO-32 and IO-62 listed in NIPCE VI-1 and the values for IO-58 and IO-62 listed in NIPCE VI-2.

CES No.	Input-Output Industry No.	NIPCE Value ($ millions)			Percent
		VI-1	VI-2	Total	
316.01	32	90	—	90	26.6
316.02	58	—	2	2	0.6
316.03	62	149	97	246	72.8
Total		239	99	338	100.0

324.00 The percentage distribution for total personal care supplies, CES 324.01–324.07, was calculated from the values for IO-29, IO-32, IO-42, IO-54, IO-64, and IO-80 listed in NIPCE III-1; and IO-24 listed in both NIPCE V-6 and NIPCE VI-1 and from the *1958 Detailed NIPCE Listing.* Because this last reference had to be used, the values cannot be given here. The value of NIPCE V-6 was adjusted for the difference between the value of cleansing tissues (SIC 2649) listed in the *1958 Detailed NIPCE Listing* and the published figure in Nancy W. Simon's article [74].

332.00 The percentage distribution for total recreation, CES 332.01–332.08, was calculated from the values for IO-34, IO-56, IO-57, IO-58, IO-64, and IO-83 listed in NIPCE IX-5 and IO-72 listed in NIPCE IX-6. Four CES components (CES 333.00 through 336.00) of the total were added and distributed according to the percentages listed under CES 332.00. The remainder of the total was distributed separately (see CES 337.00 through 347.00).

CES No.	Input-Output Industry No.	NIPCE Value ($ millions)	Percent
332.01	34	7	0.2
332.02	56	2,281	64.9
332.03	57	278	7.9
332.04	58	26	0.7
332.05	64	210	6.0
332.06	72	681	19.3
332.07	73	—	—
332.08	83	34	1.0
Total		3,517	100.0

332.06
332.07
335.04 No values were available for phonograph or musical instrument repair,
336.03 nor for rental of musical instruments.
336.04

339.00 The percentage distribution for sports events, CES 339.01–339.02, was
calculated from the values for IO-26 and IO-76 listed in NIPCE IX-8c.

CES No.	Input-Output Industry No.	NIPCE Value ($ millions)	Percent
339.01	26	4	1.6
339.02	76	245	98.4
Total		249	100.0

341.00 The percentage distribution for the remainder of recreation expenditures,
CES 341.00 through CES 347.00 (excluding pet food, CES 344.02), was
calculated from the values for the input-output industries listed in NIPCE
V-4; V-7; IX-3; IX-4; IX-10; IX-12; and the *1958 Detailed NIPCE Listing*.
Because this last reference had to be used, the values cannot be given here.
The percentages are listed under CES 341.00 in the preceding alignment.
The value for sails, which is included in CES 306.01, was subtracted from
the value for IO-19 listed in NIPCE IX-4. The information for participant
sports, CES 341.00, could not appear in the preceding alignment but is
listed here.

Title of CES Consumption Item	SIC No.	IO No.	Percent	NIPCE No.
Small arms and ammunition	1951, 1961	13	(341)	IX–3, –4
Fishing nylon	22982	17	(341)	IX–3
Pocket and folding knives	3421141	42	(341)	IX–4
Field glasses	3831034	63	(341)	IX–4
Sporting and athletic goods	3949	64	(341)	IX–3, –4
Sports	79	76	(341)	IX–12

344.02 The percentage of pet consumption expenditures, CES 344.00, allocated
to pet food was calculated from the NICB volume [59, p. 134]. The pet
food expenditures were then subtracted from the total expenditures figure
aggregated under CES 344.00 and allocated directly to IO-14, Food &
kindred products.

NICB Item	CES Category	Input-Output Industry
27 (pet supplies)	344.02	(See CES 344.00)
28 (pet food)	344.02	14

Income Distribution Group	NICB Value (dollars)			Distribution (percent)		
	27*	28*	Total	27*	28*	Total
Under $3,000	0.67	5.59	6.26	10.7	89.3	100.0
$3,000–$5,000	2.34	11.07	13.41	17.4	82.6	100.0
$5,000–$7,500	3.30	16.30	19.60	16.8	83.2	100.0
$7,500–$10,000	7.15	21.97	29.12	24.6	75.4	100.0
$10,000–$15,000	10.67	28.69	39.36	27.1	72.9	100.0
$15,000 and over	14.80	30.07	44.87	33.0	67.0	100.0
National Average	4.35	15.57	19.92	21.8	78.2	100.0

*The numbers refer to those of the NICB items included within 344.02

349.00 The percentage distribution for newspapers, CES 349.01–349.02, and magazines, CES 350.00, was calculated from the values for IO-26 and IO-83 listed in NIPCE IX-2. The value for technical and educational magazines was excluded from the values used to calculate percentages for CES 349.00 and added to the values used to calculate percentages for books, supplies, and equipment, CES 355.00.

CES No.	Input-Output Industry No.	NIPCE Value ($ millions)	Percent
349.01	26	2,081	101.4
349.02	83	–29	–1.4
Total		2,052	100.0

351.00 The percentage distribution for books other than technical or educational, CES 351.01–351.02, was calculated after subtracting the value for technical and educational books obtained from the *1958 Detailed NIPCE Listing*. Because this last reference was used, the values cannot be given here.

351.02 The value of used books, CES 351.02, was calculated by multiplying the value of IO-83, Scrap, used & secondhand goods listed in NIPCE IX-1 by the percent of total book expenditures spent on technical and educational books and magazines. The remainder of the value for IO-83 listed in NIPCE IX-1 went to CES 355.05.

355.00 The percentage distribution for books, supplies, and equipment, CES 355.01–355.02, was calculated from the values for IO-64 (part) listed in NIPCE V-4; IO-26 (part), IO-27 (part), IO-32, and IO-64 (part) listed in NIPCE V-7; IO-26 (part) and IO-83 (part) listed in NIPCE IX-1; and IO-26 (part) listed in NIPCE IX-2, and from the *1958 Detailed NIPCE Listing*. Because this last reference had to be used, no values are given here. The adjustment made to the value figures of NIPCE V-4 and V-7 are described in the comments for CES 355.04.

355.04 Since "artist brushes" was shifted to CES 343.05, the values of NIPCE V-4 and V-7 were adjusted for this value using information from the *1958 Detailed NIPCE Listing*.

355.05 The percentage distribution for IO-83, Scrap, used & secondhand goods, was obtained from the calculation described under CES 351.02.

357.00 All of CES 357.00 was allocated to IO-77, Medical, educational services, & nonprofit organizations, because no values were available for dancing lessons, SIC 7911, swimming lessons, SIC 7944, etc., all of which should have been allocated to IO-76, Amusements.

359.00 The expenditures on all-expense tours, CES 359.00, were assumed to be comprised of food, lodging, transportation, and recreation out of home city; therefore, they were distributed to the input-output industries listed under each of those CES items.

CES No.	Percent of CES 359.00	Input-Output Industry No.	Percent
10.00	32	1	3.00
		2	4.90
		3	0.80
		10	0.01
		14	87.79
		65	0.20
		69	0.50
		80	2.80
32.00	38	72	94.50
		77	5.50
305.00	24	65	100.00
346.00	6	76	100.00

Although some of the expenditures on all-expense tours may represent money spent abroad, no special adjustment was made for this because no data were available on a state basis.

360.00 The percentage distributions by income class for other miscellaneous household expenditures, CES 360.01–360.06, were calculated from the NICB volume [59, p. 142]. The following correspondences hold:

NICB Item	CES Category	Input-Output Industry
16 (legal expenses)	360.06	73
17 (funeral expenses)	360.01, 360.02, 360.04, 360.05	9, 36, 71, 72
18 (other expenses)	360.03	70

NICB item 17 was split according to the values for the four input-output categories listed in NIPCE VII-6. Items for which no specific allocation was made include: fines and court judgments, marriage licenses and fees to ministers and organists, expenses for raising food for family use, money lost or stolen, money allowances to children, etc.

Income Dis-tribution Group	NICB Value (dollars)						
	360.01	360.02	360.03	360.04	360.05	360.06	Total
Under $3,000	0.18 (0.4)*	0.88 (2.1)	16.85 (40.8)	3.57 (8.6)	15.00 (36.4)	4.83 (11.7)	41.31 (100.0)
$3,000– $5,000	0.13 (0.2)	0.66 (1.2)	34.66 (63.1)	2.68 (4.9)	11.24 (20.5)	5.53 (10.1)	54.90 (100.0)
$5,000– $7,500	0.12 (0.2)	0.63 (0.8)	53.28 (71.5)	2.55 (3.4)	10.69 (14.3)	7.29 (9.8)	74.56 (100.0)
$7,500– $10,000	0.15 (0.1)	0.76 (0.7)	76.24 (73.0)	3.08 (2.9)	12.93 (12.4)	11.30 (10.9)	104.46 (100.0)
$10,000– $15,000	0.17 (0.1)	0.84 (0.6)	105.26 (77.4)	3.42 (2.5)	14.33 (10.6)	11.95 (8.8)	135.97 (100.0)
$15,000 and over	0.09 (0.0)	0.45 (0.2)	209.41 (87.5)	1.82 (0.8)	7.66 (3.2)	19.80 (8.3)	239.23 (100.0)
National Average	7.99 (9.9)	0.14 (0.2)	0.73 (0.9)	2.96 (3.7)	12.41 (15.4)	56.37 (69.9)	80.60 (100.0)

*Numbers in parentheses are percentages.

360.04 The figures from the NICB volume [59, p. 142] were used to distribute the cemetery upkeep portion, CES 360.04, of IO-71, Real estate & rental. Independent cemetery upkeep (SIC 0731) was disregarded since no information was available, and SIC 0731 was not assigned to any input-output industry in the 1958 input-output table.

361.00 ⎫ For the percentage distribution of total personal insurance,
363.00 ⎬ CES 361.01–361.02, the consumer expenditures listed under veterans,
369.00 ⎭ CES 363.00, and social security, railroad, and government retirement, CES 369.00, were excluded since these expenditures are not included in the definition of personal consumption expenditures in the input-output accounts. The percentage distribution was calculated from the values for IO-70 and IO-80 listed in NIPCE VII-4.

CES No.	Input-Output Industry No.	NIPCE Value ($ millions)	Percent
361.01	70	3,178	99.0
361.02	80	32	1.0
Total		3,210	100.0

373.00 Cash, CES 373.00, is a transfer expenditure and is not included in the input-output accounts.

374.00 Goods and services, CES 374.00, is likely to be final demand for IO-2, IO-14, IO-18, IO-26, IO-29, IO-52, IO-56, and IO-64. The percentage distribution was calculated from the values for those input-output industries given in the personal consumption expenditures column of the 1958 input-output table [176, p. 39].

CES No.	Input-Output Industry No.	NIPCE Value ($ millions)	Percent
374.01	2	2,429	3.4
374.02	14	45,759	63.7
374.03	18	11,165	15.5
374.04	26	2,445	3.4
374.05	29	3,708	5.2
374.06	54	2,416	3.4
374.07	56	1,363	1.9
374.08	64	2,536	3.5
Total		71,821	100.0

379.00 The percentage distribution for the value of home-produced food, CES 379.01–379.03, was calculated from the values of IO-1, IO-2, and IO-14 listed in NIPCE I-4.

CES No.	Input-Output Industry No.	NIPCE Value ($ millions)	Percent
379.01	1	430	30.5
379.02	2	398	28.2
379.03	14	582	41.3
Total		1,410	100.0

Appendix C
1947, 1958, And 1963 State Estimates of Final Demands (MRIO Data Set 1)

This data set provides state estimates of final demands for the three base years, 1947, 1958, and 1963, for 87 industries. The data for each year are separated into the six major components of the gross national product:

PCE   Personal Consumption Expenditures
GPCF Gross Private Capital Formation
NINV Net Inventory Change
NEXP Net Foreign Exports
SLG   State and Local Government Net Purchases of Goods and Services
FG   Federal Government Purchases

A detailed description of these components as they are defined for the national input-output tables prepared by the Office of Business Economics (OBE) is provided in Chapter 1 of this volume. The national final demands for the six components are listed in the three OBE tables:

1.   1947: OBE computer listing of the table (dated September 1967). As of the fall of 1971 this table, which was revised by the OBE from the original 1947 Bureau of Labor Statistics (BLS) table, has not been officially published.
2.   1958: *Survey of Current Business,* September 1965 [176, p. 39].
3.   1963: *Survey of Current Business,* November 1969 [164, p. 35].

Notes about the State Estimates of Final Demand

1.   The row sums of the state final demand matrices are identical to the national final demand figures listed in the three respective OBE tables. Throughout the estimation process, an attempt was made to construct the state figures on a basis comparable with the national input-output tables. Whenever an unreconcilable discrepancy occurred between the sum of the state figures and the national controls, the discrepancy was allocated to the states in proportion to the original entries in the state tables.

213

a. The rows are the 87 industries listed in the OBE tables plus row 88 of state totals.

b. The columns are the 51 regions (50 states and the District of Columbia), arranged in alphabetical order, plus a column 52 of residuals and a column 53 of industry totals.

Only the first 49 of the 51 regional columns contain values for 1947 and 1958 (columns 50 and 51 are zero) because Alaska and Hawaii did not become states until 1958. For 1963, all 51 regional columns contain values.

c. Column 52 contains values for data that were not allocated to the states. These represent either figures for which state estimates seemed very arbitrary and were therefore not made (such as the scrap component of net inventory change) or for purchases or payments made outside the 51 regions (such as purchases for the Panama Canal, wage payments to overseas military employees, etc.). In addition, for two industries a final consistency check revealed that state allocations had not been made. The two were: IO-3, Forestry & fishery products, in the 1947 net inventory change table; and IO-6, Nonferrous metal ores mining, in the 1963 net foreign exports by state-of-exit table. The figures not allocated were so small that they were simply placed in the residual column 52. For example, in the 1947 net inventory change table, the value of –$2,000 for IO-3 had not been allocated to the states; therefore, the figure –2 appears in the residual column.

2.   The data for the three years are given in thousands of current dollars and are in producer prices.

a. Deflators. For comparisons of the sets of final demands for the three years, the figures must be deflated to constant dollars. The national final demand deflators were used for deflation in the multiregional input-output calculations. For those calculations, the national final demand deflators for 1947 (63$) and 1958 (63$), separated by component, were applied to the state final demand estimates. The 1947 deflators were obtained from the OBE, and the 1958 deflators were obtained from Jack Faucett Associates.

b. Significant digits. Some of the adjustments to the final demands were made in 1971 using single precision on the Harvard IBM 360/65. After these adjustments had been made, it was learned that certain values in the tables were so large (seven or more digits) that double precision should have been used to maintain the original number. Overall, the estimates are not affected by the use of single precision; but for any state values, the last digits will not be accurate in any row where one value is seven or more digits.[1]

---

1. An example will illustrate what occurs for individual values. The personal consumption expenditures value in the 1958 OBE input-output table for IO-77, Medical, educational services, & nonprofit organizations, is given as $20,446,683 thousand, while the value in the 1958 personal consumption expenditures state estimates table is $20,446,608 thousand. In other words, the values exactly correspond only for the first six digits. This is not

c. Producer prices. Some of the final demand estimates were made in purchaser prices and were then converted to producer prices using the transportation, trade, and insurance margins from the national input-output table.

3.   IO-11, New construction. All purchases of new construction are recorded in the final demand sector of the input-output table; that is, no purchases from this industry are considered to be intermediate purchases. The total output of the industry can therefore be obtained state by state by adding the respective state elements that appear in row 11 of the state final demand tables for gross private capital formation, gross exports, state and local government net purchases of goods and services, and federal government purchases. Because the output of new construction is assumed to be used in the region in which it is produced, the total output must equal the total consumption in each state.

4.   IO-74, Research & development. For 1947 and 1958, values appear in the state final demand matrices for IO-74 because the industry was given in the national input-output table. For 1963, this industry was eliminated in the national input-output table, and the values were included as part of the industry where the research and development was actually performed; therefore, no separate state estimates were made for IO-74 in the 1963 final demands.

To use the 1947 and 1958 final demands for the multiregional input-output calculations, IO-74 must be redistributed to the appropriate industries. This was done for the calculations at the Harvard Economic Research Project by distributing the IO-74 entries in the state final demands in proportion to the entries in column 74 of the national input-output table for the respective year.

5.   IO-78, Federal government enterprises. For this industry, a value appears in the residual column 52 in the 1958 and 1963 net export tables. The values of $41,796 thousand and $56,368 thousand represent the Panama Canal tolls. For 1947, the value of these tolls was $17,597 thousand, which was larger than the total for the industry of $8,451 thousand; therefore, no value was put into the column 52 of residuals because the Panama Canal tolls may not have been included as part of the 1947 net export figures.

6.   IO-80, Imports. No state estimates were made for imports in the net export tables. The total value for transferred (competitive) plus directly allocated

---

important for the total value, but it should be noted that the last two digits of any state value listed in row 77 will not be accurate. If the numbers had been rounded to hundreds of thousands of dollars, this problem would not have occurred, but then a zero would have been printed for some states that actually had a value listed. There was no simple way to distinguish between an actual zero and a figure smaller than a given value. For that reason, the final demands are printed in thousands of dollars rather than in hundreds of thousands of dollars.

The IBM 7094 which was used at Harvard during the first round of final demand calculations carried one more significant digit; consequently, the accuracy of large numbers was a problem in only a few rare cases.

(non-competitive) imports is given in the column 52 of residuals and in the column 53 of totals. Regional estimates for transferred imports were constructed at the 44-region level and appear in the 44-region input-output tables.

7. IO-81, Business travel, entertainment, & gifts; and IO-82, Office supplies. These two industries are especially constructed for the input-output accounts. For the multiregional input-output calculations, the national input-output table was adjusted first to provide accurate control totals for the sum of the state final demands. The adjustment was made by taking columns 81 and 82 in the national input-output transfer (secondary) matrix and calculating co-efficient vectors from them. The values in rows 81 and 82 of the national matrix were then distributed to the other elements in the respective columns in propor-tion to the coefficients formed from columns 81 and 82. Since the row sum is equal to the column sum for industries 81 and 82, none of the row and column sums of the national control matrix are changed by this adjustment. The values in rows and columns 81 and 82 were made zero.

In the final demands, values appear only for IO-82. For the multiregional input-output calculations, these values were redistributed to the appropriate industries using a procedure similar to the one used for the national control matrix; that is, the elements in row 82 of each matrix of state final demands were distributed to the other elements in each respective column according to the coefficients formed from the national column 82. For each table of state final demands, the column sums remain unchanged through this redistribution, but the row sums naturally change. (When all of the state estimates for interindustry and final demand purchases are adjusted to eliminate these two industries and summed, however, the row sum is unchanged.)

8. IO-83, Scrap, used & secondhand goods. If the output of scrap is not to be generated during the input-output calculations, special adjustments must be made to the column of scrap in the input-output tables. These adjustments, however, do not affect the final demand estimates.

9. Value added in final demand: IO-84, Government industry; IO-85, Rest of the world industry; and IO-86, Household industry. For these industries, figures appear only in the value added portion of the final demand sector of the input-output table and represent payments to government employees; purchases by foreigners and foreign interest payments and receipts; and payments to house-hold employees, respectively. The following balances exist between the values given in MRIO DATA SET 1 and MRIO DATA SET 2:

$$
\begin{aligned}
\text{IO-84 PAYROLLS} = \text{IO-84 OUTPUT} \ &= \ \text{IO-84 SLG} + \text{IO-84 FG} \\
\text{IO-85 OUTPUT} \ &= \ \text{IO-85 PCE} + \text{IO-85 NEXP} \\
&\quad + \text{IO-85 FG} \\
\text{IO-86 PAYROLLS} = \text{IO-86 OUTPUT} \ &= \ \text{IO-86 PCE}
\end{aligned}
$$

Part of the value of IO-84 represents wages paid to government employees overseas; this value appears in column 52 of the payrolls, outputs, and federal government final demand tables.[2]

10. IO-87, Inventory valuation adjustment. No state estimates were made for this; the total value appears in columns 52 and 53, and the item appears only in the net inventory change final demand tables.

11. Row 88 is the state total for the particular final demand component, obtained by summing all elements in each column.

12. Column 52 contains values for data that were not allocated to the states (explained above under 1).

13. Column 53 is the industry total for the particular final demand component. As explained under 1 above, this total was forced to equal the respective national final demand figure for the industry.

14. For certain regional analyses, three additional adjustments would have to be made to the state final demands:

a. The personal consumption expenditures column published by the OBE varies conceptually from that of the BLS. Each element in the OBE column is the same as or larger than the corresponding element in the BLS column because, in the BLS data, the purchases by foreign visitors are entirely excluded from the personal consumption expenditures column and are included in the net export column. For comparisons with the 1970 and 1980 projections of personal consumption expenditures and net exports which are described in MRIO DATA SET 3, the state data should therefore be adjusted to account for the difference between the OBE and the BLS handling of these purchases, because the projected final demands were constructed using the BLS concepts.[3] (This does not, of course, affect total final demand since the purchases are merely shifted from the personal comsumption expenditures column to the net export column.) It should be noted that if the BLS conventions are used, the IO-85 entry for personal consumption expenditures becomes zero, and the IO-85 entry in the net export column is altered by the amount of the original entry for IO-85 in the personal consumption expenditures column.

b. For the 1963 national input-output table, the OBE provides the current account purchases of the Commodity Credit Corporation and suggests that these figures be added to the federal government final demands. These current account purchases were excluded from the final demands in the 1963

---

2. For the description of MRIO DATA SET 2, refer to the second volume of this series, *State Estimates of Output, Employment, and Payrolls* [70].

3. For the description of MRIO DATA SET 3, refer to the third volume of this series, *1970 and 1980 State Projections of the Gross National Product* [73].

input-output table. The adjustment to the federal government state distribution, which is described in Chapter 6 (page 134), was not made for the figures presented in Table C.19 of this appendix. For the multiregional input-output model, the CCC figures obtained from the OBE, and listed below, must also be subtracted from the interindustry purchases of IO-78, Federal government enterprises, before those purchases are distributed to the states.

		(thousands of 1963 dollars)
IO-2	Other agricultural products	$ 636,427
IO-5	Iron & ferroalloy ores mining	−35
IO-6	Nonferrous metal ores mining	−78
IO-9	Stone & clay mining & quarrying	−26
IO-10	Chemical & fertilizer mineral mining	1
IO-14	Food & kindred products	213,688
IO-16	Broad & narrow fabrics, yarn & thread mills	15,270
IO-27	Chemicals & selected chemical products	352
IO-36	Stone & clay products	−28
IO-38	Primary nonferrous metals manufacturing	−12
IO-64	Miscellaneous manufacturing	−6
IO-65	Transportation & warehousing	641,718
IO-69	Wholesale & retail trade	24,129
IO-89	Value added	−1,531,400

c. To balance the data in the interregional trade matrices with the regional input-output tables, the inventory depletion component of net inventory change must be subtracted from the final demands and added as a row in the regional input-output tables. This adjustment is required to account for all shipments of a given commodity, regardless of the year in which it was produced.

The 19 tables of state final demand estimates follow.

MRIO Data Set 1
State Estimates of Final Demands (88 x 53)
(in thousands of current dollars)

Table No.	*Table Title*
C.1	1947 Personal Consumption Expenditures
C.2	1958 Personal Consumption Expenditures
C.3	1963 Personal Consumption Expenditures
C.4	1947 Gross Private Capital Formation
C.5	1958 Gross Private Capital Formation
C.6	1963 Gross Private Capital Formation
C.7	1947 Net Inventory Change
C.8	1958 Net Inventory Change
C.9	1963 Net Inventory Change
C.10	1947 Gross Foreign Exports by State of Production
C.11	1958 Gross Foreign Exports by State of Production
C.12	1963 Gross Foreign Exports by State of Production
C.13	1963 Gross Foreign Exports by State of Exit
C.14	1947 State and Local Government Net Purchases of Goods and Services
C.15	1958 State and Local Government Net Purchases of Goods and Services
C.16	1963 State and Local Government Net Purchases of Goods and Services
C.17	1947 Federal Government Purchases
C.18	1958 Federal Government Purchases
C.19	1963 Federal Government Purchases

TABLE C.1

STATE ESTIMATES OF 1947
PERSONAL CONSUMPTION EXPENDITURES
(THOUSANDS OF CURRENT DOLLARS)

INDUSTRY TITLE	1 ALABAMA	2 ARIZONA	3 ARKANSAS	4 CALIFORNIA	5 COLORADO	6 CONNECTICUT	7 DELAWARE	8 DISTRICT OF COLUMBIA	9 FLORIDA
1 LIVESTOCK & PRDTS.	44249	17325	30333	239575	32889	31104	6968	23718	58993
2 OTHER AGRICULTURE PRDTS.	56105	17676	39040	250384	33664	39504	6617	19700	54434
3 FORESTRY & FISHERIES	2086	715	1329	12830	1457	2271	281	1097	2277
4 AGRI.,FORES.,FISH. SERV.	0	0	0	0	0	0	0	0	0
5 IRON, FERRO. ORES MINING	0	0	0	0	0	0	0	0	0
6 NONFERROUS ORES MINING	0	0	0	0	0	0	0	0	0
7 COAL MINING	9834	2207	6802	24576	3914	9442	971	2884	8650
8 CRUDE PETRO.,NATURAL GAS	5	0	492	5538	245	0	0	0	3
9 STONE & CLAY MINING	187	69	120	1109	136	127	22	88	201
10 CHEM.&FERT. MIN. MINING	0	0	0	0	0	0	0	0	0
11 NEW CONSTRUCTION	0	0	0	0	0	0	0	0	0
12 MAINT. & REPAIR CONSTR.	0	0	0	0	0	0	0	0	0
13 ORDNANCE & ACCESSORIES	1072	716	642	12486	1423	1389	183	853	1316
14 FOOD & KINDRED PRDTS.	439755	148113	283564	2541952	310119	450019	60215	218041	494145
15 TOBACCO MANUFACTURES	42922	10903	27892	202277	22119	39841	5374	19190	42711
16 FABRICS	20273	7527	12996	120433	14536	14087	2898	10720	22578
17 TEXTILE PRDTS.	4110	2956	2464	41017	5653	7825	712	3734	5169
18 APPAREL	118316	48326	73615	791942	92817	122131	18179	75569	137067
19 MISC. TEXTILE PRDTS.	11145	4124	7033	69905	8095	10709	1593	6545	12239
20 LUMBER & WOOD PRDTS.	12353	2051	9161	27941	3724	5353	1053	2384	9529
21 WOODEN CONTAINERS	186	31	138	420	56	80	16	36	143
22 HOUSEHOLD FURNITURE	19427	5509	11760	117781	11999	21629	3194	13416	22815
23 OTHER FURNITURE	682	297	445	4785	556	636	95	347	725
24 PAPER & ALLIED PRDTS.	2986	1089	1876	18759	2146	2854	413	1634	3232
25 PAPERBOARD CONTAINERS	1551	610	835	14796	1374	2906	366	1620	2077
26 PRINTING & PUBLISHING	16017	8775	9791	149166	17003	21970	2398	11017	18820
27 CHEMICALS,SELECT. PRDTS.	2193	699	1431	11840	1371	1773	279	969	2209
28 PLASTICS & SYNTHETICS	36	14	22	237	27	42	5	21	40
29 DRUGS & COSMETICS	29429	9770	19096	164092	18991	23270	3727	13724	30196
30 PAINT & ALLIED PRDTS.	396	137	254	1994	264	472	55	234	429
31 PETROLEUM, RELATED INDS.	28215	10967	18108	184477	21729	33398	4142	14874	29403
32 RUBBER, MISC. PLASTICS	12015	4694	7622	78477	9231	9984	1766	6948	12889
33 LEATHER TANNING & PRDTS.	23	8	15	139	16	19	3	12	25
34 FOOTWEAR, LEATHER PRDTS.	31218	11533	19980	189412	22203	26471	4355	16452	33663
35 GLASS & GLASS PRDTS.	1906	779	1206	14343	1558	1941	285	1179	2088
36 STONE,& CLAY PRDTS.	2505	954	1630	14814	1835	2253	332	1242	2596
37 PRIMARY IRON, STEEL MFR.	861	219	593	2551	390	797	89	281	780
38 PRIMARY NONFERROUS MFR.	712	268	429	5077	545	866	117	481	823

#	Industry	Col 1	Col 2	Col 3	Col 4	Col 5	Col 6	Col 7	Col 8	Col 9
39	METAL CONTAINERS	259	100	166	1706	194	232	36	140	277
40	FABRICATED METAL PRDTS.	4645	832	3180	10537	1466	2166	530	1521	4042
41	SCREW MACH. PRDTS., ETC.	3273	1060	2087	20402	2191	2902	470	1925	3473
42	OTHER FAB. METAL PRDTS.	3397	1309	2172	22341	2543	3043	477	1839	3626
43	ENGINES & TURBINES	339	131	199	2926	298	267	64	340	444
44	FARM MACH. & EQUIP.	150	69	100	1037	125	127	19	66	153
45	CONSTRUC. MACH. & EQUIP.	41	19	27	281	34	34	5	18	41
46	MATERIAL HANDLING MACH.	0	0	0	0	0	0	0	0	0
47	METALWORKING MACHINERY	574	265	375	4309	496	560	83	310	616
48	SPECIAL MACH. & EQUIP.	189	87	131	1428	164	186	28	104	204
49	GENERAL MACH. & EQUIP.	200	80		1322	150	156	26	88	196
50	MACHINE SHOP PRDTS.	277	114	175	1867	223	224	42	163	296
51	OFFICE, COMPUT. MACHINES	349	161	228	2593	301	342	50	186	376
52	SERVICE IND. MACHINES	163	14	93	283	30	35	27	135	206
53	ELECT. TRANSMISS. EQUIP.	101	46	67	719	85	90	14	49	105
54	HOUSEHOLD APPLIANCES	27492	11031	18055	181970	20687	21506	3631	12155	27900
55	ELECTRIC LIGHTING EQUIP.	2763	1289	1817	20051	2384	2448	373	1350	2906
56	RADIO, TV, ETC., EQUIP.	7815	3159	4743	58356	6431	7995	1186	5350	8993
57	ELECTRONIC COMPONENTS	2364	947	1432	17575	1934	2407	358	1612	2720
58	MISC. ELECTRICAL MACH.	2378	971	1494	16333	1912	1961	356	1417	2592
59	MOTOR VEHICLES, EQUIP.	41883	16497	26154	292735	32856	37304	6894	26820	45613
60	AIRCRAFT & PARTS	155	60	91	1336	136	122	29	155	203
61	OTHER TRANSPORT. EQUIP.	3877	1502	2279	33366	3402	3051	728	3872	5066
62	PROFESS., SCIEN. INSTRU.	6888	2011	4371	36327	4195	5709	929	4118	8412
63	MEDICAL, PHOTO. EQUIP.	2147	1082	1341	19337	2219	2346	318	1344	2448
64	MISC. MANUFACTURING	23568	11885	14825	202025	23129	23232	3525	14730	26159
65	TRANSPORT. & WAREHOUSING	80731	41209	51119	720217	80777	97446	11014	47638	90414
66	COMMUNICA.,EXC. BRDCAST.	17328	7773	10379	139556	15661	21814	2577	12044	21164
67	RADIO & TV BROADCASTING	97	54	50	913	73	85	12	303	145
68	ELEC.,GAS,WATER,SAN.SER.	44379	14717	28504	248702	29275	36025	5698	21980	47628
69	WHOLESALE & RETAIL TRADE	525976	184982	338674	3145032	370600	512037	72377	271381	557120
70	FINANCE & INSURANCE	58674	21944	36400	383969	43739	65262	9353	38365	65661
71	REAL ESTATE & RENTAL	158940	72945	94463	1457517	156081	248815	23065	110568	189837
72	HOTELS; PERSONAL SERV.	62503	33347	43413	484374	58591	63443	11078	64605	143311
73	BUSINESS SERVICES	19111	6973	12604	98887	13651	13317	2238	8176	19134
74	RESEARCH & DEVELOPMENT	26507	10924	16755	178429	21348	21396	4028	15601	28300
75	AUTO. REPAIR & SERVICES	31117	13856	20915	262703	35912	31285	8966	18608	69659
76	AMUSEMENTS	97643	38081	63250	652873	74657	96315	13735	58503	109018
77	MED.,EDUC. SERVICES	3475	1629	2228	26783	3197	3678	461	2002	3840
78	FEDERAL GOV'T ENTERPRISE	1095	439	673	7588	885	812	165	674	1238
79	STATE & LOCAL GOV'T ENT.	11972	4038	7592	71994	8494	12567	1657	6250	13279
80	IMPORTS	0	0	0	0	0	0	0	0	0
81	BUS.TRAVEL, ENT., GIFTS.	0	0	0	0	0	0	0	0	0
82	OFFICE SUPPLIES	0	0	0	0	0	0	0	0	0
83	SCRAP & USED GOODS	0	0	0	0	0	0	0	0	0
84	GOVERNMENT INDUSTRY	0	0	0	0	0	0	0	0	0
85	REST OF WORLD INDUSTRY	-4379	-6067	-2861	-90181	-5280	-7491	-1197	-6156	-15064
86	HOUSEHOLD INDUSTRY	57455	11501	19527	197836	14325	43508	10065	38124	84713
87	INVENTORY VALUATION ADJ.									
88	STATE TOTAL	2240681	832127	1420123	14253419	1671656	2263472	322193	1257483	2587829

TABLE C.1

STATE ESTIMATES OF 1947
PERSONAL CONSUMPTION EXPENDITURES
(THOUSANDS OF CURRENT DOLLARS)

INDUSTRY TITLE	10 GEORGIA	11 IDAHO	12 ILLINOIS	13 INDIANA	14 IOWA	15 KANSAS	16 KENTUCKY	17 LOUISIANA	18 MAINE
1 LIVESTOCK & PRDTS.	63405	11379	161684	65784	45776	43086	53494	43613	17039
2 OTHER AGRICULTURE PRDTS.	64638	15515	190724	89484	63170	47276	59747	50679	18129
3 FORESTRY & FISHERIES	2448	610	9740	3966	2687	1923	2158	2025	905
4 AGRI.,FORES.,FISH. SERV.	0	0	0	0	0	0	0	0	0
5 IRON, FERRO. ORES MINING	0	0	0	0	0	0	0	0	0
6 NONFERROUS ORES MINING	0	0	0	0	0	0	0	0	0
7 COAL MINING	11012	2043	41077	20045	14833	10797	9978	8406	5643
8 CRUDE PETRO.,NATURAL GAS	0	0	1210	104	0	1761	291	2955	0
9 STONE & CLAY MINING	216	60	840	351	229	174	178	179	50
10 CHEM.&FERT. MIN. MINING	0	0	0	0	0	0	0	0	0
11 NEW CONSTRUCTION	0	0	0	0	0	0	0	0	0
12 MAINT. & REPAIR CONSTR.	0	0	0	0	0	0	0	0	0
13 ORDNANCE & ACCESSORIES	1267	611	7072	2668	1818	1191	1127	1171	461
14 FOOD & KINDRED PRDTS.	504992	132084	1948038	841900	549225	412705	449855	431432	184440
15 TOBACCO MANUFACTURES	48973	9180	164434	67325	45005	31345	44566	40171	14822
16 FABRICS	25241	6258	73881	30848	21701	16453	22037	19613	5749
17 TEXTILE PRDTS.	4853	2836	36799	14908	10781	7174	4390	4510	2534
18 APPAREL	145273	39241	560401	219297	149454	109679	128616	118567	43054
19 MISC. TEXTILE PRDTS.	12982	3595	47808	19194	13137	9024	11776	11077	3599
20 LUMBER & WOOD PRDTS.	13832	1769	20038	10070	7502	5579	12766	9767	4033
21 WOODEN CONTAINERS	208	27	301	151	113	84	192	147	61
22 HOUSEHOLD FURNITURE	22994	5034	99989	37840	25052	16711	21381	20412	6615
23 OTHER FURNITURE	800	242	2941	1234	883	593	735	668	229
24 PAPER & ALLIED PRDTS.	3453	918	12787	5258	3558	2501	3114	2922	1122
25 PAPERBOARD CONTAINERS	1873	614	11630	3978	2507	1576	1805	1910	738
26 PRINTING & PUBLISHING	18736	7053	100509	39931	27001	18988	16466	16414	8724
27 CHEMICALS,SELECT. PRDTS.	2518	601	8825	3692	2514	1760	2295	2061	707
28 PLASTICS & SYNTHETICS	42	12	179	72	49	34	38	36	16
29 DRUGS & COSMETICS	33816	8206	110796	45934	31179	22094	30379	27801	9916
30 PAINT & ALLIED PRDTS.	460	119	2054	819	565	396	416	382	219
31 PETROLEUM, RELATED INDS.	32737	10113	157778	69870	50837	34617	31050	27644	14697
32 RUBBER, MISC. PLASTICS	13888	4363	53029	22139	15532	10597	12978	11889	3739
33 LEATHER TANNING & PRDTS.	28	7	95	39	27	20	25	22	7
34 FOOTWEAR, LEATHER PRDTS.	37644	9430	130242	53082	36604	26915	33450	29962	9772
35 GLASS & GLASS PRDTS.	2228	668	8903	3595	2507	1697	2070	1903	653
36 STONE & CLAY PRDTS.	2897	845	11835	4971	3390	2435	2626	2400	814
37 PRIMARY IRON, STEEL MFR.	971	202	3619	1745	1293	935	878	749	467
38 PRIMARY NONFERROUS MFR.	833	233	3564	1380	922	623	765	745	299

222

#	Industry	1	2	3	4	5	6	7	8	9
39	METAL CONTAINERS	301	85	1115	458	318	217	275	254	85
40	FABRICATED METAL PRDTS.	5238	733	10741	4621	3251	2228	4942	4013	715
41	SCREW MACH. PRDTS., ETC.	3795	950	13820	5591	3859	2635	3553	3198	981
42	OTHER FAB. METAL PRDTS.	3947	1110	14611	5995	4164	2844	3607	3330	1113
43	ENGINES & TURBINES	416	1119	1784	706	493	322	367	391	93
44	FARM MACH. & EQUIP.	175	54	581	255	185	126	160	142	49
45	CONSTRUC. MACH. & EQUIP.	47	15	157	69	50	34	43	38	13
46	MATERIAL HANDLING MACH.	0	0	0	0	0	0	0	0	0
47	METALWORKING MACHINERY	676	217	2629	1081	783	518	622	570	196
48	SPECIAL MACH. & EQUIP.	223	72	875	358	259	171	205	189	65
49	GENERAL MACH. & EQUIP.	230	64	671	279	196	132	215	187	60
50	MACHINE SHOP PRDTS.	321	109	1252	528	373	254	305	276	87
51	OFFICE, COMPUT. MACHINES	411	132	1580	662	479	317	379	346	121
52	SERVICE IND. MACHINES	191	14	422	145	90	62	158	179	9
53	ELECT. TRANSMISS. EQUIP.	118	37	418	179	130	87	108	97	34
54	HOUSEHOLD APPLIANCES	31598	8793	92420	38383	26934	18238	29613	25711	8251
55	ELECTRIC LIGHTING EQUIP.	3233	1041	11495	4916	3543	2399	2946	2676	923
56	RADIO, TV, ETC., EQUIP.	9104	2757	41355	16149	10741	7464	8223	7968	2770
57	ELECTRONIC COMPONENTS	2752	827	12408	4843	3215	2237	2481	2409	829
58	MISC. ELECTRICAL MACH.	2759	907	10780	4468	3127	2130	2559	2379	747
59	MOTOR VEHICLES, EQUIP.	49081	15667	227210	89927	63023	41177	47397	42719	13555
60	AIRCRAFT & PARTS	190	54	815	322	225	147	168	178	42
61	OTHER TRANSPORT. EQUIP.	4750	1360	20343	8054	5628	3676	4192	4456	1059
62	PROFESS., SCIEN. INSTRU.	7973	1866	25469	10461	7197	4987	6851	7044	2049
63	MEDICAL, PHOTO. EQUIP.	2515	926	12776	5242	3655	2536	2260	2172	898
64	MISC. MANUFACTURING	27446	10065	119719	46913	32112	21604	25056	23813	7988
65	TRANSPORT. & WAREHOUSING	92951	31744	401632	163206	106852	77148	82152	79516	35802
66	COMMUNICA., EXC. BRDCAST.	20472	6409	102914	40290	26673	18928	17483	17856	8631
67	RADIO & TV BROADCASTING	223	33	581	126	145	67	88	118	39
68	ELEC.,GAS,WATER,SAN.SER.	51386	12459	200095	83774	57568	41119	45361	42542	15242
69	WHOLESALE & RETAIL TRADE	600810	164502	2374690	1002338	584007	479709	511692	511092	201679
70	FINANCE & INSURANCE	68873	18956	314667	122712	81311	59206	59787	59105	22359
71	REAL ESTATE & RENTAL	184767	59434	1064840	407141	262408	187633	158570	161877	97357
72	HOTELS; PERSONAL SERV.	80564	23211	362658	118532	78115	55334	67912	71113	30721
73	BUSINESS SERVICES	21821	6666	103433	45107	29664	22987	19146	17668	5468
74	RESEARCH & DEVELOPMENT	30698	10452	119633	50419	35657	24227	29148	26352	8313
75	AUTO. REPAIR & SERVICES	29189	15371	149370	74908	37658	33032	25919	36365	9353
76	AMUSEMENTS	113531	32034	490171	200414	137176	97271	103034	95932	37551
77	MED.-EDUC. SERVICES	4047	1402	17610	7393	5168	3641	3557	3380	1573
78	FEDERAL GOV'T ENTERPRISE	1274	408	4782	1957	1350	933	1154	1108	317
79	STATE & LOCAL GOV'T ENT.	13490	3697	54641	23289	15255	11052	12107	11854	4825
80	IMPORTS	0	0	0	0	0	0	0	0	0
81	BUS.TRAVEL, ENT., GIFTS.	0	0	0	0	0	0	0	0	0
82	OFFICE SUPPLIES	0	0	0	0	0	0	0	0	0
83	SCRAP & USED GOODS	0	0	0	0	0	0	0	0	0
84	GOVERNMENT INDUSTRY	0	0	0	0	0	0	0	0	0
85	REST OF WORLD INDUSTRY	-5877	-4018	-44545	-12634	-8253	-5005	-6006	-7195	-3730
86	HOUSEHOLD INDUSTRY	76212	4194	100426	37690	24135	18796	28180	51941	12688
87	INVENTORY VALUATION ADJ.	0	0	0	0	0	0	0	0	0
88	STATE TOTAL	2617179	708396	10425867	4298941	2878870	2083363	2307611	2207591	890173

223

TABLE C.1

STATE ESTIMATES OF 1947
PERSONAL CONSUMPTION EXPENDITURES
(THOUSANDS OF CURRENT DOLLARS)

INDUSTRY TITLE	19 MARYLAND	20 MASSACHUSETTS	21 MICHIGAN	22 MINNESOTA	23 MISSISSIPPI	24 MISSOURI	25 MONTANA	26 NEBRASKA	27 NEVADA
1 LIVESTOCK & PRDTS.	47946	84786	104214	51672	35442	76276	12745	29127	5895
2 OTHER AGRICULTURE PRDTS.	47946	93472	138351	67072	41026	91529	16142	32507	4562
3 FORESTRY & FISHERIES	2139	5442	6577	2958	1342	4016	653	1332	185
4 AGRI.,FORES.,FISH. SERV.	0	0	0	0	0	0	0	0	0
5 IRON, FERRO. ORES MINING	0	0	0	0	0	0	0	0	0
6 NONFERROUS ORES MINING	0	0	0	0	0	0	0	0	0
7 COAL MINING	7240	21504	29108	15663	7301	21410	2189	7590	514
8 CRUDE PETRO.,NATURAL GAS	0	0	378	0	516	4	153	0	0
9 STONE & CLAY MINING	167	300	558	248	123	387	60	116	15
10 CHEM.&FERT. MIN. MINING	0	0	0	0	0	0	0	0	0
11 NEW CONSTRUCTION	0	0	0	0	0	0	0	0	0
12 MAINT. & REPAIR CONSTR.	0	0	0	0	0	0	0	0	0
13 ORDNANCE & ACCESSORIES	1402	3028	4764	1982	592	2406	663	847	177
14 FOOD & KINDRED PRDTS.	458611	1080665	1385787	602371	289384	821285	144141	275695	42616
15 TOBACCO MANUFACTURES	40984	93413	112132	49260	27874	65269	9690	21778	2691
16 FABRICS	21737	33432	50583	23412	13487	31068	6598	11348	1927
17 TEXTILE PRDTS.	5528	17489	25145	11407	2303	14208	2967	5173	699
18 APPAREL	137888	287478	376089	164530	73798	218461	41212	75674	11904
19 MISC. TEXTILE PRDTS.	12204	24776	32496	14315	6864	18783	3786	6340	1008
20 LUMBER & WOOD PRDTS.	7462	10861	14245	7662	10402	11040	1878	3872	476
21 WOODEN CONTAINERS	112	163	214	115	156	166	28	58	7
22 HOUSEHOLD FURNITURE	24950	50550	67428	27810	10812	34888	5327	11766	1512
23 OTHER FURNITURE	722	1456	2036	936	441	1163	251	424	67
24 PAPER & ALLIED PRDTS.	3180	6712	8693	3895	1841	5284	969	1735	261
25 PAPERBOARD CONTAINERS	2847	6235	7773	2868	687	3225	702	1132	203
26 PRINTING & PUBLISHING	18524	52020	67394	29928	9536	40721	7438	13196	2043
27 CHEMICALS,SELECT. PRDTS.	2112	4147	6060	2730	1435	3664	632	1224	168
28 PLASTICS & SYNTHETICS	41	98	122	54	21	71	13	24	3
29 DRUGS & COSMETICS	28458	55075	75081	34103	19304	46604	8593	15291	2324
30 PAINT & ALLIED PRDTS.	418	1085	1369	626	259	833	122	278	30
31 PETROLEUM, RELATED INDS.	31354	74393	111325	53326	17515	67083	10797	24719	2837
32 RUBBER, MISC. PLASTICS	13415	22137	36815	16666	7368	21366	4620	7498	1210
33 LEATHER TANNING & PRDTS.	24	46	65	29	15	39	7	14	2
34 FOOTWEAR, LEATHER PRDTS.	32831	62230	88578	39803	20444	53252	9911	18572	2837
35 GLASS & GLASS PRDTS.	2154	4450	6113	2705	1160	3477	710	1204	195
36 STONE & CLAY PRDTS.	2493	5202	7997	3615	1630	5159	863	1671	219
37 PRIMARY IRON, STEEL MFR.	663	1793	2562	1364	632	1849	215	659	51
38 PRIMARY NONFERROUS MFR.	901	1972	2404	1012	404	1312	252	435	69

#	Industry	1	2	3	4	5	6	7	8	9
39	METAL CONTAINERS	277	535	764	343	163	443	90	153	24
40	FABRICATED METAL PRDTS.	3967	5052	7472	3505	3393	4518	755	1592	180
41	SCREW MACH. PRDTS., ETC.	3558	6702	9498	4193	2020	5476	1016	1862	281
42	OTHER FAB. METAL PRDTS.	3627	7012	10007	4486	2132	5799	1174	2005	316
43	ENGINES & TURBINES	494	521	1228	529	180	631	129	233	35
44	FARM MACH. & EQUIP.	145	292	407	195	101	246	56	90	15
45	CONSTRUC. MACH. & EQUIP.	39	79	110	53	27	67	15	24	4
46	MATERIAL HANDLING MACH.	0	0	0	0	0	0	0	0	0
47	METALWORKING MACHINERY	628	1258	1807	824	372	1004	229	372	61
48	SPECIAL MACH. & EQUIP.	208	416	600	273	122	332	76	123	20
49	GENERAL MACH. & EQUIP.	200	363	461	209	132	267	64	94	17
50	MACHINE SHOP PRDTS.	320	481	875	399	167	505	116	180	30
51	OFFICE, COMPUT. MACHINES	378	769	1095	504	224	612	139	228	37
52	SERVICE IND. MACHINES	213	78	269	106	85	141	15	43	4
53	ELECT. TRANSMISS. EQUIP.	102	206	290	137	67	170	39	63	10
54	HOUSEHOLD APPLIANCES	27485	49909	63502	28758	18185	36724	8755	12965	2401
55	ELECTRIC LIGHTING EQUIP.	2803	5570	7992	3748	1815	4691	1083	1713	285
56	RADIO, TV, ETC., EQUIP.	9239	18428	27648	11877	4490	16046	3001	5169	831
57	ELECTRONIC COMPONENTS	2787	5560	8292	3558	1355	4820	900	1547	249
58	MISC. ELECTRICAL MACH.	2711	4277	7469	3362	1429	4299	963	1507	254
59	MOTOR VEHICLES, EQUIP.	52844	78375	155290	67274	24726	80383	17090	29661	4479
60	AIRCRAFT & PARTS	226	238	560	241	82	288	59	106	16
61	OTHER TRANSPORT. EQUIP.	5632	5968	13995	6034	2061	7199	1470	2656	400
62	PROFESS., SCIEN. INSTRU.	7161	14140	17363	7843	4426	10273	2004	3503	524
63	MEDICAL, PHOTO. EQUIP.	2446	5404	8689	3940	1317	5200	1007	1779	268
64	MISC. MANUFACTURING	26814	52601	81107	34985	14322	44411	10667	15262	2857
65	TRANSPORT. & WAREHOUSING	84940	237059	273612	118475	51485	164510	32552	52448	9294
66	COMMUNICA.,EXC. BRDCAST.	20269	52102	68277	29960	10233	41026	6813	13020	1875
67	RADIO & TV BROADCASTING	102	446	492	141	41	230	34	84	10
68	ELEC.,GAS,WATER,SAN.SER.	43826	86076	135305	62896	28917	86154	13170	28458	3529
69	WHOLESALE & RETAIL TRADE	552204	1184170	1656543	739286	336036	969986	175550	332537	47288
70	FINANCE & INSURANCE	66666	141442	209032	89469	35922	121356	20317	39843	5594
71	REAL ESTATE & RENTAL	182181	617352	700248	300046	92822	419404	63398	127390	18104
72	HOTELS; PERSONAL SERV.	73745	163853	212651	99270	40216	141572	27262	43769	22648
73	BUSINESS SERVICES	16644	31648	68724	31487	12913	51282	6627	15143	1566
74	RESEARCH & DEVELOPMENT	30563	45975	83570	38080	15973	0	0	0	0
75	AUTO. REPAIR & SERVICES	32482	71434	142468	41709	17210	8293	11085	17193	2880
76	AMUSEMENTS	103718	228811	328811	149378	63412	53160	15070	17740	36170
77	MED.,EDUC. SERVICES	3523	8652	12042	5632	2259	205874	33823	67685	9927
78	FEDERAL GOV'T ENTERPRISE	1272	1796	3273	1467	647	7548	1488	2552	390
79	STATE & LOCAL GOV'T ENT.	12765	29760	38798	16689	7536	1916	433	654	114
80	IMPORTS	0	0	0	0	0	22468	4001	7445	1112
81	BUS.TRAVEL, ENT., GIFTS.	0	0	0	0	0	0	0	0	0
82	OFFICE SUPPLIES	0	0	0	0	0	0	0	0	0
83	SCRAP & USED GOODS	0	0	0	0	0	0	0	0	0
84	GOVERNMENT INDUSTRY									
85	REST OF WORLD INDUSTRY	-9150	-20466	-36926	-18952	-2547	-14103	-5550	-4765	-3270
86	HOUSEHOLD INDUSTRY	56251	76411	66751	23589	30913	41912	4029	11178	1985
87	INVENTORY VALUATION ADJ.	0	0	0	0	0	0	0	0	0
88	STATE TOTAL	2382758	5327155	7163017	3150135	1431495	4263431	755341	1426606	259521

225

TABLE C.1

STATE ESTIMATES OF 1947
PERSONAL CONSUMPTION EXPENDITURES
(THOUSANDS OF CURRENT DOLLARS)

INDUSTRY TITLE	28 NEW HAMPSHIRE	29 NEW JERSEY	30 NEW MEXICO	31 NEW YORK	32 NORTH CAROLINA	33 NORTH DAKOTA	34 OHIO	35 OKLAHOMA	36 OREGON
1 LIVESTOCK & PRDTS.	10718	86359	17240	287278	72715	11220	127746	43029	30279
2 OTHER AGRICULTURE PRDTS.	10977	102517	16946	331569	78946	15454	166653	50300	40803
3 FORESTRY & FISHERIES	564	5729	641	18329	2811	557	8151	1979	1805
4 AGRI.,FORES.,FISH.SERV.	0	0	0	0	0	0	0	0	0
5 IRON,FERRO.ORES MINING	0	0	0	0	0	0	0	0	0
6 NONFERROUS ORES MINING	0	0	0	0	0	0	0	0	0
7 COAL MINING	3275	21159	1999	67863	12763	3466	37730	8203	5274
8 CRUDE PETRO.,NATURAL GAS	0	0	659	171	0	0	197	2513	0
9 STONE & CLAY MINING	31	316	63	1013	227	45	717	167	167
10 CHEM.&FERT.MIN.MINING	0	0	0	0	0	0	0	0	0
11 NEW CONSTRUCTION	0	0	0	0	0	0	0	0	0
12 MAINT.& REPAIR CONSTR.	0	0	0	0	0	0	0	0	0
13 ORDNANCE & ACCESSORIES	295	3492	656	10987	1489	390	5640	1133	1840
14 FOOD & KINDRED PRDTS.	114493	1204479	134656	3888631	589325	123713	1635784	418168	365204
15 TOBACCO MANUFACTURES	9452	99756	9679	312564	57899	9035	139302	39790	27823
16 FABRICS	3541	36480	7304	111007	29650	4885	61959	19809	17753
17 TEXTILE PRDTS.	1651	19751	2946	63362	5744	2541	30205	4329	7569
18 APPAREL	27309	321096	46227	994404	171877	32198	455338	119458	112900
19 MISC. TEXTILE PRDTS.	2327	27542	3761	86208	15499	2814	39569	10943	10528
20 LUMBER & WOOD PRDTS.	2213	10869	1889	34416	16474	1793	18388	9542	4860
21 WOODEN CONTAINERS	33	163	28	517	247	27	276	143	73
22 HOUSEHOLD FURNITURE	4387	56462	4938	175916	28390	5028	80833	20645	15623
23 OTHER FURNITURE	146	1598	277	5021	977	200	2480	666	711
24 PAPER & ALLIED PRDTS.	701	7096	996	22539	4069	732	10797	2893	2718
25 PAPERBOARD CONTAINERS	509	7683	547	22894	2465	532	8844	1971	2032
26 PRINTING & PUBLISHING	5402	54981	7809	178038	21450	5572	82828	15979	21013
27 CHEMICALS,SELECT.PRDTS.	440	4382	637	13848	3005	526	7530	2050	1767
28 PLASTICS & SYNTHETICS	10	107	13	335	49	10	150	36	35
29 DRUGS & COSMETICS	6049	57575	8811	183209	39452	6378	94064	27336	24087
30 PAINT & ALLIED PRDTS.	130	1147	130	3694	546	120	1687	380	327
31 PETROLEUM,RELATED INDS.	8913	79472	9899	251933	41535	11865	136567	28404	29240
32 RUBBER, MISC. PLASTICS	2349	24601	4223	76942	17178	3482	44633	12019	12620
33 LEATHER TANNING & PRDTS.	5	51	8	155	33	6	79	22	20
34 FOOTWEAR, LEATHER PRDTS.	6141	68936	11021	211257	44378	7996	108288	30136	27263
35 GLASS & GLASS PRDTS.	421	4937	708	15527	2754	553	7370	1921	2032
36 STONE & CLAY PRDTS.	517	5661	889	17851	3455	713	10060	2377	2367
37 PRIMARY IRON, STEEL MFR.	271	1795	202	5737	1129	304	3291	731	528
38 PRIMARY NONFERROUS MFR.	192	2194	243	6820	1012	187	2911	747	714

#	Industry									
39	METAL CONTAINERS	252	253	934	69	363	1839	92	584	54
40	FABRICATED METAL PRDTS.	2010	4082	9261	703	6454	16640	813	5298	486
41	SCREW MACH. PRDTS., ETC.	2896	3244	11487	837	4713	23278	948	7396	632
42	OTHER FAB. METAL PRDTS.	3298	3314	12238	904	4756	24087	1202	7652	704
43	ENGINES & TURBINES	371	363	1458	110	507	1819	116	599	63
44	FARM MACH. & EQUIP.	157	141	502	43	211	991	64	313	31
45	CONSTRUC. MACH. & EQUIP.	43	38	136	12	57	268	17	85	8
46	MATERIAL HANDLING MACH.	0	0	0	0	0	0	0	0	0
47	METALWORKING MACHINERY	643	567	2181	181	829	4420	249	1415	125
48	SPECIAL MACH. & EQUIP.	213	187	723	60	274	1469	82	471	41
49	GENERAL MACH. & EQUIP.	188	189	564	43	284	1234	71	385	38
50	MACHINE SHOP PRDTS.	313	282	1057	85	406	1685	102	543	54
51	OFFICE, COMPUT. MACHINES	390	346	1328	110	507	2677	150	853	77
52	SERVICE IND. MACHINES	42	166	327	16	199	309	13	100	6
53	ELECT. TRANSMISS. EQUIP.	109	97	355	30	144	711	43	225	21
54	HOUSEHOLD APPLIANCES	25911	26078	77698	5927	39035	169821	9818	53008	5168
55	ELECTRIC LIGHTING EQUIP.	3035	2651	9780	813	3906	19183	1202	6060	581
56	RADIO, TV, ETC., EQUIP.	8278	7887	33848	2151	10743	63093	2776	20236	1779
57	ELECTRONIC COMPONENTS	2483	2382	10160	641	3237	19002	831	6102	533
58	MISC. ELECTRICAL MACH.	2624	2397	9030	700	3385	14943	866	4797	466
59	MOTOR VEHICLES, EQUIP.	46974	43986	184863	14168	63917	284661	15262	92146	8482
60	AIRCRAFT & PARTS	169	166	666	50	231	831	53	273	29
61	OTHER TRANSPORT. EQUIP.	4236	4143	16625	1254	5782	20824	1322	6852	721
62	PROFESS., SCIEN. INSTRU.	5467	6709	21454	1519	8893	47205	1819	14233	1338
63	MEDICAL, PHOTO. EQUIP.	2780	2132	10629	797	2977	18595	980	5875	558
64	MISC. MANUFACTURING	29849	23578	97594	6866	33109	185443	10865	58777	5115
65	TRANSPORT. & WAREHOUSING	93952	77037	333823	21725	106585	823777	36140	252923	22738
66	COMMUNICA.,EXC. BRDCAST.	19190	17145	84756	5177	22715	176520	7079	54613	5371
67	RADIO & TV BROADCASTING	99	98	593	32	163	1295	37	70	24
68	ELEC.,GAS,WATER,SAN.SER.	36213	41437	170170	11983	58867	285193	13258	88420	9377
69	WHOLESALE & RETAIL TRADE	473176	506793	1999513	151529	725198	4150079	168510	1304456	125250
70	FINANCE & INSURANCE	55519	56833	258404	18877	79639	506573	19950	153918	14130
71	REAL ESTATE & RENTAL	183793	155522	869418	48106	202838	2063016	64240	623020	61142
72	HOTELS; PERSONAL SERV.	63457	65566	262339	17905	85642	689876	25463	181951	23351
73	BUSINESS SERVICES	17380	17109	90207	5837	24807	104776	6589	32570	3385
74	RESEARCH & DEVELOPMENT	0	0	0	0	0	0	0	0	0
75	AUTO. REPAIR & SERVICES	29913	26979	100963	8131	38798	160981	9774	51860	5163
76	AMUSEMENTS	36234	32989	120111	8999	33797	482016	12440	123306	6163
77	MED.,EDUC. SERVICES	94199	94161	409585	28999	134476	794637	34156	243127	23668
78	FEDERAL GOV'T ENTERPRISE	4063	3281	14862	1118	4640	29440	1504	9020	960
79	STATE & LOCAL GOV'T ENT.	1184	1101	3993	292	1513	6225	390	1986	197
80	IMPORTS	10444	11508	45828	3390	15804	107036	3624	33399	3014
81	BUS.TRAVEL, ENT., GIFTS.	0	0	0	0	0	0	0	0	0
82	OFFICE SUPPLIES	0	0	0	0	0	0	0	0	0
83	SCRAP & USED GOODS	0	0	0	0	0	0	0	0	0
84	GOVERNMENT INDUSTRY	-6183	-5066	-31907	-3900	-5005	-149730	-3469	-23979	-3483
85	REST OF WORLD INDUSTRY	17700	22719	93418	3578	67217	357779	6034	95593	6624
86	HOUSEHOLD INDUSTRY	0	0	0	0	0	0	0	0	0
87	INVENTORY VALUATION ADJ.	0	0	0	0	0	0	0	0	0
88	STATE TOTAL	2042839	2138409	8671041	621709	3060156	18914496	751520	5838917	557646

TABLE C.1

STATE ESTIMATES OF 1947
PERSONAL CONSUMPTION EXPENDITURES
(THOUSANDS OF CURRENT DOLLARS)

INDUSTRY TITLE	37 PENNSYL-VANIA	38 RHODE ISLAND	39 SOUTH CAROLINA	40 SOUTH DAKOTA	41 TENNESSEE	42 TEXAS	43 UTAH	44 VERMONT	45 VIRGINIA
1 LIVESTOCK & PRDTS.	154227	12016	39057	12375	50022	158993	9829	5656	71723
2 OTHER AGRICULTURE PRDTS.	212569	14932	39161	15938	63878	160446	14918	7692	69696
3 FORESTRY & FISHERIES	11467	876	1399	611	2412	6919	685	369	2715
4 AGRI.,FORES.,FISH. SERV.	0	0	0	0	0	0	0	0	0
5 IRON, FERRO. ORES MINING	0	0	0	0	0	0	0	0	0
6 NONFERROUS ORES MINING	0	0	0	0	0	0	0	0	0
7 COAL MINING	52492	3759	6375	3734	10852	25658	1755	2787	10726
8 CRUDE PETRO.,NATURAL GAS	612	0	0	0	0	14613	3	0	1
9 STONE & CLAY MINING	645	49	118	51	210	583	64	21	210
10 CHEM.&FERT. MIN. MINING	0	0	0	0	0	0	0	0	0
11 NEW CONSTRUCTION	0	0	0	0	0	0	0	0	0
12 MAINT. & REPAIR CONSTR.	0	0	0	0	0	0	0	0	0
13 ORDNANCE & ACCESSORIES	6571	464	722	407	1307	4325	666	200	1566
14 FOOD & KINDRED PRDTS.	2392533	173380	299158	127044	510786	1401755	142142	75422	583150
15 TOBACCO MANUFACTURES	198753	15166	28380	9910	49395	134173	10776	6125	53049
16 FABRICS	69087	5274	15144	5426	23311	70867	6677	2228	29086
17 TEXTILE PRDTS.	36948	2692	2762	2613	5044	16577	2575	1048	6290
18 APPAREL	584767	44898	86616	35522	138745	435782	42878	16440	174388
19 MISC. TEXTILE PRDTS.	51859	3864	7484	3010	13184	38642	3907	1464	15174
20 LUMBER & WOOD PRDTS.	31527	1961	8146	1934	13334	28179	1714	2131	13094
21 WOODEN CONTAINERS	473	29	122	29	200	423	26	32	197
22 HOUSEHOLD FURNITURE	102144	7806	13292	5388	23845	75075	5969	2571	29333
23 OTHER FURNITURE	3130	235	464	209	808	2315	265	96	931
24 PAPER & ALLIED PRDTS.	14423	1083	1984	801	3498	10099	1043	470	3956
25 PAPERBOARD CONTAINERS	13057	923	1134	534	2041	7901	739	298	2940
26 PRINTING & PUBLISHING	110860	8445	10568	6094	18975	58057	7961	3663	22118
27 CHEMICALS,SELECT. PRDTS.	9011	671	1463	571	2534	6936	673	299	2757
28 PLASTICS & SYNTHETICS	210	16	24	11	42	128	13	7	50
29 DRUGS & COSMETICS	120329	8959	19410	7014	33865	93055	9179	4221	36886
30 PAINT & ALLIED PRDTS.	2471	179	265	130	462	1323	118	99	539
31 PETROLEUM, RELATED INDS.	173195	12204	19527	12399	33693	98515	10682	6671	39684
32 RUBBER, MISC. PLASTICS	49186	3492	8187	3672	14293	42184	4566	1652	16645
33 LEATHER TANNING & PRDTS.	94	7	16	6	26	78	8	3	32
34 FOOTWEAR, LEATHER PRDTS.	128296	9808	22435	8805	35930	106405	10399	3787	42976
35 GLASS & GLASS PRDTS.	9408	698	1302	584	2285	6782	767	266	2697
36 STONE & CLAY PRDTS.	11101	834	1675	779	2916	8169	877	335	3233
37 PRIMARY IRON, STEEL MFR.	4401	311	561	326	958	2324	177	231	967
38 PRIMARY NONFERROUS MFR.	4211	310	485	201	862	2732	272	124	1047

228

	Industry									
39	METAL CONTAINERS	1149	86	175	73	306	883	94	35	349
40	FABRICATED METAL PRDTS.	10228	875	3125	755	5228	13156	688	285	5621
41	SCREW MACH. PRDTS., ETC.	14101	1048	2232	891	3896	11264	1094	397	4532
42	OTHER FAB. METAL PRDTS.	15052	1122	2288	961	4005	11567	1234	463	4576
43	ENGINES & TURBINES	1230	86	235	114	432	1499	152	49	537
44	FARM MACH. & EQUIP.	638	48	101	45	175	478	59	21	195
45	CONSTRUC. MACH. & EQUIP.	173	13	27	12	47	129	16	6	53
46	MATERIAL HANDLING MACH.	0	0	0	0	0	0	0	0	0
47	METALWORKING MACHINERY	2722	202	392	186	684	1997	236	82	802
48	SPECIAL MACH. & EQUIP.	901	67	129	62	226	662	78	27	266
49	GENERAL MACH. & EQUIP.	790	61	136	45	232	639	73	25	263
50	MACHINE SHOP PRDTS.	1109	76	191	89	333	995	111	40	394
51	OFFICE, COMPUT. MACHINES	1667	124	240	114	416	1219	144	51	484
52	SERVICE IND. MACHINES	159	11	103	18	192	640	16	4	225
53	ELECT. TRANSMISS. EQUIP.	448	34	68	31	118	334	40	14	135
54	HOUSEHOLD APPLIANCES	108705	8398	18669	6263	31975	87969	10092	3391	36198
55	ELECTRIC LIGHTING EQUIP.	12167	908	1870	851	3248	9167	1129	392	3663
56	RADIO, TV, ETC., EQUIP.	39014	2913	5210	2353	9331	28398	3112	1126	11023
57	ELECTRONIC COMPONENTS	11737	879	1573	702	2820	8573	936	335	3320
58	MISC. ELECTRICAL MACH.	9687	676	1617	738	2837	8503	948	335	3313
59	MOTOR VEHICLES, EQUIP.	180691	12066	29444	14585	51187	158671	16989	6214	63993
60	AIRCRAFT & PARTS	562	39	107	52	197	684	69	22	245
61	OTHER TRANSPORT. EQUIP.	14076	988	2678	1297	4934	17085	1735	554	6121
62	PROFESS., SCIEN. INSTRU.	28194	2258	4498	1628	7987	23543	2000	809	8900
63	MEDICAL, PHOTO. EQUIP.	11637	872	1438	853	2551	7668	1028	379	3000
64	MISC. MANUFACTURING	112289	8199	15953	7261	28082	84558	11070	3355	32662
65	TRANSPORT. & WAREHOUSING	491782	37782	53007	23656	94196	266893	37469	14334	106415
66	COMMUNICA.,EXC. BRDCAST.	109310	8465	11293	5782	20468	62644	7399	3620	24189
67	RADIO & TV BROADCASTING	403	69	32	32	184	407	54	11	123
68	ELEC.,GAS,WATER,SAN.SER.	185761	14199	29130	13161	51142	142528	13830	6447	56486
69	WHOLESALE & RETAIL TRADE	2626571	190605	352951	158655	616974	1729413	178925	86061	698755
70	FINANCE & INSURANCE	306799	22786	38834	18903	69428	206088	20873	9251	77194
71	REAL ESTATE & RENTAL	1257858	100413	102004	54700	185725	564725	72826	39059	213958
72	HOTELS; PERSONAL SERV.	313890	23897	41812	18261	80531	255131	25855	13270	96197
73	BUSINESS SERVICES	68234	5255	12442	6746	21603	57485	6390	2233	22134
74	RESEARCH & DEVELOPMENT	0	0	0	0	0	0	0	0	0
75	AUTO. REPAIR & SERVICES	105987	7263	18261	8529	31816	95048	10647	3809	37696
76	AMUSEMENTS	201852	10893	19602	8271	39713	96090	17026	3725	48296
77	MED.,EDUC. SERVICES	482655	36554	65239	31590	114878	331762	36182	15705	132023
78	FEDERAL GOV'T ENTERPRISE	18846	1400	2292	1209	4035	11458	1508	690	4538
79	STATE & LOCAL GOV'T ENT.	4056	289	733	313	1300	3943	435	140	1524
80	IMPORTS	65739	4783	7905	3486	14015	38887	4086	1987	15710
81	BUS.TRAVEL, ENT., GIFTS.	0	0	0	0	0	0	0	0	0
82	OFFICE SUPPLIES	0	0	0	0	0	0	0	0	0
83	SCRAP & USED GOODS	0	0	0	0	0	0	0	0	0
84	GOVERNMENT INDUSTRY	-37372	-3189	-2402	-2144	-6249	-33677	-2267	-1750	-7421
85	REST OF WORLD INDUSTRY	155760	11757	42820	4339	50966	132116	4011	6670	55894
86	HOUSEHOLD INDUSTRY	0	0	0	0	0	0	0	0	0
87	INVENTORY VALUATION ADJ.	0	0	0	0	0	0	0	0	0
88	STATE TOTAL	11497314	850586	1525927	661596	2611877	7461235	780715	370081	3012437

TABLE C.1

STATE ESTIMATES OF 1947
PERSONAL CONSUMPTION EXPENDITURES
(THOUSANDS OF CURRENT DOLLARS)

INDUSTRY TITLE	46 WASHINGTON	47 WEST VIRGINIA	48 WISCONSIN	49 WYOMING	50 ALASKA	51 HAWAII	52 NO STATE ALLOCATION	53 NATIONAL TOTAL
1 LIVESTOCK & PRDTS.	56949	31384	57071	6524	0	0	0	2790927
2 OTHER AGRICULTURE PRDTS.	61915	43507	74897	7759	0	0	0	3250166
3 FORESTRY & FISHERIES	2897	1583	3372	336	0	0	0	151656
4 AGRI.,FORES.,FISH. SERV.	0	0	0	0	0	0	0	0
5 IRON,FERRO.ORES MINING	0	0	0	0	0	0	0	0
6 NONFERROUS ORES MINING	0	0	0	0	0	0	0	0
7 COAL MINING	7625	6737	17356	1087	0	0	0	618308
8 CRUDE PETRO.,NATURAL GAS	0	376	0	652	0	0	0	33455
9 STONE & CLAY MINING	253	125	284	30	0	0	0	11699
10 CHEM.&FERT. MIN. MINING	0	0	0	0	0	0	0	0
11 NEW CONSTRUCTION	0	0	0	0	0	0	0	0
12 MAINT. & REPAIR CONSTR.	0	0	0	0	0	0	0	0
13 ORDNANCE & ACCESSORIES	2818	913	2284	328	0	0	0	101820
14 FOOD & KINDRED PRDTS.	583855	339292	684114	72923	0	0	0	31361200
15 TOBACCO MANUFACTURES	44428	33184	56796	4991	0	0	0	2652567
16 FABRICS	28648	15706	26493	3115	0	0	0	1234871
17 TEXTILE PRDTS.	10924	3461	12916	1442	0	0	0	490734
18 APPAREL	180663	94755	188085	19829	0	0	0	8702753
19 MISC. TEXTILE PRDTS.	16120	9159	16373	1897	0	0	0	765480
20 LUMBER & WOOD PRDTS.	7237	8425	8438	942	0	0	0	454309
21 WOODEN CONTAINERS	109	127	127	14	0	0	0	6824
22 HOUSEHOLD FURNITURE	25260	17488	32382	2843	0	0	0	1454219
23 OTHER FURNITURE	1076	571	1061	123	0	0	0	47749
24 PAPER & ALLIED PRDTS.	4252	2381	4449	488	0	0	0	204660
25 PAPERBOARD CONTAINERS	3270	1674	3400	384	0	0	0	164310
26 PRINTING & PUBLISHING	32854	12604	33977	3736	0	0	0	1472563
27 CHEMICALS,SELECT. PRDTS.	2733	1728	3133	318	0	0	0	136921
28 PLASTICS & SYNTHETICS	55	30	62	6	0	0	0	2768
29 DRUGS & COSMETICS	37279	22406	38799	4322	0	0	0	1799934
30 PAINT & ALLIED PRDTS.	485	318	706	58	0	0	0	29999
31 PETROLEUM, RELATED INDS.	44660	25215	60039	5493	0	0	0	2307810
32 RUBBER, MISC. PLASTICS	19017	10319	19033	2326	0	0	0	815494
33 LEATHER TANNING & PRDTS.	32	18	33	4	0	0	0	1507
34 FOOTWEAR, LEATHER PRDTS.	43514	24234	45376	4777	0	0	0	2053004
35 GLASS & GLASS PRDTS.	3177	1669	3091	362	0	0	0	140988
36 STONE & CLAY PRDTS.	3522	2006	4115	421	0	0	0	173096
37 PRIMARY IRON, STEEL MFR.	762	603	1511	106	0	0	0	54434
38 PRIMARY NONFERROUS MFR.	1130	621	1169	130	0	0	0	55757

#	Industry	C1	C2	C3	C4	C5	C6	C7	C8
39	METAL CONTAINERS	387	213	390	45	0	0	0	17636
40	FABRICATED METAL PRDTS.	2776	3696	4013	344	0	0	0	192372
41	SCREW MACH. PRDTS., ETC.	4572	2844	4808	527	0	0	0	218408
42	OTHER FAB. METAL PRDTS.	5075	2796	5114	588	0	0	0	231022
43	ENGINES & TURBINES	609	313	608	70	0	0	0	25019
44	FARM MACH. & EQUIP.	235	121	220	27	0	0	0	9936
45	CONSTRUC. MACH. & EQUIP.	64	33	59	7	0	0	0	2687
46	MATERIAL HANDLING MACH.					0	0	0	41846
47	METALWORKING MACHINERY	969	486	931	112	0	0	0	13865
48	SPECIAL MACH. & EQUIP.	321	161	308	37	0	0	0	12173
49	GENERAL MACH. & EQUIP.	286	167	238	32	0	0	0	19053
50	MACHINE SHOP PRDTS.	467	248	455	59	0	0	0	25419
51	OFFICE, COMPUT. MACHINES	588	298	569	68	0	0	0	6072
52	SERVICE IND. MACHINES	65	119	124	8	0	0	0	6944
53	ELECT. TRANSMISS. EQUIP.	163	83	154	19	0	0	0	1675671
54	HOUSEHOLD APPLIANCES	39330	22974	32743	4348	0	0	0	190428
55	ELECTRIC LIGHTING EQUIP.	4555	2260	4228	526	0	0	0	595546
56	RADIO, TV, ETC., EQUIP.	13335	6456	13605	1591	0	0	0	179175
57	ELECTRONIC COMPONENTS	4012	1944	4077	478	0	0	0	163757
58	MISC. ELECTRICAL MACH.	3972	2050	3842	490	0	0	0	3112110
59	MOTOR VEHICLES, EQUIP.	71073	40088	77379	8637	0	0	0	11419
60	AIRCRAFT & PARTS	278	143	277	32	0	0	0	285552
61	OTHER TRANSPORT. EQUIP.	6945	3576	6932	796	0	0	0	425741
62	PROFESS., SCIEN. INSTRU.	8395	4841	8976	981	0	0	0	181413
63	MEDICAL, PHOTO. EQUIP.	4362	1742	4450	498	0	0	0	1806386
64	MISC. MANUFACTURING	45765	19758	40103	5315	0	0	0	6572247
65	TRANSPORT. & WAREHOUSING	149130	61527	135102	16312	0	0	0	1478609
66	COMMUNICA.,EXC. BRDCAST.	30689	13093	34103	3461	0	0	0	8840
67	RADIO & TV BROADCASTING	145	87	126	12	0	0	0	2910406
68	ELEC.,GAS,WATER,SAN.SER.	57121	33187	71027	6684	0	0	0	36873168
69	WHOLESALE & RETAIL TRADE	729269	429226	841159	88061	0	0	0	4440265
70	FINANCE & INSURANCE	86107	46383	104364	-10128	0	0	0	15278003
71	REAL ESTATE & RENTAL	305852	117009	343453	32773	0	0	0	5237641
72	HOTELS; PERSONAL SERV.	97405	50631	110722	16678	0	0	0	1285428
73	BUSINESS SERVICES	25276	13928	35762	3195	0	0	0	1820827
74	RESEARCH & DEVELOPMENT					0	0	0	2773861
75	AUTO. REPAIR & SERVICES	44643	23708	43459	5600	0	0	0	7215800
76	AMUSEMENTS	57236	28861	48183	6429	0	0	0	270000
77	MED.,EDUC. SERVICES	146349	77092	168812	17233	0	0	0	72662
78	FEDERAL GOV'T ENTERPRISE	6285	2633	6331	737	0	0	0	866097
79	STATE & LOCAL GOV'T ENT.	1818	909	1676	221	0	0	0	0
80	IMPORTS	16392	9430	19040	2023	0	0	0	0
81	BUS.TRAVEL, ENT., GIFTS.	0	0	0	0	0	0	0	0
82	OFFICE SUPPLIES	0	0	0	0	0	0	0	0
83	SCRAP & USED GOODS	0	0	0	0	0	0	0	0
84	GOVERNMENT INDUSTRY	0	0	0	0	0	0	0	0
85	REST OF WORLD INDUSTRY	-15242	-4106	-16060	-1733	0	0	0	-718002
86	HOUSEHOLD INDUSTRY	22121	17736	26662	2151	0	0	0	2348000
87	INVENTORY VALUATION ADJ.	0	0	0	0	0	0	0	0
88	STATE TOTAL	3206714	1751363	3589465	383366	0	0	0	1617725856

TABLE C.2

STATE ESTIMATES OF 1958
PERSONAL CONSUMPTION EXPENDITURES
(THOUSANDS OF CURRENT DOLLARS)

INDUSTRY TITLE	1 ALABAMA	2 ARIZONA	3 ARKANSAS	4 CALIFORNIA	5 COLORADO	6 CONNECTICUT	7 DELAWARE	8 DISTRICT OF COLUMBIA	9 FLORIDA
1 LIVESTOCK & PRDTS.	31594	16388	19493	206784	24226	27356	6669	16298	59675
2 OTHER AGRICULTURE PRDTS.	37564	16609	22640	229160	25599	36315	5959	11024	59661
3 FORESTRY & FISHERIES	3720	1937	2040	28868	2975	4764	650	1445	6636
4 AGRI.,FORES.,FISH. SERV.	0	0	0	0	0	0	0	0	0
5 IRON, FERRO. ORES MINING	0	0	0	0	0	0	0	0	0
6 NONFERROUS ORES MINING	0	0	0	0	0	0	0	0	0
7 COAL MINING	3800	1018	2440	10918	1500	4469	449	861	5623
8 CRUDE PETRO.,NATURAL GAS			0	0	0	0	0	0	0
9 STONE & CLAY MINING	245	136	131	2025	207	254	42	96	430
10 CHEM.&FERT. MIN. MINING	18	3	10	48	19	8	4	2	55
11 NEW CONSTRUCTION	0	0	0	0	0	0	0	0	0
12 MAINT. & REPAIR CONSTR.	0	0	0	0	0	0	0	0	0
13 ORDNANCE & ACCESSORIES	1788	1302	864	20377	2000	2657	383	883	3373
14 FOOD & KINDRED PRDTS.	618238	308656	344936	4548142	487393	758289	107547	227598	1105986
15 TOBACCO MANUFACTURES	65006	25670	36508	375469	39300	72299	10219	20781	108419
16 FABRICS	11372	5443	6145	79505	8379	9959	2013	3997	19581
17 TEXTILE PRDTS.	6976	4856	3239	76171	7515	14374	1572	3891	13657
18 APPAREL	149911	72191	77827	1091987	110130	196585	28330	63076	271306
19 MISC. TEXTILE PRDTS.	15343	7565	8156	113761	11676	18732	2817	6170	27442
20 LUMBER & WOOD PRDTS.	3143	1047	2104	13481	1581	2012	392	634	4276
21 WOODEN CONTAINERS	0	0	0	0	0	0	0	0	0
22 HOUSEHOLD FURNITURE	34343	15451	17755	243020	24178	39111	6507	14206	62660
23 OTHER FURNITURE	1832	950	991	13811	1432	2001	335	651	3162
24 PAPER & ALLIED PRDTS.	12703	5975	6913	85957	9088	13564	2170	4630	22334
25 PAPERBOARD CONTAINERS	494	243	236	3840	384	712	104	199	908
26 PRINTING & PUBLISHING	29278	17399	15128	258815	26324	42022	5561	13670	54659
27 CHEMICALS,SELECT. PRDTS.	3285	1502	1851	21302	2282	3170	533	1047	5491
28 PLASTICS & SYNTHETICS	141	70	75	1006	106	176	25	51	251
29 DRUGS & COSMETICS	59300	27005	33240	382654	40957	54124	9620	19911	100983
30 PAINT & ALLIED PRDTS.	227	93	124	1336	142	333	41	90	413
31 PETROLEUM, RELATED INDS.	99199	47694	54220	695862	73812	117661	17455	32640	168072
32 RUBBER, MISC. PLASTICS	19274	9808	10297	146864	15302	19566	3538	7397	33860
33 LEATHER TANNING & PRDTS.	0	0	0	0	0	0	0	0	0
34 FOOTWEAR, LEATHER PRDTS.	36998	18339	19941	270185	27897	41668	6471	13542	64140
35 GLASS & GLASS PRDTS.	1741	975	927	15159	1508	2137	329	700	3107
36 STONE & CLAY PRDTS.	2957	1454	1619	21247	2233	3614	520	1026	5056
37 PRIMARY IRON, STEEL MFR.	269	90	167	1093	134	317	36	73	416
38 PRIMARY NONFERROUS MFR.	160	76	82	1135	116	201	31	61	288

232

#	Industry	1	2	3	4	5	6	7	8	9
39	METAL CONTAINERS	0	0	0	0	0	0	0	0	1413
40	FABRICATED METAL PRDTS.	2213	370	204	998	628	5549	837	411	3554
41	SCREW MACH. PRDTS., ETC.	6263	1389	640	4018	2824	28301	1934	1807	5495
42	OTHER FAB. METAL PRDTS.	9580	2014	989	5846	4241	40926	2956	2774	1836
43	ENGINES & TURBINES	3695	1202	426	1480	1799	22362	878	1144	123
44	FARM MACH. & EQUIP.	207	40	21	125	95	898	69	64	0
45	CONSTRUC. MACH. & EQUIP.	0	0	0	0	0	0	0	0	0
46	MATERIAL HANDLING MACH.	0	0	0	0	0	0	0	0	0
47	METALWORKING MACHINERY	718	149	80	483	342	3344	218	226	414
48	SPECIAL MACH. & EQUIP.	447	94	50	303	214	2099	135	141	257
49	GENERAL MACH. & EQUIP.	0	0	0	0	0	0	0	0	0
50	MACHINE SHOP PRDTS.	0	0	0	0	0	0	0	0	0
51	OFFICE, COMPUT. MACHINES	1399	298	155	918	649	6339	428	430	802
52	SERVICE IND. MACHINES	12610	3564	1320	2286	1340	13005	3012	855	6507
53	ELECT. TRANSMISS. EQUIP.	359	74	39	230	167	1612	114	112	209
54	HOUSEHOLD APPLIANCES	65182	11789	6482	34380	27860	259289	22158	18618	39309
55	ELECTRIC LIGHTING EQUIP.	7594	809	809	4829	3597	34782	2395	2404	4403
56	RADIO, TV, ETC., EQUIP.	34081	8074	3356	20879	15440	152751	9641	9999	18413
57	ELECTRONIC COMPONENTS	3734	881	366	2276	1691	16709	1058	1095	2018
58	MISC. ELECTRICAL MACH.	6741	1490	710	3833	3100	29847	2003	1987	3804
59	MOTOR VEHICLES, EQUIP.	229606	50371	25095	138120	99884	979245	66213	64473	128491
60	AIRCRAFT & PARTS	800	260	92	320	389	4842	190	248	398
61	OTHER TRANSPORT. EQUIP.	21218	6895	2445	8515	10327	128282	5049	6571	10552
62	PROFESS., SCIEN. INSTRU.	9492	2249	893	5408	3955	37813	2820	2484	5204
63	MEDICAL, PHOTO. EQUIP.	10421	2390	1096	7183	5711	56499	2990	3704	5710
64	MISC. MANUFACTURING	59333	13927	6355	40608	30404	302636	17060	19879	32923
65	TRANSPORT. & WAREHOUSING	195227	47444	18778	157721	94278	939542	57584	62434	106027
66	COMMUNICA.,EXC. BRDCAST.	93460	22105	8946	66252	41769	410255	25542	27350	49042
67	RADIO & TV BROADCASTING	0	0	0	0	0	0	0	0	0
68	ELEC.,GAS,WATER,SAN.SER.	213570	43142	19898	110655	84239	782462	68365	55311	122289
69	WHOLESALE & RETAIL TRADE	1502978	312138	150943	1004277	645178	6160117	469712	415728	859764
70	FINANCE & INSURANCE	277370	66735	32399	205818	118854	1223522	76351	76645	150203
71	REAL ESTATE & RENTAL	870437	205735	83779	698602	434715	4348464	236429	281353	457935
72	HOTELS; PERSONAL SERV.	364968	80352	23996	139150	104676	953090	70798	75188	125684
73	BUSINESS SERVICES	43228	8801	4170	25449	22003	206740	14630	14207	25969
74	RESEARCH & DEVELOPMENT	0	0	0	0	0	0	0	0	0
75	AUTO. REPAIR & SERVICES	115311	24992	12255	63723	52522	499186	34941	33523	65711
76	AMUSEMENTS	85371	15620	9441	52536	40400	356882	19223	22530	36163
77	MED.,EDUC. SERVICES	520327	118058	53911	333144	211383	2091595	151330	138696	283832
78	FEDERAL GOV'T ENTERPRISE	14287	3483	1385	10339	7510	72200	4283	4890	7867
79	STATE & LOCAL GOV'T ENT.	8601	1873	876	4237	3922	37521	2504	2513	4765
80	IMPORTS	92889	18975	9098	64829	40632	386570	28275	25719	52041
81	BUS. TRAVEL, ENT., GIFTS.	0	0	0	0	0	0	0	0	0
82	OFFICE SUPPLIES	0	0	0	0	0	0	0	0	0
83	SCRAP & USED GOODS	-341	-75	-37	-203	-148	-1453	-99	-96	-191
84	GOVERNMENT INDUSTRY	0	0	0	0	0	0	0	0	0
85	REST OF WORLD INDUSTRY	-31518	-7122	-2090	-9909	-8578	-167264	-3765	-12648	-5706
86	HOUSEHOLD INDUSTRY	166266	47779	13481	62988	24096	307555	36181	21052	95071
87	INVENTORY VALUATION ADJ.									
88	STATE TOTAL	7230044	1585803	713174	4761096	3680503	29694048	2124547	1993766	3959219

TABLE C.2

STATE ESTIMATES OF 1958
PERSONAL CONSUMPTION EXPENDITURES
(THOUSANDS OF CURRENT DOLLARS)

INDUSTRY TITLE	10 GEORGIA	11 IDAHO	12 ILLINOIS	13 INDIANA	14 IOWA	15 KANSAS	16 KENTUCKY	17 LOUISIANA	18 MAINE
1 LIVESTOCK & PRDTS.	47230	7783	118349	49257	31490	29648	36356	32421	12388
2 OTHER AGRICULTURE PRDTS.	46242	9965	138132	65423	39972	31598	38261	36772	13295
3 FORESTRY & FISHERIES	4724	1035	16660	7057	4135	3383	3667	3833	1609
4 AGRI.,FORES.,FISH.SERV.	0	0	0	0	0	0	0	0	0
5 IRON,FERRO.ORES MINING	0	0	0	0	0	0	0	0	0
6 NONFERROUS ORES MINING	0	0	0	0	0	0	0	0	0
7 COAL MINING	4588	743	16576	8614	5843	4455	3803	3620	2542
8 CRUDE PETRO.,NATURAL GAS	0	0	0	0	0	0	0	0	0
9 STONE & CLAY MINING	299	74	1107	458	263	213	230	253	79
10 CHEM.&FERT.MIN.MINING	8	7	28	47	7	18	6	27	3
11 NEW CONSTRUCTION	0	0	0	0	0	0	0	0	0
12 MAINT.& REPAIR CONSTR.	0	0	0	0	0	0	0	0	0
13 ORDNANCE & ACCESSORIES	2252	718	10034	4047	2227	1802	1725	1929	765
14 FOOD & KINDRED PRDTS.	769293	173508	2648171	1173090	674090	558450	604229	639567	260994
15 TOBACCO MANUFACTURES	79909	14079	242859	105382	61312	49519	63372	65017	26056
16 FABRICS	14433	3150	39951	17686	10379	8237	11391	11573	3298
17 TEXTILE PRDTS.	8859	2656	50629	21701	12255	9702	6582	7707	3768
18 APPAREL	190069	39521	677281	280056	158383	127785	148131	156700	56242
19 MISC.TEXTILE PRDTS.	19232	4309	64209	26909	15357	12288	14995	15954	5562
20 LUMBER & WOOD PRDTS.	3799	699	6604	3278	2149	1643	3297	2878	1266
21 WOODEN CONTAINERS	0	0	0	0	0	0	0	0	0
22 HOUSEHOLD FURNITURE	43578	8356	150380	61435	34120	27840	33734	35950	11182
23 OTHER FURNITURE	2310	532	7795	3412	1976	1565	1836	1872	643
24 PAPER & ALLIED PRDTS.	15869	3324	48019	20821	12172	9737	12405	13035	4689
25 PAPERBOARD CONTAINERS	627	137	2186	910	485	397	489	522	208
26 PRINTING & PUBLISHING	36976	9518	153939	63990	36927	29652	28349	31007	13541
27 CHEMICALS,SELECT.PRDTS.	4065	860	12578	5605	3301	2634	3243	3293	1145
28 PLASTICS & SYNTHETICS	177	40	604	264	151	121	139	146	59
29 DRUGS & COSMETICS	73419	15340	210089	91962	54296	43475	58135	59984	19548
30 PAINT & ALLIED PRDTS.	288	53	1100	469	275	221	226	235	111
31 PETROLEUM,RELATED INDS.	124683	28311	436210	204898	124196	97082	100367	99652	44739
32 RUBBER,MISC.PLASTICS	24197	5837	76397	33305	19381	15366	19124	19833	6491
33 LEATHER TANNING & PRDTS.	0	0	0	0	0	0	0	0	0
34 FOOTWEAR,LEATHER PRDTS.	46462	10169	157858	67741	39020	31230	36697	37784	12976
35 GLASS & GLASS PRDTS.	2209	530	7525	3235	1848	1466	1735	1803	637
36 STONE & CLAY PRDTS.	3697	845	12934	5689	3271	2602	2940	3004	1139
37 PRIMARY IRON,STEEL MFR.	329	61	1191	594	394	302	269	261	163
38 PRIMARY NONFERROUS MFR.	202	42	630	268	150	121	157	167	64

#	Industry									
39	METAL CONTAINERS	1744	0	0	0	0	0	0	0	0
40	FABRICATED METAL PRDTS.	4489	273	3809	1656	993	784	1438	1351	365
41	SCREW MACH. PRDTS., ETC.	6888	990	14090	6082	3499	2775	3540	3645	1203
42	OTHER FAB. METAL PRDTS.	2307	1563	22445	9739	5608	4463	5436	5636	1881
43	ENGINES & TURBINES	154	532	6896	2820	1560	1250	1808	2051	559
44	FARM MACH. & EQUIP.		36	491	221	132	103	124	124	43
45	CONSTRUC. MACH. & EQUIP.	0	0	0	0	0	0	0	0	0
46	MATERIAL HANDLING MACH.		0	0	0	0	0	0	0	0
47	METALWORKING MACHINERY	523	127	1882	819	465	368	416	426	148
48	SPECIAL MACH. & EQUIP.	325	79	1182	513	290	230	259	265	92
49	GENERAL MACH. & EQUIP.	0	0	0	0	0	0	0	0	0
50	MACHINE SHOP PRDTS.	0	0	3045	0	0	0	0	0	0
51	OFFICE, COMPUT. MACHINES	1016	242	3545	1542	888	702	808	827	287
52	SERVICE IND. MACHINES	8010	511	14185	5338	2843	2372	5901	7063	523
53	ELECT. TRANSMISS. EQUIP.	264	63	895	394	229	181	211	214	74
54	HOUSEHOLD APPLIANCES	48851	10861	135554	60439	35197	27934	39502	39200	12490
55	ELECTRIC LIGHTING EQUIP.	5542	1345	18782	8202	4794	3781	4405	4507	1565
56	RADIO, TV, ETC., EQUIP.	23096	5555	86565	35839	20280	16336	17776	19330	6580
57	ELECTRONIC COMPONENTS	2528	607	9462	3918	2216	1786	1943	2118	717
58	MISC. ELECTRICAL MACH.	4782	1183	15321	6618	3838	3049	3762	3927	1274
59	MOTOR VEHICLES, EQUIP.	162931	37798	599345	251744	142266	114232	128772	137734	43929
60	AIRCRAFT & PARTS	499	115	1493	611	338	271	391	444	121
61	OTHER TRANSPORT. EQUIP.	13254	3058	39644	16219	8974	7188	10388	11778	3213
62	PROFESS., SCIEN. INSTRU.	6410	1417	19946	8391	4886	3937	4931	5556	1711
63	MEDICAL, PHOTO. EQUIP.	7220	2065	30400	12846	7427	5929	5638	6012	2261
64	MISC. MANUFACTURING	41309	10993	155599	64511	36287	29161	32251	34449	12041
65	TRANSPORT. & WAREHOUSING	132235	32103	498253	205232	117319	95417	102010	111573	47165
66	COMMUNICA.,EXC. BRDCAST.	61982	14390	240246	99484	57509	46812	47040	52287	21760
67	RADIO & TV BROADCASTING		0	0	0	0	0	0	0	0
68	ELEC.,GAS,WATER,SAN.SER.	151945	31011	514312	226798	135645	108511	119162	125124	41089
69	WHOLESALE & RETAIL TRADE	1066964	238191	3665869	1608949	931925	747325	845176	881774	334366
70	FINANCE & INSURANCE	189898	41605	761286	309107	174594	140169	145930	161101	59281
71	REAL ESTATE & RENTAL	573409	143548	2532531	1036387	591003	482535	434974	488216	228340
72	HOTELS; PERSONAL SERV.	167039	35363	564109	207354	119186	95619	124365	141989	54016
73	BUSINESS SERVICES	31821	8477	129435	56529	33004	26339	25200	26017	8544
74	RESEARCH & DEVELOPMENT		0	0	0	0	0	0	0	0
75	AUTO. REPAIR & SERVICES	82813	20491	254250	111667	65258	51616	67464	67464	21786
76	AMUSEMENTS	42057	13107	176056	79610	39097	35650	32188	42060	14015
77	MED.,EDUC. SERVICES	358091	75041	1236403	520010	301515	241065	281233	297766	100597
78	FEDERAL GOV'T ENTERPRISE	9866	2693	18080	16286	9736	7727	7654	8183	3483
79	STATE & LOCAL GOV'T ENT.	5989	1476	18278	7849	4551	3640	4656	4963	1445
80	IMPORTS	63909	14606	226689	99368	56506	45974	50131	54018	20927
81	BUS.TRAVEL, ENT., GIFTS.	0	0	0	0	0	0	0	0	0
82	OFFICE SUPPLIES	0	0	0	0	0	0	0	0	0
83	SCRAP & USED GOODS	-242	-56	-880	-369	-209	-168	-191	-197	-64
84	GOVERNMENT INDUSTRY	0	0	0	0	0	0	0	0	0
85	REST OF WORLD INDUSTRY	-8601	-6217	-54309	-16679	-9314	-6136	-8320	-10159	-7177
86	HOUSEHOLD INDUSTRY	132510	8318	144407	59194	35605	31316	43620	99282	17989
87	INVENTORY VALUATION ADJ.	0	0	0	0	0	0	0	0	0
88	STATE TOTAL	4973752	1095762	17436928	7452841	4295765	3482795	3826034	4119917	1563741

TABLE C.2

STATE ESTIMATES OF 1958
PERSONAL CONSUMPTION EXPENDITURES
(THOUSANDS OF CURRENT DOLLARS)

INDUSTRY TITLE	19 MARYLAND	20 MASSA-CHUSETTS	21 MICHIGAN	22 MINNESOTA	23 MISSISSIPPI	24 MISSOURI	25 MONTANA	26 NEBRASKA	27 NEVADA
1 LIVESTOCK & PRDTS.	38703	63638	79344	38044	22898	51619	9002	18915	6369
2 OTHER AGRICULTURE PRDTS.	39765	73632	103603	46172	24533	60512	10413	20518	4572
3 FORESTRY & FISHERIES	4474	9804	11819	5046	2167	6705	1093	2143	531
4 AGRI.,FORES.,FISH.SERV.	0	0	0	0	0	0	0	0	0
5 IRON, FERRO. ORES MINING	0	0	0	0	0	0	0	0	0
6 NONFERROUS ORES MINING	0	0	0	0	0	0	0	0	0
7 COAL MINING	2998	9301	12675	6384	2720	8715	766	3033	251
8 CRUDE PETRO.,NATURAL GAS	0	0	0	0	0	0	0	0	0
9 STONE & CLAY MINING	297	499	786	320	139	441	77	133	35
10 CHEM.&FERT. MIN. MINING	34	17	80	9	10	12	10	4	5
11 NEW CONSTRUCTION	0	0	0	0	0	0	0	0	0
12 MAINT. & REPAIR CONSTR.	0	0	0	0	0	0	0	0	0
13 ORDNANCE & ACCESSORIES	2715	5005	7093	2820	878	3563	752	1116	359
14 FOOD & KINDRED PRDTS.	740606	1559757	1947203	815259	366407	1082258	184824	348598	87829
15 TOBACCO MANUFACTURES	71240	148515	175492	74455	38824	99029	14577	31498	6460
16 FABRICS	14077	19863	29102	12419	6520	16032	3227	5301	1408
17 TEXTILE PRDTS.	11394	27088	36719	14965	3298	18754	2793	6057	1320
18 APPAREL	200846	387289	480237	195646	81515	252238	41079	80464	19028
19 MISC. TEXTILE PRDTS.	19785	37064	45822	18900	8475	24407	4450	7734	2011
20 LUMBER & WOOD PRDTS.	2560	3831	4995	2365	2447	3210	710	1104	271
21 WOODEN CONTAINERS	0	0	0	0	0	0	0	0	0
22 HOUSEHOLD FURNITURE	45796	78196	106531	42879	18215	55257	8606	17255	4103
23 OTHER FURNITURE	2323	3922	5667	2376	1041	3028	548	996	242
24 PAPER & ALLIED PRDTS.	15165	27443	34595	14716	7227	19503	3443	6193	1501
25 PAPERBOARD CONTAINERS	733	1359	1578	619	238	771	142	241	67
26 PRINTING & PUBLISHING	39234	84574	108672	45439	15727	59746	9945	18687	4534
27 CHEMICALS,SELECT. PRDTS.	3686	6415	9185	3938	1953	5215	883	1682	378
28 PLASTICS & SYNTHETICS	179	355	440	184	77	240	41	76	18
29 DRUGS & COSMETICS	66930	110823	151720	65180	35182	87128	15833	27712	6780
30 PAINT & ALLIED PRDTS.	286	649	784	334	131	439	55	140	24
31 PETROLEUM, RELATED INDS.	119715	230579	325199	144396	56633	185745	29179	63165	12733
32 RUBBER, MISC. PLASTICS	24644	37951	55363	23389	10688	30076	5990	9790	2657
33 LEATHER TANNING & PRDTS.	0	0	0	0	0	0	0	0	0
34 FOOTWEAR, LEATHER PRDTS.	45585	83016	113628	47331	21146	61292	10499	19865	4710
35 GLASS & GLASS PRDTS.	2292	4181	5417	2244	963	2856	547	925	258
36 STONE & CLAY PRDTS.	3602	7059	9445	3914	1707	5149	867	1639	376
37 PRIMARY IRON, STEEL MFR.	244	644	897	438	184	591	63	204	23
38 PRIMARY NONFERROUS MFR.	214	392	455	185	85	240	43	75	20

39 METAL CONTAINERS	1383	1909	2744	1191	915	1571	273	509	0
40 FABRICATED METAL PRDTS.	4461	7933	10141	4242	2015	5443	1021	1757	109
41 SCREW MACH. PRDTS., ETC.	6889	11544	16253	6793	3089	8751	1614	2826	481
42 OTHER FAB. METAL PRDTS.	2979	2637	4866	1951	876	2460	559	782	719
43 ENGINES & TURBINES	146	247	360	156	73	200	37	67	363
44 FARM MACH. & EQUIP.	0	0	0	0	0	0	0	0	16
45 CONSTRUC. MACH. & EQUIP.	0	0	0	0	0	0	0	0	0
46 MATERIAL HANDLING MACH.	553	928	1372	564	229	708	131	232	0
47 METALWORKING MACHINERY	347	581	861	352	142	441	82	144	59
48 SPECIAL MACH. & EQUIP.	0	0	0	0	0	0	0	0	37
49 GENERAL MACH. & EQUIP.	0	0	0	0	0	0	0	0	0
50 MACHINE SHOP PRDTS.	1070	1765	2570	1065	447	1346	250	446	0
51 OFFICE, COMPUT. MACHINES	9657	4660	9733	3751	3036	4873	520	1427	112
52 SERVICE IND. MACHINES	267	446	651	274	120	348	65	115	236
53 ELECT. TRANSMISS. EQUIP.	44542	67993	99408	42112	23393	54312	10967	17782	29
54 HOUSEHOLD APPLIANCES	5602	9367	13607	5734	2520	7324	1391	2420	4598
55 ELECTRIC LIGHTING EQUIP.	23819	41445	61223	25076	9898	32790	5781	10227	615
56 RADIO, TV, ETC., EQUIP.	2597	4524	6693	2740	1085	3587	632	1117	2681
57 ELECTRONIC COMPONENTS	4959	7366	11066	4652	2076	5981	1215	1939	292
58 MISC. ELECTRICAL MACH.	175450	262095	429859	175289	68095	221902	38883	71801	542
59 MOTOR VEHICLES, EQUIP.	645	571	1054	423	190	533	121	169	17944
60 AIRCRAFT & PARTS	17102	15184	27983	11224	5038	14150	3213	4497	79
61 OTHER TRANSPORT. EQUIP.	6345	10980	14151	5935	2961	7780	1474	2498	2084
62 PROFESS., SCIEN. INSTRU.	7666	13981	21703	9061	3110	11721	2161	3752	654
63 MEDICAL, PHOTO. EQUIP.	44636	78470	110608	45016	17630	57623	11434	18264	998
64 MISC. MANUFACTURING	132672	323476	351191	145088	60662	193220	33897	59893	5304
65 TRANSPORT. & WAREHOUSING	63555	135562	168984	71053	26579	95285	15146	29413	15879
66 COMMUNICA.-EXC. BRDCAST.	139053	228912	371633	161675	72395	216956	32303	69364	6983
67 RADIO & TV BROADCASTING	1052309	2001367	2672740	1123522	492414	1465445	247819	472682	13760
68 ELEC.,GAS,WATER,SAN.SER.	213217	388721	537677	215566	79089	281073	44274	88041	110955
69 WHOLESALE & RETAIL TRADE	600233	1436149	1775404	738689	244702	990693	151534	301199	21779
70 FINANCE & INSURANCE	159849	294197	365009	166980	72861	213733	39674	64096	72865
71 REAL ESTATE & RENTAL	28937	50357	94165	38842	15643	54164	8704	16580	69363
72 HOTELS; PERSONAL SERV.									3724
73 BUSINESS SERVICES									
74 RESEARCH & DEVELOPMENT									
75 AUTO. REPAIR & SERVICES	85156	122015	184944	78518	36137	100693	20970	32981	9197
76 AMUSEMENTS	60717	101661	143916	49448	18162	63217	13640	19625	35203
77 MED.-EDUC. SERVICES	376715	657252	877320	366182	158610	481538	78190	152641	39853
78 FEDERAL GOV'T ENTERPRISE	9724	20877	27029	11776	4534	15538	2822	4978	1260
79 STATE & LOCAL GOV'T ENT.	6155	8207	13163	5538	2587	7203	1518	2306	672
80 IMPORTS	63911	131023	165358	68645	29546	90216	15340	28670	6979
81 BUS.TRAVEL, ENT., GIFTS.	0	0	0	0	0	0	0	0	0
82 OFFICE SUPPLIES	0	0	0	0	0	0	0	0	0
83 SCRAP & USED GOODS	-260	-386	-631	-257	-101	-326	-57	-105	-27
84 GOVERNMENT INDUSTRY	0	0	0	0	0	0	0	0	0
85 REST OF WORLD INDUSTRY	-14565	-24208	-68359	-32220	-3193	-17054	-8710	-5784	-10159
86 HOUSEHOLD INDUSTRY	71787	83583	110989	48651	63845	64359	9015	19955	4452
87 INVENTORY VALUATION ADJ.	0	0	0	0	0	0	0	0	0
88 STATE TOTAL	4930402	9526052	12502984	5235663	2253138	6904563	1148360	2194570	609563

237

TABLE C.2

STATE ESTIMATES OF 1958
PERSONAL CONSUMPTION EXPENDITURES
(THOUSANDS OF CURRENT DOLLARS)

INDUSTRY TITLE	28 NEW HAMPSHIRE	29 NEW JERSEY	30 NEW MEXICO	31 NEW YORK	32 NORTH CAROLINA	33 NORTH DAKOTA	34 OHIO	35 OKLAHOMA	36 OREGON
1 LIVESTOCK & PRDTS.	8403	71894	13628	210472	54327	8346	99881	29737	20648
2 OTHER AGRICULTURE PRDTS.	8682	89880	12522	256450	55294	9114	128312	31475	27196
3 FORESTRY & FISHERIES	1081	11684	1394	33064	5208	844	15003	3283	3083
4 AGRI.,FORES.,FISH. SERV.	0	0	0	0	0	0	0	0	0
5 IRON, FERRO. ORES MINING	0	0	0	0	0	0	0	0	0
6 NONFERROUS ORES MINING	0	0	0	0	0	0	0	0	0
7 COAL MINING	1500	9845	817	29847	5502	1385	16200	3001	1741
8 CRUDE PETRO.,NATURAL GAS	0	0	0	0	0	0	0	0	0
9 STONE & CLAY MINING	54	620	99	1723	318	51	986	209	220
10 CHEM.&FERT. MIN. MINING	2	83	2	265	9	7	26	19	5
11 NEW CONSTRUCTION	0	0	0	0	0	0	0	0	0
12 MAINT. & REPAIR CONSTR.	0	0	0	0	0	0	0	0	0
13 ORDNANCE & ACCESSORIES	546	6303	933	17286	2367	427	8870	1649	2197
14 FOOD & KINDRED PRDTS.	174235	1912492	223516	5457591	861629	144253	2398477	545694	495681
15 TOBACCO MANUFACTURES	17300	173247	18058	493163	90456	12245	223526	55069	41882
16 FABRICS	2211	23902	3965	66506	16279	2155	36817	9956	9143
17 TEXTILE PRDTS.	2709	35007	3602	95557	8819	2463	46083	6579	8035
18 APPAREL	39214	483922	52261	1331127	208393	31170	602316	134580	118495
19 MISC. TEXTILE PRDTS.	3883	45685	5462	125886	21108	3034	57694	13653	12714
20 LUMBER & WOOD PRDTS.	722	4245	793	12827	4762	509	6232	2444	1836
21 WOODEN CONTAINERS	0	0	0	0	0	0	0	0	0
22 HOUSEHOLD FURNITURE	7880	95948	10805	264932	47873	6517	134249	31023	26034
23 OTHER FURNITURE	440	4762	686	13232	2621	411	7120	1618	1570
24 PAPER & ALLIED PRDTS.	3127	32418	4280	91761	17665	2435	43995	11118	9712
25 PAPERBOARD CONTAINERS	151	1663	171	4502	689	90	1994	457	425
26 PRINTING & PUBLISHING	9172	101761	12420	288691	39755	7232	137323	26474	28283
27 CHEMICALS,SELECT. PRDTS.	754	7529	1083	21320	4650	674	11690	2806	2473
28 PLASTICS & SYNTHETICS	40	421	50	1178	197	30	560	125	116
29 DRUGS & COSMETICS	12766	130143	19414	369835	82735	10956	193234	51016	44156
30 PAINT & ALLIED PRDTS.	73	801	69	2240	319	55	993	203	154
31 PETROLEUM, RELATED INDS.	29255	270569	34581	767131	145007	27289	411946	86782	81409
32 RUBBER, MISC. PLASTICS	4436	45813	7145	127806	27191	3988	69830	17085	16867
33 LEATHER TANNING & PRDTS.	0	0	0	0	0	0	0	0	0
34 FOOTWEAR, LEATHER PRDTS.	8862	101112	13272	279209	52120	7878	143198	32329	30084
35 GLASS & GLASS PRDTS.	444	5163	694	14281	2472	374	6814	1554	1609
36 STONE & CLAY PRDTS.	789	8581	1069	23763	4207	662	11903	2569	2448
37 PRIMARY IRON, STEEL MFR.	98	708	70	2100	388	92	1141	219	152
38 PRIMARY NONFERROUS MFR.	44	475	54	1313	223	29	576	144	126

	C1	C2	C3	C4	C5	C6	C7	C8	C9
39 METAL CONTAINERS	0	0	0	0	0	0	0	0	0
40 FABRICATED METAL PRDTS.	745	1168	3475	206	2105	6224	312	2187	254
41 SCREW MACH. PRDTS., ETC.	2994	3134	12807	706	5065	27057	1283	9753	836
42 OTHER FAB. METAL PRDTS.	4616	4841	20513	1137	7728	38893	1993	13960	1288
43 ENGINES & TURBINES	1832	1757	6092	303	2426	8674	835	3101	392
44 FARM MACH. & EQUIP.	104	107	453	28	178	830	47	295	29
45 CONSTRUC. MACH. & EQUIP.	0	0	0	0	0	0	0	0	0
46 MATERIAL HANDLING MACH.	0	0	0	0	0	0	0	0	0
47 METALWORKING MACHINERY	380	369	1719	96	592	3128	163	1139	104
48 SPECIAL MACH. & EQUIP.	238	230	1078	59	367	1961	102	716	65
49 GENERAL MACH. & EQUIP.	0	0	0	0	0	0	0	0	0
50 MACHINE SHOP PRDTS.	0	0	0	0	0	0	0	0	0
51 OFFICE, COMPUT. MACHINES	715	716	3211	186	1150	6006	311	2173	198
52 SERVICE IND. MACHINES	1515	6003	12205	487	7714	15674	615	5823	398
53 ELECT. TRANSMISS. EQUIP.	184	185	816	48	300	1514	81	546	51
54 HOUSEHOLD APPLIANCES	31017	33862	125846	7255	56752	227016	13496	80325	8310
55 ELECTRIC LIGHTING EQUIP.	3938	3880	17047	1006	6263	31907	1747	11467	1064
56 RADIO, TV, ETC., EQUIP.	16600	16558	77232	3917	24816	139932	7104	50254	4492
57 ELECTRONIC COMPONENTS	1815	1812	8446	427	2712	15255	777	5483	489
58 MISC. ELECTRICAL MACH.	3419	3384	13943	785	5331	24910	1447	8952	868
59 MOTOR VEHICLES, EQUIP.	110571	116355	537736	28736	182377	890134	46845	320988	30556
60 AIRCRAFT & PARTS	397	380	1319	66	525	1878	181	671	85
61 OTHER TRANSPORT. EQUIP.	10521	10092	35032	1745	13944	49952	4794	17857	2256
62 PROFESS., SCIEN. INSTRU.	4210	4670	17722	1009	6843	37169	1770	13074	1174
63 MEDICAL, PHOTO. EQUIP.	6240	5178	27255	1508	7921	47514	2635	17088	1560
64 MISC. MANUFACTURING	32987	29553	138792	7137	45207	269630	14297	97848	8440
65 TRANSPORT. & WAREHOUSING	97069	94442	438682	23135	143258	1130221	43938	397161	32339
66 COMMUNICA., EXC. BRDCAST.	43566	44691	214775	11097	65770	462254	19320	161025	14637
67 RADIO & TV BROADCASTING	0	0	0	0	0	0	0	0	0
68 ELEC.,GAS,WATER,SAN.SER.	89589	106401	472852	27829	168805	762852	39636	265160	26620
69 WHOLESALE & RETAIL TRADE	691742	754932	3342502	192994	1200398	6871030	299792	2440268	224900
70 FINANCE & INSURANCE	126615	135351	672246	34268	205460	1354700	55490	485927	41077
71 REAL ESTATE & RENTAL	449404	414751	2262176	110472	601755	4890653	194868	1699670	153369
72 HOTELS; PERSONAL SERV.	98616	116233	459797	25049	173154	1149353	48678	360054	41253
73 BUSINESS SERVICES	24178	21720	118095	6627	35953	172304	10698	61261	5673
74 RESEARCH & DEVELOPMENT	0	0	0	0	0	0	0	0	0
75 AUTO. REPAIR & SERVICES	58455	58401	233276	13536	93557	410745	24586	147212	14796
76 AMUSEMENTS	37276	34771	155165	8140	44277	513153	15893	148858	10162
77 MED.,EDUC. SERVICES	223609	255453	1100890	60957	392634	2293801	99231	817350	69322
78 FEDERAL GOV'T ENTERPRISE	7903	6968	34220	2004	10776	71439	3528	24911	2313
79 STATE & LOCAL GOV'T ENT.	4287	4262	16638	917	6565	27604	1817	9889	978
80 IMPORTS	42403	45850	205713	11657	70972	457543	18350	162069	14151
81 BUS.TRAVEL, ENT., GIFTS.	0	0	0	0	0	0	0	0	0
82 OFFICE SUPPLIES	0	0	0	0	0	0	0	0	0
83 SCRAP & USED GOODS	-164	-173	-789	-42	-271	-1310	-69	-473	-45
84 GOVERNMENT INDUSTRY	0	0	0	0	0	0	0	0	0
85 REST OF WORLD INDUSTRY	-7529	-7060	-41466	-5498	-8202	-288622	-7126	-31134	-6503
86 HOUSEHOLD INDUSTRY	25373	34219	140449	7943	110247	426124	12671	102495	10194
87 INVENTORY VALUATION ADJ.	0	0	0	0	0	0	0	0	0
88 STATE TOTAL	3235874	3468316	15704610	872647	5458007	32954064	1425051	11592079	1057018

TABLE C.2

STATE ESTIMATES OF 1958
PERSONAL CONSUMPTION EXPENDITURES
(THOUSANDS OF CURRENT DOLLARS)

INDUSTRY TITLE	37 PENNSYL-VANIA	38 RHODE ISLAND	39 SOUTH CAROLINA	40 SOUTH DAKOTA	41 TENNESSEE	42 TEXAS	43 UTAH	44 VERMONT	45 VIRGINIA
1 LIVESTOCK & PRDTS.	118547	9042	28693	9777	37120	116866	8623	3732	53685
2 OTHER AGRICULTURE PRDTS.	160882	11856	27370	9788	43492	114128	11683	5280	50758
3 FORESTRY & FISHERIES	20220	1589	2592	938	4258	12958	1367	612	5225
4 AGRI.,FORES.,FISH.SERV.	0	0	0	0	0	0	0	0	0
5 IRON,FERRO.ORES MINING	0	0	0	0	0	0	0	0	0
6 NONFERROUS ORES MINING	0	0	0	0	0	0	0	0	0
7 COAL MINING	23041	1627	2750	1525	4357	10614	647	1141	4416
8 CRUDE PETRO.,NATURAL GAS	0	0	0	0	0	0	0	0	0
9 STONE & CLAY MINING	1047	79	161	57	276	854	98	32	335
10 CHEM.&FERT. MIN. MINING	125	3	12	2	22	22	8	1	30
11 NEW CONSTRUCTION	0	0	0	0	0	0	0	0	0
12 MAINT. & REPAIR CONSTR.	0	0	0	0	0	0	0	0	0
13 ORDNANCE & ACCESSORIES	10408	755	1144	455	2031	6867	964	314	2754
14 FOOD & KINDRED PRDTS.	3325886	253532	433738	154499	711418	2073921	224480	100237	868220
15 TOBACCO MANUFACTURES	317372	24743	44407	13435	74267	211637	18680	10308	85167
16 FABRICS	41604	3143	7954	2324	13085	38740	3989	1295	16097
17 TEXTILE PRDTS.	54714	4053	4301	2620	7837	28015	3609	1504	11147
18 APPAREL	781211	60203	101601	33740	171791	538663	52064	21439	220041
19 MISC. TEXTILE PRDTS.	76055	5877	10294	3296	17558	54125	5562	2157	21986
20 LUMBER & WOOD PRDTS.	10624	622	2381	560	3623	8332	734	610	3790
21 WOODEN CONTAINERS	0	0	0	0	0	0	0	0	0
22 HOUSEHOLD FURNITURE	157633	12498	23284	7046	39424	123332	11920	4244	49863
23 OTHER FURNITURE	8314	624	1278	438	2107	6265	690	259	2618
24 PAPER & ALLIED PRDTS.	58338	4498	8659	2682	14566	43373	4298	1858	17504
25 PAPERBOARD CONTAINERS	2840	210	331	96	568	1845	194	83	746
26 PRINTING & PUBLISHING	174754	13643	19507	7979	33486	106855	12295	5336	43043
27 CHEMICALS,SELECT. PRDTS.	13901	1058	2272	739	3770	10730	1092	459	4390
28 PLASTICS & SYNTHETICS	747	58	96	33	162	494	52	23	198
29 DRUGS & COSMETICS	237775	18413	40713	12102	67928	196480	19350	7739	79389
30 PAINT & ALLIED PRDTS.	1377	102	157	61	262	796	67	46	327
31 PETROLEUM, RELATED INDS.	514386	37102	70072	29096	114760	329954	35223	18793	138655
32 RUBBER, MISC.PLASTICS	81143	5966	13152	4301	22183	66946	7302	2668	27532
33 LEATHER TANNING & PRDTS.	0	0	0	0	0	0	0	0	0
34 FOOTWEAR, LEATHER PRDTS.	171018	13153	25509	8537	42422	126804	13289	4991	52024
35 GLASS & GLASS PRDTS.	8653	656	1200	401	2009	6111	726	252	2558
36 STONE & CLAY PRDTS.	14894	1115	2056	720	3403	9958	1066	457	4144
37 PRIMARY IRON, STEEL MFR.	1552	109	193	101	309	795	60	73	332
38 PRIMARY NONFERROUS MFR.	830	62	108	31	184	572	57	25	231

39 METAL CONTAINERS	0	0	0	0	0	0	0	0	0
40 FABRICATED METAL PRDTS.	1784	158	302	4242	1630	224	1036	310	4172
41 SCREW MACH. PRDTS., ETC.	5113	470	1357	12208	4105	763	2457	1252	16348
42 OTHER FAB. METAL PRDTS.	7772	751	2037	18903	6308	1225	3767	1843	24354
43 ENGINES & TURBINES	2993	255	856	7479	2100	324	1131	396	6006
44 FARM MACH. & EQUIP.	171	18	45	406	141	30	87	40	535
45 CONSTRUC. MACH. & EQUIP.	0	0	0	0	0	0	0	0	0
46 MATERIAL HANDLING MACH.	0	0	0	0	0	0	0	0	0
47 METALWORKING MACHINERY	605	60	167	1443	476	101	288	145	1957
48 SPECIAL MACH. & EQUIP.	378	37	104	901	296	63	178	90	1222
49 GENERAL MACH. & EQUIP.	0	0	0	0	0	0	0	0	0
50 MACHINE SHOP PRDTS.	0	0	0	0	0	0	0	0	0
51 OFFICE, COMPUT. MACHINES	1180	118	313	2796	924	196	556	276	3757
52 SERVICE IND. MACHINES	9512	190	663	25835	7218	540	3856	670	8497
53 ELECT. TRANSMISS. EQUIP.	301	30	80	714	241	51	146	70	952
54 HOUSEHOLD APPLIANCES	52907	5158	13564	127688	45353	7794	27612	11139	149843
55 ELECTRIC LIGHTING EQUIP.	6315	640	1715	15082	5057	1074	3053	1477	20021
56 RADIO, TV, ETC., EQUIP.	26393	2587	7315	66450	21053	4277	12128	6655	86567
57 ELECTRONIC COMPONENTS	2882	281	801	7276	2306	467	1326	728	9452
58 MISC. ELECTRICAL MACH.	5477	528	1479	13363	4372	847	2581	1149	15838
59 MOTOR VEHICLES, EQUIP.	187951	18270	48514	458574	147872	30415	87797	40047	562864
60 AIRCRAFT & PARTS	648	55	185	1619	455	70	245	86	1300
61 OTHER TRANSPORT. EQUIP.	17190	1464	4915	42944	12068	1865	6504	2281	34568
62 PROFESS., SCIEN. INSTRU.	7133	674	1832	18593	5913	1085	3405	1775	22621
63 MEDICAL, PHOTO. EQUIP.	8371	914	2704	20568	6550	1630	3852	2205	29336
64 MISC. MANUFACTURING	48253	4826	14523	118442	37655	7672	21924	12142	162806
65 TRANSPORT. & WAREHOUSING	151626	17761	43136	372289	121458	25290	71092	52463	654941
66 COMMUNICA.,EXC. BRDCAST.	70590	8487	19421	179745	56060	12359	32605	22155	278129
67 RADIO & TV BROADCASTING	0	0	0	0	0	0	0	0	0
68 ELEC.,GAS,WATER,SAN.SER.	164764	16346	39193	411918	139912	30784	83673	38417	490552
69 WHOLESALE & RETAIL TRADE	1201460	133752	305324	2908779	988134	207134	589099	322109	4272546
70 FINANCE & INSURANCE	222995	23499	55433	558859	171307	37153	98648	59602	807026
71 REAL ESTATE & RENTAL	656997	89342	203051	1688164	521141	123999	298540	234768	2950492
72 HOTELS; PERSONAL SERV.	194027	22386	44508	486066	148321	27989	84942	43390	581810
73 BUSINESS SERVICES	34676	3446	10352	84702	29631	7438	17814	8109	108367
74 RESEARCH & DEVELOPMENT	0	0	0	0	0	0	0	0	0
75 AUTO. REPAIR & SERVICES	94615	9126	25069	228475	75771	14576	45063	19020	265013
76 AMUSEMENTS	55731	5440	18141	126535	42810	8012	23725	15573	226387
77 MED.+EDUC. SERVICES	415124	39831	99416	1013857	325989	66540	191472	103283	1349840
78 FEDERAL GOV'T ENTERPRISE	11242	1392	3452	27578	9001	2202	5330	3367	43419
79 STATE & LOCAL GOV'T ENT.	6778	597	1871	16923	5462	1000	3205	1295	17730
80 IMPORTS	72455	8156	19106	176166	59708	12427	35261	21284	278275
81 BUS.TRAVEL, ENT., GIFTS.	0	0	0	0	0	0	0	0	0
82 OFFICE SUPPLIES	0	0	0	0	0	0	0	0	0
83 SCRAP & USED GOODS	-279	-27	-72	-681	-220	-45	-130	-59	-827
84 GOVERNMENT INDUSTRY	0	0	0	0	0	0	0	0	0
85 REST OF WORLD INDUSTRY	-11270	-3224	-2958	-56006	-7866	-2434	-3976	-3334	-44698
86 HOUSEHOLD INDUSTRY	88359	9496	7088	225883	81617	9959	68255	12451	196240
87 INVENTORY VALUATION ADJ.	0	0	0	0	0	0	0	0	0
88 STATE TOTAL	5590424	619258	1433191	13661830	4519507	952475	2704532	1525060	20028096

TABLE C.2
STATE ESTIMATES OF 1958
PERSONAL CONSUMPTION EXPENDITURES
(THOUSANDS OF CURRENT DOLLARS)

INDUSTRY TITLE	46 WASHINGTON	47 WEST VIRGINIA	48 WISCONSIN	49 WYOMING	50 ALASKA	51 HAWAII	52 NO STATE ALLOCATION	53 NATIONAL TOTAL
1 LIVESTOCK & PRDTS.	40770	19139	41355	4566	0	0	0	2111188
2 OTHER AGRICULTURE PRDTS.	43800	24542	53472	5012	0	0	0	2428899
3 FORESTRY & FISHERIES	5158	2287	5949	553	0	0	0	281270
4 AGRI.,FORES.,FISH. SERV.	0	0	0	0	0	0	0	0
5 IRON, FERRO. ORES MINING	0	0	0	0	0	0	0	0
6 NONFERROUS ORES MINING	0	0	0	0	0	0	0	0
7 COAL MINING	2573	2295	7117	323	0	0	0	260969
8 CRUDE PETRO.,NATURAL GAS	0	0	0	0	0	0	0	0
9 STONE & CLAY MINING	359	144	381	39	0	0	0	17411
10 CHEM.&FERT. MIN. MINING	9	13	10	4	0	0	0	1178
11 NEW CONSTRUCTION	0	0	0	0	0	0	0	0
12 MAINT. & REPAIR CONSTR.	0	0	0	0	0	0	0	0
13 ORDNANCE & ACCESSORIES	3608	1160	3456	388	0	0	0	158309
14 FOOD & KINDRED PRDTS.	822859	387270	958094	92038	0	0	0	45758416
15 TOBACCO MANUFACTURES	67613	40441	88639	7269	0	0	0	4249840
16 FABRICS	14785	7491	14839	1607	0	0	0	712228
17 TEXTILE PRDTS.	13303	4339	18325	1421	0	0	0	742540
18 APPAREL	195063	96517	236143	20899	0	0	0	11164706
19 MISC. TEXTILE PRDTS.	20643	9770	22750	2240	0	0	0	1100557
20 LUMBER & WOOD PRDTS.	2849	1975	2688	328	0	0	0	149262
21 WOODEN CONTAINERS	0	0	0	0	0	0	0	0
22 HOUSEHOLD FURNITURE	42857	22298	52135	4532	0	0	0	2416971
23 OTHER FURNITURE	2525	1219	2861	275	0	0	0	129182
24 PAPER & ALLIED PRDTS.	15688	8012	17470	1704	0	0	0	848352
25 PAPERBOARD CONTAINERS	697	343	773	75	0	0	0	37772
26 PRINTING & PUBLISHING	46082	18444	54012	4977	0	0	0	2444837
27 CHEMICALS,SELECT. PRDTS.	3955	2085	4679	435	0	0	0	213066
28 PLASTICS & SYNTHETICS	187	91	222	20	0	0	0	10312
29 DRUGS & COSMETICS	70778	37091	77026	7769	0	0	0	3708138
30 PAINT & ALLIED PRDTS.	249	144	395	27	0	0	0	17536
31 PETROLEUM, RELATED INDS.	130580	67397	170786	14480	0	0	0	7259350
32 RUBBER, MISC. PLASTICS	27181	12634	28030	3002	0	0	0	1308586
33 LEATHER TANNING & PRDTS.	0	0	0	0	0	0	0	0
34 FOOTWEAR, LEATHER PRDTS.	49081	23757	56842	5286	0	0	0	2606967
35 GLASS & GLASS PRDTS.	2650	1149	2707	283	0	0	0	130014
36 STONE & CLAY PRDTS.	3930	1941	4712	431	0	0	0	214423
37 PRIMARY IRON, STEEL MFR.	233	165	494	28	0	0	0	18859
38 PRIMARY NONFERROUS MFR.	206	106	225	22	0	0	0	11303

39	METAL CONTAINERS	1152	910	1407	131	0	0	0	0
40	FABRICATED METAL PRDTS.	4944	2317	5092	527	0	0	0	69774
41	SCREW MACH. PRDTS., ETC.	7462	3580	8173	811	0	0	0	249125
42	OTHER FAB. METAL PRDTS.	3328	1224	2384	336	0	0	0	378913
43	ENGINES & TURBINES	166	81	185	18	0	0	0	126302
44	FARM MACH. & EQUIP.	0	0	0	0	0	0	0	8366
45	CONSTRUC. MACH. & EQUIP.	0	0	0	0	0	0	0	0
46	MATERIAL HANDLING MACH.	0	0	0	0	0	0	0	0
47	METALWORKING MACHINERY	614	282	688	67	0	0	0	30507
48	SPECIAL MACH. & EQUIP.	385	176	430	42	0	0	0	19080
49	GENERAL MACH. & EQUIP.	0	0	0	0	0	0	0	0
50	MACHINE SHOP PRDTS.	0	0	0	0	0	0	0	0
51	OFFICE, COMPUT. MACHINES	1154	541	1287	126	0	0	0	58236
52	SERVICE IND. MACHINES	2444	3722	4587	270	0	0	0	247376
53	ELECT. TRANSMISS. EQUIP.	295	140	329	32	0	0	0	14862
54	HOUSEHOLD APPLIANCES	48762	25857	50624	5412	0	0	0	2415794
55	ELECTRIC LIGHTING EQUIP.	6334	2901	6871	694	0	0	0	313468
56	RADIO, TV, ETC., EQUIP.	27222	11381	30135	2930	0	0	0	1362929
57	ELECTRONIC COMPONENTS	2976	1242	3293	320	0	0	0	148956
58	MISC. ELECTRICAL MACH.	5518	2485	5581	610	0	0	0	259937
59	MOTOR VEHICLES, EQUIP.	179213	85918	212930	19798	0	0	0	9200587
60	AIRCRAFT & PARTS	721	265	516	73	0	0	0	27347
61	OTHER TRANSPORT. EQUIP.	19106	7036	13713	1929	0	0	0	725821
62	PROFESS., SCIEN. INSTRU.	6889	3086	7065	738	0	0	0	348731
63	MEDICAL, PHOTO. EQUIP.	10143	3717	10833	1090	0	0	0	468467
64	MISC. MANUFACTURING	53854	21306	54509	5815	0	0	0	2536329
65	TRANSPORT. & WAREHOUSING	159475	64841	171303	17013	0	0	0	8659232
66	COMMUNICA.,EXC. BRDCAST.	71766	29861	83985	7603	0	0	0	3908692
67	RADIO & TV BROADCASTING	0	0	0	0	0	0	0	0
68	ELEC.,GAS,WATER,SAN.SER.	144896	74933	189837	15738	0	0	0	8060286
69	WHOLESALE & RETAIL TRADE	1121043	553526	1337562	123629	0	0	0	61562976
70	FINANCE & INSURANCE	210109	97093	259536	23085	0	0	0	11815781
71	REAL ESTATE & RENTAL	746669	275442	877116	77359	0	0	0	39960208
72	HOTELS; PERSONAL SERV.	164621	79500	186129	25436	0	0	0	9454516
73	BUSINESS SERVICES	38711	16108	46049	4293	0	0	0	1887884
74	RESEARCH & DEVELOPMENT	0	0	0	0	0	0	0	0
75	AUTO. REPAIR & SERVICES	93745	43638	94052	10458	0	0	0	4386921
76	AMUSEMENTS	61663	25447	60178	7156	0	0	0	3262088
77	MED.,EDUC. SERVICES	367525	183279	434887	40097	0	0	0	20446608
78	FEDERAL GOV'T ENTERPRISE	12916	4834	13774	1391	0	0	0	632450
79	STATE & LOCAL GOV'T ENT.	6926	3034	6627	760	0	0	0	312173
80	IMPORTS	69266	32919	81649	7677	0	0	0	3854901
81	BUS.TRAVEL, ENT., GIFTS.	0	0	0	0	0	0	0	0
82	OFFICE SUPPLIES	0	0	0	0	0	0	0	0
83	SCRAP & USED GOODS	-266	-127	-312	-29	0	0	0	-13579
84	GOVERNMENT INDUSTRY	0	0	0	0	0	0	0	0
85	REST OF WORLD INDUSTRY	-28483	-4704	-18862	-2082	0	0	0	-1152801
86	HOUSEHOLD INDUSTRY	42743	21020	42026	4802	0	0	0	3503000
87	INVENTORY VALUATION ADJ.	0	0	0	0	0	0	0	0
88	STATE TOTAL	5296258	2473070	6212755	586188	0	0	0	290065408

243

TABLE C.3

STATE ESTIMATES OF 1963
PERSONAL CONSUMPTION EXPENDITURES
(THOUSANDS OF CURRENT DOLLARS)

INDUSTRY TITLE	1 ALABAMA	2 ARIZONA	3 ARKANSAS	4 CALIFORNIA	5 COLORADO	6 CONNECTICUT	7 DELAWARE	8 DISTRICT OF COLUMBIA	9 FLORIDA
1 LIVESTOCK & PRDTS.	25613	14561	15690	181941	21412	24819	5506	12850	52784
2 OTHER AGRICULTURE PRDTS.	41754	22362	23930	297031	30905	46956	7556	11934	80493
3 FORESTRY & FISHERIES	5490	3284	2905	46044	4598	7577	1047	1827	11372
4 AGRI.,FORES.,FISH. SERV.	196	100	43	2735	231	321	65	0	1342
5 IRON,FERRO. ORES MINING	0	0	0	0	0	0	0	0	0
6 NONFERROUS ORES MINING	0	0	0	0	0	0	0	0	0
7 COAL MINING	2302	659	1451	7036	871	2921	296	495	3965
8 CRUDE PETRO.,NATURAL GAS	0	125	0	0	0	0	0	0	0
9 STONE & CLAY MINING	206	17	103	1758	173	241	41	68	427
10 CHEM.&FERT. MIN. MINING	18	0	10	235	21	31	5	15	58
11 NEW CONSTRUCTION	0	0	0	0	0	0	0	0	0
12 MAINT. & REPAIR CONSTR.	0	0	0	0	0	0	0	0	0
13 ORDNANCE & ACCESSORIES	2230	1640	1041	23494	2286	3199	513	897	4916
14 FOOD & KINDRED PRDTS.	655379	392211	352781	5452713	546643	889250	124578	223893	1362502
15 TOBACCO MANUFACTURES	74453	33391	40863	453277	46580	87337	13015	21269	148959
16 FABRICS	10194	5336	5377	72813	7460	9318	1966	2922	20716
17 TEXTILE PRDTS.	10803	7172	4790	101834	9915	22008	2590	4441	24389
18 APPAREL	183716	96661	92389	1369704	134127	257527	37863	62454	389263
19 MISC. TEXTILE PRDTS.	20862	11262	10570	157300	15705	26815	4255	7126	44147
20 LUMBER & WOOD PRDTS.	4316	1869	2678	23587	2595	3230	653	887	7290
21 WOODEN CONTAINERS	0	0	0	0	0	0	0	0	0
22 HOUSEHOLD FURNITURE	43382	21395	21843	303344	30001	52402	8940	15921	92953
23 OTHER FURNITURE	1916	1026	991	13838	1417	2172	386	577	3929
24 PAPER & ALLIED PRDTS.	18870	9526	9953	128601	13168	21160	3554	5921	39029
25 PAPERBOARD CONTAINERS	1071	537	523	7487	758	1427	227	326	2263
26 PRINTING & PUBLISHING	39679	24694	19633	348653	34159	56468	8255	15498	86057
27 CHEMICALS,SELECT. PRDTS.	6082	3090	3312	41297	4272	6229	1103	1678	12119
28 PLASTICS & SYNTHETICS	178	92	93	1220	127	221	34	52	369
29 DRUGS & COSMETICS	86839	43986	46986	579314	59825	84188	15669	25491	174965
30 PAINT & ALLIED PRDTS.	296	131	153	1775	180	503	59	98	625
31 PETROLEUM, RELATED INDS.	114041	61920	61645	847543	86718	142560	21524	32108	229743
32 RUBBER, MISC. PLASTICS	27881	15583	14362	218583	21924	29513	5584	8902	57818
33 LEATHER TANNING & PRDTS.	0	0	0	0	0	0	0	0	0
34 FOOTWEAR, LEATHER PRDTS.	42445	23519	22253	323665	32585	51092	8206	12934	87161
35 GLASS & GLASS PRDTS.	3233	1980	1645	28425	2756	4160	663	1021	6760
36 STONE & CLAY PRDTS.	3005	1625	1578	22284	2261	3905	582	853	6066
37 PRIMARY IRON, STEEL MFR.	132	52	78	631	70	169	20	35	244
38 PRIMARY NONFERROUS MFR.	187	91	94	1253	127	232	38	56	390

Code	Industry	Col 1	Col 2	Col 3	Col 4	Col 5	Col 6	Col 7	Col 8	Col 9
39	METAL CONTAINERS	1511	0	0	0	0	0	0	0	0
40	FABRICATED METAL PRDTS.	3735	620	896	7802	866	1470	242	424	2886
41	SCREW MACH. PRDTS., ETC.	8528	2201	1946	31909	3075	4605	737	1173	7757
42	OTHER FAB. METAL PRDTS.	1875	4606	4420	63069	6400	9459	1684	2615	17591
43	ENGINES & TURBINES	155	1654	861	27219	2280	1193	484	1308	4517
44	FARM MACH. & EQUIP.	0	83	83	1096	114	165	30	44	311
45	CONSTRUC. MACH. & EQUIP.	0	0	0	0	0	0	0	0	0
46	MATERIAL HANDLING MACH.	1094	602	555	8158	836	1275	227	319	2243
47	METALWORKING MACHINERY	292	161	148	2189	224	343	61	86	600
48	SPECIAL MACH. & EQUIP.	0	0	0	0	0	0	0	0	0
49	GENERAL MACH. & EQUIP.	0	0	0	0	0	0	0	0	0
50	MACHINE SHOP PRDTS.	32	18	16	245	25	32	6	10	66
51	OFFICE, COMPUT. MACHINES	1252	678	632	9317	940	1463	265	374	2584
52	SERVICE IND. MACHINES	8390	3823	3377	18005	1843	3377	1835	4039	19414
53	ELECT. TRANSMISS. EQUIP.	308	159	168	2266	232	353	90	90	629
54	HOUSEHOLD APPLIANCES	44225	22915	24533	300782	31438	43689	7894	11615	87200
55	ELECTRIC LIGHTING EQUIP.	5996	3382	3076	46018	4658	6942	1231	1820	12327
56	RADIO, TV, ETC., EQUIP.	27349	17062	13845	243148	23795	34432	5474	10463	59598
57	ELECTRONIC COMPONENTS	2306	1439	1169	20481	2006	2902	459	879	5026
58	MISC. ELECTRICAL MACH.	5493	3104	2801	43645	4365	5827	1118	1762	11483
59	MOTOR VEHICLES, EQUIP.	213800	119783	107812	1690662	168254	239603	44811	70511	452941
60	AIRCRAFT & PARTS	740	653	340	10745	900	471	191	516	1783
61	OTHER TRANSPORT. EQUIP.	14746	12997	6778	213761	17908	9403	3802	10272	35511
62	PROFESS., SCIEN. INSTRU.	5938	3149	2959	44855	4506	6575	1117	2164	12078
63	MEDICAL, PHOTO. EQUIP.	7622	5302	3812	75093	7414	9720	1599	2656	16216
64	MISC. MANUFACTURING	44016	28415	21807	402830	39427	56942	9337	15589	93804
65	TRANSPORT. & WAREHOUSING	106518	68750	55879	997040	94513	178251	21349	43641	230743
66	COMUNICA.,EXC. BRDCAST.	71390	42580	35874	601647	58906	101243	14071	27479	155346
67	RADIO & TV BROADCASTING	0	0	0	0	0	0	0	0	0
68	ELEC.,GAS,WATER,SAN.SER.	173335	85270	92957	1141934	117933	164679	31265	55527	353599
69	WHOLESALE & RETAIL TRADE	1113080	617834	586510	8582040	858173	1412696	214912	354378	2297940
70	FINANCE & INSURANCE	220706	126087	109583	1864839	176931	310884	50645	81879	470988
71	REAL ESTATE & RENTAL	646710	421327	321060	6041332	588523	1024918	129260	241859	1408083
72	HOTELS; PERSONAL SERV.	163180	101967	88714	1276433	133900	196396	33183	90300	471615
73	BUSINESS SERVICES	38910	25587	20676	353969	35710	44793	7257	11493	77555
74	RESEARCH & DEVELOPMENT	0	0	0	0	0	0	0	0	0
75	AUTO. REPAIR & SERVICES	102733	56586	52934	790831	79853	103826	20790	32029	213340
76	AMUSEMENTS	52611	38551	26877	584616	54303	85476	13150	21548	132627
77	MED.,EDUC. SERVICES	413656	214069	207951	3052028	295613	526427	86206	136616	878554
78	FEDERAL GOV'T ENTERPRISE	11146	7507	5700	105109	10406	15766	2219	4431	23884
79	STATE & LOCAL GOV'T ENT.	9950	5673	5068	79175	7964	9273	1984	3202	20911
80	IMPORTS	79717	46146	41700	648609	64130	108352	15337	25819	166330
81	BUS.TRAVEL, ENT., GIFTS.	0	0	0	0	0	0	0	0	0
82	OFFICE SUPPLIES	0	0	0	0	0	0	0	0	0
83	SCRAP & USED GOODS	-3491	-1951	-1762	-27519	-2739	-3887	-729	-1155	-7394
84	GOVERNMENT INDUSTRY	0	0	0	0	0	0	0	0	0
85	REST OF WORLD INDUSTRY	-7421	-20080	-5031	-255577	-11802	-12715	-2460	-9742	-40411
86	HOUSEHOLD INDUSTRY	99704	27229	40743	376514	27732	67637	14727	51286	189220
87	INVENTORY VALUATION ADJ.	0	0	0	0	0	0	0	0	0
88	STATE TOTAL	5118605	2892692	2645671	40535648	4025424	6612286	1010626	1779867	10842608

TABLE C.3

STATE ESTIMATES OF 1963
PERSONAL CONSUMPTION EXPENDITURES
(THOUSANDS OF CURRENT DOLLARS)

INDUSTRY TITLE	10 GEORGIA	11 IDAHO	12 ILLINOIS	13 INDIANA	14 IOWA	15 KANSAS	16 KENTUCKY	17 LOUISIANA	18 MAINE
1 LIVESTOCK & PRDTS.	37984	6195	98069	42568	24680	23676	28660	27006	9191
2 OTHER AGRICULTURE PRDTS.	52056	10988	164960	75835	42714	35728	41885	41719	14383
3 FORESTRY & FISHERIES	6948	1490	24436	10345	5579	4876	5220	5682	2202
4 AGRI.,FORES.,FISH. SERV.	161	33	617	374	224	122	96	87	49
5 IRON,FERRO.ORES MINING	0	0	0	0	0	0	0	0	0
6 NONFERROUS ORES MINING	0	0	0	0	0	0	0	0	0
7 COAL MINING	2932	404	10802	5637	3567	2795	2296	2260	1485
8 CRUDE PETRO.,NATURAL GAS	0	0	0	0	0	0	0	0	0
9 STONE & CLAY MINING	252	57	917	375	196	172	189	212	64
10 CHEM.&FERT. MIN. MINING	26	7	126	48	24	17	22	24	7
11 NEW CONSTRUCTION	0	0	0	0	0	0	0	0	0
12 MAINT. & REPAIR CONSTR.	0	0	0	0	0	0	0	0	0
13 ORDNANCE & ACCESSORIES	2764	781	10870	4437	2237	2006	2040	2355	837
14 FOOD & KINDRED PRDTS.	835224	179755	2892167	1235795	671423	579254	633713	679871	261697
15 TOBACCO MANUFACTURES	89984	16155	282100	120811	66375	56979	70877	75704	28090
16 FABRICS	12525	2652	34546	15335	8266	7103	9774	10313	2721
17 TEXTILE PRDTS.	13329	3248	62148	27819	14132	12497	9661	11686	5315
18 APPAREL	228767	44858	839496	351884	178893	159285	172681	190325	65941
19 MISC. TEXTILE PRDTS.	25892	5404	85957	36155	18837	16499	19498	21738	7167
20 LUMBER & WOOD PRDTS.	5571	1067	11134	5285	3063	2499	4428	4169	1549
21 WOODEN CONTAINERS	0	0	0	0	0	0	0	0	0
22 HOUSEHOLD FURNITURE	54678	9950	190245	77482	39850	35527	40742	45253	13869
23 OTHER FURNITURE	2386	511	8192	3576	1877	1634	1832	1951	625
24 PAPER & ALLIED PRDTS.	23469	4586	68514	29528	16052	13751	17807	19434	6427
25 PAPERBOARD CONTAINERS	1286	264	4016	1722	872	780	1005	1091	408
26 PRINTING & PUBLISHING	50991	11481	194797	81389	42575	37186	36796	41714	15849
27 CHEMICALS,SELECT. PRDTS.	7434	1525	22696	10125	5539	4727	5821	6153	1966
28 PLASTICS & SYNTHETICS	219	45	684	303	163	141	169	182	67
29 DRUGS & COSMETICS	107638	21174	301357	131420	71972	61437	82660	88621	26328
30 PAINT & ALLIED PRDTS.	385	62	1382	596	314	275	282	308	140
31 PETROLEUM, RELATED INDS.	141239	30881	475020	223427	125098	104783	111196	114276	47227
32 RUBBER, MISC. PLASTICS	34544	7619	106147	46423	24656	21328	26428	28576	8742
33 LEATHER TANNING & PRDTS.	0	0	0	0	0	0	0	0	0
34 FOOTWEAR, LEATHER PRDTS.	52093	11291	186043	80459	42077	36845	40371	43339	14322
35 GLASS & GLASS PRDTS.	4035	894	13810	6036	3107	2723	3062	3318	1117
36 STONE & CLAY PRDTS.	3699	798	12807	5728	2999	2606	2868	3036	1115
37 PRIMARY IRON, STEEL MFR.	169	28	614	301	184	147	130	132	74
38 PRIMARY NONFERROUS MFR.	228	44	660	283	148	130	175	191	67

Industry									
39 METAL CONTAINERS	0	0	0	0	0	0	0	0	0
40 FABRICATED METAL PRDTS.	512	1493	1515	1010	1176	2197	4941	360	1930
41 SCREW MACH. PRDTS., ETC.	1239	3830	3552	2960	3401	6539	14849	974	4660
42 OTHER FAB. METAL PRDTS.	2724	8724	8091	6843	7876	14939	34277	2250	10527
43 ENGINES & TURBINES	410	2086	1732	1051	1165	2379	5560	579	2597
44 FARM MACH. & EQUIP.	50	157	149	130	152	282	633	42	194
45 CONSTRUC. MACH. & EQUIP.	0	0	0	0	0	0	0	0	0
46 MATERIAL HANDLING MACH.	361	1109	1044	960	1094	2122	4823	304	1348
47 METALWORKING MACHINERY	96	296	279	257	292	569	1295	81	360
48 SPECIAL MACH. & EQUIP.	0	0	0	0	0	0	0	0	0
49 GENERAL MACH. & EQUIP.	10	33	30	24	27	51	116	9	39
50 MACHINE SHOP PRDTS.	409	1277	1190	1076	1225	2379	5505	338	1553
51 OFFICE, COMPUT. MACHINES	736	9150	7436	3458	3745	7705	19616	676	10275
52 SERVICE IND. MACHINES	101	313	295	267	306	588	1339	84	383
53 ELECT. TRANSMISS. EQUIP.	14041	44289	43079	32934	38231	71835	156772	11723	54067
54 HOUSEHOLD APPLIANCES	1967	6125	5705	5125	5879	11252	25910	1672	7463
55 ELECTRIC LIGHTING EQUIP.	9733	28909	25423	25469	28890	56370	134494	7837	34539
56 RADIO, TV, ETC., EQUIP.	821	2440	2140	2153	2442	4766	11364	661	2905
57 ELECTRONIC COMPONENTS	1717	5637	5195	4198	4840	9145	21147	1510	6788
58 MISC. ELECTRICAL MACH.	69157	219892	203757	193917	218889	429348	1011262	57917	266813
59 MOTOR VEHICLES, EQUIP.	162	824	684	415	460	939	2195	229	1025
60 AIRCRAFT & PARTS	3230	16406	13626	8281	9184	18739	43795	4554	20424
61 OTHER TRANSPORT. EQUIP.	1814	6290	5324	4600	5219	10093	24175	1538	7747
62 PROFESS., SCIEN. INSTRU.	2736	7931	7171	7414	8500	16137	38644	2547	9705
63 MEDICAL, PHOTO. EQUIP.	15036	45793	41039	37978	42885	83939	201290	13339	54469
64 MISC. MANUFACTURING	44670	113327	98529	95218	108600	208380	524068	29680	139050
65 TRANSPORT. & WAREHOUSING	28748	75675	65995	62419	71691	134329	328298	18867	93585
66 COMMUNICA., EXC. BRDCAST.	52752	178782	163853	147378	173079	314194	715693	41218	220326
67 RADIO & TV BROADCASTING	410065	1142954	1062141	955074	1110014	2075647	4783901	294194	1387010
68 ELEC.,GAS,WATER,SAN.SER.	300066	232236	207400	192262	222975	429058	1044142	55877	279338
69 WHOLESALE & RETAIL TRADE	289850	685007	592043	608923	696903	1321774	3224776	184625	822359
70 FINANCE & INSURANCE	62280	179018	154123	122443	141299	268495	699798	41079	214581
71 REAL ESTATE & RENTAL	12679	39405	36623	39547	45810	86428	198273	12517	47505
72 HOTELS; PERSONAL SERV.	31546	104911	97932	75920	88105	164733	374474	28100	126852
73 BUSINESS SERVICES	21344	58159	52432	48969	55470	107746	276379	16948	65903
74 RESEARCH & DEVELOPMENT	135991	429277	389328	336144	382530	738840	1755776	95872	520604
75 AUTO. REPAIR & SERVICES	4518	11743	10419	10140	11915	21739	52076	3428	14588
76 AMUSEMENTS	2802	10282	9335	7181	8278	15561	36148	2749	12391
77 MED.,EDUC. SERVICES	30396	82471	75449	69279	80434	150852	354233	21397	99128
78 FEDERAL GOV'T ENTERPRISE									
79 STATE & LOCAL GOV'T ENT.									
80 IMPORTS									
81 BUS.TRAVEL, ENT., GIFTS.	0	0	0	0	0	0	0	0	0
82 OFFICE SUPPLIES	-1119	-3592	-3324	-3132	-3536	-6933	-16340	-942	-4354
83 SCRAP & USED GOODS									
84 GOVERNMENT INDUSTRY	0	0	0	0	0	0	0	0	0
85 REST OF WORLD INDUSTRY	-8001	-11321	-10256	-7358	-10678		-62697	-7035	-11894
86 HOUSEHOLD INDUSTRY	18016	101618	46393	33022	39229	62554	145791	8663	149186
87 INVENTORY VALUATION ADJ.									
88 STATE TOTAL	1882705	5313581	4799254	4361476	5025688	9477210	22304032	1330707	6474776

TABLE C.3

STATE ESTIMATES OF 1963
PERSONAL CONSUMPTION EXPENDITURES
(THOUSANDS OF CURRENT DOLLARS)

INDUSTRY TITLE	19 MARYLAND	20 MASSA-CHUSETTS	21 MICHIGAN	22 MINNESOTA	23 MISSISSIPPI	24 MISSOURI	25 MONTANA	26 NEBRASKA	27 NEVADA
1 LIVESTOCK & PRDTS.	31971	51867	68900	31494	17728	40736	7390	15141	5766
2 OTHER AGRICULTURE PRDTS.	50328	86418	123021	52519	25889	67781	11158	22182	6456
3 FORESTRY & FISHERIES	7178	14041	17729	7216	3095	9430	1520	2915	946
4 AGRI.,FORES.,FISH. SERV.	191	421	567	210	51	217	28	52	7
5 IRON, FERRO. ORES MINING	0	0	0	0	0	0	0	0	0
6 NONFERROUS ORES MINING	0	0	0	0	0	0	0	0	0
7 COAL MINING	1953	5667	8513	4029	1626	5408	417	1838	175
8 CRUDE PETRO.,NATURAL GAS		0	0		0	0	0	0	0
9 STONE & CLAY MINING	288	424	657	258	110	342	57	101	35
10 CHEM.&FERT. MIN. MINING	35	65	80	35	10	42	9	15	6
11 NEW CONSTRUCTION	0	0	0	0	0	0	0	0	0
12 MAINT. & REPAIR CONSTR.	0	0	0	0	0	0	0	0	0
13 ORDNANCE & ACCESSORIES	3583	5505	7827	3021	1095	3844	771	1147	479
14 FOOD & KINDRED PRDTS.	851992	1660043	2097858	863225	375756	1124857	184962	352206	114328
15 TOBACCO MANUFACTURES	90022	164605	206951	84633	42720	110513	16179	34402	9044
16 FABRICS	13521	16751	25701	10457	5687	13413	2611	4253	1480
17 TEXTILE PRDTS.	18571	37666	46891	18210	5014	23149	3241	7151	2030
18 APPAREL	264592	456711	607379	237050	97395	305321	44608	92060	27523
19 MISC. TEXTILE PRDTS.	29650	47621	62354	24722	11135	31771	5356	9639	3171
20 LUMBER & WOOD PRDTS.	4368	5701	8444	3667	3132	4798	1047	1565	529
21 WOODEN CONTAINERS		0	0	0	0	0	0	0	0
22 HOUSEHOLD FURNITURE	62097	92910	137028	53399	22843	68286	9806	20518	5956
23 OTHER FURNITURE	2653	3809	6056	2417	1054	3082	503	960	284
24 PAPER & ALLIED PRDTS.	24590	38609	50262	20479	10480	26730	4582	8243	2583
25 PAPERBOARD CONTAINERS	1568	2481	2977	1151	540	1457	258	446	153
26 PRINTING & PUBLISHING	57688	103225	140297	55951	20885	73050	11519	21794	7005
27 CHEMICALS,SELECT. PRDTS.	7563	11340	16928	6938	3498	9049	1514	2847	839
28 PLASTICS & SYNTHETICS	236	404	512	207	97	268	45	84	25
29 DRUGS & COSMETICS	108056	155296	222360	91035	49906	119756	21174	36994	11739
30 PAINT & ALLIED PRDTS.	410	876	1009	406	165	534	62	161	35
31 PETROLEUM, RELATED INDS.	145570	254304	360806	152723	64583	196166	30701	64244	17505
32 RUBBER, MISC. PLASTICS	38496	52020	78306	31594	15114	40528	7543	12626	4439
33 LEATHER TANNING & PRDTS.	0	0	0	0	0	0	0	0	0
34 FOOTWEAR, LEATHER PRDTS.	56980	91449	136844	54357	23479	70021	11169	21649	6531
35 GLASS & GLASS PRDTS.	4574	7312	10203	4025	1742	5140	886	1579	553
36 STONE & CLAY PRDTS.	3983	6900	9608	3805	1680	4935	786	1522	451
37 PRIMARY IRON, STEEL MFR.	137	316	471	215	87	285	29	95	14
38 PRIMARY NONFERROUS MFR.	261	410	486	192	99	247	44	76	25

#	Industry									
39	METAL CONTAINERS	0	0	0	0	0	0	0	0	0
40	FABRICATED METAL PRDTS.	174	605	347	1945	972	1493	3686	2536	1614
41	SCREW MACH. PRDTS., ETC.	614	1730	969	5611	2057	4375	10985	8178	5084
42	OTHER FAB. METAL PRDTS.	1277	4025	2225	13000	4662	10426	25331	16835	11617
43	ENGINES & TURBINES	498	593	578	1984	936	1554	4087	2014	3286
44	FARM MACH. & EQUIP.	23	78	42	246	88	192	471	293	205
45	CONSTRUC. MACH. & EQUIP.	0	0	0	0	0	0	0	0	0
46	MATERIAL HANDLING MACH.	169	0	298	1794	590	1414	3589	2212	1555
47	METALWORKING MACHINERY	45	556	80	480	157	379	964	594	418
48	SPECIAL MACH. & EQUIP.	0	149	0	0	0	0	0	0	0
49	GENERAL MACH. & EQUIP.	5	0	9	45	17	35	86	56	44
50	MACHINE SHOP PRDTS.	193	14	332	2023	673	1593	4045	2502	1816
51	OFFICE, COMPUT. MACHINES	378	625	657	6809	3844	5230	13970	6090	13420
52	SERVICE IND. MACHINES	47	1920	83	502	170	394	991	613	432
53	ELECT. TRANSMISS. EQUIP.	6167	156	11445	61743	25947	47914	118536	77194	53490
54	HOUSEHOLD APPLIANCES	947	19563	1652	9694	3282	7592	19065	12039	8469
55	ELECTRIC LIGHTING EQUIP.	4822	3005	7856	49449	14400	38135	97320	60744	38510
56	RADIO, TV, ETC., EQUIP.	405	14776	662	4179	1214	3222	8229	5114	3235
57	ELECTRONIC COMPONENTS	886	1249	1498	8006	2937	6241	15512	10177	7726
58	MISC. ELECTRICAL MACH.	34823	2481	57317	369118	112348	288749	732152	419084	309665
59	MOTOR VEHICLES, EQUIP.	197	112668	228	783	369	614	1614	795	1297
60	AIRCRAFT & PARTS	3911	234	4546	15634	7364	12247	32194	15885	25828
61	OTHER TRANSPORT. EQUIP.	904	4671	1529	8941	3235	6904	17337	11922	7926
62	PROFESS., SCIEN. INSTRU.	1521	2690	2529	14333	4060	11157	27938	17116	11042
63	MEDICAL, PHOTO. EQUIP.	8127	4356	13261	72992	22957	56973	145368	99688	64922
64	MISC. MANUFACTURING	19279	21961	30353	190806	58184	146186	368367	329636	150584
65	TRANSPORT. & WAREHOUSING	11709	55997	19190	124868	38310	94386	234580	188381	98864
66	COMMUNICA., EXC. BRDCAST.	0	37005	0	0	0	0	0	0	0
67	RADIO & TV BROADCASTING	23016	0	41497	288363	99584	217983	528674	307179	216657
68	ELEC., GAS, WATER, SAN. SER.	174013	88992	294466	1841420	620104	1422715	3508737	2552614	1483230
69	WHOLESALE & RETAIL TRADE	39111	570413	57432	379501	116602	292428	748400	538329	338287
70	FINANCE & INSURANCE	117988	115123	187168	1220412	340189	922963	2309464	1895834	914766
71	REAL ESTATE & RENTAL	91778	358737	43697	257310	90392	201295	472018	374129	226469
72	HOTELS; PERSONAL SERV.	7240	75271	12372	77281	22177	57967	146746	79178	50010
73	BUSINESS SERVICES	0	23224	0	0	0	0	0	0	0
74	RESEARCH & DEVELOPMENT	16198	0	27819	143951	55449	112371	276784	181425	142971
75	AUTO. REPAIR & SERVICES	44394	45163	16715	96154	26656	75208	194206	156561	89272
76	AMUSEMENTS	65147	29703	96152	653643	222120	501893	1270768	930305	596921
77	MED.,EDUC. SERVICES	2074	195748	3472	20115	6142	15443	37279	28874	15547
78	FEDERAL GOV'T ENTERPRISE	1597	6135	2731	13801	5326	10672	26507	16313	13766
79	STATE & LOCAL GOV'T ENT.	13014	4250	21576	134968	44001	104054	257765	198005	106517
80	IMPORTS	0	41413	0	0	0	0	0	0	0
81	BUS.TRAVEL, ENT., GIFTS.	0	0	0	0	0	0	0	0	0
82	OFFICE SUPPLIES	0	0	0	0	0	0	0	0	0
83	SCRAP & USED GOODS	-566	-1819	-932	-5963	-1837	-4665	-11834	-6794	-5042
84	GOVERNMENT INDUSTRY	0	0	0	0	0	0	0	0	0
85	REST OF WORLD INDUSTRY	-16564	-7021	8325	-20071	-4164	-34999	-76258	-30197	-18325
86	HOUSEHOLD INDUSTRY	6846	21766		67734	73454	49273	118488	86259	75073
87	INVENTORY VALUATION ADJ.	0	0	0	0	0	0	0	0	0
88	STATE TOTAL	912519	2596709	1350150	8494759	2831562	6511345	16151185	11972878	6950272

249

TABLE C.3

STATE ESTIMATES OF 1963
PERSONAL CONSUMPTION EXPENDITURES
(THOUSANDS OF CURRENT DOLLARS)

INDUSTRY TITLE	28 NEW HAMPSHIRE	29 NEW JERSEY	30 NEW MEXICO	31 NEW YORK	32 NORTH CAROLINA	33 NORTH DAKOTA	34 OHIO	35 OKLAHOMA	36 OREGON
1 LIVESTOCK & PRDTS.	6822	61668	10881	173814	43515	6311	85067	22505	17874
2 OTHER AGRICULTURE PRDTS.	10366	111310	14714	294557	62529	9218	153736	35042	31990
3 FORESTRY & FISHERIES	1613	18175	2084	47763	7692	1102	22178	4762	4610
4 AGRI.,FORES.,FISH.SERV.	60	607	24	955	241	17	1114	146	373
5 IRON,FERRO.ORES MINING	0	0	0	0	0	0	0	0	0
6 NONFERROUS ORES MINING	0	0	0	0	0	0	0	0	0
7 COAL MINING	934	6439	468	18577	3542	846	10607	1805	994
8 CRUDE PETRO.,NATURAL GAS	0	0	0	0	0	0	0	0	0
9 STONE & CLAY MINING	48	567	79	1447	269	36	821	177	177
10 CHEM.&FERT.MIN.MINING	6	86	9	256	28	6	105	19	21
11 NEW CONSTRUCTION	0	0	0	0	0	0	0	0	0
12 MAINT. & REPAIR CONSTR.	0	0	0	0	0	0	0	0	0
13 ORDNANCE & ACCESSORIES	648	7373	1041	18816	2863	406	9760	2006	2429
14 FOOD & KINDRED PRDTS.	191060	2137893	249031	5672670	934754	135925	2628658	568643	550320
15 TOBACCO MANUFACTURES	19823	208806	21011	555542	105054	12999	258465	63547	48535
16 FABRICS	1985	21834	3427	56296	14492	1653	32053	8791	7874
17 TEXTILE PRDTS.	4218	51266	4536	128485	12761	2734	58067	10063	10254
18 APPAREL	50378	612776	61293	1562160	249906	33400	761287	161909	138781
19 MISC. TEXTILE PRDTS.	5433	63179	7144	161207	28122	3560	78095	18412	16429
20 LUMBER & WOOD PRDTS.	971	7033	1264	19436	6662	682	10400	3435	2887
21 WOODEN CONTAINERS	0	0	0	0	0	0	0	0	0
22 HOUSEHOLD FURNITURE	10635	121489	13257	312309	59444	7289	170551	38633	31167
23 OTHER FURNITURE	467	4960	658	12813	2688	370	7535	1673	1525
24 PAPER & ALLIED PRDTS.	4642	49480	6054	130067	26365	3138	62946	16365	13707
25 PAPERBOARD CONTAINERS	309	3239	334	8244	1468	161	3706	950	809
26 PRINTING & PUBLISHING	11797	133394	15589	352202	53368	8047	176759	35111	35412
27 CHEMICALS,SELECT. PRDTS.	1398	14518	1978	38190	8686	1110	21127	5177	4489
28 PLASTICS & SYNTHETICS	48	519	58	1361	251	32	639	155	134
29 DRUGS & COSMETICS	18676	198481	27658	523582	122821	14243	278391	74232	62485
30 PAINT & ALLIED PRDTS.	105	1157	84	2977	414	62	1270	260	187
31 PETROLEUM,RELATED INDS.	33511	322260	39542	851215	168095	26786	449807	98116	91428
32 RUBBER, MISC. PLASTICS	6476	67322	9909	175327	38881	4861	97776	24286	22919
33 LEATHER TANNING & PRDTS.	0	0	0	0	0	0	0	0	0
34 FOOTWEAR, LEATHER PRDTS.	10602	120214	15035	308901	59226	8134	170792	36750	34150
35 GLASS & GLASS PRDTS.	849	9674	1237	24804	4478	601	12736	2829	2806
36 STONE & CLAY PRDTS.	831	9038	1042	23232	4248	589	11942	2576	2386
37 PRIMARY IRON, STEEL MFR.	48	376	35	1048	197	42	588	108	76
38 PRIMARY NONFERROUS MFR.	50	536	57	1374	258	28	606	164	134

#	Industry	1	2	3	4	5	6	7	8	9
39	METAL CONTAINERS	0	0	0	0	0	0	0	0	0
40	FABRICATED METAL PRDTS.	379	3093	417	8166	2342	237	4598	1261	994
41	SCREW MACH. PRDTS., ETC.	937	10790	1367	27761	5233	662	13754	3246	3076
42	OTHER FAB. METAL PRDTS.	2021	21916	2930	56799	11876	1537	31599	7428	6764
43	ENGINES & TURBINES	305	2547	1009	6625	2484	214	5094	1723	2134
44	FARM MACH. & EQUIP.	37	378	54	985	221	31	586	134	123
45	CONSTRUC. MACH. & EQUIP.	0	0	0	0	0	0	0	0	0
46	MATERIAL HANDLING MACH.	0	0	0	0	0	0	0	0	0
47	METALWORKING MACHINERY	273	2891	386	7419	1524	214	4463	958	910
48	SPECIAL MACH. & EQUIP.	73	777	103	1989	406	57	1198	256	244
49	GENERAL MACH. & EQUIP.	0	0	0	0	0	0	0	0	0
50	MACHINE SHOP PRDTS.	7	73	11	190	45	5	107	28	26
51	OFFICE, COMPUT. MACHINES	311	3286	436	8414	1733	239	5032	1095	1015
52	SERVICE IND. MACHINES	591	8442	831	21057	9916	635	17444	7795	2025
53	ELECT. TRANSMISS. EQUIP.	75	803	109	2067	431	61	1233	268	251
54	HOUSEHOLD APPLIANCES	10098	98798	14734	258066	64893	7743	147846	37686	33803
55	ELECTRIC LIGHTING EQUIP.	1475	15827	2182	40736	8315	1157	23736	5231	5004
56	RADIO, TV, ETC., EQUIP.	7296	78628	10658	203804	36768	5400	122117	24374	24300
57	ELECTRONIC COMPONENTS	615	6619	898	17135	3094	456	10322	2054	2047
58	MISC. ELECTRICAL MACH.	1276	13226	1970	34337	7609	946	19384	4807	4552
59	MOTOR VEHICLES, EQUIP.	51826	546786	76091	1424817	298036	41932	921063	190628	175781
60	AIRCRAFT & PARTS	120	1005	398	2615	981	85	2011	680	843
61	OTHER TRANSPORT. EQUIP.	2404	20086	7924	52245	19547	1690	40126	13550	16773
62	PROFESS., SCIEN. INSTRU.	1356	15489	1981	40215	7687	1004	21823	5071	4699
63	MEDICAL, PHOTO. EQUIP.	2058	22439	3356	57958	10449	1631	34876	6734	7853
64	MISC. MANUFACTURING	11447	133419	17978	340040	58968	8009	182164	38932	41233
65	TRANSPORT. & WAREHOUSING	34144	435314	42694	1146077	142017	20008	464131	93857	95154
66	COMMUNICA.-EXC. BRDCAST.	21282	240589	26538	646662	96771	13525	295763	63308	59195
67	RADIO & TV BROADCASTING	37240	386143	54296	1033504	243339	34792	662021	148876	122474
68	ELEC.,GAS,WATER,SAN.SER.	301181	3318827	391052	8676761	1563475	219860	4390033	963318	891950
69	WHOLESALE & RETAIL TRADE	60813	711144	77958	1853799	301966	42801	928607	194496	179473
70	FINANCE & INSURANCE	215282	2417961	259542	6450960	853846	128684	2916490	572962	591104
71	REAL ESTATE & RENTAL	50475	482146	59673	1393409	224187	28811	592242	146115	124398
72	HOTELS; PERSONAL SERV.	9328	104793	16454	269527	53738	8919	181991	32779	37632
73	BUSINESS SERVICES	0	0	0	0	0	0	0	0	0
74	RESEARCH & DEVELOPMENT	23271	233932	36089	611117	144389	17524	345521	89758	83731
75	AUTO. REPAIR & SERVICES	18312	214538	23525	590075	70083	9988	247819	48331	53919
76	AMUSEMENTS	104419	1243861	133861	3206020	562159	73453	1589526	363966	300144
77	MED.,EDUC. SERVICES	3342	36859	4747	98821	15143	2347	47029	9797	10548
78	FEDERAL GOV'T ENTERPRISE	2060	21085	3589	54935	13687	1610	33134	8717	8295
79	STATE & LOCAL GOV'T ENT.	22464	258701	28895	676417	110558	15693	322908	69282	65832
80	IMPORTS	258701								
81	BUS.TRAVEL, ENT., GIFTS.	0	0	0	0	0	0	0	0	0
82	OFFICE SUPPLIES	-839	-8867	-1238	-23075	-4862	-676	-14879	-3111	-2861
83	SCRAP & USED GOODS	0	0	0	0	0	0	0	0	0
84	GOVERNMENT INDUSTRY	-7609	-39638	-9912	-294006	-11841	-6063	-48296	-8361	-10234
85	REST OF WORLD INDUSTRY	11328	119459	14220	451466	129142	8109	143230	37888	27685
86	HOUSEHOLD INDUSTRY	0	0	0	0	0	0	0	0	0
87	INVENTORY VALUATION ADJ.									
88	STATE TOTAL	1396312	15549125	1817338	40935424	7083672	977718	20289344	4427563	4110250

TABLE C.3

STATE ESTIMATES OF 1963
PERSONAL CONSUMPTION EXPENDITURES
(THOUSANDS OF CURRENT DOLLARS)

INDUSTRY TITLE	37 PENNSYLVANIA	38 RHODE ISLAND	39 SOUTH CAROLINA	40 SOUTH DAKOTA	41 TENNESSEE	42 TEXAS	43 UTAH	44 VERMONT	45 VIRGINIA
1 LIVESTOCK & PRDTS.	95834	7743	21243	6942	29291	93948	7696	3331	42420
2 OTHER AGRICULTURE PRDTS.	178534	13574	30373	9809	48285	135961	14237	5847	59104
3 FORESTRY & FISHERIES	28477	2233	3788	1184	6242	19401	2139	887	7896
4 AGRI.,FORES.,FISH. SERV.	1393	74	62	15	234	354	38	18	225
5 IRON, FERRO. ORES MINING	0	0	0	0	0	0	0	0	0
6 NONFERROUS ORES MINING	0	0	0	0	0	0	0	0	0
7 COAL MINING	13977	984	1778	913	2687	6633	375	648	2850
8 CRUDE PETRO.,NATURAL GAS	0	0	0	0	0	0	0	0	0
9 STONE & CLAY MINING	860	65	135	40	231	- 740	83	26	296
10 CHEM.&FERT. MIN. MINING	120	9	12	6	23	81	0	3	31
11 NEW CONSTRUCTION	0	0	0	0	0	0	0	0	0
12 MAINT. & REPAIR CONSTR.	0	0	0	0	0	0	0	0	0
13 ORDNANCE & ACCESSORIES	11158	817	1396	424	2476	8469	1122	346	3388
14 FOOD & KINDRED PRDTS.	3367590	263609	457980	145420	750036	2298979	251696	105792	946656
15 TOBACCO MANUFACTURES	345386	27019	50892	13925	85502	253918	22239	11380	102169
16 FABRICS	34677	2620	7053	1736	11637	35035	3603	1101	14615
17 TEXTILE PRDTS.	73652	5533	6202	2808	11811	43560	4905	2171	16634
18 APPAREL	907446	69688	122010	35076	207347	663973	64077	26636	271115
19 MISC. TEXTILE PRDTS.	96426	7375	13711	3761	23575	75490	7601	2923	30509
20 LUMBER & WOOD PRDTS.	14561	894	3366	736	5021	12634	1220	697	5636
21 WOODEN CONTAINERS	0	0	0	0	0	0	0	0	0
22 HOUSEHOLD FURNITURE	187698	14413	28868	7677	49127	157917	14914	5682	63977
23 OTHER FURNITURE	7951	588	1314	384	2174	6691	697	258	2777
24 PAPER & ALLIED PRDTS.	80849	6173	12877	3364	21543	65875	6303	2618	26869
25 PAPERBOARD CONTAINERS	5237	380	706	165	1210	3857	383	168	1563
26 PRINTING & PUBLISHING	208349	16276	26295	8606	44736	145282	16153	6454	59371
27 CHEMICALS,SELECT. PRDTS.	24156	1819	4229	1182	6975	20526	2059	803	8451
28 PLASTICS & SYNTHETICS	848	65	122	34	204	621	62	27	254
29 DRUGS & COSMETICS	327312	25160	60320	15324	99450	296095	28548	10707	121252
30 PAINT & ALLIED PRDTS.	1797	133	206	65	337	1050	87	58	436
31 PETROLEUM, RELATED INDS.	552944	40019	81210	27848	131464	382620	41543	19499	162288
32 RUBBER, MISC. PLASTICS	108972	8008	18856	5108	31710	97916	10520	3601	40374
33 LEATHER TANNING & PRDTS.	0	0	0	0	0	0	0	0	0
34 FOOTWEAR, LEATHER PRDTS.	187108	14228	28865	8554	48277	148365	15756	5782	60942
35 GLASS & GLASS PRDTS.	14909	1120	2183	624	3668	11434	1339	458	4755
36 STONE & CLAY PRDTS.	14386	1069	2076	617	3424	10256	1098	458	4290
37 PRIMARY IRON, STEEL MFR.	744	53	98	45	153	411	32	32	175
38 PRIMARY NONFERROUS MFR.	859	64	125	29	212	661	63	28	270

#	Category	1	2	3	4	5	6	7	8	9
39	METAL CONTAINERS	0	0	0	0	0	0	0	0	0
40	FABRICATED METAL PRDTS.	2024	213	428	4803	1762	249	1145	393	5471
41	SCREW MACH. PRDTS., ETC.	5446	506	1482	13053	4263	691	2543	1263	16629
42	OTHER FAB. METAL PRDTS.	12289	1116	3118	29880	9695	1609	5784	2624	35001
43	ENGINES & TURBINES	3130	172	1102	7367	2082	222	1219	300	4383
44	FARM MACH. & EQUIP.	222	21	55	529	177	32	109	46	619
45	CONSTRUC. MACH. & EQUIP.	0	0	0	0	0	0	0	0	0
46	MATERIAL HANDLING MACH.	1592	149	416	3832	1236	220	744	337	4625
47	METALWORKING MACHINERY	426	40	112	1025	330	58	198	90	1239
48	SPECIAL MACH. & EQUIP.	0	0	0	0	0	0	0	0	0
49	GENERAL MACH. & EQUIP.	46	4	12	112	36	6	22	9	119
50	MACHINE SHOP PRDTS.	1837	170	462	4410	1412	246	848	377	5212
51	OFFICE, COMPUT. MACHINES	12620	294	923	34332	9295	669	4845	930	11456
52	SERVICE IND. MACHINES	447	42	114	1073	349	63	211	93	1279
53	ELECT. TRANSMISS. EQUIP.	61292	5770	15525	146272	51041	8041	31531	12159	165837
54	HOUSEHOLD APPLIANCES	8731	813	2272	21057	6781	1204	4078	1833	25038
55	ELECTRIC LIGHTING EQUIP.	40432	3981	11337	100957	31062	5699	17931	9415	125119
56	RADIO, TV, ETC., EQUIP.	3402	336	956	8519	2620	482	1508	793	10551
57	ELECTRONIC COMPONENTS	8004	709	2093	19483	6238	996	3695	1552	21327
58	MISC. ELECTRICAL MACH.	313480	28524	81213	771846	242547	43217	143836	63395	877369
59	MOTOR VEHICLES, EQUIP.	1236	68	435	2908	822	88	481	118	1730
60	AIRCRAFT & PARTS	24613	1352	8659	57923	16375	1748	9587	2364	34553
61	OTHER TRANSPORT. EQUIP.	8252	740	2116	21109	6616	1054	3860	1877	24143
62	PROFESS., SCIEN. INSTRU.	11269	1129	3573	27400	8597	1724	5141	2631	35278
63	MEDICAL, PHOTO. EQUIP.	65074	6169	19106	160476	49524	8387	28692	15112	201693
64	MISC. MANUFACTURING	159101	18043	43821	389389	120359	21556	70588	51825	641446
65	TRANSPORT. & WAREHOUSING	105545	11692	27591	260692	80835	14636	48223	30030	377645
66	COMMUNICA.,EXC. BRDCAST.	243614	21488	55476	596723	197969	37492	120972	50220	645647
67	RADIO & TV BROADCASTING	1596695	168004	409416	3879032	1270821	232145	762512	400584	5266727
68	ELEC.,GAS,WATER,SAN.SER.	331440	32886	83567	816265	250261	45054	145533	80123	1075456
69	WHOLESALE & RETAIL TRADE	949744	118543	277262	2388310	729587	139757	424612	301514	3831456
70	FINANCE & INSURANCE	252735	29012	56882	623777	188979	31107	110841	54991	730649
71	REAL ESTATE & RENTAL	54493	5193	17134	132666	44179	9590	26458	12289	163883
72	HOTELS; PERSONAL SERV.	149336	13038	38215	360659	117042	18411	69782	27705	384045
73	BUSINESS SERVICES	80791	9680	25189	200665	61072	11473	34249	24590	299993
74	RESEARCH & DEVELOPMENT	608618	56005	140424	1483791	466814	77515	277154	141446	1853978
75	AUTO. REPAIR & SERVICES	16609	1846	4860	40307	12625	2527	7525	4541	58421
76	AMUSEMENTS	14368	1154	3827	35464	11288	1710	6697	2515	34407
77	MED.,EDUC. SERVICES	114158	12399	30422	280512	90890	16691	54042	31256	402769
78	FEDERAL GOV'T ENTERPRISE	0	0	0	0	0	0	0	0	0
79	STATE & LOCAL GOV'T ENT.	0	0	0	0	0	0	0	0	0
80	IMPORTS	-5116	-461	-1324	-12599	-3961	-698	-2347	-1028	-14211
81	BUS.TRAVEL, ENT., GIFTS.	0	0	0	0	0	0	0	0	0
82	OFFICE SUPPLIES	0	0	0	0	0	0	0	0	0
83	SCRAP & USED GOODS	0	0	0	0	0	0	0	0	0
84	GOVERNMENT INDUSTRY	0	0	0	0	0	0	0	0	0
85	REST OF WORLD INDUSTRY	-14489	-4694	-4015	-76829	-10620	-3079	-5333	-4084	-52682
86	HOUSEHOLD INDUSTRY	101545	12126	8979	247775	86632	10416	72732	13830	188151
87	INVENTORY VALUATION ADJ.	0	0	0	0	0	0	0	0	0
88	STATE TOTAL	7406538	776711	1893830	18083680	5796693	1045429	3480593	1871862	24390528

TABLE C.3

STATE ESTIMATES OF 1963
PERSONAL CONSUMPTION EXPENDITURES
(THOUSANDS OF CURRENT DOLLARS)

INDUSTRY TITLE	46 WASHINGTON	47 WEST VIRGINIA	48 WISCONSIN	49 WYOMING	50 ALASKA	51 HAWAII	52 NO STATE ALLOCATION	53 NATIONAL TOTAL
1 LIVESTOCK & PRDTS.	32439	14409	34751	4034	5645	10090	0	1762471
2 OTHER AGRICULTURE PRDTS.	51913	25072	62800	5635	4552	9801	0	2867800
3 FORESTRY & FISHERIES	7668	3082	8685	794	614	1458	0	419519
4 AGRI.,FORES.,FISH. SERV.	323	59	292	8	1	58	0	15231
5 IRON, FERRO. ORES MINING	0	0	0	0	0	0	0	0
6 NONFERROUS ORES MINING	0	0	0	0	0	0	0	0
7 COAL MINING	1471	1349	4549	176	191	323	0	164916
8 CRUDE PETRO.,NATURAL GAS	0	0	0	0	0	0	0	0
9 STONE & CLAY MINING	292	112	315	30	20	50	0	14764
10 CHEM.&FERT. MIN. MINING	32	11	47	4	3	9	0	1943
11 NEW CONSTRUCTION	0	0	0	0	0	0	0	0
12 MAINT. & REPAIR CONSTR.	0	0	0	0	0	0	0	0
13 ORDNANCE & ACCESSORIES	3997	1251	3780	414	275	626	0	181096
14 FOOD & KINDRED PRDTS.	909958	373661	1040551	95459	75525	175401	0	49920912
15 TOBACCO MANUFACTURES	78214	42600	101625	8258	5720	14804	0	4942621
16 FABRICS	12779	6017	12790	1351	939	2199	0	629768
17 TEXTILE PRDTS.	17023	5718	23055	1741	1152	2645	0	1010774
18 APPAREL	229296	104783	295583	23528	16872	38873	0	13696666
19 MISC. TEXTILE PRDTS.	26853	11801	30503	2798	1911	4577	0	1482003
20 LUMBER & WOOD PRDTS.	4570	2571	4339	514	424	786	0	229860
21 WOODEN CONTAINERS	0	0	0	0	0	0	0	0
22 HOUSEHOLD FURNITURE	51065	24997	66139	5263	3146	8654	0	3024931
23 OTHER FURNITURE	2449	1128	2992	262	172	418	0	132598
24 PAPER & ALLIED PRDTS.	22189	10794	24728	2333	1671	4133	0	1240991
25 PAPERBOARD CONTAINERS	1312	636	1448	139	87	216	0	73821
26 PRINTING & PUBLISHING	58098	22266	68452	5972	4388	10244	0	3159909
27 CHEMICALS,SELECT. PRDTS.	7225	3529	8391	771	545	1326	0	394344
28 PLASTICS & SYNTHETICS	216	104	253	23	16	39	0	12322
29 DRUGS & COSMETICS	100702	49784	109596	10674	7822	19136	0	5428011
30 PAINT & ALLIED PRDTS.	304	168	497	31	22	52	0	22981
31 PETROLEUM, RELATED INDS.	147877	69202	184028	15692	11424	26145	0	8232114
32 RUBBER, MISC. PLASTICS	37358	16212	38776	3915	2711	6415	0	1863488
33 LEATHER TANNING & PRDTS.	0	0	0	0	0	0	0	0
34 FOOTWEAR, LEATHER PRDTS.	55819	24504	67187	5833	4105	9658	0	3031966
35 GLASS & GLASS PRDTS.	4647	1882	5020	473	298	801	0	238384
36 STONE & CLAY PRDTS.	3863	1771	4718	407	269	653	0	216724
37 PRIMARY IRON, STEEL MFR.	118	77	247	13	12	23	0	9610
38 PRIMARY NONFERROUS MFR.	218	109	237	23	15	38	0	12392

		C1	C2	C3	C4	C5		C6		C7
39	METAL CONTAINERS	1549	0	0	0	0	0	0	0	0
40	FABRICATED METAL PRDTS.	5127	910	1824	174	120	0	233	0	88008
41	SCREW MACH. PRDTS., ETC.	10947	2171	5423	516	327	0	904	0	265915
42	OTHER FAB. METAL PRDTS.	3834	4960	12482	1155	776	0	1912	0	579939
43	ENGINES & TURBINES	196	1083	1979	345	199	0	543	0	124575
44	FARM MACH. & EQUIP.	0	91	235	21	14	0	35	0	10459
45	CONSTRUC. MACH. & EQUIP.	1462	0	0	0	0	0	0	0	0
46	MATERIAL HANDLING MACH.	392	651	1771	156	102	0	240	0	77222
47	METALWORKING MACHINERY	0	174	475	42	27	0	64	0	20690
48	SPECIAL MACH. & EQUIP.	42	0	0	0	0	0	0	0	0
49	GENERAL MACH. & EQUIP.	1641	19	43	4	3	0	7	0	2076
50	MACHINE SHOP PRDTS.	3271	736	1990	175	115	0	268	0	87719
51	OFFICE, COMPUT. MACHINES	403	4282	6578	351	225	0	501	0	336447
52	SERVICE IND. MACHINES	53395	181	490	43	29	0	67	0	21514
53	ELECT. TRANSMISS. EQUIP.	8079	26515	59017	5847	3813	0	9907	0	2792890
54	HOUSEHOLD APPLIANCES	40086	3496	9409	860	583	0	1359	0	421549
55	ELECTRIC LIGHTING EQUIP.	3376	15154	47204	4096	2923	0	7141	0	2088724
56	RADIO, TV, ETC., EQUIP.	7431	1274	3989	345	245	0	604	0	176108
57	ELECTRONIC COMPONENTS	288555	3180	7662	777	545	0	1284	0	368322
58	MISC. ELECTRICAL MACH.	1514	124549	359800	30207	22455	0	47546	0	15380552
59	MOTOR VEHICLES, EQUIP.	30123	427	781	136	78	0	214	0	49177
60	AIRCRAFT & PARTS	7688	8518	15590	2715	1562	0	4266	0	979990
61	OTHER TRANSPORT. EQUIP.	12827	3152	8506	794	533	0	1280	0	402574
62	PROFESS., SCIEN. INSTRU.	67685	4375	13678	1324	923	0	2103	0	603597
63	MEDICAL, PHOTO. EQUIP.	157437	25053	70810	7010	4762	0	11319	0	3327281
64	MISC. MANUFACTURING	97927	58494	177829	15841	11201	0	29951	0	8945875
65	TRANSPORT. & WAREHOUSING	198414	39335	113750	9866	7205	0	18356	0	5542297
66	COMMUNICA.,EXC. BRDCAST.	1454850	97732	261551	20764	15997	0	37702	0	11358165
67	RADIO & TV BROADCASTING	297401	644613	1738419	151907	108477	0	256830	0	80790432
68	ELEC.,GAS,WATER,SAN.SER.	979674	125789	359733	30720	21497	0	51288	0	16879152
69	WHOLESALE & RETAIL TRADE	197396	352497	1111570	97642	67037	0	179587	0	53878208
70	FINANCE & INSURANCE	61067	92720	237456	28698	17151	0	49435	0	12074448
71	REAL ESTATE & RENTAL	0	22135	70989	6412	4423	0	9801	0	2966765
72	HOTELS; PERSONAL SERV.	136104	0	0	0	0	0	0	0	0
73	BUSINESS SERVICES	89449	60251	137544	14347	10146	0	23516	0	6693099
74	RESEARCH & DEVELOPMENT	496582	32589	92588	9208	6229	0	15869	0	4712202
75	AUTO. REPAIR & SERVICES	17399	236024	619242	51183	35444	0	86369	0	29335248
76	AMUSEMENTS	13517	6197	18456	1770	1331	0	3207	0	888069
77	MED.,EDUC. SERVICES	107984	5670	13044	1411	983	0	2370	0	638427
78	FEDERAL GOV'T ENTERPRISE	0	45536	127166	11169	7862	0	19382	0	6004080
79	STATE & LOCAL GOV'T ENT.	0	0	0	0	0	0	0	0	0
80	IMPORTS	-4694	0	0	0	0	0	0	0	0
81	BUS.TRAVEL, ENT., GIFTS.	0	-2032	-5812	-491	-361	0	-777	0	-249671
82	OFFICE SUPPLIES	0	0	0	0	0	0	0	0	0
83	SCRAP & USED GOODS	-30937	-5490	-21824	-2622	-1723	0	-5433	0	-1381897
84	GOVERNMENT INDUSTRY	45668	19738	46432	4550	3287	0	13025	0	3823959
85	REST OF WORLD INDUSTRY	0	0	0	0	0	0	0	0	0
86	HOUSEHOLD INDUSTRY									
87	INVENTORY VALUATION ADJ.	0	0	0	0	0	0	0	0	0
88	STATE TOTAL	6735152	2882407	7940242	705986	507092	0	1231925	0	375540224

255

TABLE C.4

STATE ESTIMATES OF 1947

GROSS PRIVATE CAPITAL FORMATION

(THOUSANDS OF CURRENT DOLLARS)

INDUSTRY TITLE	1 ALABAMA	2 ARIZONA	3 ARKANSAS	4 CALIFORNIA	5 COLORADO	6 CONNECTICUT	7 DELAWARE	8 DISTRICT OF COLUMBIA	9 FLORIDA
1 LIVESTOCK & PRDTS.	674	181	753	329	334	28	28	0	138
2 OTHER AGRICULTURE PRDTS.	0	0	0	0	0	0	0	0	0
3 FORESTRY & FISHERIES	0	0	0	0	0	0	0	0	0
4 AGRI.,FORES.,FISH.SERV.	0	0	0	0	0	0	0	0	0
5 IRON, FERRO. ORES MINING	0	0	0	0	0	0	0	0	0
6 NONFERROUS ORES MINING	0	0	0	0	0	0	0	0	0
7 COAL MINING	0	0	0	0	0	0	0	0	0
8 CRUDE PETRO.,NATURAL GAS	0	0	0	0	0	0	0	0	0
9 STONE & CLAY MINING	0	0	0	0	0	0	0	0	0
10 CHEM.&FERT. MIN. MINING	0	0	0	0	0	0	0	0	0
11 NEW CONSTRUCTION*	181189	76324	165821	2109399	167034	176101	30302	65041	491738
12 MAINT. & REPAIR CONSTR.	0	0	0	0	0	0	0	0	0
13 ORDNANCE & ACCESSORIES	2	0	1	4	8	347	1	0	4
14 FOOD & KINDRED PRDTS.	0	0	0	0	0	0	0	0	0
15 TOBACCO MANUFACTURES	0	0	0	0	0	0	0	0	0
16 FABRICS	36	14	23	265	29	42	7	24	53
17 TEXTILE PRDTS.	188	72	111	1626	168	278	47	162	285
18 APPAREL	0	0	0	1	0	0	0	0	0
19 MISC. TEXTILE PRDTS.	722	1850	119	2559	222	93	90	0	43
20 LUMBER & WOOD PRDTS.	184	11	102	276	21	268	61	2	332
21 WOODEN CONTAINERS	799	289	441	6717	675	1371	203	5	1168
22 HOUSEHOLD FURNITURE	4387	1610	2327	35322	3434	8761	1061	649	5929
23 OTHER FURNITURE	16	8	10	182	15	24	4	3306	36
24 PAPER & ALLIED PRDTS.	0	0	0	0	0	0	0	27	0
25 PAPERBOARD CONTAINERS	2	1	2	20	2	3	0	0	6
26 PRINTING & PUBLISHING	1	0	1	11	2	1	0	3	2
27 CHEMICALS,SELECT. PRDTS.	0	0	0	0	2	0	0	0	0
28 PLASTICS & SYNTHETICS	0	0	0	0	0	0	0	0	0
29 DRUGS & COSMETICS	0	0	0	0	0	0	0	0	0
30 PAINT & ALLIED PRDTS.	0	0	0	0	0	0	0	0	0
31 PETROLEUM, RELATED INDS.	0	0	6	72	3	0	0	0	0
32 RUBBER, MISC. PLASTICS	92	32	58	624	68	109	19	55	130
33 LEATHER TANNING & PRDTS.	425	39	0	0	73	111	0	0	0
34 FOOTWEAR, LEATHER PRDTS.	243	95	55	3600	196	281	72	83	241
35 GLASS & GLASS PRDTS.	0	0	155	1774	0	0	46	160	354
36 STONE & CLAY PRDTS.	0	0	0	0	0	0	0	0	0
37 PRIMARY IRON, STEEL MFR.	0	0	0	0	0	0	0	0	0
38 PRIMARY NONFERROUS MFR.	1	0	0	5	20	48	0	5	1

#	Industry									
39	METAL CONTAINERS	212	65	156	2309	307	174	93	82	316
40	FABRICATED METAL PRDTS.	4688	914	2004	25601	1223	5783	834	1473	3218
41	SCREW MACH. PRDTS., ETC.	28	11	18	207	23	33	5	19	41
42	OTHER FAB. METAL PRDTS.	1456	635	718	10034	676	1614	387	469	1145
43	ENGINES & TURBINES	1985	706	925	11277	559	2639	337	805	1733
44	FARM MACH. & EQUIP.	52953	681	1551	121154	1316	2117	4500	1125	2976
45	CONSTRUC. MACH. & EQUIP.	13275	13848	6912	73526	6006	6651	1213	479	9299
46	MATERIAL HANDLING MACH.	4594	2126	1697	20707	2141	7127	856	799	3725
47	METALWORKING MACHINERY	11888	1296	1397	31227	2853	26649	1641	269	1867
48	SPECIAL MACH. & EQUIP.	18669	2333	8370	76266	6546	23210	5188	3276	15459
49	GENERAL MACH. & EQUIP.	11630	1722	4349	47704	3248	13512	3559	787	5881
50	MACHINE SHOP PRDTS.	0	0	0	0	0	0	0	0	0
51	OFFICE, COMPUT. MACHINES	4120	1173	1909	36436	2854	13568	1532	2932	5113
52	SERVICE IND. MACHINES	6951	2527	3956	54430	5437	8490	1557	4916	10107
53	ELECT. TRANSMISS. EQUIP.	12116	3534	5525	73331	5981	25579	2035	6565	11293
54	HOUSEHOLD APPLIANCES	2178	561	840	12516	1146	1935	323	1263	2225
55	ELECTRIC LIGHTING EQUIP.	309	118	179	2651	238	462	63	235	450
56	RADIO, TV, ETC., EQUIP.	2908	1216	1379	24008	12318	28814	601	4495	3879
57	ELECTRONIC COMPONENTS	487	154	194	4834	389	2318	125	350	612
58	MISC. ELECTRICAL MACH.	604	336	263	4337	522	896	125	500	572
59	MOTOR VEHICLES, EQUIP.	61557	10278	15916	288338	21791	37076	9275	17321	37327
60	AIRCRAFT & PARTS	1934	647	909	14037	1141	2183	545	645	1867
61	OTHER TRANSPORT. EQUIP.	15063	4660	6304	87075	7416	6705	3995	3441	13591
62	PROFESS., SCIEN. INSTRU.	2560	857	1387	22732	2050	4052	791	2546	2785
63	MEDICAL, PHOTO. EQUIP.	590	248	316	8409	516	1221	175	808	1133
64	MISC. MANUFACTURING	1597	601	926	22894	1222	2015	375	1238	2856
65	TRANSPORT. & WAREHOUSING	7352	1596	1982	34062	2611	7107	1160	1892	4196
66	COMMUNICA.,EXC. BRDCAST.	0	0	0	362	5970	13706	0	1446	0
67	RADIO & TV BROADCASTING	0	0	0	0	0	0	0	0	0
68	ELEC.,GAS,WATER,SAN.SER.	0	0	0	0	0	0	0	0	0
69	WHOLESALE & RETAIL TRADE	47611	8873	12296	217559	15742	40871	7714	12242	26677
70	FINANCE & INSURANCE	0	0	0	0	0	0	0	0	0
71	REAL ESTATE & RENTAL	9548	2708	3694	75203	6300	25122	5255	8215	13513
72	HOTELS; PERSONAL SERV.	0	0	0	0	0	0	0	0	0
73	BUSINESS SERVICES	0	0	0	0	0	0	0	0	0
74	RESEARCH & DEVELOPMENT	0	0	0	0	0	0	0	0	0
75	AUTO. REPAIR & SERVICES	0	0	0	0	0	0	0	0	0
76	AMUSEMENTS	0	0	0	0	0	0	0	0	0
77	MED.,EDUC. SERVICES	113	35	48	991	96	147	29	131	194
78	FEDERAL GOV'T ENTERPRISE	0	0	0	0	0	0	0	0	0
79	STATE & LOCAL GOV'T ENT.	0	0	0	0	0	0	0	0	0
80	IMPORTS	0	0	0	0	0	0	0	0	0
81	BUS.TRAVEL, ENT., GIFTS.	0	0	0	0	0	0	0	0	0
82	OFFICE SUPPLIES	0	0	0	0	0	0	0	0	0
83	SCRAP & USED GOODS	17956	4011	5246	85379	7242	18946	3277	4992	11287
84	GOVERNMENT INDUSTRY	0	0	0	0	0	0	0	0	0
85	REST OF WORLD INDUSTRY	0	0	0	0	0	0	0	0	0
86	HOUSEHOLD INDUSTRY	0	0	0	0	0	0	0	0	0
87	INVENTORY VALUATION ADJ.	0	0	0	0	0	0	0	0	0
88	STATE TOTAL	505890	148997	261350	3652363	298184	518588	89508	155273	695796

*The data for this industry could not be made entirely consistent with the 1947 state output estimates. (See page 215.)

TABLE C.4

STATE ESTIMATES OF 1947
GROSS PRIVATE CAPITAL FORMATION
(THOUSANDS OF CURRENT DOLLARS)

INDUSTRY TITLE	10 GEORGIA	11 IDAHO	12 ILLINOIS	13 INDIANA	14 IOWA	15 KANSAS	16 KENTUCKY	17 LOUISIANA	18 MAINE
1 LIVESTOCK & PRDTS.	717	271	587	347	761	600	883	615	74
2 OTHER AGRICULTURE PRDTS.	0	0	0	0	0	0	0	0	0
3 FORESTRY & FISHERIES	0	0	0	0	0	0	0	0	0
4 AGRI.,FORES.,FISH. SERV.	0	0	0	0	0	0	0	0	0
5 IRON, FERRO. ORES MINING	0	0	0	0	0	0	0	0	0
6 NONFERROUS ORES MINING	0	0	0	0	0	0	0	0	0
7 COAL MINING	0	0	0	0	0	0	0	0	0
8 CRUDE PETRO.,NATURAL GAS	0	0	0	0	0	0	0	0	0
9 STONE & CLAY MINING	0	0	0	0	0	0	0	0	0
10 CHEM.&FERT. MIN. MINING	0	0	0	0	0	0	0	0	0
11 NEW CONSTRUCTION*	239494	59652	924101	481275	348542	247054	204076	376411	53310
12 MAINT. & REPAIR CONSTR.	1	1	1	0	0	0	0	0	0
13 ORDNANCE & ACCESSORIES	0	1	1	27	0	0	1	5	3
14 FOOD & KINDRED PRDTS.	0	0	0	0	0	0	0	0	0
15 TOBACCO MANUFACTURES	0	0	0	0	0	0	0	0	0
16 FABRICS	48	11	232	77	54	38	37	45	15
17 TEXTILE PRDTS.	305	54	1360	416	272	213	205	251	76
18 APPAREL	0	0	0	0	0	0	0	0	0
19 MISC. TEXTILE PRDTS.	0	0	1	0	0	0	0	0	0
20 LUMBER & WOOD PRDTS.	18	1087	584	397	2837	86	91	591	578
21 WOODEN CONTAINERS	242	0	423	210	17	15	33	470	0
22 HOUSEHOLD FURNITURE	1244	210	5742	1920	1066	840	849	994	318
23 OTHER FURNITURE	6559	1249	30100	11388	5428	3990	4502	5325	1829
24 PAPER & ALLIED PRDTS.	24	5	154	36	22	17	17	22	7
25 PAPERBOARD CONTAINERS	3	1	17	5	3	2	3	2	1
26 PRINTING & PUBLISHING	2	0	11	3	3	2	3	4	0
27 CHEMICALS,SELECT. PRDTS.	0	0	0	3	0	0	0	0	0
28 PLASTICS & SYNTHETICS	0	0	0	0	0	0	0	0	0
29 DRUGS & COSMETICS	0	0	0	0	0	0	0	0	0
30 PAINT & ALLIED PRDTS.	0	0	0	0	0	0	0	0	0
31 PETROLEUM, RELATED INDS.	0	0	14	1	0	23	0	35	0
32 RUBBER, MISC. PLASTICS	123	26	545	180	120	87	89	120	46
33 LEATHER TANNING & PRDTS.	26	0	0	0	0	0	0	0	0
34 FOOTWEAR, LEATHER PRDTS.	98	329	652	171	1495	73	96	395	30
35 GLASS & GLASS PRDTS.	325	72	1553	512	359	255	248	301	99
36 STONE & CLAY PRDTS.	0	0	0	0	0	0	0	0	0
37 PRIMARY IRON, STEEL MFR.	0	0	0	0	0	0	0	0	0
38 PRIMARY NONFERROUS MFR.	78	0	49	14	0	1	1	1	1

#	Industry									
39	METAL CONTAINERS	89	651	536	391	634	711	2293	100	438
40	FABRICATED METAL PRDTS.	1693	7243	3316	3925	5549	10219	20339	1263	3904
41	SCREW MACH. PRDTS., ETC.	11	34	29	29	41	63	183	8	38
42	OTHER FAB. METAL PRDTS.	441	2903	1278	1511	1690	3087	7052	462	1313
43	ENGINES & TURBINES	735	2609	1601	1776	2682	4311	9185	600	1793
44	FARM MACH. & EQUIP.	1102	46174	1686	1681	9062	3533	9846	34754	2948
45	CONSTRUC. MACH. & EQUIP.	2675	29682	15101	14714	9104	25550	42855	6253	9117
46	MATERIAL HANDLING MACH.	1190	4231	4392	3116	3251	9635	20602	1692	3943
47	METALWORKING MACHINERY	871	2102	5971	1287	2391	40089	56272	1096	2802
48	SPECIAL MACH. & EQUIP.	13575	22580	14143	7364	19286	31407	74795	5088	28122
49	GENERAL MACH. & EQUIP.	3328	17875	6695	6922	7164	24471	39624	2190	7727
50	MACHINE SHOP PRDTS.	0	0	0	0	0	1	1	0	0
51	OFFICE, COMPUT. MACHINES	1843	5685	4125	3459	4823	12095	33788	1126	6028
52	SERVICE IND. MACHINES	2615	8836	7370	6875	13874	15060	44864	2539	8970
53	ELECT. TRANSMISS. EQUIP.	4187	13336	10968	11585	14437	34792	72545	2724	18031
54	HOUSEHOLD APPLIANCES	625	2206	1496	1314	3233	2942	9030	858	2148
55	ELECTRIC LIGHTING EQUIP.	120	385	319	347	427	689	1944	87	528
56	RADIO, TV, ETC. EQUIP.	1090	3501	2860	2955	4036	12415	39620	899	44982
57	ELECTRONIC COMPONENTS	163	656	485	444	626	3332	9516	103	921
58	MISC. ELECTRICAL MACH.	195	711	568	562	975	1099	2890	256	995
59	MOTOR VEHICLES, EQUIP.	10787	66210	29777	28126	118239	64257	177963	32571	42564
60	AIRCRAFT & PARTS	583	2740	1888	2818	2754	4031	10423	706	2091
61	OTHER TRANSPORT. EQUIP.	4661	21991	13987	18746	19964	23410	66250	5177	13987
62	PROFESS., SCIEN. INSTRU.	1047	4490	2750	2722	3420	6843	15475	648	2821
63	MEDICAL, PHOTO. EQUIP.	223	804	619	559	756	1548	5707	166	814
64	MISC. MANUFACTURING	603	2002	1623	1426	2390	3353	10188	534	1962
65	TRANSPORT. & WAREHOUSING	1513	8290	3910	3594	11058	10319	23807	3373	5871
66	COMMUNICA.,EXC. BRDCAST.	0	0	0	127	0	3380	13199	0	23688
67	RADIO & TV BROADCASTING	0	0	0	0	0	0	3380	0	0
68	ELEC.,GAS,WATER,SAN.SER.	0	0	0	0	0	0	0	0	0
69	WHOLESALE & RETAIL TRADE	9310	52612	23564	21736	75335	60043	145076	22581	33068
70	FINANCE & INSURANCE	0	0	0	0	0	0	0	0	0
71	REAL ESTATE & RENTAL	3121	10041	8035	6541	10798	16979	70585	1517	15431
72	HOTELS; PERSONAL SERV.	0	0	0	0	0	0	0	0	0
73	BUSINESS SERVICES	0	0	0	0	0	0	0	0	0
74	RESEARCH & DEVELOPMENT	0	0	0	0	0	0	0	0	0
75	AUTO. REPAIR & SERVICES	0	0	0	0	0	0	0	0	0
76	AMUSEMENTS	0	0	0	0	0	0	0	0	0
77	MED.,EDUC. SERVICES	60	189	102	96	132	314	759	29	98
78	FEDERAL GOV'T ENTERPRISE	0	0	0	0	0	0	0	0	0
79	STATE & LOCAL GOV'T ENT.	0	0	0	0	0	0	0	0	0
80	IMPORTS	0	0	0	0	0	0	0	0	0
81	BUS.TRAVEL, ENT., GIFTS.	0	0	0	0	0	0	0	0	0
82	OFFICE SUPPLIES	0	0	0	0	0	0	0	0	0
83	SCRAP & USED GOODS	4204	20471	10277	9515	26352	26090	63179	7758	17418
84	GOVERNMENT INDUSTRY	0	0	0	0	0	0	0	0	0
85	REST OF WORLD INDUSTRY	0	0	0	0	0	0	0	0	0
86	HOUSEHOLD INDUSTRY	0	0	0	0	0	0	0	0	0
87	INVENTORY VALUATION ADJ.	0	0	0	0	0	0	0	0	0
88	STATE TOTAL	129049	746823	390514	419557	825461	953046	2065970	200124	55384

*The data for this industry could not be made entirely consistent with the 1947 state output estimates. (See page 215.)

TABLE C.4

STATE ESTIMATES OF 1947
GROSS PRIVATE CAPITAL FORMATION
(THOUSANDS OF CURRENT DOLLARS)

INDUSTRY TITLE	19 MARYLAND	20 MASSA-CHUSETTS	21 MICHIGAN	22 MINNESOTA	23 MISSISSIPPI	24 MISSOURI	25 MONTANA	26 NEBRASKA	27 NEVADA
1 LIVESTOCK & PRDTS.	140	36	322	778	1028	1240	426	692	94
2 OTHER AGRICULTURE PRDTS.	0	0	0	0	0	0	0	0	0
3 FORESTRY & FISHERIES	0	0	0	0	0	0	0	0	0
4 AGRI.,FORES.,FISH. SERV.	0	0	0	0	0	0	0	0	0
5 IRON, FERRO. ORES MINING	0	0	0	0	0	0	0	0	0
6 NONFERROUS ORES MINING	0	0	0	0	0	0	0	0	0
7 COAL MINING	0	0	0	0	0	0	0	0	0
8 CRUDE PETRO.,NATURAL GAS	0	0	0	0	0	0	0	0	0
9 STONE & CLAY MINING	0	0	0	0	0	0	0	0	0
10 CHEM.&FERT. MIN. MINING	0	0	0	0	0	0	0	0	0
11 NEW CONSTRUCTION*	238205	392523	738460	321454	123255	333039	56047	152057	33515
12 MAINT. & REPAIR CONSTR.	0	0	0	0	0	0	0	0	0
13 ORDNANCE & ACCESSORIES	2	213	6	1	1	1	0	0	0
14 FOOD & KINDRED PRDTS.	0	0	0	0	0	0	0	0	0
15 TOBACCO MANUFACTURES	0	0	0	0	0	0	0	0	0
16 FABRICS	44	109	133	73	23	96	12	30	4
17 TEXTILE PRDTS.	268	674	693	367	105	545	64	163	26
18 APPAREL	0	1	1	0	0	1	0	0	0
19 MISC. TEXTILE PRDTS.	0	0	0	0	0	0	0	0	0
20 LUMBER & WOOD PRDTS.	71	581	195	6	796	418	462	1649	321
21 WOODEN CONTAINERS	140	735	860	153	154	95	0	4	1
22 HOUSEHOLD FURNITURE	1188	2866	3406	1435	424	2192	249	631	107
23 OTHER FURNITURE	6427	16298	20703	7549	2185	11285	1277	3066	539
24 PAPER & ALLIED PRDTS.	26	67	79	28	10	46	5	12	4
25 PAPERBOARD CONTAINERS	3	8	9	4	1	0	0	0	0
26 PRINTING & PUBLISHING	3	3	9	4	1	6	1	2	1
27 CHEMICALS,SELECT. PRDTS.	2	3	3	4	1	4	0	1	0
28 PLASTICS & SYNTHETICS	0	0	0	0	0	0	0	0	0
29 DRUGS & COSMETICS	0	0	0	0	0	0	0	0	0
30 PAINT & ALLIED PRDTS.	0	0	0	0	0	0	0	0	0
31 PETROLEUM, RELATED INDS.	108	271	4	164	8	219	2	65	10
32 RUBBER, MISC. PLASTICS	0	0	321	0	58	0	28	0	0
33 LEATHER TANNING & PRDTS.	156	467	354	134	430	197	25	865	88
34 FOOTWEAR, LEATHER PRDTS.	294	732	890	488	151	642	80	200	27
35 GLASS & GLASS PRDTS.	0	0	0	0	0	0	0	0	0
36 STONE & CLAY PRDTS.	0	0	0	0	0	0	0	0	0
37 PRIMARY IRON, STEEL MFR.	0	0	0	1	0	0	0	0	0
38 PRIMARY NONFERROUS MFR.	17	81	44	44	0	77	0	22	0

Industry									
39 METAL CONTAINERS	476	691	826	752	132	831	74	244	17
40 FABRICATED METAL PRDTS., ETC.	5019	11417	14969	3826	2532	5640	1220	2256	241
41 SCREW MACH. PRDTS., ETC.	34	86	107	56	17	74	9	23	3
42 OTHER FAB. METAL PRDTS.	1578	3108	4050	2236	811	2176	454	950	164
43 ENGINES & TURBINES	2194	5331	6568	1865	958	2717	659	907	186
44 FARM MACH. & EQUIP.	2400	13369	6127	2876	58655	4455	528	75621	292
45 CONSTRUC. MACH. & EQUIP.	9276	12446	33463	39107	7103	14782	5819	4882	3393
46 MATERIAL HANDLING MACH.	4597	9414	18246	11648	1343	6862	1390	1480	689
47 METALWORKING MACHINERY	15358	23946	62452	4207	564	9318	1115	601	228
48 SPECIAL MACH. & EQUIP.	19204	58747	57321	16389	9676	24396	2105	8048	719
49 GENERAL MACH. & EQUIP.	13277	20799	38614	6137	5147	9907	1753	3712	512
50 MACHINE SHOP PRDTS.	0	0	0	0	0	0	0	0	0
51 OFFICE, COMPUT. MACHINES	6590	18245	24170	6587	1807	10313	983	2636	319
52 SERVICE IND. MACHINES	8841	20532	25317	12374	4324	16922	2083	7213	960
53 ELECT. TRANSMISS. EQUIP.	17400	44085	61511	14259	4666	26391	3938	5754	959
54 HOUSEHOLD APPLIANCES	1947	5068	5074	2556	1651	3601	436	2062	208
55 ELECTRIC LIGHTING EQUIP.	427	1084	1136	500	160	839	113	238	60
56 RADIO, TV, ETC., EQUIP.	12842	49438	27763	4611	1369	46420	910	13885	395
57 ELECTRONIC COMPONENTS	1600	2879	3538	864	187	1337	126	403	38
58 MISC. ELECTRICAL MACH.	777	1918	1800	1261	363	1609	213	689	82
59 MOTOR VEHICLES, EQUIP.	36502	90562	103487	48741	53223	69865	8454	77339	3476
60 AIRCRAFT & PARTS	2522	3556	4445	2668	989	4077	731	1689	264
61 OTHER TRANSPORT. EQUIP.	14248	20183	28793	21117	7751	26133	5165	12812	2067
62 PROFESS., SCIEN. INSTRU.	4297	9067	10661	4579	1316	5597	760	1587	201
63 MEDICAL, PHOTO. EQUIP.	1163	2664	3515	1004	304	1621	171	378	147
64 MISC. MANUFACTURING	2257	5181	6356	2565	938	3674	458	1317	638
65 TRANSPORT. & WAREHOUSING	5510	13361	17052	6280	5466	8878	1176	7379	495
66 COMMUNICA.,EXC. BRDCAST.	4896	23679	10118	95	0	23136	0	6757	0
67 RADIO & TV BROADCASTING	0	0	0	0	0	0	0	0	0
68 ELEC.,GAS,WATER,SAN.SER.	0	0	0	0	0	0	0	0	0
69 WHOLESALE & RETAIL TRADE	32554	78982	100503	37892	37460	52301	6845	50212	2828
70 FINANCE & INSURANCE	0	0	0	0	0	0	0	0	0
71 REAL ESTATE & RENTAL	12822	42474	17911	16434	3471	22596	1870	7531	521
72 HOTELS; PERSONAL SERV.	0	0	0	0	0	0	0	0	0
73 BUSINESS SERVICES	0	0	0	0	0	0	0	0	0
74 RESEARCH & DEVELOPMENT	0	0	0	0	0	0	0	0	0
75 AUTO. REPAIR & SERVICES	0	0	0	0	0	0	0	0	0
76 AMUSEMENTS	0	0	0	0	0	0	0	0	0
77 MED.,EDUC. SERVICES	227	402	424	187	60	253	30	65	7
78 FEDERAL GOV'T ENTERPRISE	0	0	0	0	0	0	0	0	0
79 STATE & LOCAL GOV'T ENT.	0	0	0	0	0	0	0	0	0
80 IMPORTS	0	0	0	0	0	0	0	0	0
81 BUS.TRAVEL, ENT., GIFTS.	0	0	0	0	0	0	0	0	0
82 OFFICE SUPPLIES	0	0	0	0	0	0	0	0	0
83 SCRAP & USED GOODS	14627	36138	42416	16648	12698	24759	3034	17886	1244
84 GOVERNMENT INDUSTRY	0	0	0	0	0	0	0	0	0
85 REST OF WORLD INDUSTRY	0	0	0	0	0	0	0	0	0
86 HOUSEHOLD INDUSTRY	0	0	0	0	0	0	0	0	0
87 INVENTORY VALUATION ADJ.	0	0	0	0	0	0	0	0	0
88 STATE TOTAL	502551	1044511	1505207	622921	353771	781578	111301	476015	56088

*The data for this industry could not be made entirely consistent with the 1947 state output estimates. (See page 215.)

TABLE C.4

STATE ESTIMATES OF 1947
GROSS PRIVATE CAPITAL FORMATION
(THOUSANDS OF CURRENT DOLLARS)

INDUSTRY TITLE	28 NEW HAMPSHIRE	29 NEW JERSEY	30 NEW MEXICO	31 NEW YORK	32 NORTH CAROLINA	33 NORTH DAKOTA	34 OHIO	35 OKLAHOMA	36 OREGON
1 LIVESTOCK & PRDTS.	28	36	240	431	878	429	408	679	204
2 OTHER AGRICULTURE PRDTS.	0	0	0	0	0	0	0	0	0
3 FORESTRY & FISHERIES	0	0	0	0	0	0	0	0	0
4 AGRI.,FORES.,FISH. SERV.	0	0	0	0	0	0	0	0	0
5 IRON, FERRO. ORES MINING	0	0	0	0	0	0	0	0	0
6 NONFERROUS ORES MINING	0	0	0	0	0	0	0	0	0
7 COAL MINING	0	0	0	0	0	0	0	0	0
8 CRUDE PETRO.,NATURAL GAS	0	0	0	0	0	0	0	0	0
9 STONE & CLAY MINING	0	0	0	0	0	0	0	0	0
10 CHEM.&FERT. MIN. MINING	0	0	0	0	0	0	0	0	0
11 NEW CONSTRUCTION*	39584	510421	116797	886708	287062	87587	895702	327995	196575
12 MAINT. & REPAIR CONSTR.	0	0	0	0	0	0	1	1	0
13 ORDNANCE & ACCESSORIES	0	27	0	180	1	0	0	0	2
14 FOOD & KINDRED PRDTS.	0	0	0	0	0	0	0	0	0
15 TOBACCO MANUFACTURES	0	0	0	0	0	0	0	0	0
16 FABRICS	9	97	10	495	51	12	176	38	37
17 TEXTILE PRDTS.	51	589	53	3033	244	54	969	218	185
18 APPAREL	0	0	0	0	0	0	0	0	0
19 MISC. TEXTILE PRDTS.	0	1	0	3	0	0	1	0	0
20 LUMBER & WOOD PRDTS.	266	1078	355	639	1540	0	116	1274	12
21 WOODEN CONTAINERS	226	580	0	1186	492	0	787	7	197
22 HOUSEHOLD FURNITURE	1422	2765	213	12189	1040	205	4375	851	735
23 OTHER FURNITURE	5	16020	1154	62246	6779	1020	25269	4010	4046
24 PAPER & ALLIED PRDTS.	0	67	6	376	24	4	91	21	18
25 PAPERBOARD CONTAINERS	1	0	1	0	4	1	0	0	0
26 PRINTING & PUBLISHING	0	9	0	34	2	0	11	3	2
27 CHEMICALS,SELECT. PRDTS.	0	4	0	9	0	0	5	1	1
28 PLASTICS & SYNTHETICS	0	0	0	0	0	0	0	0	0
29 DRUGS & COSMETICS	0	0	0	0	0	0	0	0	0
30 PAINT & ALLIED PRDTS.	0	0	0	0	0	0	0	0	0
31 PETROLEUM, RELATED INDS.	0	0	9	0	0	0	416	30	0
32 RUBBER, MISC. PLASTICS	27	265	23	1143	135	26	0	85	110
33 LEATHER TANNING & PRDTS.	45	0	26	0	0	0	443	0	0
34 FOOTWEAR, LEATHER PRDTS.	57	588	68	1759	827	20	1177	653	80
35 GLASS & GLASS PRDTS.	0	649	0	3316	345	82	0	252	250
36 STONE & CLAY PRDTS.	0	0	0	1	0	0	0	0	0
37 PRIMARY IRON, STEEL MFR.	0	0	0	0	0	0	0	0	0
38 PRIMARY NONFERROUS MFR.	1	33	0	168	5	0	37	0	1

#	Industry									
39	METAL CONTAINERS	58	862	45	2533	385	48	1144	202	284
40	FABRICATED METAL PRDTS.	1245	16197	1234	33970	6386	459	20579	4946	2258
41	SCREW MACH. PRDTS., ETC.	7	79	8	385	40	9	139	29	29
42	OTHER FAB. METAL PRDTS.	271	5085	474	12603	1664	165	5588	2062	718
43	ENGINES & TURBINES	557	6247	719	16998	2293	257	9152	1926	1188
44	FARM MACH. & EQUIP.	610	29657	485	19985	124471	458	6907	72036	2037
45	CONSTRUC. MACH. & EQUIP.	1434	19883	9662	39375	13679	387	36588	21450	6171
46	MATERIAL HANDLING MACH.	938	10893	1289	30186	4099	494	20410	3074	3142
47	METALWORKING MACHINERY	1350	35455	581	56803	3931	125	79265	1586	2814
48	SPECIAL MACH. & EQUIP.	10689	58464	2195	142848	62630	1030	70234	7526	17849
49	GENERAL MACH. & EQUIP.	2073	40450	2490	49690	13521	333	52124	10190	3390
50	MACHINE SHOP PRDTS.	0	1	0	1	1		1		0
51	OFFICE, COMPUT. MACHINES	1520	19092	994	71478	6849	754	28329	3564	3225
52	SERVICE IND. MACHINES	1748	21039	1796	88016	10202	1785	32847	7971	6481
53	ELECT. TRANSMISS. EQUIP.	3516	43433	3893	132246	12437	2032	74260	10772	7501
54	HOUSEHOLD APPLIANCES	472	5009	388	22322	4754	392	6718	2317	1367
55	ELECTRIC LIGHTING EQUIP.	89	955	103	4217	374	81	1592	356	269
56	RADIO, TV, ETC., EQUIP.	784	23139	823	118291	6491	691	29879	3139	2558
57	ELECTRONIC COMPONENTS	99	5624	109	10090	874	98	3743	436	353
58	MISC. ELECTRICAL MACH.	135	1521	159	6644	731	130	2399	730	423
59	MOTOR VEHICLES, EQUIP.	6999	101346	7710	345188	118548	6431	134008	78029	27961
60	AIRCRAFT & PARTS	288	4131	586	19325	1725	388	8382	3535	1358
61	OTHER TRANSPORT. EQUIP.	1823	26858	4226	118458	13818	2448	50559	25985	9195
62	PROFESS., SCIEN. INSTRU.	786	10879	708	29820	2905	508	14025	2500	2090
63	MEDICAL, PHOTO. EQUIP.	203	2635	210	14164	831	129	3763	650	653
64	MISC. MANUFACTURING	547	5396	441	23650	2735	390	7621	1683	1479
65	TRANSPORT. & WAREHOUSING	1129	15162	1263	43113	12977	613	21426	8459	2940
66	COMMUNICA.,EXC. BRDCAST.	0	8657	0	49292	946		9302		40
67	RADIO & TV BROADCASTING	0	0	0	0	0	0	0	0	0
68	ELEC.,GAS,WATER,SAN.SER.	0	0	0	0	0	0	0	0	0
69	WHOLESALE & RETAIL TRADE	6698	92680	6975	269947	88142	4072	126437	55895	19109
70	FINANCE & INSURANCE	0	0	0	0	0	0	0	0	0
71	REAL ESTATE & RENTAL	2567	37159	1264	203208	11397	1799	40001	6545	6720
72	HOTELS; PERSONAL SERV.	0	0	0	0	0	0	0	0	0
73	BUSINESS SERVICES	0	0	0	0	0	0	0	0	0
74	RESEARCH & DEVELOPMENT	0	0	0	0	0	0	0	0	0
75	AUTO. REPAIR & SERVICES	0	0	0	0	0	0	0	0	0
76	AMUSEMENTS	0	0	0	0	0	0	0	0	0
77	MED.,EDUC. SERVICES	32	402	42	1372	85	24	523	72	98
78	FEDERAL GOV'T ENTERPRISE	0	0	0	0	0	0	0	0	0
79	STATE & LOCAL GOV'T ENT.	0	0	0	0	0	0	0	0	0
80	IMPORTS	0	0	0	0	0	0	0	0	0
81	BUS.TRAVEL, ENT., GIFTS.	0	0	0	0	0	0	0	0	0
82	OFFICE SUPPLIES	0	0	0	0	0	0	0	0	0
83	SCRAP & USED GOODS	2992	39348	3091	120858	31892	1637	54588	20209	8168
84	GOVERNMENT INDUSTRY	0	0	0	0	0	0	0	0	0
85	REST OF WORLD INDUSTRY	0	0	0	0	0	0	0	0	0
86	HOUSEHOLD INDUSTRY	0	0	0	0	0	0	0	0	0
87	INVENTORY VALUATION ADJ.	0	0	0	0	0	0	0	0	0
88	STATE TOTAL	93383	1220960	172915	3070978	861237	117602	1882502	693991	344322

*The data for this industry could not be made entirely consistent with the 1947 state output estimates. (See page 215.)

TABLE C.4

STATE ESTIMATES OF 1947
GROSS PRIVATE CAPITAL FORMATION
(THOUSANDS OF CURRENT DOLLARS)

INDUSTRY TITLE	37 PENNSYLVANIA	38 RHODE ISLAND	39 SOUTH CAROLINA	40 SOUTH DAKOTA	41 TENNESSEE	42 TEXAS	43 UTAH	44 VERMONT	45 VIRGINIA
1 LIVESTOCK & PRDTS.	368	3	452	503	914	1396	158	84	538
2 OTHER AGRICULTURE PRDTS.	0	0	0	0	0	0	0	0	0
3 FORESTRY & FISHERIES	0	0	0	0	0	0	0	0	0
4 AGRI.,FORES.,FISH. SERV.	0	0	0	0	0	0	0	0	0
5 IRON, FERRO. ORES MINING	0	0	0	0	0	0	0	0	0
6 NONFERROUS ORES MINING	0	0	0	0	0	0	0	0	0
7 COAL MINING	0	0	0	0	0	0	0	0	0
8 CRUDE PETRO.,NATURAL GAS	0	0	0	0	0	0	0	0	0
9 STONE & CLAY MINING	0	0	0	0	0	0	0	0	0
10 CHEM.&FERT. MIN.* MINING	0	0	0	0	0	0	0	0	0
11 NEW CONSTRUCTION*	901385	66247	119994	70087	210502	1985766	82109	26179	314670
12 MAINT. & REPAIR CONSTR.	0	0	0	0	0	0	0	0	0
13 ORDNANCE & ACCESSORIES	2	0	0	0	1	27	0	4	4
14 FOOD & KINDRED PRDTS.	0	0	0	0	0	0	0	0	0
15 TOBACCO MANUFACTURES	0	0	0	0	0	0	0	0	0
16 FABRICS	207	17	25	12	59	14	6	47	57
17 TEXTILE PRDTS.	1264	89	118	53	268	71	33	270	300
18 APPAREL	1	0	0	0	0	0	0	0	0
19 MISC. TEXTILE PRDTS.	535	44	0	191	1064	1635	195	54	66
20 LUMBER & WOOD PRDTS.	809	49	280	0	189	285	65	588	586
21 WOODEN CONTAINERS	5458	392	486	206	1087	0	139	1118	1204
22 HOUSEHOLD FURNITURE	30430	2447	3037	1050	6034	1594	753	6483	6330
23 OTHER FURNITURE	115	9	10	4	23	6	3	25	27
24 PAPER & ALLIED PRDTS.	0	1	2	1	3	0	0	0	0
25 PAPERBOARD CONTAINERS	14	2	1	0	2	3	0	4	4
26 PRINTING & PUBLISHING	6	1	0	0	0	1	0	2	2
27 CHEMICALS,SELECT. PRDTS.	0	0	0	0	0	0	0	0	0
28 PLASTICS & SYNTHETICS	0	0	0	0	0	0	0	0	0
29 DRUGS & COSMETICS	0	0	0	0	0	0	0	0	0
30 PAINT & ALLIED PRDTS.	3	0	0	0	0	0	0	0	0
31 PETROLEUM, RELATED INDS.	497	50	71	26	137	177	16	125	156
32 RUBBER, MISC. PLASTICS	557	0	0	0	0	31	0	0	0
33 LEATHER TANNING & PRDTS.	1385	100	44	24	575	37	105	122	128
34 FOOTWEAR, LEATHER PRDTS.	0	111	167	81	393	91	41	316	383
35 GLASS & GLASS PRDTS.	0	0	0	0	0	0	0	0	0
36 STONE & CLAY PRDTS.	0	0	0	0	0	0	0	0	0
37 PRIMARY IRON, STEEL MFR.	0	0	0	0	0	0	0	0	0
38 PRIMARY NONFERROUS MFR.	82	1	1	0	1	0	0	14	2

39 METAL CONTAINERS	1390	84	181	60	463	139	49	363	429
40 FABRICATED METAL PRDTS.	26335	2155	2503	463	2945	1097	792	4765	3557
41 SCREW MACH. PRDTS., ETC.	163	13	19	9	45	10	5	37	44
42 OTHER FAB. METAL PRDTS.	8124	487	613	195	1461	714	187	1535	1314
43 ENGINES & TURBINES	11951	973	1089	281	969	685	412	2179	1728
44 FARM MACH. & EQUIP.	8569	1847	1263	545	61926	522	3770	2920	3104
45 CONSTRUC. MACH. & EQUIP.	65548	1438	4402	2068	10976	13581	1084	10259	7864
46 MATERIAL HANDLING MACH.	25792	1570	1939	704	4489	2380	635	4961	4495
47 METALWORKING MACHINERY	90103	6667	1050	135	6256	2968	568	5768	4511
48 SPECIAL MACH. & EQUIP.	84080	13110	33331	1405	23129	2930	3375	34085	23446
49 GENERAL MACH. & EQUIP.	61780	3738	4374	421	12402	2778	1073	16555	6477
50 MACHINE SHOP PRDTS.	0	0	0	0	0	0	0	0	0
51 OFFICE, COMPUT. MACHINES	31368	2650	2923	740	5650	1299	826	7310	5617
52 SERVICE IND. MACHINES	39575	3125	4513	1833	10838	2478	1464	9061	10049
53 ELECT. TRANSMISS. EQUIP.	91018	7036	6093	2110	6196	3612	2395	14536	11106
54 HOUSEHOLD APPLIANCES	9312	872	1423	400	3022	504	306	2137	2112
55 ELECTRIC LIGHTING EQUIP.	2068	154	178	82	331	111	58	438	420
56 RADIO, TV, ETC., EQUIP.	56561	1176	1855	742	4227	1227	403	10560	4674
57 ELECTRONIC COMPONENTS	5087	205	238	101	545	165	103	774	710
58 MISC. ELECTRICAL MACH.	3794	202	242	143	730	316	104	763	766
59 MOTOR VEHICLES, EQUIP.	167604	12531	19009	6789	78241	10455	8336	38473	40623
60 AIRCRAFT & PARTS	11058	378	683	351	1995	722	282	2272	2734
61 OTHER TRANSPORT. EQUIP.	74767	2285	4676	2203	15040	5426	2017	16959	17885
62 PROFESS., SCIEN. INSTRU.	19660	1369	1529	532	3375	915	498	4482	3524
63 MEDICAL, PHOTO. EQUIP.	4475	370	371	137	919	226	83	1144	1000
64 MISC. MANUFACTURING	9534	971	1038	414	2229	581	281	2234	2296
65 TRANSPORT. & WAREHOUSING	27347	2017	2540	711	8184	1696	894	5406	4553
66 COMMUNICA.,EXC. BRDCAST.	23394	0	0	0	198	0	0	3906	311
67 RADIO & TV BROADCASTING	0	0	0	0	0	0	0	0	0
68 ELEC.,GAS,WATER,SAN.SER.	0	0	0	0	0	0	0	0	0
69 WHOLESALE & RETAIL TRADE	158005	12188	15606	4495	55411	9419	5768	33395	29294
70 FINANCE & INSURANCE	62522	5064	6167	1754	11676	2807	1573	12252	13172
71 REAL ESTATE & RENTAL	0	0	0	0	0	0	0	0	0
72 HOTELS; PERSONAL SERV.	0	0	0	0	0	0	0	0	0
73 BUSINESS SERVICES	0	0	0	0	0	0	0	0	0
74 RESEARCH & DEVELOPMENT	0	0	0	0	0	0	0	0	0
75 AUTO. REPAIR & SERVICES	0	0	0	0	0	0	0	0	0
76 AMUSEMENTS	0	0	0	0	0	0	0	0	0
77 MED.,EDUC. SERVICES	993	51	53	24	124	28	20	272	188
78 FEDERAL GOV'T ENTERPRISE	0	0	0	0	0	0	0	0	0
79 STATE & LOCAL GOV'T ENT.	0	0	0	0	0	0	0	0	0
80 IMPORTS	0	0	0	0	0	0	0	0	0
81 BUS.TRAVEL, ENT., GIFTS.	0	0	0	0	0	0	0	0	0
82 OFFICE SUPPLIES	0	0	0	0	0	0	0	0	0
83 SCRAP & USED GOODS	71703	5206	7413	1845	20149	4310	2269	15197	12732
84 GOVERNMENT INDUSTRY	0	0	0	0	0	0	0	0	0
85 REST OF WORLD INDUSTRY	0	0	0	0	0	0	0	0	0
86 HOUSEHOLD INDUSTRY	0	0	0	0	0	0	0	0	0
87 INVENTORY VALUATION ADJ.	0	0	0	0	0	0	0	0	0
88 STATE TOTAL	2196785	159489	251998	103931	575393	2065204	123250	300429	545192

*The data for this industry could not be made entirely consistent with the 1947 state output estimates. (See page 215.)

TABLE C.4

STATE ESTIMATES OF 1947

GROSS PRIVATE CAPITAL FORMATION

(THOUSANDS OF CURRENT DOLLARS)

INDUSTRY TITLE	46 WASHINGTON	47 WEST VIRGINIA	48 WISCONSIN	49 WYOMING	50 ALASKA	51 HAWAII	52 NO STATE ALLOCATION	53 NATIONAL TOTAL
1 LIVESTOCK & PRDTS.	163	242	676	209	0	0	0	21116
2 OTHER AGRICULTURE PRDTS.	0	0	0	0	0	0	0	0
3 FORESTRY & FISHERIES	0	0	0	0	0	0	0	0
4 AGRI.,FORES.,FISH. SERV.	0	0	0	0	0	0	0	0
5 IRON, FERRO. ORES MINING	0	0	0	0	0	0	0	0
6 NONFERROUS ORES MINING	0	0	0	0	0	0	0	0
7 COAL MINING	0	0	0	0	0	0	0	0
8 CRUDE PETRO.,NATURAL GAS	0	0	0	0	0	0	0	0
9 STONE & CLAY MINING	0	0	0	0	0	0	0	0
10 CHEM.&FERT. MIN. MINING	0	0	0	0	0	0	0	0
11 NEW CONSTRUCTION*	325846	171698	359300	63282	0	0	0	16830896
12 MAINT. & REPAIR CONSTR.	0	0	0	0	0	0	0	0
13 ORDNANCE & ACCESSORIES	1	1	27	1	0	0	0	906
14 FOOD & KINDRED PRDTS.	0	0	0	0	0	0	0	0
15 TOBACCO MANUFACTURES	0	0	0	0	0	0	0	0
16 FABRICS	29	70	6	73	0	0	0	3120
17 TEXTILE PRDTS.	154	370	40	367	0	0	0	17786
18 APPAREL	0	0	0	0	0	0	0	0
19 MISC. TEXTILE PRDTS.	0	0	0	0	0	0	0	17
20 LUMBER & WOOD PRDTS.	317	29	1	6	0	0	0	25042
21 WOODEN CONTAINERS	75	717	153	153	0	0	0	12416
22 HOUSEHOLD FURNITURE	670	1579	686	1435	0	0	0	74802
23 OTHER FURNITURE	3972	8859	0	7549	0	0	0	407026
24 PAPER & ALLIED PRDTS.	12	31	3	28	0	0	0	1807
25 PAPERBOARD CONTAINERS	0	0	0	0	0	0	0	0
26 PRINTING & PUBLISHING	2	4	0	4	0	0	0	216
27 CHEMICALS,SELECT. PRDTS.	0	0	0	0	0	0	0	109
28 PLASTICS & SYNTHETICS	0	0	0	0	0	0	0	0
29 DRUGS & COSMETICS	0	0	0	0	0	0	0	0
30 PAINT & ALLIED PRDTS.	0	0	0	0	0	0	0	0
31 PETROLEUM, RELATED INDS.	0	0	0	10	0	0	0	401
32 RUBBER, MISC. PLASTICS	78	172	14	164	0	0	0	7536
33 LEATHER TANNING & PRDTS.	0	0	0	0	0	0	0	0
34 FOOTWEAR, LEATHER PRDTS.	221	141	14	134	0	0	0	17397
35 GLASS & GLASS PRDTS.	194	466	40	488	0	0	0	20884
36 STONE & CLAY PRDTS.	0	0	0	0	0	0	0	0
37 PRIMARY IRON, STEEL MFR.	0	0	0	0	0	0	0	4
38 PRIMARY NONFERROUS MFR.	7	15	0	1	0	0	0	835

39	METAL CONTAINERS	120	815	24	752	0	0	0	24030
40	FABRICATED METAL PRDTS.	4971	6082	675	3826	0	0	0	297750
41	SCREW MACH. PRDTS., ETC.	22	57	5	56	0	0	0	2441
42	OTHER FAB. METAL PRDTS.	1686	1718	422	2236	0	0	0	101721
43	ENGINES & TURBINES	2451	2774	254	1865	0	0	0	134589
44	FARM MACH. & EQUIP.	8341	2949	295	2876	0	0	0	909053
45	CONSTRUC. MACH. & EQUIP.	24619	11791	6309	39107	0	0	0	764204
46	MATERIAL HANDLING MACH.	5429	6878	824	11648	0	0	0	297761
47	METALWORKING MACHINERY	9040	14478	150	4207	0	0	0	637564
48	SPECIAL MACH. & EQUIP.	14203	28610	822	16389	0	0	0	1224657
49	GENERAL MACH. & EQUIP.	16222	10974	1903	6137	0	0	0	627336
50	MACHINE SHOP PRDTS.	0	0	0	0	0	0	0	0
51	OFFICE, COMPUT. MACHINES	3546	8663	568	6587	0	0	0	427811
52	SERVICE IND. MACHINES	5633	13068	1221	12374	0	0	0	595059
53	ELECT. TRANSMISS. EQUIP.	14025	22125	1603	14219	0	0	0	993648
54	HOUSEHOLD APPLIANCES	1165	2658	223	2556	0	0	0	139869
55	ELECTRIC LIGHTING EQUIP.	309	554	64	500	0	0	0	27408
56	RADIO, TV, ETC., EQUIP.	5593	10761	573	4611	0	0	0	638364
57	ELECTRONIC COMPONENTS	353	822	79	864	0	0	0	68150
58	MISC. ELECTRICAL MACH.	605	947	125	1261	0	0	0	47990
59	MOTOR VEHICLES, EQUIP.	31364	51077	5736	48741	0	0	0	2906207
60	AIRCRAFT & PARTS	1696	2244	855	2668	0	0	0	140537
61	OTHER TRANSPORT. EQUIP.	15994	13546	6249	21117	0	0	0	926131
62	PROFESS., SCIEN. INSTRU.	3047	5107	431	4579	0	0	0	231309
63	MEDICAL, PHOTO. EQUIP.	522	1168	99	1004	0	0	0	70335
64	MISC. MANUFACTURING	1339	2722	251	2565	0	0	0	151589
65	TRANSPORT. & WAREHOUSING	5123	6875	801	6280	0	0	0	378797
66	COMMUNICA., EXC. BRDCAST.	1849	3691	0	95	0	0	0	232240
67	RADIO & TV BROADCASTING	0	0	0	0	0	0	0	0
68	ELEC., GAS, WATER, SAN.SER.	0	0	0	0	0	0	0	0
69	WHOLESALE & RETAIL TRADE	29083	41405	4673	37892	0	0	0	2339064
70	FINANCE & INSURANCE	0	0	0	0	0	0	0	0
71	REAL ESTATE & RENTAL	4486	15235	722	16434	0	0	0	882760
72	HOTELS; PERSONAL SERV.	0	0	0	0	0	0	0	0
73	BUSINESS SERVICES	0	0	0	0	0	0	0	0
74	RESEARCH & DEVELOPMENT	0	0	0	0	0	0	0	2
75	AUTO. REPAIR & SERVICES	0	0	0	0	0	0	0	0
76	AMUSEMENTS	0	0	0	0	0	0	0	0
77	MED., EDUC. SERVICES	84	233	10	187	0	0	0	10134
78	FEDERAL GOV'T ENTERPRISE	0	0	0	0	0	0	0	0
79	STATE & LOCAL GOV'T ENT.	0	0	0	0	0	0	0	0
80	IMPORTS	0	0	0	0	0	0	0	0
81	BUS.TRAVEL, ENT., GIFTS.	0	0	0	0	0	0	0	0
82	OFFICE SUPPLIES	0	0	0	0	0	0	0	0
83	SCRAP & USED GOODS	12806	17731	2162	16648	0	0	0	0
84	GOVERNMENT INDUSTRY	0	0	0	0	0	0	0	985999
85	REST OF WORLD INDUSTRY	0	0	0	0	0	0	0	0
86	HOUSEHOLD INDUSTRY	0	0	0	0	0	0	0	0
87	INVENTORY VALUATION ADJ.	0	0	0	0	0	0	0	0
88	STATE TOTAL	557464	492154	399090	364191	0	0	0	34656784

*The data for this industry could not be made entirely consistent with the 1947 state output estimates. (See page 215.)

TABLE C.5

STATE ESTIMATES OF 1958
GROSS PRIVATE CAPITAL FORMATION
(THOUSANDS OF CURRENT DOLLARS)

INDUSTRY TITLE	1 ALABAMA	2 ARIZONA	3 ARKANSAS	4 CALIFORNIA	5 COLORADO	6 CONNECTICUT	7 DELAWARE	8 DISTRICT OF COLUMBIA	9 FLORIDA
1 LIVESTOCK & PRDTS.	0	0	0	0	0	0	0	0	0
2 OTHER AGRICULTURE PRDTS.	0	0	0	0	0	0	0	0	0
3 FORESTRY & FISHERIES	0	0	0	0	0	0	0	0	0
4 AGRI.,FORES.,FISH. SERV.	0	0	0	0	0	0	0	0	0
5 IRON, FERRO. ORES MINING	0	0	0	0	0	0	0	0	0
6 NONFERROUS ORES MINING	0	0	0	0	0	0	0	0	0
7 COAL MINING	0	0	0	0	0	0	0	0	0
8 CRUDE PETRO.,NATURAL GAS	0	0	0	0	0	0	0	0	0
9 STONE & CLAY MINING	0	0	0	0	0	0	0	0	0
10 CHEM.&FERT. MIN. MINING	0	0	0	0	0	0	0	0	0
11 NEW CONSTRUCTION	549443	445040	283795	443949	534454	550943	116706	164702	1556064
12 MAINT. & REPAIR CONSTR.	0	0	0	0	0	0	0	0	0
13 ORDNANCE & ACCESSORIES	0	0	0	0	0	0	0	0	0
14 FOOD & KINDRED PRDTS.	0	0	0	0	0	0	0	0	0
15 TOBACCO MANUFACTURES	0	0	0	0	0	0	0	0	0
16 FABRICS	507	302	298	4500	516	624	121	339	1150
17 TEXTILE PRDTS.	0	0	0	0	0	0	0	0	0
18 APPAREL	0	0	0	0	0	0	0	0	0
19 MISC. TEXTILE PRDTS.	0	0	0	0	0	0	0	0	0
20 LUMBER & WOOD PRDTS.	177	312	16	710	199	23	26	0	22
21 WOODEN CONTAINERS	0	0	0	0	0	0	0	0	0
22 HOUSEHOLD FURNITURE	1469	813	780	12742	1366	2026	353	864	3143
23 OTHER FURNITURE	9225	4653	4526	81781	8036	13580	2207	5328	18133
24 PAPER & ALLIED PRDTS.	0	0	0	0	0	0	0	0	0
25 PAPERBOARD CONTAINERS	0	0	0	0	0	0	0	0	0
26 PRINTING & PUBLISHING	0	0	0	0	0	0	0	0	0
27 CHEMICALS,SELECT. PRDTS.	0	0	0	0	0	0	0	0	0
28 PLASTICS & SYNTHETICS	0	0	0	0	0	0	0	0	0
29 DRUGS & COSMETICS	0	0	0	0	0	0	0	0	0
30 PAINT & ALLIED PRDTS.	0	0	0	0	0	0	0	0	0
31 PETROLEUM, RELATED INDS.	0	0	0	0	0	0	0	0	0
32 RUBBER, MISC. PLASTICS	685	332	392	5120	543	754	163	305	1463
33 LEATHER TANNING & PRDTS.	0	0	0	0	0	0	0	0	0
34 FOOTWEAR, LEATHER PRDTS.	116	15	12	871	47	23	25	27	101
35 GLASS & GLASS PRDTS.	0	0	0	0	0	0	0	0	0
36 STONE & CLAY PRDTS.	0	0	0	0	0	0	0	0	0
37 PRIMARY IRON, STEEL MFR.	0	0	0	0	0	0	0	0	0
38 PRIMARY NONFERROUS MFR.	0	0	0	0	0	0	0	0	0

Industry									
39 METAL CONTAINERS	115	49	60	1028	106	82	34	39	215
40 FABRICATED METAL PRDTS.	16210	6294	5697	60808	8241	19368	2481	6565	12864
41 SCREW MACH. PRDTS., ETC.	0	0	0	0	0	0	0	0	0
42 OTHER FAB. METAL PRDTS.	2808	1398	1299	15150	2073	2564	560	831	3173
43 ENGINES & TURBINES	13186	6779	4736	49920	8091	17310	1864	6547	11837
44 FARM MACH. & EQUIP.	80176	2514	3763	223649	3211	3651	14069	1847	8258
45 CONSTRUC. MACH. & EQUIP.	24053	22547	11235	108306	29183	11475	2606	4213	32021
46 MATERIAL HANDLING MACH.	6102	3243	2542	33047	4426	5369	917	680	7189
47 METALWORKING MACHINERY	27425	4055	3356	103905	5758	33751	2650	661	9066
48 SPECIAL MACH. & EQUIP.	29066	6175	12415	111285	8504	25795	5226	6751	31190
49 GENERAL MACH. & EQUIP.	24791	4296	6387	82828	8543	20003	4273	2105	16760
50 MACHINE SHOP PRDTS.	0	0	0	0	0	0	0	0	0
51 OFFICE, COMPUT. MACHINES	10905	4728	5149	106734	8603	22428	3160	6406	19231
52 SERVICE IND. MACHINES	12478	6227	6121	98984	9841	13038	2807	6511	26709
53 ELECT. TRANSMISS. EQUIP.	29531	14964	10731	151165	21355	46493	4597	17859	29161
54 HOUSEHOLD APPLIANCES	1426	528	506	9231	847	1231	296	627	2402
55 ELECTRIC LIGHTING EQUIP.	340	209	181	2616	341	434	69	234	639
56 RADIO, TV, ETC., EQUIP.	4294	2569	2287	97993	18047	12239	906	4803	8139
57 ELECTRONIC COMPONENTS	175	144	97	3595	166	687	47	145	375
58 MISC. ELECTRICAL MACH.	1057	721	586	7797	1182	1073	220	470	1533
59 MOTOR VEHICLES, EQUIP.	71341	21265	20687	387585	33763	41067	13838	19530	77981
60 AIRCRAFT & PARTS	6059	4174	4774	33933	5090	3926	943	685	8641
61 OTHER TRANSPORT. EQUIP.	21959	14085	16141	99192	17770	6994	3299	1386	30146
62 PROFESS., SCIEN. INSTRU.	6966	2768	2864	47778	5432	8930	1660	3256	9429
63 MEDICAL, PHOTO. EQUIP.	1300	873	673	19690	1421	2418	400	2025	3740
64 MISC. MANUFACTURING	2853	1548	1447	37450	3350	3256	876	2072	7953
65 TRANSPORT. & WAREHOUSING	10083	3287	2926	51115	5196	8004	1786	2683	9391
66 COMMUNICA.,EXC. BRDCAST.	0	0	0	29434	8089	3464	617	617	0
67 RADIO & TV BROADCASTING	0	0	0	0	0	0	0	0	0
68 ELEC.,GAS,WATER,SAN.SER.	0	0	0	0	0	0	0	0	0
69 WHOLESALE & RETAIL TRADE	75654	22590	21514	384638	35694	56099	14115	19270	71743
70 FINANCE & INSURANCE	0	0	0	0	0	0	0	0	0
71 REAL ESTATE & RENTAL	11746	5992	5517	125162	12496	25967	4094	10494	27516
72 HOTELS; PERSONAL SERV.	0	0	0	0	0	0	0	0	0
73 BUSINESS SERVICES	0	0	0	0	0	0	0	0	0
74 RESEARCH & DEVELOPMENT	0	0	0	0	0	0	0	0	0
75 AUTO. REPAIR & SERVICES	0	0	0	0	0	0	0	0	0
76 AMUSEMENTS	0	0	0	0	0	0	0	0	0
77 MED.,EDUC. SERVICES	0	0	0	0	0	0	0	0	0
78 FEDERAL GOV'T ENTERPRISE	0	0	0	0	0	0	0	0	0
79 STATE & LOCAL GOV'T ENT.	0	0	0	0	0	0	0	0	0
80 IMPORTS	203	1	4	1136	18	521	190	0	50
81 BUS.TRAVEL, ENT., GIFTS.	0	0	0	0	0	0	0	0	0
82 OFFICE SUPPLIES	0	0	0	0	0	0	0	0	0
83 SCRAP & USED GOODS	-15794	-5336	-5000	-81114	-8689	-12982	-2845	-4263	-15384
84 GOVERNMENT INDUSTRY	0	0	0	0	0	0	0	0	0
85 REST OF WORLD INDUSTRY	0	0	0	0	0	0	0	0	0
86 HOUSEHOLD INDUSTRY	0	0	0	0	0	0	0	0	0
87 INVENTORY VALUATION ADJ.	0	0	0	0	0	0	0	0	0
88 STATE TOTAL	1038128	610153	438512	6945689	603305	952626	204739	296611	2032028

TABLE C.5

STATE ESTIMATES OF 1958
GROSS PRIVATE CAPITAL FORMATION
(THOUSANDS OF CURRENT DOLLARS)

INDUSTRY TITLE	10 GEORGIA	11 IDAHO	12 ILLINOIS	13 INDIANA	14 IOWA	15 KANSAS	16 KENTUCKY	17 LOUISIANA	18 MAINE
1 LIVESTOCK & PRDTS.	0	0	0	0	0	0	0	0	0
2 OTHER AGRICULTURE PRDTS.	0	0	0	0	0	0	0	0	0
3 FORESTRY & FISHERIES	0	0	0	0	0	0	0	0	0
4 AGRI.,FORES.,FISH. SERV.	0	0	0	0	0	0	0	0	0
5 IRON, FERRO. ORES MINING	0	0	0	0	0	0	0	0	0
6 NONFERROUS ORES MINING	0	0	0	0	0	0	0	0	0
7 COAL MINING	0	0	0	0	0	0	0	0	0
8 CRUDE PETRO.,NATURAL GAS	0	0	0	0	0	0	0	0	0
9 STONE & CLAY MINING	0	0	0	0	0	0	0	0	0
10 CHEM.&FERT. MIN. MINING	0	0	0	0	0	0	0	0	0
11 NEW CONSTRUCTION	687984	174789	1739843	772369	363072	565334	526460	1224802	162252
12 MAINT. & REPAIR CONSTR.	0	0	0	0	0	0	0	0	0
13 ORDNANCE & ACCESSORIES	0	0	0	0	0	0	0	0	0
14 FOOD & KINDRED PRDTS.	0	0	0	0	0	0	0	0	0
15 TOBACCO MANUFACTURES	0	0	0	0	0	0	0	0	0
16 FABRICS	0	0	0	0	0	0	0	0	0
17 TEXTILE PRDTS.	867	181	3275	1037	697	545	496	659	188
18 APPAREL	0	0	0	0	0	0	0	0	0
19 MISC. TEXTILE PRDTS.	1	0	0	0	0	0	0	0	0
20 LUMBER & WOOD PRDTS.	1	167	45	18	648	1	8	165	1
21 WOODEN CONTAINERS	0	0	0	0	0	0	0	0	0
22 HOUSEHOLD FURNITURE	2378	475	9155	3278	1814	1480	1378	1758	507
23 OTHER FURNITURE	14542	2408	59227	21691	10474	7952	9128	11658	3253
24 PAPER & ALLIED PRDTS.	0	0	0	0	0	0	0	0	0
25 PAPERBOARD CONTAINERS	0	0	0	0	0	0	0	0	0
26 PRINTING & PUBLISHING	0	0	0	0	0	0	0	0	0
27 CHEMICALS,SELECT. PRDTS.	0	0	0	0	0	0	0	0	0
28 PLASTICS & SYNTHETICS	0	0	0	0	0	0	0	0	0
29 DRUGS & COSMETICS	0	0	0	0	0	0	0	0	0
30 PAINT & ALLIED PRDTS.	0	0	0	0	0	0	0	0	0
31 PETROLEUM, RELATED INDS.	0	0	0	0	0	0	0	0	0
32 RUBBER, MISC. PLASTICS	1045	203	3636	1174	793	537	606	953	301
33 LEATHER TANNING & PRDTS.	0	0	0	0	0	0	0	0	0
34 FOOTWEAR, LEATHER PRDTS.	32	91	180	42	399	18	27	131	7
35 GLASS & GLASS PRDTS.	0	0	0	0	0	0	0	0	0
36 STONE & CLAY PRDTS.	0	0	0	0	0	0	0	0	0
37 PRIMARY IRON, STEEL MFR.	0	0	0	0	0	0	0	0	0
38 PRIMARY NONFERROUS MFR.	0	0	0	0	0	0	0	0	0

Table of industry outputs by final-demand category (industry codes 39–88). No column headers appear on this page.

Code	Industry									
39	METAL CONTAINERS	296	64	788	293	307	119	168	163	50
40	FABRICATED METAL PRDTS.	12604	8608	39668	28713	11860	9525	8541	21341	3078
41	SCREW MACH. PRDTS., ETC.	0	0	0	0	2907	2688	1969	7281	667
42	OTHER FAB. METAL PRDTS.	2528	1085	10137	5438	9090	6851	7616	13319	2328
43	ENGINES & TURBINES	10446	7989	29063	21238	18494	3152	3021	96081	2174
44	FARM MACH. & EQUIP.	8181	61870	17305	6139	17649	21285	25264	114613	4871
45	CONSTRUC. MACH. & EQUIP.	19426	8581	46388	23483	5818	4704	4707	6860	1495
46	MATERIAL HANDLING MACH.	6057	1641	24723	12518	8597	4837	10783	5461	1304
47	METALWORKING MACHINERY	8407	962	110587	98570	27035	10261	17973	27916	14651
48	SPECIAL MACH. & EQUIP.	50867	6105	90452	40623	15743	11533	14839	48453	4520
49	GENERAL MACH. & EQUIP.	13739	4665	68957	53588	12019	9091	13260	14165	0
50	MACHINE SHOP PRDTS.									
51	OFFICE, COMPUT. MACHINES	16629	2695	75376	28351	20691	10600	11414	15059	3914
52	SERVICE IND. MACHINES	18362	4681	68657	22756	17780	17522	19764	22543	4240
53	ELECT. TRANSMISS. EQUIP.	32311	16549	95227	62795	2105	791	1025	1625	4646
54	HOUSEHOLD APPLIANCES	2055	528	6003	1799	338	307	287	368	386
55	ELECTRIC LIGHTING EQUIP.	503	175	1548	626	5574	4874	3866	5555	97
56	RADIO, TV, ETC., EQUIP.	43820	1405	44945	15841	370	228	263	272	1533
57	ELECTRONIC COMPONENTS	322	51	2894	985	1747	1142	909	1239	67
58	MISC. ELECTRICAL MACH.	1662	468	5105	1734	150654	35424	36063	93333	339
59	MOTOR VEHICLES, EQUIP.	60537	40376	204216	71768	10446	11114	4319	7660	13589
60	AIRCRAFT & PARTS	7581	3521	21301	11224	37881	36130	15607	32829	2057
61	OTHER TRANSPORT. EQUIP.	23838	12960	66148	34675	7652	5681	6893	12852	7232
62	PROFESS., SCIEN. INSTRU.	8173	1766	39172	16671	1691	1403	1366	1879	2060
63	MEDICAL, PHOTO. EQUIP.	2152	309	13709	3641	3830	2377	3074	4331	456
64	MISC. MANUFACTURING	4319	897	18222	5850	15883	4972	5399	14243	1016
65	TRANSPORT. & WAREHOUSING	8903	4872	29535	14208	0	0	0	0	1860
66	COMMUNICA.,EXC. BRDCAST.	21261	0	10157	3756	0	0	0	0	0
67	RADIO & TV BROADCASTING	0	0	0	0	0	0	0	0	0
68	ELEC.,GAS,WATER,SAN.SER.	0	0	0	0	0	0	0	0	0
69	WHOLESALE & RETAIL TRADE	62345	37581	218733	98849	129396	36294	39573	104050	14087
70	FINANCE & INSURANCE	0	0	0	0	0	0	0	0	0
71	REAL ESTATE & RENTAL	20102	2614	87675	24290	13090	9058	9352	13393	3943
72	HOTELS; PERSONAL SERV.	0	0	0	0	0	0	0	0	0
73	BUSINESS SERVICES	0	0	0	0	0	0	0	0	0
74	RESEARCH & DEVELOPMENT	0	0	0	0	0	0	0	0	0
75	AUTO. REPAIR & SERVICES	0	0	0	0	0	0	0	0	0
76	AMUSEMENTS	0	0	0	0	0	0	0	0	0
77	MED.,EDUC. SERVICES	0	0	0	0	0	0	0	0	0
78	FEDERAL GOV'T ENTERPRISE	0	0	0	0	0	0	0	0	0
79	STATE & LOCAL GOV'T ENT.	0	0	0	0	0	0	0	0	0
80	IMPORTS	209	0	0	0	0	0	0	0	133
81	BUS.,TRAVEL, ENT., GIFTS.	0	1284	0	514	127	63	54	50	0
82	OFFICE SUPPLIES	0	0	0	0	0	0	0	0	0
83	SCRAP & USED GOODS	-15231	-7406	-47697	-23111	-23907	-8533	-8737	-21986	-3164
84	GOVERNMENT INDUSTRY	0	0	0	0	0	0	0	0	0
85	REST OF WORLD INDUSTRY	0	0	0	0	0	0	0	0	0
86	HOUSEHOLD INDUSTRY	0	0	0	0	0	0	0	0	0
87	INVENTORY VALUATION ADJ.	0	0	0	0	0	0	0	0	0
88	STATE TOTAL	1152744	403924	3215621	1487426	1102759	829358	796795	1905051	260139

TABLE C.5

STATE ESTIMATES OF 1958
GROSS PRIVATE CAPITAL FORMATION
(THOUSANDS OF CURRENT DOLLARS)

INDUSTRY TITLE	19 MARYLAND	20 MASSA-CHUSETTS	21 MICHIGAN	22 MINNESOTA	23 MISSISSIPPI	24 MISSOURI	25 MONTANA	26 NEBRASKA	27 NEVADA
1 LIVESTOCK & PRDTS.	0	0	0	0	0	0	0	0	0
2 OTHER AGRICULTURE PRDTS.	0	0	0	0	0	0	0	0	0
3 FORESTRY & FISHERIES	0	0	0	0	0	0	0	0	0
4 AGRI.,FORES.,FISH. SERV.	0	0	0	0	0	0	0	0	0
5 IRON, FERRO. ORES MINING	0	0	0	0	0	0	0	0	0
6 NONFERROUS ORES MINING	0	0	0	0	0	0	0	0	0
7 COAL MINING	0	0	0	0	0	0	0	0	0
8 CRUDE PETRO.,NATURAL GAS	0	0	0	0	0	0	0	0	0
9 STONE & CLAY MINING	0	0	0	0	0	0	0	0	0
10 CHEM.&FERT. MIN. MINING	0	0	0	0	0	0	0	0	0
11 NEW CONSTRUCTION	645981	894670	1172227	622432	223925	841292	183799	244353	111251
12 MAINT. & REPAIR CONSTR.	0	0	0	0	0	0	0	0	0
13 ORDNANCE & ACCESSORIES	0	0	0	0	0	0	0	0	0
14 FOOD & KINDRED PRDTS.	0	0	0	0	0	0	0	0	0
15 TOBACCO MANUFACTURES	0	0	0	0	0	0	0	0	0
16 FABRICS	0	0	0	0	0	0	0	0	0
17 TEXTILE PRDTS.	657	1417	1842	935	307	1218	201	430	133
18 APPAREL	0	0	0	0	0	0	0	0	0
19 MISC. TEXTILE PRDTS.	0	0	0	0	0	0	0	0	0
20 LUMBER & WOOD PRDTS.	4	140	26	7	230	28	39	382	32
21 WOODEN CONTAINERS	0	0	0	0	0	0	0	0	0
22 HOUSEHOLD FURNITURE	1895	3957	5467	2456	846	3360	511	1142	365
23 OTHER FURNITURE	11729	25487	36386	14436	4854	20545	2655	6257	1907
24 PAPER & ALLIED PRDTS.	0	0	0	0	0	0	0	0	0
25 PAPERBOARD CONTAINERS	0	0	0	0	0	0	0	0	0
26 PRINTING & PUBLISHING	0	0	0	0	0	0	0	0	0
27 CHEMICALS,SELECT. PRDTS.	0	0	0	0	0	0	0	0	0
28 PLASTICS & SYNTHETICS	0	0	0	0	0	0	0	0	0
29 DRUGS & COSMETICS	0	0	0	0	0	0	0	0	0
30 PAINT & ALLIED PRDTS.	0	0	0	0	0	0	0	0	0
31 PETROLEUM, RELATED INDS.	0	0	0	0	0	0	0	0	0
32 RUBBER, MISC. PLASTICS	791	1597	2232	1096	403	1426	221	450	109
33 LEATHER TANNING & PRDTS.	0	0	0	0	0	0	0	0	0
34 FOOTWEAR, LEATHER PRDTS.	49	108	104	34	142	51	6	235	81
35 GLASS & GLASS PRDTS.	0	0	0	0	0	0	0	0	0
36 STONE & CLAY PRDTS.	0	0	0	0	0	0	0	0	0
37 PRIMARY IRON, STEEL MFR.	0	0	0	0	0	0	0	0	0
38 PRIMARY NONFERROUS MFR.	0	0	0	0	0	0	0	0	0

Code	Industry									
39	METAL CONTAINERS	154	241	386	297	76	283	26	126	10
40	FABRICATED METAL PRDTS.	9308	13398	25453	8521	11952	11995	1975	6301	853
41	SCREW MACH. PRDTS., ETC.	0	0	0	0	0	0	0	0	0
42	OTHER FAB. METAL PRDTS.	1874	3718	6285	3028	1881	3207	954	1931	356
43	ENGINES & TURBINES	7898	10911	20196	7176	9603	10077	1473	4363	1147
44	FARM MACH. & EQUIP.	4785	22981	10127	5767	123559	7482	1368	142744	1423
45	CONSTRUC. MACH. & EQUIP.	11576	21521	52819	35873	14887	23830	11332	12724	3308
46	MATERIAL HANDLING MACH.	3974	7787	20034	9482	2694	8299	2296	3059	942
47	METALWORKING MACHINERY	17997	32070	70077	9236	2787	22649	1546	5252	457
48	SPECIAL MACH. & EQUIP.	18999	48850	60151	23457	16397	27288	4527	13277	1249
49	GENERAL MACH. & EQUIP.	14223	20766	45761	11242	11973	16960	3245	9603	902
50	MACHINE SHOP PRDTS.	0	0	0	0	0	0	0	0	0
51	OFFICE, COMPUT. MACHINES	13563	33885	48020	17995	5874	23483	2647	7290	1241
52	SERVICE IND. MACHINES	13912	29215	39988	19154	7777	25306	3652	11357	3141
53	ELECT. TRANSMISS. EQUIP.	22338	35551	69353	20032	19496	36335	2942	9145	2330
54	HOUSEHOLD APPLIANCES	1340	3036	3415	1610	1193	2265	274	1287	284
55	ELECTRIC LIGHTING EQUIP.	355	634	953	434	234	635	100	214	131
56	RADIO, TV, ETC., EQUIP.	12140	24454	28742	6333	2485	41108	1597	16198	1131
57	ELECTRONIC COMPONENTS	726	1143	1075	358	132	500	56	330	31
58	MISC. ELECTRICAL MACH.	1245	2299	3395	1944	783	2317	474	1223	188
59	MOTOR VEHICLES, EQUIP.	43310	93867	122080	58655	72869	78337	13282	93520	7004
60	AIRCRAFT & PARTS	3559	5187	12949	9769	5126	9757	4754	6838	1621
61	OTHER TRANSPORT. EQUIP.	9710	15066	42365	33991	18928	30065	16803	25171	6179
62	PROFESS., SCIEN. INSTRU.	9547	17001	23558	10595	3553	12419	1608	4204	569
63	MEDICAL, PHOTO. EQUIP.	2204	5543	7568	2546	633	3708	414	924	826
64	MISC. MANUFACTURING	4298	7922	11153	4346	1680	6197	788	2366	3377
65	TRANSPORT. & WAREHOUSING	6072	12660	18907	7627	8886	10599	1742	10081	998
66	COMMUNICA.,EXC. BRDCAST.	3861	8060	7596	0	0	17954	0	7233	0
67	RADIO & TV BROADCASTING	0	0	0	0	0	0	0	0	0
68	ELEC.,GAS,WATER,SAN.SER.	0	0	0	0	0	0	0	0	0
69	WHOLESALE & RETAIL TRADE	44891	96157	139245	57790	70086	77218	12850	81623	7299
70	FINANCE & INSURANCE	15402	54129	38290	21669	4950	28864	2828	10707	1351
71	REAL ESTATE & RENTAL	0	0	0	0	0	0	0	0	0
72	HOTELS; PERSONAL SERV.	0	0	0	0	0	0	0	0	0
73	BUSINESS SERVICES	0	0	0	0	0	0	0	0	0
74	RESEARCH & DEVELOPMENT	0	0	0	0	0	0	0	0	0
75	AUTO. REPAIR & SERVICES	0	0	0	0	0	0	0	0	0
76	AMUSEMENTS	0	0	0	0	0	0	0	0	0
77	MED.,EDUC. SERVICES	0	0	0	0	0	0	0	0	0
78	FEDERAL GOV'T ENTERPRISE	0	0	0	0	0	0	0	0	0
79	STATE & LOCAL GOV'T ENT.	0	0	0	0	0	0	0	0	0
80	IMPORTS	76	1524	409	290	68	76	0	12	0
81	BUS.TRAVEL, ENT., GIFTS.	0	0	0	0	0	0	0	0	0
82	OFFICE SUPPLIES	0	0	0	0	0	0	0	0	0
83	SCRAP & USED GOODS	-9845	-20735	-30569	-12779	-13379	-17715	-3105	-15591	-1596
84	GOVERNMENT INDUSTRY	0	0	0	0	0	0	0	0	0
85	REST OF WORLD INDUSTRY	0	0	0	0	0	0	0	0	0
86	HOUSEHOLD INDUSTRY	0	0	0	0	0	0	0	0	0
87	INVENTORY VALUATION ADJ.	0	0	0	0	0	0	0	0	0
88	STATE TOTAL	950597	1536209	2118051	1017834	637885	1389408	279879	726763	160630

TABLE C.5

STATE ESTIMATES OF 1958
GROSS PRIVATE CAPITAL FORMATION
(THOUSANDS OF CURRENT DOLLARS)

INDUSTRY TITLE	28 NEW HAMPSHIRE	29 NEW JERSEY	30 NEW MEXICO	31 NEW YORK	32 NORTH CAROLINA	33 NORTH DAKOTA	34 OHIO	35 OKLAHOMA	36 OREGON
1 LIVESTOCK & PRDTS.	0	0	0	0	0	0	0	0	0
2 OTHER AGRICULTURE PRDTS.	0	0	0	0	0	0	0	0	0
3 FORESTRY & FISHERIES	0	0	0	0	0	0	0	0	0
4 AGRI.,FORES.,FISH. SERV.	0	0	0	0	0	0	0	0	0
5 IRON, FERRO. ORES MINING	0	0	0	0	0	0	0	0	0
6 NONFERROUS ORES MINING	0	0	0	0	0	0	0	0	0
7 COAL MINING	0	0	0	0	0	0	0	0	0
8 CRUDE PETRO.,NATURAL GAS	0	0	0	0	0	0	0	0	0
9 STONE & CLAY MINING	0	0	0	0	0	0	0	0	0
10 CHEM.&FERT. MIN. MINING	0	0	0	0	0	0	0	0	0
11 NEW CONSTRUCTION	132096	1370613	456901	2966486	547972	217669	2255565	770166	388978
12 MAINT. & REPAIR CONSTR.	0	0	0	0	0	0	0	0	0
13 ORDNANCE & ACCESSORIES	0	0	0	0	0	0	0	0	0
14 FOOD & KINDRED PRDTS.	0	0	0	0	0	0	0	0	0
15 TOBACCO MANUFACTURES	0	0	0	0	0	0	0	0	0
16 FABRICS	0	0	0	0	0	0	0	0	0
17 TEXTILE PRDTS.	130	1502	213	7410	737	183	2332	558	471
18 APPAREL	0	0	0	0	0	0	0	0	0
19 MISC. TEXTILE PRDTS.	0	0	0	0	0	0	0	0	0
20 LUMBER & WOOD PRDTS.	18	183	739	106	85	216	28	134	96
21 WOODEN CONTAINERS	0	0	0	0	0	0	0	0	0
22 HOUSEHOLD FURNITURE	382	4430	559	19820	2137	463	7241	1495	1265
23 OTHER FURNITURE	2380	29625	3646	125313	13875	2249	48626	8302	8240
24 PAPER & ALLIED PRDTS.	0	0	0	0	0	0	0	0	0
25 PAPERBOARD CONTAINERS	0	0	0	0	0	0	0	0	0
26 PRINTING & PUBLISHING	0	0	0	0	0	0	0	0	0
27 CHEMICALS,SELECT. PRDTS.	0	0	0	0	0	0	0	0	0
28 PLASTICS & SYNTHETICS	0	0	0	0	0	0	0	0	0
29 DRUGS & COSMETICS	0	0	0	0	0	0	0	0	0
30 PAINT & ALLIED PRDTS.	0	0	0	0	0	0	0	0	0
31 PETROLEUM, RELATED INDS.	0	0	0	0	0	0	0	0	0
32 RUBBER, MISC. PLASTICS	165	1869	226	7222	1029	173	2744	572	737
33 LEATHER TANNING & PRDTS.	0	0	0	0	0	0	0	0	0
34 FOOTWEAR, LEATHER PRDTS.	10	123	12	788	74	129	133	95	47
35 GLASS & CLAY PRDTS.	0	0	0	0	0	0	0	0	0
36 STONE & CLAY PRDTS.	0	0	0	0	0	0	0	0	0
37 PRIMARY IRON, STEEL MFR.	0	0	0	0	0	0	0	0	0
38 PRIMARY NONFERROUS MFR.	0	0	0	0	0	0	0	0	0

#	Sector	1	2	3	4	5	6	7	8	9
39	METAL CONTAINERS	27	411	28	1043	176	25	514	93	115
40	FABRICATED METAL PRDTS.	3018	35682	6150	57939	15442	5919	44713	11437	14726
41	SCREW MACH. PRDTS., ETC.	450	6981	2665	17332	2280	1330	8787	3583	0
42	OTHER FAB. METAL PRDTS.	2732	26340	7362	53644	13579	3409	33972	8658	1919
43	ENGINES & TURBINES	964	14730	5248	42305	14792	163063	12925	18129	13658
44	FARM MACH. & EQUIP.	3196	30747	72134	71602	12476	12396	57058	43624	43620
45	CONSTRUC. MACH. & EQUIP.	946	11063	4867	27409	5149	1458	23823	4364	15373
46	MATERIAL HANDLING MACH.	2225	48312	1115	88173	9174	700	135654	5503	4944
47	METALWORKING MACHINERY	7194	63890	4884	135206	64485	2437	89839	11226	11836
48	SPECIAL MACH. & EQUIP.	2513	53170	11892	66435	14272	6908	86241	17393	24571
49	GENERAL MACH. & EQUIP.									12839
50	MACHINE SHOP PRDTS.	0	0	0	0	0	0	0	0	0
51	OFFICE, COMPUT. MACHINES	3000	38911	3623	171134	16385	2537	69497	9600	9389
52	SERVICE IND. MACHINES	2726	34641	4128	129370	18374	3583	51758	12891	9994
53	ELECT. TRANSMISS. EQUIP.	6553	67171	12146	218587	31907	5820	107484	20000	30191
54	HOUSEHOLD APPLIANCES	86	3295	346	13645	2589	980	4379	943	1039
55	ELECTRIC LIGHTING EQUIP.	945	859	158	4078	451	109	1264	336	350
56	RADIO, TV, ETC., EQUIP.	95	23179	2272	420570	9632	1389	32485	4972	3967
57	ELECTRONIC COMPONENTS	238	1459	67	4101	489	47	1619	234	187
58	MISC. ELECTRICAL MACH.	8797	2274	866	13421	1141	662	3818	1145	828
59	MOTOR VEHICLES, EQUIP.	1104	108692	21117	424721	59339	74821	160057	51806	50975
60	AIRCRAFT & PARTS	3476	7410	4336	19963	6243	4696	18052	10207	5248
61	OTHER TRANSPORT. EQUIP.	1674	22763	17012	49650	20840	18118	52828	36030	20755
62	PROFESS., SCIEN. INSTRU.	352	23530	3412	68593	7632	1589	32418	6265	5555
63	MEDICAL, PHOTO. EQUIP.	827	5638	624	33732	1686	277	9397	1346	1349
64	MISC. MANUFACTURING	1375	9544	1057	52138	4720	891	14218	2757	2562
65	TRANSPORT. & WAREHOUSING		16853	4656	60190	8268	8491	27294	6900	7178
66	COMMUNICA.,EXC. BRDCAST.		7435		205279	1798		7123		86
67	RADIO & TV BROADCASTING	0	0	0	0	0	0	0	0	0
68	ELEC.,GAS,WATER,SAN.SER.	0	0	0	0	0	0	0	0	0
69	WHOLESALE & RETAIL TRADE	9884	123537	28864	430862	61573	70027	197396	50366	53044
70	FINANCE & INSURANCE	0	0	0	0	0	0	0	0	0
71	REAL ESTATE & RENTAL	3731	41275	3153	290968	15346	2727	50255	10758	9457
72	HOTELS; PERSONAL SERV.	0	0	0	0	0	0	0	0	0
73	BUSINESS SERVICES	0	0	0	0	0	0	0	0	0
74	RESEARCH & DEVELOPMENT	0	0	0	0	0	0	0	0	0
75	AUTO. REPAIR & SERVICES	0	0	0	0	0	0	0	0	0
76	AMUSEMENTS	0	0	0	0	0	0	0	0	0
77	MED.,EDUC. SERVICES	0	0	0	0	0	0	0	0	0
78	FEDERAL GOV'T ENTERPRISE	0	0	0	0	0	0	0	0	0
79	STATE & LOCAL GOV'T ENT.	0	0	0	0	0	0	0	0	0
80	IMPORTS	345	1155	0	1880	410	0	1940	53	57
81	BUS.TRAVEL, ENT., GIFTS.	0	0	0	0	0	0	0	0	0
82	OFFICE SUPPLIES	0	0	0	0	0	0	0	0	0
83	SCRAP & USED GOODS	-2249	-27196	-7188	-104400	-13731	-12455	-43766	-11326	-11480
84	GOVERNMENT INDUSTRY	0	0	0	0	0	0	0	0	0
85	REST OF WORLD INDUSTRY	0	0	0	0	0	0	0	0	0
86	HOUSEHOLD INDUSTRY	0	0	0	0	0	0	0	0	0
87	INVENTORY VALUATION ADJ.	0	0	0	0	0	0	0	0	0
88	STATE TOTAL	201673	2212079	679289	6196702	972827	603034	3609691	1120606	744167

TABLE C.5

STATE ESTIMATES OF 1958
GROSS PRIVATE CAPITAL FORMATION
(THOUSANDS OF CURRENT DOLLARS)

INDUSTRY TITLE	37 PENNSYL- VANIA	38 RHODE ISLAND	39 SOUTH CAROLINA	40 SOUTH DAKOTA	41 TENNESSEE	42 TEXAS	43 UTAH	44 VERMONT	45 VIRGINIA
1 LIVESTOCK & PRDTS.	0	0	0	0	0	0	0	0	0
2 OTHER AGRICULTURE PRDTS.	0	0	0	0	0	0	0	0	0
3 FORESTRY & FISHERIES	0	0	0	0	0	0	0	0	0
4 AGRI.,FORES.,FISH. SERV.	0	0	0	0	0	0	0	0	0
5 IRON, FERRO. ORES MINING	0	0	0	0	0	0	0	0	0
6 NONFERROUS ORES MINING	0	0	0	0	0	0	0	0	0
7 COAL MINING	0	0	0	0	0	0	0	0	0
8 CRUDE PETRO.,NATURAL GAS	0	0	0	0	0	0	0	0	0
9 STONE & CLAY MINING	0	0	0	0	0	0	0	0	0
10 CHEM.&FERT. MIN. MINING	0	0	0	0	0	0	0	0	0
11 NEW CONSTRUCTION	1537893	102486	366096	148587	319221	2761444	335693	73603	778689
12 MAINT. & REPAIR CONSTR.	0	0	0	0	0	0	0	0	0
13 ORDNANCE & ACCESSORIES	0	0	0	0	0	0	0	0	0
14 FOOD & KINDRED PRDTS.	0	0	0	0	0	0	0	0	0
15 TOBACCO MANUFACTURES	0	0	0	0	0	0	0	0	0
16 FABRICS	0	0	0	0	0	0	0	0	0
17 TEXTILE PRDTS.	2727	188	315	170	637	196	77	685	725
18 APPAREL	0	0	0	0	0	0	0	0	0
19 MISC. TEXTILE PRDTS.	0	0	0	0	0	0	0	0	0
20 LUMBER & WOOD PRDTS.	187	7	118	3	125	133	39	135	7
21 WOODEN CONTAINERS	0	0	0	0	0	0	0	0	0
22 HOUSEHOLD FURNITURE	7848	517	881	431	1785	527	216	1901	1990
23 OTHER FURNITURE	52623	3354	5864	2116	11440	3186	1300	12431	11989
24 PAPER & ALLIED PRDTS.	0	0	0	0	0	0	0	0	0
25 PAPERBOARD CONTAINERS	0	0	0	0	0	0	0	0	0
26 PRINTING & PUBLISHING	0	0	0	0	0	0	0	0	0
27 CHEMICALS,SELECT. PRDTS.	0	0	0	0	0	0	0	0	0
28 PLASTICS & SYNTHETICS	0	0	0	0	0	0	0	0	0
29 DRUGS & COSMETICS	0	0	0	0	0	0	0	0	0
30 PAINT & ALLIED PRDTS.	0	0	0	0	0	0	0	0	0
31 PETROLEUM, RELATED INDS.	0	0	0	0	0	0	0	0	0
32 RUBBER, MISC. PLASTICS	3202	243	439	171	889	228	99	912	967
33 LEATHER TANNING & PRDTS.	111	19	79	7	89	11	25	94	35
34 FOOTWEAR, LEATHER PRDTS.	0	0	0	0	0	0	0	0	0
35 GLASS & GLASS PRDTS.	0	0	0	0	0	0	0	0	0
36 STONE & CLAY PRDTS.	0	0	0	0	0	0	0	0	0
37 PRIMARY IRON, STEEL MFR.	0	0	0	0	0	0	0	0	0
38 PRIMARY NONFERROUS MFR.	0	0	0	0	0	0	0	0	0

#	Sector	1	2	3	4	5	6	7	8	9
39	METAL CONTAINERS	638	37	54	167	33	43	16	152	164
40	FABRICATED METAL PRDTS.	52896	2474	7040	7011	1169	2943	678	14078	15693
41	SCREW MACH. PRDTS., ETC.	10769	525	1294	2118	479	1273	232	2943	0
42	OTHER FAB. METAL PRDTS.	42169	2115	4687	5055	1146	2573	601	11520	3511
43	ENGINES & TURBINES	13911	1783	89796	16599	1162	1210	4891	92725	10727
44	FARM MACH. & EQUIP.	74492	1954	10303	9686	4814	24384	1063	34703	6499
45	CONSTRUC. MACH. & EQUIP.	25673	1083	2455	5264	1301	2432	639	6522	7705
46	MATERIAL HANDLING MACH.	148057	4795	2500	11966	558	5571	995	8856	5480
47	METALWORKING MACHINERY	100876	7169	36364	33220	2134	3399	3523	37565	9890
48	SPECIAL MACH. & EQUIP.	92057	3035	9489	20953	1020	6703	1187	23334	22456
49	GENERAL MACH. & EQUIP.	64197	4080	6639	13803	1963	3323	1562	16888	15437
50	MACHINE SHOP PRDTS.	57730	4089	7707	16192	3192	4237	2126	15539	0
51	OFFICE, COMPUT. MACHINES	118453	5676	8967	12638	3005	5631	1233	25751	14733
52	SERVICE IND. MACHINES	5854	426	1369	1634	246	343	173	1936	15362
53	ELECT. TRANSMISS. EQUIP.	1496	97	166	293	88	105	34	400	25052
54	HOUSEHOLD APPLIANCES	37328	1272	2835	6188	1147	1661	563	11747	1307
55	ELECTRIC LIGHTING EQUIP.	1282	54	97	350	38	58	25	363	404
56	RADIO, TV, ETC., EQUIP.	5129	301	659	1053	375	455	178	1479	8161
57	ELECTRONIC COMPONENTS	178767	11999	57893	52187	10415	15267	8480	84605	365
58	MISC. ELECTRICAL MACH.	18323	762	3670	4989	3423	2543	926	5726	1219
59	MOTOR VEHICLES, EQUIP.	58742	2305	14031	17732	11595	9501	3274	23313	47921
60	AIRCRAFT & PARTS	42723	2381	3632	8003	1390	2308	971	8686	8048
61	OTHER TRANSPORT. EQUIP.	9377	581	720	2120	290	506	187	2363	26958
62	PROFESS., SCIEN. INSTRU.	14817	1264	1963	3614	719	1104	436	4040	7887
63	MEDICAL, PHOTO. EQUIP.	30465	1643	7193	6498	1184	2448	875	11323	2255
64	MISC. MANUFACTURING	8865	0	0	454	0	0	0	3537	4104
65	TRANSPORT. & WAREHOUSING	0	0	0	0	0	0	0	0	6513
66	COMMUNICA., EXC. BRDCAST.	0	0	0	0	0	0	0	0	1003
67	RADIO & TV BROADCASTING	0	0	0	0	0	0	0	0	0
68	ELEC., GAS, WATER, SAN. SER.	0	0	0	0	0	0	0	0	0
69	WHOLESALE & RETAIL TRADE	216670	12464	57015	50730	9043	16854	7126	86700	49110
70	FINANCE & INSURANCE	0	0	0	0	0	0	0	0	0
71	REAL ESTATE & RENTAL	72483	6353	7347	14454	2415	4135	1937	15573	17250
72	HOTELS; PERSONAL SERV.	0	0	0	0	0	0	0	0	0
73	BUSINESS SERVICES	0	0	0	0	0	0	0	0	0
74	RESEARCH & DEVELOPMENT	0	0	0	0	0	0	0	0	0
75	AUTO. REPAIR & SERVICES	0	0	0	0	0	0	0	0	0
76	AMUSEMENTS	0	0	0	0	0	0	0	0	0
77	MED., EDUC. SERVICES	0	0	0	0	0	0	0	0	0
78	FEDERAL GOV'T ENTERPRISE	0	0	0	0	50	0	0	0	0
79	STATE & LOCAL GOV'T ENT.	0	0	0	0	0	0	0	0	0
80	IMPORTS	1224	72	252	50	1	8	28	52	34
81	BUS. TRAVEL, ENT., GIFTS.	0	0	0	0	0	0	0	0	0
82	OFFICE SUPPLIES	0	0	0	0	0	0	0	0	0
83	SCRAP & USED GOODS	-49221	-2665	-11078	-10644	-2105	-3923	-1431	-17801	-10988
84	GOVERNMENT INDUSTRY	0	0	0	0	0	0	0	0	0
85	REST OF WORLD INDUSTRY	0	0	0	0	0	0	0	0	0
86	HOUSEHOLD INDUSTRY	0	0	0	0	0	0	0	0	0
87	INVENTORY VALUATION ADJ.	0	0	0	0	0	0	0	0	0
88	STATE TOTAL	3060815	184938	708847	648562	213722	2882805	379978	624376	1118655

278

TABLE C.5

STATE ESTIMATES OF 1958
GROSS PRIVATE CAPITAL FORMATION
(THOUSANDS OF CURRENT DOLLARS)

INDUSTRY TITLE	46 WASHINGTON	47 WEST VIRGINIA	48 WISCONSIN	49 WYOMING	50 ALASKA	51 HAWAII	52 NO STATE ALLOCATION	53 NATIONAL TOTAL
1 LIVESTOCK & PRDTS.	0	0	0	0	0	0	0	0
2 OTHER AGRICULTURE PRDTS.	0	0	0	0	0	0	0	0
3 FORESTRY & FISHERIES	0	0	0	0	0	0	0	0
4 AGRI.,FORES.,FISH.SERV.	0	0	0	0	0	0	0	0
5 IRON,FERRO. ORES MINING	0	0	0	0	0	0	0	0
6 NONFERROUS ORES MINING	0	0	0	0	0	0	0	0
7 COAL MINING	0	0	0	0	0	0	0	0
8 CRUDE PETRO.,NATURAL GAS	0	0	0	0	0	0	0	0
9 STONE & CLAY MINING	0	0	0	0	0	0	0	0
10 CHEM.&FERT. MIN. MINING	0	0	0	0	0	0	0	0
11 NEW CONSTRUCTION	477995	305088	705276	144774	0	0	0	36956992
12 MAINT. & REPAIR CONSTR.	0	0	0	0	0	0	0	0
13 ORDNANCE & ACCESSORIES	0	0	0	0	0	0	0	0
14 FOOD & KINDRED PRDTS.	0	0	0	0	0	0	0	0
15 TOBACCO MANUFACTURES	0	0	0	0	0	0	0	0
16 FABRICS	0	0	0	0	0	0	0	0
17 TEXTILE PRDTS.	338	924	103	935	0	0	0	45000
18 APPAREL	0	0	0	0	0	0	0	0
19 MISC. TEXTILE PRDTS.	0	0	0	0	0	0	0	0
20 LUMBER & WOOD PRDTS.	61	40	107	7	0	0	0	6000
21 WOODEN CONTAINERS	0	0	0	0	0	0	0	0
22 HOUSEHOLD FURNITURE	1008	2600	269	2456	0	0	0	126000
23 OTHER FURNITURE	7075	16487	1388	14436	0	0	0	797999
24 PAPER & ALLIED PRDTS.	0	0	0	0	0	0	0	0
25 PAPERBOARD CONTAINERS	0	0	0	0	0	0	0	0
26 PRINTING & PUBLISHING	0	0	0	0	0	0	0	0
27 CHEMICALS,SELECT. PRDTS.	0	0	0	0	0	0	0	0
28 PLASTICS & SYNTHETICS	0	0	0	0	0	0	0	0
29 DRUGS & COSMETICS	0	0	0	0	0	0	0	0
30 PAINT & ALLIED PRDTS.	0	0	0	0	0	0	0	0
31 PETROLEUM, RELATED INDS.	0	0	0	0	0	0	0	0
32 RUBBER, MISC. PLASTICS	503	1096	89	1096	0	0	0	52000
33 LEATHER TANNING & PRDTS.	0	0	0	0	0	0	0	0
34 FOOTWEAR, LEATHER PRDTS.	53	57	3	34	0	0	0	5000
35 GLASS & GLASS PRDTS.	0	0	0	0	0	0	0	0
36 STONE & CLAY PRDTS.	0	0	0	0	0	0	0	0
37 PRIMARY IRON, STEEL MFR.	0	0	0	0	0	0	0	0
38 PRIMARY NONFERROUS MFR.	0	0	0	0	0	0	0	0

#	Industry	1	2	3	4	5	6	7	8
39	METAL CONTAINERS	57	328	9	297	0	0	0	10000
40	FABRICATED METAL PRDTS.	13497	13179	1579	8521	0	0	0	708001
41	SCREW MACH. PRDTS., ETC.	0	0	0	0	0	0	0	166000
42	OTHER FAB. METAL PRDTS.	2914	2892	909	3028	0	0	0	576001
43	ENGINES & TURBINES	12082	10412	1332	7176	0	0	0	1669993
44	FARM MACH. & EQUIP.	9083	32375	641	5767	0	0	0	1318998
45	CONSTRUC. MACH. & EQUIP.	41759	20430	18167	35873	0	0	0	351999
46	MATERIAL HANDLING MACH.	7065	8434	1540	9482	0	0	0	1152997
47	METALWORKING MACHINERY	20325	25102	257	9236	0	0	0	1468001
48	SPECIAL MACH. & EQUIP.	22256	33977	1396	23457	0	0	0	1050998
49	GENERAL MACH. & EQUIP.	32794	17436	3954	11242	0	0	0	0
50	MACHINE SHOP PRDTS.	0	0	0	0	0	0	0	1015998
51	OFFICE, COMPUT. MACHINES	8196	20337	1369	17995	0	0	0	954999
52	SERVICE IND. MACHINES	7730	19892	1905	19154	0	0	0	1616999
53	ELECT. TRANSMISS. EQUIP.	24704	31231	2260	20032	0	0	0	93000
54	HOUSEHOLD APPLIANCES	587	1777	139	1610	0	0	0	25000
55	ELECTRIC LIGHTING EQUIP.	268	463	58	434	0	0	0	1008999
56	RADIO, TV, ETC., EQUIP.	6315	12201	958	6333	0	0	0	27000
57	ELECTRONIC COMPONENTS	107	340	32	358	0	0	0	83000
58	MISC. ELECTRICAL MACH.	947	1710	304	1944	0	0	0	3574997
59	MOTOR VEHICLES, EQUIP.	33709	71237	7614	58655	0	0	0	357999
60	AIRCRAFT & PARTS	4964	7656	2938	9769	0	0	0	1177998
61	OTHER TRANSPORT. EQUIP.	23016	24703	10760	33991	0	0	0	531999
62	PROFESS., SCIEN. INSTRU.	7259	11299	1144	10595	0	0	0	163000
63	MEDICAL, PHOTO. EQUIP.	1216	2727	200	2546	0	0	0	279000
64	MISC. MANUFACTURING	2034	4587	409	4346	0	0	0	506999
65	TRANSPORT. & WAREHOUSING	6800	9931	1376	7627	0	0	0	362000
66	COMMUNICA.,EXC. BRDCAST.	1699	3242	0	0	0	0	0	0
67	RADIO & TV BROADCASTING	0	0	0	0	0	0	0	3746999
68	ELEC.,GAS,WATER,SAN.SER.	45563	73894	9115	57790	0	0	0	0
69	WHOLESALE & RETAIL TRADE	0	0	0	0	0	0	0	1208997
70	FINANCE & INSURANCE	4952	20822	1252	21669	0	0	0	0
71	REAL ESTATE & RENTAL	0	0	0	0	0	0	0	0
72	HOTELS; PERSONAL SERV.	0	0	0	0	0	0	0	0
73	BUSINESS SERVICES	0	0	0	0	0	0	0	0
74	RESEARCH & DEVELOPMENT	0	0	0	0	0	0	0	0
75	AUTO. REPAIR & SERVICES	0	0	0	0	0	0	0	0
76	AMUSEMENTS	0	0	0	0	0	0	0	0
77	MED.,EDUC. SERVICES	0	0	0	0	0	0	0	0
78	FEDERAL GOV'T ENTERPRISE	0	0	0	0	0	0	0	0
79	STATE & LOCAL GOV'T ENT.	0	0	0	0	0	0	0	0
80	IMPORTS	13	623	0	290	0	0	0	15500
81	BUS.TRAVEL, ENT., GIFTS.	0	0	0	0	0	0	0	0
82	OFFICE SUPPLIES	0	0	0	0	0	0	0	0
83	SCRAP & USED GOODS	-10987	-15793	-2304	-12779	0	0	0	-822004
84	GOVERNMENT INDUSTRY	0	0	0	0	0	0	0	0
85	REST OF WORLD INDUSTRY	0	0	0	0	0	0	0	0
86	HOUSEHOLD INDUSTRY	0	0	0	0	0	0	0	0
87	INVENTORY VALUATION ADJ.	0	0	0	0	0	0	0	0
88	STATE TOTAL	817945	793732	776548	540176	0	0	0	62391232

TABLE C.6

STATE ESTIMATES OF 1963
GROSS PRIVATE CAPITAL FORMATION
(THOUSANDS OF CURRENT DOLLARS)

INDUSTRY TITLE	1 ALABAMA	2 ARIZONA	3 ARKANSAS	4 CALIFORNIA	5 COLORADO	6 CONNECTICUT	7 DELAWARE	8 DISTRICT OF COLUMBIA	9 FLORIDA
1 LIVESTOCK & PRDTS.	0	0	0	0	0	0	0	0	0
2 OTHER AGRICULTURE PRDTS.	0	0	0	0	0	0	0	0	0
3 FORESTRY & FISHERIES	0	0	0	0	0	0	0	0	0
4 AGRI.,FORES.,FISH. SERV.	0	0	0	0	0	0	0	0	0
5 IRON, FERRO. ORES MINING	0	0	0	0	0	0	0	0	0
6 NONFERROUS ORES MINING	0	0	0	0	0	0	0	0	0
7 COAL MINING	0	0	0	0	0	0	0	0	0
8 CRUDE PETRO.,NATURAL GAS	0	0	0	0	0	0	0	0	0
9 STONE & CLAY MINING	0	0	0	0	0	0	0	0	0
10 CHEM.&FERT. MIN. MINING	0	0	0	0	0	0	0	0	0
11 NEW CONSTRUCTION	526895	549203	249210	9562994	606202	780963	134682	257991	2035853
12 MAINT. & REPAIR CONSTR.	0	0	0	0	0	0	0	0	0
13 ORDNANCE & ACCESSORIES	0	0	0	0	0	0	0	0	0
14 FOOD & KINDRED PRDTS.	0	0	0	0	0	0	0	0	0
15 TOBACCO MANUFACTURES	0	0	0	0	0	0	0	0	0
16 FABRICS	0	0	0	0	0	0	0	0	0
17 TEXTILE PRDTS.	616	426	367	7666	593	1181	188	586	1548
18 APPAREL	0	0	0	0	0	0	0	0	0
19 MISC. TEXTILE PRDTS.	0	0	0	0	0	0	0	0	0
20 LUMBER & WOOD PRDTS.	58	31	49	662	107	34	101	8	152
21 WOODEN CONTAINERS	0	0	0	0	0	0	0	0	0
22 HOUSEHOLD FURNITURE	1260	992	738	14420	1349	2024	345	1383	3954
23 OTHER FURNITURE	11734	8395	6866	127487	11251	20497	3606	10198	28240
24 PAPER & ALLIED PRDTS.	0	0	0	0	0	0	0	0	0
25 PAPERBOARD CONTAINERS	0	0	0	0	0	0	0	0	0
26 PRINTING & PUBLISHING	0	0	0	0	0	0	0	0	0
27 CHEMICALS,SELECT. PRDTS.	0	0	0	0	0	0	0	0	0
28 PLASTICS & SYNTHETICS	0	0	0	0	0	0	0	0	0
29 DRUGS & COSMETICS	0	0	0	0	0	0	0	0	0
30 PAINT & ALLIED PRDTS.	0	0	0	0	0	0	0	0	0
31 PETROLEUM, RELATED INDS.	0	0	0	0	0	0	0	0	0
32 RUBBER, MISC. PLASTICS	273	409	183	1562	239	242	47	94	660
33 LEATHER TANNING & PRDTS.	0	0	0	0	0	0	0	0	0
34 FOOTWEAR, LEATHER PRDTS.	0	0	0	0	0	0	0	0	0
35 GLASS & GLASS PRDTS.	0	0	0	0	0	0	0	0	0
36 STONE & CLAY PRDTS.	0	0	0	0	0	0	0	0	0
37 PRIMARY IRON, STEEL MFR.	0	0	0	0	0	0	0	0	0
38 PRIMARY NONFERROUS MFR.	310	186	197	3153	206	358	77	166	656

#	Industry									
39	METAL CONTAINERS	99	54	77	1083	161	72	140	23	252
40	FABRICATED METAL PRDTS.	7478	6150	4119	51732	5492	8970	2120	2760	14298
41	SCREW MACH. PRDTS., ETC.	0	0	0	0	0	0	0	0	0
42	OTHER FAB. METAL PRDTS.	2560	2469	1605	26024	2305	4613	882	1925	5975
43	ENGINES & TURBINES	5669	8874	3923	33921	5097	5212	1076	1896	13639
44	FARM MACH. & EQUIP.	29509	22851	3780	170593	30360	9058	5243	1810	48450
45	CONSTRUC. MACH. & EQUIP.	20680	23425	12828	232089	22853	22056	4166	9277	50571
46	MATERIAL HANDLING MACH.	7214	6125	5349	74171	5642	13388	2415	3400	14466
47	METALWORKING MACHINERY	17715	13309	11526	163092	9872	41728	8477	3423	28323
48	SPECIAL MACH. & EQUIP.	33406	12609	20581	173907	14811	32376	9255	7652	44424
49	GENERAL MACH. & EQUIP.	18156	13302	10019	139054	11369	28156	6600	6455	30433
50	MACHINE SHOP PRDTS.	93	62	59	613	67	88	28	23	149
51	OFFICE, COMPUT. MACHINES	14977	10309	9260	199281	14199	35853	5316	12490	35835
52	SERVICE IND. MACHINES	12585	7675	7484	126476	11552	17386	4007	7436	29738
53	ELECT. TRANSMISS. EQUIP.	26250	31001	18262	218275	20958	29291	5658	12362	63010
54	HOUSEHOLD APPLIANCES	1488	835	837	12841	1161	1767	323	892	3053
55	ELECTRIC LIGHTING EQUIP.	704	699	576	5558	661	694	209	341	1527
56	RADIO, TV, ETC., EQUIP.	26234	17612	17378	286053	19772	28206	5222	17319	61537
57	ELECTRONIC COMPONENTS	787	609	644	13086	718	1703	219	744	1948
58	MISC. ELECTRICAL MACH.	2248	1670	1622	21184	1767	3461	890	1411	4381
59	MOTOR VEHICLES, EQUIP.	64187	45467	53097	593460	69394	71000	23691	42633	152841
60	AIRCRAFT & PARTS	4007	1597	4095	32335	5705	4133	3623	2247	11019
61	OTHER TRANSPORT. EQUIP.	15129	7009	14373	111271	19723	9820	11425	7366	39117
62	PROFESS., SCIEN. INSTRU.	6833	6621	4333	79436	5586	17148	1739	5297	14451
63	MEDICAL, PHOTO. EQUIP.	3115	2261	1769	40131	3248	6706	893	4089	8232
64	MISC. MANUFACTURING	4553	3234	2952	62259	4902	7893	1851	4746	13351
65	TRANSPORT. & WAREHOUSING	6945	5370	5454	61199	6580	7996	2193	3491	15105
66	COMMUNICA., EXC. BRDCAST.	5792	4349	4379	54315	5263	7460	1742	3190	12647
67	RADIO & TV BROADCASTING	0	0	0	0	0	0	0	0	0
68	ELEC.,GAS,WATER,SAN.SER.	57360	43130	46767	523757	55328	69909	17512	31275	124556
69	WHOLESALE & RETAIL TRADE	9	6	6	77	8	10	3	5	19
70	FINANCE & INSURANCE	14153	8381	6902	139673	13564	26935	3543	9309	33459
71	REAL ESTATE & RENTAL	0	0	0	0	0	0	0	0	0
72	HOTELS; PERSONAL SERV.	0	0	0	0	0	0	0	0	0
73	BUSINESS SERVICES	0	0	0	0	0	0	0	0	0
74	RESEARCH & DEVELOPMENT	0	0	0	0	0	0	0	0	0
75	AUTO.REPAIR & SERVICES	0	0	0	0	0	0	0	0	0
76	AMUSEMENTS	0	0	0	0	0	0	0	0	0
77	MED.,EDUC. SERVICES	0	0	0	0	0	0	0	0	0
78	FEDERAL GOV'T ENTERPRISE	0	0	0	0	0	0	0	0	0
79	STATE & LOCAL GOV'T ENT.	0	0	0	0	0	0	0	0	0
80	IMPORTS	2112	1446	1406	17281	1842	2327	708	1018	4312
81	BUS.TRAVEL, ENT., GIFTS.	0	0	0	0	0	0	0	0	0
82	OFFICE SUPPLIES	0	0	0	0	0	0	0	0	0
83	SCRAP & USED GOODS	-12377	-8478	-8243	-101305	-10796	-13641	-4150	-5967	-25281
84	GOVERNMENT INDUSTRY	0	0	0	0	0	0	0	0	0
85	REST OF WORLD INDUSTRY	0	0	0	0	0	0	0	0	0
86	HOUSEHOLD INDUSTRY	0	0	0	0	0	0	0	0	0
87	INVENTORY VALUATION ADJ.	0	0	0	0	0	0	0	0	0
88	STATE TOTAL	942613	859676	558885	13280816	979109	1307061	266067	470764	2926875

TABLE C.6

STATE ESTIMATES OF 1963
GROSS PRIVATE CAPITAL FORMATION
(THOUSANDS OF CURRENT DOLLARS)

INDUSTRY TITLE	10 GEORGIA	11 IDAHO	12 ILLINOIS	13 INDIANA	14 IOWA	15 KANSAS	16 KENTUCKY	17 LOUISIANA	18 MAINE
1 LIVESTOCK & PRDTS.	0	0	0	0	0	0	0	0	0
2 OTHER AGRICULTURE PRDTS.	0	0	0	0	0	0	0	0	0
3 FORESTRY & FISHERIES	0	0	0	0	0	0	0	0	0
4 AGRI.,FORES.,FISH. SERV.	0	0	0	0	0	0	0	0	0
5 IRON, FERRO. ORES MINING	0	0	0	0	0	0	0	0	0
6 NONFERROUS ORES MINING	0	0	0	0	0	0	0	0	0
7 COAL MINING	0	0	0	0	0	0	0	0	0
8 CRUDE PETRO.,NATURAL GAS	0	0	0	0	0	0	0	0	0
9 STONE & CLAY MINING	0	0	0	0	0	0	0	0	0
10 CHEM.&FERT. MIN. MINING	0	0	0	0	0	0	0	0	0
11 NEW CONSTRUCTION	840568	82298	2173708	793027	385662	409662	353457	1174726	93633
12 MAINT. & REPAIR CONSTR.	0	0	0	0	0	0	0	0	0
13 ORDNANCE & ACCESSORIES	0	0	0	0	0	0	0	0	0
14 FOOD & KINDRED PRDTS.	0	0	0	0	0	0	0	0	0
15 TOBACCO MANUFACTURES	0	0	0	0	0	0	0	0	0
16 FABRICS	0	0	0	0	0	0	0	0	0
17 TEXTILE PRDTS.	1013	174	4514	1470	715	569	639	979	255
18 APPAREL	0	0	0	0	0	0	0	0	0
19 MISC. TEXTILE PRDTS.	0	0	0	0	0	0	0	0	0
20 LUMBER & WOOD PRDTS.	101	35	482	133	173	55	73	132	25
21 WOODEN CONTAINERS	0	0	0	0	0	0	0	0	0
22 HOUSEHOLD FURNITURE	2023	350	8689	2702	1602	1135	1392	1641	562
23 OTHER FURNITURE	18867	3289	79355	27876	13897	10647	12980	16205	4605
24 PAPER & ALLIED PRDTS.	0	0	0	0	0	0	0	0	0
25 PAPERBOARD CONTAINERS	0	0	0	0	0	0	0	0	0
26 PRINTING & PUBLISHING	0	0	0	0	0	0	0	0	0
27 CHEMICALS,SELECT. PRDTS.	0	0	0	0	0	0	0	0	0
28 PLASTICS & SYNTHETICS	0	0	0	0	0	0	0	0	0
29 DRUGS & COSMETICS	0	0	0	0	0	0	0	0	0
30 PAINT & ALLIED PRDTS.	0	0	0	0	0	0	0	0	0
31 PETROLEUM, RELATED INDS.	0	0	0	0	0	0	0	0	0
32 RUBBER, MISC. PLASTICS	529	49	949	434	173	249	441	590	62
33 LEATHER TANNING & PRDTS.	0	0	0	0	0	0	0	0	0
34 FOOTWEAR, LEATHER PRDTS.	0	0	0	0	0	0	0	0	0
35 GLASS & GLASS PRDTS.	0	0	0	0	0	0	0	0	0
36 STONE & CLAY PRDTS.	0	0	0	0	0	0	0	0	0
37 PRIMARY IRON, STEEL MFR.	0	0	0	0	0	0	0	0	0
38 PRIMARY NONFERROUS MFR.	546	108	1244	527	281	232	253	362	68

39 METAL CONTAINERS	173	52	776	219	257	91	118	201	41
40 FABRICATED METAL PRDTS.	10344	1776	29999	14593	5795	7152	10313	22950	2392
41 SCREW MACH. PRDTS., ETC.	0	0	0	0	0	0	0	0	0
42 OTHER FAB. METAL PRDTS.	3969	829	17094	6962	2324	2428	3365	4524	1033
43 ENGINES & TURBINES	10905	1215	20886	9748	4085	5312	9084	11989	1321
44 FARM MACH. & EQUIP.	41841	23458	122634	67597	131892	57683	40191	27036	9891
45 CONSTRUC. MACH. & EQUIP.	26391	6146	101566	34928	17972	24972	33376	98294	4060
46 MATERIAL HANDLING MACH.	11661	2315	44339	20763	7341	5975	8719	12214	3589
47 METALWORKING MACHINERY	21362	4388	130759	78039	20290	12859	22730	11922	6409
48 SPECIAL MACH. & EQUIP.	64937	7282	129416	49769	22737	17128	28310	39845	23350
49 GENERAL MACH. & EQUIP.	24533	4778	85614	46765	14380	14676	23356	33977	6837
50 MACHINE SHOP PRDTS.	125	29	421	252	140	88	122	145	30
51 OFFICE, COMPUT. MACHINES	23674	4472	118074	43590	16288	14329	16775	25991	5885
52 SERVICE IND. MACHINES	22250	3841	30045	26612	15028	10642	12387	16816	5322
53 ELECT. TRANSMISS. EQUIP.	49095	7049	105436	49019	21101	21198	32224	32526	5607
54 HOUSEHOLD APPLIANCES	2494	393	7953	2602	1820	1176	1317	1659	848
55 ELECTRIC LIGHTING EQUIP.	1205	315	3503	1525	1140	805	904	1127	239
56 RADIO, TV, ETC., EQUIP.	47468	10147	110558	40432	25719	20360	19680	25519	3502
57 ELECTRONIC COMPONENTS	1370	359	5621	3071	809	732	775	877	232
58 MISC. ELECTRICAL MACH.	3601	874	13263	6170	2094	2007	2285	2592	799
59 MOTOR VEHICLES, EQUIP.	105474	32281	403827	134137	114286	79134	74250	114145	23157
60 AIRCRAFT & PARTS	9379	3492	41208	9384	2921	6087	3555	14057	1167
61 OTHER TRANSPORT. EQUIP.	31265	11827	122350	28337	14174	23136	14253	59560	5092
62 PROFESS., SCIEN. INSTRU.	9961	1609	42836	19953	5943	6605	10323	16647	2599
63 MEDICAL, PHOTO. EQUIP.	4474	934	24069	7787	3558	3069	3980	6371	1320
64 MISC. MANUFACTURING	7356	1573	33722	11074	5306	4341	5505	7343	2115
65 TRANSPORT. & WAREHOUSING	11282	3001	38824	14902	11386	7939	8321	13053	2535
66 COMMUNICA.,EXC. BRDCAST.	9430	2392	32775	12840	9054	6180	6610	9232	2020
67 RADIO & TV BROADCASTING	0	0	0	0	0	0	0	0	0
68 ELEC.,GAS,WATER,SAN.SER.	0	0	0	0	0	0	0	0	0
69 WHOLESALE & RETAIL TRADE	90613	26285	331744	129886	109600	69327	69356	95948	21076
70 FINANCE & INSURANCE	14	3	50	23	13	9	11	15	3
71 REAL ESTATE & RENTAL	23665	2689	83843	25934	14038	10689	11224	15943	3854
72 HOTELS; PERSONAL SERV.	0	0	0	0	0	0	0	0	0
73 BUSINESS SERVICES	0	0	0	0	0	0	0	0	0
74 RESEARCH & DEVELOPMENT	0	0	0	0	0	0	0	0	0
75 AUTO. REPAIR & SERVICES	0	0	0	0	0	0	0	0	0
76 AMUSEMENTS	0	0	0	0	0	0	0	0	0
77 MED.,EDUC. SERVICES	0	0	0	0	0	0	0	0	0
78 FEDERAL GOV'T ENTERPRISE	0	0	0	0	0	0	0	0	0
79 STATE & LOCAL GOV'T ENT.	0	0	0	0	0	0	0	0	0
80 IMPORTS	3228	758	11265	5111	2922	2106	2522	3364	637
81 BUS.TRAVEL, ENT., GIFTS.	0	0	0	0	0	0	0	0	0
82 OFFICE SUPPLIES	0	0	0	0	0	0	0	0	0
83 SCRAP & USED GOODS	-18926	-4445	-66038	-29960	-17127	-12341	-14785	-19724	-3733
84 GOVERNMENT INDUSTRY	0	0	0	0	0	0	0	0	0
85 REST OF WORLD INDUSTRY	0	0	0	0	0	0	0	0	0
86 HOUSEHOLD INDUSTRY	0	0	0	0	0	0	0	0	0
87 INVENTORY VALUATION ADJ.	0	0	0	0	0	0	0	0	0
88 STATE TOTAL	1518248	248419	4497336	1698214	989782	848439	830386	1900768	242433

TABLE C.6

STATE ESTIMATES OF 1963
GROSS PRIVATE CAPITAL FORMATION
(THOUSANDS OF CURRENT DOLLARS)

INDUSTRY TITLE	19 MARYLAND	20 MASSA-CHUSETTS	21 MICHIGAN	22 MINNESOTA	23 MISSISSIPPI	24 MISSOURI	25 MONTANA	26 NEBRASKA	27 NEVADA
1 LIVESTOCK & PRDTS.	0	0	0	0	0	0	0	0	0
2 OTHER AGRICULTURE PRDTS.	0	0	0	0	0	0	0	0	0
3 FORESTRY & FISHERIES	0	0	0	0	0	0	0	0	0
4 AGRI.,FORES.,FISH. SERV.	0	0	0	0	0	0	0	0	0
5 IRON, FERRO. ORES MINING	0	0	0	0	0	0	0	0	0
6 NONFERROUS ORES MINING	0	0	0	0	0	0	0	0	0
7 COAL MINING	0	0	0	0	0	0	0	0	0
8 CRUDE PETRO.,NATURAL GAS	0	0	0	0	0	0	0	0	0
9 STONE & CLAY MINING	0	0	0	0	0	0	0	0	0
10 CHEM.&FERT. MIN. MINING	0	0	0	0	0	0	0	0	0
11 NEW CONSTRUCTION	1193287	1408899	1695170	757328	215050	814904	88579	219684	486783
12 MAINT. & REPAIR CONSTR.	0	0	0	0	0	0	0	0	0
13 ORDNANCE & ACCESSORIES	0	0	0	0	0	0	0	0	0
14 FOOD & KINDRED PRDTS.	0	0	0	0	0	0	0	0	0
15 TOBACCO MANUFACTURES	0	0	0	0	0	0	0	0	0
16 FABRICS	0	0	0	0	0	0	0	0	0
17 TEXTILE PRDTS.	942	2176	2832	1130	359	1568	172	393	0
18 APPAREL	0	0	0	0	0	0	0	0	209
19 MISC. TEXTILE PRDTS.	0	0	0	0	0	0	0	0	0
20 LUMBER & WOOD PRDTS.	68	101	186	135	36	164	13	73	3
21 WOODEN CONTAINERS	0	0	0	0	0	0	0	0	0
22 HOUSEHOLD FURNITURE	1966	4441	5021	2285	710	3103	368	857	869
23 OTHER FURNITURE	17755	40573	51733	21374	6412	29497	3414	7846	3494
24 PAPER & ALLIED PRDTS.	0	0	0	0	0	0	0	0	0
25 PAPERBOARD CONTAINERS	0	0	0	0	0	0	0	0	0
26 PRINTING & PUBLISHING	0	0	0	0	0	0	0	0	0
27 CHEMICALS,SELECT. PRDTS.	0	0	0	0	0	0	0	0	0
28 PLASTICS & SYNTHETICS	0	0	0	0	0	0	0	0	0
29 DRUGS & COSMETICS	0	0	0	0	0	0	0	0	0
30 PAINT & ALLIED PRDTS.	0	0	0	0	0	0	0	0	0
31 PETROLEUM, RELATED INDS.	0	0	0	0	0	0	0	0	0
32 RUBBER, MISC. PLASTICS	281	302	590	228	223	593	86	39	156
33 LEATHER TANNING & PRDTS.	0	0	0	0	0	0	0	0	0
34 FOOTWEAR, LEATHER PRDTS.	0	0	0	0	0	0	0	0	0
35 GLASS & GLASS PRDTS.	0	0	0	0	0	0	0	0	0
36 STONE & CLAY PRDTS.	0	0	0	0	0	0	0	0	0
37 PRIMARY IRON, STEEL MFR.	0	0	0	0	0	0	0	0	0
38 PRIMARY NONFERROUS MFR.	396	598	705	385	202	606	98	162	204

#	Industry									
39	METAL CONTAINERS	8	112	23	272	60	218	326	193	120
40	FABRICATED METAL PRDTS.	2241	2882	2501	12402	5143	7588	24408	12682	8341
41	SCREW MACH. PRDTS., ETC.	0	0	0	0	0	0	0	0	0
42	OTHER FAB. METAL PRDTS.	1050	1236	968	6235	1621	4111	10919	7753	3604
43	ENGINES & TURBINES	3176	1102	2026	12418	4819	4853	13044	6609	5929
44	FARM MACH. & EQUIP.	4075	63526	22044	63381	38305	80838	46883	12862	16715
45	CONSTRUC. MACH. & EQUIP.	10522	11149	11423	36631	14283	26734	61929	37047	26068
46	MATERIAL HANDLING MACH.	2301	3423	2443	14521	5819	9383	42540	19995	9112
47	METALWORKING MACHINERY	3197	7222	4030	39233	12157	21351	154207	52062	24534
48	SPECIAL MACH. & EQUIP.	4031	10985	5531	38137	21591	31685	91046	57140	27164
49	GENERAL MACH. & EQUIP.	4669	6987	5227	32481	11244	20206	77356	40280	21991
50	MACHINE SHOP PRDTS.	20	65	35	151	72	128	330	136	95
51	OFFICE, COMPUT. MACHINES	4044	9242	4567	38559	9111	26912	87179	55813	22236
52	SERVICE IND. MACHINES	3062	8434	3430	29798	7265	21631	50180	34260	17094
53	ELECT. TRANSMISS. EQUIP.	16889	9053	6754	56734	17743	26237	57275	45096	33309
54	HOUSEHOLD APPLIANCES	347	981	369	2938	918	2255	5129	4011	1762
55	ELECTRIC LIGHTING EQUIP.	297	530	271	1648	589	1084	2677	1272	894
56	RADIO, TV, ETC., EQUIP.	20215	15180	6493	57405	14191	33767	56703	52422	36884
57	ELECTRONIC COMPONENTS	434	495	225	2044	519	1092	11557	2689	1290
58	MISC. ELECTRICAL MACH.	896	1078	660	5494	1545	3118	13561	6221	3468
59	MOTOR VEHICLES, EQUIP.	24166	58513	29327	182216	51325	133697	220029	145019	81414
50	AIRCRAFT & PARTS	2821	1234	1518	24800	2395	10835	22684	5185	5121
61	OTHER TRANSPORT. EQUIP.	8904	7510	7293	75937	10941	37247	63011	15410	17687
52	PROFESS., SCIEN. INSTRU.	2057	2688	1964	14287	4457	8787	35318	23357	9247
53	MEDICAL, PHOTO. EQUIP.	1389	1996	951	7728	1724	5861	14617	13544	5286
64	MISC. MANUFACTURING	4745	2977	1398	12195	2722	8523	21832	16345	7761
65	TRANSPORT. & WAREHOUSING	2519	5738	2897	16701	5404	12331	23876	14130	8144
66	COMMUNICA.,EXC. BRDCAST.	2195	4619	2217	13654	4269	10007	20464	13041	7124
57	RADIO & TV BROADCASTING	0	0	0	0	0	0	0	0	0
58	ELEC.,GAS,WATER,SAN.SER.									
59	WHOLESALE & RETAIL TRADE	20005	55131	25037	138494	46273	109904	202419	124628	67674
70	FINANCE & INSURANCE	3	6	3	21	7	15	32	18	11
71	REAL ESTATE & RENTAL	2938	10730	2885	31486	6380	24884	38074	49588	16523
72	HOTELS; PERSONAL SERV.	0	0	0	0	0	0	0	0	0
73	BUSINESS SERVICES	0	0	0	0	0	0	0	0	0
74	RESEARCH & DEVELOPMENT	0	0	0	0	0	0	0	0	0
75	AUTO. REPAIR & SERVICES	0	0	0	0	0	0	0	0	0
76	AMUSEMENTS	0	0	0	0	0	0	0	0	0
77	MED.,EDUC. SERVICES	0	0	0	0	0	0	0	0	0
78	FEDERAL GOV'T ENTERPRISE	0	0	0	0	0	0	0	0	0
79	STATE & LOCAL GOV'T ENT.	733	1448	741	4726	1497	3383	7309	4122	2550
80	IMPORTS	0	0	0	0	0	0	0	0	0
81	BUS.TRAVEL, ENT., GIFTS.	0	0	0	0	0	0	0	0	0
82	OFFICE SUPPLIES	-4298	-8488	-4341	-27708	-8776	-19832	-42842	-24166	-14946
83	SCRAP & USED GOODS	0	0	0	0	0	0	0	0	0
84	GOVERNMENT INDUSTRY	0	0	0	0	0	0	0	0	0
85	REST OF WORLD INDUSTRY	0	0	0	0	0	0	0	0	0
86	HOUSEHOLD INDUSTRY	0	0	0	0	0	0	0	0	0
87	INVENTORY VALUATION ADJ.	0	0	0	0	0	0	0	0	0
88	STATE TOTAL	641369	526834	243639	1795437	518602	1451682	3190284	2305829	1688885

285

TABLE C.6

STATE ESTIMATES OF 1963
GROSS PRIVATE CAPITAL FORMATION
(THOUSANDS OF CURRENT DOLLARS)

INDUSTRY TITLE	28 NEW HAMPSHIRE	29 NEW JERSEY	30 NEW MEXICO	31 NEW YORK	32 NORTH CAROLINA	33 NORTH DAKOTA	34 OHIO	35 OKLAHOMA	36 OREGON
1 LIVESTOCK & PRDTS.	0	0	0	0	0	0	0	0	0
2 OTHER AGRICULTURE PRDTS.	0	0	0	0	0	0	0	0	0
3 FORESTRY & FISHERIES	0	0	0	0	0	0	0	0	0
4 AGRI.,FORES.,FISH. SERV.	0	0	0	0	0	0	0	0	0
5 IRON, FERRO. ORES MINING	0	0	0	0	0	0	0	0	0
6 NONFERROUS ORES MINING	0	0	0	0	0	0	0	0	0
7 COAL MINING	0	0	0	0	0	0	0	0	0
8 CRUDE PETRO.,NATURAL GAS	0	0	0	0	0	0	0	0	0
9 STONE & CLAY MINING	0	0	0	0	0	0	0	0	0
10 CHEM.&FERT. MIN. MINING	0	0	0	0	0	0	0	0	0
11 NEW CONSTRUCTION	100305	1579805	277258	2927360	727598	93209	2218821	646552	452142
12 MAINT. & REPAIR CONSTR.	0	0	0	0	0	0	0	0	0
13 ORDNANCE & ACCESSORIES	0	0	0	0	0	0	0	0	0
14 FOOD & KINDRED PRDTS.	0	0	0	0	0	0	0	0	0
15 TOBACCO MANUFACTURES	0	0	0	0	0	0	0	0	0
16 FABRICS	0	0	0	0	0	0	0	0	0
17 TEXTILE PRDTS.	183	2319	221	9056	1147	150	3496	609	625
18 APPAREL	0	0	0	0	0	0	0	0	0
19 MISC. TEXTILE PRDTS.	0	0	0	0	0	0	0	0	0
20 LUMBER & WOOD PRDTS.	7	246	11	367	90	25	224	49	60
21 WOODEN CONTAINERS	0	0	0	0	0	0	0	0	0
22 HOUSEHOLD FURNITURE	468	4525	479	18041	2331	310	6328	1202	1241
23 OTHER FURNITURE	3473	42415	4098	158711	21483	2929	62153	10922	11167
24 PAPER & ALLIED PRDTS.	0	0	0	0	0	0	0	0	0
25 PAPERBOARD CONTAINERS	0	0	0	0	0	0	0	0	0
26 PRINTING & PUBLISHING	0	0	0	0	0	0	0	0	0
27 CHEMICALS,SELECT. PRDTS.	0	0	0	0	0	0	0	0	0
28 PLASTICS & SYNTHETICS	0	0	0	0	0	0	0	0	0
29 DRUGS & COSMETICS	0	0	0	0	0	0	0	0	0
30 PAINT & ALLIED PRDTS.	0	0	0	0	0	0	0	0	0
31 PETROLEUM, RELATED INDS.	0	0	0	0	0	0	0	0	0
32 RUBBER, MISC. PLASTICS	38	606	145	1456	565	71	761	404	263
33 LEATHER TANNING & PRDTS.	0	0	0	0	0	0	0	0	0
34 FOOTWEAR, LEATHER PRDTS.	0	0	0	0	0	0	0	0	0
35 GLASS & GLASS PRDTS.	0	0	0	0	0	0	0	0	0
36 STONE & CLAY PRDTS.	0	0	0	0	0	0	0	0	0
37 PRIMARY IRON, STEEL MFR.	0	0	0	0	0	0	0	0	0
38 PRIMARY NONFERROUS MFR.	76	901	99	2742	487	64	1058	224	211

286

Code	Sector	1	2	3	4	5	6	7	8	9
39	METAL CONTAINERS	14	398	22	763	156	39	392	84	101
40	FABRICATED METAL PRDTS.	1325	25502	4223	46403	12077	1462	30182	8769	5372
41	SCREW MACH. PRDTS., ETC.	0	0	1020	0	0	0	0	0	2114
42	OTHER FAB. METAL PRDTS.	679	9810	3313	29795	4695	507	13865	2483	5637
43	ENGINES & TURBINES	809	13366	12243	30765	11915	1517	17010	8179	20931
44	FARM MACH. & EQUIP.	2961	18255	2946	68668	59469	31802	64881	32742	17162
45	CONSTRUC. MACH. & EQUIP.	3363	53000	3951	165332	26140	6797	88300	37358	8209
46	MATERIAL HANDLING MACHINERY	1908	27700	4686	68256	15370	1330	42409	6657	11884
47	METALWORKING MACHINERY	5105	68906	5993	148870	22687	1132	141799	12477	30494
48	SPECIAL MACH. & EQUIP.	7605	96849	7600	174405	97339	3572	119391	14522	13062
49	GENERAL MACH. & EQUIP.	3893	65014	5400	131727	31010	2497	88770	14028	9070
50	MACHINE SHOP PRDTS.	16	194	37	498	173	31	396	79	68
51	OFFICE, COMPUT. MACHINES	4352	64947	4852	230706	27550	3129	94222	14374	12371
52	SERVICE IND. MACHINES	3068	43160	3969	150354	22204	3192	59375	10895	12106
53	ELECT. TRANSMISS. EQUIP.	5391	65896	10828	198920	47573	6045	86758	29231	21454
54	HOUSEHOLD APPLIANCES	430	4588	449	16664	4064	374	5859	1190	1186
55	ELECTRIC LIGHTING EQUIP.	141	1703	307	5086	1344	289	2971	814	613
56	RADIO, TV, ETC., EQUIP.	6618	68561	9837	257223	37043	6253	89969	21526	17767
57	ELECTRONIC COMPONENTS	235	3825	311	12263	1318	165	6398	692	588
58	MISC. ELECTRICAL MACH.	624	7504	672	20612	3796	410	13796	1883	2179
59	MOTOR VEHICLES, EQUIP.	15040	159330	28016	583221	124301	29349	309076	68451	65346
60	AIRCRAFT & PARTS	979	5765	1559	31023	10629	1418	31578	5782	4362
61	OTHER TRANSPORT. EQUIP.	2845	20318	8021	100193	34493	6126	92241	22295	19974
62	PROFESS., SCIEN. INSTRU.	1768	33129	2735	74950	13297	1348	40002	7228	5569
63	MEDICAL, PHOTO. EQUIP.	1105	13820	1262	50708	5615	727	19055	3122	3050
64	MISC. MANUFACTURING	1719	17959	1528	76863	8849	1061	27021	4160	4724
65	TRANSPORT. & WAREHOUSING	1495	17965	3260	57396	13389	2821	30685	7423	6363
66	COMMUNICA.-EXC. BRDCAST.	1337	16309	2391	52760	10813	2141	26022	5699	5022
67	RADIO & TV BROADCASTING	0	0	0	0	0	0	0	0	0
68	ELEC.,GAS,WATER,SAN.SER.	0	0	0	0	0	0	0	0	0
69	WHOLESALE & RETAIL TRADE	12743	151234	24514	504880	109563	26261	256507	59369	50904
70	FINANCE & INSURANCE	2	22	4	76	17	3	42	9	8
71	REAL ESTATE & RENTAL	3300	40200	3924	236533	19569	2611	53063	12906	10316
72	HOTELS; PERSONAL SERV.	0	0	0	0	0	0	0	0	0
73	BUSINESS SERVICES	0	0	0	0	0	0	0	0	0
74	RESEARCH & DEVELOPMENT	0	0	0	0	0	0	0	0	0
75	AUTO. REPAIR & SERVICES	0	0	0	0	0	0	0	0	0
76	AMUSEMENTS	0	0	0	0	0	0	0	0	0
77	MED.-EDUC. SERVICES	0	0	0	0	0	0	0	0	0
78	FEDERAL GOV'T ENTERPRISE	0	0	0	0	0	0	0	0	0
79	STATE & LOCAL GOV'T ENT.	438	4994	819	17068	3782	691	9384	1988	1744
80	IMPORTS	-2565	-29275	-4799	-100058	-22173	-4048	-55013	-11651	-10220
81	BUS.TRAVEL, ENT., GIFTS.	0	0	0	0	0	0	0	0	0
82	OFFICE SUPPLIES	0	0	0	0	0	0	0	0	0
83	SCRAP & USED GOODS	0	0	0	0	0	0	0	0	0
84	GOVERNMENT INDUSTRY	0	0	0	0	0	0	0	0	0
85	REST OF WORLD INDUSTRY	0	0	0	0	0	0	0	0	0
86	HOUSEHOLD INDUSTRY	0	0	0	0	0	0	0	0	0
87	INVENTORY VALUATION ADJ.	0	0	0	0	0	0	0	0	0
88	STATE TOTAL	193291	2721736	452935	6560599	1511753	237805	4099215	1064720	816165

TABLE C.6

STATE ESTIMATES OF 1963
GROSS PRIVATE CAPITAL FORMATION
(THOUSANDS OF CURRENT DOLLARS)

INDUSTRY TITLE	37 PENNSYL-VANIA	38 RHODE ISLAND	39 SOUTH CAROLINA	40 SOUTH DAKOTA	41 TENNESSEE	42 TEXAS	43 UTAH	44 VERMONT	45 VIRGINIA
1 LIVESTOCK & PRDTS.	0	0	0	0	0	0	0	0	0
2 OTHER AGRICULTURE PRDTS.	0	0	0	0	0	0	0	0	0
3 FORESTRY & FISHERIES	0	0	0	0	0	0	0	0	0
4 AGRI.,FORES.,FISH. SERV.	0	0	0	0	0	0	0	0	0
5 IRON, FERRO. ORES MINING	0	0	0	0	0	0	0	0	0
6 NONFERROUS ORES MINING	0	0	0	0	0	0	0	0	0
7 COAL MINING	0	0	0	0	0	0	0	0	0
8 CRUDE PETRO.,NATURAL GAS	0	0	0	0	0	0	0	0	0
9 STONE & CLAY MINING	0	0	0	0	0	0	0	0	0
10 CHEM.&FERT. MIN. MINING	0	0	0	0	0	0	0	0	0
11 NEW CONSTRUCTION	1380231	157896	168669	69193	516961	3106622	326653	22542	1247057
12 MAINT. & REPAIR CONSTR.	0	0	0	0	0	0	0	0	0
13 ORDNANCE & ACCESSORIES	0	0	0	0	0	0	0	0	0
14 FOOD & KINDRED PRDTS.	0	0	0	0	0	0	0	0	0
15 TOBACCO MANUFACTURES	0	0	0	0	0	0	0	0	0
16 FABRICS	0	0	0	0	0	0	0	0	0
17 TEXTILE PRDTS.	3758	263	468	140	921	260	122	983	879
18 APPAREL	0	0	0	0	0	0	0	0	0
19 MISC. TEXTILE PRDTS.	0	0	0	0	0	0	0	0	0
20 LUMBER & WOOD PRDTS.	299	16	33	19	90	22	7	77	72
21 WOODEN CONTAINERS	0	0	0	0	0	0	0	0	0
22 HOUSEHOLD FURNITURE	7365	587	912	316	1899	547	287	2054	1829
23 OTHER FURNITURE	68415	5083	8348	2817	17951	5183	2198	18324	16434
24 PAPER & ALLIED PRDTS.	0	0	0	0	0	0	0	0	0
25 PAPERBOARD CONTAINERS	0	0	0	0	0	0	0	0	0
26 PRINTING & PUBLISHING	0	0	0	0	0	0	0	0	0
27 CHEMICALS,SELECT. PRDTS.	0	0	0	0	0	0	0	0	0
28 PLASTICS & SYNTHETICS	0	0	0	0	0	0	0	0	0
29 DRUGS & COSMETICS	0	0	0	0	0	0	0	0	0
30 PAINT & ALLIED PRDTS.	0	0	0	0	0	0	0	0	0
31 PETROLEUM, RELATED INDS.	0	0	0	0	0	0	0	0	0
32 RUBBER, MISC. PLASTICS	1211	38	274	24	131	244	25	460	188
33 LEATHER TANNING & PRDTS.	0	0	0	0	0	0	0	0	0
34 FOOTWEAR, LEATHER PRDTS.	0	0	0	0	0	0	0	0	0
35 GLASS & GLASS PRDTS.	0	0	0	0	0	0	0	0	0
36 STONE & CLAY PRDTS.	0	0	0	0	0	0	0	0	0
37 PRIMARY IRON, STEEL MFR.	0	0	0	0	0	0	0	0	0
38 PRIMARY NONFERROUS MFR.	973	82	284	54	391	111	49	444	307

Sector	1	2	3	4	5	6	7	8	9
39 METAL CONTAINERS	126	133	13	38	151	31	58	29	502
40 FABRICATED METAL PRDTS.	6630	13079	867	3855	9942	1007	5844	1717	35856
41 SCREW MACH. PRDTS., ETC.	3086	4726	413	1302	3872	0	0	0	0
42 OTHER FAB. METAL PRDTS.	4186	9789	571	5147	3270	417	2165	922	16332
43 ENGINES & TURBINES	31236	26602	6228	8372	32419	661	5819	819	25644
44 FARM MACH. & EQUIP.	25757	36513	2235	17251	25374	35610	20483	1708	49900
45 CONSTRUC. MACH. & EQUIP.	9187	12039	1172	3230	9889	5761	10041	4516	98852
46 MATERIAL HANDLING MACH.	17640	20400	2731	6428	26543	1138	7315	2417	42936
47 METALWORKING MACHINERY	32285	55182	3627	6386	35829	1503	10598	7186	118457
48 SPECIAL MACH. & EQUIP.	17806	30167	2296	7162	26917	2111	10582	9267	120904
49 GENERAL MACH. & EQUIP.	84	120	11	36	105	32	15829	5528	93420
50 MACHINE SHOP PRDTS.	18777	25275	2483	5856	24005	2805	84	20	426
51 OFFICE, COMPUT. MACHINES	17014	18801	1818	4671	18477	2953	11734	6543	102428
52 SERVICE IND. MACHINES	22047	40316	3388	17274	21918	3494	9883	4583	64945
53 ELECT. TRANSMISS. EQUIP.	1670	1822	234	469	2301	377	24669	5586	101159
54 HOUSEHOLD APPLIANCES	717	1014	117	367	789	260	1317	541	7479
55 ELECTRIC LIGHTING EQUIP.	26220	36782	4505	10384	31940	5604	643	159	3087
56 RADIO, TV, ETC., EQUIP.	871	1239	132	317	1395	155	20319	6876	75164
57 ELECTRONIC COMPONENTS	2703	3139	417	871	3058	363	658	303	5400
58 MISC. ELECTRICAL MACH.	90969	97529	12148	25557	89512	29127	1939	771	11925
59 MOTOR VEHICLES, EQUIP.	6585	7389	472	886	6692	843	41287	18599	330012
60 AIRCRAFT & PARTS	25476	24732	1526	4543	21735	4416	1938	1107	34739
61 OTHER TRANSPORT. EQUIP.	6902	13439	1200	3839	9869	929	6880	3342	102294
62 PROFESS., SCIEN. INSTRU.	4524	5611	755	1432	5308	728	6022	2321	48245
63 MEDICAL, PHOTO. EQUIP.	6890	7910	1057	1901	7411	1126	2235	1525	21789
64 MISC. MANUFACTURING	8528	10384	1127	3019	8974	2758	3648	2236	28986
65 TRANSPORT. & WAREHOUSING	6937	8645	972	2404	7746	2106	5607	1855	32455
66 COMMUNICA.-EXC. BRDCAST.	0	972	0	0	0	0	4658	1669	27101
67 RADIO & TV BROADCASTING	0	0	0	0	0	0	0	0	0
68 ELEC.,GAS,WATER,SAN.SER.	70946	83523	10229	23265	76898	26854	44208	15881	267932
69 WHOLESALE & RETAIL TRADE	10	13	0	4	12	3	0	2	46
70 FINANCE & INSURANCE	16651	18302	1790	4695	18025	2757	9436	6019	68009
71 REAL ESTATE & RENTAL	0	0	0	0	0	0	0	0	0
72 HOTELS; PERSONAL SERV.	0	0	0	0	0	0	0	0	0
73 BUSINESS SERVICES	0	0	0	0	0	0	0	0	0
74 RESEARCH & DEVELOPMENT	0	0	0	0	0	0	0	0	0
75 AUTO. REPAIR & SERVICES	0	0	0	0	0	0	0	0	0
76 AMUSEMENTS	0	0	0	0	0	0	0	0	0
77 MED.,EDUC. SERVICES	0	0	0	0	0	0	0	0	0
78 FEDERAL GOV'T ENTERPRISE	0	0	0	0	0	0	0	0	0
79 STATE & LOCAL GOV'T ENT.	0	0	0	0	0	0	0	0	0
80 IMPORTS	2319	2963	304	862	2641	662	1633	561	10301
81 BUS.TRAVEL, ENT., GIFTS.	0	0	0	0	0	0	0	0	0
82 OFFICE SUPPLIES	0	0	0	0	0	0	0	0	0
83 SCRAP & USED GOODS	-13591	-17364	-1781	-5052	-15479	-3882	-9569	-3288	-60390
84 GOVERNMENT INDUSTRY	0	0	0	0	0	0	0	0	0
85 REST OF WORLD INDUSTRY	0	0	0	0	0	0	0	0	0
86 HOUSEHOLD INDUSTRY	0	0	0	0	0	0	0	0	0
87 INVENTORY VALUATION ADJ.	0	0	0	0	0	0	0	0	0
88 STATE TOTAL	1737935	645093	392395	3279741	1055875	208467	516954	275282	3348553

TABLE C.6

STATE ESTIMATES OF 1963
GROSS PRIVATE CAPITAL FORMATION
(THOUSANDS OF CURRENT DOLLARS)

INDUSTRY TITLE	46 WASHINGTON	47 WEST VIRGINIA	48 WISCONSIN	49 WYOMING	50 ALASKA	51 HAWAII	52 NO STATE ALLOCATION	53 NATIONAL TOTAL
1 LIVESTOCK & PRDTS.	0	0	0	0	0	0	0	0
2 OTHER AGRICULTURE PRDTS.	0	0	0	0	0	0	0	0
3 FORESTRY & FISHERIES	0	0	0	0	0	0	0	0
4 AGRI.,FORES.,FISH. SERV.	0	0	0	0	0	0	0	0
5 IRON, FERRO. ORES MINING	0	0	0	0	0	0	0	0
6 NONFERROUS ORES MINING	0	0	0	0	0	0	0	0
7 COAL MINING	0	0	0	0	0	0	0	0
8 CRUDE PETRO.,NATURAL GAS	0	0	0	0	0	0	0	0
9 STONE & CLAY MINING	0	0	0	0	0	0	0	0
10 CHEM.&FERT. MIN. MINING	0	0	0	0	0	0	0	0
11 NEW CONSTRUCTION	861635	114224	849896	99862	64632	249917	0	46150992
12 MAINT. & REPAIR CONSTR.	0	0	0	0	0	0	0	0
13 ORDNANCE & ACCESSORIES	0	0	0	0	0	0	0	0
14 FOOD & KINDRED PRDTS.	0	0	0	0	0	0	0	0
15 TOBACCO MANUFACTURES	0	0	0	0	0	0	0	0
16 FABRICS	0	0	0	0	0	0	0	0
17 TEXTILE PRDTS.	468	1228	97	88	192	1568	0	62520
18 APPAREL	0	0	0	0	0	0	0	0
19 MISC. TEXTILE PRDTS.	0	0	0	0	0	0	0	0
20 LUMBER & WOOD PRDTS.	16	220	5	7	51	164	0	5367
21 WOODEN CONTAINERS	0	0	0	0	0	0	0	0
22 HOUSEHOLD FURNITURE	848	2339	228	150	482	3103	0	124055
23 OTHER FURNITURE	8656	21910	1629	1232	3419	29497	0	1126537
24 PAPER & ALLIED PRDTS.	0	0	0	0	0	0	0	0
25 PAPERBOARD CONTAINERS	0	0	0	0	0	0	0	0
26 PRINTING & PUBLISHING	0	0	0	0	0	0	0	0
27 CHEMICALS,SELECT. PRDTS.	0	0	0	0	0	0	0	0
28 PLASTICS & SYNTHETICS	0	0	0	0	0	0	0	0
29 DRUGS & COSMETICS	0	0	0	0	0	0	0	0
30 PAINT & ALLIED PRDTS.	0	0	0	0	0	0	0	0
31 PETROLEUM, RELATED INDS.	0	0	0	0	0	0	0	0
32 RUBBER, MISC. PLASTICS	314	380	94	23	114	593	0	18106
33 LEATHER TANNING & PRDTS.	0	0	0	0	0	0	0	0
34 FOOTWEAR, LEATHER PRDTS.	0	0	0	0	0	0	0	0
35 GLASS & GLASS PRDTS.	0	0	0	0	0	0	0	0
36 STONE & CLAY PRDTS.	0	0	0	0	0	0	0	0
37 PRIMARY IRON, STEEL MFR.	0	0	0	0	0	0	0	0
38 PRIMARY NONFERROUS MFR.	159	413	43	6	85	606	0	22155

39	METAL CONTAINERS	31	328	9	12	73	272	0	9000
40	FABRICATED METAL PRDTS.	7679	10505	2237	902	1819	12402	0	536275
41	SCREW MACH. PRDTS., ETC.	0	0	0	0	0	0	0	0
42	OTHER FAB. METAL PRDTS.	3241	4659	572	340	730	6235	0	242362
43	ENGINES & TURBINES	6524	8110	2012	549	2329	12418	0	388186
44	FARM MACH. & EQUIP.	7650	58428	8310	506	12578	63381	0	1901909
45	CONSTRUC. MACH. & EQUIP.	36851	27203	13394	7011	6247	36631	0	1760247
46	MATERIAL HANDLING MACH.	6844	16350	1384	1202	1826	14521	0	664856
47	METALWORKING MACHINERY	20728	53660	1292	953	1791	39233	0	1670157
48	SPECIAL MACH. & EQUIP.	12836	57343	2224	2780	6316	38137	0	2024850
49	GENERAL MACH. & EQUIP.	20106	28798	2857	1741	3427	32481	0	1385532
50	MACHINE SHOP PRDTS.	85	153	20	8	22	151	0	6415
51	OFFICE, COMPUT. MACHINES	13325	33775	2559	1967	4519	38559	0	1614965
52	SERVICE IND. MACHINES	7742	23775	1705	1286	3433	29798	0	1111638
53	ELECT. TRANSMISS. EQUIP.	22150	38010	4902	911	9458	56734	0	1861526
54	HOUSEHOLD APPLIANCES	659	2429	194	112	383	2938	0	119896
55	ELECTRIC LIGHTING EQUIP.	690	1218	170	86	254	1648	0	55478
56	RADIO, TV, ETC., EQUIP.	14303	31438	3124	795	7988	57405	0	1923611
57	ELECTRONIC COMPONENTS	617	2266	103	64	234	2044	0	96241
58	MISC. ELECTRICAL MACH.	2464	4169	311	394	559	5494	0	198412
59	MOTOR VEHICLES, EQUIP.	77376	115292	18131	16321	23064	182216	0	5671411
60	AIRCRAFT & PARTS	16334	7559	2226	3752	1234	24800	0	446250
61	OTHER TRANSPORT. EQUIP.	48994	22892	8770	13428	4533	75937	0	1465163
62	PROFESS., SCIEN. INSTRU.	6881	14697	1379	599	2089	14287	0	672807
63	MEDICAL, PHOTO. EQUIP.	2662	6179	543	426	1044	7728	0	340053
64	MISC. MANUFACTURING	4907	8937	781	825	1560	12195	0	496829
65	TRANSPORT. & WAREHOUSING	7151	12335	1860	1287	2226	16701	0	574378
66	COMMUNICA., EXC. BRDCAST.	5173	10392	1263	794	1808	13654	0	485078
67	RADIO & TV BROADCASTING	0	0	0	0	0	0	0	0
68	ELEC.,GAS,WATER,SAN.SER.	52129	106416	14006	8733	19057	138494	0	4857513
69	WHOLESALE & RETAIL TRADE	10	15	2	1	3	21	0	733
70	FINANCE & INSURANCE	5286	20665	1299	909	4970	31486	0	1224003
71	REAL ESTATE & RENTAL	0	0	0	0	0	0	0	0
72	HOTELS; PERSONAL SERV.	0	0	0	0	0	0	0	0
73	BUSINESS SERVICES	0	0	0	0	0	0	0	0
74	RESEARCH & DEVELOPMENT	0	0	0	0	0	0	0	0
75	AUTO. REPAIR & SERVICES	0	0	0	0	0	0	0	0
76	AMUSEMENTS	0	0	0	0	0	0	0	0
77	MED.,EDUC. SERVICES	0	0	0	0	0	0	0	0
78	FEDERAL GOV'T ENTERPRISE	0	0	0	0	0	0	0	0
79	STATE & LOCAL GOV'T ENT.	0	0	0	0	0	0	0	0
80	IMPORTS	2225	3399	451	305	612	4726	0	165746
81	BUS.TRAVEL, ENT., GIFTS.	0	0	0	0	0	0	0	0
82	OFFICE SUPPLIES	0	0	0	0	0	0	0	0
83	SCRAP & USED GOODS	-13039	-19929	-2644	-1785	-3584	-27708	0	-971601
84	GOVERNMENT INDUSTRY	0	0	0	0	0	0	0	0
85	REST OF WORLD INDUSTRY	0	0	0	0	0	0	0	0
86	HOUSEHOLD INDUSTRY	0	0	0	0	0	0	0	0
87	INVENTORY VALUATION ADJ.	0	0	0	0	0	0	0	0
88	STATE TOTAL	1272720	851774	947438	168581	191573	1230457	0	80509744

TABLE C.7

STATE ESTIMATES OF 1947
NET INVENTORY CHANGE
(THOUSANDS OF CURRENT DOLLARS)

INDUSTRY TITLE	1 ALABAMA	2 ARIZONA	3 ARKANSAS	4 CALIFORNIA	5 COLORADO	6 CONNECTICUT	7 DELAWARE	8 DISTRICT OF COLUMBIA	9 FLORIDA
1 LIVESTOCK & PRDTS.	-12115	-8967	-22706	-33175	13503	-631	-176	0	-68
2 OTHER AGRICULTURE PRDTS.	-21251	4057	-45976	28383	31905	3433	-1378	0	2304
3 FORESTRY & FISHERIES	0	0	0	0	0	0	0	0	0
4 AGRI.,FORES.,FISH.SERV.	0	0	0	0	0	0	0	0	0
5 IRON,FERRO.ORES MINING	966	1	2	75	4	0	0	0	0
6 NONFERROUS ORES MINING	0	1048	67	160	126	0	0	0	24
7 COAL MINING	457	0	55	0	126	0	0	0	0
8 CRUDE PETRO.,NATURAL GAS	0	0	0	0	0	0	0	0	0
9 STONE & CLAY MINING	133	30	39	825	60	61	9	0	168
10 CHEM.&FERT.MIN.MINING	0	6	66	121	26	0	0	0	915
11 NEW CONSTRUCTION	0	0	0	0	0	0	0	0	0
12 MAINT.& REPAIR CONSTR.	0	0	0	0	0	0	0	0	0
13 ORDNANCE & ACCESSORIES	0	0	0	1	0	92	0	0	0
14 FOOD & KINDRED PRDTS.	1599	412	1408	19158	2113	948	722	579	1893
15 TOBACCO MANUFACTURES	133	0	62	826	2	153	221	0	1715
16 FABRICS	3320	0	75	120	22	1760	49	0	1
17 TEXTILE PRDTS.	1338	0	66	380	10	1205	60	0	19
18 APPAREL	1147	24	235	5598	139	2757	169	94	207
19 MISC.TEXTILE PRDTS.	-124	-2	-5	-397	-31	-141	-2	-11	-20
20 LUMBER & WOOD PRDTS.	8465	848	6262	15560	655	550	196	53	3390
21 WOODEN CONTAINERS	70	11	152	505	19	49	37	2	179
22 HOUSEHOLD FURNITURE	55	9	131	730	20	60	2	3	58
23 OTHER FURNITURE	-2	-1	-1	-47	-3	-6	0	-1	-4
24 PAPER & ALLIED PRDTS.	417	26	231	432	32	-300	62	16	582
25 PAPERBOARD CONTAINERS	-46	-6	-26	-967	-106	-540	-51	-54	-161
26 PRINTING & PUBLISHING	-116	-48	-61	-1517	-133	-408	-20	-327	-193
27 CHEMICALS,SELECT.PRDTS.	1823	94	996	4425	258	975	799	41	1309
28 PLASTICS & SYNTHETICS	0	0	-1048	-1440	0	-921	-3055	0	-546
29 DRUGS & COSMETICS	23	10	5	1275	23	377	7	16	19
30 PAINT & ALLIED PRDTS.	161	38	17	6354	245	412	18	35	179
31 PETROLEUM,RELATED INDS.	153	56	973	19034	224	45	85	0	83
32 RUBBER,MISC.PLASTICS	2451	2	111	6443	198	4906	455	8	194
33 LEATHER TANNING & PRDTS.	0	0	0	190	2	63	260	0	41
34 FOOTWEAR,LEATHER PRDTS.	77	11	200	1104	302	304	0	0	48
35 GLASS & GLASS PRDTS.	7	1	176	874	69	229	0	0	6
36 STONE & CLAY PRDTS.	1535	161	294	5428	399	994	50	32	646
37 PRIMARY IRON,STEEL MFR.	11791	74	14	4870	1475	2381	315	0	9
38 PRIMARY NONFERROUS MFR.	1339	1301	995	3079	419	6256	11	0	125

Code & Industry									
39 METAL CONTAINERS	181	0	9	12	19	1014	26	0	25
40 FABRICATED METAL PRDTS.	439	87	184	1886	528	7776	107	248	2104
41 SCREW MACH. PRDTS., ETC.	13	13	358	4724	15	2545	5	0	394
42 OTHER FAB. METAL PRDTS.	219	35	110	8816	229	5550	122	28	756
43 ENGINES & TURBINES	1	0	0	203	11	1093	0	0	1
44 FARM MACH. & EQUIP.	109	0	8	142	266	1768	305	7	385
45 CONSTRUC. MACH. & EQUIP.	49	0	8	240	379	1738	41	0	83
46 MATERIAL HANDLING MACH.	5	0	0	67	55	158	26	0	22
47 METALWORKING MACHINERY	3	0	111	1762	5	362	0	3	8
48 SPECIAL MACH. & EQUIP.	76	1	271	1069	108	1202	22	7	80
49 GENERAL MACH. & EQUIP.	148	25	34	4948	148	2602	29	0	233
50 MACHINE SHOP PRDTS.	36	3	36	451	62	1141	11	12	43
51 OFFICE, COMPUT. MACHINES	2	1	36	1906	11	423	0	0	1
52 SERVICE IND. MACHINES	3	28	28	1126	42	2135	51	107	93
53 ELECT. TRANSMISS. EQUIP.	30	5	5	1463	56	2272	41	96	81
54 HOUSEHOLD APPLIANCES	26	0	33	9335	21	5331	9	8	399
55 ELECTRIC LIGHTING EQUIP.	40	1	0	4916	61	2814	0	7	225
56 RADIO, TV, ETC., EQUIP.	16	31	0	1362	75	1107	0	4	124
57 ELECTRONIC COMPONENTS	9	16	0	541	4	443	0	0	66
58 MISC. ELECTRICAL MACH.	202	28	0	654	53	1470	34	0	28
59 MOTOR VEHICLES, EQUIP.	324	6	137	1354	121	14134	1	168	234
60 AIRCRAFT & PARTS	1	0	0	550	10	1423	1	0	36
61 OTHER TRANSPORT. EQUIP.	31	0	9	13	1	125	1	-2	-3
62 PROFESS., SCIEN. INSTRU.	-4	-5	-3	-239	-4	-151	-2	-2	-60
63 MISC., PHOTO. EQUIP.	-116	-4	-185	68	-26	-154	-2	-2	0
64 MISC. MANUFACTURING	-60	-21	415	-3648	-197	-1650	-88	-12	0
65 TRANSPORT. & WAREHOUSING	1406	427	415	745	881	8760	667	431	1350
66 COMMUNICA.,EXC. BRDCAST.	0	0	0	0	0	0	0	0	0
67 RADIO & TV BROADCASTING	0	0	0	0	0	0	0	0	0
68 ELEC.,GAS,WATER,SAN.SER.	1974	890	257	1569	1096	9894	862	530	1357
69 WHOLESALE & RETAIL TRADE	0	0	0	0	0	0	0	0	0
70 FINANCE & INSURANCE	0	0	0	0	0	0	0	0	0
71 REAL ESTATE & RENTAL	0	0	0	0	0	0	0	0	0
72 HOTELS; PERSONAL SERV.	-4	-4	0	-3	-2	-29	-1	-1	-2
73 BUSINESS SERVICES	0	0	0	0	0	0	-1	-1	0
74 RESEARCH & DEVELOPMENT	0	0	0	0	0	0	0	0	0
75 AUTO. REPAIR & SERVICES	0	0	0	0	0	0	0	0	0
76 AMUSEMENTS	95	33	11	44	29	991	22	15	30
77 MED.,EDUC. SERVICES	0	0	0	0	0	0	0	0	0
78 FEDERAL GOV'T ENTERPRISE	0	0	0	0	0	0	0	0	0
79 STATE & LOCAL GOV'T ENT.	0	0	0	0	0	0	0	0	0
80 IMPORTS	0	0	0	0	0	0	0	0	0
81 BUS.TRAVEL, ENT., GIFTS.	0	0	0	0	0	0	0	0	0
82 OFFICE SUPPLIES	0	0	0	0	0	0	0	0	0
83 SCRAP & USED GOODS	0	0	0	0	0	0	0	0	0
84 GOVERNMENT INDUSTRY	0	0	0	0	0	0	0	0	0
85 REST OF WORLD INDUSTRY	0	0	0	0	0	0	0	0	0
86 HOUSEHOLD INDUSTRY	0	0	0	0	0	0	0	0	0
87 INVENTORY VALUATION ADJ.	0	0	0	0	0	0	0	0	0
88 STATE TOTAL	18437	2044	677	71741	56209	165001	-54896	854	11898

TABLE C.7

STATE ESTIMATES OF 1947
NET INVENTORY CHANGE
(THOUSANDS OF CURRENT DOLLARS)

INDUSTRY TITLE	10 GEORGIA	11 IDAHO	12 ILLINOIS	13 INDIANA	14 IOWA	15 KANSAS	16 KENTUCKY	17 LOUISIANA	18 MAINE
1 LIVESTOCK & PRDTS.	-9585	3404	-61280	-27651	-157525	-54639	9028	-21606	-1381
2 OTHER AGRICULTURE PRDTS.	-15346	-13571	-200576	-59266	-408191	67199	-78997	-11231	-5856
3 FORESTRY & FISHERIES	0	0	0	0	0	0	0	0	0
4 AGRI.,FORES.,FISH. SERV.	29	4	0	0	0	0	0	0	0
5 IRON, FERRO. ORES MINING	0	0	0	0	0	48	0	0	0
6 NONFERROUS ORES MINING	4	269	9	0	0	40	1619	0	0
7 COAL MINING	1	0	0	359	28	0	0	0	0
8 CRUDE PETRO.,NATURAL GAS	0	0	935	0	0	0	0	0	0
9 STONE & CLAY MINING	476	37	601	341	216	138	174	50	38
10 CHEM.&FERT. MIN. MINING	18	113	171	0	0	159	75	818	0
11 NEW CONSTRUCTION	0	0	0	0	0	0	0	0	0
12 MAINT.& REPAIR CONSTR.	0	0	0	0	0	0	0	0	0
13 ORDNANCE & ACCESSORIES	0	29	9	4	0	0	0	0	0
14 FOOD & KINDRED PRDTS.	3503	1144	25615	7141	9897	6350	5645	6154	630
15 TOBACCO MANUFACTURES	202	0	151	311	3	0	10369	177	4
16 FABRICS	6703	0	222	78	16	2	172	44	1756
17 TEXTILE PRDTS.	2207	0	1614	129	1	4	60	121	411
18 APPAREL	2859	-2	7463	2331	454	144	1339	546	228
19 MISC. TEXTILE PRDTS.	-359	0	-446	-97	-37	-65	-41	-185	-168
20 LUMBER & WOOD PRDTS.	7807	2946	4646	3353	1786	325	2714	6520	2407
21 WOODEN CONTAINERS	170	6	293	97	23	17	229	157	116
22 HOUSEHOLD FURNITURE	207	2	1022	801	75	32	268	49	8
23 OTHER FURNITURE	-6	0	-106	-23	-9	-2	-3	-2	-2
24 PAPER & ALLIED PRDTS.	469	0	903	323	45	62	29	1108	1244
25 PAPERBOARD CONTAINERS	-226	-6	-2116	-904	-150	-126	-114	-384	-19
26 PRINTING & PUBLISHING	-192	-26	-3300	-491	-327	-147	-168	-129	-53
27 CHEMICALS,SELECT. PRDTS.	2353	58	6131	1273	225	831	440	3729	255
28 PLASTICS & SYNTHETICS	-1317	0	-1030	-393	-158	0	-807	-2781	-58
29 DRUGS & COSMETICS	141	6	2649	3063	201	593	20	31	5
30 PAINT & ALLIED PRDTS.	535	1	9933	1425	812	53	1850	369	45
31 PETROLEUM, RELATED INDS.	198	48	9644	6467	42	5110	1005	9413	23
32 RUBBER, MISC. PLASTICS	310	0	2986	3026	1175	515	957	15	37
33 LEATHER TANNING & PRDTS.	56	0	1000	89	0	0	71	5	87
34 FOOTWEAR, LEATHER PRDTS.	526	7	6401	559	189	32	840	77	3414
35 GLASS & GLASS PRDTS.	4	0	2032	1545	17	1	22	119	14
36 STONE & CLAY PRDTS.	1368	107	4911	2489	1302	889	664	464	128
37 PRIMARY IRON, STEEL MFR.	608	4	22957	26225	309	56	2130	30	12
38 PRIMARY NONFERROUS MFR.	215	489	7808	3667	110	227	978	299	51

	C1	C2	C3	C4	C5	C6	C7	C8	C9
39 METAL CONTAINERS	9	0	1622	163	26	0	6	137	25
40 FABRICATED METAL PRDTS.	562	49	7954	4254	1329	1056	2304	611	228
41 SCREW MACH. PRDTS., ETC.	272	0	13024	3400	125	50	182	96	18
42 OTHER FAB. METAL PRDTS.	153	1	16973	3504	720	73	691	389	178
43 ENGINES & TURBINES	0	0	2433	2509	40	14	0	0	0
44 FARM MACH. & EQUIP.	460	76	27325	3868	5637	685	665	100	17
45 CONSTRUC. MACH. & EQUIP.	230	12	4041	926	1412	337	93	107	33
46 MATERIAL HANDLING MACH.	62	1	991	124	116	42	78	4	4
47 METALWORKING MACHINERY	9	0	3518	643	182	18	60	5	7
48 SPECIAL MACH. & EQUIP.	319	0	2853	730	283	133	78	61	826
49 GENERAL MACH. & EQUIP.	77	17	5370	3266	359	35	316	61	2
50 MACHINE SHOP PRDTS.	11	5	1596	1568	160	125	116	44	12
51 OFFICE, COMPUT. MACHINES	3	0	1295	33	3	0	12	0	1
52 SERVICE IND. MACHINES	245	0	6239	10972	365	174	271	50	16
53 ELECT. TRANSMISS. EQUIP.	191	0	4573	4103	378	64	72	0	0
54 HOUSEHOLD APPLIANCES	293	0	25993	9933	5431	1126	575	33	36
55 ELECTRIC LIGHTING EQUIP.	36	0	10539	3710	105	181	473	0	0
56 RADIO, TV, ETC., EQUIP.	192	0	17475	4296	364	17	9	2	0
57 ELECTRONIC COMPONENTS	66	0	4417	2576	153	8	450	0	0
58 MISC. ELECTRICAL MACH.	572	0	3138	6538	626	160	178	30	8
59 MOTOR VEHICLES, EQUIP.	1261	5	8879	26283	325	1389	1149	49	3
60 AIRCRAFT & PARTS	0	1	42	228	26	108	8	40	15
61 OTHER TRANSPORT. EQUIP.	-6	0	312	115	9	12	-6	-2	-5
62 PROFESS., SCIEN. INSTRU.	0	-4	-504	-82	-6	-5	1	1	-8
63 MEDICAL, PHOTO. EQUIP.	0	0	990	-32	-30	-5	-2	-8	-6
64 MISC. MANUFACTURING	-176	-17	-4553	-1250	-638	-87	-157	-83	-358
65 TRANSPORT. & WAREHOUSING	1662	367	8029	2699	1484	2370	1506	1961	433
66 COMMUNICA.-EXC. BRDCAST.	0	0	0	0	0	0	0	0	0
67 RADIO & TV BROADCASTING	0	0	0	0	0	0	0	0	0
68 ELEC.,GAS,WATER,SAN.SER.	0	0	0	0	0	0	0	0	0
69 WHOLESALE & RETAIL TRADE	1810	400	8662	2857	2004	1423	1384	1675	552
70 FINANCE & INSURANCE	0	0	0	0	0	0	0	0	0
71 REAL ESTATE & RENTAL	0	0	0	0	0	0	0	0	0
72 HOTELS; PERSONAL SERV.	0	0	0	0	0	0	0	0	0
73 BUSINESS SERVICES	-3	-1	-25	-4	-3	-2	-2	-3	-1
74 RESEARCH & DEVELOPMENT	0	0	0	0	0	0	0	0	0
75 AUTO. REPAIR & SERVICES	0	0	0	0	0	0	0	0	0
76 AMUSEMENTS	39	11	257	67	42	29	38	41	12
77 MED.,EDUC. SERVICES	0	0	0	0	0	0	0	0	0
78 FEDERAL GOV'T ENTERPRISE	0	0	0	0	0	0	0	0	0
79 STATE & LOCAL GOV'T ENT.	0	0	0	0	0	0	0	0	0
80 IMPORTS	0	0	0	0	0	0	0	0	0
81 BUS.TRAVEL,ENT., GIFTS.	0	0	0	0	0	0	0	0	0
82 OFFICE SUPPLIES	0	0	0	0	0	0	0	0	0
83 SCRAP & USED GOODS	0	0	0	0	0	0	0	0	0
84 GOVERNMENT INDUSTRY	0	0	0	0	0	0	0	0	0
85 REST OF WORLD INDUSTRY	0	0	0	0	0	0	0	0	0
86 HOUSEHOLD INDUSTRY	0	0	0	0	0	0	0	0	0
87 INVENTORY VALUATION ADJ.	0	0	0	0	0	0	0	0	0
88 STATE TOTAL	12297	-4002	34711	74332	-528382	37383	-28881	-617	5447

TABLE C.7

STATE ESTIMATES OF 1947
NET INVENTORY CHANGE
(THOUSANDS OF CURRENT DOLLARS)

INDUSTRY TITLE	19 MARYLAND	20 MASSA-CHUSETTS	21 MICHIGAN	22 MINNESOTA	23 MISSISSIPPI	24 MISSOURI	25 MONTANA	26 NEBRASKA	27 NEVADA
1 LIVESTOCK & PRDTS.	1025	-2073	-27555	-86263	-12681	-35432	-3144	-29149	1282
2 OTHER AGRICULTURE PRDTS.	-6520	66	-7652	-69075	-17069	-118801	10621	-113592	1025
3 FORESTRY & FISHERIES	0	0	0	0	0	0	0	0	0
4 AGRI.,FORES.,FISH. SERV.	0	0	0	0	0	0	0	0	0
5 IRON,FERRO.ORES MINING	0	0	1927	8531	0	24	173	0	122
6 NONFERROUS ORES MINING	0	0	60	0	0	234	262	0	182
7 COAL MINING	43	12	3	0	0	59	29	0	0
8 CRUDE PETRO.,NATURAL GAS	0	0	0	0	0	0	0	0	0
9 STONE & CLAY MINING	142	170	458	136	24	282	39	47	84
10 CHEM.&FERT.MIN. MINING	0	0	98	0	0	67	44	0	13
11 NEW CONSTRUCTION	0	0	0	0	0	0	0	0	0
12 MAINT. & REPAIR CONSTR.	0	0	0	0	0	0	0	0	0
13 ORDNANCE & ACCESSORIES	1	25	1	9	0	0	0	0	0
14 FOOD & KINDRED PRDTS.	3990	4897	6324	11466	1214	9282	674	5124	96
15 TOBACCO MANUFACTURES	36	925	356	5	0	1537	0	0	0
16 FABRICS	159	7734	101	61	267	49	0	4	0
17 TEXTILE PRDTS.	127	4002	861	187	103	298	4	15	0
18 APPAREL	3683	6228	1016	1395	1137	4521	0	69	0
19 MISC. TEXTILE PRDTS.	-116	-400	-171	-151	-9	-387	0	-69	-1
20 LUMBER & WOOD PRDTS.	977	1770	4824	2338	7139	1927	1666	104	254
21 WOODEN CONTAINERS	78	193	240	71	168	126	2	10	0
22 HOUSEHOLD FURNITURE	80	382	479	99	38	179	0	48	0
23 OTHER FURNITURE	-7	-19	-70	-6	-1	-21	0	-4	0
24 PAPER & ALLIED PRDTS.	195	1404	1591	548	390	232	0	21	2
25 PAPERBOARD CONTAINERS	-351	-1481	-1106	-386	-22	-714	0	-38	0
26 PRINTING & PUBLISHING	-329	-1069	-800	-588	-41	-647	-32	-122	-12
27 CHEMICALS,SELECT. PRDTS.	2404	2187	5491	319	750	2604	114	95	105
28 PLASTICS & SYNTHETICS	-3377	-2972	-1294	0	0	0	0	-5	0
29 DRUGS & COSMETICS	601	1213	1316	322	37	952	0	314	0
30 PAINT & ALLIED PRDTS.	783	1618	5019	242	7	2565	0	15	0
31 PETROLEUM, RELATED INDS.	1357	1067	1881	1226	82	746	577	147	0
32 RUBBER, MISC. PLASTICS	1692	9007	8575	2133	842	822	0	205	0
33 LEATHER TANNING & PRDTS.	48	3527	410	60	4	53	0	30	0
34 FOOTWEAR, LEATHER PRDTS.	655	15989	452	340	1	11347	2	55	0
35 GLASS & GLASS PRDTS.	235	205	294	150	56	316	1	1	1
36 STONE & CLAY PRDTS.	1080	2546	3749	665	212	2525	175	280	147
37 PRIMARY IRON, STEEL MFR.	7716	3679	12932	1155	8	1701	248	24	0
38 PRIMARY NONFERROUS MFR.	1258	1612	4299	430	10	1299	1267	208	205

Industry	(1)	(2)	(3)	(4)	(5)	(6)	(7)	(8)	(9)
39 METAL CONTAINERS	568	99	22	65	7	243	0	25	0
40 FABRICATED METAL PRDTS.	1547	2144	6623	1674	84	2842	76	390	26
41 SCREW MACH. PRDTS., ETC.	2229	3032	13487	858	0	871	21	4	0
42 OTHER FAB. METAL PRDTS.	555	6955	13941	631	112	2577	20	145	0
43 ENGINES & TURBINES	3	1058	4121	295	0	371	0	11	0
44 FARM MACH. & EQUIP.	520	146	5817	3196	37	660	9	551	4
45 CONSTRUC. MACH. & EQUIP.	113	71	1552	823	40	210	12	53	0
46 MATERIAL HANDLING MACH.	29	185	752	117	1	35	21	13	0
47 METALWORKING MACHINERY	153	1508	4650	224	0	215	0	6	0
48 SPECIAL MACH. & EQUIP.	383	4059	1408	337	65	463	1	56	0
49 GENERAL MACH. & EQUIP.	282	2250	3983	262	77	600	0	9	9
50 MACHINE SHOP PRDTS.	415	505	2772	195	6	761	5		0
51 OFFICE, COMPUT. MACHINES	1	197	904	4	0	27	0	217	0
52 SERVICE IND. MACHINES	559	3569	9604	2888	0	2305	10	87	0
53 ELECT.TRANSMISS. EQUIP.	262	6950	2817	2178	11	2736	0	233	0
54 HOUSEHOLD APPLIANCES	781	3096	15099	3305	0	3648	24	79	0
55 ELECTRIC LIGHTING EQUIP.	233	6171	1519	75	190	2356	0	285	0
56 RADIO, TV, ETC., EQUIP.	1390	2062	1104	840	0	160	0	44	0
57 ELECTRONIC COMPONENTS	378	1871	519	63	0	41	0	57	0
58 MISC. ELECTRICAL MACH.	194	1163	1152	640	0	402	0	184	0
59 MOTOR VEHICLES, EQUIP.	1721	2409	173480	1157	206	15134	10		5
60 AIRCRAFT & PARTS	270	119	38	23	16	22	0	2	0
61 OTHER TRANSPORT. EQUIP.	-23	52	68	18	-1	46	0	-4	0
62 PROFESS., SCIEN. INSTRU.	7	-180	-132	-41	-1	-49	-1	-16	0
63 MEDICAL, PHOTO. EQUIP.		-623	144	-45		73			0
64 MISC. MANUFACTURING	-465	-4402	-1716	-574	-47	-1002	-21	-115	-11
65 TRANSPORT. & WAREHOUSING	1600	2260	2815	2089	563	3253	603	1041	212
66 COMMUNICA.,EXC. BRDCAST.	0	0	0	0	0	0	0	0	0
67 RADIO & TV BROADCASTING	0	0	0	0	0	0	0	0	0
68 ELEC.,GAS,WATER,SAN.SER.	0	0	0	0	0	0	0	0	0
69 WHOLESALE & RETAIL TRADE	1638	4082	4958	2723	841	3579	448	1117	149
70 FINANCE & INSURANCE	0	0	0	0	0	0	0	0	0
71 REAL ESTATE & RENTAL	0	0	0	0	0	0	0	0	0
72 HOTELS; PERSONAL SERV.	0	0	0	0	0	0	-1	0	0
73 BUSINESS SERVICES	-3	-10	-12	-3	0	-6	-1	-1	0
74 RESEARCH & DEVELOPMENT	0	0	0	0	0	0	0	0	0
75 AUTO. REPAIR & SERVICES	0	0	0	0	0	0	0	0	0
76 AMUSEMENTS	61	133	139	53	16	78	10	22	35
77 MED.,EDUC. SERVICES	0	0	0	0	0	0	0	0	0
78 FEDERAL GOV'T ENTERPRISE	0	0	0	0	0	0	0	0	0
79 STATE & LOCAL GOV'T ENT.	0	0	0	0	0	0	0	0	0
80 IMPORTS	0	0	0	0	0	0	0	0	0
81 BUS.TRAVEL, ENT., GIFTS.	0	0	0	0	0	0	0	0	0
82 OFFICE SUPPLIES	0	0	0	0	0	0	0	0	0
83 SCRAP & USED GOODS	0	0	0	0	0	0	0	0	0
84 GOVERNMENT INDUSTRY	0	0	0	0	0	0	0	0	0
85 REST OF WORLD INDUSTRY	0	0	0	0	0	0	0	0	0
86 HOUSEHOLD INDUSTRY	0	0	0	0	0	0	0	0	0
87 INVENTORY VALUATION ADJ.	0	0	0	0	0	0	0	0	0
88 STATE TOTAL	33138	114620	295740	-100422	-15110	-69607	13949	-131633	3934

TABLE C.7

STATE ESTIMATES OF 1947
NET INVENTORY CHANGE
(THOUSANDS OF CURRENT DOLLARS)

INDUSTRY TITLE	28 NEW HAMPSHIRE	29 NEW JERSEY	30 NEW MEXICO	31 NEW YORK	32 NORTH CAROLINA	33 NORTH DAKOTA	34 OHIO	35 OKLAHOMA	36 OREGON
1 LIVESTOCK & PRDTS.	-1474	1496	-5643	-4978	-956	-20227	-18471	-30831	-7424
2 OTHER AGRICULTURE PRDTS.	1059	-2250	9207	-11631	-12292	51008	-68124	4628	-4997
3 FORESTRY & FISHERIES	0	0	0	0	0	0	0	0	0
4 AGRI.,FORES.,FISH. SERV.	0	0	0	0	0	0	0	0	0
5 IRON. FERRO. ORES MINING	0	152	18	555	31	0	0	0	0
6 NONFERROUS ORES MINING	0	67	201	48	4	0	0	68	6
7 COAL MINING	0	29	29	0	0	23	576	66	0
8 CRUDE PETRO.,NATURAL GAS	0	0	0	0	0	0	0	0	6
9 STONE & CLAY MINING	9	0	20	574	240	11	771	0	165
10 CHEM.&FERT. MIN. MINING	0	356	483	195	0	0	0	105	0
11 NEW CONSTRUCTION	0	0	0	0	0	0	0	0	0
12 MAINT. & REPAIR CONSTR.	0	0	0	0	0	0	0	0	0
13 ORDNANCE & ACCESSORIES	0	3	0	23	0	0	1	0	0
14 FOOD & KINDRED PRDTS.	267	8027	209	21085	1758	913	10595	2524	2194
15 TOBACCO MANUFACTURES	132	3129	0	752	66484	0	1136	0	0
16 FABRICS	1234	2872	1	2628	10755	0	485	38	59
17 TEXTILE PRDTS.	228	2571	0	4912	2471	16	993	13	41
18 APPAREL	386	7524	18	82233	5796		4657	179	318
19 MISC. TEXTILE PRDTS.	-16	-569	-5	-2347	-821	-1	-269	-12	-42
20 LUMBER & WOOD PRDTS.	1447	2490	607	5355	7051	11	3670	938	25564
21 WOODEN CONTAINERS	120	175	3	278	154	0	262	7	97
22 HOUSEHOLD FURNITURE	46	285	9	1170	998	0	538	29	123
23 OTHER FURNITURE	-1	-17	0	-143	-13	0	-124	-2	-5
24 PAPER & ALLIED PRDTS.	361	1004	0	2820	528	0	1485	17	398
25 PAPERBOARD CONTAINERS	-28	-1698	0	-3415	-241	0	-2012	-87	-68
26 PRINTING & PUBLISHING	-57	-650	-20	-7307	-149	-25	-1860	-142	-135
27 CHEMICALS,SELECT. PRDTS.	-79	12784	131	8635	932	30	5799	173	254
28 PLASTICS & SYNTHETICS	-60	-7027	0	-3117	-1541		-3595		
29 DRUGS & COSMETICS	11	4575	0	4190	110	38	1929	9	22
30 PAINT & ALLIED PRDTS.	15	9016	0	8142	273	16	7283	158	346
31 PETROLEUM, RELATED INDS.	3	11599	246	3511	11	0	5576	5295	151
32 RUBBER, MISC. PLASTICS	221	5586	0	5208	320	0	26410	940	65
33 LEATHER TANNING & PRDTS.	201	656	0	1664	230	0	534	534	6
34 FOOTWEAR, LEATHER PRDTS.	5409	1771	19	18252	98	0	3692	47	83
35 GLASS & GLASS PRDTS.	0	1390	0	1452	65	1	2811	517	8
36 STONE & CLAY PRDTS.	173	4078	54	7401	841	0	8088	466	311
37 PRIMARY IRON, STEEL MFR.	30	4355	3	15970	64	32	52670	344	1122
38 PRIMARY NONFERROUS MFR.	96	10228	421	9525	244	0	4245	1148	360

39	METAL CONTAINERS	0	626	0	427	0	0	668	26	22
40	FABRICATED METAL PRDTS.	105	3283	96	8374	611	36	12545	1156	804
41	SCREW MACH. PRDTS., ETC.	206	2024	0	7574	21	2	16918	66	39
42	OTHER FAB. METAL PRDTS.	131	7086	0	9269	265	14	12262	226	230
43	ENGINES & TURBINES	1	804	0	1884	1	0	2746	11	0
44	FARM MACH. & EQUIP.	6	552	7	3711	279	29	5550	165	110
45	CONSTRUC. MACH. & EQUIP.	113	696	0	464	49	0	5185	696	127
46	MATERIAL HANDLING MACH.	6	577	4	691	31	0	1208	13	233
47	METALWORKING MACHINERY	134	1145	0	1814	12	0	5781	12	24
48	SPECIAL MACH. & EQUIP.	510	1941	10	3780	269	0	3862	19	143
49	GENERAL MACH. & EQUIP.	34	4565	0	6088	50	4	8681	257	83
50	MACHINE SHOP PRDTS.	29	980	0	1261	84	0	1472	36	194
51	OFFICE, COMPUT. MACHINES	0	356	0	3093	1	0	2391	3	0
52	SERVICE IND. MACHINES	14	1588	0	6191	89	330	14349	77	63
53	ELECT. TRANSMISS. EQUIP.	232	4053	0	7116	22	0	13175	50	129
54	HOUSEHOLD APPLIANCES	12	5708	0	8570	79	0	28459	146	358
55	ELECTRIC LIGHTING EQUIP.	22	6982	0	11089	31	0	9296	22	16
56	RADIO, TV, ETC., EQUIP.	0	8658	0	7385	370	0	1943	0	13
57	ELECTRONIC COMPONENTS	0	3190	0	4092	197	0	809	0	7
58	MISC. ELECTRICAL MACH.	84	3619	0	4553	110	28	8637	56	160
59	MOTOR VEHICLES, EQUIP.	3	11097	106	18912	249	0	30557	188	162
60	AIRCRAFT & PARTS	0	231	0	298	2	0	338	3	0
61	OTHER TRANSPORT. EQUIP.	0	103	0	223	-3	0	102	3	12
62	PROFESS., SCIEN. INSTRU.	-9	-384	0	-899	0	0	-200	-13	-4
63	MEDICAL, PHOTO. EQUIP.	7	-436	0	4933	0	0	184	4	12
64	MISC. MANUFACTURING	-265	-4861	-35	-13478	-84	-8	-3842	-96	-147
65	TRANSPORT. & WAREHOUSING	185	2428	440	14776	942	320	5936	2859	1030
66	COMMUNICA., EXC. BRDCAST.	0	0	0	0	0	0	0	0	0
67	RADIO & TV BROADCASTING	0	0	0	0	0	0	0	0	0
68	ELEC.,GAS,WATER,SAN.SER.	0	0	0	0	0	0	0	0	0
69	WHOLESALE & RETAIL TRADE	320	3608	376	18492	1921	456	6560	1405	1394
70	FINANCE & INSURANCE	0	0	0	0	0	0	0	0	0
71	REAL ESTATE & RENTAL	0	0	0	0	0	0	0	0	0
72	HOTELS; PERSONAL SERV.	0	0	0	0	0	0	0	0	0
73	BUSINESS SERVICES	0	-7	-1	-72	-2	0	-12	-3	-2
74	RESEARCH & DEVELOPMENT	0	0	0	0	0	0	0	0	0
75	AUTO. REPAIR & SERVICES	0	0	0	0	0	0	0	0	0
76	AMUSEMENTS	18	141	10	692	41	8	174	34	31
77	MED.,EDUC. SERVICES	0	0	0	0	0	0	0	0	0
78	FEDERAL GOV'T ENTERPRISE	0	0	0	0	0	0	0	0	0
79	STATE & LOCAL GOV'T ENT.	0	0	0	0	0	0	0	0	0
80	IMPORTS	0	0	0	0	0	0	0	0	0
81	BUS.TRAVEL, ENT., GIFTS.	0	0	0	0	0	0	0	0	0
82	OFFICE SUPPLIES	0	0	0	0	0	0	0	0	0
83	SCRAP & USED GOODS	0	0	0	0	0	0	0	0	0
84	GOVERNMENT INDUSTRY	0	0	0	0	0	0	0	0	0
85	REST OF WORLD INDUSTRY	0	0	0	0	0	0	0	0	0
86	HOUSEHOLD INDUSTRY	0	0	0	0	0	0	0	0	0
87	INVENTORY VALUATION ADJ.	0	0	0	0	0	0	0	0	0
88	STATE TOTAL	11634	155202	7023	314941	89082	33065	245485	-5943	24265

299

TABLE C.7

STATE ESTIMATES OF 1947
NET INVENTORY CHANGE
(THOUSANDS OF CURRENT DOLLARS)

INDUSTRY TITLE	37 PENNSYL-VANIA	38 RHODE ISLAND	39 SOUTH CAROLINA	40 SOUTH DAKOTA	41 TENNESSEE	42 TEXAS	43 UTAH	44 VERMONT	45 VIRGINIA
1 LIVESTOCK & PRDTS.	-6718	-185	-2292	-28501	-7196	-62363	-1863	-4937	-4516
2 OTHER AGRICULTURE PRDTS.	-15653	919	-20118	-55571	-27901	64794	7304	611	-21020
3 FORESTRY & FISHERIES	0	0	0	0	0	0	0	0	0
4 AGRI.,FORES.,FISH.SERV.	0	0	0	0	0	0	0	0	0
5 IRON,FERRO.ORES MINING	525	0	0	0	133	40	120	0	3
6 NONFERROUS ORES MINING	0	0	0	108	55	0	927	4	22
7 COAL MINING	4549	0	0	1	131	0	128	0	427
8 CRUDE PETRO.,NATURAL GAS	0	0	0	0	0	0	0	0	0
9 STONE & CLAY MINING	899	7	107	124	299	303	34	164	337
10 CHEM.&FERT. MIN. MINING	0	0	0	0	224	1941	3	0	0
11 NEW CONSTRUCTION	0	0	0	0	0	0	0	0	0
12 MAINT. & REPAIR CONSTR.	0	0	0	0	0	0	0	0	0
13 ORDNANCE & ACCESSORIES	6	0	0	0	0	1	0	0	0
14 FOOD & KINDRED PRDTS.	12248	487	803	1412	4162	9527	1071	635	2279
15 TOBACCO MANUFACTURES	5758	4	501	0	937	367	1	0	28660
16 FABRICS	3958	4097	8308	0	838	396	15	235	1971
17 TEXTILE PRDTS.	4736	1555	2142	0	237	310	0	22	592
18 APPAREL	19731	346	757	0	3148	2179	185	285	2252
19 MISC. TEXTILE PRDTS.	-472	-62	-297	-2	-174	-335	-4	-8	-328
20 LUMBER & WOOD PRDTS.	4109	133	5450	261	3975	7800	174	1374	5055
21 WOODEN CONTAINERS	258	15	77	2	226	133	4	47	130
22 HOUSEHOLD FURNITURE	566	17	75	0	296	167	15	43	546
23 OTHER FURNITURE	-34	-3	-1	0	-2	-18	-1	-3	-3
24 PAPER & ALLIED PRDTS.	1567	77	324	0	294	234	0	203	740
25 PAPERBOARD CONTAINERS	-2162	-113	-179	-9	-233	-328	-13	-44	-207
26 PRINTING & PUBLISHING	-2085	-93	-56	-29	-279	-529	-54	-27	-171
27 CHEMICALS,SELECT. PRDTS.	6502	150	805	13	2616	5002	147	46	2290
28 PLASTICS & SYNTHETICS	-6217	-181	-2	0	-7052	-4634	0	-74	-12595
29 DRUGS & COSMETICS	1513	63	12	5	240	374	11	27	167
30 PAINT & ALLIED PRDTS.	4966	294	50	5	445	1509	42	17	284
31 PETROLEUM, RELATED INDS.	12349	293	64	9	215	33189	661	55	89
32 RUBBER, MISC. PLASTICS	7410	1408	109	0	2381	543	3	296	360
33 LEATHER TANNING & PRDTS.	1592	41	3	0	85	45	5	15	173
34 FOOTWEAR, LEATHER PRDTS.	6101	121	10	0	3029	338	5	61	821
35 GLASS & GLASS PRDTS.	3794	44	8	0	179	208	1	14	149
36 STONE & CLAY PRDTS.	9184	51	358	89	1273	2244	262	553	788
37 PRIMARY IRON, STEEL MFR.	73685	1071	149	1	1690	1884	1978	18	532
38 PRIMARY NONFERROUS MFR.	5664	990	6	0	1207	1834	1047	8	137

#	Industry									
39	METAL CONTAINERS	549	0	0	0	38	424	38	0	17
40	FABRICATED METAL PRDTS.	13588	304	92	116	2288	2917	204	135	1013
41	SCREW MACH. PRDTS., ETC.	13181	941	0	0	312	169	2	5	5
42	OTHER FAB. METAL PRDTS.	11805	1351	20	17	350	1211	21	112	387
43	ENGINES & TURBINES	2626	0	0	0	3	24	0	120	12
44	FARM MACH. & EQUIP.	3535	17	17	76	387	766	14	6	87
45	CONSTRUC. MACH. & EQUIP.	2580	0	2	2	124	2384	116	0	49
46	MATERIAL HANDLING MACH.	571	4	6	0	75	22	26	0	24
47	METALWORKING MACHINERY	2237	685	2	3	9	31	4	0	2
48	SPECIAL MACH. & EQUIP.	3142	598	156	8	121	342	10	122	116
49	GENERAL MACH. & EQUIP.	5272	75	58	3	206	478	0	6	40
50	MACHINE SHOP PRDTS.	2084	357	3	1	109	236	5	26	37
51	OFFICE, COMPUT. MACHINES	33	1	0	0	2	2	30	146	1
52	SERVICE IND. MACHINES	7545	184	0	19	426	720	0	0	15
53	ELECT. TRANSMISS. EQUIP.	16121	41	0	18	87	155	12	6	156
54	HOUSEHOLD APPLIANCES	11129	132	0	22	1440	928	16	71	242
55	ELECTRIC LIGHTING EQUIP.	6359	1189	4	0	222	354	7	23	28
56	RADIO, TV, ETC., EQUIP.	3893	48	0	0	75	25	0	48	127
57	ELECTRONIC COMPONENTS	3542	26	0	0	0	9	0	26	66
58	MISC. ELECTRICAL MACH.	2787	815	2	0	301	757	10	2	60
59	MOTOR VEHICLES, EQUIP.	11877	49	58	5	1907	1095	3	3	328
60	AIRCRAFT & PARTS	87	0	0	0	9	230	1	0	86
61	OTHER TRANSPORT. EQUIP.	315	1	3	0	9	28	-1	-3	-3
62	PROFESS., SCIEN. INSTRU.	-524	-18	-1	0	-42	-11	-1	0	89
63	MEDICAL, PHOTO. EQUIP.	156	109	-2	-15	-315	-25	-46	-86	-167
64	MISC. MANUFACTURING	-4542	-2749	-102	-15	1327	-366	506	171	1812
65	TRANSPORT. & WAREHOUSING	8403	215	471	263	9046	9046	506	0	0
66	COMMUNICA.,EXC. BRDCAST.	0	0	0	0	0	0	0	0	0
67	RADIO & TV BROADCASTING	0	0	0	0	0	0	0	0	0
68	ELEC.,GAS,WATER,SAN.SER.	0	0	0	0	0	0	0	0	0
69	WHOLESALE & RETAIL TRADE	7720	617	929	455	2189	5721	506	227	1759
70	FINANCE & INSURANCE	0	0	0	0	0	0	0	0	0
71	REAL ESTATE & RENTAL	0	0	0	0	0	0	0	0	0
72	HOTELS; PERSONAL SERV.	0	0	0	0	0	0	0	0	0
73	BUSINESS SERVICES	-15	-1	-1	0	-2	-14	-1	0	-2
74	RESEARCH & DEVELOPMENT	0	0	0	0	0	0	0	0	0
75	AUTO. REPAIR & SERVICES	0	0	0	0	0	0	0	0	0
76	AMUSEMENTS	219	32	17	9	39	122	15	5	48
77	MED.,EDUC. SERVICES	0	0	0	0	0	0	0	0	0
78	FEDERAL GOV'T ENTERPRISE	0	0	0	0	0	0	0	0	0
79	STATE & LOCAL GOV'T ENT.	0	0	0	0	0	0	0	0	0
80	IMPORTS	0	0	0	0	0	0	0	0	0
81	BUS.TRAVEL, ENT., GIFTS.	0	0	0	0	0	0	0	0	0
82	OFFICE SUPPLIES	0	0	0	0	0	0	0	0	0
83	SCRAP & USED GOODS	0	0	0	0	0	0	0	0	0
84	GOVERNMENT INDUSTRY	0	0	0	0	0	0	0	0	0
85	REST OF WORLD INDUSTRY	0	0	0	0	0	0	0	0	0
86	HOUSEHOLD INDUSTRY	0	0	0	0	0	0	0	0	0
87	INVENTORY VALUATION ADJ.	0	0	0	0	0	0	0	0	0
88	STATE TOTAL	294600	16565	-1092	-81068	-2835	94984	13703	1174	16398

TABLE C.7

STATE ESTIMATES OF 1947
NET INVENTORY CHANGE
(THOUSANDS OF CURRENT DOLLARS)

INDUSTRY TITLE	46 WASHINGTON	47 WEST VIRGINIA	48 WISCONSIN	49 WYOMING	50 ALASKA	51 HAWAII	52 NO STATE ALLOCATION	53 NATIONAL TOTAL
1 LIVESTOCK & PRDTS.	-9120	-3789	-44921	-2414	0	0	0	-846881
2 OTHER AGRICULTURE PRDTS.	-12490	-247	-4370	-445	0	0	0	-1162922
3 FORESTRY & FISHERIES	0	0	0	0	0	0	-2	0
4 AGRI.,FORES.,FISH. SERV.	0	0	0	0	0	0	0	0
5 IRON, FERRO. ORES MINING	0	0	216	91	0	0	0	13742
6 NONFERROUS ORES MINING	37	0	13	0	0	0	0	4056
7 COAL MINING	29	3457	0	119	0	0	0	13301
8 CRUDE PETRO.,NATURAL GAS	0	0	0	0	0	0	0	0
9 STONE & CLAY MINING	179	219	363	48	0	0	0	10110
10 CHEM.&FERT. MIN. MINING	0	5	0	8	0	0	0	5569
11 NEW CONSTRUCTION	0	0	0	0	0	0	0	0
12 MAINT. & REPAIR CONSTR.	0	0	0	0	0	0	0	0
13 ORDNANCE & ACCESSORIES	0	0	0	0	0	0	0	207
14 FOOD & KINDRED PRDTS.	3429	667	13152	197	0	0	0	235618
15 TOBACCO MANUFACTURES	0	350	138	0	0	0	0	125537
16 FABRICS	13	106	124	0	0	0	0	60847
17 TEXTILE PRDTS.	25	0	342	0	0	0	0	34424
18 APPAREL	303	341	1769	0	0	0	0	176194
19 MISC. TEXTILE PRDTS.	-57	-2	-102	0	0	0	0	-9358
20 LUMBER & WOOD PRDTS.	21059	1745	4821	343	0	0	0	192911
21 WOODEN CONTAINERS	57	32	179	1	0	0	0	5277
22 HOUSEHOLD FURNITURE	129	32	420	2	0	0	0	10349
23 OTHER FURNITURE	-4	-1	-16	0	0	0	0	-737
24 PAPER & ALLIED PRDTS.	1259	95	1919	0	0	0	0	23990
25 PAPERBOARD CONTAINERS	-341	-122	-951	0	0	0	0	-22352
26 PRINTING & PUBLISHING	-227	-75	-571	-13	0	0	0	-25850
27 CHEMICALS,SELECT. PRDTS.	507	5632	711	56	0	0	0	93221
28 PLASTICS & SYNTHETICS	-89	-2788	-79	0	0	0	0	-70251
29 DRUGS & COSMETICS	39	30	336	0	0	0	0	26884
30 PAINT & ALLIED PRDTS.	250	37	1722	20	0	0	0	67635
31 PETROLEUM, RELATED INDS.	160	688	492	1354	0	0	0	135712
32 RUBBER, MISC. PLASTICS	21	93	1606	1	0	0	0	100047
33 LEATHER TANNING & PRDTS.	2	256	1199	0	0	0	0	12698
34 FOOTWEAR, LEATHER PRDTS.	108	111	4417	2	0	0	0	87727
35 GLASS & GLASS PRDTS.	79	2425	63	0	0	0	0	19583
36 STONE & CLAY PRDTS.	717	1775	1158	76	0	0	0	73211
37 PRIMARY IRON, STEEL MFR.	746	6852	3583	0	0	0	0	267467
38 PRIMARY NONFERROUS MFR.	2064	598	1583	0	0	0	0	79364

	Col1	Col2	Col3	Col4	Col5	Col6	Col7	Col8
39 METAL CONTAINERS	91	151	51	0	0	0	0	7429
40 FABRICATED METAL PRDTS.	698	1156	5541	21	0	0	0	102193
41 SCREW MACH. PRDTS., ETC.	67	1261	4213	0	0	0	0	92705
42 OTHER FAB. METAL PRDTS.	307	477	2250	0	0	0	0	111277
43 ENGINES & TURBINES	22	0	4432	0	0	0	0	24850
44 FARM MACH. & EQUIP.	182	116	8049	14	0	0	0	76438
45 CONSTRUC. MACH. & EQUIP.	346	331	3615	2	0	0	0	29476
46 MATERIAL HANDLING MACH.	50	11	230	0	0	0	0	6677
47 METALWORKING MACHINERY	54	6	1163	0	0	0	0	26946
48 SPECIAL MACH. & EQUIP.	163	43	1794	0	0	0	0	31989
49 GENERAL MACH. & EQUIP.	97	16	2685	0	0	0	0	53879
50 MACHINE SHOP PRDTS.	148	46	507	3	0	0	0	17725
51 OFFICE, COMPUT. MACHINES	2	0	29	0	0	0	0	10889
52 SERVICE IND. MACHINES	67	16	1735	8	0	0	0	74541
53 ELECT. TRANSMISS. EQUIP.	87	44	4728	11	0	0	0	74552
54 HOUSEHOLD APPLIANCES	629	149	5791	9	0	0	0	148771
55 ELECTRIC LIGHTING EQUIP.	104	464	811	0	0	0	0	70773
56 RADIO, TV, ETC., EQUIP.	81	0	110	0	0	0	0	53700
57 ELECTRONIC COMPONENTS	7	134	56	0	0	0	0	23828
58 MISC. ELECTRICAL MACH.	158	23	1742	0	0	0	0	41185
59 MOTOR VEHICLES, EQUIP.	573	327	12422	0	0	0	0	340087
60 AIRCRAFT & PARTS	133	10	14	0	0	0	0	4190
61 OTHER TRANSPORT. EQUIP.	36	-1	45	0	0	0	0	1997
62 PROFESS., SCIEN. INSTRU.	-5	-5	-224	0	0	0	0	-3807
63 MEDICAL, PHOTO. EQUIP.	-4	-162	34	0	0	0	0	8245
64 MISC. MANUFACTURING	-152	1220	-1048	-4	0	0	0	-54221
65 TRANSPORT. & WAREHOUSING	2073	0	1553	790	0	0	0	106795
66 COMMUNICA.,EXC. BRDCAST.	0	0	0	0	0	0	0	0
67 RADIO & TV BROADCASTING	0	0	0	0	0	0	0	0
68 ELEC.,GAS,WATER,SAN.SER.	0	0	0	0	0	0	0	119427
69 WHOLESALE & RETAIL TRADE	2139	1076	2602	225	0	0	0	0
70 FINANCE & INSURANCE	0	0	0	0	0	0	0	0
71 REAL ESTATE & RENTAL	0	0	0	0	0	0	0	0
72 HOTELS; PERSONAL SERV.	0	-1	-4	0	0	0	0	0
73 BUSINESS SERVICES	-3	0	0	0	0	0	0	-274
74 RESEARCH & DEVELOPMENT	0	0	0	0	0	0	0	0
75 AUTO. REPAIR & SERVICES	0	0	0	0	0	0	0	0
76 AMUSEMENTS	51	31	55	0	0	0	0	4150
77 MED.,EDUC. SERVICES	0	0	0	0	0	0	0	0
78 FEDERAL GOV'T ENTERPRISE	0	0	0	0	0	0	0	0
79 STATE & LOCAL GOV'T ENT.	0	0	0	0	0	0	0	0
80 IMPORTS	0	0	0	0	0	0	-85441	-85441
81 BUS.TRAVEL, ENT., GIFTS.	0	0	0	0	0	0	0	0
82 OFFICE SUPPLIES	0	0	0	0	0	0	0	0
83 SCRAP & USED GOODS	0	0	0	0	0	0	0	0
84 GOVERNMENT INDUSTRY	0	0	0	0	0	0	-956017	-956017
85 REST OF WORLD INDUSTRY	0	0	0	0	0	0	0	0
86 HOUSEHOLD INDUSTRY	0	0	0	0	0	0	0	0
87 INVENTORY VALUATION ADJ.	0	0	0	0	0	0	-763965	-763965
88 STATE TOTAL	17096	25473	54297	533	0	0	-1805425	-461996

TABLE C.8

STATE ESTIMATES OF 1958
NET INVENTORY CHANGE
(THOUSANDS OF CURRENT DOLLARS)

	INDUSTRY TITLE	1 ALABAMA	2 ARIZONA	3 ARKANSAS	4 CALIFORNIA	5 COLORADO	6 CONNECTICUT	7 DELAWARE	8 DISTRICT OF COLUMBIA	9 FLORIDA
1	LIVESTOCK & PRDTS.	-4041	4167	-7818	51049	25475	-1017	-904	0	-11911
2	OTHER AGRICULTURE PRDTS.	9048	-13096	-23650	2906	12526	-1216	6315	0	29
3	FORESTRY & FISHERIES	464	56	325	2276	18	45	37	0	900
4	AGRI.,FORES.,FISH. SERV.	762	406	1136	2163	119	108	101	0	611
5	IRON, FERRO. ORES MINING	-407	-17	-14	-906	-1753	-11	0	0	0
6	NONFERROUS ORES MINING	-25	-9490	-522	-182	-1957	0	0	0	-214
7	COAL MINING	-823	-3	-23	-1	-220	0	0	0	0
8	CRUDE PETRO.,NATURAL GAS	-78	-2	-268	-3872	-474	0	0	0	-8
9	STONE & CLAY MINING	55	24	68	366	35	29	2	0	103
10	CHEM.&FERT. MIN. MINING	0	0	-6	-164	-3	0	0	0	-236
11	NEW CONSTRUCTION	0	0	0	0	0	0	0	0	0
12	MAINT. & REPAIR CONSTR.	0	0	0	0	0	0	0	0	0
13	ORDNANCE & ACCESSORIES	1345	1559	2	46618	641	2228	0	0	3952
14	FOOD & KINDRED PRDTS.	2737	888	2821	26259	3416	1498	725	447	5405
15	TOBACCO MANUFACTURES	-97	0	0	-3	0	-49	0	0	-433
16	FABRICS	-4977	-2	-149	-233	-3	-1756	-466	0	-88
17	TEXTILE PRDTS.	-686	-2	-230	-1282	-8	-596	-124	0	-20
18	APPAREL	-2309	-162	-538	-5583	-106	-1294	-335	0	-731
19	MISC. TEXTILE PRDTS.	-13	-1	0	-68	-3	-11	-1	0	-5
20	LUMBER & WOOD PRDTS.	1583	352	1805	7846	218	208	79	9	971
21	WOODEN CONTAINERS	-175	-36	-336	-1606	-49	-86	-14	0	-436
22	HOUSEHOLD FURNITURE	-63	-15	-149	-664	-23	-61	-1	0	-118
23	OTHER FURNITURE	3	1	6	60	-3	10	-1	0	-6
24	PAPER & ALLIED PRDTS.	-76	-3	-41	-99	-5	-25	-2	0	-81
25	PAPERBOARD CONTAINERS	-5	-1	-11	-118	73	-20	-3	0	-19
26	PRINTING & PUBLISHING	54	41	33	810	-69	182	16	163	161
27	CHEMICALS,SELECT. PRDTS.	-479	-49	-65	-1366	-3	-384	-126	-3	-559
28	PLASTICS & SYNTHETICS	-882	0	-7	3363	63	-643	-1478	0	-1083
29	DRUGS & COSMETICS	18	28	2	-432	-14	1614	95	0	130
30	PAINT & ALLIED PRDTS.	-11	-4	-5	-14	-14	-12	-1	0	-60
31	PETROLEUM, RELATED INDS.	-530	-47	-1338	-22478	-750	-180	-1487	0	-343
32	RUBBER, MISC. PLASTICS	-726	-22	-156	-2435	-429	-1088	-239	0	-88
33	LEATHER TANNING & PRDTS.	0	0	0	-61	-3	-7	-69	0	-5
34	FOOTWEAR, LEATHER PRDTS.	87	4	672	512	372	233	57	0	190
35	GLASS & GLASS PRDTS.	-13	-1	-26	-335	-3	-25	-1	0	-31
36	STONE & CLAY PRDTS.	489	210	153	2910	290	377	58	0	761
37	PRIMARY IRON, STEEL MFR.	-6563	-62	-20	-5325	-1132	-1542	-1052	62	-203
38	PRIMARY NONFERROUS MFR.	-187	-338	-99	-488	-8	-503	-14	0	-41

#	Industry									
39	METAL CONTAINERS	423	0	0	18	115	2152	50	0	-48
40	FABRICATED METAL PRDTS.	-1504	-37	-180	-749	-380	-6480	-324	-265	-1361
41	SCREW MACH. PRDTS., ETC.	-175	0	-117	-3060	-25	-3610	-135	-13	-420
42	OTHER FAB. METAL PRDTS.	-239	0	-44	-2405	-199	-3847	-172	-38	-436
43	ENGINES & TURBINES	-50	0	0	-1596	-120	-2222	0	0	0
44	FARM MACH. & EQUIP.	-78	0	-6	-18	-66	-549	-40	-41	-157
45	CONSTRUC. MACH. & EQUIP.	-41	0	-6	-27	-1583	-2373	-10	-3	-185
46	MATERIAL HANDLING MACH.	-63	0	0	-83	-57	-1284	-142	-3	-97
47	METALWORKING MACHINERY	-366	0	-136	-7609	-48	-5443	-183	-86	-139
48	SPECIAL MACH. & EQUIP.	-664	0	-555	-2880	-226	-5080	-87	-27	-570
49	GENERAL MACH. & EQUIP.	-176	0	-11	-6288	-320	-6658	-169	-37	-178
50	MACHINE SHOP PRDTS.	-99	-8	-13	-329	-76	-1463	-22	-66	-56
51	OFFICE, COMPUT. MACHINES	-167	0	0	-818	-7	-2175	-33	-436	-1
52	SERVICE IND. MACHINES	-127	0	-45	-327	-25	-1613	-206	-364	-203
53	ELECT. TRANSMISS. EQUIP.	-176	0	-3	-3273	-961	-10175	-1186	-453	-453
54	HOUSEHOLD APPLIANCES	-36	0	-68	-3010	-7	-3106	-1956	-3	-3
55	ELECTRIC LIGHTING EQUIP.	-70	0	-28	-1515	-37	-1874	-232	-2	-314
56	RADIO, TV, ETC., EQUIP.	-1115	0	-1	-733	-12	-11611	-567	-7	-52
57	ELECTRONIC COMPONENTS	-320	0	0	-1748	-20	-8190	-2	-496	-195
58	MISC. ELECTRICAL MACH.	-338	0	-8	-429	-87	-1033	-3	-853	-162
59	MOTOR VEHICLES, EQUIP.	-198	0	-74	-3050	-298	-32980	-188	-6	-902
60	AIRCRAFT & PARTS	-3030	0	-6012	-26256	-2464	-64583	-22	-106	-10360
61	OTHER TRANSPORT. EQUIP.	-1986	0	-140	-1271	-111	-6614	-500	-2456	-1615
62	PROFESS., SCIEN. INSTRU.	-43	0	-35	-495	-26	-616	-76	-75	-4
63	MEDICAL, PHOTO. EQUIP.	42	0	-14	98	11	298	2	-63	0
64	MISC. MANUFACTURING	199	11	98	1787	125	2443	217	42	115
65	TRANSPORT. & WAREHOUSING	4202	1475	352	1378	1701	15599	898	737	1612
66	COMMUNICA.,EXC. BRDCAST.	0	0	0	0	0	0	0	0	0
67	RADIO & TV BROADCASTING	0	0	0	0	0	0	0	0	0
68	ELEC.,GAS,WATER,SAN.SER.	0	0	0	0	0	0	0	0	0
69	WHOLESALE & RETAIL TRADE	1884	437	197	979	715	7391	446	485	798
70	FINANCE & INSURANCE	0	0	0	0	0	0	0	0	0
71	REAL ESTATE & RENTAL	0	0	0	0	0	0	0	0	0
72	HOTELS; PERSONAL SERV.	0	0	0	0	0	0	0	0	0
73	BUSINESS SERVICES	0	0	0	0	0	0	0	0	0
74	RESEARCH & DEVELOPMENT	0	0	0	0	0	0	0	0	0
75	AUTO. REPAIR & SERVICES	0	0	0	0	0	0	0	0	0
76	AMUSEMENTS	712	156	67	164	202	4427	93	122	99
77	MED.,EDUC. SERVICES	0	0	0	0	0	0	0	0	0
78	FEDERAL GOV'T ENTERPRISE	0	0	0	0	0	0	0	0	0
79	STATE & LOCAL GOV'T ENT.	0	0	0	0	0	0	0	0	0
80	IMPORTS	0	0	0	0	0	0	0	0	0
81	BUS.TRAVEL, ENT., GIFTS.	0	0	0	0	0	0	0	0	0
82	OFFICE SUPPLIES	0	0	0	0	0	0	0	0	0
83	SCRAP & USED GOODS	0	0	0	0	0	0	0	0	0
84	GOVERNMENT INDUSTRY	0	0	0	0	0	0	0	0	0
85	REST OF WORLD INDUSTRY	0	0	0	0	0	0	0	0	0
86	HOUSEHOLD INDUSTRY	0	0	0	0	0	0	0	0	0
87	INVENTORY VALUATION ADJ.	0	0	0	0	0	0	0	0	0
88	STATE TOTAL	-7093	2712	-5703	-67539	31946	-52741	-33005	-19710	-21712

TABLE C.8

STATE ESTIMATES OF 1958
NET INVENTORY CHANGE
(THOUSANDS OF CURRENT DOLLARS)

INDUSTRY TITLE	10 GEORGIA	11 IDAHO	12 ILLINOIS	13 INDIANA	14 IOWA	15 KANSAS	16 KENTUCKY	17 LOUISIANA	18 MAINE
1 LIVESTOCK & PRDTS.	-4227	12209	20325	9881	117728	70096	5385	-14104	-807
2 OTHER AGRICULTURE PRDTS.	14235	-3685	52465	20823	-41900	137834	33889	-4082	-1464
3 FORESTRY & FISHERIES	728	127	62	40	17	4	96	1035	594
4 AGRI.,FORES.,FISH. SERV.	1131	126	743	412	604	286	127	347	171
5 IRON, FERRO. ORES MINING	-45	-13	0	0	0	0	0	0	0
6 NONFERROUS ORES MINING	-6	-1002	-369	0	0	-3	0	0	-2
7 COAL MINING	-1		-1775	-493	0	-69	-3002	0	0
8 CRUDE PETRO.,NATURAL GAS	0		-841	-120	-38	-1578	-303	-8873	0
9 STONE & CLAY MINING	206	14	181	96	82	46	95	40	4
10 CHEM.&FERT. MIN. MINING	-5	-12	-19	0	0	-3	-12	-180	0
11 NEW CONSTRUCTION									
12 MAINT. & REPAIR CONSTR.									
13 ORDNANCE & ACCESSORIES	42	62	1640	2016	1177	0	0	1266	190
14 FOOD & KINDRED PRDTS.	5312	1352	20886	7047	11401	4380	3925	4758	1091
15 TOBACCO MANUFACTURES	-61		-73	-58	0	0	-4586	-30	0
16 FABRICS	-11684		-409	0	-33	-2	-247	0	-2064
17 TEXTILE PRDTS.	-6286		-874	-111	-2	-2	-25	-67	-115
18 APPAREL	-4069	-5	-2802	-907	-191	-212	-1528	-382	-265
19 MISC. TEXTILE PRDTS.	-45		-56	-11	-3	-4	-8	-9	-4
20 LUMBER & WOOD PRDTS.	1667	1462	1233	1430	365	73	626	1174	972
21 WOODEN CONTAINERS	-589	-23	-323	-99	-56	-21	-453	-188	-48
22 HOUSEHOLD FURNITURE	-151	-3	-355	-453	-34	-23	-106	-24	-9
23 OTHER FURNITURE	4		64	21	-8	4	3	1	0
24 PAPER & ALLIED PRDTS.	-110	-7	-88	-33	-14	-4	-8	-88	-103
25 PAPERBOARD CONTAINERS	-41	-1	-118	-39	144	-16	-12	-16	-2
26 PRINTING & PUBLISHING	106	11	1183	218	-81	71	81	53	19
27 CHEMICALS,SELECT. PRDTS.	-462	-53	-1361	-411	-687	-154	-413	-1054	-30
28 PLASTICS & SYNTHETICS	-456		-807	-321	323	-138	-1757	-1436	-3
29 DRUGS & COSMETICS	641		6487	3800	-53	833	14	69	3
30 PAINT & ALLIED PRDTS.	-83		-554	-63	-96	-11	-117	-16	-1
31 PETROLEUM, RELATED INDS.	-463	-4	-12102	-8117	-678	-5672	-1484	-15285	-35
32 RUBBER, MISC. PLASTICS	-241	-1	-2095	-1643	62	-306	-200	-17	-109
33 LEATHER TANNING & PRDTS.	-26		-164	-7		-16	-16	-2	-137
34 FOOTWEAR, LEATHER PRDTS.	420	6	1417	322		15	284	1	2225
35 GLASS & GLASS PRDTS.	-46		-445	-279		-2	-46	-47	-2
36 STONE & CLAY PRDTS.	515	54	1703	1000	472	517	283	407	55
37 PRIMARY IRON, STEEL MFR.	-1096	-8	-13338	-17356	-429	-153	-1643	-156	-8
38 PRIMARY NONFERROUS MFR.	-52	-76	-745	-611	-81	-20	-67	-85	-5

39 METAL CONTAINERS	196	8	-2159	236	2	36	25	299	86
40 FABRICATED METAL PRDTS.	-1104	-81	-4673	-3015	-873	-713	-860	-714	-117
41 SCREW MACH. PRDTS., ETC.	-593	0	-10310	-3077	-251	-67	-487	-71	-10
42 OTHER FAB. METAL PRDTS.	-173	-3	-6020	-1896	-432	-140	-727	-239	-41
43 ENGINES & TURBINES	-6	-6	-6136	-2075	-1104	0	0	-17	0
44 FARM MACH. & EQUIP.	-279	-47	-4747	-907	-4382	-300	-526	-88	-7
45 CONSTRUC. MACH. & EQUIP.	-547	-24	-23812	-1812	-3036	-527	-32	-423	-219
46 MATERIAL HANDLING MACH.	-207	-12	-2780	-217	-208	-196	-373	-29	0
47 METALWORKING MACHINERY	-192	-5	-15960	-3550	-820	-234	-314	-27	-66
48 SPECIAL MACH. & EQUIP.	-1604	-25	-9198	-1811	-851	-584	-548	-380	-241
49 GENERAL MACH. & EQUIP.	-187	0	-7700	-5583	-590	-411	-944	-50	-53
50 MACHINE SHOP PRDTS.	-47	-9	-829	-590	-39	-139	-145	-73	-13
51 OFFICE, COMPUT. MACHINES	-13	0	-905	-11	-1	-1	-226	-3	0
52 SERVICE IND. MACHINES	-210	-9	-2936	-1423	-587	-319	-871	-78	-37
53 ELECT. TRANSMISS. EQUIP.	-2196	0	-10704	-6193	-489	-67	-1423	-42	-53
54 HOUSEHOLD APPLIANCES	-62	0	-9821	-4937	-2384	-6	-4514	-12	-4
55 ELECTRIC LIGHTING EQUIP.	-235	0	-3330	-1504	-9	-16	-561	-9	-69
56 RADIO, TV, ETC., EQUIP.	-8	0	-10489	-4742	-550	-34	-77	-2	-19
57 ELECTRONIC COMPONENTS	-31	-6	-3754	-2018	-590	-173	-335	-5	-220
58 MISC. ELECTRICAL MACH.	-276	0	-1736	-5478	-180	-214	-101	-23	-35
59 MOTOR VEHICLES, EQUIP.	-10737	-27	-13410	-26903	-444	-3229	-3315	-225	-10
60 AIRCRAFT & PARTS	-4092	-53	-2253	-8565	-122	-13271	-22	-2162	-328
61 OTHER TRANSPORT. EQUIP.	-1083	-234	-6063	-5451	-425	-878	-312	-2650	-1332
62 PROFESS., SCIEN. INSTRU.	-48	0	-1157	-215	-106	-8	-35	-10	-1
63 MEDICAL, PHOTO. EQUIP.	1	0	469	71	5	2	3	4	0
64 MISC. MANUFACTURING	357	16	3028	794	443	42	144	90	85
65 TRANSPORT. & WAREHOUSING	3046	450	12439	3313	1607	2009	1903	3268	520
66 COMMUNICA.,EXC. BRDCAST.	0	0	0	0	0	0	0	0	0
67 RADIO & TV BROADCASTING	0	0	0	0	0	0	0	0	0
68 ELEC.,GAS,WATER,SAN.SER.	0	0	0	0	0	0	0	0	0
69 WHOLESALE & RETAIL TRADE	1371	216	4800	1590	968	683	769	931	278
70 FINANCE & INSURANCE	0	0	0	0	0	0	0	0	0
71 REAL ESTATE & RENTAL	0	0	0	0	0	0	0	0	0
72 HOTELS; PERSONAL SERV.	0	0	0	0	0	0	0	0	0
73 BUSINESS SERVICES	0	0	0	0	0	0	0	0	0
74 RESEARCH & DEVELOPMENT	0	0	0	0	0	0	0	0	0
75 AUTO. REPAIR & SERVICES	0	0	0	0	0	0	0	0	0
76 AMUSEMENTS	202	39	1187	260	161	124	189	207	51
77 MED.,EDUC. SERVICES	0	0	0	0	0	0	0	0	0
78 FEDERAL GOV'T ENTERPRISE	0	0	0	0	0	0	0	0	0
79 STATE & LOCAL GOV'T ENT.	0	0	0	0	0	0	0	0	0
80 IMPORTS	0	0	0	0	0	0	0	0	0
81 BUS.TRAVEL, ENT., GIFTS.	0	0	0	0	0	0	0	0	0
82 OFFICE SUPPLIES	0	0	0	0	0	0	0	0	0
83 SCRAP & USED GOODS	0	0	0	0	0	0	0	0	0
84 GOVERNMENT INDUSTRY	0	0	0	0	0	0	0	0	0
85 REST OF WORLD INDUSTRY	0	0	0	0	0	0	0	0	0
86 HOUSEHOLD INDUSTRY	0	0	0	0	0	0	0	0	0
87 INVENTORY VALUATION ADJ.	0	0	0	0	0	0	0	0	0
88 STATE TOTAL	-23995	10724	-65955	-69735	72711	187135	15060	-39523	-1743

TABLE C.8

STATE ESTIMATES OF 1958
NET INVENTORY CHANGE
(THOUSANDS OF CURRENT DOLLARS)

INDUSTRY TITLE	19 MARYLAND	20 MASSA-CHUSETTS	21 MICHIGAN	22 MINNESOTA	23 MISSISSIPPI	24 MISSOURI	25 MONTANA	26 NEBRASKA	27 NEVADA
1 LIVESTOCK & PRDTS.	-190	-1735	4255	27212	-21831	33547	7275	74261	584
2 OTHER AGRICULTURE PRDTS.	25837	233	49739	-7523	-35181	23530	25432	45767	2939
3 FORESTRY & FISHERIES	311	924	173	114	451	100	79	3	0
4 AGRI.,FORES.,FISH. SERV.	344	53	244	574	1020	604	76	260	13
5 IRON,FERRO.ORES MINING	-19	0	-3131	-12502	0	-380	-49	0	-119
6 NONFERROUS ORES MINING	0	0	-909	-84	0	-425	-2046	-1	-1279
7 COAL MINING	-43	0	0	0	0	-111	-19	0	0
8 CRUDE PETRO.,NATURAL GAS	-2	0	-230	0	-734	-2	-287	-225	-1
9 STONE & CLAY MINING	79	45	144	48	22	112	11	34	28
10 CHEM.&FERT.MIN. MINING	0	0	-14	0	0	-14	-20	0	-3
11 NEW CONSTRUCTION	0	0	0	0	0	0	0	0	0
12 MAINT.& REPAIR CONSTR.	0	0	0	0	0	0	0	0	0
13 ORDNANCE & ACCESSORIES	275	1535	1514	1927	0	2279	0	17	0
14 FOOD & KINDRED PRDTS.	4102	5143	7015	9283	1833	8023	655	5532	118
15 TOBACCO MANUFACTURES	-17	-11	-55	0	0	-73	0	-4	0
16 FABRICS	-442	-4592	-50	-138	-258	-187	0	0	0
17 TEXTILE PRDTS.	-13	-2044	-620	-139	-398	-246	0	0	0
18 APPAREL	-2086	-4859	-487	-625	-1867	-2314	0	-85	-2
19 MISC. TEXTILE PRDTS.	-12	-46	-144	-10	-6	-22	0	-1	0
20 LUMBER & WOOD PRDTS.	428	548	1290	843	1739	581	1185	139	64
21 WOODEN CONTAINERS	-186	-187	-147	-100	-555	-207	0	-16	0
22 HOUSEHOLD FURNITURE	-59	-216	-196	-40	-150	-70	-1	-18	-2
23 OTHER FURNITURE	11	12	71	7	7	13	-1	-3	0
24 PAPER & ALLIED PRDTS.	-19	-119	-128	-69	-17	-26	-1	-2	0
25 PAPERBOARD CONTAINERS	-31	-55	-67	-20	-3	-37	0	-4	0
26 PRINTING & PUBLISHING	147	418	313	199	17	279	12	50	11
27 CHEMICALS,SELECT. PRDTS.	-348	-295	-1039	-208	-114	-595	-11	-43	-43
28 PLASTICS & SYNTHETICS	-424	-1702	-896	-109	-34	-29	0	0	0
29 DRUGS & COSMETICS	1607	1154	2376	893	193	2099	2	264	14
30 PAINT & ALLIED PRDTS.	-65	-91	-263	-29	-1	-157	2	-2	-2
31 PETROLEUM, RELATED INDS.	-1059	-752	-3327	-1497	-772	-1669	-1284	-112	-13
32 RUBBER, MISC. PLASTICS	-696	-2387	-1491	-243	-215	-392	-1	-171	0
33 LEATHER TANNING & PRDTS.	-11	-537	-76	-25	201	-22	0	0	0
34 FOOTWEAR, LEATHER PRDTS.	178	4693	278	137	-23	3239	1	6	0
35 GLASS & GLASS PRDTS.	-89	-7	-266	-31	233	-113	69	0	0
36 STONE & CLAY PRDTS.	452	708	1107	557	-54	714	-9	163	145
37 PRIMARY IRON, STEEL MFR.	-3306	-1302	-14854	-1207	-10	-1202	-152	-27	-4
38 PRIMARY NONFERROUS MFR.	-253	-207	-522	-22	0	-103	0	-59	-54

Industry									
39 METAL CONTAINERS	0	75	0	549	1	305	64	130	657
40 FABRICATED METAL PRDTS.	-47	-626	-53	-1784	-419	-751	-3286	-1359	-934
41 SCREW MACH. PRDTS., ETC.	-2	-33	0	-784	-305	-779	-9406	-2097	-592
42 OTHER FAB. METAL PRDTS.	-2	-61	-2	-1013	-196	-471	-5746	-2505	-410
43 ENGINES & TURBINES	0	0	0	-319	0	-559	-12723	-5439	0
44 FARM MACH. & EQUIP.	-6	-284	-7	-467	-225	-1048	-1861	-11	-6
45 CONSTRUC. MACH. & EQUIP.	0	-79	-3	-674	-262	-1739	-2717	-88	-80
46 MATERIAL HANDLING MACH.	-4	-18	-2	-234	-210	-365	-3391	-568	-184
47 METALWORKING MACHINERY	0	-38	0	-1426	-5	-906	-27368	-6231	-1854
48 SPECIAL MACH. & EQUIP.	-5	-26	0	-1416	-354	-1061	-6213	-10945	-2138
49 GENERAL MACH. & EQUIP.	0	-380	0	-852	-41	-889	-5374	-2746	-290
50 MACHINE SHOP PRDTS.	-9	-13	-8	-456	-38	-205	-1135	-326	-153
51 OFFICE, COMPUT. MACHINES	-13	-1	0	-85	0	-1283	-1171	-511	-36
52 SERVICE IND. MACHINES	0	-22	0	-1835	-142	-1670	-3627	-1114	-458
53 ELECT. TRANSMISS. EQUIP.	-24	-16	0	-3665	-269	-1942	-4181	-5181	-769
54 HOUSEHOLD APPLIANCES	-2	-19	0	-739	-322	-1994	-4019	-491	-143
55 ELECTRIC LIGHTING EQUIP.	-6	0	0	-1004	-472	-193	-468	-1845	-40
56 RADIO, TV, ETC., EQUIP.	-2	-609	0	-689	-54	-684	-437	-5569	-2805
57 ELECTRONIC COMPONENTS	-1	-246	0	-102	-88	-530	-748	-4326	-201
58 MISC. ELECTRICAL MACH.	0	-39	0	-392	-34	-254	-2525	-700	-334
59 MOTOR VEHICLES, EQUIP.	0	-731	-6	-33913	-676	-3850	-206081	-4084	-9121
60 AIRCRAFT & PARTS	0	-2	0	-6609	0	-762	-3104	-3852	-4231
61 OTHER TRANSPORT. EQUIP.	0	-541	-18	-1479	-119	-360	-4013	-1791	-4246
62 PROFESS., SCIEN. INSTRU.	0	-51	-4	-84	-13	-109	-530	-624	-48
63 MEDICAL, PHOTO. EQUIP.	0	0	0	38	0	57	29	530	17
64 MISC. MANUFACTURING	17	86	17	463	183	460	1289	2132	250
65 TRANSPORT. & WAREHOUSING	401	1360	584	4733	740	2743	4459	3725	2583
66 COMMUNICA.,EXC. BRDCAST.	0	0	0	0	0	0	0	0	0
67 RADIO & TV BROADCASTING	0	0	0	0	0	0	0	0	0
68 ELEC.,GAS,WATER,SAN.SER.	0	0	0	0	0	0	0	0	0
69 WHOLESALE & RETAIL TRADE	151	568	223	1890	446	1375	2864	2125	1088
70 FINANCE & INSURANCE	0	0	0	0	0	0	0	0	0
71 REAL ESTATE & RENTAL	0	0	0	0	0	0	0	0	0
72 HOTELS; PERSONAL SERV.	0	0	0	0	0	0	0	0	0
73 BUSINESS SERVICES	0	0	0	0	0	0	0	0	0
74 RESEARCH & DEVELOPMENT	0	0	0	0	0	0	0	0	0
75 AUTO. REPAIR & SERVICES	0	0	0	0	0	0	0	0	0
76 AMUSEMENTS	0	116	36	323	62	229	608	478	355
77 MED.,EDUC. SERVICES	0	0	0	0	0	0	0	0	0
78 FEDERAL GOV'T ENTERPRISE	0	0	0	0	0	0	0	0	0
79 STATE & LOCAL GOV'T ENT.	0	0	0	0	0	0	0	0	0
80 IMPORTS	0	0	0	0	0	0	0	0	0
81 BUS.TRAVEL, ENT., GIFTS.	0	0	0	0	0	0	0	0	0
82 OFFICE SUPPLIES	0	0	0	0	0	0	0	0	0
83 SCRAP & USED GOODS	0	0	0	0	0	0	0	0	0
84 GOVERNMENT INDUSTRY	0	0	0	0	0	0	0	0	0
85 REST OF WORLD INDUSTRY	0	0	0	0	0	0	0	0	0
86 HOUSEHOLD INDUSTRY	0	0	0	0	0	0	0	0	0
87 INVENTORY VALUATION ADJ.	0	0	0	0	0	0	0	0	0
88 STATE TOTAL	3548	124095	31674	14699	-59324	-112	-261204	-58961	278

INDUSTRY TITLE	28 NEW HAMPSHIRE	29 NEW JERSEY	30 NEW MEXICO	31 NEW YORK	32 NORTH CAROLINA	33 NORTH DAKOTA	34 OHIO	35 OKLAHOMA	36 OREGON
1 LIVESTOCK & PRDTS.	-924	-2771	11706	-8604	870	-3809	-332	44710	10988
2 OTHER AGRICULTURE PRDTS.	656	16435	20510	19276	9768	38607	42295	17293	-4774
3 FORESTRY & FISHERIES	54	269	24	377	662	1	93	27	3095
4 AGRI.,FORES.,FISH. SERV.	45	93	107	220	720	129	368	346	166
5 IRON, FERRO. ORES MINING	0	-144	-64	-948	-76	-30	-7	-51	-58
6 NONFERROUS ORES MINING	0	-144	-3967	-466	-5	-78	-7	-45	-9
7 COAL MINING	0	0	-78	0	0	-276	-1435	-2887	0
8 CRUDE PETRO.,NATURAL GAS	0	0	-1708	-34	0		-95	39	-2
9 STONE & CLAY MINING	6	125	21	186	77	8	191	0	51
10 CHEM.&FERT. MIN. MINING	0	0	-220	-27	-8		-30	0	-2
11 NEW CONSTRUCTION	0	0	0	0	0	0	0	0	0
12 MAINT. & REPAIR CONSTR.	0	0	0	0	0	0	0	0	0
13 ORDNANCE & ACCESSORIES	365	34	1211	1344	598	534	2781	5	6
14 FOOD & KINDRED PRDTS.	0	9940	437	17574	3577		10942	2004	2404
15 TOBACCO MANUFACTURES	-1365	-132	0	-40	-12682		-128	0	0
16 FABRICS	-108	-2507	-1	-2377	-29706		-229	-12	-403
17 TEXTILE PRDTS.	-377	-1262	-1	-1837	-1591		-1079	-229	-56
18 APPAREL	-2	-5814	-17	-43980	-8475		-2756	-327	-362
19 MISC. TEXTILE PRDTS.	433	-78	-1	-229	-52	12	-17	-2	-9
20 LUMBER & WOOD PRDTS.	-112	533	202	1658	2069		1092	194	11640
21 WOODEN CONTAINERS	-34	-306	-2	-365	-235		-269	0	-127
22 HOUSEHOLD FURNITURE	-3	-182	-2	-444	-953		-230	-19	-53
23 OTHER FURNITURE	16	16	1	83	18		59	2	1
24 PAPER & ALLIED PRDTS.	-35	-109	0	-207	-67	10	-146	-3	-46
25 PAPERBOARD CONTAINERS	-3	-85	0	-116	-23	-5	-88	-4	-5
26 PRINTING & PUBLISHING	29	388	13	2669	87		660	54	53
27 CHEMICALS,SELECT. PRDTS.	-23	-2872	-18	-1203	-242		-1153	-41	-92
28 PLASTICS & SYNTHETICS	-134	-2304	0	-1923	-1320		-2253	-7	-38
29 DRUGS & COSMETICS	14	9839	0	8351	409		3490	24	44
30 PAINT & ALLIED PRDTS.	-1	-428	-1	-205	-33		-343	-9	-17
31 PETROLEUM, RELATED INDS.	-16	-12619	-548	-2365	-76	-328	-8563	-6838	-186
32 RUBBER, MISC. PLASTICS	-183	-1974	-18	-1729	-271		-6864	-336	-32
33 LEATHER TANNING & PRDTS.	-93	-172	0	-251	-22		-87	0	-4
34 FOOTWEAR, LEATHER PRDTS.	1852	1056	13	5552	157		845	40	41
35 GLASS & GLASS PRDTS.	-3	-443	0	-324	-93		-793	-126	-16
36 STONE & CLAY PRDTS.	126	1297	96	1929	368	30	2319	246	201
37 PRIMARY IRON, STEEL MFR.	-119	-1953	0	-6799	-210	-1	-28047	-195	-425
38 PRIMARY NONFERROUS MFR.	-15	-813	-28	-886	-69	0	-741	-59	-85

Code	Industry								
39	METAL CONTAINERS	107	16	757	0	3	689	0	1483	0
40	FABRICATED METAL PRDTS.	-639	-1225	-7292	-47	-821	-4746	-54	-2723	-94
41	SCREW MACH. PRDTS., ETC.	-55	-92	-9724	-4	-259	-4740	-20	-3123	-107
42	OTHER FAB. METAL PRDTS.	-166	-229	-5371	-1	-376	-3454	-4	-2997	-84
43	ENGINES & TURBINES	-17	-3	-1529	0	-3	-5718	0	-115	-3
44	FARM MACH. & EQUIP.	-57	-55	-1276	-56	-160	-394	-3	-29	-1
45	CONSTRUC. MACH. & EQUIP.	-186	-2521	-7749	-2	-30	-654	-27	-862	-451
46	MATERIAL HANDLING MACH.	-603	-38	-3349	-5	-28	-2247	-38	-2252	-343
47	METALWORKING MACHINERY	-58	-61	-24275	-42	-242	-8477	-25	-3578	-1654
48	SPECIAL MACH. & EQUIP.	-1299	-282	-11254	-12	-3939	-9558	-2	-7254	-408
49	GENERAL MACH. & EQUIP.	-97	-850	-11589	-2	-113	-8177	-30	-5667	-25
50	MACHINE SHOP PRDTS.	-1	-65	-966	-6	-66	-951	-3	-374	-17
51	OFFICE, COMPUT. MACHINES	-71	-6	-890	0	-32	-4044	-14	-536	-62
52	SERVICE IND. MACHINES	0	-222	-3623	0	-276	-4496	-5	-1513	0
53	ELECT. TRANSMISS. EQUIP.	-1162	-430	-18199	0	-2250	-14817	0	-6176	-1426
54	HOUSEHOLD APPLIANCES	-64	-33	-15186	0	-711	-2222	-19	-731	-2
55	ELECTRIC LIGHTING EQUIP.	-18	-5	-3481	-5	-240	-3503	-15	-2703	-32
56	RADIO, TV, ETC., EQUIP.	-10	-1081	-2317	0	-1457	-10643	-37	-7647	-349
57	ELECTRONIC COMPONENTS	-10	-59	-1786	0	-535	-6529	-2	-3846	-569
58	MISC. ELECTRICAL MACH.	-100	-75	-2837	0	-789	-1654	-9	-1078	-10
59	MOTOR VEHICLES, EQUIP.	-1171	-833	-70431	0	-514	-25104	-7	-10031	-3
60	AIRCRAFT & PARTS	-349	-9273	-19428	-6	-357	-21728	0	-6644	0
61	OTHER TRANSPORT. EQUIP.	-970	-248	-2864	0	-383	-3723	0	-2885	-32
62	PROFESS., SCIEN. INSTRU.	-16	-20	-330	0	-69	-929	0	-517	-7
63	MEDICAL, PHOTO. EQUIP.	23	0	21	0	48	3006	0	277	15
64	MISC. MANUFACTURING	114	88	1667	25	203	8012	21	2370	127
65	TRANSPORT. & WAREHOUSING	1922	1827	7666	378	2358	19720	602	6356	203
66	COMMUNICA., EXC. BRDCAST.	0	0	0	0	0	0	0	0	0
67	RADIO & TV BROADCASTING	0	0	0	0	0	0	0	0	0
68	ELEC.,GAS,WATER,SAN.SER.	0	0	0	0	0	0	0	0	0
69	WHOLESALE & RETAIL TRADE	779	713	3438	223	1340	9518	262	2599	189
70	FINANCE & INSURANCE	0	0	0	0	0	0	0	0	0
71	REAL ESTATE & RENTAL	0	0	0	0	0	0	0	0	0
72	HOTELS; PERSONAL SERV.	0	0	0	0	0	0	0	0	0
73	BUSINESS SERVICES	0	0	0	0	0	0	0	0	0
74	RESEARCH & DEVELOPMENT	0	0	0	0	0	0	0	0	0
75	AUTO. REPAIR & SERVICES	0	0	0	0	0	0	0	0	0
76	AMUSEMENTS	130	131	816	30	200	5749	63	665	85
77	MED.,EDUC. SERVICES	0	0	0	0	0	0	0	0	0
78	FEDERAL GOV'T ENTERPRISE	0	0	0	0	0	0	0	0	0
79	STATE & LOCAL GOV'T ENT.	0	0	0	0	0	0	0	0	0
80	IMPORTS	0	0	0	0	0	0	0	0	0
81	BUS.TRAVEL, ENT., GIFTS.	0	0	0	0	0	0	0	0	0
82	OFFICE SUPPLIES	0	0	0	0	0	0	0	0	0
83	SCRAP & USED GOODS	0	0	0	0	0	0	0	0	0
84	GOVERNMENT INDUSTRY	0	0	0	0	0	0	0	0	0
85	REST OF WORLD INDUSTRY	0	0	0	0	0	0	0	0	0
86	HOUSEHOLD INDUSTRY	0	0	0	0	0	0	0	0	0
87	INVENTORY VALUATION ADJ.	0	0	0	0	0	0	0	0	0
88	STATE TOTAL	17750	39090	-201931	35277	-46327	-117954	28300	-56618	-5024

TABLE C.8

STATE ESTIMATES OF 1958
NET INVENTORY CHANGE
(THOUSANDS OF CURRENT DOLLARS)

INDUSTRY TITLE	37 PENNSYL-VANIA	38 RHODE ISLAND	39 SOUTH CAROLINA	40 SOUTH DAKOTA	41 TENNESSEE	42 TEXAS	43 UTAH	44 VERMONT	45 VIRGINIA
1 LIVESTOCK & PRDTS.	-620	-244	-2676	32825	566	106741	2135	-1633	1747
2 OTHER AGRICULTURE PRDTS.	91469	611	8929	-46329	23874	-146238	-4959	2562	51521
3 FORESTRY & FISHERIES	176	92	459	9	131	857	8	44	783
4 AGRI.,FORES.,FISH. SERV.	409	42	253	156	229	2802	63	9	291
5 IRON, FERRO. ORES MINING	-1213	0	-1	-1	-3	-205	-347	0	-25
6 NONFERROUS ORES MINING	-84	0	-7	-656	-364	-124	-5818	0	-147
7 COAL MINING	-5781	0	0	-1	-231	-11	-284	0	-1353
8 CRUDE PETRO.,NATURAL GAS	-184	0	0	-1		-15041	-390	0	-2
9 STONE & CLAY MINING	190	5	56	20	100	127	15	22	114
10 CHEM.&FERT. MIN. MINING	-11	0	-1	0	-77	-148	-20	0	-1
11 NEW CONSTRUCTION	0	0	0	0	0	0	0	0	0
12 MAINT. & REPAIR CONSTR.	0	0	0	0	0	0	0	0	0
13 ORDNANCE & ACCESSORIES	1744	1	0	0	1024	894	0	0	12
14 FOOD & KINDRED PRDTS.	13073	564	1307	1619	5029	11089	2100	600	3299
15 TOBACCO MANUFACTURES	-1367		-341		-207	-19	1218		-4983
16 FABRICS	-4744	-3053	-24455	0	-2095	-948	-6	-64	-3918
17 TEXTILE PRDTS.	-2444	-469	-1985	0	-572	-126	-4	-25	-682
18 APPAREL	-12983	-414	-1865	0	-5148	-2822	-168	-151	-2075
19 MISC. TEXTILE PRDTS.	-47	-2	-13	0	-17	-21	-1	0	-10
20 LUMBER & WOOD PRDTS.	1364	35	1175	71	1290	1640	100	277	1672
21 WOODEN CONTAINERS	-251	-11	-218	-3	-467	-211	-211	-39	-333
22 HOUSEHOLD FURNITURE	-330	-3	-62	-1	-322	-169	-14	-38	-464
23 OTHER FURNITURE	53	4	-2	0	9	18	1	0	13
24 PAPER & ALLIED PRDTS.	-155	-4	-47	0	-64	-47	-1	-14	-71
25 PAPERBOARD CONTAINERS	-92	-5	-17	0	-17	-27	-1	-3	-14
26 PRINTING & PUBLISHING	714	37	30	13	139	279	29	18	97
27 CHEMICALS,SELECT. PRDTS.	-953	-71	-101	-5	-773	-4354	-29	-8	-452
28 PLASTICS & SYNTHETICS	-3127	-339	-1648	0	-4201	-3595		-29	-5607
29 DRUGS & COSMETICS	4150	57	238	6	716	766	19	3	575
30 PAINT & ALLIED PRDTS.	-241	-11	-5	-5	-34	-176	-3	-6	-17
31 PETROLEUM, RELATED INDS.	-12149	-275	-186	-4	-407	-51662	-1466	-4	-672
32 RUBBER, MISC. PLASTICS	-1804	-557	-216	-12	-614	-699	-41	-79	-286
33 LEATHER TANNING & PRDTS.	-181	-1	-3	0	-104	-9	5	-11	-35
34 FOOTWEAR, LEATHER PRDTS.	2859	122		0	1816	305	0	52	443
35 GLASS & GLASS PRDTS.	-756	-63	-103	0	-209	-65	0	0	-41
36 STONE & CLAY PRDTS.	2047	39	182	46	475	1563	201	121	537
37 PRIMARY IRON, STEEL MFR.	-37728	-493	-163	-1	-739	-2433	-1134	-23	-611
38 PRIMARY NONFERROUS MFR.	-553	-156	-13	0	-230	-423	-101	-9	-63

	C1	C2	C3	C4	C5	C6	C7	C8	C9
39 METAL CONTAINERS	927	0	4	0	74	628	38	0	58
40 FABRICATED METAL PRDTS.	-7327	-134	-389	-98	-1582	-3332	-449	-42	-1177
41 SCREW MACH. PRDTS., ETC.	-6609	-493	-163	0	-551	-378	-12	-11	-53
42 OTHER FAB. METAL PRDTS.	-3829	-358	-143	-11	-464	-1217	-24	-28	-394
43 ENGINES & TURBINES	-8246	-3	0	0	-3	-504	0	0	0
44 FARM MACH. & EQUIP.	-803	-1	-22	-34	-497	-210	-13	-4	-63
45 CONSTRUC. MACH. & EQUIP.	-3041	-6	-8	0	-133	-8424	-617	-33	-110
46 MATERIAL HANDLING MACH.	-2617	-11	-86	-70	-389	-374	-4	0	-89
47 METALWORKING MACHINERY	-10039	-1651	-903	-96	-280	-705	-43	-2030	-54
48 SPECIAL MACH. & EQUIP.	-8403	-1546	-2493	-8	-649	-2296	-114	-122	-372
49 GENERAL MACH. & EQUIP.	-7311	-270	-282	-54	-412	-1427	-146	-13	-274
50 MACHINE SHOP PRDTS.	-527	-45	-43	-15	-88	-302	-19	-8	-49
51 OFFICE, COMPUT. MACHINES	-716	-1	-39	0	-447	-37	-1	-101	-190
52 SERVICE IND. MACHINES	-2806	-37	-31	0	-1459	-1796	-122	-55	-297
53 ELECT. TRANSMISS. EQUIP.	-17192	-121	-649	0	-2159	-1238	-132	-41	-2596
54 HOUSEHOLD APPLIANCES	-1535	-50	-111	0	-224	-368	0	0	-9
55 ELECTRIC LIGHTING EQUIP.	-3260	-542	-9	0	-876	-192	-8	-74	-14
56 RADIO, TV, ETC., EQUIP.	-1725	-87	-464	-1	-205	-1760	-91	0	-714
57 ELECTRONIC COMPONENTS	-6414	-280	-5	-26	-199	-575	-117	-182	-1073
58 MISC. ELECTRICAL MACH.	-1361	-128	-84	0	-1221	-413	-3	-86	-53
59 MOTOR VEHICLES, EQUIP.	-13518	-166	0	-13	-1281	-8965	-47	0	-3226
60 AIRCRAFT & PARTS	-15225	-160	-219	0	-1069	-12641	-4577	-1425	-455
61 OTHER TRANSPORT. EQUIP.	-8679	-131	-49	-48	-100	-2625	-144	0	-1893
62 PROFESS., SCIEN. INSTRU.	-938	-69	33	0	1	-120	-3	-20	-20
63 MEDICAL, PHOTO. EQUIP.	94	27	278	11	483	21	1	11	57
64 MISC. MANUFACTURING	2510	1413	817	250	2168	376	69	38	361
65 TRANSPORT. & WAREHOUSING	9721	446	0	0	0	8697	825	219	3164
66 COMMUNICA.,EXC. BRDCAST.	0	0	0	0	0	0	0	0	0
67 RADIO & TV BROADCASTING	0	0	0	0	0	0	0	0	0
68 ELEC.,GAS,WATER,SAN.SER.	3820	303	532	208	1131	3461	314	112	1140
69 WHOLESALE & RETAIL TRADE	0	0	0	0	0	0	0	0	0
70 FINANCE & INSURANCE	0	0	0	0	0	0	0	0	0
71 REAL ESTATE & RENTAL	0	0	0	0	0	0	0	0	0
72 HOTELS; PERSONAL SERV.	0	0	0	0	0	0	0	0	0
73 BUSINESS SERVICES	0	0	0	0	0	0	0	0	0
74 RESEARCH & DEVELOPMENT	0	0	0	0	0	0	0	0	0
75 AUTO. REPAIR & SERVICES	0	0	0	0	0	0	0	0	0
76 AMUSEMENTS	0	0	0	0	0	0	0	0	0
77 MED.,EDUC. SERVICES	682	106	83	52	173	560	82	42	191
78 FEDERAL GOV'T ENTERPRISE	0	0	0	0	0	0	0	0	0
79 STATE & LOCAL GOV'T ENT.	0	0	0	0	0	0	0	0	0
80 IMPORTS	0	0	0	0	0	0	0	0	0
81 BUS.TRAVEL, ENT., GIFTS.	0	0	0	0	0	0	0	0	0
82 OFFICE SUPPLIES	0	0	0	0	0	0	0	0	0
83 SCRAP & USED GOODS	0	0	0	0	0	0	0	0	0
84 GOVERNMENT INDUSTRY	0	0	0	0	0	0	0	0	0
85 REST OF WORLD INDUSTRY	0	0	0	0	0	0	0	0	0
86 HOUSEHOLD INDUSTRY	0	0	0	0	0	0	0	0	0
87 INVENTORY VALUATION ADJ.	0	0	0	0	0	0	0	0	0
88 STATE TOTAL	-83917	-8557	-25952	-12202	8245	-138648	-14255	-2287	31038

313

TABLE C.8

STATE ESTIMATES OF 1958
NET INVENTORY CHANGE
(THOUSANDS OF CURRENT DOLLARS)

INDUSTRY TITLE	46 WASHINGTON	47 WEST VIRGINIA	48 WISCONSIN	49 WYOMING	50 ALASKA	51 HAWAII	52 NO STATE ALLOCATION	53 NATIONAL TOTAL
1 LIVESTOCK & PRDTS.	10570	-1259	56	5773	0	0	0	600679
2 OTHER AGRICULTURE PRDTS.	-12619	4695	-39824	2951	0	0	0	428459
3 FORESTRY & FISHERIES	1753	87	155	9	1105	59	0	19308
4 AGRI.,FORES.,FISH. SERV.	205	112	239	-25	1	426	0	19997
5 IRON, FERRO. ORES MINING	-21	0	-25	-482	-10	0	0	-22977
6 NONFERROUS ORES MINING	-272	0	-46	-1570	-154	0	0	-32448
7 COAL MINING	-40	-6263	0	-88	-24	0	0	-22333
8 CRUDE PETRO.,NATURAL GAS	-30	-280	0	-1415	-54	0	0	-40297
9 STONE & CLAY MINING	40	42	95	35	3	13	0	3550
10 CHEM.&FERT. MIN. MINING	0	0	0	-39	0	0	0	-1273
11 NEW CONSTRUCTION	0	0	0	0	0	0	0	0
12 MAINT. & REPAIR CONSTR.	0	0	0	0	0	0	0	0
13 ORDNANCE & ACCESSORIES	134	1606	303	0	0	0	0	84082
14 FOOD & KINDRED PRDTS.	3865	697	9383	269	299	1878	0	248018
15 TOBACCO MANUFACTURES	0	-90	-2	0	0	0	0	-25537
16 FABRICS	-89	-52	-103	0	0	-2	0	-103913
17 TEXTILE PRDTS.	-23	-1	-367	0	0	-3	0	-26526
18 APPAREL	-354	-300	-993	0	0	-166	0	-123291
19 MISC. TEXTILE PRDTS.	-6	-1	-5	0	0	-1	0	-997
20 LUMBER & WOOD PRDTS.	5862	444	1547	116	96	61	0	62473
21 WOODEN CONTAINERS	-229	-24	-277	0	0	-1	0	-9419
22 HOUSEHOLD FURNITURE	-46	-12	-82	0	0	-10	0	-6474
23 OTHER FURNITURE	4	2	14	0	0	-1	0	617
24 PAPER & ALLIED PRDTS.	-142	-6	-223	0	0	-2	0	-2549
25 PAPERBOARD CONTAINERS	-16	-3	-45	0	0	-1	0	-1223
26 PRINTING & PUBLISHING	81	33	236	-6	3	16	0	10559
27 CHEMICALS,SELECT. PRDTS.	-369	-2001	-125	-2	0	-34	0	-24284
28 PLASTICS & SYNTHETICS	-141	-2477	-175	0	0	0	0	-43579
29 DRUGS & COSMETICS	34	54	1058	0	0	0	0	55944
30 PAINT & ALLIED PRDTS.	-24	-3	-66	0	0	11	0	-3668
31 PETROLEUM, RELATED INDS.	-2026	-630	-512	-3323	0	0	0	-186034
32 RUBBER, MISC. PLASTICS	-39	-24	-625	0	0	-283	0	-32475
33 LEATHER TANNING & PRDTS.	-2	-36	-343	0	0	-3	0	-2526
34 FOOTWEAR, LEATHER PRDTS.	28	40	1379	0	0	0	0	32234
35 GLASS & GLASS PRDTS.	-14	-470	-8	0	0	17	0	-5359
36 STONE & CLAY PRDTS.	343	238	509	60	18	-1	0	27534
37 PRIMARY IRON, STEEL MFR.	-353	-3576	-2656	0	0	79	0	-159747
38 PRIMARY NONFERROUS MFR.	-324	-167	-116	0	0	-37	0	-9653

314

No.	Industry								
39	METAL CONTAINERS	277	86	549	0	0	116	0	-13456
40	FABRICATED METAL PRDTS.	-675	-565	-2399	-6	0	-49	0	-68554
41	SCREW MACH. PRDTS., ETC.	-100	-279	-3399	-8	0	0	0	-66600
42	OTHER FAB. METAL PRDTS.	-126	-379	-918	-3	0	-5	0	-48038
43	ENGINES & TURBINES	-9	0	-11551	0	0	-5	0	-60070
44	FARM MACH. & EQUIP.	-56	-71	-2281	0	0	-5	0	-22238
45	CONSTRUC. MACH. & EQUIP.	-508	-844	-6933	-15	0	-2	0	-73462
46	MATERIAL HANDLING MACH.	-376	-69	-548	0	0	0	0	-23880
47	METALWORKING MACHINERY	-219	-466	-4777	0	0	-6	0	-131394
48	SPECIAL MACH. & EQUIP.	-826	-78	-6821	0	0	-149	0	-106642
49	GENERAL MACH. & EQUIP.	-112	-16	-4246	-2	0	-2	0	-81401
50	MACHINE SHOP PRDTS.	-124	-46	-249	-5	0	-7	0	-10462
51	OFFICE, COMPUT. MACHINES	-21	0	-37	0	0	0	0	-14556
52	SERVICE IND. MACHINES	-109	-53	-1544	0	0	-3	0	-35834
53	ELECT. TRANSMISS. EQUIP.	-387	-511	-10718	-12	0	-3	0	-132992
54	HOUSEHOLD APPLIANCES	-106	-24	-2551	0	0	-3	0	-63517
55	ELECTRIC LIGHTING EQUIP.	-120	-814	-256	-1	0	-3	0	-29335
56	RADIO, TV, ETC., EQUIP.	-94	-3	-1182	0	0	-1	0	-71445
57	ELECTRONIC COMPONENTS	-29	-97	-421	0	0	-1	0	-47994
58	MISC. ELECTRICAL MACH.	-24		-1112	0	0	0	0	-24385
59	MOTOR VEHICLES, EQUIP.	-890	-358	-31599	0	0	-12	0	-528725
60	AIRCRAFT & PARTS	-9352	-2	-110	-35	0	0	0	-261785
61	OTHER TRANSPORT. EQUIP.	-3604	-659	-1915	-1	0	-25	0	-75341
62	PROFESS., SCIEN. INSTRU.	-5	-24	-245	-3	0	0	0	-7872
63	MEDICAL, PHOTO. EQUIP.	5	9	11	0	0	0	0	5338
64	MISC. MANUFACTURING	147	58	726	0	0	13	0	33953
65	TRANSPORT. & WAREHOUSING	3019	1423	2323	339	450	773	0	153503
66	COMMUNICA.,EXC. BRDCAST.	0	0	0	0	0	0	0	0
67	RADIO & TV BROADCASTING	0	0	0	0	0	0	0	0
68	ELEC.,GAS,WATER,SAN.SER.	0	0	0	0	0	0	0	0
69	WHOLESALE & RETAIL TRADE	1108	406	1335	102	69	198	0	68968
70	FINANCE & INSURANCE	0	0	0	0	0	0	0	0
71	REAL ESTATE & RENTAL	0	0	0	0	0	0	0	0
72	HOTELS; PERSONAL SERV.	0	0	0	0	0	0	0	0
73	BUSINESS SERVICES	0	0	0	0	0	0	0	0
74	RESEARCH & DEVELOPMENT	0	0	0	0	0	0	0	0
75	AUTO. REPAIR & SERVICES	0	0	0	0	0	0	0	0
76	AMUSEMENTS	224	135	235	26	19	64	0	21922
77	MED.,EDUC. SERVICES	0	0	0	0	0	0	0	0
78	FEDERAL GOV'T ENTERPRISE	0	0	0	0	0	0	0	0
79	STATE & LOCAL GOV'T ENT.	0	0	0	0	0	0	0	0
80	IMPORTS	0	0	0	0	0	0	8000	8000
81	BUS.TRAVEL, ENT., GIFTS.	0	0	0	0	0	0	0	0
82	OFFICE SUPPLIES	0	0	0	0	0	0	0	0
83	SCRAP & USED GOODS	0	0	0	0	0	0	-205513	-205513
84	GOVERNMENT INDUSTRY	0	0	0	0	0	0	0	0
85	REST OF WORLD INDUSTRY	0	0	0	0	0	0	0	0
86	HOUSEHOLD INDUSTRY	0	0	0	0	0	0	0	0
87	INVENTORY VALUATION ADJ.	0	0	0	0	0	0	-311000	-311000
88	STATE TOTAL	-7352	-12866	-122278	2701	1821	2909	-508513	-1491000

TABLE C.9

STATE ESTIMATES OF 1963
NET INVENTORY CHANGE
(THOUSANDS OF CURRENT DOLLARS)

INDUSTRY TITLE	1 ALABAMA	2 ARIZONA	3 ARKANSAS	4 CALIFORNIA	5 COLORADO	6 CONNECTICUT	7 DELAWARE	8 DISTRICT OF COLUMBIA	9 FLORIDA
1 LIVESTOCK & PRDTS.	5868	-3941	11477	18342	-369	-1451	-764	0	10311
2 OTHER AGRICULTURE PRDTS.	33991	-33184	-27750	-31682	-14443	5935	-5607	0	3128
3 FORESTRY & FISHERIES	1066	128	747	5233	41	103	85	0	2070
4 AGRI.,FORES.,FISH. SERV.	0	0	0	0	0	0	0	0	0
5 IRON, FERRO. ORES MINING	-978	-40	-34	-2177	-4214	0	0	0	0
6 NONFERROUS ORES MINING	-3	-995	-55	-19	-205	-1	0	0	-22
7 COAL MINING	2	0	0	0	1	0	0	0	0
8 CRUDE PETRO.,NATURAL GAS	30	0	104	1507	185	0	0	0	3
9 STONE & CLAY MINING	19	8	23	125	12	0	1	0	35
10 CHEM.&FERT. MIN. MINING	0	0	-3	-84	-2	0	0	0	-121
11 NEW CONSTRUCTION	0	0	0	0	0	0	0	0	0
12 MAINT. & REPAIR CONSTR.	0	0	0	0	0	0	0	0	0
13 ORDNANCE & ACCESSORIES	-417	-484	-1	-14458	-199	-691	0	0	-1226
14 FOOD & KINDRED PRDTS.	6436	2089	6634	61751	8032	3523	1706	0	12710
15 TOBACCO MANUFACTURES	87	0	0	3	0	44	0	1050	389
16 FABRICS	1561	1	47	73	1	551	146	0	27
17 TEXTILE PRDTS.	2136	6	716	3995	24	1857	386	0	62
18 APPAREL	1255	88	292	3034	57	703	182	0	397
19 MISC. TEXTILE PRDTS.	512	55	9	2691	117	421	59	14	214
20 LUMBER & WOOD PRDTS.	1584	353	1806	7852	218	209	79	9	972
21 WOODEN CONTAINERS	15	3	29	137	4	7	1	0	37
22 HOUSEHOLD FURNITURE	712	168	1678	7502	264	685	6	0	1328
23 OTHER FURNITURE	76	32	140	1348	41	213	12	0	134
24 PAPER & ALLIED PRDTS.	2683	92	1439	3469	99	876	78	0	2840
25 PAPERBOARD CONTAINERS	141	34	294	3138	130	533	68	0	517
26 PRINTING & PUBLISHING	556	424	338	8355	757	1882	164	1686	1660
27 CHEMICALS,SELECT. PRDTS.	1740	178	236	3305	253	1395	456	13	2033
28 PLASTICS & SYNTHETICS	515	0	4	798	2	376	864	0	633
29 DRUGS & COSMETICS	52	81	6	9622	179	4619	271	0	371
30 PAINT & ALLIED PRDTS.	119	45	58	4565	153	172	11	0	633
31 PETROLEUM, RELATED INDS.	505	72	1274	21404	714	172	1416	0	327
32 RUBBER, MISC. PLASTICS	2358	0	507	7909	1394	3535	775	0	287
33 LEATHER TANNING & PRDTS.	0	0	0	-188	-4	-21	-214	0	-14
34 FOOTWEAR, LEATHER PRDTS.	-128	-6	-992	-755	-549	-343	-85	0	-280
35 GLASS & GLASS PRDTS.	168	16	332	4286	36	324	15	0	399
36 STONE & CLAY PRDTS.	1251	539	391	7451	742	966	149	160	1948
37 PRIMARY IRON, STEEL MFR.	4209	40	13	3414	726	989	674	0	130
38 PRIMARY NONFERROUS MFR.	2353	4257	1250	6146	106	6326	176	0	513

	(1)	(2)	(3)	(4)	(5)	(6)	(7)	(8)	(9)
39 METAL CONTAINERS	99	0	103	4433	237	36	0	0	872
40 FABRICATED METAL PRDTS.	1715	334	408	8167	480	944	227	47	1896
41 SCREW MACH. PRDTS., ETC.	352	11	114	3026	21	2564	98	0	146
42 OTHER FAB. METAL PRDTS.	842	73	331	7425	385	4642	85	0	461
43 ENGINES & TURBINES	0	0	0	1006	54	722	13	0	23
44 FARM MACH. & EQUIP.	326	85	83	1137	138	36	36	0	162
45 CONSTRUC. MACH. & EQUIP.	132	2	7	1687	1126	19	4	0	29
46 MATERIAL HANDLING MACH.	49	1	71	645	29	42	0	0	32
47 METALWORKING MACHINERY	59	37	80	2309	20	3228	58	0	155
48 SPECIAL MACH. & EQUIP.	134	6	20	1194	53	677	131	0	156
49 GENERAL MACH. & EQUIP.	94	19	89	3513	169	3317	6	0	93
50 MACHINE SHOP PRDTS.	47	56	19	1240	65	279	11	0	84
51 OFFICE, COMPUT. MACHINES	2	1227	93	6123	20	2303	0	0	472
52 SERVICE IND. MACHINES	293	526	298	2330	36	472	64	0	184
53 ELECT. TRANSMISS. EQUIP.	78	7	203	1745	165	562	1	0	30
54 HOUSEHOLD APPLIANCES	10	8	6502	10326	22	10008	227	0	120
55 ELECTRIC LIGHTING EQUIP.	292	6	216	1747	34	1413	26	0	65
56 RADIO, TV, ETC., EQUIP.	109	1050	1200	24561	26	1551	1	0	2358
57 ELECTRONIC COMPONENTS	-38	-165		-1582	-4	-338	-2	0	-62
58 MISC. ELECTRICAL MACH.	187	7	3	1191	100	495	85	0	390
59 MOTOR VEHICLES, EQUIP.	1043	123	218	38128	344	3527	6950	0	229
60 AIRCRAFT & PARTS	13520	3206	28	84283	3215	34265	183	0	3954
61 OTHER TRANSPORT. EQUIP.	981	46	304	4020	67	773	21	0	1207
62 PROFESS., SCIEN. INSTRU.	28	450	543	4383	185	3521	101	0	303
63 MEDICAL, PHOTO. EQUIP.		6	1	771	28	253	0	0	108
64 MISC. MANUFACTURING	167	61	316	3557	182	2602	11	16	290
65 TRANSPORT. & WAREHOUSING	1597	730	890	15462	1686	1366	349	1462	4165
66 COMMUNICA.,EXC. BRDCAST.	0	0	0	0	0	0	0	0	0
67 RADIO & TV BROADCASTING	0	0	0	0	0	0	0	0	0
68 ELEC.,GAS,WATER,SAN.SER.	0	0	0	0	0	0	0	0	0
69 WHOLESALE & RETAIL TRADE	3756	2282	2101	34801	3369	4610	930	2058	8873
70 FINANCE & INSURANCE	0	0	0	0	0	0	0	0	0
71 REAL ESTATE & RENTAL	0	0	0	0	0	0	0	0	0
72 HOTELS; PERSONAL SERV.	0	0	0	0	0	0	0	0	0
73 BUSINESS SERVICES	0	0	0	0	0	0	0	0	0
74 RESEARCH & DEVELOPMENT	0	0	0	0	0	0	0	0	0
75 AUTO. REPAIR & SERVICES	0	0	0	0	0	0	0	0	0
76 AMUSEMENTS	27	33	25	1212	55	45	18	43	195
77 MED.,EDUC. SERVICES	0	0	0	0	0	0	0	0	0
78 FEDERAL GOV'T ENTERPRISE	0	0	0	0	0	0	0	0	0
79 STATE & LOCAL GOV'T ENT.	0	0	0	0	0	0	0	0	0
80 IMPORTS	0	0	0	0	0	0	0	0	0
81 BUS.TRAVEL, ENT., GIFTS.	0	0	0	0	0	0	0	0	0
82 OFFICE SUPPLIES	0	0	0	0	0	0	0	0	0
83 SCRAP & USED GOODS	0	0	0	0	0	0	0	0	0
84 GOVERNMENT INDUSTRY	0	0	0	0	0	0	0	0	0
85 REST OF WORLD INDUSTRY	0	0	0	0	0	0	0	0	0
86 HOUSEHOLD INDUSTRY	0	0	0	0	0	0	0	0	0
87 INVENTORY VALUATION ADJ.	0	0	0	0	0	0	0	0	0
88 STATE TOTAL	96375	-19668	15275	417232	5610	117808	10708	6565	69435

TABLE C.9

STATE ESTIMATES OF 1963
NET INVENTORY CHANGE
(THOUSANDS OF CURRENT DOLLARS)

INDUSTRY TITLE	10 GEORGIA	11 IDAHO	12 ILLINOIS	13 INDIANA	14 IOWA	15 KANSAS	16 KENTUCKY	17 LOUISIANA	18 MAINE
1 LIVESTOCK & PRDTS.	11200	15710	2565	2151	7384	28158	19992	10936	-1837
2 OTHER AGRICULTURE PRDTS.	65367	10728	63230	72157	317949	-34837	143689	16098	-4839
3 FORESTRY & FISHERIES	1673	292	143	92	39	8	222	2379	1365
4 AGRI.,FORES.,FISH. SERV.	0	0	0	0	0	0	0	0	0
5 IRON, FERRO. ORES MINING	-108	-31	0	0	0	0	0	0	0
6 NONFERROUS ORES MINING	-1	-105	-39	0	0	0	0	0	0
7 COAL MINING	0	0	4	1	0	0	7	0	0
8 CRUDE PETRO.,NATURAL GAS	0	0	327	47	0	615	118	3455	0
9 STONE & CLAY MINING	70	5	62	33	28	16	32	14	1
10 CHEM.&FERT. MIN. MINING	-3	-6	-10	0	0	-1	-6	-92	0
11 NEW CONSTRUCTION	0	0	0	0	0	0	0	0	0
12 MAINT. & REPAIR CONSTR.	0	0	0	0	0	0	0	0	0
13 ORDNANCE & ACCESSORIES	-13	-19	-509	-625	-365	0	0	-393	-59
14 FOOD & KINDRED PRDTS.	12492	3180	49116	16571	26812	10300	9231	11190	2566
15 TOBACCO MANUFACTURES	55	0	66	52	0	0	4116	27	0
16 FABRICS	3664	0	128		10	1	78		647
17 TEXTILE PRDTS.	19582	0	2722	347	7	6	78	208	359
18 APPAREL	2212	0	1523	493	104	115	830	208	144
19 MISC. TEXTILE PRDTS.	1800	10	2234	435	116	150	314	366	142
20 LUMBER & WOOD PRDTS.	1669	1463	1234	1431	365	73	627	1175	973
21 WOODEN CONTAINERS	50	2	28	8	5	2	39	16	4
22 HOUSEHOLD FURNITURE	1707	38	4014	5121	381	256	1203	267	106
23 OTHER FURNITURE	98	6	1435	480	150	91	78	25	30
24 PAPER & ALLIED PRDTS.	3871	246	3095	1173	298	158	297	3075	3631
25 PAPERBOARD CONTAINERS	1089	22	3140	1030	376	416	331	437	54
26 PRINTING & PUBLISHING	1096	116	12207	2246	1487	729	835	544	437
27 CHEMICALS,SELECT. PRDTS.	1679	192	4946	1493	296	558	1499	3831	193
28 PLASTICS & SYNTHETICS	266	0	472	187	401	81	1027	839	111
29 DRUGS & COSMETICS	1833	0	18557	10870	923	2383	40	197	8
30 PAINT & ALLIED PRDTS.	876	4	5855	665	560	115	1235	172	8
31 PETROLEUM, RELATED INDS.	441	4	11524	7729	91	5401	1413	14555	33
32 RUBBER, MISC. PLASTICS	783	3	6803	5336	2201	995	649	55	353
33 LEATHER TANNING & PRDTS.	-79	0	-505	-21	0	0	-48	-5	-420
34 FOOTWEAR, LEATHER PRDTS.	-620	-9	-2091	-475	-91	-22	-419	-1	-3283
35 GLASS & GLASS PRDTS.	583	0	5681	3560	4	21	588	605	29
36 STONE & CLAY PRDTS.	1318	137	4359	2561	1209	1325	726	1042	140
37 PRIMARY IRON, STEEL MFR.	703	5	8553	11130	275	98	1054	100	5
38 PRIMARY NONFERROUS MFR.	660	962	9376	7691	1024	248	839	1069	59

#	Industry									
39	METAL CONTAINERS	404	17	4468	485	5	73	51	615	177
40	FABRICATED METAL PRDTS.	1391	102	5890	3800	1101	898	1084	899	147
41	SCREW MACH. PRDTS., ETC.	497	0	8640	2578	210	56	408	59	8
42	OTHER FAB. METAL PRDTS.	333	5	11620	3660	833	271	1403	461	79
43	ENGINES & TURBINES	3	0	2778	939	500	0	0	8	0
44	FARM MACH. & EQUIP.	577	98	9835	1880	9079	622	1091	183	15
45	CONSTRUC. MACH. & EQUIP.	389	17	16934	1289	2159	375	23	301	156
46	MATERIAL HANDLING MACH.	104	6	1396	109	104	98	187	15	0
47	METALWORKING MACHINERY	81	2	6770	1506	348	99	133	11	28
48	SPECIAL MACH. & EQUIP.	377	6	2161	426	200	137	129	89	57
49	GENERAL MACH. & EQUIP.	99	0	4062	2945	311	217	498	27	28
50	MACHINE SHOP PRDTS.	39	7	703	500	33	118	123	62	11
51	OFFICE, COMPUT. MACHINES	37	0	2548	31	1	3	637	8	.
52	SERVICE IND. MACHINES	304	13	4241	2056	848	460	1258	112	53
53	ELECT. TRANSMISS. EQUIP.	377	0	1836	1062	84	11	244	7	9
54	HOUSEHOLD APPLIANCES	205	0	32649	16414	7926	19	15006	40	12
55	ELECTRIC LIGHTING EQUIP.	219	0	3105	1402	8	15	523	8	65
56	RADIO, TV, ETC., EQUIP.	18	0	22188	10031	1164	72	163	4	41
57	ELECTRONIC COMPONENTS	-6	-1	-725	-390	-114	-33	-65	-1	-42
58	MISC. ELECTRICAL MACH.	319	-1	2001	6312	208	247	116	26	41
59	MOTOR VEHICLES, EQUIP.	12413	31	15503	31102	514	3733	3832	260	11
60	AIRCRAFT & PARTS	5341	69	2940	11178	159	17319	28	2822	428
61	OTHER TRANSPORT. EQUIP.	658	142	3685	3313	258	534	190	1611	810
62	PROFESS., SCIEN. INSTRU.	344	2	8231	1530	755	54	246	69	10
63	MEDICAL, PHOTO. EQUIP.	3	0	1214	185	13	5	8	11	123
64	MISC. MANUFACTURING	519	23	4410	1156	645	61	210	131	515
65	TRANSPORT. & WAREHOUSING	3019	446	12329	3283	1593	1992	1886	3239	
66	COMMUNICA.,EXC. BRDCAST.	0	0	0	0	0	0	0	0	0
67	RADIO & TV BROADCASTING	0	0	0	0	0	0	0	0	0
68	ELEC.,GAS,WATER,SAN.SER.	0	0	0	0	0	0	0	0	0
69	WHOLESALE & RETAIL TRADE	6456	1018	22599	7488	4560	3217	3622	4383	1308
70	FINANCE & INSURANCE	0	0	0	0	0	0	0	0	0
71	REAL ESTATE & RENTAL	0	0	0	0	0	0	0	0	0
72	HOTELS; PERSONAL SERV.	0	0	0	0	0	0	0	0	0
73	BUSINESS SERVICES	0	0	0	0	0	0	0	0	0
74	RESEARCH & DEVELOPMENT	0	0	0	0	0	0	0	0	0
75	AUTO. REPAIR & SERVICES	0	0	0	0	0	0	0	0	0
76	AMUSEMENTS	55	11	325	71	44	34	52	57	14
77	MED.,EDUC. SERVICES	0	0	0	0	0	0	0	0	0
78	FEDERAL GOV'T ENTERPRISE	0	0	0	0	0	0	0	0	0
79	STATE & LOCAL GOV'T ENT.	0	0	0	0	0	0	0	0	0
80	IMPORTS	0	0	0	0	0	0	0	0	0
81	BUS.TRAVEL, ENT., GIFTS.	0	0	0	0	0	0	0	0	0
82	OFFICE SUPPLIES	0	0	0	0	0	0	0	0	0
83	SCRAP & USED GOODS	0	0	0	0	0	0	0	0	0
84	GOVERNMENT INDUSTRY	0	0	0	0	0	0	0	0	0
85	REST OF WORLD INDUSTRY	0	0	0	0	0	0	0	0	0
86	HOUSEHOLD INDUSTRY	0	0	0	0	0	0	0	0	0
87	INVENTORY VALUATION ADJ.	0	0	0	0	0	0	0	0	0
88	STATE TOTAL	170588	34972	434581	270310	395588	48166	223800	87911	4629

TABLE C.9

STATE ESTIMATES OF 1963
NET INVENTORY CHANGE
(THOUSANDS OF CURRENT DOLLARS)

INDUSTRY TITLE	19 MARYLAND	20 MASSA-CHUSETTS	21 MICHIGAN	22 MINNESOTA	23 MISSISSIPPI	24 MISSOURI	25 MONTANA	26 NEBRASKA	27 NEVADA
1 LIVESTOCK & PRDTS.	-2580	-1403	-2164	16617	8005	17444	18992	45837	4181
2 OTHER AGRICULTURE PRDTS.	-10418	-978	25274	207533	84157	-20132	-16050	-15656	4038
3 FORESTRY & FISHERIES	715	2125	397	262	1038	230	181	7	1
4 AGRI.,FORES.,FISH. SERV.	0	0	0	0	0	0	0	0	0
5 IRON,FERRO.ORES MINING	-47	0	-7525	-30048	0	-913	-119	0	-286
6 NONFERROUS ORES MINING	0	0	-95	-9	0	-45	-215	0	-134
7 COAL MINING	0	0	0	0	0	0	0	0	0
8 CRUDE PETRO.,NATURAL GAS	1	0	89	0	286	1	112	88	0
9 STONE & CLAY MINING	27	15	49	17	8	38	4	12	10
10 CHEM.&FERT.MIN. MINING	0	0	-7	0	0	-7	-11	0	-1
11 NEW CONSTRUCTION	0	0	0	0	0	0	0	0	0
12 MAINT. & REPAIR CONSTR.	0	0	0	0	0	0	0	0	0
13 ORDNANCE & ACCESSORIES	-85	-476	-470	-598	0	-707	0	-5	0
14 FOOD & KINDRED PRDTS.	9647	12095	16498	21830	4310	18866	1539	13009	277
15 TOBACCO MANUFACTURES	16	10	50	0	0	66	0	1	0
16 FABRICS	139	1440	16	43	81	59	0	1	0
17 TEXTILE PRDTS.	42	6367	1931	433	1241	768	0	1	0
18 APPAREL	1134	2640	265	339	1014	1257	0	46	1
19 MISC. TEXTILE PRDTS.	473	1811	5701	407	250	874	2	26	6
20 LUMBER & WOOD PRDTS.	428	548	1291	844	1741	581	1186	139	64
21 WOODEN CONTAINERS	16	16	13	9	47	18	11	1	0
22 HOUSEHOLD FURNITURE	668	2439	2214	447	1698	797	11	208	19
23 OTHER FURNITURE	237	263	1581	165	43	285	4	72	2
24 PAPER & ALLIED PRDTS.	662	4162	4485	2412	602	897	39	72	1
25 PAPERBOARD CONTAINERS	835	1475	1783	521	91	982	0	107	0
26 PRINTING & PUBLISHING	1513	4308	3229	2056	178	2878	124	520	116
27 CHEMICALS,SELECT. PRDTS.	1264	1072	3777	756	415	2162	41	156	158
28 PLASTICS & SYNTHETICS	248	994	524	64	20	17	0	0	0
29 DRUGS & COSMETICS	4599	3301	6796	2555	551	6006	6	756	39
30 PAINT & ALLIED PRDTS.	687	958	2781	304	11	1663	0	24	4
31 PETROLEUM, RELATED INDS.	1008	716	3168	1425	735	1589	1223	107	12
32 RUBBER, MISC. PLASTICS	2259	7752	4841	788	697	1274	3	555	0
33 LEATHER TANNING & PRDTS.	-34	-1651	-233	-78	0	-67	0	-15	0
34 FOOTWEAR, LEATHER PRDTS.	-263	-6926	-410	-203	-297	-4779	-1	-8	0
35 GLASS & GLASS PRDTS.	1134	94	3395	391	295	1446	0	-4	0
36 STONE & CLAY PRDTS.	1158	1813	2835	1427	597	1829	178	416	371
37 PRIMARY IRON, STEEL MFR.	2120	835	9525	774	35	771	6	18	2
38 PRIMARY NONFERROUS MFR.	3184	2607	6576	277	126	1300	1912	745	674

#	Sector	C1	C2	C3	C4	C5	C6	C7	C8	C9
39	METAL CONTAINERS	1352	268	132	629	2	1131	0	155	0
40	FABRICATED METAL PRDTS.	1177	1713	4141	946	529	2248	67	789	59
41	SCREW MACH. PRDTS., ETC.	496	1757	7883	653	256	657	0	27	2
42	OTHER FAB. METAL PRDTS.	792	4834	11090	909	378	1954	4	117	4
43	ENGINES & TURBINES	13	2462	5759	253	467	144	0	588	0
44	FARM MACH. & EQUIP.	57	22	3857	2172	186	968	15	57	4
45	CONSTRUC. MACH. & EQUIP.	92	63	1932	1236	105	479	2	9	0
46	MATERIAL HANDLING MACH.	787	285	1703	183	2	117	0	16	1
47	METALWORKING MACHINERY	502	2643	11609	384	83	605	0	6	1
48	SPECIAL MACH. & EQUIP.	153	2572	1460	249	21	333	0	201	4
49	GENERAL MACH. & EQUIP.	130	1449	2835	469	32	450	6	11	13
50	MACHINE SHOP PRDTS.	101	277	962	174	205	387	0	2	2
51	OFFICE, COMPUT. MACHINES	661	1438	3296	3613	46	238	0	32	0
52	SERVICE IND. MACHINES	132	1609	5240	2412	1071	2650	0	3	50
53	ELECT. TRANSMISS. EQUIP.	477	889	717	333	440	629	0	64	2
54	HOUSEHOLD APPLIANCES	38	1632	13363	6629	115	2456	0	1289	7
55	ELECTRIC LIGHTING EQUIP.	5934	1720	436	180	-17	936	0	-48	3
56	RADIO, TV, ETC., EQUIP.	-39	11779	925	1447	39	1457	0	45	1
57	ELECTRONIC COMPONENTS	385	-836	-144	-112	781	-20	7	845	0
58	MISC. ELECTRICAL MACH.	10544	806	2909	292	0	452	11	328	25
59	MOTOR VEHICLES, EQUIP.	5521	4722	238249	4450	72	39206	28	364	397
60	AIRCRAFT & PARTS	2580	5027	4051	995	91	8624	0	2	0
61	OTHER TRANSPORT. EQUIP.	339	1088	2439	219	1	899	24	126	0
62	PROFESS., SCIEN. INSTRU.	43	4436	3767	773	267	600	579	1348	0
63	MEDICAL, PHOTO. EQUIP.	364	1371	76	149	733	99	0	0	0
64	MISC. MANUFACTURING	2560	3104	1878	670	0	674	0	0	0
65	TRANSPORT. & WAREHOUSING	0	3692	4419	2719	0	4691	0	0	0
66	COMMUNICA.,EXC. BRDCAST.	0	0	0	0	0	0	0	0	0
67	RADIO & TV BROADCASTING	0	0	0	0	0	-8902	0	0	0
68	ELEC.,GAS,WATER,SAN.SER.	0	0	0	0	0	0	0	0	0
69	WHOLESALE & RETAIL TRADE	5125	10007	13487	6473	2101	0	1049	2673	713
70	FINANCE & INSURANCE	0	0	0	0	0	0	0	0	0
71	REAL ESTATE & RENTAL	0	0	0	0	0	0	0	0	0
72	HOTELS; PERSONAL SERV.	0	0	0	0	0	0	0	0	0
73	BUSINESS SERVICES	0	0	0	0	0	0	0	0	0
74	RESEARCH & DEVELOPMENT	0	0	0	0	0	0	0	0	0
75	AUTO. REPAIR & SERVICES	0	0	0	0	0	0	0	0	0
76	AMUSEMENTS	97	131	166	63	17	88	10	194	0
77	MED.,EDUC. SERVICES	0	0	0	0	0	0	0	0	0
78	FEDERAL GOV'T ENTERPRISE	0	0	0	0	0	0	0	0	0
79	STATE & LOCAL GOV'T ENT.	0	0	0	0	0	0	0	0	0
80	IMPORTS	0	0	0	0	0	0	0	0	0
81	BUS.TRAVEL, ENT., GIFTS.	0	0	0	0	0	0	0	0	0
82	OFFICE SUPPLIES	0	0	0	0	0	0	0	0	0
83	SCRAP & USED GOODS	0	0	0	0	0	0	0	0	0
84	GOVERNMENT INDUSTRY	0	0	0	0	0	0	0	0	0
85	REST OF WORLD INDUSTRY	0	0	0	0	0	0	0	0	0
86	HOUSEHOLD INDUSTRY	0	0	0	0	0	0	0	0	0
87	INVENTORY VALUATION ADJ.	0	0	0	0	0	0	0	0	0
88	STATE TOTAL	61200	119382	446817	271322	116008	119502	10970	56326	11037

TABLE C.9

STATE ESTIMATES OF 1963
NET INVENTORY CHANGE
(THOUSANDS OF CURRENT DOLLARS)

INDUSTRY TITLE	28 NEW HAMPSHIRE	29 NEW JERSEY	30 NEW MEXICO	31 NEW YORK	32 NORTH CAROLINA	33 NORTH DAKOTA	34 OHIO	35 OKLAHOMA	36 OREGON
1 LIVESTOCK & PRDTS.	-994	-3971	6143	-12197	3801	31763	-12686	23649	11625
2 OTHER AGRICULTURE PRDTS.	-3423	-2415	11	58183	9622	-92476	43198	-37101	18066
3 FORESTRY & FISHERIES	124	618	56	868	1523	2	213	62	7116
4 AGRI.,FORES.,FISH. SERV.	0	0	0	0	0	0	0	0	0
5 IRON. FERRO. ORES MINING	0	-346	-154	-2277	-182	0	-1	-5	-139
6 NONFERROUS ORES MINING	0	-15	-416	-49	-1	-3	-1	0	-1
7 COAL MINING	0	0	0	0	0	0	3	0	0
8 CRUDE PETRO.,NATURAL GAS	0	0	665	13	0	107	37	1124	1
9 STONE & CLAY MINING	2	43	7	64	26	3	65	13	17
10 CHEM.&FERT. MIN. MINING	0	0	-113	-14	-4	0	-15	0	0
11 NEW CONSTRUCTION	0	0	0	0	0	0	0	0	0
12 MAINT. & REPAIR CONSTR.	0	0	0	0	0	0	0	0	0
13 ORDNANCE & ACCESSORIES	0	-11	-376	-417	-185	0	-863	-1	-2
14 FOOD & KINDRED PRDTS.	859	23375	1027	41327	8412	1256	25731	4713	5654
15 TOBACCO MANUFACTURES	0	119	0	36	11384	0	115	0	0
16 FABRICS	428	786	0	745	9317	0	72	4	126
17 TEXTILE PRDTS.	335	3931	0	5722	4956	0	3362	6	176
18 APPAREL	205	3160	9	23901	4606	0	1498	178	197
19 MISC. TEXTILE PRDTS.	99	3085	37	9071	2081	0	691	63	362
20 LUMBER & WOOD PRDTS.	433	534	203	1659	2071	5	1093	195	11649
21 WOODEN CONTAINERS	10	26	0	31	20	12	23	0	11
22 HOUSEHOLD FURNITURE	381	2061	27	5022	10769	0	2597	215	603
23 OTHER FURNITURE	62	362	17	1871	412	4	1322	38	32
24 PAPER & ALLIED PRDTS.	1215	3840	0	7266	2364	1	5117	96	1625
25 PAPERBOARD CONTAINERS	82	2270	1	3088	610	0	2350	114	132
26 PRINTING & PUBLISHING	302	4000	138	27535	902	1	6813	553	549
27 CHEMICALS,SELECT. PRDTS.	82	10439	65	4373	881	107	4190	148	334
28 PLASTICS & SYNTHETICS	79	1346	0	1123	771	19	1317	0	22
29 DRUGS & COSMETICS	40	28147	2	23889	1169	0	9984	68	124
30 PAINT & ALLIED PRDTS.	8	4532	8	2172	349	0	3625	98	184
31 PETROLEUM, RELATED INDS.	15	12016	522	2252	72	312	8154	6511	177
32 RUBBER, MISC. PLASTICS	593	6411	58	5616	880	0	22294	1093	104
33 LEATHER TANNING & PRDTS.	-286	-530	0	-770	-67	0	-268	0	-13
34 FOOTWEAR, LEATHER PRDTS.	-2733	-1558	-20	-8193	-231	0	-1246	-59	-60
35 GLASS & GLASS PRDTS.	33	5655	4	4145	1186	0	10126	1614	204
36 STONE & CLAY PRDTS.	321	3320	245	4939	943	77	5938	629	514
37 PRIMARY IRON, STEEL MFR.	76	1253	0	4360	135	0	17986	125	272
38 PRIMARY NONFERROUS MFR.	189	10240	355	11156	874	0	9332	743	1066

39 METAL CONTAINERS	0	3054	0	1419	6	0	1558	33	221
40 FABRICATED METAL PRDTS.	119	3432	68	5982	1035	59	9191	1544	806
41 SCREW MACH. PRDTS., ETC.	89	2617	17	3973	217	3	8149	77	46
42 OTHER FAB. METAL PRDTS.	162	5784	7	6666	726	3	10366	441	321
43 ENGINES & TURBINES	1	52	0	2588	1	0	692	1	8
44 FARM MACH. & EQUIP.	2	61	6	816	332	116	2644	113	118
45 CONSTRUC. MACH. & EQUIP.	320	613	19	465	21	2	5511	1793	132
46 MATERIAL HANDLING MACH.	0	1131	0	1129	14	2	1682	19	303
47 METALWORKING MACHINERY	146	1518	16	3596	102	18	10297	26	25
48 SPECIAL MACH. & EQUIP.	389	1705	6	2246	926	3	2644	66	305
49 GENERAL MACH. & EQUIP.	215	2990	1	4314	60	1	6114	449	51
50 MACHINE SHOP PRDTS.	21	317	25	807	56	5	819	55	83
51 OFFICE, COMPUT. MACHINES	47	1511	8	11386	91	0	2507	18	2
52 SERVICE IND. MACHINES	90	2186	20	6496	398	0	5233	321	102
53 ELECT. TRANSMISS. EQUIP.	245	1059	1	2542	386	0	3122	74	199
54 HOUSEHOLD APPLIANCES	8	2430	0	7389	2363	0	50488	110	212
55 ELECTRIC LIGHTING EQUIP.	30	2520	0	3267	223	0	3246	4	17
56 RADIO, TV, ETC., EQUIP.	737	16175	40	22513	3083	0	4902	2287	22
57 ELECTRONIC COMPONENTS	-110	-743	-3	-1261	-103	0	-345	-11	-2
58 MISC. ELECTRICAL MACH.	11	1242	4	1906	910	0	3268	87	116
59 MOTOR VEHICLES, EQUIP.	4	11597	42	29023	594	0	81425	963	1354
60 AIRCRAFT & PARTS	0	8670	3	28355	466	0	25354	12101	455
61 OTHER TRANSPORT. EQUIP.	19	1753	5	2263	233	4	1740	151	589
62 PROFESS., SCIEN. INSTRU.	48	3674	53	6607	487	1	2349	140	112
63 MEDICAL, PHOTO. EQUIP.	38	718	0	7778	125	0	55	1	59
64 MISC. MANUFACTURING	185	3452	31	11666	295	37	2427	128	165
65 TRANSPORT. & WAREHOUSING	201	6300	596	19547	2337	375	7599	1811	1905
66 COMMUNICA., EXC. BRDCAST.	0	0	0	0	0	0	0	0	0
67 RADIO & TV BROADCASTING	0	0	0	0	0	0	0	0	0
68 ELEC.,GAS,WATER,SAN.SER.	0	0	0	0	0	0	0	0	0
69 WHOLESALE & RETAIL TRADE	891	12239	1233	44819	6309	1051	16189	3355	3667
70 FINANCE & INSURANCE	0	0	0	0	0	0	0	0	0
71 REAL ESTATE & RENTAL	0	0	0	0	0	0	0	0	0
72 HOTELS; PERSONAL SERV.	0	0	0	0	0	0	0	0	0
73 BUSINESS SERVICES	0	0	0	0	0	0	0	0	0
74 RESEARCH & DEVELOPMENT	0	0	0	0	0	0	0	0	0
75 AUTO. REPAIR & SERVICES	0	0	0	0	0	0	0	0	0
76 AMUSEMENTS	23	182	17	1574	55	8	223	36	36
77 MED.,EDUC. SERVICES	0	0	0	0	0	0	0	0	0
78 FEDERAL GOV'T ENTERPRISE	0	0	0	0	0	0	0	0	0
79 STATE & LOCAL GOV'T ENT.	0	0	0	0	0	0	0	0	0
80 IMPORTS	0	0	0	0	0	0	0	0	0
81 BUS.TRAVEL, ENT., GIFTS.	0	0	0	0	0	0	0	0	0
82 OFFICE SUPPLIES	0	0	0	0	0	0	0	0	0
83 SCRAP & USED GOODS	0	0	0	0	0	0	0	0	0
84 GOVERNMENT INDUSTRY	0	0	0	0	0	0	0	0	0
85 REST OF WORLD INDUSTRY	0	0	0	0	0	0	0	0	0
86 HOUSEHOLD INDUSTRY	0	0	0	0	0	0	0	0	0
87 INVENTORY VALUATION ADJ.	0	0	0	0	0	0	0	0	0
88 STATE TOTAL	2468	220962	10736	466381	101214	-57122	441616	31083	72156

323

TABLE C.9

STATE ESTIMATES OF 1963
NET INVENTORY CHANGE
(THOUSANDS OF CURRENT DOLLARS)

INDUSTRY TITLE	37 PENNSYL-VANIA	38 RHODE ISLAND	39 SOUTH CAROLINA	40 SOUTH DAKOTA	41 TENNESSEE	42 TEXAS	43 UTAH	44 VERMONT	45 VIRGINIA
1 LIVESTOCK & PRDTS.	-9943	-269	1380	57921	10743	8328	3197	-3352	-14189
2 OTHER AGRICULTURE PRDTS.	29506	-178	15282	22975	72379	-208119	2221	-1357	-89557
3 FORESTRY & FISHERIES	404	212	1054	21	302	1969	18	102	1799
4 AGRI.,FORES.,FISH. SERV.	0	0	0	0	0	0	0	0	0
5 IRON, FERRO. ORES MINING	-2914	0	-1	-2	-7	-492	-834	0	-59
6 NONFERROUS ORES MINING	-9	0	0	-69	-38	-13	-610	0	-15
7 COAL MINING	14	0	0	0	1	0	1	0	3
8 CRUDE PETRO.,NATURAL GAS	72	2	0	7	0	5856	152	8	1
9 STONE & CLAY MINING	65	0	19	0	34	43	5	5	39
10 CHEM.&FERT. MIN. MINING	-6	0	-1	0	-39	-76	-10	0	-1
11 NEW CONSTRUCTION	0	0	0	0	0	0	0	0	0
12 MAINT. & REPAIR CONSTR.	0	0	0	0	0	0	0	0	0
13 ORDNANCE & ACCESSORIES	-541	0	0	0	-318	-277	-651	0	-4
14 FOOD & KINDRED PRDTS.	30742	1327	3073	3807	11827	26077	2864	1410	7757
15 TOBACCO MANUFACTURES	1227		306		186	17	0	0	4473
16 FABRICS	1488	957	7670	0	657	297	2	20	1229
17 TEXTILE PRDTS.	7615	1462	6183	0	1782	392	13	78	2125
18 APPAREL	7056	225	1014	0	2797	1534	91	82	1128
19 MISC. TEXTILE PRDTS.	1856	77	524	13	664	850	23	6	378
20 LUMBER & WOOD PRDTS.	1365	36	1176	71	1291	1641	100	278	1674
21 WOODEN CONTAINERS	21	1	19	0	40	18	0	3	28
22 HOUSEHOLD FURNITURE	3727	29	696	16	3634	1907	155	425	5243
23 OTHER FURNITURE	1188	97	42	1	202	407	29	1	282
24 PAPER & ALLIED PRDTS.	5460	142	1667	1	2252	1649	34	487	2494
25 PAPERBOARD CONTAINERS	2447	130	462	6	444	722	18	71	365
26 PRINTING & PUBLISHING	7370	385	306	132	1439	2875	304	190	1000
27 CHEMICALS,SELECT. PRDTS.	3465	257	366	20	2808	15825	106	28	1643
28 PLASTICS & SYNTHETICS	1827	198	963	0	2454	2101	0	17	3276
29 DRUGS & COSMETICS	11871	164	682	18	2049	2192	54	8	1645
30 PAINT & ALLIED PRDTS.	2549	115	57	0	358	1863	28	64	185
31 PETROLEUM, RELATED INDS.	11568	262	177	4	388	49193	1396	4	640
32 RUBBER, MISC. PLASTICS	5859	1810	702	40	1995	2270	134	255	929
33 LEATHER TANNING & PRDTS.	-556	-2	-9	0	-321	-27	-4	-33	-106
34 FOOTWEAR, LEATHER PRDTS.	-4219	-180	0	0	-2680	-450	-7	-77	-654
35 GLASS & GLASS PRDTS.	9657	800	1318	0	2665	831	6	0	528
36 STONE & CLAY PRDTS.	5241	101	467	119	1217	4002	515	310	1376
37 PRIMARY IRON, STEEL MFR.	24193	316	105	0	474	1560	727	14	392
38 PRIMARY NONFERROUS MFR.	6958	1958	159	0	2889	5320	1277	112	790

#	Industry	(1)	(2)	(3)	(4)	(5)	(6)	(7)	(8)	(9)
39	METAL CONTAINERS	1909	0	8	0	153	1294	79	0	120
40	FABRICATED METAL PRDTS.	9235	169	490	124	1994	4200	566	53	1483
41	SCREW MACH. PRDTs., ETC.	5538	413	137	0	462	317	10	10	45
42	OTHER FAB. METAL PRDTS.	7391	691	276	22	896	2349	45	55	760
43	ENGINES & TURBINES	3733	1	0	0	1	228	0	0	0
44	FARM MACH. & EQUIP.	1664	2	45	70	1030	435	27	7	131
45	CONSTRUC. MACH. & EQUIP.	2163	4	6	0	95	5991	439	24	78
46	MATERIAL HANDLING MACH.	1314	5	43	35	195	188	2	0	45
47	METALWORKING MACHINERY	4258	700	383	41	119	299	18	861	23
48	SPECIAL MACH. & EQUIP.	1975	363	586	2	153	539	27	29	87
49	GENERAL MACH. & EQUIP.	3857	142	149	29	218	753	77	7	145
50	MACHINE SHOP PRDTS.	447	38	36	13	75	256	16	7	42
51	OFFICE, COMPUT. MACHINES	2017	3	109	0	646	104	3	284	534
52	SERVICE IND. MACHINES	4054	53	45	0	250	2595	176	80	429
53	ELECT. TRANSMISS. EQUIP.	2949	21	111	0	7179	212	23	7	445
54	HOUSEHOLD APPLIANCES	5102	165	368	0	208	1222	0	0	31
55	ELECTRIC LIGHTING EQUIP.	3040	505	12	-1	1853	179	8	69	13
56	RADIO, TV, ETC., EQUIP.	3650	184	19	-5	-40	3723	193	0	1511
57	ELECTRONIC COMPONENTS	-1239	-54	-90	15	229	-111	-23	-35	-207
58	MISC. ELECTRICAL MACH.	1569	147	6	29	1412	476	4	99	61
59	MOTOR VEHICLES, EQUIP.	15628	192	97	2	1672	10364	55	0	3730
60	AIRCRAFT & PARTS	19869	209	133	15	650	16497	5973	1859	594
61	OTHER TRANSPORT. EQUIP.	5274	79	348	247	710	1595	88	4	1150
62	PROFESS., SCIEN. INSTRU.	6668	491	85	0	2	850	18	140	140
63	MEDICAL, PHOTO. EQUIP.	245	69	405	0	703	53	2	30	149
64	MISC. MANUFACTURING	3654	2057	810	0	2149	548	101	55	526
65	TRANSPORT. & WAREHOUSING	9635	442	0	0	0	8620	818	217	3136
66	COMMUNICA.,EXC. BRDCAST.	0	0	0	0	0	0	0	0	0
67	RADIO & TV BROADCASTING	0	0	0	0	0	0	0	0	0
68	ELEC.,GAS,WATER,SAN.SER.	0	0	0	0	0	0	0	0	0
69	WHOLESALE & RETAIL TRADE	17987	1425	2506	981	5324	16297	1476	528	5370
70	FINANCE & INSURANCE	0	0	0	0	0	0	0	0	0
71	REAL ESTATE & RENTAL	0	0	0	0	0	0	0	0	0
72	HOTELS; PERSONAL SERV.	0	0	0	0	0	0	0	0	0
73	BUSINESS SERVICES	0	0	0	0	0	0	0	0	0
74	RESEARCH & DEVELOPMENT	0	0	0	0	0	0	0	0	0
75	AUTO. REPAIR & SERVICES	0	0	0	0	0	0	0	0	0
76	AMUSEMENTS	0	0	0	0	0	0	0	0	0
77	MED.,EDUC. SERVICES	187	29	23	14	47	153	23	11	52
78	FEDERAL GOV'T ENTERPRISE	0	0	0	0	0	0	0	0	0
79	STATE & LOCAL GOV'T ENT.	0	0	0	0	0	0	0	0	0
80	IMPORTS	0	0	0	0	0	0	0	0	0
81	BUS.TRAVEL, ENT., GIFTS.	0	0	0	0	0	0	0	0	0
82	OFFICE SUPPLIES	0	0	0	0	0	0	0	0	0
83	SCRAP & USED GOODS	0	0	0	0	0	0	0	0	0
84	GOVERNMENT INDUSTRY	0	0	0	0	0	0	0	0	0
85	REST OF WORLD INDUSTRY	0	0	0	0	0	0	0	0	0
86	HOUSEHOLD INDUSTRY	0	0	0	0	0	0	0	0	0
87	INVENTORY VALUATION ADJ.	0	0	0	0	0	0	0	0	0
88	STATE TOTAL	310396	18979	53004	86736	152953	10511	21598	3555	-42540

TABLE C.9

STATE ESTIMATES OF 1963
NET INVENTORY CHANGE
(THOUSANDS OF CURRENT DOLLARS)

INDUSTRY TITLE	46 WASHINGTON	47 WEST VIRGINIA	48 WISCONSIN	49 WYOMING	50 ALASKA	51 HAWAII	52 NO STATE ALLOCATION	53 NATIONAL TOTAL
1 LIVESTOCK & PRDTS.	8568	-2076	-6429	18430	130	1347	0	374438
2 OTHER AGRICULTURE PRDTS.	12051	-3669	-105740	10028	-3	-3240	0	584252
3 FORESTRY & FISHERIES	4031	200	357	20	2540	135	0	44388
4 AGRI.,FORES.,FISH. SERV.	0	0	0	0	0	0	0	-55218
5 IRON, FERRO. ORES MINING	-50	0	-60	-1158	-24	0	0	-3404
6 NONFERROUS ORES MINING	-29	0	-5	-165	-16	0	0	52
7 COAL MINING	0	15	0	0	0	0	0	15689
8 CRUDE PETRO.,NATURAL GAS	11	109	0	551	21	4	0	1214
9 STONE & CLAY MINING	14	14	33	12	1	0	0	-653
10 CHEM.&FERT. MIN. MINING	0	0	0	-20	0	0	0	0
11 NEW CONSTRUCTION	0	0	0	0	0	0	0	0
12 MAINT. & REPAIR CONSTR.	-41	-498	-94	0	0	0	0	-26079
13 ORDNANCE & ACCESSORIES	9089	1640	22064	633	704	4415	0	583243
14 FOOD & KINDRED PRDTS.	0	81	2	0	0	0	0	22927
15 TOBACCO MANUFACTURES	0	0	0	0	0	0	0	32589
16 FABRICS	28	16	32	0	0	1	0	82639
17 TEXTILE PRDTS.	72	3	1143	0	0	10	0	67002
18 APPAREL	192	163	540	0	0	90	0	39584
19 MISC. TEXTILE PRDTS.	225	24	215	1	0	25	0	62527
20 LUMBER & WOOD PRDTS.	5867	444	1548	116	96	61	0	804
21 WOODEN CONTAINERS	20	2	24	0	0	0	0	73137
22 HOUSEHOLD FURNITURE	514	140	921	1	0	113	0	13881
23 OTHER FURNITURE	95	37	315	1	0	26	0	89509
24 PAPER & ALLIED PRDTS.	4983	195	7815	0	0	55	0	32602
25 PAPERBOARD CONTAINERS	431	92	1195	0	0	27	0	108962
26 PRINTING & PUBLISHING	840	344	2433	58	26	164	0	88263
27 CHEMICALS,SELECT. PRDTS.	1342	7273	454	8	0	122	0	25463
28 PLASTICS & SYNTHETICS	82	1447	102	0	0	0	0	160037
29 DRUGS & COSMETICS	98	154	3028	0	0	30	0	38811
30 PAINT & ALLIED PRDTS.	259	28	696	0	0	0	0	177143
31 PETROLEUM, RELATED INDS.	1929	599	487	3164	0	270	0	105471
32 RUBBER, MISC. PLASTICS	125	77	2030	1	0	11	0	-7763
33 LEATHER TANNING & PRDTS.	-7	-112	-1055	0	0	0	0	-47564
34 FOOTWEAR, LEATHER PRDTS.	-42	-60	-2034	0	0	-25	0	68473
35 GLASS & GLASS PRDTS.	183	5999	101	0	0	12	0	70506
36 STONE & CLAY PRDTS.	877	610	1304	154	47	202	0	102438
37 PRIMARY IRON, STEEL MFR.	226	2293	1703	0	0	24	0	121510
38 PRIMARY NONFERROUS MFR.	4077	2100	1455	3	0	1	0	

	Code	Description								
39	METAL CONTAINERS	571	177	1131	0	0	239	0	27716
40	FABRICATED METAL PRDTS.	851	712	3024	8	0	62	0	86406
41	SCREW MACH. PRDTS., ETC.	84	234	2848	7	0	0	0	55812
42	OTHER FAB. METAL PRDTS.	243	731	1772	6	0	10	0	92714
43	ENGINES & TURBINES	4	0	5229	0	0	0	0	27190
44	FARM MACH. & EQUIP.	116	147	4726	0	0	11	0	46081
45	CONSTRUC. MACH. & EQUIP.	361	600	4930	11	0	1	0	52243
46	MATERIAL HANDLING MACH.	189	35	275	0	0	1	0	11990
47	METALWORKING MACHINERY	93	197	2026	0	0	2	0	55734
48	SPECIAL MACH. & EQUIP.	194	18	1603	1	0	35	0	25060
49	GENERAL MACH. & EQUIP.	59	9	2240	4	0	1	0	42948
50	MACHINE SHOP PRDTS.	105	39	211	4	0	6	0	8870
51	OFFICE, COMPUT. MACHINES	58		105	0	0	0	0	40980
52	SERVICE IND. MACHINES	158	77	2231	0	0	5	0	51765
53	ELECT. TRANSMISS. EQUIP.	66	88	1839	2	0	5	0	22814
54	HOUSEHOLD APPLIANCES	353	80	8481	1	0	1	0	211167
55	ELECTRIC LIGHTING EQUIP.	112	759	238	1	0	0	0	27347
56	RADIO, TV, ETC. EQUIP.	199	7	2500	0	0	2	0	151135
57	ELECTRONIC COMPONENTS	-6	-19	-81	0	0	3	0	-9272
58	MISC. ELECTRICAL MACH.	28	0	1282	0	0	0	0	28103
59	MOTOR VEHICLES, EQUIP.	1029	414	36532	0	0	14	0	611256
60	AIRCRAFT & PARTS	12205	3	143	46	0	0	0	341636
61	OTHER TRANSPORT. EQUIP.	2190	400	1164	1	0	15	0	45786
62	PROFESS., SCIEN. INSTRU.	33	170	1747	19	0	0	0	55960
63	MEDICAL, PHOTO. EQUIP.	12	23	28	0	0	1	0	13820
64	MISC. MANUFACTURING	214	85	1057	1	0	20	0	49439
65	TRANSPORT. & WAREHOUSING	2992	1411	2302	336	446	766	0	152145
66	COMMUNICA.,EXC. BRDCAST.	0	0	0	0	0	0	0	0
67	RADIO & TV BROADCASTING	0	0	0	0	0	0	0	0
68	ELEC.,GAS,WATER,SAN.SER.	0	0	0	0	0	0	0	0
69	WHOLESALE & RETAIL TRADE	5216	1912	6285	482	327	933	0	324763
70	FINANCE & INSURANCE	0	0	0	0	0	0	0	0
71	REAL ESTATE & RENTAL	0	0	0	0	0	0	0	0
72	HOTELS; PERSONAL SERV.	0	0	0	0	0	0	0	0
73	BUSINESS SERVICES	0	0	0	0	0	0	0	0
74	RESEARCH & DEVELOPMENT	0	0	0	0	0	0	0	0
75	AUTO. REPAIR & SERVICES	0	0	0	0	0	0	0	0
76	AMUSEMENTS	61	37	64	7	5	18	0	5999
77	MED.,EDUC. SERVICES	0	0	0	0	0	0	0	0
78	FEDERAL GOV'T ENTERPRISE	0	0	0	0	0	0	0	0
79	STATE & LOCAL GOV'T ENT.	0	0	0	0	0	0	0	0
80	IMPORTS	0	0	0	0	0	0	21000	21000
81	BUS.TRAVEL, ENT., GIFTS.	0	0	0	0	0	0	0	0
82	OFFICE SUPPLIES	0	0	0	0	0	0	0	0
83	SCRAP & USED GOODS	0	0	0	0	0	0	105518	105518
84	GOVERNMENT INDUSTRY	0	0	0	0	0	0	0	0
85	REST OF WORLD INDUSTRY	0	0	0	0	0	0	0	0
86	HOUSEHOLD INDUSTRY	0	0	0	0	0	0	0	0
87	INVENTORY VALUATION ADJ.	0	0	0	0	0	0	-502000	-502000
88	STATE TOTAL	83850	26030	43370	32770	4300	6025	-375482	5329000

TABLE C.10

STATE ESTIMATES OF 1947
NET FOREIGN EXPORTS BY STATE OF PRODUCTION
(THOUSANDS OF CURRENT DOLLARS)

	INDUSTRY TITLE	1 ALABAMA	2 ARIZONA	3 ARKANSAS	4 CALIFORNIA	5 COLORADO	6 CONNECTICUT	7 DELAWARE	8 DISTRICT OF COLUMBIA	9 FLORIDA
1	LIVESTOCK & PRDTS.	841	162	578	4307	719	71	355	0	182
2	OTHER AGRICULTURE PRDTS.	28324	33387	65748	199808	13714	3076	2435	0	22429
3	FORESTRY & FISHERIES	661	592	709	2392	657	61	25	0	728
4	AGRI.,FORES.,FISH. SERV.	0	0	0	484	0	0	0	0	0
5	IRON, FERRO. ORES MINING	782	111	0	6026	2355	0	0	0	0
6	NONFERROUS ORES MINING	0	2467	16381	16642	3101	0	0	0	0
7	COAL MINING	9191	0	893	2241	615	0	0	0	0
8	CRUDE PETRO.,NATURAL GAS	0	0	1404	1067	173	0	0	0	0
9	STONE & CLAY MINING	196	0	0	0	0	0	0	0	6357
10	CHEM.&FERT. MIN. MINING	0	0	116	0	0	0	0	0	0
11	NEW CONSTRUCTION	0	0	0	0	0	0	0	0	0
12	MAINT. & REPAIR CONSTR.	0	0	0	0	0	0	0	0	0
13	ORDNANCE & ACCESSORIES	0	3426	0	903	65	4534	3098	3446	0
14	FOOD & KINDRED PRDTS.	8981	0	24887	158101	18714	3778	56	0	9008
15	TOBACCO MANUFACTURES	33	0	16	831	264	574	795	2	733
16	FABRICS	49995	0	1286	2658	437	26293	135	0	75
17	TEXTILE PRDTS.	1997	0	37	2582	264	5805	389	0	136
18	APPAREL	1842	10	305	9745	188	3328	11	41	303
19	MISC. TEXTILE PRDTS.	1394	21	15	1870	617	633	185	68	167
20	LUMBER & WOOD PRDTS.	7634	758	7608	13452	40	216	0	7	2774
21	WOODEN CONTAINERS	137	52	55	733	25	89	2	0	414
22	HOUSEHOLD FURNITURE	142	14	183	1618	20	148	7	7	114
23	OTHER FURNITURE	12	5	4	333		27	1	5	23
24	PAPER & ALLIED PRDTS.	1799	75	1052	2748	86	2023	302	150	2214
25	PAPERBOARD CONTAINERS	228	0	106	1379	10	748	48	107	101
26	PRINTING & PUBLISHING	322	143	166	4589	362	1068	85	1036	570
27	CHEMICALS,SELECT. PRDTS.	9723	241	4389	21554	1568	3512	2098	20	7326
28	PLASTICS & SYNTHETICS	0	0	892	1597	0	1156	4075	0	272
29	DRUGS & COSMETICS	118	24	59	10174	220	4259	40	142	196
30	PAINT & ALLIED PRDTS.	126	23	11	3556	191	418	11	21	108
31	PETROLEUM, RELATED INDS.	326	200	3373	67169	872	57	235	69	69
32	RUBBER, MISC. PLASTICS	3939	1	193	11810	411	8158	555	6	392
33	LEATHER TANNING & PRDTS.	0	0	0	777	4	158	1542	0	102
34	FOOTWEAR, LEATHER PRDTS.	57	15	132	929	245	883	0	0	25
35	GLASS & GLASS PRDTS.	8	3	479	3172	242	464	0	0	147
36	STONE & CLAY PRDTS.	1924	100	431	7008	506	1501	61	35	272
37	PRIMARY IRON, STEEL MFR.	23065	228	14	16022	3629	4689	1030	0	10
38	PRIMARY NONFERROUS MFR.	4337	9721	2281	6620	1225	16483	0	0	28

#	Industry	1	2	3	4	5	6	7	8	9
39	METAL CONTAINERS	70	0	54	2496	49	24	18	0	189
40	FABRICATED METAL PRDTS.	1742	378	173	9117	551	3549	429	135	466
41	SCREW MACH. PRDTS., ETC.	219	2	2	1352	0	3138	172	0	3
42	OTHER FAB. METAL PRDTS.	1289	32	67	6531	290	16747	118	77	140
43	ENGINES & TURBINES	0	0	0	6851	66	4767	0	0	0
44	FARM MACH. & EQUIP.	569	17	711	4045	343	308	17	0	248
45	CONSTRUC. MACH. & EQUIP.	1079	0	738	23114	3410	2542	0	0	376
46	MATERIAL HANDLING MACH.	223	0	422	1931	188	153	0	0	8
47	METALWORKING MACHINERY	7	5	0	1997	0	19175	538	0	3
48	SPECIAL MACH. & EQUIP.	802	92	113	14668	1669	9612	1676	6	1096
49	GENERAL MACH. & EQUIP.	825	0	74	8238	171	12436	46	2	289
50	MACHINE SHOP PRDTS.	6	2	1	166	9	63	4	0	4
51	OFFICE, COMPUT. MACHINES	70	0	52	3334	44	15410	6	6	10
52	SERVICE IND. MACHINES	345	127	0	2442	12	292	30	0	30
53	ELECT. TRANSMISS. EQUIP.	233	83	24	3939	124	2542	20	0	59
54	HOUSEHOLD APPLIANCES	184	6	7	4270	20	7557	22	0	31
55	ELECTRIC LIGHTING EQUIP.	335	16	0	2930	74	4244	0	82	26
56	RADIO, TV, ETC., EQUIP.	130	6	0	2415	208	2908	0	31	45
57	ELECTRONIC COMPONENTS	14	0	0	1141	6	1035	0	14	17
58	MISC. ELECTRICAL MACH.	0	0	453	1187	37	977	377	0	790
59	MOTOR VEHICLES, EQUIP.	916	522	0	22386	418	3322	0	0	981
60	AIRCRAFT & PARTS	0	47	260	46643	93	13144	28	0	28
61	OTHER TRANSPORT. EQUIP.	5173	344	151	15461	1320	1607	1238	103	2279
62	PROFESS., SCIEN. INSTRU.	44	93	0	5312	132	8224	79	11	73
63	MEDICAL, PHOTO. EQUIP.	63	0	0	1605	255	602	0	0	29
64	MISC. MANUFACTURING	4	4	120	4291	452	6373	334	36	336
65	TRANSPORT. & WAREHOUSING	43087	3212	9574	146785	7064	7130	877	226	51971
66	COMMUNICA., EXC. BRDCAST.	25	9	14	1022	16	96	11	14	24
67	RADIO & TV BROADCASTING	0	0	0	0	0	0	0	0	0
68	ELEC., GAS, WATER, SAN. SER.	139	139	0	405	0	0	0	0	0
69	WHOLESALE & RETAIL TRADE	16529	2605	7126	55591	3691	22766	1698	371	3972
70	FINANCE & INSURANCE	810	324	737	6335	554	1009	158	316	1460
71	REAL ESTATE & RENTAL	531	51	162	2418	174	1149	111	60	212
72	HOTELS; PERSONAL SERV.	0	0	0	0	0	0	0	0	0
73	BUSINESS SERVICES	229	87	87	6126	269	585	68	355	644
74	RESEARCH & DEVELOPMENT	0	0	0	0	0	0	0	0	0
75	AUTO. REPAIR & SERVICES	0	0	0	0	0	0	0	0	0
76	AMUSEMENTS	30	19	0	29142	1948	392	0	1796	1192
77	MED., EDUC. SERVICES	0	0	0	0	0	0	0	0	0
78	FEDERAL GOV'T ENTERPRISE	118	28	89	563	78	104	17	135	129
79	STATE & LOCAL GOV'T ENT.	0	0	0	0	0	0	0	0	0
80	IMPORTS	0	0	0	0	0	0	0	0	0
81	BUS. TRAVEL, ENT., GIFTS.	0	0	0	0	0	0	0	0	0
82	OFFICE SUPPLIES	0	0	0	0	0	0	0	0	0
83	SCRAP & USED GOODS	11655	1481	4521	48367	3532	20389	1751	492	2915
84	GOVERNMENT INDUSTRY	0	0	0	0	0	0	0	0	0
85	REST OF WORLD INDUSTRY	0	0	0	0	0	0	0	0	0
86	HOUSEHOLD INDUSTRY	0	0	0	0	0	0	0	0	0
87	INVENTORY VALUATION ADJ.	0	0	0	0	0	0	0	0	0
88	STATE TOTAL	245493	61508	159535	1079512	78813	288591	27406	9361	125350

TABLE C.10

STATE ESTIMATES OF 1947
NET FOREIGN EXPORTS BY STATE OF PRODUCTION
(THOUSANDS OF CURRENT DOLLARS)

INDUSTRY TITLE	10 GEORGIA	11 IDAHO	12 ILLINOIS	13 INDIANA	14 IOWA	15 KANSAS	16 KENTUCKY	17 LOUISIANA	18 MAINE
1 LIVESTOCK & PRDTS.	1175	213	1003	628	2371	578	628	253	91
2 OTHER AGRICULTURE PRDTS.	40244	15828	99455	45819	51522	56136	16469	48702	1922
3 FORESTRY & FISHERIES	762	790	108	120	85	43	371	635	639
4 AGRI.,FORES.,FISH. SERV.	118	236	0	0	0	0	0	0	0
5 IRON, FERRO. ORES MINING	0	0	0	0	0	0	0	0	0
6 NONFERROUS ORES MINING	0	2745	0	0	0	0	0	0	0
7 COAL MINING	0	0	32539	12528	885	1327	39170	0	0
8 CRUDE PETRO.,NATURAL GAS	0	0	4703	420	0	5753	1084	8899	0
9 STONE & CLAY MINING	168	169	312	201	174	0	196	0	0
10 CHEM.&FERT. MIN. MINING	0	951	178	0	0	0	79	4620	0
11 NEW CONSTRUCTION	0	0	0	0	0	0	0	0	0
12 MAINT. & REPAIR CONSTR.	0	0	0	0	0	0	0	0	0
13 ORDNANCE & ACCESSORIES	0	868	868	13	0	0	0	0	0
14 FOOD & KINDRED PRDTS.	21739	17066	182541	51229	67754	104106	22913	56640	8730
15 TOBACCO MANUFACTURES	942	0	99	117	1	0	29802	37	1
16 FABRICS	93741	0	3243	1150	48	337	3411	1430	17700
17 TEXTILE PRDTS.	2096	0	2729	1392	110	598	298	1557	1210
18 APPAREL	4923	6	13072	3282	649	289	1890	845	585
19 MISC. TEXTILE PRDTS.	4567	9	3998	549	431	329	410	467	1741
20 LUMBER & WOOD PRDTS.	5430	2856	2023	2715	458	134	2879	6532	3366
21 WOODEN CONTAINERS	342	14	536	200	56	27	360	348	256
22 HOUSEHOLD FURNITURE	368	2	3238	1827	107	63	619	72	72
23 OTHER FURNITURE	40	3	820	247	44	43	17	9	7
24 PAPER & ALLIED PRDTS.	1869	0	5625	2142	313	273	116	5220	7187
25 PAPERBOARD CONTAINERS	525	0	3165	792	100	151	105	352	286
26 PRINTING & PUBLISHING	538	81	10139	1445	735	424	533	345	136
27 CHEMICALS,SELECT. PRDTS.	9685	48	23922	3719	937	4362	1848	17839	377
28 PLASTICS & SYNTHETICS	892	0	802	520	520	1527	948	1562	1562
29 DRUGS & COSMETICS	731	35	23402	26411	2523	30	140	246	106
30 PAINT & ALLIED PRDTS.	245	0	5808	925	263	0	1017	257	31
31 PETROLEUM, RELATED INDS.	367	200	36575	45538	210	14824	3123	46508	67
32 RUBBER, MISC. PLASTICS	585	0	4824	6185	2616	1364	1858	0	81
33 LEATHER TANNING & PRDTS.	164	0	3296	218	111	0	177	18	319
34 FOOTWEAR, LEATHER PRDTS.	380	14	4039	357	22	21	467	21	2252
35 GLASS & GLASS PRDTS.	8	0	5248	5461	0	0	158	209	23
36 STONE & CLAY PRDTS.	1911	81	6979	3125	1294	1008	1042	589	173
37 PRIMARY IRON, STEEL MFR.	1069	3	51820	61214	523	70	5755	53	11
38 PRIMARY NONFERROUS MFR.	1063	1125	19644	6427	139	100	4351	456	230

#	Industry									
39	METAL CONTAINERS	87	0	4694	253	95	0	13	0	49
40	FABRICATED METAL PRDTS.	697	48	8167	5277	1886	750	1029	0	170
41	SCREW MACH. PRDTS., ETC.	106	0	7686	2292	51	18	304	0	4
42	OTHER FAB. METAL PRDTS.	232	0	24698	4768	1417	72	1318	0	5469
43	ENGINES & TURBINES	0	0	17849	12941	538	66	0	0	0
44	FARM MACH. & EQUIP.	850	238	85541	9047	20231	1254	1572	366	41
45	CONSTRUC. MACH. & EQUIP.	1752	121	65060	8780	18678	3290	1281	740	300
46	MATERIAL HANDLING MACH.	587	0	11886	1201	575	182	576	41	18
47	METALWORKING MACHINERY	18	0	22092	4841	629	47	1143	61	37
48	SPECIAL MACH. & EQUIP.	2850	0	31896	6712	3701	1215	564	0	9372
49	GENERAL MACH. & EQUIP.	195	72	14462	4692	1438	45	509	982	5
50	MACHINE SHOP PRDTS.	13	1	218	194	28	14	14	1719	1
51	OFFICE, COMPUT. MACHINES	260	0	7582	251	16	0	59	7	226
52	SERVICE IND. MACHINES	288	0	4306	11647	219	188	74	500	20
53	ELECT. TRANSMISS. EQUIP.	236	0	11013	7968	797	142	48	63	0
54	HOUSEHOLD APPLIANCES	24	0	16823	7823	2237	394	704	5	23
55	ELECTRIC LIGHTING EQUIP.	527	0	10071	4845	73	147	404	52	0
56	RADIO, TV, ETC., EQUIP.	130	0	37921	8371	893	39	13	22	0
57	ELECTRONIC COMPONENTS	949	0	7701	3534	267	522	522	0	0
58	MISC. ELECTRICAL MACH.	3613	25	7106	5600	438	14	777	2	15
59	MOTOR VEHICLES, EQUIP.	0	0	25509	84562	1069	108	3225	15	215
60	AIRCRAFT & PARTS	1257	344	1017	6064	549	4029	1111	215	0
61	OTHER TRANSPORT. EQUIP.	85	1	57071	14980	2033	5827	213	4862	1970
62	PROFESS., SCIEN. INSTRU.	0	39	12624	1491	85	2044	316	26	81
63	MEDICAL, PHOTO. EQUIP.	603	23	8845	3222	294	85	0	11	41
64	MISC. MANUFACTURING	12482	4631	16007	3022	3202	0	0	201	770
65	TRANSPORT. & WAREHOUSING	28	9	76137	33509	10166	150	33048	106560	7122
66	COMMUNICA.,EXC. BRDCAST.	0	0	219	76	33	14685	21	25	24
67	RADIO & TV BROADCASTING	0	4	0	0	0	24	0	0	0
68	ELEC.,GAS,WATER,SAN.SER.	20154	2034	0	0	0	0	11889	16075	5
69	WHOLESALE & RETAIL TRADE	1253	235	70508	38528	10414	0	994	1144	6067
70	FINANCE & INSURANCE	615	67	4514	1608	1025	8954	450	420	474
71	REAL ESTATE & RENTAL	0	0	4045	1798	406	1041	0	0	260
72	HOTELS; PERSONAL SERV.	570	77	0	0	0	279	274	405	0
73	BUSINESS SERVICES	0	0	11224	707	457	0	0	0	0
74	RESEARCH & DEVELOPMENT	0	0	0	0	0	121	0	0	0
75	AUTO. REPAIR & SERVICES	0	0	0	0	0	0	0	0	0
76	AMUSEMENTS	1600	0	0	0	0	0	30	1188	0
77	MED.,EDUC. SERVICES	0	0	4142	681	509	0	0	0	10
78	FEDERAL GOV'T ENTERPRISE	150	31	0	0	0	61	139	101	0
79	STATE & LOCAL GOV'T ENT.	0	0	634	197	166	0	0	0	63
80	IMPORTS	0	0	0	0	0	131	0	0	0
81	BUS.TRAVEL, ENT., GIFTS.	0	0	0	0	0	0	0	0	0
82	OFFICE SUPPLIES	0	0	0	0	0	0	0	0	0
83	SCRAP & USED GOODS	14918	2052	82369	39463	12448	13214	8800	13328	5587
84	GOVERNMENT INDUSTRY	0	0	0	0	0	0	0	0	0
85	REST OF WORLD INDUSTRY	0	0	0	0	0	0	0	0	0
86	HOUSEHOLD INDUSTRY	0	0	0	0	0	0	0	0	0
87	INVENTORY VALUATION ADJ.	0	0	0	0	0	0	0	0	0
88	STATE TOTAL	263817	53395	1328390	624861	232164	252548	213668	353858	85768

TABLE C.10

STATE ESTIMATES OF 1947
NET FOREIGN EXPORTS BY STATE OF PRODUCTION
(THOUSANDS OF CURRENT DOLLARS)

INDUSTRY TITLE	19 MARYLAND	20 MASSACHUSETTS	21 MICHIGAN	22 MINNESOTA	23 MISSISSIPPI	24 MISSOURI	25 MONTANA	26 NEBRASKA	27 NEVADA
1 LIVESTOCK & PRDTS.	345	10	882	2321	719	983	71	1226	0
2 OTHER AGRICULTURE PRDTS.	7626	2627	27555	41333	60109	45690	29606	38898	192
3 FORESTRY & FISHERIES	104	167	622	574	568	536	892	36	126
4 AGRI.,FORES.,FISH. SERV.	0	0	0	0	0	0	0	0	0
5 IRON, FERRO. ORES MINING	0	0	1034	6068	0	0	324	0	708
6 NONFERROUS ORES MINING	0	0	0	0	0	0	1965	0	1247
7 COAL MINING	979	0	0	0	0	1989	1614	0	0
8 CRUDE PETRO.,NATURAL GAS	0	0	1194	0	1184	0	556	0	0
9 STONE & CLAY MINING	0	0	87	0	0	350	0	0	0
10 CHEM.&FERT. MIN. MINING	0	0	0	0	0	117	299	0	0
11 NEW CONSTRUCTION	0	0	0	0	0	0	0	0	0
12 MAINT. & REPAIR CONSTR.	0	0	0	0	0	0	0	0	0
13 ORDNANCE & ACCESSORIES	0	1720	46	868	0	0	0	0	0
14 FOOD & KINDRED PRDTS.	27426	25208	50352	117233	6831	92706	9466	53351	264
15 TOBACCO MANUFACTURES	312	886	145	1	1	1117	0	0	0
16 FABRICS	4182	89093	699	770	3798	2084	0	112	0
17 TEXTILE PRDTS.	792	12230	1428	1170	178	3537	0	350	0
18 APPAREL	4417	9832	2081	2173	1477	6297	0	180	0
19 MISC. TEXTILE PRDTS.	775	2687	768	507	38	1525	0	136	4
20 LUMBER & WOOD PRDTS.	764	1292	4725	1112	6246	1665	1499	29	33
21 WOODEN CONTAINERS	194	408	412	136	327	222	6	22	0
22 HOUSEHOLD FURNITURE	191	870	1609	102	71	673	30	30	0
23 OTHER FURNITURE	36	196	1013	77	6	230	3	43	0
24 PAPER & ALLIED PRDTS.	1813	9433	8765	3198	2023	1025	0	0	0
25 PAPERBOARD CONTAINERS	179	2660	1993	429	16	1013	0	0	0
26 PRINTING & PUBLISHING	933	3218	2355	2031	114	1939	107	317	40
27 CHEMICALS,SELECT. PRDTS.	6578	8283	22080	935	11074	8588	1004	244	630
28 PLASTICS & SYNTHETICS	1783	5640	2228	2634	935	0	0	0	0
29 DRUGS & COSMETICS	2568	5850	17225	510	186	10599	0	1818	0
30 PAINT & ALLIED PRDTS.	532	1196	2829	3861	5	1561	0	11	0
31 PETROLEUM, RELATED INDS.	4978	2951	6188	2438	299	2380	2017	581	0
32 RUBBER, MISC. PLASTICS	2746	14125	14270	151	1640	1713	0	360	0
33 LEATHER TANNING & PRDTS.	131	7849	1576	260	15	141	0	76	0
34 FOOTWEAR, LEATHER PRDTS.	382	10347	312	271	151	5917	5	40	0
35 GLASS & GLASS PRDTS.	1039	1083	465	449	260	708	1	1	0
36 STONE & CLAY PRDTS.	933	6613	4028	2847	207	3435	126	277	59
37 PRIMARY IRON, STEEL MFR.	24847	7301	34556	199	242	5168	55	30	0
38 PRIMARY NONFERROUS MFR.	3290	4571	12683	0	13	2779	5762	136	1492

	39–88	(1)	(2)	(3)	(4)	(5)	(6)	(7)	(8)	(9)
39	METAL CONTAINERS	1255	195	140	131	35	876	0	61	0
40	FABRICATED METAL PRDTS.	1942	3310	4670	2014	102	3069	80	633	38
41	SCREW MACH. PRDTS., ETC.	1350	2305	7066	476	143	427	20	2	0
42	OTHER FAB. METAL PRDTS.	502	10241	17721	1562	0	2836	0	175	0
43	ENGINES & TURBINES	1447	6132	27738	1966	0	1970	22	66	0
44	FARM MACH. & EQUIP.	1469	161	8865	7673	75	780	121	1375	0
45	CONSTRUC. MACH. & EQUIP.	270	653	15749	9545	567	2155	108	534	14
46	MATERIAL HANDLING MACH.	1189	1453	8887	947	0	727	0	72	0
47	METALWORKING MACHINERY	6374	10611	27126	1622	0	2490	0	180	0
48	SPECIAL MACH. & EQUIP.	1293	47401	11001	3276	378	6134	5	301	0
49	GENERAL MACH. & EQUIP.	5	7616	10472	539	167	1930	0	147	1
50	MACHINE SHOP PRDTS.	454	85	397	27	1	113	1	1	0
51	OFFICE, COMPUT. MACHINES	512	5859	8220	22	0	219	0	0	0
52	SERVICE IND. MACHINES	454	3435	9735	2602	0	1896	12	294	0
53	ELECT. TRANSMISS. EQUIP.	202	12867	6624	4000	18	6112	9	260	0
54	HOUSEHOLD APPLIANCES	2146	3272	10075	2280	0	2792	9	200	0
55	ELECTRIC LIGHTING EQUIP.	758	5636	1203	45	194	1917	0	48	0
56	RADIO, TV, ETC., EQUIP.	949	6095	2633	1753	0	399	0	581	0
57	ELECTRONIC COMPONENTS	4769	3982	908	126	0	72	0	76	0
58	MISC. ELECTRICAL MACH.	5057	749	1146	434	0	231	0	28	0
59	MOTOR VEHICLES, EQUIP.	9989	5120	560069	3299	695	26870	51	616	26
60	AIRCRAFT & PARTS	1523	3091	1936	562	0	517	3	160	0
61	OTHER TRANSPORT. EQUIP.	18	6693	6982	2603	2398	6904	45	200	0
62	PROFESS., SCIEN. INSTRU.	869	6145	2540	433	9	683	10	152	0
63	MEDICAL, PHOTO. EQUIP.	18	4469	1491	423	18	608	10	161	21
64	MISC. MANUFACTURING	869	9473	5457	4853	50	2707	10	247	247
65	TRANSPORT. & WAREHOUSING	218480	18448	40215	16988	7808	15501	6739	6024	247
66	COMMUNICA., EXC. BRDCAST.	40	1018	109	37	18	48	16	16	2
67	RADIO & TV BROADCASTING	0	0	0	0	0	0	0	0	0
68	ELEC.,GAS,WATER,SAN.SER.	0	0	37	0	10	0	6	6	0
69	WHOLESALE & RETAIL TRADE	12587	40270	76881	12124	6947	17361	2631	4328	269
70	FINANCE & INSURANCE	932	2233	2391	1080	609	1692	333	584	114
71	REAL ESTATE & RENTAL	689	2031	3148	618	183	981	55	158	10
72	HOTELS; PERSONAL SERV.	0	0	0	0	0	0	0	0	0
73	BUSINESS SERVICES	728	2244	6504	1080	109	2053	42	0	39
74	RESEARCH & DEVELOPMENT	0	0	0	0	0	0	0	0	0
75	AUTO. REPAIR & SERVICES	0	0	0	0	0	0	0	0	0
76	AMUSEMENTS	95	1790	2474	888	0	1886	0	219	0
77	MED.,EDUC. SERVICES	0	0	0	0	0	0	0	0	0
78	FEDERAL GOV'T ENTERPRISE	107	310	300	189	86	276	37	97	10
79	STATE & LOCAL GOV'T ENT.	0	0	0	0	0	0	0	0	0
80	IMPORTS	0	0	0	0	0	0	0	0	0
81	BUS.TRAVEL, ENT., GIFTS.	0	0	0	0	0	0	0	0	0
82	OFFICE SUPPLIES	0	0	0	0	0	0	0	0	0
83	SCRAP & USED GOODS	12027	35417	83898	17381	3489	20467	1807	5671	231
84	GOVERNMENT INDUSTRY	0	0	0	0	0	0	0	0	0
85	REST OF WORLD INDUSTRY	0	0	0	0	0	0	0	0	0
86	HOUSEHOLD INDUSTRY	0	0	0	0	0	0	0	0	0
87	INVENTORY VALUATION ADJ.	0	0	0	0	0	0	0	0	0
88	STATE TOTAL	391446	509156	1201013	298256	121495	342586	67521	121724	5817

TABLE C.10

STATE ESTIMATES OF 1947
NET FOREIGN EXPORTS BY STATE OF PRODUCTION
(THOUSANDS OF CURRENT DOLLARS)

INDUSTRY TITLE	28 NEW HAMPSHIRE	29 NEW JERSEY	30 NEW MEXICO	31 NEW YORK	32 NORTH CAROLINA	33 NORTH DAKOTA	34 OHIO	35 OKLAHOMA	36 OREGON
1 LIVESTOCK & PRDTS.	0	486	122	1398	790	91	1338	274	162
2 OTHER AGRICULTURE PRDTS.	513	4934	9484	20250	134188	34540	44793	35117	16213
3 FORESTRY & FISHERIES	163	87	566	497	697	18	176	294	2654
4 AGRI.,FORES.,FISH. SERV.	0	77	0	493	0	0	0	0	0
5 IRON, FERRO. ORES MINING	0	0	0	0	0	0	0	0	0
6 NONFERROUS ORES MINING	0	623	705	0	0	0	19140	1533	0
7 COAL MINING	0	0	0	786	0	691	752	8117	0
8 CRUDE PETRO.,NATURAL GAS	0	0	1817	207	1147	0	397	196	0
9 STONE & CLAY MINING	0	0	0	0	0	0	0	0	0
10 CHEM.&FERT. MIN. MINING	0	0	1113	0	0	0	0	0	0
11 NEW CONSTRUCTION	0	0	0	0	0	0	0	0	0
12 MAINT. & REPAIR CONSTR.	0	0	0	0	0	0	0	0	0
13 ORDNANCE & ACCESSORIES	0	13	0	1452	0	0	0	0	0
14 FOOD & KINDRED PRDTS.	749	31673	2274	139065	14679	11396	66466	38967	30474
15 TOBACCO MANUFACTURES	33	1889	0	1118	121293	1	1587	1	1
16 FABRICS	15024	49629	0	32939	162660	0	3533	646	666
17 TEXTILE PRDTS.	775	16231	0	19209	3032	55	7055	0	688
18 APPAREL	633	14700	33	100955	10351	0	6833	110	360
19 MISC. TEXTILE PRDTS.	161	1893	46	13088	7220	5	2098	74	192
20 LUMBER & WOOD PRDTS.	1384	2577	478	4225	6110	1	1779	387	21588
21 WOODEN CONTAINERS	261	364	30	591	406	6	506	0	272
22 HOUSEHOLD FURNITURE	82	663	8	3177	1521	1	2016	43	290
23 OTHER FURNITURE	11	250	2	2447	124	1	3188	10	34
24 PAPER & ALLIED PRDTS.	1881	6273	0	15655	3309	0	9349	50	2007
25 PAPERBOARD CONTAINERS	273	1973	0	6121	186	0	2555	45	122
26 PRINTING & PUBLISHING	196	2146	58	17968	427	70	4885	411	428
27 CHEMICALS,SELECT. PRDTS.	222	57931	1639	38575	1402	122	21643	1335	968
28 PLASTICS & SYNTHETICS	132	15640	0	6119	1164	0	2476	0	0
29 DRUGS & COSMETICS	100	42422	0	42207	1234	25	10313	97	122
30 PAINT & ALLIED PRDTS.	10	5313	1025	4865	164	23	4980	105	175
31 PETROLEUM, RELATED INDS.	0	48297	0	12056	0	74	17070	22932	298
32 RUBBER, MISC. PLASTICS	378	11494	0	8444	592	0	60975	1837	208
33 LEATHER TANNING & PRDTS.	744	2253	0	3216	550	0	1317	0	14
34 FOOTWEAR, LEATHER PRDTS.	2901	1486	24	11573	49	1	2556	41	74
35 GLASS & GLASS PRDTS.	0	5078	0	7187	82	0	12138	1140	17
36 STONE & CLAY PRDTS.	398	6182	57	12949	1202	10	11451	404	408
37 PRIMARY IRON, STEEL MFR.	260	10437	3	36577	115	0	121670	1321	3441
38 PRIMARY NONFERROUS MFR.	63	35588	2983	21468	586	0	7171	4830	546

	C1	C2	C3	C4	C5	C6	C7	C8	C9
39 METAL CONTAINERS	83	54	3591	0	0	1343	0	1538	0
40 FABRICATED METAL PRDTS.	1656	1332	10484	34	1117	9286	298	3955	81
41 SCREW MACH. PRDTS., ETC.	18	21	12302	1	11	4540	0	1188	138
42 OTHER FAB. METAL PRDTS.	629	303	18019	20	240	16632	0	9917	429
43 ENGINES & TURBINES	276	66	12539	0	0	7668	0	5157	14
44 FARM MACH. & EQUIP.	812	190	7254	65	458	9637	16	391	1044
45 CONSTRUC. MACH. & EQUIP.	1361	10704	46508	0	376	4531	0	6683	1801
46 MATERIAL HANDLING MACH.	197	385	15764	0	473	3735	0	4244	4817
47 METALWORKING MACHINERY	1189	53	50861	0	53	14947	5	8146	92
48 SPECIAL MACH. & EQUIP.	322	159	29479	0	2547	42738	32	16854	3
49 GENERAL MACH. & EQUIP.	32	1006	19570	11	276	16103	0	15698	20
50 MACHINE SHOP PRDTS.	0	5	203	0	15	187	0	114	1557
51 OFFICE, COMPUT. MACHINES	27	13	17736	0	104	30631	0	1673	13
52 SERVICE IND. MACHINES	216	35	17617	88	153	6017	0	1839	23
53 ELECT. TRANSMISS. EQUIP.	241	55	31283	0	50	18651	0	11198	0
54 HOUSEHOLD APPLIANCES	21	62	18644	0	7	5442	0	11928	0
55 ELECTRIC LIGHTING EQUIP.	32	16	10008	0	1004	10414	0	9097	70
56 RADIO, TV, ETC., EQUIP.	13	0	4610	0	389	19002	0	22311	23
57 ELECTRONIC COMPONENTS	72	28	1922	0	207	8141	0	8444	2
58 MISC. ELECTRICAL MACH.	760	794	9952	14	983	4291	166	3475	242
59 MOTOR VEHICLES, EQUIP.	33202	9962	103464	5629	18422	307396	2552	21607	1454
60 AIRCRAFT & PARTS	102		10459	6	30	33679	5	294	19
61 OTHER TRANSPORT. EQUIP.	1761	83	11236	1	602	39132	39	0	393
62 PROFESS., SCIEN. INSTRU.	174	588	4993	0	58	31653	1053	68020	74
63 MEDICAL, PHOTO. EQUIP.	115	23	1321	0		51384	248	2469	19
64 MISC. MANUFACTURING	302	345	7142	0	46	38631	19	2534	3
65 TRANSPORT. & WAREHOUSING	1761	31	53412	0	18422	307396	111	22031	4176
66 COMMUNICA.-EXC. BRDCAST.	34		164	6	30	33679	2552	21607	280
67 RADIO & TV BROADCASTING	0	0	0	1		68	5	294	186
68 ELEC.,GAS,WATER,SAN.SER.	6459	7227	91333	2287	43842	96738	39	0	0
69 WHOLESALE & RETAIL TRADE	950	1038	3123	344	1325	11298	1053	68020	19
70 FINANCE & INSURANCE	409	206	3849	18	996	5845	248	2469	0
71 REAL ESTATE & RENTAL	0	0	0	0	0	0	19	2534	0
72 HOTELS; PERSONAL SERV.	570	496	3454	0	193	27813	0	822	0
73 BUSINESS SERVICES	0	0	0	0	0	0	59	822	0
74 RESEARCH & DEVELOPMENT	0	0	0	0	0	0	0	0	0
75 AUTO. REPAIR & SERVICES	118	372	3521	0	1093	64806	0	1033	0
76 AMUSEMENTS	0	0	0	0	0	0	0	1033	0
77 MED.,EDUC. SERVICES	0	0	0	0	0	0	0	0	0
78 FEDERAL GOV'T ENTERPRISE	76	121	413	54	143	1258	27	218	34
79 STATE & LOCAL GOV'T ENT.	0	0	0	0	0	0	0	0	0
80 IMPORTS	0	0	0	0	0	0	0	0	0
81 BUS.TRAVEL, ENT., GIFTS.	0	0	0	0	0	0	0	0	0
82 OFFICE SUPPLIES	0	0	0	0	0	0	0	0	0
83 SCRAP & USED GOODS	6484	8024	75883	1058	30582	90158	817	52868	3300
84 GOVERNMENT INDUSTRY	0	0	0	0	0	0	0	0	0
85 REST OF WORLD INDUSTRY	0	0	0	0	0	0	0	0	0
86 HOUSEHOLD INDUSTRY	0	0	0	0	0	0	0	0	0
87 INVENTORY VALUATION ADJ.	0	0	0	0	0	0	0	0	0
88 STATE TOTAL	141033	164215	1164318	56760	581080	1687529	27915	757030	47654

TABLE C.10

STATE ESTIMATES OF 1947

NET FOREIGN EXPORTS BY STATE OF PRODUCTION

(THOUSANDS OF CURRENT DOLLARS)

INDUSTRY TITLE	37 PENNSYLVANIA	38 RHODE ISLAND	39 SOUTH CAROLINA	40 SOUTH DAKOTA	41 TENNESSEE	42 TEXAS	43 UTAH	44 VERMONT	45 VIRGINIA
1 LIVESTOCK & PRDTS.	1287	0	203	507	902	1520	284	71	760
2 OTHER AGRICULTURE PRDTS.	12688	256	44217	17046	29606	160526	4229	320	22172
3 FORESTRY & FISHERIES	500	16	424	69	388	1098	243	136	542
4 AGRI.,FORES.,FISH. SERV.	0	0	0	0	0	0	0	0	0
5 IRON, FERRO. ORES MINING	141	0	0	5688	0	106	334	0	0
6 NONFERROUS ORES MINING	0	0	0	691	0	0	6883	0	0
7 COAL MINING	133238	0	0	0	3262	0	3628	0	9604
8 CRUDE PETRO.,NATURAL GAS	2886	0	0	0	0	44182	0	0	0
9 STONE & CLAY MINING	206	0	0	71	0	196	196	125	0
10 CHEM.&FERT. MIN. MINING	0	0	0	0	1579	18480	0	0	0
11 NEW CONSTRUCTION	0	0	0	0	0	0	0	0	0
12 MAINT. & REPAIR CONSTR.	0	0	0	0	0	0	0	0	0
13 ORDNANCE & ACCESSORIES	868	0	0	0	0	882	0	0	0
14 FOOD & KINDRED PRDTS.	63376	1864	5062	10019	28658	122802	12512	1592	19101
15 TOBACCO MANUFACTURES	5291	1	2343	0	1885	89	0	0	53727
16 FABRICS	57154	46266	135756	0	15147	9293	59	1085	28860
17 TEXTILE PRDTS.	10973	5318	345	0	1465	2391	0	40	870
18 APPAREL	32190	612	1787	11	5312	3093	147	168	3091
19 MISC. TEXTILE PRDTS.	3192	213	2694	0	1173	1170	41	34	2674
20 LUMBER & WOOD PRDTS.	3407	57	4452	162	5209	5965	100	1555	4038
21 WOODEN CONTAINERS	430	42	151	0	426	320	0	115	308
22 HOUSEHOLD FURNITURE	1428	42	133	0	478	276	23	88	819
23 OTHER FURNITURE	532	21	3	0	11	102	7	5	32
24 PAPER & ALLIED PRDTS.	9341	380	1656	0	1343	1457	11	644	3375
25 PAPERBOARD CONTAINERS	2706	212	382	0	234	281	10	202	331
26 PRINTING & PUBLISHING	5363	285	155	84	756	1509	146	80	489
27 CHEMICALS,SELECT. PRDTS.	23283	912	1658	36	9819	27680	460	379	8109
28 PLASTICS & SYNTHETICS	10512	96	83	0	8223	1896	0	193	13149
29 DRUGS & COSMETICS	12085	348	42	64	3514	1259	78	200	2363
30 PAINT & ALLIED PRDTS.	3017	229	221	0	321	657	23	10	171
31 PETROLEUM, RELATED INDS.	62067	1390	0	40	458	134390	2310	50	288
32 RUBBER, MISC. PLASTICS	12998	2710	206	0	3392	972	0	366	352
33 LEATHER TANNING & PRDTS.	4588	132	11	0	198	124	2	0	407
34 FOOTWEAR, LEATHER PRDTS.	3145	162	4	0	1416	327	10	35	523
35 GLASS & GLASS PRDTS.	15775	493	151	0	369	652	0	29	193
36 STONE & CLAY PRDTS.	16123	114	379	98	1819	2310	529	800	599
37 PRIMARY IRON, STEEL MFR.	218758	906	80	0	1696	3195	4052	34	1453
38 PRIMARY NONFERROUS MFR.	19424	3157	31	0	4220	12126	3124	35	391

Sector									
39 METAL CONTAINERS	1752	0	0	0	79	904	97	0	36
40 FABRICATED METAL PRDTS.	15007	425	93	275	2288	3243	223	55	1627
41 SCREW MACH. PRDTS., ETC.	9856	832	5	0	516	87	0	0	4
42 OTHER FAB. METAL PRDTS.	17397	2690	0	34	474	564	6	218	360
43 ENGINES & TURBINES	13908	0	33	0	0	638	0	737	0
44 FARM MACH. & EQUIP.	6240	0	0	176	1074	2104	35	14	189
45 CONSTRUC. MACH. & EQUIP.	26429	0	0	36	940	41483	900	0	376
46 MATERIAL HANDLING MACH.	6513	75	28	0	164	339	108	0	393
47 METALWORKING MACHINERY	14727	9949	1720	0	17	170	5	4542	0
48 SPECIAL MACH. & EQUIP.	34488	7749	82	105	960	2485	253	1873	544
49 GENERAL MACH. & EQUIP.	12763	232	0	11	268	1293	0	21	124
50 MACHINE SHOP PRDTS.	269	34	30	0	13	30	1	3	5
51 OFFICE, COMPUT. MACHINES	662	226	19	0	0	10	22	591	0
52 SERVICE IND. MACHINES	8900	334	0	0	370	639	5	0	5
53 ELECT. TRANSMISS. EQUIP.	31153	77	0	39	376	307	0	11	0
54 HOUSEHOLD APPLIANCES	9591	1065	0	8	926	546	8	23	134
55 ELECTRIC LIGHTING EQUIP.	4584	879	0	0	218	311	21	90	15
56 RADIO, TV, ETC., EQUIP.	7457	90	0	0	203	83	11	0	339
57 ELECTRONIC COMPONENTS	5908	35	0	0	0	23	0	35	130
58 MISC. ELECTRICAL MACH.	2668	259	0	0	152	309	0	0	192
59 MOTOR VEHICLES, EQUIP.	33939	148	387	26	5419	3412	51	23	992
60 AIRCRAFT & PARTS	2015	0	522	0	47	4063	0	0	229
61 OTHER TRANSPORT. EQUIP.	66994	64	9	10	1222	3643	0	28	13501
62 PROFESS., SCIEN. INSTRU.	14469	192	11	33	787	519	13	36	74
63 MEDICAL, PHOTO. EQUIP.	969	690	0	147	11	223	0	0	462
64 MISC. MANUFACTURING	10043	8008	388	47	1579	719	102	285	471
65 TRANSPORT. & WAREHOUSING	253411	2317	32111	3743	10360	244684	4498	1169	295040
66 COMMUNICA., EXC. BRDCAST	345	23	13	6	28	89	18	12	37
67 RADIO & TV BROADCASTING	0	0	0	0	0	0	0	0	0
68 ELEC.,GAS,WATER,SAN.SER.	0	0	0	0	0	467	0	2	0
69 WHOLESALE & RETAIL TRADE	94023	14088	21388	1493	13706	41215	1839	1515	15453
70 FINANCE & INSURANCE	3825	338	680	346	1059	3912	211	119	1037
71 REAL ESTATE & RENTAL	4192	399	481	31	582	1045	77	91	636
72 HOTELS; PERSONAL SERV.	0	0	0	0	0	0	0	0	0
73 BUSINESS SERVICES	4196	303	54	31	547	1609	184	14	449
74 RESEARCH & DEVELOPMENT	0	0	0	0	0	0	0	0	0
75 AUTO. REPAIR & SERVICES	0	0	0	0	0	0	0	0	0
76 AMUSEMENTS	2656	0	15	0	571	2204	518	0	24
77 MED.,EDUC. SERVICES	0	0	0	0	0	0	0	0	0
78 FEDERAL GOV'T ENTERPRISE	532	38	74	51	143	341	33	31	162
79 STATE & LOCAL GOV'T ENT.	0	0	0	0	0	0	0	0	0
80 IMPORTS	0	0	0	0	0	0	0	0	0
81 BUS.TRAVEL, ENT., GIFTS.	0	0	0	0	0	0	0	0	0
82 OFFICE SUPPLIES	0	0	0	0	0	0	0	0	0
83 SCRAP & USED GOODS	84166	8799	14174	1008	10174	35485	2244	1438	14596
84 GOVERNMENT INDUSTRY	0	0	0	0	0	0	0	0	0
85 REST OF WORLD INDUSTRY	0	0	0	0	0	0	0	0	0
86 HOUSEHOLD INDUSTRY	0	0	0	0	0	0	0	0	0
87 INVENTORY VALUATION ADJ.	0	0	0	0	0	0	0	0	0
88 STATE TOTAL	1555019	126592	274946	42242	188558	960524	50928	21390	526432

TABLE C.10

STATE ESTIMATES OF 1947
NET FOREIGN EXPORTS BY STATE OF PRODUCTION
(THOUSANDS OF CURRENT DOLLARS)

INDUSTRY TITLE	46 WASHINGTON	47 WEST VIRGINIA	48 WISCONSIN	49 WYOMING	50 ALASKA	51 HAWAII	52 NO STATE ALLOCATION	53 NATIONAL TOTAL
1 LIVESTOCK & PRDTS.	395	111	3516	20	0	0	0	34949
2 OTHER AGRICULTURE PRDTS.	38257	1538	8779	2051	0	0	0	1640371
3 FORESTRY & FISHERIES	1883	304	522	287	0	0	0	24567
4 AGRI.,FORES.,FISH. SERV.	0	0	0	0	0	0	0	0
5 IRON, FERRO. ORES MINING	0	0	119	0	0	0	0	11135
6 NONFERROUS ORES MINING	485	0	0	3891	0	0	0	46865
7 COAL MINING	563	85982	0	1795	0	0	0	367144
8 CRUDE PETRO.,NATURAL GAS	0	1456	0	0	0	0	0	104245
9 STONE & CLAY MINING	0	131	0	56	0	0	0	7139
10 CHEM.&FERT. MIN. MINING	0	0	0	0	0	0	0	35012
11 NEW CONSTRUCTION	0	0	0	0	0	0	0	0
12 MAINT. & REPAIR CONSTR.	0	0	0	0	0	0	0	0
13 ORDNANCE & ACCESSORIES	0	0	13	0	0	0	0	13113
14 FOOD & KINDRED PRDTS.	54296	3672	69640	1165	0	0	0	1878496
15 TOBACCO MANUFACTURES	1	92	96	0	0	0	0	225149
16 FABRICS	117	1299	1121	0	0	0	0	864420
17 TEXTILE PRDTS.	330	0	898	0	0	0	0	110479
18 APPAREL	522	437	3152	0	0	0	0	252711
19 MISC. TEXTILE PRDTS.	190	26	818	0	0	0	0	60321
20 LUMBER & WOOD PRDTS.	17468	1979	3450	274	0	0	0	163654
21 WOODEN CONTAINERS	123	41	422	0	0	0	0	10194
22 HOUSEHOLD FURNITURE	235	50	934	0	0	0	0	24425
23 OTHER FURNITURE	25	5	123	0	0	0	0	10197
24 PAPER & ALLIED PRDTS.	5908	272	10081	0	0	0	0	132643
25 PAPERBOARD CONTAINERS	346	133	1329	0	0	0	0	31934
26 PRINTING & PUBLISHING	684	232	1559	41	0	0	0	71743
27 CHEMICALS,SELECT. PRDTS.	1337	19321	2626	477	0	0	0	392518
28 PLASTICS & SYNTHETICS	184	2121	1353	0	0	0	0	86145
29 DRUGS & COSMETICS	288	370	3143	0	0	0	0	231548
30 PAINT & ALLIED PRDTS.	259	21	859	11	0	0	0	40940
31 PETROLEUM, RELATED INDS.	608	2058	1535	8163	0	0	0	558298
32 RUBBER, MISC. PLASTICS	31	52	2853	1	0	0	0	188144
33 LEATHER TANNING & PRDTS.	6	521	3461	0	0	0	0	34291
34 FOOTWEAR, LEATHER PRDTS.	69	57	2194	5	0	0	0	53856
35 GLASS & GLASS PRDTS.	264	10591	125	0	0	0	0	73702
36 STONE & CLAY PRDTS.	852	3625	1044	96	0	0	0	105651
37 PRIMARY IRON, STEEL MFR.	2181	16968	7514	0	0	0	0	674683
38 PRIMARY NONFERROUS MFR.	6986	3549	2593	0	0	0	0	234013

39 METAL CONTAINERS	252	219	154	0	0	0	0	21252
40 FABRICATED METAL PRDTS.	1004	855	6952	27	0	0	0	111479
41 SCREW MACH. PRDTS., ETC.	66	1390	2089	0	0	0	0	60076
42 OTHER FAB. METAL PRDTS.	256	817	4047	0	0	0	0	169583
43 ENGINES & TURBINES	132	0	26305	0	0	0	0	148200
44 FARM MACH. & EQUIP.	494	412	25486	35	0	0	0	201005
45 CONSTRUC. MACH. & EQUIP.	4122	4070	43423	24	0	0	0	355494
46 MATERIAL HANDLING MACH.	311	28	1340	0	0	0	0	65689
47 METALWORKING MACHINERY	532	4	12627	0	0	0	0	212398
48 SPECIAL MACH. & EQUIP.	1462	282	17364	0	0	0	0	328514
49 GENERAL MACH. & EQUIP.	146	265	7707	0	0	0	0	141716
50 MACHINE SHOP PRDTS.	24	4	72	0	0	0	0	2462
51 OFFICE, COMPUT. MACHINES	16	0	229	0	0	0	0	93107
52 SERVICE IND. MACHINES	57	90	1786	0	0	0	0	76212
53 ELECT. TRANSMISS. EQUIP.	161	735	9876	18	0	0	0	163533
54 HOUSEHOLD APPLIANCES	406	119	3544	3	0	0	0	112344
55 ELECTRIC LIGHTING EQUIP.	122	484	852	0	0	0	0	69375
56 RADIO, TV, ETC., EQUIP.	224	0	839	0	0	0	0	123677
57 ELECTRONIC COMPONENTS	13	261	171	0	0	0	0	45941
58 MISC. ELECTRICAL MACH.	775	13	3947	0	0	0	0	47973
59 MOTOR VEHICLES, EQUIP.	2137	989	36745	0	0	0	0	1020501
60 AIRCRAFT & PARTS	2762	47	229	47	0	0	0	122313
61 OTHER TRANSPORT. EQUIP.	5193	1497	5620	0	0	0	0	314623
62 PROFESS., SCIEN. INSTRU.	87	23	2922	0	0	0	0	114242
63 MEDICAL, PHOTO. EQUIP.	41	41	261	0	0	0	0	78528
64 MISC. MANUFACTURING	182	574	6539	8	0	0	0	157850
65 TRANSPORT. & WAREHOUSING	33089	65694	18087	4509	0	0	0	2321064
66 COMMUNICA.-EXC. BRDCAST.	45	27	37	4	0	0	0	37930
67 RADIO & TV BROADCASTING	29	0	0	0	0	0	0	0
68 ELEC.,GAS,WATER,SAN.SER.	0	0	0	0	0	0	0	1215
69 WHOLESALE & RETAIL TRADE	9031	17745	24439	1143	0	0	0	1050583
70 FINANCE & INSURANCE	1360	601	1154	122	0	0	0	69798
71 REAL ESTATE & RENTAL	529	402	1370	21	0	0	0	44999
72 HOTELS; PERSONAL SERV.	0	0	0	0	0	0	0	0
73 BUSINESS SERVICES	709	125	1509	21	0	0	0	78261
74 RESEARCH & DEVELOPMENT	0	0	0	0	0	0	0	0
75 AUTO. REPAIR & SERVICES	0	0	0	0	0	0	0	0
76 AMUSEMENTS	723	0	452	0	0	0	0	128198
77 MED.,EDUC. SERVICES	0	0	0	0	0	0	0	0
78 FEDERAL GOV'T ENTERPRISE	126	89	184	16	0	0	0	8449
79 STATE & LOCAL GOV'T ENT.	0	0	0	0	0	0	0	0
80 IMPORTS	0	0	0	0	0	0	-8208000	-8208000
81 BUS.-TRAVEL, ENT., GIFTS.	0	0	0	0	0	0	0	0
82 OFFICE SUPPLIES	0	0	0	0	0	0	0	0
83 SCRAP & USED GOODS	10054	7100	30268	914	0	0	0	957266
84 GOVERNMENT INDUSTRY	0	0	0	0	0	0	0	0
85 REST OF WORLD INDUSTRY	0	0	0	0	0	0	1837000	1837000
86 HOUSEHOLD INDUSTRY	0	0	0	0	0	0	0	0
87 INVENTORY VALUATION ADJ.	0	0	0	0	0	0	0	0
88 STATE TOTAL	211565	262016	434498	25245	0	0	-6371000	11480000

TABLE C.11

STATE ESTIMATES OF 1958
NET FOREIGN EXPORTS BY STATE OF PRODUCTION
(THOUSANDS OF CURRENT DOLLARS)

INDUSTRY TITLE	1 ALABAMA	2 ARIZONA	3 ARKANSAS	4 CALIFORNIA	5 COLORADO	6 CONNECTICUT	7 DELAWARE	8 DISTRICT OF COLUMBIA	9 FLORIDA
1 LIVESTOCK & PRDTS.	696	141	640	3988	1041	56	380	0	225
2 OTHER AGRICULTURE PRDTS.	24275	29352	76148	191710	20583	2631	2677	0	29029
3 FORESTRY & FISHERIES	980	202	318	4440	0	50	311	4	2914
4 AGRI.,FORES.,FISH. SERV.	56	53	58	524	26	56	17	0	223
5 IRON, FERRO. ORES MINING	3097	126	0	2271	7082	0	0	0	0
6 NONFERROUS ORES MINING	0	0	2107	0	598	0	0	0	0
7 COAL MINING	11015	0	0	0	0	0	0	0	0
8 CRUDE PETRO.,NATURAL GAS	0	0	396	2705	2526	0	0	0	294
9 STONE & CLAY MINING	1017	299	222	1816	423	55	0	0	0
10 CHEM.&FERT. MIN. MINING	0	0	62	0	164	0	0	2000	17158
11 NEW CONSTRUCTION	0	0	0	0	0	0	0	0	0
12 MAINT. & REPAIR CONSTR.	0	0	0	0	0	0	0	0	0
13 ORDNANCE & ACCESSORIES	82	292	13	6511	266	623	4	0	709
14 FOOD & KINDRED PRDTS.	8631	2466	42396	156305	10717	3509	3320	1518	17546
15 TOBACCO MANUFACTURES	0	0	0	0	0	191	0	0	1527
16 FABRICS	11372	109	219	875	109	3280	656	0	109
17 TEXTILE PRDTS.	800	0	267	1733	0	1066	533	0	133
18 APPAREL	3852	90	448	4479	179	1791	358	0	806
19 MISC. TEXTILE PRDTS.	250	0	0	1001	0	250	0	0	125
20 LUMBER & WOOD PRDTS.	4266	465	4188	11091	388	310	233	0	1706
21 WOODEN CONTAINERS	57	0	114	256	0	28	0	0	114
22 HOUSEHOLD FURNITURE	210	70	419	1187	70	140	0	0	419
23 OTHER FURNITURE	0	0	222	1551	0	222	0	0	443
24 PAPER & ALLIED PRDTS.	5009	0	1391	2504	93	1206	0	93	30517
25 PAPERBOARD CONTAINERS	27	0	82	769	0	330	0	0	1704
26 PRINTING & PUBLISHING	211	211	141	3524	352	1269	70	3242	564
27 CHEMICALS,SELECT. PRDTS.	15246	410	1149	40256	3201	6737	1776	0	44804
28 PLASTICS & SYNTHETICS	1785	0	0	8825	0	3680	1317	0	4902
29 DRUGS & COSMETICS	0	0	0	10751	0	7455	4236	0	564
30 PAINT & ALLIED PRDTS.	402	0	0	1089	0	0	0	0	0
31 PETROLEUM, RELATED INDS.	0	0	666	137586	500	0	0	0	0
32 RUBBER, MISC. PLASTICS	5295	96	481	9628	3659	4332	1637	0	193
33 LEATHER TANNING & PRDTS.	0	0	0	913	0	304	2436	0	0
34 FOOTWEAR, LEATHER PRDTS.	79	0	949	553	237	949	79	0	79
35 GLASS & GLASS PRDTS.	0	0	0	1475	0	568	0	0	0
36 STONE & CLAY PRDTS.	193	0	0	6785	0	2735	0	0	0
37 PRIMARY IRON, STEEL MFR.	14897	0	0	22563	8646	1070	0	0	485
38 PRIMARY NONFERROUS MFR.	2953	3052	1191	11523	969	2587	1191	0	670

#	Industry	C1	C2	C3	C4	C5	C6	C7	C8	C9
39	METAL CONTAINERS	0	0	0	8273	0	0	0	0	0
40	FABRICATED METAL PRDTS.	4038	0	565	13411	0	564	2606	0	1463
41	SCREW MAC., PRDTS., ETC.	54	0	0	725	1901	1246	76	0	85
42	OTHER FAB. METAL PRDTS.	483	0	0	16047	253	21021	0	0	1011
43	ENGINES & TURBINES	0	0	0	1429	11033	874	0	0	0
44	FARM MACH. & EQUIP.	394	0	0	5072	1187	0	0	0	0
45	CONSTRUC. MACH. & EQUIP.	1135	0	2464	20042	0	0	0	0	0
46	MATERIAL HANDLING MACH.	122	0	265	2157	208	17855	0	0	0
47	METALWORKING MACHINERY	0	0	0	2827	0	16645	0	0	0
48	SPECIAL MACH. & EQUIP.	1678	0	0	17183	0	16221	658	0	0
49	GENERAL MACH. & EQUIP.	275	0	546	22011	0	0	228	0	0
50	MACHINE SHOP PRDTS.	0	0	0	1645	0	7038	0	0	0
51	OFFICE, COMPUT. MACHINES	2388	244	0	7949	0	860	688	0	167
52	SERVICE IND. MACHINES	110	1868	81	7725	1662	2138	0	0	0
53	ELECT. TRANSMISS. EQUIP.	0	0	0	32816	0	8103	0	0	0
54	HOUSEHOLD APPLIANCES	0	0	0	3297	0	3010	0	0	0
55	ELECTRIC LIGHTING EQUIP.	645	0	663	1127	0	2561	0	0	1165
56	RADIO, TV, ETC., EQUIP.	0	663	0	8522	0	1091	0	0	120
57	ELECTRONIC COMPONENTS	1139	258	0	8042	0	0	0	0	0
58	MISC. ELECTRICAL MACH.	263	386	0	0	0	3651	331	0	0
59	MOTOR VEHICLES, EQUIP.	1051	0	231	27106	125	68079	231	0	771
60	AIRCRAFT & PARTS	62	3889	0	221297	520	3198	0	0	1647
61	OTHER TRANSPORT. EQUIP.	62	0	0	0	0	8148	0	0	1296
62	PROFESS., SCIEN. INSTRU.	52	1235	155	18101	155	1246	309	0	1392
63	MEDICAL, PHOTO. EQUIP.	0	0	0	4392	0	13647	0	0	1128
64	MISC. MANUFACTURING	348	139	836	6963	139	7114	0	0	975
65	TRANSPORT. & WAREHOUSING	25853	4048	11515	140220	9130	171	1152	244	64347
66	COMMUNICA., EXC. BRDCAST.	39	20	26	1203	39	88	25	28	83
67	RADIO & TV BROADCASTING	273	122	147	551	147	0	25	40	381
68	ELEC.,GAS,WATER,SAN.SER.	0	1218	0	7320	0	12927	0	0	0
69	WHOLESALE & RETAIL TRADE	14196	6041	5792	128903	14704	412	4001	8339	27427
70	FINANCE & INSURANCE	217	112	136	2127	194	5820	49	108	511
71	REAL ESTATE & RENTAL	3221	655	1077	21911	1422	0	764	360	2566
72	HOTELS; PERSONAL SERV.	0	0	0	0	0	1108	0	0	0
73	BUSINESS SERVICES	462	396	167	19965	912	0	122	1019	2100
74	RESEARCH & DEVELOPMENT	0	0	0	0	0	0	0	0	0
75	AUTO. REPAIR & SERVICES	0	0	0	0	0	790	0	0	0
76	AMUSEMENTS	61	38	0	58798	3929	77	102	3623	2404
77	MED.,EDUC. SERVICES	11	5	11	194	45	281	34	69	19
78	FEDERAL GOV'T ENTERPRISE	227	97	152	1609	196	0	0	361	415
79	STATE & LOCAL GOV'T ENT.	281	281	0	592	0	0	0	0	0
80	IMPORTS	0	0	0	0	0	0	0	0	0
81	BUS.TRAVEL, ENT., GIFTS.	0	0	0	0	0	4909	0	0	0
82	OFFICE SUPPLIES	0	0	0	0	0	0	0	0	0
83	SCRAP & USED GOODS	1424	402	953	18617	1021	0	315	86	2199
84	GOVERNMENT INDUSTRY	0	0	0	0	0	0	0	0	0
85	REST OF WORLD INDUSTRY	0	0	0	0	0	0	0	0	0
86	HOUSEHOLD INDUSTRY	0	0	0	0	0	0	0	0	0
87	INVENTORY VALUATION ADJ.	0	0	0	0	0	0	0	0	0
88	STATE TOTAL	176974	58891	160069	1511355	110751	278373	33040	21134	271634

TABLE C.11

STATE ESTIMATES OF 1958

NET FOREIGN EXPORTS BY STATE OF PRODUCTION

(THOUSANDS OF CURRENT DOLLARS)

INDUSTRY TITLE	10 GEORGIA	11 IDAHO	12 ILLINOIS	13 INDIANA	14 IOWA	15 KANSAS	16 KENTUCKY	17 LOUISIANA	18 MAINE
1 LIVESTOCK & PRDTS.	957	260	1273	760	3348	971	626	169	190
2 OTHER AGRICULTURE PRDTS.	33875	19799	131391	57319	75410	97701	16937	33967	3923
3 FORESTRY & FISHERIES	1103	283	68	81	37	0	23	1951	1329
4 AGRI.,FORES.,FISH.SERV.	104	16	138	0	83	41	42	41	20
5 IRON, FERRO.ORES MINING	0	1691	0	0	0	0	0	0	0
6 NONFERROUS ORES MINING	0	0	0	0	0	0	0	0	0
7 COAL MINING	0	0	23958	7832	0	0	46797	0	0
8 CRUDE PETRO.,NATURAL GAS	0	0	414	608	624	430	474	5993	0
9 STONE & CLAY MINING	2920	0	664	799	538	399	406	387	97
10 CHEM.&FERT.MIN.MINING	0	0	171	0	0	0	0	0	0
11 NEW CONSTRUCTION	0	0	0	0	0	0	0	0	0
12 MAINT.& REPAIR CONSTR.	0	0	0	0	0	0	0	0	0
13 ORDNANCE & ACCESSORIES	26	13	787	245	305	9	13	86	64
14 FOOD & KINDRED PRDTS.	20866	3794	137525	32058	53398	36041	9390	35282	5406
15 TOBACCO MANUFACTURES	95	0	477	191	0	0	2673	0	0
16 FABRICS	24821	0	656	267	269	109	219	219	2515
17 TEXTILE PRDTS.	6531	0	2399	896	125	0	0	133	133
18 APPAREL	7255	0	3045	250	776	269	1254	179	269
19 MISC.TEXTILE PRDTS.	1126	0	876	0	0	125	125	125	0
20 LUMBER & WOOD PRDTS.	3335	2017	1629	2017	70	155	1396	2792	2327
21 WOODEN CONTAINERS	199	0	85	57	222	0	142	57	28
22 HOUSEHOLD FURNITURE	349	0	838	978	93	70	279	70	0
23 OTHER FURNITURE	222	0	1329	665	55	222	0	0	0
24 PAPER & ALLIED PRDTS.	31352	1020	2133	649	916	0	835	7050	8719
25 PAPERBOARD CONTAINERS	2858	27	632	220	0	27	357	330	27
26 PRINTING & PUBLISHING	352	70	13463	1692	1940	282	352	211	70
27 CHEMICALS,SELECT.PRDTS.	19693	2216	19043	1123	925	2052	3291	44760	1642
28 PLASTICS & SYNTHETICS	379	0	5028	533	0	0	31975	22651	0
29 DRUGS & COSMETICS	9331	0	15002	16501	0	0	0	0	0
30 PAINT & ALLIED PRDTS.	1122	0	3759	0	0	0	147	1071	0
31 PETROLEUM,RELATED INDS.	0	0	6496	4830	0	2499	0	99941	0
32 RUBBER,MISC.PLASTICS	289	0	12516	5680	2407	3755	866	0	289
33 LEATHER TANNING & PRDTS.	304	0	2131	0	0	0	0	289	913
34 FOOTWEAR,LEATHER PRDTS.	316	0	1502	316	79	0	237	913	2688
35 GLASS & GLASS PRDTS.	100	0	3748	515	0	0	874	0	0
36 STONE & CLAY PRDTS.	193	0	3922	3173	808	1351	5047	0	0
37 PRIMARY IRON,STEEL MFR.	0	0	25453	14550	0	0	4756	0	0
38 PRIMARY NONFERROUS MFR.	2382	0	2311	9078	1340	670	86	32007	74

#	Sector	(1)	(2)	(3)	(4)	(5)	(6)	(7)	(8)	(9)
39	METAL CONTAINERS	0	0	5867	252	0	0	0	190	357
40	FABRICATED METAL PRDTS.	4184	0	10858	13752	872	3953	2958	3162	0
41	SCREW MACH. PRDTS., ETC.	384	0	4434	870	61	0	607	1170	0
42	OTHER FAB. METAL PRDTS.	228	0	31413	5678	5059	457	2884	1253	0
43	ENGINES & TURBINES	0	0	21597	25683	1892	2393	4704	135	255
44	FARM MACH. & EQUIP.	1900	0	47468	2866	65429	257	0	0	27
45	CONSTRUC. MACH. & EQUIP.	6717	0	343517	14141	18260	324	8909	858	0
46	MATERIAL HANDLING MACH.	723	0	36967	1522	1965	955	2947	2430	3106
47	METALWORKING MACHINERY	0	0	35336	4336	1056	272	1880	0	231
48	SPECIAL MACH. & EQUIP.	3468	0	25958	7447	367	163	296	487	338
49	GENERAL MACH. & EQUIP.	284	0	17153	12585	540	551	2139	93188	138
50	MACHINE SHOP PRDTS.	0	0	920	736	0	1984	5771	67	0
51	OFFICE, COMPUT. MACHINES	0	0	5017	68	184	13288	979	210	1656
52	SERVICE IND. MACHINES	0	0	6016	4659	1339	618	10756	20276	823
53	ELECT. TRANSMISS. EQUIP.	2123	0	13017	4716	11912	155	1404	297	0
54	HOUSEHOLD APPLIANCES	0	0	27242	13714	17148	59	0	2601	348
55	ELECTRIC LIGHTING EQUIP.	0	0	6963	3091	1650	70	954	1129	3452
56	RADIO, TV, ETC., EQUIP.	0	0	32221	17843	145	14095	260	0	29
57	ELECTRONIC COMPONENTS	0	0	5979	8184	103	41	7476	2397	67
58	MISC. ELECTRICAL MACH.	0	0	2239	15410	183	124	619	28	587
59	MOTOR VEHICLES, EQUIP.	1092	77	21832	64175	576	14773	279	224	4219
60	AIRCRAFT & PARTS	14909	432	24468	7868	1186	247	34860	0	91
61	OTHER TRANSPORT. EQUIP.	0	0	75607	509	59	2130	39		1142
62	PROFESS., SCIEN. INSTRU.	155	139	15987	3352	2298	404	208		110
63	MEDICAL, PHOTO. EQUIP.	766	4466	8072	475	15665	123	12758		0
64	MISC. MANUFACTURING	15301	16	10932	3551	52	7	238		20
65	TRANSPORT. & WAREHOUSING	71	82	128504	24819	168	269	3217		5
66	COMMUNICA., EXC. BRDCAST.	316	730	439	127	22371		612		116
67	RADIO & TV BROADCASTING	0	3329	299	187	305		62		4
68	ELEC.,GAS,WATER,SAN.SER.	28566	65	117250	26028	3063		10		0
69	WHOLESALE & RETAIL TRADE	326	465	1369	587	976		249		
70	FINANCE & INSURANCE	3823	115	21212	10006	1026				
71	REAL ESTATE & RENTAL	1399	0	37693	1419	17				
72	HOTELS; PERSONAL SERV.	0	1	8356	1374	291				
73	BUSINESS SERVICES	3227	60	277	91					
74	RESEARCH & DEVELOPMENT	110	47	1374	405					
75	AUTO. REPAIR & SERVICES	322								
76	AMUSEMENTS									
77	MED., EDUC. SERVICES									
78	FEDERAL GOV'T ENTERPRISE									
79	STATE & LOCAL GOV'T ENT.									
80	IMPORTS									
81	BUS. TRAVEL, ENT., GIFTS.									
82	OFFICE SUPPLIES									
83	SCRAP & USED GOODS	2933	156	23631	5598	3334	1290	2067	3541	522
84	GOVERNMENT INDUSTRY	0	0	0	0	0	0	0	0	0
85	REST OF WORLD INDUSTRY	0	0	0	0	0	0	0	0	0
86	HOUSEHOLD INDUSTRY	0	0	0	0	0	0	0	0	0
87	INVENTORY VALUATION ADJ.	0	0	0	0	0	0	0	0	0
88	STATE TOTAL	265782	41387	1602345	472007	323320	207585	239761	439903	48366

343

TABLE C.11

STATE ESTIMATES OF 1958
NET FOREIGN EXPORTS BY STATE OF PRODUCTION
(THOUSANDS OF CURRENT DOLLARS)

INDUSTRY TITLE	19 MARYLAND	20 MASSA- CHUSETTS	21 MICHIGAN	22 MINNESOTA	23 MISSISSIPPI	24 MISSOURI	25 MONTANA	26 NEBRASKA	27 NEVADA
1 LIVESTOCK & PRDTS.	387	7	914	2884	619	1273	70	1576	7
2 OTHER AGRICULTURE PRDTS.	9092	2169	29444	53304	53396	61288	29721	52150	508
3 FORESTRY & FISHERIES	874	1980	213	230	926	14	0	0	0
4 AGRI.,FORES.,FISH. SERV.	57	77	87	67	34	75	0	37	8
5 IRON,FERRO. ORES MINING	0	0	3328	16194	0	96	1142	0	283
6 NONFERROUS ORES MINING	0	0	0	0	0	0	0	0	0
7 COAL MINING	712	0	0	0	0	0	193	0	0
8 CRUDE PETRO.,NATURAL GAS	0	0	0	0	460	1531	207	210	178
9 STONE & CLAY MINING	112	61	398	107	234	811	44	32	0
10 CHEM.&FERT. MIN. MINING	0	0	0	0	0	0	730	0	0
11 NEW CONSTRUCTION	0	0	0	0	0	0	0	0	0
12 MAINT. & REPAIR CONSTR.	0	0	0	0	0	0	0	0	0
13 ORDNANCE & ACCESSORIES	181	804	417	383	9	662	0	21	0
14 FOOD & KINDRED PRDTS.	19254	13847	27695	31963	12425	47707	1043	19538	190
15 TOBACCO MANUFACTURES	95	0	477	477	0	668	0	0	0
16 FABRICS	219	11153	0	109	109	656	0	0	0
17 TEXTILE PRDTS.	267	4932	0	133	533	533	0	0	0
18 APPAREL	1075	6180	1200	1971	1881	2150	0	179	0
19 MISC. TEXTILE PRDTS.	125	1001	1075	626	125	250	0	0	0
20 LUMBER & WOOD PRDTS.	931	1008	2628	1086	3257	1318	1396	155	78
21 WOODEN CONTAINERS	0	57	2017	28	199	57	0	0	0
22 HOUSEHOLD FURNITURE	210	489	419	70	349	140	0	70	70
23 OTHER FURNITURE	886	222	1772	222	70	222	0	0	0
24 PAPER & ALLIED PRDTS.	278	7421	2504	6864	20778	928	0	222	0
25 PAPERBOARD CONTAINERS	137	797	330	467	275	247	0	27	0
26 PRINTING & PUBLISHING	634	2608	1128	916	70	1269	70	211	0
27 CHEMICALS,SELECT. PRDTS.	8766	5653	29854	6365	8027	16674	70	0	328
28 PLASTICS & SYNTHETICS	4814	10842	11402	0	1674	0	0	0	0
29 DRUGS & COSMETICS	7763	2736	43496	350	1086	2320	0	304	0
30 PAINT & ALLIED PRDTS.	678	616	1275	0	0	0	0	0	0
31 PETROLEUM, RELATED INDS.	999	333	1499	999	0	833	0	0	0
32 RUBBER, MISC. PLASTICS	4140	18967	6643	2022	193	963	0	674	0
33 LEATHER TANNING & PRDTS.	0	6394	1522	304	0	0	0	0	0
34 FOOTWEAR, LEATHER PRDTS.	237	7907	237	79	158	3163	0	0	0
35 GLASS & GLASS PRDTS.	1805	0	6972	0	0	1504	0	0	0
36 STONE & CLAY PRDTS.	3475	9847	5163	808	772	7337	0	0	0
37 PRIMARY IRON, STEEL MFR.	62147	2350	45740	0	81	4399	0	193	193
38 PRIMARY NONFERROUS MFR.	1340	2004	2830	0	0	935	3201	447	2977

	C1	C2	C3	C4	C5	C6	C7	C8	C9
39 METAL CONTAINERS	2530	0	0	156		0	0	153	0
40 FABRICATED METAL PRDTS.	1835	203	4122	185	6689	3287	0	908	0
41 SCREW MACH. PRDTS., ETC.	699	355	4042	194	53	219	0	188	0
42 OTHER FAB. METAL PRDTS.	519	25063	17080	2112	1103	3405	0	0	0
43 ENGINES & TURBINES	0	21296	27212	1491	0	1070	0	229	0
44 FARM MACH. & EQUIP.	0	0	15542	9748	946	1139	0	2223	0
45 CONSTRUC. MACH. & EQUIP.	2501	100	22150	4522	1486	3280	0	239	0
46 MATERIAL HANDLING MACH.	269	11	2384	487	160	353	0	0	0
47 METALWORKING MACHINERY	2911	27317	23145	1139	0	2586	0	0	0
48 SPECIAL MACH. & EQUIP.	12309	49432	8156	1087	575	2021	0	4158	0
49 GENERAL MACH. & EQUIP.	525	6818	5686	1844	0	1455	0	0	0
50 MACHINE SHOP PRDTS.	598	365	3405	199	0	181	0	0	0
51 OFFICE, COMPUT. MACHINES	0	1445	13002	4857	0	6018	0	0	0
52 SERVICE IND. MACHINES	4838	957	21845	6255	109	2030	0	0	0
53 ELECT. TRANSMISS. EQUIP.	0	22683	1861	3848	0	5141	0	0	0
54 HOUSEHOLD APPLIANCES	162	4640	14283	1392	562	400	0	0	0
55 ELECTRIC LIGHTING EQUIP.	553	4341	437	3691	512	1934	0	0	0
56 RADIO, TV. ETC. EQUIP.	16197	3033	2271	166	121	430	0	0	0
57 ELECTRONIC COMPONENTS	0	10548	2004	373	0	0	0	0	0
58 MISC. ELECTRICAL MACH.	11008	2114	2780	154	3090	116	77	116	0
59 MOTOR VEHICLES, EQUIP.	0	1845	345233	275	316	5266	0	0	0
60 AIRCRAFT & PARTS	368	2158	0	0	0	1340	0	0	0
61 OTHER TRANSPORT. EQUIP.	4346	627	9180	11088	557	301	0	972	0
62 PROFESS., SCIEN. INSTRU.	1135	14698	5209	594	0	1186	0	567	0
63 MEDICAL, PHOTO. EQUIP.	178	8368	1128	2855	0	297	0	119	0
64 MISC. MANUFACTURING	487	11697	2089		9744	2089	6557	139	390
65 TRANSPORT. & WAREHOUSING	51292	15286	41702	164794	35	14231	14	7049	5
66 COMMUNICA., EXC. BRDCAST.	81	2865	49	49	168	105	86	21	46
67 RADIO & TV BROADCASTING	101	170	255	156		208	650	93	
68 ELEC.,GAS,WATER,SAN.SER.	0	0	4079	1299	6911	47733	3797	14773	990
69 WHOLESALE & RETAIL TRADE	16485	43180	57719	32532	144	508	75	156	33
70 FINANCE & INSURANCE	309	794	956	410	1168	5912	347	975	124
71 REAL ESTATE & RENTAL	4354	9328	1521	3728					
72 HOTELS; PERSONAL SERV.	1508	0	19293	4263	184	5254	55	771	105
73 BUSINESS SERVICES	0	4521	0	0				0	
74 RESEARCH & DEVELOPMENT	0	0	0	0		3805		0	
75 AUTO. REPAIR & SERVICES	192	3611	4991	1791				442	
76 AMUSEMENTS	39	138	276	85	2	108	71	22	25
77 MED.,EDUC. SERVICES	217	703	662	431	140	655	90	172	26
78 FEDERAL GOV'T ENTERPRISE		152	152	87					
79 STATE & LOCAL GOV'T ENT.									
80 IMPORTS	0	0	0	0	0	0	0	0	0
81 BUS.TRAVEL, ENT., GIFTS.	0	0	0	0	0	0	0	0	0
82 OFFICE SUPPLIES	0	0	0	0	0	0	0	0	0
83 SCRAP & USED GOODS	2961	5489	12966	2090	1064	2457	101	510	67
84 GOVERNMENT INDUSTRY	0	0	0	0	0	0	0	0	0
85 REST OF WORLD INDUSTRY	0	0	0	0	0	0	0	0	0
86 HOUSEHOLD INDUSTRY	0	0	0	0	0	0	0	0	0
87 INVENTORY VALUATION ADJ.	0	0	0	0	0	0	0	0	0
88 STATE TOTAL	273197	428762	945465	398978	143509	286543	49745	110626	6561

TABLE C.11

STATE ESTIMATES OF 1958
NET FOREIGN EXPORTS BY STATE OF PRODUCTION
(THOUSANDS OF CURRENT DOLLARS)

INDUSTRY TITLE	28 NEW HAMPSHIRE	29 NEW JERSEY	30 NEW MEXICO	31 NEW YORK	32 NORTH CAROLINA	33 NORTH DAKOTA	34 OHIO	35 OKLAHOMA	36 OREGON
1 LIVESTOCK & PRDTS.	0	478	127	1351	633	98	1449	345	176
2 OTHER AGRICULTURE PRDTS.	462	4938	10522	20399	112007	38905	50258	46243	18368
3 FORESTRY & FISHERIES	120	572	0	733	430	2	104	1	1602
4 AGRI.,FORES.,FISH. SERV.	15	77	13	211	64	8	120	33	34
5 IRON, FERRO. ORES MINING	0	363	180	891	0	0	0	0	297
6 NONFERROUS ORES MINING	0	0	522	0	0	0	0	0	0
7 COAL MINING	0	0	101	0	0	0	21377	0	0
8 CRUDE PETRO.,NATURAL GAS	0	0	1386	0	0	148	131	1453	0
9 STONE & CLAY MINING	97	303	222	968	1873	0	969	1538	53
10 CHEM.&FERT. MIN. MINING	0	0	0	0	0	0	0	126	0
11 NEW CONSTRUCTION	0	0	0	0	0	0	0	0	0
12 MAINT. & REPAIR CONSTR.	0	0	0	0	0	0	0	0	0
13 ORDNANCE & ACCESSORIES	4	181	159	1307	125	0	456	0	9
14 FOOD & KINDRED PRDTS.	664	44387	1423	108028	12140	854	36136	12709	15175
15 TOBACCO MANUFACTURES	0	382	0	95	258970	0	955	0	0
16 FABRICS	1749	6451	0	4374	51938	0	765	328	219
17 TEXTILE PRDTS.	0	2932	0	3599	2399	0	2932	0	0
18 APPAREL	448	6718	0	30813	19437	0	2418	358	448
19 MISC. TEXTILE PRDTS.	0	1627	0	3629	876	0	375	0	125
20 LUMBER & WOOD PRDTS.	776	853	310	2870	4809	0	1241	310	18149
21 WOODEN CONTAINERS	57	85	0	85	114	0	85	0	0
22 HOUSEHOLD FURNITURE	70	349	0	1117	2584	0	419	70	85
23 OTHER FURNITURE	0	443	0	2658	886	0	1772	0	70
24 PAPER & ALLIED PRDTS.	3247	4267	0	7699	11316	0	5009	0	7050
25 PAPERBOARD CONTAINERS	27	1017	0	1401	852	0	742	27	247
26 PRINTING & PUBLISHING	141	2890	70	34256	423	70	4370	211	211
27 CHEMICALS,SELECT. PRDTS.	0	84288	1642	18556	1756	0	20341	739	903
28 PLASTICS & SYNTHETICS	0	18586	0	6607	5777	0	21935	0	0
29 DRUGS & COSMETICS	0	50400	0	105543	271	0	2430	0	0
30 PAINT & ALLIED PRDTS.	0	6592	0	1708	0	0	2751	0	0
31 PETROLEUM, RELATED INDS.	0	77787	0	9994	0	0	3165	12826	0
32 RUBBER, MISC. PLASTICS	289	14345	0	11842	866	0	66431	5199	0
33 LEATHER TANNING & PRDTS.	1218	1827	0	1827	304	0	1218	0	0
34 FOOTWEAR, LEATHER PRDTS.	2135	1186	0	4744	158	0	1344	0	0
35 GLASS & GLASS PRDTS.	0	4974	0	8457	301	0	19177	1304	0
36 STONE & CLAY PRDTS.	97	7182	0	15994	0	0	7413	0	386
37 PRIMARY IRON, STEEL MFR.	375	2399	0	43584	0	0	85748	0	2255
38 PRIMARY NONFERROUS MFR.	5089	39846	8932	12929	2977	0	7441	11612	2389

#	Industry									
39	METAL CONTAINERS	0	4623	0	1338	0	0	0	0	238
40	FABRICATED METAL PRDTS.	0	5286	0	9192	9223	0	48169	6314	0
41	SCREW MACH. PRDTS., ETC.	0	1916	0	1822	0	0	4045	0	0
42	OTHER FAB. METAL PRDTS.	0	14743	0	7995	683	0	32720	187	0
43	ENGINES & TURBINES	0	0	0	20369	0	0	10090	0	0
44	FARM MACH. & EQUIP.	0	0	0	2918	0	0	2926	0	0
45	CONSTRUC. MACH. & EQUIP.	2563	4732	0	2886	0	0	61046	11053	2805
46	MATERIAL HANDLING MACH.	276	515	0	311	0	0	6569	1189	302
47	METALWORKING MACHINERY	556	3787	0	28051	0	0	94850	0	0
48	SPECIAL MACH. & EQUIP.	16359	15079	0	40042	1691	0	35641	1866	356
49	GENERAL MACH. & EQUIP.	2985	34588	0	52981	1186	0	47959	0	0
50	MACHINE SHOP PRDTS.	0	566	0	154	324	0	2672	0	159
51	OFFICE, COMPUT. MACHINES	404	3069	0	40859	5530	0	35068	0	0
52	SERVICE IND. MACHINES	0	4571	0	21726	0	0	11014	0	0
53	ELECT. TRANSMISS. EQUIP.	948	12748	0	38694	3560	0	35402	185	10709
54	HOUSEHOLD APPLIANCES	0	3911	0	8106	2256	0	43250	0	0
55	ELECTRIC LIGHTING EQUIP.	159	8750	0	7386	161	0	8254	0	0
56	RADIO, TV, ETC., EQUIP.	300	23765	0	44950	5011	0	619	0	0
57	ELECTRONIC COMPONENTS	540	9733	0	14853	437	0	4364	0	0
58	MISC. ELECTRICAL MACH.	0	4375	110	9559	1472	0	18546	0	0
59	MOTOR VEHICLES, EQUIP.	0	92104	0	58748	193	0	199577	0	1281
60	AIRCRAFT & PARTS	0	13590	0	12004	114	0	18079	2238	0
61	OTHER TRANSPORT. EQUIP.	216	12730	0	64458	0	0	2446	0	299
62	PROFESS., SCIEN. INSTRU.	0	22433	52	31923	619	0	7684	155	0
63	MEDICAL, PHOTO. EQUIP.	178	4273	0	55611	0	0	534	0	712
64	MISC. MANUFACTURING	139	5152	70	17546	70	0	5988	139	70
65	TRANSPORT. & WAREHOUSING	1685	29536	2021	238382	25824	6849	250889	8919	24956
66	COMMUNICA., EXC. BROCAST.	28	635	19	56153	68	10	306	59	53
67	RADIO & TV BROADCASTING	46	63	103	406	398	57	309	141	168
68	ELEC.,GAS,WATER,SAN.SER.	379	0	419	6532	0	279	0	0	0
69	WHOLESALE & RETAIL TRADE	1970	4180	3309	273142	25008	4996	71721	13256	16216
70	FINANCE & INSURANCE	82	820	84	2664	355	67	1085	252	202
71	REAL ESTATE & RENTAL	893	13640	196	28901	5598	115	20865	1318	2222
72	HOTELS; PERSONAL SERV.	0	0	0	105581	0	0	0	0	0
73	BUSINESS SERVICES	74	2721	124	130755	575	42	8863	710	1189
74	RESEARCH & DEVELOPMENT	0	0	0	0	0	0	0	0	0
75	AUTO. REPAIR & SERVICES	0	0	0	0	0	0	0	0	0
76	AMUSEMENTS	0	2084	0	3412	2205	0	7105	750	237
77	MED.,EDUC. SERVICES	7	114	79	2742	58	0	273	47	11
78	FEDERAL GOV'T ENTERPRISE	64	537	26	136	291	84	1002	229	175
79	STATE & LOCAL GOV'T ENT.	1	0	0	0	0	69	0	0	0
80	IMPORTS	0	0	0	0	0	0	0	0	0
81	BUS.TRAVEL, ENT., GIFTS.	0	0	0	0	0	0	0	0	0
82	OFFICE SUPPLIES	0	0	0	0	0	0	0	0	0
83	SCRAP & USED GOODS	674	10726	274	16858	5991	0	17799	1212	1097
84	GOVERNMENT INDUSTRY	0	0	0	0	0	14	0	0	0
85	REST OF WORLD INDUSTRY	0	0	0	0	0	0	0	0	0
86	HOUSEHOLD INDUSTRY	0	0	0	0	0	0	0	0	0
87	INVENTORY VALUATION ADJ.	0	0	0	0	0	0	0	0	0
88	STATE TOTAL	48606	799925	32495	1928414	593187	52667	1489206	145722	131708

347

TABLE C.11

STATE ESTIMATES OF 1958
NET FOREIGN EXPORTS BY STATE OF PRODUCTION
(THOUSANDS OF CURRENT DOLLARS)

INDUSTRY TITLE	37 PENNSYL-VANIA	38 RHODE ISLAND	39 SOUTH CAROLINA	40 SOUTH DAKOTA	41 TENNESSEE	42 TEXAS	43 UTAH	44 VERMONT	45 VIRGINIA
1 LIVESTOCK & PRDTS.	1456	0	148	366	1069	1773	281	56	732
2 OTHER AGRICULTURE PRDTS.	14953	231	34290	12876	36321	194802	4338	277	22106
3 FORESTRY & FISHERIES	326	181	929	2	19	2205	0	0	1590
4 AGRI.,FORES.,FISH. SERV.	122	11	28	21	55	182	13	16	62
5 IRON, FERRO. ORES MINING	727	0	0	619	876	150	1023	0	81
6 NONFERROUS ORES MINING	0	0	0	0	0	0	763	0	0
7 COAL MINING	81380	0	0	0	3778	0	6389	0	19741
8 CRUDE PETRO.,NATURAL GAS	594	0	0	0	0	9762	199	0	0
9 STONE & CLAY MINING	1167	0	621	79	990	1468	661	153	747
10 CHEM.&FERT. MIN. MINING	0	0	0	0	2518	16788	162	0	0
11 NEW CONSTRUCTION	0	0	0	0	0	0	0	0	0
12 MAINT. & REPAIR CONSTR.	0	0	0	0	0	0	0	0	0
13 ORDNANCE & ACCESSORIES	701	17	95	0	64	219	258	129	43
14 FOOD & KINDRED PRDTS.	33575	1423	3889	3983	30919	157443	3699	948	14037
15 TOBACCO MANUFACTURES	2482	0	286	0	1241	0	0	0	164470
16 FABRICS	8529	6998	49314	0	3718	1968	0	109	16073
17 TEXTILE PRDTS.	4265	1999	2133	0	1066	400	0	0	2399
18 APPAREL	18810	717	2956	0	6897	2329	269	269	4926
19 MISC. TEXTILE PRDTS.	1001	125	125	0	250	375	0	0	250
20 LUMBER & WOOD PRDTS.	2172	78	2792	310	2637	2947	155	620	3490
21 WOODEN CONTAINERS	57	0	85	0	114	114	0	0	142
22 HOUSEHOLD FURNITURE	768	0	210	0	768	349	0	70	908
23 OTHER FURNITURE	1551	0	0	0	222	886	0	70	443
24 PAPER & ALLIED PRDTS.	5565	0	4360	0	8997	5565	0	371	12337
25 PAPERBOARD CONTAINERS	962	27	659	0	714	522	0	27	577
26 PRINTING & PUBLISHING	11207	141	141	70	705	1128	70	70	634
27 CHEMICALS,SELECT. PRDTS.	23228	361	6244	0	19835	149156	410	0	15803
28 PLASTICS & SYNTHETICS	25913	402	8691	0	28256	65640	0	0	29487
29 DRUGS & COSMETICS	36114	0	315	0	1927	2173	0	0	394
30 PAINT & ALLIED PRDTS.	3742	0	0	0	0	2324	0	0	0
31 PETROLEUM, RELATED INDS.	51470	333	167	0	0	240525	0	0	0
32 RUBBER, MISC. PLASTICS	11553	2407	481	0	6836	1829	193	481	2118
33 LEATHER TANNING & PRDTS.	2436	158	0	0	304	0	0	0	304
34 FOOTWEAR, LEATHER PRDTS.	2846	702	0	0	1344	158	0	79	395
35 GLASS & GLASS PRDTS.	9617	0	1003	0	903	711	97	0	386
36 STONE & CLAY PRDTS.	11885	0	676	0	0	570	1113	97	0
37 PRIMARY IRON, STEEL MFR.	166194	1157	0	0	8894	1623	12299	0	1131
38 PRIMARY NONFERROUS MFR.	7707	1688	0	0	517	48452	0	74	149

#	Industry								
39	METAL CONTAINERS	2023	0	0	0	0	0	0	0	0
40	FABRICATED METAL PRDTS.	59975	0	0	0	10817	5735	0	0	2223
41	SCREW MACH. PRDTS., ETC.	3713	115	74	0	0	100	0	0	86
42	OTHER FAB. METAL PRDTS.	33417	1706	219	0	640	12775	0	0	512
43	ENGINES & TURBINES	48073	0	0	0	1613	782	0	0	0
44	FARM MACH. & EQUIP.	3469	0	0	430	1852	103	0	0	0
45	CONSTRUC. MACH. & EQUIP.	41562	1775	147	0	199	57125	11301	0	0
46	MATERIAL HANDLING MACH.	473	0	16	46	793	6147	1216	11523	0
47	METALWORKING MACHINERY	48879	0	384	0	0	0	0	2780	0
48	SPECIAL MACH. & EQUIP.	36809	9750	7593	0	908	4490	262	0	948
49	GENERAL MACH. & EQUIP.	28884	0	588	0	620	1075	0	0	0
50	MACHINE SHOP PRDTS.	619	450	0	279	0	0	0	0	0
51	OFFICE, COMPUT. MACHINES	737	523	0	0	1327	61	1204	0	1815
52	SERVICE IND. MACHINES	12721	0	0	0	670	1100	0	0	1904
53	ELECT. TRANSMISS. EQUIP.	55065	0	677	0	1639	0	0	985	7037
54	HOUSEHOLD APPLIANCES	2752	1284	0	0	0	0	0	0	0
55	ELECTRIC LIGHTING EQUIP.	10098	731	0	0	983	7850	433	0	637
56	RADIO, TV, ETC., EQUIP.	11029	345	0	0	1115	2634	196	0	115
57	ELECTRONIC COMPONENTS	12073	248	270	0	267	282	441	0	0
58	MISC. ELECTRICAL MACH.	6029	0	0	0	100	1100	294	0	0
59	MOTOR VEHICLES, EQUIP.	24258	539	0	0	1618	4220	77	0	6474
60	AIRCRAFT & PARTS	12186	0	0	0	0	0	0	0	0
61	OTHER TRANSPORT. EQUIP.	101516	980	413	0	1512	1186	0	258	1728
62	PROFESS., SCIEN. INSTRU.	20732	356	59	0	1289	2166	0	253	155
63	MEDICAL, PHOTO. EQUIP.	1484	0	0	0	59	237	0	0	356
64	MISC. MANUFACTURING	5709	5570	0	3652	766	1114	487	696	1810
65	TRANSPORT. & WAREHOUSING	111444	1879	9118	0	14620	166636	6199	1034	264720
66	COMMUNICA.-EXC. BRDCAST.	362	34	30	11	56	206	17	82	82
67	RADIO & TV BROADCASTING	438	40	191	53	271	640	67	29	240
68	ELEC.,GAS.,WATER,SAN.SER.	0	0	0	0	25540	6331	0	146	0
69	WHOLESALE & RETAIL TRADE	81141	5001	7986	4742	300	0	5956	1149	17361
70	FINANCE & INSURANCE	1237	104	169	65	4014	1018	72	41	316
71	REAL ESTATE & RENTAL	20774	1375	2473	207	0	9175	758	429	3861
72	HOTELS; PERSONAL SERV.	0	0	0	0	0	0	0	0	0
73	BUSINESS SERVICES	10396	574	320	69	1323	4444	428	51	698
74	RESEARCH & DEVELOPMENT	0	0	0	0	0	0	0	0	0
75	AUTO. REPAIR & SERVICES	0	0	0	0	0	0	0	0	0
76	AMUSEMENTS	5358	0	31	0	1152	4448	1045	0	48
77	MED.,EDUC. SERVICES	371	12	16	0	23	252	1	1	28
78	FEDERAL GOV'T ENTERPRISE	1251	76	141	82	307	825	57	57	286
79	STATE & LOCAL GOV'T ENT.	0	0	0	0	0	298	3	0	0
80	IMPORTS	0	0	0	0	0	0	0	0	0
81	BUS.TRAVEL, ENT., GIFTS.	0	0	0	0	0	0	0	0	0
82	OFFICE SUPPLIES	0	0	0	0	0	0	0	0	0
83	SCRAP & USED GOODS	15631	715	1422	86	2599	12370	855	343	4586
84	GOVERNMENT INDUSTRY	0	0	0	0	0	0	0	0	0
85	REST OF WORLD INDUSTRY	0	0	0	0	0	0	0	0	0
86	HOUSEHOLD INDUSTRY	0	0	0	0	0	0	0	0	0
87	INVENTORY VALUATION ADJ.	0	0	0	0	0	0	0	0	0
88	STATE TOTAL	1351762	58050	152975	28048	251846	1301112	62866	24386	633981

TABLE C.11

STATE ESTIMATES OF 1958
NET FOREIGN EXPORTS BY STATE OF PRODUCTION
(THOUSANDS OF CURRENT DOLLARS)

INDUSTRY TITLE	46 WASHINGTON	47 WEST VIRGINIA	48 WISCONSIN	49 WYOMING	50 ALASKA	51 HAWAII	52 NO STATE ALLOCATION	53 NATIONAL TOTAL
1 LIVESTOCK & PRDTS.	401	134	2961	28	0		0	37520
2 OTHER AGRICULTURE PRDTS.	40566	1800	7707	3000	0		0	1813168
3 FORESTRY & FISHERIES	2383	0	374	485	0		0	30304
4 AGRI.,FORES.,FISH.SERV.	52	11	77	4	0		0	3262
5 IRON,FERRO.ORES MINING	0	0	367	148	0		0	41032
6 NONFERROUS ORES MINING	0	0	0	221	0		0	4211
7 COAL MINING	325	100707	0	798	0		0	332063
8 CRUDE PETRO.,NATURAL GAS	0	930	0	747	0		0	27948
9 STONE & CLAY MINING	358	140	151	0	0		0	22849
10 CHEM.&FERT.MIN.MINING	0	0	0	162	0		0	55276
11 NEW CONSTRUCTION	0	0	0	0	0		0	2000
12 MAINT. & REPAIR CONSTR.	0	0	0	0	0		0	0
13 ORDNANCE & ACCESSORIES	9	0	421	0	0		0	16743
14 FOOD & KINDRED PRDTS.	30540	1138	30445	379	0		0	1297764
15 TOBACCO MANUFACTURES	0	573	0	0	0		0	435848
16 FABRICS	0	0	219	0	0		0	210266
17 TEXTILE PRDTS.	0	0	400	0	0		0	46117
18 APPAREL	537	448	1344	0	0		0	140092
19 MISC. TEXTILE PRDTS.	250	0	125	0	0		0	18266
20 LUMBER & WOOD PRDTS.	10703	1163	3180	155	0		0	110057
21 WOODEN CONTAINERS	57	28	85	0	0		0	2728
22 HOUSEHOLD FURNITURE	140	140	140	0	0		0	15088
23 OTHER FURNITURE	0	222	886	0	0		0	18391
24 PAPER & ALLIED PRDTS.	50182	93	3525	0	0		0	261113
25 PAPERBOARD CONTAINERS	1484	27	220	0	0		0	19257
26 PRINTING & PUBLISHING	423	141	1692	0	0		0	92962
27 CHEMICALS,SELECT.PRDTS.	4055	44866	815	0	0		0	676064
28 PLASTICS & SYNTHETICS	0	14734	1123	0	0		0	339202
29 DRUGS & COSMETICS	264	1241	1585	0	0		0	325173
30 PAINT & ALLIED PRDTS.	0	0	0	0	0		0	27276
31 PETROLEUM,RELATED INDS.	666	500	0	333	0		0	654947
32 RUBBER, MISC. PLASTICS	96	0	1637	0	0		0	211328
33 LEATHER TANNING & PRDTS.	0	304	3045	0	0		0	28008
34 FOOTWEAR, LEATHER PRDTS.	79	79	1502	0	0		0	36051
35 GLASS & GLASS PRDTS.	0	3775	0	0	0		0	68485
36 STONE & CLAY PRDTS.	483	807	3475	0	0		0	99734
37 PRIMARY IRON, STEEL MFR.	170	5738	5947	0	0		0	535081
38 PRIMARY NONFERROUS MFR.	39890	16822	626	0	0		0	305257

#	Industry								
39	METAL CONTAINERS	108	0	0	0	0	0	0	26108
40	FABRICATED METAL PRDTS.	642	1084	6818	0	0	0	0	225093
41	SCREW MACH. PRDTS., ETC.	665	378	1974	0	0	0	0	28327
42	OTHER FAB. METAL PRDTS.	0	1264	7408	0	0	0	0	251299
43	ENGINES & TURBINES	0	0	28754	0	0	0	0	210865
44	FARM MACH. & EQUIP.	2118	4128	16889	0	0	0	0	187940
45	CONSTRUC. MACH. & EQUIP.	228	0	52128	0	0	0	0	709270
46	MATERIAL HANDLING MACH.	106	5945	5610	0	0	0	0	76327
47	METALWORKING MACHINERY	3092	0	7345	0	0	0	0	331276
48	SPECIAL MACH. & EQUIP.	0	0	41451	0	0	0	0	369805
49	GENERAL MACH. & EQUIP.	0	0	8139	0	0	0	0	274565
50	MACHINE SHOP PRDTS.	0	0	342	0	0	0	0	15033
51	OFFICE, COMPUT. MACHINES	0	0	285	0	0	0	0	135772
52	SERVICE IND. MACHINES	222	4323	8070	0	0	0	0	135540
53	ELECT. TRANSMISS. EQUIP.	0	0	17351	0	0	0	0	280977
54	HOUSEHOLD APPLIANCES	0	1860	3553	0	0	0	0	163214
55	ELECTRIC LIGHTING EQUIP.	1860	0	123	0	0	0	0	63956
56	RADIO, TV, ETC., EQUIP.	0	0	464	0	0	0	0	201289
57	ELECTRONIC COMPONENTS	0	0	4084	0	0	0	0	90187
58	MISC. ELECTRICAL MACH.	0	0	5245	0	0	0	0	71421
59	MOTOR VEHICLES, EQUIP.	5712	154	29737	0	0	0	0	918343
60	AIRCRAFT & PARTS	133497	0	0	0	0	0	0	559159
61	OTHER TRANSPORT. EQUIP.	7860	864	2409	0	0	0	0	298139
62	PROFESS., SCIEN. INSTRU.	52	155	9128	52	0	0	0	183133
63	MEDICAL, PHOTO. EQUIP.	0	0	297	0	0	0	0	90271
64	MISC. MANUFACTURING	139	348	8007	1869	0	0	0	115550
65	TRANSPORT. & WAREHOUSING	37711	67119	119943	9	0	0	0	2302073
66	COMMUNICA. EXC. BRDCAST.	76	44	63	55	0	0	0	64298
67	RADIO & TV BROADCASTING	204	141	212	0	0	0	0	8996
68	ELEC.,GAS.WATER,SAN.SER.	4089	0	0	0	0	0	0	34058
69	WHOLESALE & RETAIL TRADE	21476	6573	22570	1050	0	0	0	1420065
70	FINANCE & INSURANCE	297	141	418	32	0	0	0	20597
71	REAL ESTATE & RENTAL	3941	2308	7202	113	0	0	0	256981
72	HOTELS; PERSONAL SERV.	0	177	2887	0	0	0	0	0
73	BUSINESS SERVICES	1669	0	0	22	0	0	0	248999
74	RESEARCH & DEVELOPMENT	0	0	0	0	0	0	0	0
75	AUTO. REPAIR & SERVICES	1459	0	912	0	0	0	0	258649
76	AMUSEMENTS	17	9	75	0	0	0	0	6502
77	MED., EDUC. SERVICES	271	159	363	1	0	0	41796	60700
78	FEDERAL GOV'T ENTERPRISE	1040	0	73	0	0	0	0	2399
79	STATE & LOCAL GOV'T ENT.	0	0	0	36	0	0	0	-21081104
80	IMPORTS	0	0	0	0	0	0	-21081104	0
81	BUS. TRAVEL, ENT., GIFTS.	0	0	0	0	0	0	0	0
82	OFFICE SUPPLIES	0	0	0	0	0	0	0	208696
83	SCRAP & USED GOODS	6577	1919	6233	12	0	0	0	0
84	GOVERNMENT INDUSTRY	0	0	0	0	0	0	0	4019800
85	REST OF WORLD INDUSTRY	0	0	0	0	0	0	4019800	0
86	HOUSEHOLD INDUSTRY	0	0	0	0	0	0	0	0
87	INVENTORY VALUATION ADJ.	0	0	0	0	0	0	0	0
88	STATE TOTAL	417381	295654	500636	9711	0	0	-17215488	2206000

TABLE C.12

STATE ESTIMATES OF 1963
NET FOREIGN EXPORTS BY STATE OF PRODUCTION
(THOUSANDS OF CURRENT DOLLARS)

INDUSTRY TITLE	1 ALABAMA	2 ARIZONA	3 ARKANSAS	4 CALIFORNIA	5 COLORADO	6 CONNECTICUT	7 DELAWARE	8 DISTRICT OF COLUMBIA	9 FLORIDA
1 LIVESTOCK & PRDTS.	605	109	589	2755	736	33	355	0	251
2 OTHER AGRICULTURE PRDTS.	32774	34933	108619	204891	22477	2325	3820	0	50323
3 FORESTRY & FISHERIES	1147	781	458	4477	0	117	120	0	3620
4 AGRI.,FORES.,FISH.SERV.	156	135	186	1720	84	191	59	11	716
5 IRON,FERRO. ORES MINING	1463	0	0	8403	29734	0	0	0	0
6 NONFERROUS ORES MINING	0	0	407	0	82	0	0	0	0
7 COAL MINING	11320	0	179	0	2806	0	0	0	0
8 CRUDE PETRO.,NATURAL GAS	0	0	0	910	0	0	0	0	688
9 STONE & CLAY MINING	566	360	258	6185	614	0	0	0	25101
10 CHEM.&FERT. MIN. MINING	0	0	0	0	0	0	0	2000	0
11 NEW CONSTRUCTION	0	0	0	0	0	0	0	0	0
12 MAINT. & REPAIR CONSTR.	0	0	0	0	0	0	0	0	0
13 ORDNANCE & ACCESSORIES	1449	8455	0	102188	3322	7912	0	0	10931
14 FOOD & KINDRED PRDTS.	11759	4145	53975	198744	13301	5205	4145	2410	24867
15 TOBACCO MANUFACTURES	0	0	0	0	0	204	0	0	1019
16 FABRICS	13426	0	324	647	0	4368	971	0	162
17 TEXTILE PRDTS.	640	0	240	1360	279	640	160	0	0
18 APPAREL	4085	279	557	4920	279	1671	371	0	836
19 MISC. TEXTILE PRDTS.	207	0	0	2277	0	414	0	207	207
20 LUMBER & WOOD PRDTS.	7225	744	7650	16362	744	531	425	0	3400
21 WOODEN CONTAINERS	65	0	108	195	0	22	0	0	43
22 HOUSEHOLD FURNITURE	117	58	292	817	58	0	0	0	219
23 OTHER FURNITURE	0	0	236	1649	0	471	0	0	295
24 PAPER & ALLIED PRDTS.	5999	0	1800	5899	200	4500	100	200	47295
25 PAPERBOARD CONTAINERS	0	0	0	2528	0	632	0	0	0
26 PRINTING & PUBLISHING	387	291	194	6102	581	2034	97	5037	969
27 CHEMICALS,SELECT. PRDTS.	41435	728	2789	54396	11883	10112	3092	0	58907
28 PLASTICS & SYNTHETICS	2062	0	0	12168	0	6201	2528	0	18525
29 DRUGS & COSMETICS	0	0	0	9670	0	7566	5141	101	2354
30 PAINT & ALLIED PRDTS.	204	0	0	2712	0	0	0	0	0
31 PETROLEUM, RELATED INDS.	0	0	1266	118729	475	0	0	0	0
32 RUBBER, MISC. PLASTICS	6771	115	1033	14116	6771	5853	1836	0	230
33 LEATHER TANNING & PRDTS.	0	0	0	1280	0	0	3414	0	0
34 FOOTWEAR, LEATHER PRDTS.	34	0	414	276	103	310	69	0	34
35 GLASS & GLASS PRDTS.	0	0	0	1325	0	656	0	0	0
36 STONE & CLAY PRDTS.	315	0	0	8671	0	2820	0	0	0
37 PRIMARY IRON, STEEL MFR.	22473	0	0	19254	6444	2469	0	0	473
38 PRIMARY NONFERROUS MFR.	7256	8034	4161	14184	1342	11688	2726	0	877

#	Sector	C1	C2	C3	C4	C5	C6	C7	C8	C9
39	METAL CONTAINERS	0	0	0	8224	0	0	0	0	175
40	FABRICATED METAL PRDTS.	6942	124	249	16602	0	347	4424	0	2675
41	SCREW MACH. PRDTS., ETC.	84	0	0	2446	1754	1144	152	0	147
42	OTHER FAB. METAL PRDTS.	719	0	0	13855	195	19277	162	0	1885
43	ENGINES & TURBINES	0	0	0	679	392	1471	0	0	0
44	FARM MACH. & EQUIP.	655	630	630	2725	15020	0	0	0	0
45	CONSTRUC. MACH. & EQUIP.	1373	64	64	18401	1537	0	0	0	0
46	MATERIAL HANDLING MACH.	141	0	0	1883	0	0	0	0	0
47	METALWORKING MACHINERY	0	0	0	1318	656	19334	536	0	303
48	SPECIAL MACH. & EQUIP.	4530	0	0	24921	0	31407	232	0	0
49	GENERAL MACH. & EQUIP.	658	151	151	38732	0	20668	0	0	0
50	MACHINE SHOP PRDTS.	0	0	0	0	0	0	0	0	0
51	OFFICE, COMPUT. MACHINES	5490	2657	330	21310	3665	13326	599	0	29200
52	SERVICE IND. MACHINES	135	1205	4709	6709	0	1637	0	0	0
53	ELECT. TRANSMISS. EQUIP.	0	0	582	24622	0	3926	0	0	0
54	HOUSEHOLD APPLIANCES	799	0	0	2029	108	5337	0	0	0
55	ELECTRIC LIGHTING EQUIP.	0	117	383	4646	141	3318	0	0	0
56	RADIO, TV, ETC., EQUIP.	2466	474	0	41098	0	2803	0	0	2431
57	ELECTRONIC COMPONENTS	316	2011	0	48725	157	5269	340	0	244
58	MISC. ELECTRICAL MACH.	1006	0	0	276	836	1049	895	0	0
59	MOTOR VEHICLES, EQUIP.	0	6526	0	31450	0	4717	195	0	1194
60	AIRCRAFT & PARTS	109	0	418	403113	259	112755	0	0	3636
61	OTHER TRANSPORT. EQUIP.	0	0	0	0	0	1239	691	0	430
62	PROFESS., SCIEN. INSTRU.	86	4232	259	49697	0	14587	0	0	4836
63	MEDICAL, PHOTO. EQUIP.	0	0	0	3836	946	3156	53	0	0
64	MISC. MANUFACTURING	210	525	893	9508	34	12292	1555	0	1261
65	TRANSPORT. & WAREHOUSING	33899	4269	13935	198666	426	10801	14	329	90894
66	COMMUNICA.,EXC. BRDCAST.	29	18	20	897	0	110	62	19	67
67	RADIO & TV BROADCASTING	789	374	446	1858	17542	270	0	93	1157
68	ELEC.,GAS,WATER,SAN.SER.	0	1001	0	6817	368	0	5278	0	0
69	WHOLESALE & RETAIL TRADE	16438	8672	7485	171330	2467	16830	89	9969	36250
70	FINANCE & INSURANCE	403	245	256	4179	44	658	1359	243	1007
71	REAL ESTATE & RENTAL	5196	1295	1985	35459	774	9289	8	535	4859
72	HOTELS; PERSONAL SERV.	0	38	25	5432	0	49	85	41	169
73	BUSINESS SERVICES	369	460	163	15654	0	932	0	879	1831
74	RESEARCH & DEVELOPMENT	0	0	0	0	1932	0	0	0	0
75	AUTO. REPAIR & SERVICES	0	0	0	0	216	0	425	0	0
76	AMUSEMENTS	25	70	70	79276	366	923	71	4536	2086
77	MED.,EDUC. SERVICES	37	26	26	962	0	374	0	281	121
78	FEDERAL GOV'T ENTERPRISE	394	200	200	3152	0	479	0	791	836
79	STATE & LOCAL GOV'T ENT.	0	0	0	0	0	0	0	0	0
80	IMPORTS	0	0	0	0	0	0	0	0	0
81	BUS.TRAVEL, ENT., GIFTS.	0	0	0	0	1701	0	0	0	0
82	OFFICE SUPPLIES	2597	891	1620	28833	0	7428	539	154	4333
83	SCRAP & USED GOODS	0	0	0	0	0	0	0	0	0
84	GOVERNMENT INDUSTRY	0	0	0	0	0	0	0	0	0
85	REST OF WORLD INDUSTRY	0	0	0	0	0	0	0	0	0
86	HOUSEHOLD INDUSTRY	0	0	0	0	0	0	0	0	0
87	INVENTORY VALUATION ADJ.	0	0	0	0	0	0	0	0	0
88	STATE TOTAL	259874	94597	220613	2154130	166516	406147	47193	27836	444369

TABLE C.12

STATE ESTIMATES OF 1963
NET FOREIGN EXPORTS BY STATE OF PRODUCTION
(THOUSANDS OF CURRENT DOLLARS)

INDUSTRY TITLE	10 GEORGIA	11 IDAHO	12 ILLINOIS	13 INDIANA	14 IOWA	15 KANSAS	16 KENTUCKY	17 LOUISIANA	18 MAINE
1 LIVESTOCK & PRDTS.	971	316	1642	1096	4069	1124	693	175	136
2 OTHER AGRICULTURE PRDTS.	53368	37037	262467	127773	141780	175052	29175	53534	4429
3 FORESTRY & FISHERIES	896	82	87	10	11		189	4267	2319
4 AGRI.,FORES.,FISH. SERV.	316	50	440	236	251	147	144	132	56
5 IRON,FERRO. ORES MINING	268	0	0	0	0	0	0	0	0
6 NONFERROUS ORES MINING	0	0	0	0	0	0	0	0	0
7 COAL MINING	0	0	24415	6781	520	411	41290	0	0
8 CRUDE PETRO.,NATURAL GAS	0	0	160	458		602	559	3221	0
9 STONE & CLAY MINING	6831	0	740	0	1221	239	0	557	0
10 CHEM.&FERT. MIN. MINING	0	1026	168		0	0	0	13067	0
11 NEW CONSTRUCTION	0	0	0		0	0	0	0	0
12 MAINT. & REPAIR CONSTR.	0	0	0		0	0		1570	0
13 ORDNANCE & ACCESSORIES		181	5556	3443	3201				785
14 FOOD & KINDRED PRDTS.	28433	5398	172142	39132	51083	59083	2700	54746	7325
15 TOBACCO MANUFACTURES	102	0	611	407	0	0	18217		0
16 FABRICS	31058	0	1132	160	0		2241	0	3397
17 TEXTILE PRDTS.	4321	0	1360	1021	279		162	240	80
18 APPAREL	7056	0	3435	414	207		1578	279	186
19 MISC. TEXTILE PRDTS.	1656	0	1863	3825	1275		207	0	207
20 LUMBER & WOOD PRDTS.	6268	3719	3187	22	22		2762	5100	4356
21 WOODEN CONTAINERS	173	0	43	700	0		108	65	22
22 HOUSEHOLD FURNITURE	233	0	467	707	471		175	58	0
23 OTHER FURNITURE	236	0	1885	2000	400		0	0	
24 PAPER & ALLIED PRDTS.	45096	2200	6299	632	1550	162	2700	10599	11199
25 PAPERBOARD CONTAINERS	632	0	3161	3003	537	279	0	0	0
26 PRINTING & PUBLISHING	678	97	30318	2976	3656	207	581	387	194
27 CHEMICALS,SELECT. PRDTS.	24868	4001	39101	2433	1784	212	10902	84378	1698
28 PLASTICS & SYNTHETICS	602	0	25266	13143	0	58	43965	24909	0
29 DRUGS & COSMETICS	5819	0	3148	211	2066	236	501	0	0
30 PAINT & ALLIED PRDTS.	1252	0	6649	3324	34	200	1033	1084	0
31 PETROLEUM, RELATED INDS.	459	0	18477	11706	0	484	427	112397	0
32 RUBBER, MISC. PLASTICS	0	0	2134	138	0	4520	103	0	0
33 LEATHER TANNING & PRDTS.	172	0	758	969		803	998	0	689
34 FOOTWEAR, LEATHER PRDTS.	171	0	5800	2774		163	5582	0	1707
35 GLASS & CLAY PRDTS.	280	0				1108		0	1241
36 STONE & CLAY PRDTS.	0	0	6373			4131		0	0
37 PRIMARY IRON, STEEL MFR.		0	22402	24099	749	2098	2123		
38 PRIMARY NONFERROUS MFR.	4017	0	7648	10438	3336	1148	150	41031	143

354

No.	Industry									
39	METAL CONTAINERS	0	0	8017	165	0	0	0	144	244
40	FABRICATED METAL PRDTS.	7975	0	7155	8943	881	2986	1768	4705	0
41	SCREW MACH. PRDTS., ETC.	928	0	5331	3057	73	0	437	0	0
42	OTHER FAB. METAL PRDTS.	305	0	29563	7135	4658	0	3427	1425	0
43	ENGINES & TURBINES		0	26356	33543	5350	0	0	0	436
44	FARM MACH. & EQUIP.	1761	0	71497	4746	87471	1056	6792	311	45
45	CONSTRUC. MACH. & EQUIP.	11808	0	461889	18168	24006	1106	0	1174	2835
46	MATERIAL HANDLING MACH.	1209	0	47276	1860	2457	113	134	120	174
47	METALWORKING MACHINERY		0	40927	7193	679	0	5747	0	0
48	SPECIAL MACH. & EQUIP.	6839	0	51992	3868	1058	663	3059	1369	0
49	GENERAL MACH. & EQUIP.	482	0	32664	18657	1268	397	0	0	0
50	MACHINE SHOP PRDTS.		0		0	0	0			0
51	OFFICE, COMPUT. MACHINES	1384	0	6465	188	303	285	14022	0	0
52	SERVICE IND. MACHINES	5627	0	9970	5129	1382	0	8688	0	0
53	ELECT. TRANSMISS. EQUIP.		0	12749	6969	9828	0	1022	0	0
54	HOUSEHOLD APPLIANCES		0	21755	11872		0	9308	0	547
55	ELECTRIC LIGHTING EQUIP.		0	11111	3832	16008	0	1310	0	0
56	RADIO, TV, ETC., EQUIP.		0	51885	17549	2405	380	0	0	542
57	ELECTRONIC COMPONENTS		0	4455	8218	135	681	1734	0	0
58	MISC. ELECTRICAL MACH.		0	3727	16456	149	448	239	0	0
59	MOTOR VEHICLES, EQUIP.	5062	0	27608	108698	455	25888	10117	0	0
60	AIRCRAFT & PARTS	13736	0	5015	20853	251	125	1094	0	2376
61	OTHER TRANSPORT. EQUIP.		264	42968	214	3195	518	725	0	276
62	PROFESS., SCIEN. INSTRU.	518		21078	4089		0	0	0	0
63	MEDICAL, PHOTO. EQUIP.		105	16049	7530	3730	210	1814	0	683
64	MISC. MANUFACTURING	1103	6282	23271	3782	21569	20307	263	420	3896
65	TRANSPORT. & WAREHOUSING	21414	12	183564	68175	35	30	44179	179617	17
66	COMMUNICA.,EXC. BRDCAST.	49	260	175	77	452	369	42	42	202
67	RADIO & TV BROADCASTING	929	559	924	607	0	0	586	540	0
68	ELEC.,GAS,WATER,SAN.SER.			0	0	22872	16414	0	0	458
69	WHOLESALE & RETAIL TRADE	39218	3772	141065	31239	506	407	15547	22262	4745
70	FINANCE & INSURANCE	623	112	2321	916	4725	3016	422	526	154
71	REAL ESTATE & RENTAL	6723	756	30246	15964	42	32	5266	3958	1624
72	HOTELS; PERSONAL SERV.	63	12	235	75	585	216	42	47	18
73	BUSINESS SERVICES	1840	131	28701	1106	0	0	465	576	63
74	RESEARCH & DEVELOPMENT				0	0	0	0	0	0
75	AUTO. REPAIR & SERVICES		15	0	0	0	0	0	0	0
76	AMUSEMENTS	2602	6	10967	1247	745	0	59	2077	16
77	MED.,EDUC. SERVICES	449	99	1441	345	92	40	58	69	0
78	FEDERAL GOV'T ENTERPRISE	597		2472	753	503	417	442	382	199
79	STATE & LOCAL GOV'T ENT.							0	0	0
80	IMPORTS							0	0	0
81	BUS.TRAVEL, ENT., GIFTS.							0	0	0
82	OFFICE SUPPLIES							0	0	0
83	SCRAP & USED GOODS	4211	295	37161	9365	5067	2251	3185	5389	805
84	GOVERNMENT INDUSTRY	0	0	0	0	0	0	0	0	0
85	REST OF WORLD INDUSTRY	0	0	0	0	0	0	0	0	0
86	HOUSEHOLD INDUSTRY	0	0	0	0	0	0	0	0	0
87	INVENTORY VALUATION ADJ.	0	0	0	0	0	0	0	0	0
88	STATE TOTAL	363687	66787	2141954	716614	441437	330827	306990	638611	60524

TABLE C.12

STATE ESTIMATES OF 1963
NET FOREIGN EXPORTS BY STATE OF PRODUCTION
(THOUSANDS OF CURRENT DOLLARS)

INDUSTRY TITLE	19 MARYLAND	20 MASSA-CHUSETTS	21 MICHIGAN	22 MINNESOTA	23 MISSISSIPPI	24 MISSOURI	25 MONTANA	26 NEBRASKA	27 NEVADA
1 LIVESTOCK & PRDTS.	409	5	1069	3164	605	1265	109	1855	5
2 OTHER AGRICULTURE PRDTS.	14781	2214	53423	90515	80827	93948	69866	94778	554
3 FORESTRY & FISHERIES	1796	3309	951	125	1329	41	1	9	0
4 AGRI.,FORES.,FISH. SERV.	230	239	299	189	98	282	27	112	34
5 IRON, FERRO. ORES MINING	0	0	10421	48022	0	332	396	0	600
6 NONFERROUS ORES MINING	0	0	0	0	0	0	0	0	0
7 COAL MINING	602	0	0	0	0	1772	0	0	0
8 CRUDE PETRO.,NATURAL GAS	0	0	0	0	136	0	0	0	0
9 STONE & CLAY MINING	284	137	1976	85	581	931	448	61	795
10 CHEM.&FERT. MIN. MINING	0	0	0	0	0	0	2016	0	0
11 NEW CONSTRUCTION	0	0	0	0	0	0	0	0	0
12 MAINT. & REPAIR CONSTR.	0	0	0	0	0	0	0	0	0
13 ORDNANCE & ACCESSORIES	2959	5254	1570	5496	0	9361	0	60	0
14 FOOD & KINDRED PRDTS.	25831	20241	37975	37879	16385	56385	1446	23903	386
15 TOBACCO MANUFACTURES	102	0	407	0	0	815	0	0	0
16 FABRICS	647	14720	324	162	0	647	0	0	0
17 TEXTILE PRDTS.	0	3201	800	240	800	560	0	0	0
18 APPAREL	1300	7148	650	2321	2785	2135	0	186	0
19 MISC. TEXTILE PRDTS.	207	2070	6416	1035	207	621	0	319	0
20 LUMBER & WOOD PRDTS.	1487	1912	3825	2019	6268	2337	2550	0	106
21 WOODEN CONTAINERS	43	43	22	22	130	65	0	0	0
22 HOUSEHOLD FURNITURE	117	292	292	58	175	0	0	0	0
23 OTHER FURNITURE	471	471	1649	236	236	707	0	236	0
24 PAPER & ALLIED PRDTS.	900	13899	5399	7099	30097	2500	0	200	0
25 PAPERBOARD CONTAINERS	632	1264	1264	0	0	632	0	0	0
26 PRINTING & PUBLISHING	1066	4553	1937	1453	194	2422	97	387	0
27 CHEMICALS,SELECT. PRDTS.	16747	6886	48972	8041	17654	28404	0	2324	606
28 PLASTICS & SYNTHETICS	7764	14498	17259	2382	2382	0	0	0	0
29 DRUGS & COSMETICS	7607	2290	54891	573	1852	5520	0	386	0
30 PAINT & ALLIED PRDTS.	978	585	1721	0	0	0	0	0	0
31 PETROLEUM, RELATED INDS.	2375	317	2691	475	0	633	0	1262	0
32 RUBBER, MISC. PLASTICS	5050	25936	9296	1836	230	1492	0	0	0
33 LEATHER TANNING & PRDTS.	427	9816	3841	427	0	427	0	0	0
34 FOOTWEAR, LEATHER PRDTS.	69	4102	620	34	69	1310	0	0	0
35 GLASS & GLASS PRDTS.	2846	0	10124	0	0	3947	0	0	0
36 STONE & CLAY PRDTS.	4384	10699	6926	105	1049	10092	0	0	210
37 PRIMARY IRON, STEEL MFR.	46269	4548	35613	677	97	1796	0	0	210
38 PRIMARY NONFERROUS MFR.	2076	2863	7988	0	0	1066	17503	574	6886

#	Industry									
39	METAL CONTAINERS	2087	0	0	175	11686	5524	0	206	0
40	FABRICATED METAL PRDTS.	1369	347	7625	179	73	227	0	2106	0
41	SCREW MACH. PRDTS., ETC.	626	499	7507	221	1716	2758	0	0	0
42	OTHER FAB. METAL PRDTS.	402	23507	18105	1733	1108	553	0	371	0
43	ENGINES & TURBINES	0	28475	36579	934	1857	1777	0	0	0
44	FARM MACH. & EQUIP.	3710	0	46466	5279	190	2730	0	724	0
45	CONSTRUC. MACH. & EQUIP.	380	894	26427	6521	0	279	0	0	0
46	MATERIAL HANDLING MACH.	7489	92	2705	667	696	2577	0	0	0
47	METALWORKING MACHINERY	14896	30657	33562	1746	0	1860	0	0	0
48	SPECIAL MACH. & EQUIP.	1110	60908	10252	1571	0	1040	0	0	0
49	GENERAL MACH. & EQUIP.	0	7493	17896	2230	112	0	0	3921	0
50	MACHINE SHOP PRDTS.	4612	0	0	0	551	543	0	0	0
51	OFFICE, COMPUT. MACHINES	0	10504	15207	19250	552	12960	0	0	0
52	SERVICE IND. MACHINES	323	5931	27947	19219	112	3603	0	0	0
53	ELECT. TRANSMISS. EQUIP.	1036	21616	2951	4798	0	1325	0	0	0
54	HOUSEHOLD APPLIANCES	37153	3306	10165	1218	0	2940	0	0	0
55	ELECTRIC LIGHTING EQUIP.	0	4696	349	457	0	1739	0	0	0
56	RADIO, TV, ETC., EQUIP.	10850	60672	2124	298	0	0	0	0	0
57	ELECTRONIC COMPONENTS	472	19439	3388	134	3612	291	0	239	0
58	MISC. ELECTRICAL MACH.	1433	1857	2898	353	1650	9541	0	0	0
59	MOTOR VEHICLES, EQUIP.	1727	5108	541699	448	152	2984	0	502	0
60	AIRCRAFT & PARTS	238	7658	5760	0	0	110	0	0	0
61	OTHER TRANSPORT. EQUIP.	3677	520	2462	38170	0	4232	0	2159	0
62	PROFESS., SCIEN. INSTRU.	59003	33106	18826	0	735	0	0	0	0
63	MEDICAL, PHOTO. EQUIP.	56	11038	0	0	0	0	0	368	0
64	MISC. MANUFACTURING	353	16600	5726	3257	12717	3047	0	10276	780
65	TRANSPORT. & WAREHOUSING	0	20745	55118	149048	26	18648	11151	16	5
66	COMMUNICA., EXC. BRDCAST.	21662	2043	137	32	462	67	10	311	130
67	RADIO & TV BROADCASTING	576	488	867	452	8652	659	244	0	0
68	ELEC.,GAS,WATER,SAN.SER.	6200	0	3434	1198	271	648	648	16476	1888
69	WHOLESALE & RETAIL TRADE	52	50316	68051	40622	2101	59587	4086	266	80
70	FINANCE & INSURANCE	1181	1344	1777	711	25	838	123	1543	219
71	REAL ESTATE & RENTAL	0	13231	27044	5797	134	8876	488	25	47
72	HOTELS; PERSONAL SERV.	382	106	137	60	0	84	13	599	167
73	BUSINESS SERVICES	153	3267	14224	3148	64	4174	36	0	0
74	RESEARCH & DEVELDPMENT	398	0	0	0	9	0	0	0	0
75	AUTO. REPAIR & SERVICES	0	3122	4825	1504	233	3567	0	408	0
76	AMUSEMENTS	0	546	1431	472	0	510	1	78	94
77	MED.,EDUC. SERVICES	0	1329	1144	753	0	1060	115	309	67
78	FEDERAL GOV'T ENTERPRISE	0	0	0	0	0	0	0	0	0
79	STATE & LOCAL GOV'T ENT.	0	0	0	0	0	0	0	0	0
80	IMPORTS	0	0	0	0	0	0	0	0	0
81	BUS.TRAVEL, ENT., GIFTS.	0	0	0	0	0	0	0	0	0
82	OFFICE SUPPLIES	0	0	0	0	0	0	0	0	0
83	SCRAP & USED GOODS	4362	10036	21235	3825	1979	3953	308	769	114
84	GOVERNMENT INDUSTRY	0	0	0	0	0	0	0	0	0
85	REST OF WORLD INDUSTRY	0	0	0	0	0	0	0	0	0
86	HOUSEHOLD INDUSTRY	0	0	0	0	0	0	0	0	0
87	INVENTORY VALUATION ADJ.	0	0	0	0	0	0	0	0	0
88	STATE TOTAL	338424	625008	1376661	528768	215661	397108	111682	168324	13773

357

TABLE C.12

STATE ESTIMATES OF 1963
NET FOREIGN EXPORTS BY STATE OF PRODUCTION
(THOUSANDS OF CURRENT DOLLARS)

INDUSTRY TITLE	28 NEW HAMPSHIRE	29 NEW JERSEY	30 NEW MEXICO	31 NEW YORK	32 NORTH CAROLINA	33 NORTH DAKOTA	34 OHIO	35 OKLAHOMA	36 OREGON
1 LIVESTOCK & PRDTS.	0	447	98	1287	627	175	1751	338	224
2 OTHER AGRICULTURE PRDTS.	554	7197	12788	30061	171564	105518	93726	70364	35985
3 FORESTRY & FISHERIES	90	1022	0	1738	650	1	177	2	2168
4 AGRI.,FORES.,FISH. SERV.	65	277	44	683	215	24	374	121	104
5 IRON, FERRO. ORES MINING	0	822	604	4767	982	0	0	0	982
6 NONFERROUS ORES MINING	0	0	141	0	0	0	0	0	0
7 COAL MINING	0	0	0	0	0	0	19737	684	0
8 CRUDE PETRO.,NATURAL GAS	0	0	518	0	0	0	0	799	0
9 STONE & CLAY MINING	0	339	454	2128	1416	0	961	435	228
10 CHEM.&FERT. MIN. MINING	0	0	0	0	0	0	0	0	0
11 NEW CONSTRUCTION	0	0	0	0	0	0	0	0	0
12 MAINT. & REPAIR CONSTR.	0	0	0	0	0	0	0	0	0
13 ORDNANCE & ACCESSORIES	0	0	2476	3201	1208	0	3443	0	0
14 FOOD & KINDRED PRDTS.	964	49059	2120	106890	16578	1349	51276	24289	19277
15 TOBACCO MANUFACTURES	0	509	0	102	311765	0	1120	0	0
16 FABRICS	2426	8088	0	5176	72793	0	1132	162	324
17 TEXTILE PRDTS.	80	1440	0	1760	1680	0	2160	0	0
18 APPAREL	371	7427	0	32771	19774	0	2785	464	464
19 MISC. TEXTILE PRDTS.	0	3105	0	7037	1656	0	621	0	414
20 LUMBER & WOOD PRDTS.	1381	1594	637	5312	8925	0	2550	531	29961
21 WOODEN CONTAINERS	43	65	0	65	87	0	43	0	22
22 HOUSEHOLD FURNITURE	58	233	0	700	1867	0	408	58	58
23 OTHER FURNITURE	0	471	0	2827	707	0	1178	0	0
24 PAPER & ALLIED PRDTS.	3300	9899	0	14199	14499	0	9199	600	7499
25 PAPERBOARD CONTAINERS	0	1896	0	3161	632	0	1896	0	0
26 PRINTING & PUBLISHING	194	5231	97	62574	678	97	6974	387	291
27 CHEMICALS,SELECT. PRDTS.	0	145171	2546	34285	3083	0	53994	935	1819
28 PLASTICS & SYNTHETICS	0	9880	0	8525	10782	0	21535	0	0
29 DRUGS & COSMETICS	0	54755	0	94471	285	0	5161	0	0
30 PAINT & ALLIED PRDTS.	0	9059	0	1801	0	0	1278	177	0
31 PETROLEUM, RELATED INDS.	0	76145	0	8707	0	0	3483	20421	0
32 RUBBER, MISC. PLASTICS	344	19739	0	17329	1148	0	72644	6427	0
33 LEATHER TANNING & PRDTS.	2134	2561	0	2561	427	0	1707	0	0
34 FOOTWEAR, LEATHER PRDTS.	1172	517	0	2241	69	0	655	0	0
35 GLASS & GLASS PRDTS.	0	4493	0	9591	1253	0	26242	1538	0
36 STONE & CLAY PRDTS.	210	10484	0	19214	128	0	9785	0	524
37 PRIMARY IRON, STEEL MFR.	387	2939	0	26301	0	0	83738	182	3672
38 PRIMARY NONFERROUS MFR.	287	67515	15638	23527	717	0	24955	6759	3302

#	Industry									
39	METAL CONTAINERS	0	1909	0	1050	0	0	46834	0	0
40	FABRICATED METAL PRDTS.	0	4957	0	9105	10837	0	5944	12746	560
41	SCREW MACH. PRDTS., ETC.	0	2187	0	3161	647	0	34587	0	164
42	OTHER FAB. METAL PRDTS.	0	16531	0	9593	0	0	6310	1486	0
43	ENGINES & TURBINES	0	0	0	76291	0	0	5582	0	0
44	FARM MACH. & EQUIP.	3622	14923	0	1352	0	0	94415	15431	3666
45	CONSTRUC. MACH. & EQUIP.	371	1527	0	5101	0	0	9664	1579	375
46	MATERIAL HANDLING MACH.	1003	4983	0	522	0	0	112377	0	0
47	METALWORKING MACHINERY	20197	28259	0	31121	0	0	47300	0	1705
48	SPECIAL MACH. & EQUIP.	867	30867	0	43161	19799	0	63037	1472	0
49	GENERAL MACH. & EQUIP.	0	0	0	58744	1905	0	0	0	0
50	MACHINE SHOP PRDTS.	0	0	0	0	0	0	0	0	0
51	OFFICE, COMPUT. MACHINES	634	8358	0	73561	278	0	61383	288	0
52	SERVICE IND. MACHINES	0	7089	0	30838	0	0	13303	388	0
53	ELECT. TRANSMISS. EQUIP.	1910	17490	0	57289	7611	0	39876	0	12863
54	HOUSEHOLD APPLIANCES	92	4913	0	3378	694	0	35749	0	96
55	ELECTRIC LIGHTING EQUIP.	222	6378	0	11464	357	0	11739	0	115
56	RADIO, TV, ETC., EQUIP.	561	37122	194	56298	242	0	786	0	0
57	ELECTRONIC COMPONENTS	1905	18912	0	21176	1576	0	9819	0	0
58	MISC. ELECTRICAL MACH.	0	3643	0	9348	2967	0	16946	0	1600
59	MOTOR VEHICLES, EQUIP.	0	134128	0	83394	439	0	294133	5093	0
60	AIRCRAFT & PARTS	0	19912	0	22636	223	0	97212	0	149
61	OTHER TRANSPORT. EQUIP.	259	4398	0	58089	0	0	3122	173	104
62	PROFESS., SCIEN. INSTRU.	0	31955	173	35425	1295	0	21652	0	642
63	MEDICAL, PHOTO. EQUIP.	210	13733	0	98271	788	53	195	420	210
64	MISC. MANUFACTURING	0	7354	158	36982	31939	12913	6724	0	0
65	TRANSPORT. & WAREHOUSING	1755	37759	2279	296036	54	8	368436	11731	37161
66	COMMUNICA.,EXC. BRDCAST.	18	425	13	37399	1183	171	206	45	37
67	RADIO & TV BROADCASTING	140	239	306	1183	0	199	1012	420	524
68	ELEC.,GAS,WATER,SAN.SER.	281	0	350	5886	33810	5907	88159	16777	21536
69	WHOLESALE & RETAIL TRADE	2445	61824	3772	320563	0	112	1772	422	356
70	FINANCE & INSURANCE	139	1464	150	4460	643	149	32036	2023	3198
71	REAL ESTATE & RENTAL	1314	20571	310	40409	9435	9	168	39	37
72	HOTELS; PERSONAL SERV.	16	136	19	478	69	29	7090	569	713
73	BUSINESS SERVICES	86	2096	125	87349	723	0	0	0	0
74	RESEARCH & DEVELOPMENT	0	0	0	0	0	0	4159	452	0
75	AUTO. REPAIR & SERVICES	19	984	0	171388	1626	0	1299	196	447
76	AMUSEMENTS	27	606	6	17847	315	0	1800	400	55
77	MED.,EDUC. SERVICES	115	1115	0	4660	544	0	0	0	309
78	FEDERAL GOV'T ENTERPRISE	0	0	133	0	0	141	0	0	0
79	STATE & LOCAL GOV'T ENT.	0	0	0	0	0	0	0	0	0
80	IMPORTS	0	0	0	0	0	0	29015	2058	0
81	BUS.TRAVEL, ENT., GIFTS.	0	0	0	0	0	0	0	0	0
82	OFFICE SUPPLIES	0	0	0	0	0	0	0	0	0
83	SCRAP & USED GOODS	832	16334	394	27654	9189	30	0	0	1756
84	GOVERNMENT INDUSTRY	0	0	0	0	0	0	0	0	0
85	REST OF WORLD INDUSTRY	0	0	0	0	0	0	0	0	0
86	HOUSEHOLD INDUSTRY	0	0	0	0	0	0	0	0	0
87	INVENTORY VALUATION ADJ.	0	0	0	0	0	0	0	0	0
88	STATE TOTAL	53100	1067460	46543	2387654	785378	126885	2080528	209881	195696

TABLE C.12

STATE ESTIMATES OF 1963
NET FOREIGN EXPORTS BY STATE OF PRODUCTION
(THOUSANDS OF CURRENT DOLLARS)

INDUSTRY TITLE	37 PENNSYLVANIA	38 RHODE ISLAND	39 SOUTH CAROLINA	40 SOUTH DAKOTA	41 TENNESSEE	42 TEXAS	43 UTAH	44 VERMONT	45 VIRGINIA
1 LIVESTOCK & PRDTS.	1511	0	142	660	895	1489	289	65	665
2 OTHER AGRICULTURE PRDTS.	23971	166	50711	36040	47168	252723	6976	443	31058
3 FORESTRY & FISHERIES	267	315	1191	6	96	3780	0	0	1903
4 AGRI.,FORES.,FISH. SERV.	483	39	105	61	199	570	36	46	187
5 IRON, FERRO. ORES MINING	4219	0	0	0	0	737	1366	0	114
6 NONFERROUS ORES MINING	0	0	0	0	0	0	107	0	0
7 COAL MINING	80286	0	0	0	3184	0	4577	0	18611
8 CRUDE PETRO.,NATURAL GAS	114	0	0	0	0	4569	0	0	0
9 STONE & CLAY MINING	919	0	1079	438	821	1511	165	451	542
10 CHEM.&FERT. MIN. MINING	0	0	0	0	4943	14996	672	0	0
11 NEW CONSTRUCTION	0	0	0	0	0	0	0	0	0
12 MAINT. & REPAIR CONSTR.	0	0	0	0	0	0	0	0	0
13 ORDNANCE & ACCESSORIES	2537	0	0	0	0	3201	4167	0	1087
14 FOOD & KINDRED PRDTS.	47132	2120	5687	5783	35855	187660	4337	1735	19084
15 TOBACCO MANUFACTURES	2648	0	407	0	1528	0	0	0	183331
16 FABRICS	11000	10029	66808	0	4044	2912	0	162	23294
17 TEXTILE PRDTS.	2240	960	1600	0	320	240	0	0	1360
18 APPAREL	18764	928	2785	0	6406	2507	279	186	5106
19 MISC. TEXTILE PRDTS.	1631	207	207	0	414	414	0	0	414
20 LUMBER & WOOD PRDTS.	3931	212	5100	531	4887	5631	212	1062	6375
21 WOODEN CONTAINERS	43	0	87	0	108	43	0	0	130
22 HOUSEHOLD FURNITURE	525	0	408	0	583	292	0	22	642
23 OTHER FURNITURE	1649	0	0	0	236	707	0	236	471
24 PAPER & ALLIED PRDTS.	13099	100	8899	0	11199	6901	0	600	13299
25 PAPERBOARD CONTAINERS	1896	632	0	0	0	623	0	0	0
26 PRINTING & PUBLISHING	11527	291	291	97	1162	1937	194	97	1066
27 CHEMICALS,SELECT. PRDTS.	54243	970	10499	0	32527	241188	728	0	26969
28 PLASTICS & SYNTHETICS	61398	1586	16230	0	46006	110475	0	0	55192
29 DRUGS & COSMETICS	25323	0	273	0	1282	2231	0	0	393
30 PAINT & ALLIED PRDTS.	3321	0	0	0	0	2682	0	0	0
31 PETROLEUM, RELATED INDS.	47175	317	475	0	0	267537	0	0	0
32 RUBBER, MISC. PLASTICS	16181	3328	574	0	7574	2295	574	918	2869
33 LEATHER TANNING & PRDTS.	2561	0	0	0	427	0	0	0	427
34 FOOTWEAR, LEATHER PRDTS.	1379	69	0	0	586	69	0	34	172
35 GLASS & GLASS PRDTS.	15240	801	2019	0	2143	332	0	0	0
36 STONE & CLAY PRDTS.	8404	393	551	0	135	3399	105	105	524
37 PRIMARY IRON, STEEL MFR.	161053	1624	97	0	1281	7854	1176	0	774
38 PRIMARY NONFERROUS MFR.	15827	1607	0	0	5703	35116	24652	287	861

#	Industry									
39	METAL CONTAINERS	0	0	0	0	0	0	0	0	2342
40	FABRICATED METAL PRDTS.	5183	0	0	18199	542	0	0	0	37191
41	SCREW MACH. PRDTS., ETC.	79	0	0	76	4455	0	225	95	7235
42	OTHER FAB. METAL PRDTS.	1184	0	0	8906	2074	0	723	1221	37120
43	ENGINES & TURBINES	0	0	0	505	2483	0	0	0	47463
44	FARM MACH. & EQUIP.	0	0	12285	811	254	650	331	0	1454
45	CONSTRUC. MACH. & EQUIP.	0	0	1257	60935	1117	67	34	0	55068
46	MATERIAL HANDLING MACH.	0	19478	0	6237	1040	0	953	2531	5636
47	METALWORKING MACHINERY	1874	0	0	131	0	0	12638	21706	86997
48	SPECIAL MACH. & EQUIP.	0	0	556	1868	0	0	1385	350	53514
49	GENERAL MACH. & EQUIP.	0	0	0	6778	1601	0	0	0	45205
50	MACHINE SHOP PRDTS.	3827	0	0	396	2138	0	377	377	35377
51	OFFICE, COMPUT. MACHINES	3224	566	566	876	1364	0	753	277	23877
52	SERVICE IND. MACHINES	11973	1281	0	1023	820	0	56	568	71357
53	ELECT. TRANSMISS. EQUIP.	0	0	0	0	1781	0	1230	1230	10917
54	HOUSEHOLD APPLIANCES	1098	459	759	19295	465	0	68	693	13081
55	ELECTRIC LIGHTING EQUIP.	287	456	0	11508	139	0	357	904	20430
56	RADIO, TV, ETC., EQUIP.	0	272	0	747	2496	0	0	324	4316
57	ELECTRONIC COMPONENTS	3660	80	0	2079	1154	0	732	732	35551
58	MISC. ELECTRICAL MACH.	0	0	0	10224	2936	0	0	0	20565
59	MOTOR VEHICLES, EQUIP.	3076	605	0	672	1154	0	907	2303	38543
60	AIRCRAFT & PARTS	864	0	0	4619	2936	0	208	198	44973
61	OTHER TRANSPORT. EQUIP.	0	3887	420	1101	1051	6254	1786	5043	905
62	PROFESS., SCIEN. INSTRU.	1366	1623	6566	1418	17003	9	13172	2623	13395
63	MEDICAL, PHOTO. EQUIP.	261048	10	187	206138	804	176	21	23	163331
64	MISC. MANUFACTURING	57	93	187	157	42	176	586	119	233
65	TRANSPORT. & WAREHOUSING	799	77	0	1936	804	0	0	0	1261
66	COMMUNICA.,EXC. BRDCAST.	0	1278	7117	5800	32328	4721	9650	5805	0
67	RADIO & TV BROADCASTING	21188	65	139	88628	589	112	313	174	87365
68	ELEC.,GAS,WATER,SAN.SER.	605	638	1469	1801	6824	289	4361	1981	2048
69	WHOLESALE & RETAIL TRADE	6293	9	16	14640	56	10	30	15	29015
70	FINANCE & INSURANCE	67	32	349	193	1220	43	248	594	197
71	REAL ESTATE & RENTAL	658	0	0	3749	0	0	0	0	7666
72	HOTELS; PERSONAL SERV.	0	925	925	0	836	0	59	0	0
73	BUSINESS SERVICES	70	3	7	4352	111	1	84	3	4662
74	RESEARCH & DEVELOPMENT	108	95	158	1157	538	139	267	47	1487
75	AUTO. REPAIR & SERVICES	507	0	0	1482	0	0	0	154	2159
76	AMUSEMENTS	0	0	0	0	0	0	0	0	0
77	MED.,EDUC. SERVICES	0	0	0	0	0	0	0	0	0
78	FEDERAL GOV'T ENTERPRISE	0	0	0	0	0	0	0	0	0
79	STATE & LOCAL GOV'T ENT.	7000	657	1169	18401	3633	162	2200	1123	24725
80	IMPORTS	0	0	0	0	0	0	0	0	0
81	BUS.TRAVEL, ENT., GIFTS.	0	0	0	0	0	0	0	0	0
82	OFFICE SUPPLIES	0	0	0	0	0	0	0	0	0
83	SCRAP & USED GOODS	0	0	0	0	0	0	0	0	0
84	GOVERNMENT INDUSTRY	0	0	0	0	0	0	0	0	0
85	REST OF WORLD INDUSTRY	0	0	0	0	0	0	0	0	0
86	HOUSEHOLD INDUSTRY	0	0	0	0	0	0	0	0	0
87	INVENTORY VALUATION ADJ.	0	0	0	0	0	0	0	0	0
88	STATE TOTAL	733015	37547	84671	1673458	314391	56249	228272	77275	1683377

TABLE C.12

STATE ESTIMATES OF 1963
NET FOREIGN EXPORTS BY STATE OF PRODUCTION
(THOUSANDS OF CURRENT DOLLARS)

INDUSTRY TITLE	46 WASHINGTON	47 WEST VIRGINIA	48 WISCONSIN	49 WYOMING	50 ALASKA	51 HAWAII	52 NO STATE ALLOCATION	53 NATIONAL TOTAL
1 LIVESTOCK & PRDTS.	485	93	3044	22	0	0	0	38448
2 OTHER AGRICULTURE PRDTS.	76288	1938	12235	3931	0	166	0	2917254
3 FORESTRY & FISHERIES	2693	231	281	9	3418	113	0	46008
4 AGRI.,FORES.,FISH. SERV.	172	35	2291	1848	0	28	0	10698
5 IRON, FERRO. ORES MINING	0	0	0	77	0	0	0	118371
6 NONFERROUS ORES MINING	181	0	0		688	0	0	814
7 COAL MINING	0	86150	0	1212	0	0	0	305406
8 CRUDE PETRO.,NATURAL GAS	0	202	0	330	0	0	0	11561
9 STONE & CLAY MINING	521	317	203	336	0	0	0	37502
10 CHEM.&FERT. MIN. MINING	0	0	0		0	0	0	62325
11 NEW CONSTRUCTION	0	0			0	0	0	2000
12 MAINT. & REPAIR CONSTR.	0	0						
13 ORDNANCE & ACCESSORIES	0	0	1329		0	0	0	197127
14 FOOD & KINDRED PRDTS.	32963	1735	42120	578	1639	13590	0	1648361
15 TOBACCO MANUFACTURES	162	611	162		0	0	0	507929
16 FABRICS	0	0	320		0	0	0	280983
17 TEXTILE PRDTS.	464	464	1578		0	186	0	28962
18 APPAREL	414	0	207		0	0	0	147345
19 MISC. TEXTILE PRDTS.		2337	5737		0	106	0	35370
20 LUMBER & WOOD PRDTS.	18062	117	87	319	425	0	0	194426
21 WOODEN CONTAINERS	58	0	175		0	58	0	2058
22 HOUSEHOLD FURNITURE	236	200	471		0	0	0	10426
23 OTHER FURNITURE		0	5499		0	0	0	19381
24 PAPER & ALLIED PRDTS.	87191	291	632		35396	200	0	448558
25 PAPERBOARD CONTAINERS			3487		0	0	0	22745
26 PRINTING & PUBLISHING			1168		0	0	0	162734
27 CHEMICALS,SELECT. PRDTS.	0	54939	191		0	0	0	1160237
28 PLASTICS & SYNTHETICS	678	49139	3689		0	0	0	553270
29 DRUGS & COSMETICS	9216	2650	529		0	0	0	334639
30 PAINT & ALLIED PRDTS.	0	0	0		0	0	0	31243
31 PETROLEUM, RELATED INDS.	0	1108	2984	633	633	1108	0	678181
32 RUBBER, MISC. PLASTICS	633	115	4268		0	0	0	275546
33 LEATHER TANNING & PRDTS.	115	427	620		0	0	0	41400
34 FOOTWEAR, LEATHER PRDTS.	34	34	0		0	0	0	17541
35 GLASS & GLASS PRDTS.	0	5699	8811		0	1259	0	96187
36 STONE & CLAY PRDTS.	1049	266	7289		0	0	0	127724
37 PRIMARY IRON, STEEL MFR.	406	4537	949		0	0	0	492796
38 PRIMARY NONFERROUS MFR.	77873	28274			0	0	0	490984

#	Industry								
39	METAL CONTAINERS	0	0	0	0	0	0	0	24738
40	FABRICATED METAL PRDTS.	415	1100	9241	0	0	249	0	251771
41	SCREW MACH. PRDTS., ETC.	0	453	1868	0	0	0	0	44275
42	OTHER FAB. METAL PRDTS.	183	1131	8140	0	0	0	0	258828
43	ENGINES & TURBINES	0	0	38059	0	0	0	0	302763
44	FARM MACH. & EQUIP.	0	1751	39617	0	0	0	0	285401
45	CONSTRUC. MACH. & EQUIP.	4849	0	66054	0	0	0	0	935963
46	MATERIAL HANDLING MACH.	496	0	6761	0	0	0	0	95798
47	METALWORKING MACHINERY	151	10494	6430	0	0	0	0	422801
48	SPECIAL MACH. & EQUIP.	3930	0	76445	0	0	1444	0	560904
49	GENERAL MACH. & EQUIP.	0	0	14336	0	0	0	0	377898
50	MACHINE SHOP PRDTS.	0	0	0	0	0	0	0	0
51	OFFICE, COMPUT. MACHINES	0	0	311	0	0	0	0	317127
52	SERVICE IND. MACHINES	676	0	9021	0	0	155	0	208668
53	ELECT. TRANSMISS. EQUIP.	0	3357	20118	0	0	0	0	343463
54	HOUSEHOLD APPLIANCES	0	0	4343	0	0	0	0	132490
55	ELECTRIC LIGHTING EQUIP.	0	1281	232	0	0	0	0	80850
56	RADIO, TV, ETC., EQUIP.	0	0	588	0	0	0	0	366420
57	ELECTRONIC COMPONENTS	0	0	10284	0	0	0	0	198553
58	MISC. ELECTRICAL MACH.	0	0	7980	0	0	0	0	75081
59	MOTOR VEHICLES, EQUIP.	2171	174	62591	0	0	0	0	1386469
60	AIRCRAFT & PARTS	65113	0	0	0	0	0	0	856617
61	OTHER TRANSPORT. EQUIP.	2555	293	1441	0	0	0	0	165272
62	PROFESS., SCIEN. INSTRU.	0	288	20553	86	0	0	0	373249
63	MEDICAL, PHOTO. EQUIP.	99	99	0	0	0	0	0	157199
64	MISC. MANUFACTURING	263	263	11242	0	0	0	0	185698
65	TRANSPORT. & WAREHOUSING	57575	81383	161561	3001	3096	1741	0	3039905
66	COMMUNICA.,EXC. BRDCAST.	53	27	41	6	109	1	0	42963
67	RADIO & TV BROADCASTING	628	363	654	171	0	161	0	27530
68	ELEC.,GAS,WATER,SAN.SER.	3692	0	0	0	0	0	0	30400
69	WHOLESALE & RETAIL TRADE	25046	6759	26639	1206	876	3559	0	1735226
70	FINANCE & INSURANCE	546	218	749	55	45	101	0	36499
71	REAL ESTATE & RENTAL	6258	3899	11080	169	176	539	0	397297
72	HOTELS; PERSONAL SERV.	54	24	66	11	0	19	0	3703
73	BUSINESS SERVICES	1055	134	1935	12	0	264	0	198499
74	RESEARCH & DEVELOPMENT	0	0	0	0	0	0	0	0
75	AUTO. REPAIR & SERVICES	0	0	0	0	0	0	0	312900
76	AMUSEMENTS	1532	11	932	9	0	0	0	32300
77	MED.,EDUC. SERVICES	103	9	360	6	1	186	0	90455
78	FEDERAL GOV'T ENTERPRISE	501	267	622	62	38	76	0	0
79	STATE & LOCAL GOV'T ENT.	0	0	0	0	0	0	56368	0
80	IMPORTS	0	0	0	0	0	0	-26638016	-26638016
81	BUS.TRAVEL, ENT., GIFTS.	0	0	0	0	0	0	0	0
82	OFFICE SUPPLIES	0	0	0	0	0	0	0	0
83	SCRAP & USED GOODS	5829	2935	10913	27	714	343	0	329499
84	GOVERNMENT INDUSTRY	0	0	0	0	0	0	0	0
85	REST OF WORLD INDUSTRY	0	0	0	0	0	0	6208000	6208000
86	HOUSEHOLD INDUSTRY	0	0	0	0	0	0	0	0
87	INVENTORY VALUATION ADJ.	0	0	0	0	0	0	0	0
88	STATE TOTAL	493568	358391	741794	14116	45626	25652	-20377648	5812000

TABLE C.13

STATE ESTIMATES OF 1963
NET FOREIGN EXPORTS BY STATE OF EXIT
(THOUSANDS OF CURRENT DOLLARS)

INDUSTRY TITLE	1 ALABAMA	2 ARIZONA	3 ARKANSAS	4 CALIFORNIA	5 COLORADO	6 CONNECTICUT	7 DELAWARE	8 DISTRICT OF COLUMBIA	9 FLORIDA
1 LIVESTOCK & PRDTS.	0	0	0	5059	0	0	0	0	2024
2 OTHER AGRICULTURE PRDTS.	79061	4003	0	261202	0	0	0	0	76059
3 FORESTRY & FISHERIES	0	0	0	2937	0	0	0	0	3916
4 AGRI.,FORES.,FISH.SERV.	0	0	0	2378	0	0	0	0	0
5 IRON, FERRO. ORES MINING	1012	2023	0	43505	0	0	0	0	1012
6 NONFERROUS ORES MINING	0	0	0	0	0	0	0	0	0
7 COAL MINING	0	0	0	0	0	0	0	0	0
8 CRUDE PETRO.,NATURAL GAS	0	0	0	1156	0	0	0	0	0
9 STONE & CLAY MINING	1022	0	0	4054	0	0	0	0	3041
10 CHEM.&FERT. MIN. MINING	0	0	0	7152	0	0	0	0	5109
11 NEW CONSTRUCTION	0	0	0	0	0	0	0	2000	0
12 MAINT. & REPAIR CONSTR.	0	0	0	0	0	0	0	0	14009
13 ORDNANCE & ACCESSORIES	2001	11007	0	132086	0	10007	0	0	35008
14 FOOD & KINDRED PRDTS.	25005	3001	0	182039	0	0	0	0	17997
15 TOBACCO MANUFACTURES	0	0	0	18997	0	0	0	0	15053
16 FABRICS	0	0	0	5018	0	0	0	0	2146
17 TEXTILE PRDTS.	0	0	0	1073	0	0	0	0	8960
18 APPAREL	0	0	0	12942	0	0	0	0	3121
19 MISC. TEXTILE PRDTS.	0	0	0	2081	0	0	0	0	5116
20 LUMBER & WOOD PRDTS.	1023	0	0	46048	0	0	0	0	0
21 WOODEN CONTAINERS	0	0	0	0	0	0	0	0	1304
22 HOUSEHOLD FURNITURE	0	0	0	1304	0	0	0	0	2769
23 OTHER FURNITURE	0	0	0	1384	0	0	0	0	0
24 PAPER & ALLIED PRDTS.	6021	0	0	72251	0	0	0	0	56195
25 PAPERBOARD CONTAINERS	0	0	0	2166	0	0	0	0	1083
26 PRINTING & PUBLISHING	0	0	0	6946	0	0	0	0	1985
27 CHEMICALS,SELECT. PRDTS.	9002	2000	0	74015	0	0	0	0	61012
28 PLASTICS & SYNTHETICS	2001	0	0	16008	0	0	0	0	7003
29 DRUGS & COSMETICS	1011	0	0	18198	0	0	0	0	9099
30 PAINT & ALLIED PRDTS.	0	0	0	2155	0	0	0	0	1077
31 PETROLEUM, RELATED INDS.	9029	3010	0	80258	0	0	0	0	9029
32 RUBBER, MISC. PLASTICS	1002	0	0	17034	0	0	0	0	6012
33 LEATHER TANNING & PRDTS.	0	0	0	4246	0	0	0	0	1061
34 FOOTWEAR, LEATHER PRDTS.	0	0	0	2339	0	0	0	0	1170
35 GLASS & GLASS PRDTS.	0	0	0	3967	0	0	0	0	1983
36 STONE & CLAY PRDTS.	1006	0	0	6034	0	0	0	0	4023
37 PRIMARY IRON, STEEL MFR.	2993	998	0	23941	0	0	0	0	5985
38 PRIMARY NONFERROUS MFR.	3000	1000	0	54998	0	0	0	0	5000

Code	Industry	1	2	3	4	5	6	7	8	9
39	METAL CONTAINERS	0	0	0	2151	0	0	0	0	1076
40	FABRICATED METAL PRDTS.	995	995	0	19903	0	0	0	0	8956
41	SCREW MACH. PRDTS., ETC.	1011	0	0	1054	0	0	0	0	4044
42	OTHER FAB. METAL PRDTS.	996	0	0	19210	0	0	0	0	6972
43	ENGINES & TURBINES	998	0	0	21911	0	0	0	0	5987
44	FARM MACH. & EQUIP.	0	0	0	16964	0	0	0	0	23048
45	CONSTRUC. MACH. & EQUIP.	5011	1002	0	66139	0	0	0	0	988
46	MATERIAL HANDLING MACH.	0	0	0	6913	0	0	0	0	2009
47	METALWORKING MACHINERY	1004	1004	0	23098	0	0	0	0	8998
48	SPECIAL MACH. & EQUIP.	1000	1000	0	31995	0	0	0	0	4985
49	GENERAL MACH. & EQUIP.	997	997	0	31907	0	0	0	0	0
50	MACHINE SHOP PRDTS.	0	0	0	0	0	0	0	0	0
51	OFFICE, COMPUT. MACHINES	0	1004	0	25089	0	0	0	0	2007
52	SERVICE IND. MACHINES	0	0	0	12097	0	0	0	0	5040
53	ELECT. TRANSMISS. EQUIP.	0	1004	0	29124	0	0	0	0	4017
54	HOUSEHOLD APPLIANCES	0	0	0	6068	0	0	0	0	6068
55	ELECTRIC LIGHTING EQUIP.	1007	0	0	6140	0	0	0	0	1023
56	RADIO, TV, ETC., EQUIP.	1007	1007	0	44292	0	0	0	0	8053
57	ELECTRONIC COMPONENTS	0	993	0	23826	0	0	0	0	1986
58	MISC. ELECTRICAL MACH.	0	0	0	8776	0	0	0	0	975
59	MOTOR VEHICLES, EQUIP.	2001	1000	0	34012	0	0	0	0	10003
60	AIRCRAFT & PARTS	998	8985	0	287535	0	0	0	0	23961
61	OTHER TRANSPORT. EQUIP.	1014	1009	0	13181	0	0	0	0	5070
62	PROFESS., SCIEN. INSTRU.	0	0	0	37325	0	0	0	0	5044
63	MEDICAL, PHOTO. EQUIP.	0	0	0	8954	0	0	0	0	1990
64	MISC. MANUFACTURING	0	0	0	15057	0	0	0	0	5019
65	TRANSPORT. & WAREHOUSING	25016	2001	0	215135	2001	3002	0	2001	95060
66	COMMUNICA.,EXC. BRDCAST.	1197	0	0	1074	0	0	0	0	1197
67	RADIO & TV BROADCASTING	0	0	0	2394	0	0	0	0	0
68	ELEC.,GAS,WATER,SAN.SER.	14018	1013	0	7093	1001	1001	1008	0	45058
69	WHOLESALE & RETAIL TRADE	5006	5006	0	163209	0	1043	0	0	1043
70	FINANCE & INSURANCE	0	0	0	4171	0	9075	0	0	5042
71	REAL ESTATE & RENTAL	5042	1008	2017	35293	2017	9075	0	1008	5042
72	HOTELS; PERSONAL SERV.	0	0	0	0	0	997	0	0	0
73	BUSINESS SERVICES	0	0	0	15960	997	997	0	997	1995
74	RESEARCH & DEVELOPMENT	0	0	0	0	0	0	0	0	0
75	AUTO. REPAIR & SERVICES	0	0	0	0	0	1000	0	0	0
76	AMUSEMENTS	0	0	0	78975	1999	1000	0	4998	1999
77	MED.,EDUC. SERVICES	0	0	0	1404	0	0	0	0	0
78	FEDERAL GOV'T ENTERPRISE	406	406	406	3246	406	406	0	812	812
79	STATE & LOCAL GOV'T ENT.	0	0	0	0	0	0	0	0	0
80	IMPORTS	0	0	0	0	0	0	0	0	0
81	BUS.TRAVEL, ENT., GIFTS.	0	0	0	0	0	0	0	0	0
82	OFFICE SUPPLIES	1588	823	0	0	0	221	0	0	0
83	SCRAP & USED GOODS	0	0	0	31721	0	0	0	0	8522
84	GOVERNMENT INDUSTRY	0	0	0	0	0	0	0	0	0
85	REST OF WORLD INDUSTRY	0	0	0	0	0	0	0	0	0
86	HOUSEHOLD INDUSTRY	0	0	0	0	0	0	0	0	0
87	INVENTORY VALUATION ADJ.	0	0	0	0	0	0	0	0	0
88	STATE TOTAL	207481	57301	2423	2467350	7421	27750	1008	9816	676404

TABLE C.13

STATE ESTIMATES OF 1963
NET FOREIGN EXPORTS BY STATE OF EXIT
(THOUSANDS OF CURRENT DOLLARS)

INDUSTRY TITLE	10 GEORGIA	11 IDAHO	12 ILLINOIS	13 INDIANA	14 IOWA	15 KANSAS	16 KENTUCKY	17 LOUISIANA	18 MAINE
1 LIVESTOCK & PRDTS.	1012	0	1012	0	0	0	0	3035	0
2 OTHER AGRICULTURE PRDTS.	22017	0	36028	0	0	0	0	896693	1001
3 FORESTRY & FISHERIES	979	0	979	0	0	0	0	4895	0
4 AGRI.,FORES.,FISH. SERV.	0	0	4047	0	0	0	0	1189	0
5 IRON, FERRO. ORES MINING	0	0	0	0	0	0	0	9106	0
6 NONFERROUS ORES MINING	0	0	0	0	0	0	0	0	0
7 COAL MINING	0	0	9012	0	0	0	0	0	0
8 CRUDE PETRO.,NATURAL GAS	0	0	0	0	0	0	0	2312	0
9 STONE & CLAY MINING	1014	0	1014	0	0	0	0	4054	0
10 CHEM.&FERT. MIN. MINING	1022	0	1022	0	0	0	0	6130	0
11 NEW CONSTRUCTION	0	0	0	0	0	0	0	0	0
12 MAINT. & REPAIR CONSTR.	0	0	0	0	0	0	0	0	0
13 ORDNANCE & ACCESSORIES	0	0	30007	0	0	0	0	2001	1001
14 FOOD & KINDRED PRDTS.	10002	0	0	0	0	0	0	292063	3001
15 TOBACCO MANUFACTURES	4999	0	0	0	0	0	0	1000	0
16 FABRICS	4014	0	2007	0	0	0	0	4014	1004
17 TEXTILE PRDTS.	0	0	0	0	0	0	0	1073	0
18 APPAREL	2987	0	996	0	0	0	0	2987	0
19 MISC. TEXTILE PRDTS.	1040	0	0	0	0	0	0	1040	0
20 LUMBER & WOOD PRDTS.	1023	0	2047	0	0	0	0	9210	1023
21 WOODEN CONTAINERS	0	0	0	0	0	0	0	0	0
22 HOUSEHOLD FURNITURE	0	0	0	0	0	0	0	0	0
23 OTHER FURNITURE	0	0	0	0	0	0	0	0	0
24 PAPER & ALLIED PRDTS.	16056	0	2007	0	0	0	0	69240	2007
25 PAPERBOARD CONTAINERS	0	0	0	0	0	0	0	2166	0
26 PRINTING & PUBLISHING	992	0	2977	0	0	0	0	992	992
27 CHEMICALS,SELECT. PRDTS.	18004	0	9002	0	0	0	0	111023	1000
28 PLASTICS & SYNTHETICS	2001	0	5002	0	0	0	0	26013	1000
29 DRUGS & COSMETICS	3033	0	2022	0	0	0	0	16176	0
30 PAINT & ALLIED PRDTS.	0	0	0	0	0	0	0	2155	0
31 PETROLEUM, RELATED INDS.	2006	0	4013	0	0	0	0	110355	0
32 RUBBER, MISC. PLASTICS	2004	0	5010	0	0	0	0	8016	1002
33 LEATHER TANNING & PRDTS.	0	0	1061	0	0	0	0	2123	0
34 FOOTWEAR, LEATHER PRDTS.	0	0	0	0	0	0	0	0	0
35 GLASS & GLASS PRDTS.	992	0	1983	0	0	0	0	3967	0
36 STONE & CLAY PRDTS.	1006	0	2011	0	0	0	0	6034	0
37 PRIMARY IRON, STEEL MFR.	1995	0	6983	0	0	0	0	30924	998
38 PRIMARY NONFERROUS MFR.	1000	0	4000	0	0	0	0	39999	1000

Code	Industry	(1)	(2)	(3)	(4)	(5)	(6)	(7)	(8)	(9)
39	METAL CONTAINERS	0	0	1076	0	0	0	0	1076	0
40	FABRICATED METAL PRDTS.	2985	0	3981	0	0	0	0	12937	995
41	SCREW MACH. PRDTS., ETC.	1011	0	3162	0	0	0	0	1054	1011
42	OTHER FAB. METAL PRDTS.	1992	0	4044	0	0	0	0	9099	0
43	ENGINES & TURBINES	1996	0	13971	0	0	0	0	15935	0
44	FARM MACH. & EQUIP.	7015	0	20042	0	0	0	0	11975	1002
45	CONSTRUC. MACH. & EQUIP.	1004	0	1975	0	0	0	0	63132	0
46	MATERIAL HANDLING MACH.	2999	0	7030	0	0	0	0	2963	0
47	METALWORKING MACHINERY	997	0	7999	0	0	0	0	6026	1004
48	SPECIAL MACH. & EQUIP.	0	0	5983	0	0	0	0	17997	2999
49	GENERAL MACH. & EQUIP.	0	0	3011	0	0	0	0	11965	997
50	MACHINE SHOP PRDTS.	0	0	0	0	0	0	0	0	0
51	OFFICE, COMPUT. MACHINES	1008	0	3024	0	0	0	0	1004	2007
52	SERVICE IND. MACHINES	1004	0	5021	0	0	0	0	6048	0
53	ELECT. TRANSMISS. EQUIP.	2023	0	3034	0	0	0	0	6026	1004
54	HOUSEHOLD APPLIANCES	0	0	1023	0	0	0	0	5057	0
55	ELECTRIC LIGHTING EQUIP.	0	0	5033	0	0	0	0	2047	0
56	RADIO, TV, ETC., EQUIP.	2013	0	2978	0	0	0	0	7047	1007
57	ELECTRONIC COMPONENTS	993	0	975	0	0	0	0	1986	993
58	MISC. ELECTRICAL MACH.	0	0	0	0	0	0	0	975	0
59	MOTOR VEHICLES, EQUIP.	3001	0	83028	0	0	0	0	29010	0
60	AIRCRAFT & PARTS	6989	0	2995	0	0	0	0	12979	4992
61	OTHER TRANSPORT. EQUIP.	2028	0	2028	0	0	0	0	7098	0
62	PROFESS., SCIEN. INSTRU.	1009	0	4035	0	0	0	0	4035	2018
63	MEDICAL, PHOTO. EQUIP.	995	0	995	0	0	0	0	995	995
64	MISC. MANUFACTURING	1004	0	2008	0	0	0	0	4015	1004
65	TRANSPORT. & WAREHOUSING	12008	2001	149093	0	0	0	0	282177	3002
66	COMMUNICA..EXC. BRDCAST.	0	0	1197	0	0	0	0	0	0
67	RADIO & TV BROADCASTING	1197	1013	0	1197	0	0	1197	1197	0
68	ELEC.,GAS,WATER,SAN.SER.	0	0	0	0	0	0	0	0	0
69	WHOLESALE & RETAIL TRADE	13017	1008	29037	1043	0	0	0	165212	4005
70	FINANCE & INSURANCE	1043	0	2086	0	1043	0	0	1043	0
71	REAL ESTATE & RENTAL	7059	0	30251	16134	5042	3025	5042	4034	2017
72	HOTELS; PERSONAL SERV.	0	0	28927	0	0	0	0	0	0
73	BUSINESS SERVICES	1995	0	0	997	997	0	0	997	0
74	RESEARCH & DEVELOPMENT	0	0	0	0	0	0	0	0	0
75	AUTO. REPAIR & SERVICES	0	0	0	0	0	0	0	0	0
76	AMUSEMENTS	2999	0	10996	1000	1000	0	0	1999	0
77	MED.,EDUC. SERVICES	0	0	1404	0	0	0	0	0	0
78	FEDERAL GOV'T ENTERPRISE	812	0	2435	812	406	406	406	406	0
79	STATE & LOCAL GOV'T ENT.	0	0	0	0	0	0	0	0	0
80	IMPORTS	0	0	0	0	0	0	0	0	0
81	BUS.TRAVEL, ENT., GIFTS.	0	0	0	0	0	0	0	0	0
82	OFFICE SUPPLIES	0	0	0	0	0	0	0	0	0
83	SCRAP & USED GOODS	2313	0	5571	0	0	0	0	19774	724
84	GOVERNMENT INDUSTRY	0	0	0	0	0	0	0	0	0
85	REST OF WORLD INDUSTRY	0	0	0	0	0	0	0	0	0
86	HOUSEHOLD INDUSTRY	0	0	0	0	0	0	0	0	0
87	INVENTORY VALUATION ADJ.	0	0	0	0	0	0	0	0	0
88	STATE TOTAL	183703	4023	591656	21183	8488	3431	6645	2389272	46804

TABLE C.13

STATE ESTIMATES OF 1963
NET FOREIGN EXPORTS BY STATE OF EXIT
(THOUSANDS OF CURRENT DOLLARS)

INDUSTRY TITLE	19 MARYLAND	20 MASSA-CHUSETTS	21 MICHIGAN	22 MINNESOTA	23 MISSISSIPPI	24 MISSOURI	25 MONTANA	26 NEBRASKA	27 NEVADA
1 LIVESTOCK & PRDTS.	1012	0	3035	0	0	0	0	0	0
2 OTHER AGRICULTURE PRDTS.	122094	3002	173134	28022	64049	0	22017	0	0
3 FORESTRY & FISHERIES	979	0	2937	979	0	0	0	0	0
4 AGRI.,FORES.,FISH. SERV.	0	0	2378	0	0	0	0	0	0
5 IRON, FERRO. ORES MINING	1012	1012	18211	3035	1012	0	0	0	0
6 NONFERROUS ORES MINING	0	0	0	7009	0	0	0	0	0
7 COAL MINING	74099	0	42056	0	0	0	0	0	0
8 CRUDE PETRO.,NATURAL GAS	0	0	1156	0	0	0	0	0	0
9 STONE & CLAY MINING	1014	0	2027	0	0	0	0	0	0
10 CHEM.&FERT. MIN. MINING	1022	0	4087	1022	0	0	0	0	0
11 NEW CONSTRUCTION	0	0	0	0	0	0	0	0	0
12 MAINT. & REPAIR CONSTR.	0	0	0	0	0	0	0	0	0
13 ORDNANCE & ACCESSORIES	4003	7005	0	0	0	0	0	0	0
14 FOOD & KINDRED PRDTS.	32007	9002	147032	24005	21005	0	13003	0	0
15 TOBACCO MANUFACTURES	38995	1000	0	0	0	0	2000	0	0
16 FABRICS	7025	3011	8028	1004	0	0	0	0	0
17 TEXTILE PRDTS.	1073	0	1073	0	0	0	0	0	0
18 APPAREL	4978	996	3982	996	0	0	0	0	0
19 MISC. TEXTILE PRDTS.	2081	0	1040	0	0	0	0	0	0
20 LUMBER & WOOD PRDTS.	5116	4093	8186	1023	1023	0	5116	0	0
21 WOODEN CONTAINERS	0	0	0	0	0	0	0	0	0
22 HOUSEHOLD FURNITURE	0	0	1304	0	0	0	0	0	0
23 OTHER FURNITURE	0	0	1384	0	0	0	0	0	0
24 PAPER & ALLIED PRDTS.	7024	6021	9031	1003	5017	0	4014	0	0
25 PAPERBOARD CONTAINERS	1083	1083	1083	1985	0	0	0	0	0
26 PRINTING & PUBLISHING	2977	1985	12899	7001	0	0	992	0	0
27 CHEMICALS,SELECT. PRDTS.	24005	3001	43009	7001	7001	0	3001	0	0
28 PLASTICS & SYNTHETICS	28014	2001	26013	4002	1000	0	1000	0	0
29 DRUGS & COSMETICS	6066	1011	12132	2022	1011	0	1011	0	0
30 PAINT & ALLIED PRDTS.	1077	0	1077	0	0	0	0	0	0
31 PETROLEUM, RELATED INDS.	23074	1003	21068	3010	7023	0	2006	0	0
32 RUBBER, MISC. PLASTICS	3006	3006	23045	4008	1002	0	1002	0	0
33 LEATHER TANNING & PRDTS.	1061	1061	3184	0	0	0	0	0	0
34 FOOTWEAR, LEATHER PRDTS.	0	0	1170	0	0	0	0	0	0
35 GLASS & GLASS PRDTS.	1983	992	9916	1983	0	0	0	0	0
36 STONE & CLAY PRDTS.	3017	1006	12068	2011	0	0	0	0	0
37 PRIMARY IRON, STEEL MFR.	25937	2993	33917	4988	1995	0	998	0	0
38 PRIMARY NONFERROUS MFR.	16999	2000	19999	3000	3000	0	5000	0	0

	C1	C2	C3	C4	C5	C6	C7	C8
39 METAL CONTAINERS	0	0	0	0	0	3227	0	0
40 FABRICATED METAL PRDTS.	0	995	0	995	2985	18908	1990	4976
41 SCREW MACH. PRDTS., ETC.	0	0	0	1011	2108	15812	0	0
42 OTHER FAB. METAL PRDTS.	0	1011	0	996	3033	21232	2022	4044
43 ENGINES & TURBINES	0	1992	0	998	5976	37846	996	3984
44 FARM MACH. & EQUIP.	0	998	0	4008	10977	68855	998	3992
45 CONSTRUC. MACH. & EQUIP.	0	5011	0	0	16034	99208	1002	15032
46 MATERIAL HANDLING MACH.	0	988	0	1000	1975	9876	988	1975
47 METALWORKING MACHINERY	0	1004	0	997	6026	36154	3013	9038
48 SPECIAL MACH. & EQUIP.	0	2000	0	0	5999	36994	6999	9998
49 GENERAL MACH. & EQUIP.	0	1994	0	0	3988	26921	2991	4985
50 MACHINE SHOP PRDTS.	0	0	0	0	0	0	0	0
51 OFFICE, COMPUT. MACHINES	0	1004	0	0	2007	15054	6021	1004
52 SERVICE IND. MACHINES	0	1008	0	0	2016	14113	1008	4032
53 ELECT. TRANSMISS. EQUIP.	0	2009	0	0	4017	23093	3013	4017
54 HOUSEHOLD APPLIANCES	0	0	0	0	2023	13143	1011	2023
55 ELECTRIC LIGHTING EQUIP.	0	0	0	0	1023	6140	1023	1023
56 RADIO, TV, ETC. EQUIP.	0	2013	0	0	4027	25166	2013	5033
57 ELECTRONIC COMPONENTS	0	993	0	0	1986	12906	1986	1986
58 MISC. ELECTRICAL MACH.	0	975	0	0	975	4875	975	975
59 MOTOR VEHICLES, EQUIP.	0	3001	0	2001	65022	405137	1000	24008
60 AIRCRAFT & PARTS	0	0	0	998	1997	15974	14976	1997
61 OTHER TRANSPORT. EQUIP.	0	1014	0	0	2028	12167	1014	2028
62 PROFESS., SCIEN. INSTRU.	0	2018	0	0	3026	20175	4035	3026
63 MEDICAL, PHOTO. EQUIP.	0	995	0	0	995	4975	1990	995
64 MISC. MANUFACTURING	0	1004	0	0	2008	11041	2008	2008
65 TRANSPORT. & WAREHOUSING	0	5003	3002	9006	146092	113071	11007	138087
66 COMMUNICA.,EXC. BROCAST.	0	0	1197	0	0	0	2148	0
67 RADIO & TV BROADCASTING	0	0	0	0	0	1197	0	0
68 ELEC.,GAS,WATER,SAN.SER.	0	1013	0	0	1013	3040	0	0
69 WHOLESALE & RETAIL TRADE	0	9012	0	11014	22028	139179	11014	48062
70 FINANCE & INSURANCE	0	0	1043	1043	1043	2086	1043	1043
71 REAL ESTATE & RENTAL	0	0	9075	2017	6050	27226	13109	6050
72 HOTELS; PERSONAL SERV.	0	0	0	0	2992	13965	0	997
73 BUSINESS SERVICES	0	0	3990	0	0	0	2992	0
74 RESEARCH & DEVELOPMENT	0	0	0	0	0	0	0	0
75 AUTO. REPAIR & SERVICES	0	0	0	0	0	0	0	0
76 AMUSEMENTS	0	0	3999	0	1999	4998	2999	2999
77 MED.,EDUC. SERVICES	0	0	0	0	0	1404	0	0
78 FEDERAL GOV'T ENTERPRISE	0	0	1217	406	812	1217	1217	406
79 STATE & LOCAL GOV'T ENT.	0	406	0	0	0	0	0	0
80 IMPORTS	0	0	0	0	0	0	0	0
81 BUS.TRAVEL, ENT., GIFTS.	0	0	0	0	0	0	0	0
82 OFFICE SUPPLIES	0	0	0	0	0	0	0	0
83 SCRAP & USED GOODS	0	1429	0	1246	4302	27313	2315	7082
84 GOVERNMENT INDUSTRY	0	0	0	0	0	0	0	0
85 REST OF WORLD INDUSTRY	0	0	0	0	0	0	0	0
86 HOUSEHOLD INDUSTRY	0	0	0	0	0	0	0	0
87 INVENTORY VALUATION ADJ.	0	0	0	0	0	0	0	0
88 STATE TOTAL	0	109641	23523	150831	440688	1944352	167198	755735

TABLE C.13

STATE ESTIMATES OF 1963
NET FOREIGN EXPORTS BY STATE OF EXIT
(THOUSANDS OF CURRENT DOLLARS)

INDUSTRY TITLE	28 NEW HAMPSHIRE	29 NEW JERSEY	30 NEW MEXICO	31 NEW YORK	32 NORTH CAROLINA	33 NORTH DAKOTA	34 OHIO	35 OKLAHOMA	36 OREGON
1 LIVESTOCK & PRDTS.	0	0	0	10118	1012	1012	1012	0	1012
2 OTHER AGRICULTURE PRDTS.	0	2002	0	75058	19015	31024	30023	0	61047
3 FORESTRY & FISHERIES	0	0	0	12726	979	979	979	0	0
4 AGRI.,FORES.,FISH. SERV.	0	0	0	2378	0	0	0	0	0
5 IRON,FERRO. ORES MINING	0	0	0	13153	0	3035	3035	0	1012
6 NONFERROUS ORES MINING	0	0	0	0	0	0	0	0	0
7 COAL MINING	0	2003	0	6008	0	7009	7009	0	0
8 CRUDE PETRO.-NATURAL GAS	0	0	0	2312	0	0	0	0	0
9 STONE & CLAY MINING	0	0	0	10135	1014	0	0	0	1014
10 CHEM.&FERT. MIN. MINING	0	0	0	16348	1022	1022	1022	0	1022
11 NEW CONSTRUCTION	0	0	0	0	0	0	0	0	0
12 MAINT. & REPAIR CONSTR.	0	0	0	0	0	0	0	0	0
13 ORDNANCE & ACCESSORIES	0	1000	0	4003	2001	0	0	0	0
14 FOOD & KINDRED PRDTS.	0	1000	0	236051	9002	26006	26006	0	38008
15 TOBACCO MANUFACTURES	0	0	0	308957	4999	0	0	0	5999
16 FABRICS	0	0	0	198694	4014	1004	1004	0	1004
17 TEXTILE PRDTS.	0	0	0	18237	0	0	0	0	996
18 APPAREL	0	0	0	85618	1991	996	996	0	996
19 MISC. TEXTILE PRDTS.	0	0	0	17685	1040	0	0	0	0
20 LUMBER & WOOD PRDTS.	0	0	0	36839	1023	1023	1023	0	14326
21 WOODEN CONTAINERS	0	0	0	2056	0	0	0	0	0
22 HOUSEHOLD FURNITURE	0	0	0	6518	0	0	0	0	0
23 OTHER FURNITURE	0	0	0	12459	0	0	0	0	0
24 PAPER & ALLIED PRDTS.	0	0	0	91317	14049	2007	2007	0	10035
25 PAPERBOARD CONTAINERS	0	0	0	8666	0	0	0	0	0
26 PRINTING & PUBLISHING	0	0	0	103195	903	1985	1985	0	1985
27 CHEMICALS,SELECT. PRDTS.	0	0	0	375077	15003	8002	8002	0	8002
28 PLASTICS & SYNTHETICS	0	1000	0	237117	2001	5002	5002	0	2001
29 DRUGS & COSMETICS	0	0	0	193100	2022	2022	2022	0	3033
30 PAINT & ALLIED PRDTS.	0	0	0	17237	0	0	0	0	0
31 PETROLEUM, RELATED INDS.	0	0	0	92297	2006	4013	4013	0	5016
32 RUBBER, MISC. PLASTICS	0	0	0	159314	2004	4008	4008	0	3006
33 LEATHER TANNING & PRDTS.	0	0	0	21229	0	0	0	0	1061
34 FOOTWEAR, LEATHER PRDTS.	0	0	0	12867	0	0	0	0	0
35 GLASS & GLASS PRDTS.	0	0	0	51565	1006	1983	1983	0	992
36 STONE & CLAY PRDTS.	0	0	0	63359	1995	2011	2011	0	1006
37 PRIMARY IRON, STEEL MFR.	0	998	0	226446	1995	5985	5985	0	2993
38 PRIMARY NONFERROUS MFR.	0	0	0	202993	1000	4000	4000	0	13000

Code	Sector								
39	METAL CONTAINERS	0	0	0	13983	0	0	0	0
40	FABRICATED METAL PRDTS.	0	0	0	112451	1990	2985	2985	2985
41	SCREW MACH. PRDTS., ETC.	0	0	0	11596	1011	3162	3162	0
42	OTHER FAB. METAL PRDTS.	0	0	0	129415	1992	4044	4044	3033
43	ENGINES & TURBINES	0	0	0	131463	1996	6972	6972	4980
44	FARM MACH. & EQUIP.	0	0	0	81828	6013	11975	11975	3992
45	CONSTRUC. MACH. & EQUIP.	0	0	0	355746	0	18038	17036	15032
46	MATERIAL HANDLING MACH.	0	0	0	45430	0	1975	1975	988
47	METALWORKING MACHINERY	0	0	0	253077	0	6026	6026	3013
48	SPECIAL MACH. & EQUIP.	0	0	0	312946	2000	6999	5999	5999
49	GENERAL MACH. & EQUIP.	0	0	0	182468	997	4985	4985	4985
50	MACHINE SHOP PRDTS.	0	0	0	0	0	0	0	0
51	OFFICE, COMPUT. MACHINES	0	0	0	224800	1008	3011	3011	4014
52	SERVICE IND. MACHINES	0	0	0	117942	1004	3024	2016	2016
53	ELECT. TRANSMISS. EQUIP.	0	0	0	206881	2023	4017	4017	4017
54	HOUSEHOLD APPLIANCES	0	0	0	70796	0	2023	2023	1011
55	ELECTRIC LIGHTING EQUIP.	0	0	0	48100	0	1023	1023	1023
56	RADIO, TV, ETC., EQUIP.	0	0	0	197303	2013	4027	4027	7047
57	ELECTRONIC COMPONENTS	0	0	0	113176	0	1986	1986	3971
58	MISC. ELECTRICAL MACH.	0	0	0	42903	0	975	975	975
59	MOTOR VEHICLES, EQUIP.	0	0	0	400136	3001	72024	70024	8003
60	AIRCRAFT & PARTS	0	0	0	281545	5990	2995	2995	33945
61	OTHER TRANSPORT. EQUIP.	0	0	0	77060	1014	2028	2028	3042
62	PROFESS., SCIEN. INSTRU.	0	0	0	231000	1009	4035	3026	6053
63	MEDICAL, PHOTO. EQUIP.	0	0	0	117402	1004	995	995	995
64	MISC. MANUFACTURING	0	0	0	114429	8005	2008	2008	2008
65	TRANSPORT. & WAREHOUSING	1001	3002	0	485304	0	21013	316198	43027
66	COMMUNICA., EXC. BRDCAST.	0	0	0	39744	1197	0	0	1197
67	RADIO & TV BROADCASTING	0	0	0	1197	0	1197	1197	0
68	ELEC.,GAS,WATER,SAN.SER.	0	1001	0	6080	11014	25032	24031	26033
69	WHOLESALE & RETAIL TRADE	1008	1043	0	588756	1043	0	2086	3025
70	FINANCE & INSURANCE	0	21176	0	5214	9075	0	0	0
71	REAL ESTATE & RENTAL	0	0	0	40335	0	0	0	0
72	HOTELS; PERSONAL SERV.	0	1995	0	3700	997	997	6982	997
73	BUSINESS SERVICES	0	0	0	87779	0	0	0	0
74	RESEARCH & DEVELOPMENT	0	0	0	0	0	0	0	0
75	AUTO. REPAIR & SERVICES	0	0	0	170945	0	0	0	0
76	AMUSEMENTS	0	1000	0	22470	1999	0	3999	0
77	MED.,EDUC. SERVICES	0	1404	0	4870	0	0	1404	0
78	FEDERAL GOV'T ENTERPRISE	0	1217	0	0	406	0	2029	406
79	STATE & LOCAL GOV'T ENT.	0	0	0	0	0	0	0	0
80	IMPORTS	0	0	0	0	0	0	0	0
81	BUS.TRAVEL, ENT., GIFTS.	0	0	0	0	0	0	0	0
82	OFFICE SUPPLIES	0	0	0	0	0	0	0	0
83	SCRAP & USED GOODS	0	80	0	133626	2012	4845	4725	4729
84	GOVERNMENT INDUSTRY	0	0	0	0	0	0	0	0
85	REST OF WORLD INDUSTRY	0	0	0	0	0	0	0	0
86	HOUSEHOLD INDUSTRY	0	0	0	0	0	0	0	0
87	INVENTORY VALUATION ADJ.	0	0	0	0	0	0	0	0
88	STATE TOTAL	2009	39921	0	8395005	159003	336348	673356	380106

TABLE C.13

STATE ESTIMATES OF 1963
NET FOREIGN EXPORTS BY STATE OF EXIT
(THOUSANDS OF CURRENT DOLLARS)

INDUSTRY TITLE	37 PENNSYL-VANIA	38 RHODE ISLAND	39 SOUTH CAROLINA	40 SOUTH DAKOTA	41 TENNESSEE	42 TEXAS	43 UTAH	44 VERMONT	45 VIRGINIA
1 LIVESTOCK & PRDTS.	0	0	1012	0	0	4047	0	0	1012
2 OTHER AGRICULTURE PRDTS.	79061	0	19015	0	0	501387	0	3002	161124
3 FORESTRY & FISHERIES	979	0	979	0	0	5873	0	0	979
4 AGRI.,FORES.,FISH. SERV.	1012	0	0	0	0	1189	0	0	0
5 IRON, FERRO. ORES MINING	0	0	0	0	0	6070	0	1012	2023
6 NONFERROUS ORES MINING	49066	0	0	0	0	0	0	0	0
7 COAL MINING	0	0	0	0	0	1001	0	0	98131
8 CRUDE PETRO.,NATURAL GAS	1014	0	1014	0	0	4625	0	0	0
9 STONE & CLAY MINING	1022	0	1022	0	0	5068	0	0	1014
10 CHEM.&FERT. MIN. MINING	0	0	0	0	0	8174	0	0	2043
11 NEW CONSTRUCTION	0	0	0	0	0	0	0	0	0
12 MAINT. & REPAIR CONSTR.	0	0	0	0	0	0	0	0	0
13 ORDNANCE & ACCESSORIES	3002	0	0	0	0	4003	0	0	1001
14 FOOD & KINDRED PRDTS.	21005	0	9002	0	0	296064	0	8002	43009
15 TOBACCO MANUFACTURES	24997	0	4999	0	0	5999	0	1000	50993
16 FABRICS	5018	0	4014	0	0	1004	0	3011	9032
17 TEXTILE PRDTS.	1073	0	0	0	0	1073	0	0	2146
18 APPAREL	2987	0	1991	0	0	2987	0	996	5973
19 MISC. TEXTILE PRDTS.	1040	0	1040	0	0	1040	0	0	3121
20 LUMBER & WOOD PRDTS.	4093	0	1023	0	0	2047	0	4093	7163
21 HOUSEHOLD FURNITURE	0	0	0	0	0	0	0	0	0
22 WOODEN CONTAINERS	0	0	0	0	0	0	0	0	0
23 OTHER FURNITURE	0	0	0	0	0	1384	0	0	0
24 PAPER & ALLIED PRDTS.	5017	0	14049	0	0	15052	0	6021	9031
25 PAPERBOARD CONTAINERS	1083	0	0	0	0	1083	0	1083	1083
26 PRINTING & PUBLISHING	1985	0	992	0	0	3969	0	992	3969
27 CHEMICALS,SELECT. PRDTS.	16003	0	16003	0	0	285058	0	3001	32007
28 PLASTICS & SYNTHETICS	18009	0	2001	0	0	116057	0	2001	36018
29 DRUGS & COSMETICS	4044	0	2022	0	0	35385	0	1011	8088
30 PAINT & ALLIED PRDTS.	0	0	0	0	0	4309	0	0	1077
31 PETROLEUM, RELATED INDS.	15048	0	2006	0	0	233752	0	1003	30097
32 RUBBER, MISC. PLASTICS	2004	0	2004	0	0	10020	0	3006	4008
33 LEATHER TANNING & PRDTS.	0	0	0	0	0	1061	0	1061	1061
34 FOOTWEAR, LEATHER PRDTS.	0	0	0	0	0	0	0	0	0
35 GLASS & GLASS PRDTS.	992	0	0	0	0	3967	0	992	2975
36 STONE & CLAY PRDTS.	2011	0	1006	0	0	9051	0	1006	3017
37 PRIMARY IRON, STEEL MFR.	16958	0	1995	0	0	38905	0	1995	34915
38 PRIMARY NONFERROUS MFR.	11000	0	1000	0	0	38999	0	2000	21999

#	Sector	1	2	3	4	5	6	7	8	9
39	METAL CONTAINERS	0	0	0	0	0	1076	0	0	0
40	FABRICATED METAL PRDTS.	2985	0	1990	0	0	23383	0	1990	6966
41	SCREW MACH. PRDTS., ETC.	0	0	1011	0	0	2108	0	2022	0
42	OTHER FAB. METAL PRDTS.	3033	0	1992	0	0	25276	0	996	6066
43	ENGINES & TURBINES	2988	0	1996	0	0	17927	0	998	4980
44	FARM MACH. & EQUIP.	2994	0	6013	0	0	11975	0	1002	4989
45	CONSTRUC. MACH. & EQUIP.	10021	0	0	0	0	121254	0	1002	19040
46	MATERIAL HANDLING MACH.	988	0	0	0	0	7901	0	988	2963
47	METALWORKING MACHINERY	6026	0	2000	0	0	29124	0	3013	12051
48	SPECIAL MACH. & EQUIP.	5999	0	997	0	0	45992	0	6999	12998
49	GENERAL MACH. & EQUIP.	2991	0	0	0	0	53843	0	1994	5983
50	MACHINE SHOP PRDTS.	0	0	0	0	0	5018	0	0	1004
51	OFFICE, COMPUT. MACHINES	1004	0	1008	0	0	17137	0	6021	5040
52	SERVICE IND. MACHINES	3024	0	1004	0	0	19081	0	1008	5021
53	ELECT. TRANSMISS. EQUIP.	2009	0	2023	0	0	5057	0	2009	2023
54	HOUSEHOLD APPLIANCES	1011	0	0	0	0	5117	0	1011	1023
55	ELECTRIC LIGHTING EQUIP.	1023	0	2013	0	0	14093	0	1023	7047
56	RADIO, TV, ETC., EQUIP.	3020	0	0	0	0	8935	0	2013	1986
57	ELECTRONIC COMPONENTS	993	0	0	0	0	3900	0	1986	975
58	MISC. ELECTRICAL MACH.	0	0	0	0	0	80027	0	975	31011
59	MOTOR VEHICLES, EQUIP.	15005	0	3001	0	0	27955	0	1000	2995
60	AIRCRAFT & PARTS	1997	0	5990	0	0	18251	0	13977	2028
61	OTHER TRANSPORT. EQUIP.	1014	0	1014	0	0	16140	0	1014	4035
62	PROFESS., SCIEN. INSTRU.	2018	0	1009	0	0	6965	0	4035	995
63	MEDICAL, PHOTO. EQUIP.	0	0	1004	0	0	4015	0	995	3011
64	MISC. MANUFACTURING	2008	0	10006	2001	0	249156	0	2008	348218
65	TRANSPORT. & WAREHOUSING	104065	1001	1197	0	0	2394	0	5003	1197
66	COMMUNICA.-EXC. BRDCAST.	0	0	0	0	1197	6080	0	0	0
67	RADIO & TV BROADCASTING	1197	0	11014	0	0	0	0	0	0
68	ELEC.,GAS,WATER,SAN.SER.	0	0	0	0	0	192247	0	0	63081
69	WHOLESALE & RETAIL TRADE	31040	0	4034	0	0	2086	0	9012	1043
70	FINANCE & INSURANCE	2086	0	0	0	1043	15126	0	0	6050
71	REAL ESTATE & RENTAL	29243	2017	0	0	7059	3990	1008	1008	0
72	HOTELS; PERSONAL SERV.	0	0	0	0	0	0	0	0	0
73	BUSINESS SERVICES	7980	997	997	0	997	3999	0	0	997
74	RESEARCH & DEVELOPMENT	0	0	0	0	0	0	0	0	0
75	AUTO. REPAIR & SERVICES	0	0	0	0	0	0	0	0	0
76	AMUSEMENTS	4998	0	0	0	1000	1404	1000	0	0
77	MED.,EDUC. SERVICES	1404	0	0	0	0	1623	0	0	0
78	FEDERAL GOV'T ENTERPRISE	2029	0	406	0	406	33810	0	0	406
79	STATE & LOCAL GOV'T ENT.	0	0	0	0	0	0	0	0	0
80	IMPORTS	0	0	0	0	0	0	0	0	0
81	BUS.TRAVEL, ENT., GIFTS.	0	0	0	0	0	0	0	0	0
82	OFFICE SUPPLIES	0	0	0	0	0	0	0	0	0
83	SCRAP & USED GOODS	4607	0	1992	0	0	33810	0	2034	9154
84	GOVERNMENT INDUSTRY	0	0	0	0	0	0	0	0	0
85	REST OF WORLD INDUSTRY	0	0	0	0	0	0	0	0	0
86	HOUSEHOLD INDUSTRY	0	0	0	0	0	0	0	0	0
87	INVENTORY VALUATION ADJ.	0	0	0	0	0	0	0	0	0
88	STATE TOTAL	550318	4015	150901	2001	11702	2733644	2008	122421	1152478

TABLE C.13

STATE ESTIMATES OF 1963
NET FOREIGN EXPORTS BY STATE OF EXIT
(THOUSANDS OF CURRENT DOLLARS)

INDUSTRY TITLE	46 WASHINGTON	47 WEST VIRGINIA	48 WISCONSIN	49 WYOMING	50 ALASKA	51 HAWAII	52 NO STATE ALLOCATION	53 NATIONAL TOTAL
1 LIVESTOCK & PRDTS.	2024	0	0	0	0	0	0	38449
2 OTHER AGRICULTURE PRDTS.	137106	0	10008	0	0	0	0	2917243
3 FORESTRY & FISHERIES	979	0	0	0	1958	0	0	46009
4 AGRI.,FORES.,FISH. SERV.	1189	0	1012	0	0	0	0	107C0
5 IRON, FERRO. ORES MINING	2023	0	0	0	0	0	0	118373
6 NONFERROUS ORES MINING	0	0	0	0	0	0	814	814
7 COAL MINING	0	0	2003	0	1001	0	0	305407
8 CRUDE PETRO.,NATURAL GAS	0	0	0	0	0	0	0	11562
9 STONE & CLAY MINING	1014	0	0	0	0	0	0	37501
10 CHEM.&FERT. MIN. MINING	2043	0	0	0	0	0	0	62325
11 NEW CONSTRUCTION	0	0	0	0	0	0	0	2000
12 MAINT. & REPAIR CONSTR.	0	0	0	0	0	0	0	0
13 ORDNANCE & ACCESSORIES	0	0	0	0	0	0	0	197128
14 FOOD & KINDRED PRDTS.	84018	0	9002	0	2000	14003	0	1648350
15 TOBACCO MANUFACTURES	13998	0	0	0	0	0	0	507928
16 FABRICS	2007	0	1004	0	0	0	0	280982
17 TEXTILE PRDTS.	0	0	0	0	0	0	0	28965
18 APPAREL	1991	0	0	0	0	0	0	147342
19 MISC. TEXTILE PRDTS.	0	0	0	0	0	0	0	35369
20 LUMBER & WOOD PRDTS.	31722	0	0	0	0	0	0	194426
21 WOODEN CONTAINERS	0	0	0	0	0	0	0	2056
22 HOUSEHOLD FURNITURE	0	0	0	0	0	0	0	10429
23 OTHER FURNITURE	0	0	0	0	0	0	0	19380
24 PAPER & ALLIED PRDTS.	23080	0	1003	0	0	0	0	448556
25 PAPERBOARD CONTAINERS	1083	0	0	0	0	0	0	22747
26 PRINTING & PUBLISHING	3969	0	992	0	0	0	0	162731
27 CHEMICALS,SELECT. PRDTS.	19004	0	3001	0	0	0	0	1160233
28 PLASTICS & SYNTHETICS	4002	0	2001	0	0	0	0	553271
29 DRUGS & COSMETICS	8088	0	1011	0	0	0	0	334639
30 PAINT & ALLIED PRDTS.	1077	0	0	0	0	0	0	31242
31 PETROLEUM, RELATED INDS.	12039	0	1003	0	0	1003	0	678181
32 RUBBER, MISC. PLASTICS	6012	0	1002	0	0	0	0	275543
33 LEATHER TANNING & PRDTS.	2123	0	0	0	0	0	0	41397
34 FOOTWEAR, LEATHER PRDTS.	0	0	0	0	0	0	0	17546
35 GLASS & GLASS PRDTS.	1983	0	992	0	0	0	0	96188
36 STONE & CLAY PRDTS.	2011	0	1006	0	0	1006	0	127723
37 PRIMARY IRON, STEEL MFR.	5985	0	1995	0	0	0	0	492793
38 PRIMARY NONFERROUS MFR.	29999	0	1000	0	0	0	0	490982

#	Industry	1	2	3	4	5	6	7	8
39	METAL CONTAINERS	24739	0	0	0	0	0	0	1076
40	FABRICATED METAL PRDTS.	251770	0	0	0	0	995	0	6966
41	SCREW MACH. PRDTS., ETC.	44275	0	0	0	0	1054	0	7077
42	OTHER FAB. METAL PRDTS.	258828	0	0	0	0	1011	0	11951
43	ENGINES & TURBINES	302763	0	0	0	0	1992	0	7983
44	FARM MACH. & EQUIP.	285399	0	0	0	0	3992	0	34071
45	CONSTRUC. MACH. & EQUIP.	935963	0	0	0	0	6013	0	2963
46	MATERIAL HANDLING MACH.	95799	0	0	0	0	988	0	6026
47	METALWORKING MACHINERY	422799	0	0	0	0	2009	0	11998
48	SPECIAL MACH. & EQUIP.	560903	0	1000	0	0	2000	0	10968
49	GENERAL MACH. & EQUIP.	377897	0	0	0	0	1994	0	0
50	MACHINE SHOP PRDTS.	0	0	0	0	0	0	0	0
51	OFFICE, COMPUT. MACHINES	317129	0	0	0	0	1004	0	9032
52	SERVICE IND. MACHINES	208667	0	0	0	0	1008	0	5040
53	ELECT. TRANSMISS. EQUIP.	343461	0	0	0	0	1004	0	10043
54	HOUSEHOLD APPLIANCES	132489	0	0	0	0	1011	0	2023
55	ELECTRIC LIGHTING EQUIP.	80849	0	0	0	0	0	0	15100
56	RADIO, TV, ETC., EQUIP.	366418	0	0	0	0	1007	0	8935
57	ELECTRONIC COMPONENTS	198554	0	0	0	0	993	0	2925
58	MISC. ELECTRICAL MACH.	75081	0	0	0	0	0	0	0
59	MOTOR VEHICLES, EQUIP.	1386465	0	0	0	0	24008	0	17006
60	AIRCRAFT & PARTS	856615	0	0	0	0	998	0	88856
61	OTHER TRANSPORT. EQUIP.	165273	0	0	0	0	1014	0	7098
62	PROFESS., SCIEN. INSTRU.	373246	0	0	0	0	1009	0	13114
63	MEDICAL, PHOTO. EQUIP.	157199	0	0	0	0	0	0	2985
64	MISC. MANUFACTURING	185697	0	0	0	0	1004	0	5019
65	TRANSPORT. & WAREHOUSING	3039894	0	1001	3002	1001	151095	0	71045
66	COMMUNICA., EXC. BRDCAST.	42966	0	0	0	0	0	0	1197
67	RADIO & TV BROADCASTING	27534	0	0	0	0	1197	0	4053
68	ELEC.,GAS,WATER,SAN.SER.	30400	0	2003	4005	0	0	0	59076
69	WHOLESALE & RETAIL TRADE	1735219	0	0	0	0	8010	0	1043
70	FINANCE & INSURANCE	36500	0	1008	0	0	1043	0	6050
71	REAL ESTATE & RENTAL	397300	0	0	0	0	11092	4034	997
72	HOTELS; PERSONAL SERV.	3700	0	0	0	0	0	0	0
73	BUSINESS SERVICES	198499	0	0	0	0	1995	0	1999
74	RESEARCH & DEVELOPMENT	0	0	0	0	0	0	0	0
75	AUTO. REPAIR & SERVICES	312899	0	0	0	0	0	0	0
76	AMUSEMENTS	32300	0	0	0	0	1000	0	0
77	MED.,EDUC. SERVICES	90455	0	0	0	0	0	0	0
78	FEDERAL GOV'T ENTERPRISE	0	56368	0	0	0	812	406	406
79	STATE & LOCAL GOV'T ENT.	-26638016	-26638016	0	0	0	0	0	0
80	IMPORTS	0	0	0	0	0	0	0	0
81	BUS.TRAVEL, ENT., GIFTS.	0	0	0	0	0	0	0	0
82	OFFICE SUPPLIES	0	0	0	0	0	0	0	0
83	SCRAP & USED GOODS	329498	0	341	40	0	1628	0	10930
84	GOVERNMENT INDUSTRY	0	0	0	0	0	0	0	0
85	REST OF WORLD INDUSTRY	6209000	6208000	0	0	0	0	0	0
86	HOUSEHOLD INDUSTRY	0	0	0	0	0	0	0	0
87	INVENTORY VALUATION ADJ.	-20372832	0	0	0	0	0	0	0
88	STATE TOTAL	5812000	-20372832	21365	12007	1001	272011	4439	847666

TABLE C.14

STATE ESTIMATES OF 1947

STATE AND LOCAL GOVERNMENT NET PURCHASES OF GOODS AND SERVICES

(THOUSANDS OF CURRENT DOLLARS)

INDUSTRY TITLE	1 ALABAMA	2 ARIZONA	3 ARKANSAS	4 CALIFORNIA	5 COLORADO	6 CONNECTICUT	7 DELAWARE	8 DISTRICT OF COLUMBIA	9 FLORIDA
1 LIVESTOCK & PRDTS.	113	52	57	1208	109	200	21	117	251
2 OTHER AGRICULTURE PRDTS.	128	61	79	1309	146	214	23	158	305
3 FORESTRY & FISHERIES	31	17	17	284	30	43	5	17	56
4 AGRI.,FORES.,FISH. SERV.	-3	-2	-2	-24	-3	-3	-1	-1	-6
5 IRON, FERRO. ORES MINING	0	0	0	0	0	0	0	0	0
6 NONFERROUS ORES MINING	0	0	0	0	0	0	0	0	0
7 COAL MINING	743	388	419	7135	744	1120	131	582	1507
8 CRUDE PETRO.,NATURAL GAS	0	0	0	0	0	0	0	0	0
9 STONE & CLAY MINING	3	2	2	25	3	3	1	1	6
10 CHEM.&FERT. MIN. MINING	0	0	0	0	0	0	0	0	0
11 NEW CONSTRUCTION*	43195	29556	27875	223020	33312	35842	3980	14773	56363
12 MAINT. & REPAIR CONSTR.	14776	8777	9468	121472	14887	16979	2505	6866	29248
13 ORDNANCE & ACCESSORIES	9	4	3	99	7	17	2	8	19
14 FOOD & KINDRED PRDTS.	1698	848	941	16968	1730	2732	301	1563	3559
15 TOBACCO MANUFACTURES	0	0	0	0	0	0	0	0	0
16 FABRICS	28	13	15	295	27	48	5	28	62
17 TEXTILE PRDTS.	7	3	4	66	7	11	1	7	15
18 APPAREL	369	176	197	3816	365	621	67	367	816
19 MISC. TEXTILE PRDTS.	35	17	16	367	30	60	6	26	70
20 LUMBER & WOOD PRDTS.	14	8	8	124	14	19	1	9	29
21 WOODEN CONTAINERS	3	2	2	30	4	4	1	2	7
22 HOUSEHOLD FURNITURE	74	39	41	685	70	104	13	48	151
23 OTHER FURNITURE	253	144	151	2222	251	328	43	138	489
24 PAPER & ALLIED PRDTS.	384	223	201	3398	350	512	65	122	590
25 PAPERBOARD CONTAINERS	177	106	118	1429	182	196	30	84	363
26 PRINTING & PUBLISHING	1777	1035	1033	15278	1706	2231	301	746	3184
27 CHEMICALS,SELECT. PRDTS.	153	86	95	1330	155	194	26	94	314
28 PLASTICS & SYNTHETICS	0	0	0	0	0	0	0	0	0
29 DRUGS & COSMETICS	584	289	347	5813	639	939	103	617	1280
30 PAINT & ALLIED PRDTS.	14	8	9	120	14	18	2	8	28
31 PETROLEUM, RELATED INDS.	844	444	464	8018	791	1234	150	577	1749
32 RUBBER, MISC. PLASTICS	84	39	38	894	72	146	16	71	178
33 LEATHER TANNING & PRDTS.	3	3	1	28	4	4	1	2	6
34 FOOTWEAR, LEATHER PRDTS.	85	39	43	923	82	154	16	91	191
35 GLASS & GLASS PRDTS.	48	27	28	427	47	64	8	25	91
36 STONE & CLAY PRDTS.	60	31	32	583	55	91	11	42	123
37 PRIMARY IRON, STEEL MFR.	6	3	4	50	6	7	1	3	12
38 PRIMARY NONFERROUS MFR.	14	8	8	125	14	19	2	7	26

	Col1	Col2	Col3	Col4	Col5	Col6	Col7	Col8	Col9
39 METAL CONTAINERS	3	2	2	27	3	4	1	2	6
40 FABRICATED METAL PRDTS.	55	31	32	491	54	73	9	29	104
41 SCREW MACH. PRDTS., ETC.	231	132	143	1987	228	286	40	128	477
42 OTHER FAB. METAL PRDTS.	-11	-6	-7	-97	-11	-14	-2	-6	-21
43 ENGINES & TURBINES	31	19	21	254	32	35	5	15	64
44 FARM MACH. & EQUIP.	93	53	56	808	93	119	16	50	179
45 CONSTRUC. MACH. & EQUIP.	655	392	435	5279	671	723	111	312	1341
46 MATERIAL HANDLING MACH.	42	23	23	374	41	57	7	22	74
47 METALWORKING MACHINERY	74	44	49	598	76	82	13	36	151
48 SPECIAL MACH. & EQUIP.	21	11	11	199	20	31	4	14	42
49 GENERAL MACH. & EQUIP.	118	66	68	1058	114	158	20	64	227
50 MACHINE SHOP PRDTS.	10	6	5	93	9	14	2	4	17
51 OFFICE, COMPUT. MACHINES	225	129	122	2000	210	301	38	92	375
52 SERVICE IND. MACHINES	24	14	15	206	24	30	4	13	48
53 ELECT. TRANSMISS. EQUIP.	22	13	14	187	23	26	4	12	46
54 HOUSEHOLD APPLIANCES	42	25	28	350	44	49	7	23	87
55 ELECTRIC LIGHTING EQUIP.	186	107	99	1643	171	247	31	65	296
56 RADIO, TV, ETC., EQUIP.	18	10	11	164	18	24	3	11	38
57 ELECTRONIC COMPONENTS	2	1	1	14	2	2	0	1	4
58 MISC. ELECTRICAL MACH.	55	32	29	483	50	73	18	18	85
59 MOTOR VEHICLES, EQUIP.	1258	678	686	11754	1179	1803	221	762	2444
60 AIRCRAFT & PARTS	4	2	3	32	4	4	1	2	8
61 OTHER TRANSPORT. EQUIP.	47	28	31	378	48	52	8	22	96
62 PROFESS., SCIEN. INSTRU.	414	233	257	3640	427	539	71	264	833
63 MEDICAL, PHOTO. EQUIP.	128	72	73	1143	123	171	22	69	243
64 MISC. MANUFACTURING	661	382	380	5735	634	844	112	287	1179
65 TRANSPORT. & WAREHOUSING	3069	1722	1678	27777	2898	4217	526	1502	5413
66 COMMUNICA.,EXC. BRDCAST.	875	473	475	8165	821	1254	153	519	1672
67 RADIO & TV BROADCASTING	0	0	0	0	0	0	0	0	0
68 ELEC.,GAS,WATER,SAN.SER.	1813	1044	948	16154	1649	2441	307	629	2866
69 WHOLESALE & RETAIL TRADE	1971	988	1203	19077	2011	2941	359	1914	4842
70 FINANCE & INSURANCE	659	386	380	5653	630	826	111	259	1152
71 REAL ESTATE & RENTAL	1187	682	746	10147	1197	1461	204	665	2419
72 HOTELS; PERSONAL SERV.	842	367	587	8855	1053	1450	155	1395	2476
73 BUSINESS SERVICES	350	192	211	3173	358	480	61	243	713
74 RESEARCH & DEVELOPMENT	0	0	0	0	0	0	0	0	0
75 AUTO. REPAIR & SERVICES	307	153	159	3079	281	488	56	241	653
76 AMUSEMENTS	44	25	22	390	39	59	7	13	65
77 MED.,EDUC. SERVICES	309	148	190	3146	354	515	55	379	718
78 FEDERAL GOV'T ENTERPRISE	365	204	225	3229	371	478	63	236	751
79 STATE & LOCAL GOV'T ENT.	0	0	0	0	0	0	0	0	0
80 IMPORTS	62	37	41	503	64	69	11	30	128
81 BUS.TRAVEL, ENT., GIFTS.	0	0	0	0	0	0	0	0	0
82 OFFICE SUPPLIES	0	0	0	0	0	0	0	0	0
83 SCRAP & USED GOODS	401	242	270	3188	415	433	68	186	816
84 GOVERNMENT INDUSTRY	72096	38929	39393	646416	65693	94522	13119	37192	125620
85 REST OF WORLD INDUSTRY	0	0	0	0	0	0	0	0	0
86 HOUSEHOLD INDUSTRY	0	0	0	0	0	0	0	0	0
87 INVENTORY VALUATION ADJ.	0	0	0	0	0	0	0	0	0
88 STATE TOTAL	154467	90536	90831	1215269	137970	181518	23849	74912	259829

*The data for this industry could not be made entirely consistent with the 1947 state output estimates. (See page 215.)

TABLE C.14

STATE ESTIMATES OF 1947

STATE AND LOCAL GOVERNMENT NET PURCHASES OF GOODS AND SERVICES
(THOUSANDS OF CURRENT DOLLARS)

INDUSTRY TITLE	10 GEORGIA	11 IDAHO	12 ILLINOIS	13 INDIANA	14 IOWA	15 KANSAS	16 KENTUCKY	17 LOUISIANA	18 MAINE
1 LIVESTOCK & PRDTS.	193	31	797	286	156	108	115	182	50
2 OTHER AGRICULTURE PRDTS.	265	39	986	356	218	138	144	210	59
3 FORESTRY & FISHERIES	44	10	165	69	48	36	31	47	14
4 AGRI.,FORES.,FISH. SERV.	-4	-1	-14	-5	-5	-4	-3	-5	-2
5 IRON,FERRO.ORES MINING	0	0	0	0	0	0	0	0	0
6 NONFERROUS ORES MINING	0	0	0	0	0	0	0	0	0
7 COAL MINING	1203	232	4571	1772	1147	821	760	1158	342
8 CRUDE PETRO.,NATURAL GAS	4	1	0	5	5	4	0	0	0
9 STONE & CLAY MINING	4	1	15	5	5	3	3	5	2
10 CHEM.&FERT. MIN. MINING	0	0	0	0	0	0	0	0	0
11 NEW CONSTRUCTION*	40291	14734	122694	43502	44923	50491	44588	36150	16115
12 MAINT. & REPAIR CONSTR.	19565	5343	70451	26468	22542	19492	13764	22729	9142
13 ORDNANCE & ACCESSORIES	12	2	58	20	9	7	8	14	4
14 FOOD & KINDRED PRDTS.	2964	511	11338	4349	2656	1791	1790	2675	730
15 TOBACCO MANUFACTURES	0	0	0	0	0	0	0	0	0
16 FABRICS	47	8	194	69	39	28	28	45	13
17 TEXTILE PRDTS.	13	2	48	18	12	7	7	11	3
18 APPAREL	626	107	2531	908	525	372	375	592	172
19 MISC. TEXTILE PRDTS.	48	10	211	78	43	34	33	55	16
20 LUMBER & WOOD PRDTS.	20	5	77	28	20	17	13	22	8
21 WOODEN CONTAINERS	5	1	19	7	5	4	3	5	2
22 HOUSEHOLD FURNITURE	101	24	406	146	100	84	69	115	41
23 OTHER FURNITURE	359	86	1320	521	390	310	246	388	134
24 PAPER & ALLIED PRDTS.	511	124	1822	881	613	440	384	553	140
25 PAPERBOARD CONTAINERS	233	66	837	300	269	241	163	275	118
26 PRINTING & PUBLISHING	2372	606	8590	3614	2743	2180	1710	2660	890
27 CHEMICALS,SELECT. PRDTS.	219	53	813	299	231	191	146	238	90
28 PLASTICS & SYNTHETICS	0	0	0	0	0	0	0	0	0
29 DRUGS & COSMETICS	1132	180	4170	1591	993	634	647	932	250
30 PAINT & ALLIED PRDTS.	20	5	74	28	21	17	13	22	8
31 PETROLEUM,RELATED INDS.	1169	265	4769	1705	1131	941	787	1324	461
32 RUBBER, MISC. PLASTICS	117	23	531	185	96	77	77	133	40
33 LEATHER TANNING & PRDTS.	4	1	16	7		4	3	5	2
34 FOOTWEAR, LEATHER PRDTS.	146	23	612	218	116	79	87	138	37
35 GLASS & GLASS PRDTS.	68	16	251	101	73	57	47	73	24
36 STONE & CLAY PRDTS.	83	18	346	125	79	64	56	94	31
37 PRIMARY IRON, STEEL MFR.	8	2	30	11	9	8	6	9	4
38 PRIMARY NONFERROUS MFR.	20	5	73	29	21	17	14	21	7

378

		1		6	5	4	3	5	2
39 METAL CONTAINERS	4	1	16	6	5	4	3	5	2
40 FABRICATED METAL PRDTS.	78	18	288	116	85	66	54	84	28
41 SCREW MACH. PRDTS., ETC.	306	80	1166	413	330	291	211	360	145
42 OTHER FAB. METAL PRDTS.	-16	-4	-58	-24	-18	-14	-11	-17	-6
43 ENGINES & TURBINES	42	12	149	53	48	43	29	49	21
44 FARM MACH. & EQUIP.	132	32	480	190	144	115	90	142	50
45 CONSTRUC. MACH. & EQUIP.	862	242	3093	1108	994	888	602	1017	435
46 MATERIAL HANDLING MACH.	62	14	222	96	67	49	42	62	18
47 METALWORKING MACHINERY	98	27	351	126	112	100	68	115	49
48 SPECIAL MACH. & EQUIP.	30	6	120	45	29	23	20	32	10
49 GENERAL MACH. & EQUIP.	164	39	618	243	176	141	114	181	62
50 MACHINE SHOP PRDTS.	14	3	51	23	16	12	10	15	4
51 OFFICE, COMPUT. MACHINES	307	73	1114	502	352	260	223	331	93
52 SERVICE IND. MACHINES	34	8	124	48	37	30	23	37	14
53 ELECT. TRANSMISS. EQUIP.	30	8	110	39	33	29	21	35	14
54 HOUSEHOLD APPLIANCES	58	15	210	76	65	56	40	66	27
55 ELECTRIC LIGHTING EQUIP.	249	60	893	418	294	215	185	270	73
56 RADIO, TV, ETC., EQUIP.	24	6	96	34	25	22	17	29	11
57 ELECTRONIC COMPONENTS	2	1	8	3	2	2	2	3	1
58 MISC. ELECTRICAL MACH.	73	18	260	124	87	63	54	79	21
59 MOTOR VEHICLES, EQUIP.	1752	398	6887	2660	1785	1413	1202	1934	626
60 AIRCRAFT & PARTS	5	1	19	7	6	5	4	6	3
61 OTHER TRANSPORT. EQUIP.	62	17	221	79	71	63	43	73	31
62 PROFESS., SCIEN. INSTRU.	629	142	2278	879	659	512	411	641	224
63 MEDICAL, PHOTO. EQUIP.	179	42	670	267	192	152	124	195	65
64 MISC. MANUFACTURING	895	223	3244	1375	1025	801	641	988	321
65 TRANSPORT. & WAREHOUSING	4314	992	15949	6851	4738	3526	3038	4584	1336
66 COMMUNICA.,EXC. BRDCAST.	1226	277	4778	1882	1261	981	843	1339	422
67 RADIO & TV BROADCASTING	0	0	0	0	0	0	0	0	0
68 ELEC.,GAS,WATER,SAN.SER.	2410	584	8722	4104	2843	2070	1798	2630	692
69 WHOLESALE & RETAIL TRADE	3050	632	12619	3816	2581	2267	1832	3268	1317
70 FINANCE & INSURANCE	877	225	3148	1360	1029	807	638	980	319
71 REAL ESTATE & RENTAL	1646	417	6078	2234	1787	1513	1119	1844	717
72 HOTELS; PERSONAL SERV.	1929	264	7404	2226	1378	941	937	1491	539
73 BUSINESS SERVICES	543	117	2007	767	548	418	350	545	183
74 RESEARCH & DEVELOPMENT	0	0	0	0	0	0	0	0	0
75 AUTO. REPAIR & SERVICES	436	91	1855	649	389	318	287	487	160
76 AMUSEMENTS	58	14	207	103	70	49	44	63	15
77 MED.,EDUC. SERVICES	651	95	2386	888	544	332	354	502	133
78 FEDERAL GOV'T ENTERPRISE	539	124	2001	743	557	449	354	569	207
79 STATE & LOCAL GOV'T ENT.	0	0	0	0	0	0	0	0	0
80 IMPORTS	82	23	294	105	95	85	57	97	41
81 BUS.TRAVEL, ENT., GIFTS.	0	0	0	0	0	0	0	0	0
82 OFFICE SUPPLIES	0	0	0	0	0	0	0	0	0
83 SCRAP & USED GOODS	532	150	1877	681	621	551	371	621	266
84 GOVERNMENT INDUSTRY	97294	25742	372105	165144	105024	81637	67609	101075	36532
85 REST OF WORLD INDUSTRY	0	0	0	0	0	0	0	0	0
86 HOUSEHOLD INDUSTRY	0	0	0	0	0	0	0	0	0
87 INVENTORY VALUATION ADJ.	0	0	0	0	0	0	0	0	0
88 STATE TOTAL	193520	53762	702861	288150	209319	179975	149967	197701	74168

*The data for this industry could not be made entirely consistent with the 1947 state output estimates. (See page 215.)

TABLE C.14

STATE ESTIMATES OF 1947
STATE AND LOCAL GOVERNMENT NET PURCHASES OF GOODS AND SERVICES
(THOUSANDS OF CURRENT DOLLARS)

INDUSTRY TITLE	19 MARYLAND	20 MASSA-CHUSETTS	21 MICHIGAN	22 MINNESOTA	23 MISSISSIPPI	24 MISSOURI	25 MONTANA	26 NEBRASKA	27 NEVADA
1 LIVESTOCK & PRDTS.	206	579	662	232	68	229	38	70	23
2 OTHER AGRICULTURE PRDTS.	229	694	864	330	98	263	47	86	30
3 FORESTRY & FISHERIES	42	96	144	62	21	56	13	23	5
4 AGRI.,FORES.,FISH.SERV.	-3	-7	-10	-6	-3	-5	-2	-3	-1
5 IRON,FERRO.ORES MINING	0	0	0	0	0	0	0	0	0
6 NONFERROUS ORES MINING	0	0	0	0	0	0	0	0	0
7 COAL MINING	1138	2938	3920	1583	519	1413	292	527	143
8 CRUDE PETRO.,NATURAL GAS	0	0	0	0	0	0	0	0	0
9 STONE & CLAY MINING	3	7	11	6	3	5	2	3	1
10 CHEM.&FERT.MIN.MINING	0	0	0	0	0	0	0	0	0
11 NEW CONSTRUCTION*	46813	48282	90105	49651	32581	42874	18499	29756	9036
12 MAINT.& REPAIR CONSTR.	16808	35858	54745	27953	12973	25540	7287	13479	3009
13 ORDNANCE & ACCESSORIES	17	46	44	13	4	18	3	5	2
14 FOOD & KINDRED PRDTS.	2809	7648	9871	3802	1140	3328	623	1125	335
15 TOBACCO MANUFACTURES	0	0	0	0	0	0	0	0	0
16 FABRICS	50	139	159	57	18	56	10	18	6
17 TEXTILE PRDTS.	11	33	43	17	5	13	2	4	1
18 APPAREL	641	1790	2099	769	242	735	132	244	78
19 MISC. TEXTILE PRDTS.	59	147	168	59	19	68	12	23	6
20 LUMBER & WOOD PRDTS.	19	47	61	27	11	25	6	12	3
21 WOODEN CONTAINERS	5	11	15	7	3	6	2	3	1
22 HOUSEHOLD FURNITURE	104	253	315	133	54	135	31	58	15
23 OTHER FURNITURE	325	740	1094	501	197	453	113	206	48
24 PAPER & ALLIED PRDTS.	484	930	1701	760	234	674	156	267	51
25 PAPERBOARD CONTAINERS	195	419	627	333	165	305	91	170	38
26 PRINTING & PUBLISHING	2165	4486	7263	3421	1327	3111	797	1430	306
27 CHEMICALS,SELECT.PRDTS.	196	466	645	299	128	274	71	131	32
28 PLASTICS & SYNTHETICS	0	0	0	0	0	0	0	0	0
29 DRUGS & COSMETICS	987	2828	3719	1452	425	1164	215	389	123
30 PAINT & ALLIED PRDTS.	18	42	60	28	12	25	6	12	3
31 PETROLEUM,RELATED INDS.	1235	3057	3701	1509	602	1569	351	651	170
32 RUBBER, MISC. PLASTICS	146	386	409	138	46	165	29	54	16
33 LEATHER TANNING & PRDTS.	4	9	14	6	2	6	1	2	1
34 FOOTWEAR, LEATHER PRDTS.	159	451	507	175	50	174	28	52	18
35 GLASS & GLASS PRDTS.	63	142	210	94	36	86	21	38	9
36 STONE & CLAY PRDTS.	91	227	272	106	40	113	24	44	12
37 PRIMARY IRON, STEEL MFR.	7	17	24	11	5	10	3	5	1
38 PRIMARY NONFERROUS MFR.	18	41	61	28	10	25	6	11	3

39	METAL CONTAINERS	4	9	13	6	2	5	1	2	1
40	FABRICATED METAL PRDTS.	72	163	242	109	41	99	24	43	10
41	SCREW MACH. PRDTS., ETC.	286	656	877	419	196	408	110	205	49
42	OTHER FAB. METAL PRDTS.	-14	-32	-50	-23	-9	-20	-5	-9	-2
43	ENGINES & TURBINES	35	75	112	59	29	54	16	30	7
44	FARM MACH. & EQUIP.	118	265	399	185	73	166	42	76	18
45	CONSTRUC. MACH. & EQUIP.	722	1551	2318	1228	609	1125	335	625	141
46	MATERIAL HANDLING MACH.	56	125	199	87	29	75	17	30	7
47	METALWORKING MACHINERY	82	178	264	139	68	127	38	70	16
48	SPECIAL MACH. & EQUIP.	31	76	97	39	14	39	8	15	4
49	GENERAL MACH. & EQUIP.	156	354	507	226	88	213	52	94	22
50	MACHINE SHOP PRDTS.	14	27	46	20	6	18	4	7	1
51	OFFICE, COMPUT. MACHINES	290	598	999	444	147	399	93	163	34
52	SERVICE IND. MACHINES	30	69	101	48	20	43	11	21	5
53	ELECT. TRANSMISS. EQUIP.	26	59	83	42	20	39	11	21	5
54	HOUSEHOLD APPLIANCES	49	111	161	81	38	74	21	39	9
55	ELECTRIC LIGHTING EQUIP.	235	463	817	366	118	327	77	132	26
56	RADIO, TV, ETC., EQUIP.	24	57	73	33	15	33	8	16	4
57	ELECTRONIC COMPONENTS	2	4	6	3	2	1	1	2	0
58	MISC. ELECTRICAL MACH.	69	134	241	108	34	96	22	38	7
59	MOTOR VEHICLES, EQUIP.	1785	4227	5620	2345	867	2311	518	943	232
60	AIRCRAFT & PARTS	4	9	14	7	4	7	2	4	1
61	OTHER TRANSPORT. EQUIP.	52	111	166	88	43	80	24	45	10
62	PROFESS., SCIEN. INSTRU.	545	1311	1902	866	337	750	186	340	83
63	MEDICAL, PHOTO. EQUIP.	169	384	557	248	94	230	55	100	23
64	MISC. MANUFACTURING	820	1720	2773	1286	484	1163	292	521	112
65	TRANSPORT. & WAREHOUSING	4110	9021	13981	6082	2054	5526	1266	2236	498
66	COMMUNICA., EXC. BROCAST.	1239	2910	3957	1653	595	1606	358	647	158
67	RADIO & TV BROADCASTING									
68	ELEC.,GAS,WATER,SAN-SER.	2318	4568	7991	3540	1117	3198	738	1270	250
69	WHOLESALE & RETAIL TRADE	3080	8700	9166	3680	1663	3797	857	1665	502
70	FINANCE & INSURANCE	797	1614	2706	1277	483	1151	294	524	109
71	REAL ESTATE & RENTAL	1463	3365	4757	2280	1012	2103	563	1044	247
72	HOTELS; PERSONAL SERV.	1637	5557	5979	2243	800	1809	328	653	262
73	BUSINESS SERVICES	486	1208	1680	733	274	645	151	276	70
74	RESEARCH & DEVELOPMENT				0	0	0	0	0	0
75	AUTO. REPAIR & SERVICES	491	1269	1437	539	201	588	118	221	62
76	AMUSEMENTS	56	106	197	87	25	77	17	29	5
77	MED.,EDUC. SERVICES	552	1666	2139	821	233	633	111	202	70
78	FEDERAL GOV'T ENTERPRISE	483	1173	1616	732	299	662	165	304	75
79	STATE & LOCAL GOV'T ENT.				0		0	0	0	0
80	IMPORTS	69	147	221	117	58	107	32	60	13
81	BUS.TRAVEL, ENT., GIFTS.	0	0	0	0	0	0	0	0	0
82	OFFICE SUPPLIES	0	0	0	0	0	0	0	0	0
83	SCRAP & USED GOODS	432	917	1422	766	378	685	207	386	86
84	GOVERNMENT INDUSTRY	94631	221460	338807	149288	50408	121517	29899	56149	12156
85	REST OF WORLD INDUSTRY	0	0	0	0	0	0	0	0	0
86	HOUSEHOLD INDUSTRY	0	0	0	0	0	0	0	0	0
87	INVENTORY VALUATION ADJ.	0	0	0	0	0	0	0	0	0
88	STATE TOTAL	192550	389187	598115	275853	114003	234881	65975	118134	28911

*The data for this industry could not be made entirely consistent with the 1947 state output estimates. (See page 215.)

381

TABLE C.14

STATE ESTIMATES OF 1947
STATE AND LOCAL GOVERNMENT NET PURCHASES OF GOODS AND SERVICES
(THOUSANDS OF CURRENT DOLLARS)

INDUSTRY TITLE	28 NEW HAMPSHIRE	29 NEW JERSEY	30 NEW MEXICO	31 NEW YORK	32 NORTH CAROLINA	33 NORTH DAKOTA	34 OHIO	35 OKLAHOMA	36 OREGON
1 LIVESTOCK & PRDTS.	45	568	35	2259	162	30	605	99	110
2 OTHER AGRICULTURE PRDTS.	59	616	46	3070	206	36	745	113	120
3 FORESTRY & FISHERIES	10	106	13	394	48	12	142	32	31
4 AGRI.,FORES.,FISH. SERV.	-1	-8	-1	-32	-5	-1	-12	-3	-3
5 IRON, FERRO. ORES MINING	0	0	0	0	0	0	0	-3	-0
6 NONFERROUS ORES MINING	0	0	0	0	0	0	0	0	0
7 COAL MINING	270	2959	282	12261	1149	255	3694	720	730
8 CRUDE PETRO.,NATURAL GAS	0	0	0	0	0	0	0	0	0
9 STONE & CLAY MINING	1	9	1	33	5	1	13	3	3
10 CHEM.&FERT. MIN. MINING	0	0	0	0	0	0	0	0	0
11 NEW CONSTRUCTION*	4908	55999	18617	270148	52799	14850	97594	51044	34711
12 MAINT. & REPAIR CONSTR.	5109	41463	6217	157803	23223	6528	61817	15554	15685
13 ORDNANCE & ACCESSORIES	3	48	2	150	11	2	43	7	9
14 FOOD & KINDRED PRDTS.	648	7412	621	32007	2625	529	8931	1589	1630
15 TOBACCO MANUFACTURES	0	0	0	0	0	0	0	0	0
16 FABRICS	11	137	9	543	40	8	148	25	27
17 TEXTILE PRDTS.	3	30	3	147	11	2	37	6	6
18 APPAREL	147	1752	121	7140	541	105	1940	330	360
19 MISC. TEXTILE PRDTS.	12	161	11	516	48	11	167	33	36
20 LUMBER & WOOD PRDTS.	5	49	5	195	21	5	63	14	14
21 WOODEN CONTAINERS	1	12	1	48	1	1	16	1	4
22 HOUSEHOLD FURNITURE	26	277	27	985	108	27	332	72	76
23 OTHER FURNITURE	86	813	104	3153	397	103	1131	261	260
24 PAPER & ALLIED PRDTS.	98	1123	171	3849	612	160	1671	419	379
25 PAPERBOARD CONTAINERS	64	485	74	1876	279	80	733	186	191
26 PRINTING & PUBLISHING	545	5239	758	18979	2793	752	7628	1886	1822
27 CHEMICALS,SELECT. PRDTS.	56	501	61	1997	237	62	682	154	159
28 PLASTICS & SYNTHETICS	0	0	0	0	0	0	0	0	0
29 DRUGS & COSMETICS	242	2591	219	12483	941	179	3245	539	547
30 PAINT & ALLIED PRDTS.	5	45	6	182	22	6	62	14	14
31 PETROLEUM, RELATED INDS.	301	3313	298	11707	1222	296	3859	813	873
32 RUBBER, MISC. PLASTICS	30	411	25	1351	111	23	407	75	85
33 LEATHER TANNING & PRDTS.	1	10	1	38	5	1	14	3	3
34 FOOTWEAR, LEATHER PRDTS.	34	440	26	1748	121	21	461	74	82
35 GLASS & GLASS PRDTS.	16	157	20	593	75	19	215	50	49
36 STONE & CLAY PRDTS.	21	245	21	855	86	20	278	57	61
37 PRIMARY IRON, STEEL MFR.	2	18	2	72	9	2	26	6	6
38 PRIMARY NONFERROUS MFR.	5	46	6	173	22	6	63	14	14

#	Industry									
39	METAL CONTAINERS	1	10	1	37	5	1	14	3	3
40	FABRICATED METAL PRDTS.	18	180	23	682	86	22	247	57	56
41	SCREW MACH. PRDTS., ETC.	83	739	90	2703	349	95	986	234	245
42	OTHER FAB. METAL PRDTS.	-4	-34	-5	-139	-18	-5	-50	-12	-11
43	ENGINES & TURBINES	11	86	13	335	49	14	130	33	34
44	FARM MACH. & EQUIP.	31	292	39	1144	146	38	413	96	95
45	CONSTRUC. MACH. & EQUIP.	236	1792	275	6937	1029	295	2705	688	705
46	MATERIAL HANDLING MACH.	13	136	18	539	67	16	192	43	41
47	METALWORKING MACHINERY	27	204	31	794	116	33	307	77	79
48	SPECIAL MACH. & EQUIP.	7	82	8	299	31	7	97	20	21
49	GENERAL MACH. & EQUIP.	39	394	47	1453	182	47	526	121	122
50	MACHINE SHOP PRDTS.	3	32	4	110	16	4	45	11	10
51	OFFICE, COMPUT. MACHINES	64	694	97	2482	354	92	993	239	224
52	SERVICE IND. MACHINES	8	75	10	298	38	10	106	25	25
53	ELECT. TRANSMISS. EQUIP.	8	67	9	252	35	10	95	23	24
54	HOUSEHOLD APPLIANCES	15	124	17	494	66	18	181	44	45
55	ELECTRIC LIGHTING EQUIP.	50	552	82	1919	295	77	810	201	184
56	RADIO, TV, ETC., EQUIP.	7	64	7	227	27	7	80	18	19
57	ELECTRONIC COMPONENTS	1	5	1	19	3	1	7	2	2
58	MISC. ELECTRICAL MACH.	14	161	24	553	87	23	238	59	54
59	MOTOR VEHICLES, EQUIP.	419	4637	475	16574	1876	461	5727	1251	1281
60	AIRCRAFT & PARTS	17	11	2	42	6	2	16	4	4
61	OTHER TRANSPORT. EQUIP.	1	128	20	497	74	21	193	49	50
62	PROFESS., SCIEN. INSTRU.	149	1369	170	5781	658	165	1915	421	421
63	MEDICAL, PHOTO. EQUIP.	42	425	52	1586	197	50	571	131	130
64	MISC. MANUFACTURING	202	1987	281	7268	1040	276	2869	699	673
65	TRANSPORT. & WAREHOUSING	928	10104	1275	37184	4791	1207	13845	3196	3064
66	COMMUNICA.,EXC. BRDCAST.	287	3193	335	11488	1314	322	3994	875	886
67	RADIO & TV BROADCASTING	0	0	0	0	0	0	0	0	0
68	ELEC.,GAS,WATER,SAN.SER.	477	5464	791	18647	2860	745	7908	1956	1796
69	WHOLESALE & RETAIL TRADE	868	8703	621	34570	2811	633	9582	1757	2075
70	FINANCE & INSURANCE	196	1905	285	6862	1042	281	2823	706	673
71	REAL ESTATE & RENTAL	425	3712	480	14445	1843	494	5172	1216	1247
72	HOTELS; PERSONAL SERV.	487	4688	248	24655	1316	197	5241	649	810
73	BUSINESS SERVICES	128	1243	139	5207	550	133	1658	349	353
74	RESEARCH & DEVELOPMENT	0	0	0	0	0	0	0	0	0
75	AUTO. REPAIR & SERVICES	112	1349	100	4703	430	96	1457	284	315
76	AMUSEMENTS	11	128	20	435	70	18	191	48	43
77	MED.,EDUC. SERVICES	139	1466	113	7475	505	88	1815	275	284
78	FEDERAL GOV'T ENTERPRISE	134	1239	145	5024	568	144	1667	366	376
79	STATE & LOCAL GOV'T ENT.	0	0	0	0	0	0	0	0	0
80	IMPORTS	22	170	26	660	98	28	258	66	67
81	BUS.TRAVEL, ENT., GIFTS.	0	0	0	0	0	0	0	0	0
82	OFFICE SUPPLIES	0	0	0	0	0	0	0	0	0
83	SCRAP & USED GOODS	144	1059	171	4216	637	183	1654	424	431
84	GOVERNMENT INDUSTRY	21166	217400	29948	896897	114055	27988	328143	73719	72111
85	REST OF WORLD INDUSTRY	0	0	0	0	0	0	0	0	0
86	HOUSEHOLD INDUSTRY	0	0	0	0	0	0	0	0	0
87	INVENTORY VALUATION ADJ.	0	0	0	0	0	0	0	0	0
88	STATE TOTAL	39749	403062	64290	1672077	227633	58468	601571	164615	147160

*The data for this industry could not be made entirely consistent with the 1947 state output estimates. (See page 215.)

TABLE C.14

STATE ESTIMATES OF 1947
STATE AND LOCAL GOVERNMENT NET PURCHASES OF GOODS AND SERVICES
(THOUSANDS OF CURRENT DOLLARS)

INDUSTRY TITLE	37 PENNSYL-VANIA	38 RHODE ISLAND	39 SOUTH CAROLINA	40 SOUTH DAKOTA	41 TENNESSEE	42 TEXAS	43 UTAH	44 VERMONT	45 VIRGINIA
1 LIVESTOCK & PRDTS.	730	71	96	30	135	366	45	20	171
2 OTHER AGRICULTURE PRDTS.	880	75	130	37	171	389	54	26	210
3 FORESTRY & FISHERIES	168	13	28	11	40	118	15	6	45
4 AGRI.,FORES.,FISH. SERV.	-16	-1	-3	-2	-5	-12	-1	-1	-4
5 IRON, FERRO. ORES MINING	0	0	0	0	0	0	0	0	0
6 NONFERROUS ORES MINING	0	0	0	0	0	0	0	0	0
7 COAL MINING	4407	367	685	249	964	2622	331	142	1110
8 CRUDE PETRO.,NATURAL GAS	0	0	0	0	0	0	0	0	0
9 STONE & CLAY MINING	17	1	3	2	5	13	1	1	5
10 CHEM.&FERT. MIN. MINING	0	0	0	0	0	0	0	0	0
11 NEW CONSTRUCTION*	161644	7166	48034	10574	57905	152128	12318	6616	54203
12 MAINT. & REPAIR CONSTR.	78695	5300	14552	6807	23321	59403	6367	3239	21068
13 ORDNANCE & ACCESSORIES	54	6	6	2	9	29	3	1	12
14 FOOD & KINDRED PRDTS.	10532	912	1565	512	2115	5686	750	317	2595
15 TOBACCO MANUFACTURES	0	0	0	0	0	0	0	0	0
16 FABRICS	179	17	24	8	35	92	11	5	42
17 TEXTILE PRDTS.	44	4	7	2	9	21	3	1	11
18 APPAREL	2350	218	325	106	463	1217	149	68	559
19 MISC. TEXTILE PRDTS.	205	20	27	10	41	127	15	6	50
20 LUMBER & WOOD PRDTS.	80	6	13	6	21	52	6	3	20
21 WOODEN CONTAINERS	20	1	3	1	5	13	1	1	5
22 HOUSEHOLD FURNITURE	418	35	65	28	103	276	30	15	105
23 OTHER FURNITURE	1384	102	240	103	361	976	114	52	365
24 PAPER & ALLIED PRDTS.	1896	138	336	140	452	1519	203	68	534
25 PAPERBOARD CONTAINERS	952	62	179	85	294	718	74	40	254
26 PRINTING & PUBLISHING	9226	659	1648	730	2461	7043	839	352	2507
27 CHEMICALS,SELECT. PRDTS.	858	63	148	64	231	584	64	32	222
28 PLASTICS & SYNTHETICS	0	0	0	0	0	0	0	0	0
29 DRUGS & COSMETICS	3783	314	578	175	751	1865	260	114	928
30 PAINT & ALLIED PRDTS.	78	6	14	6	21	53	6	3	20
31 PETROLEUM, RELATED INDS.	4858	422	734	306	1160	3135	340	164	1207
32 RUBBER, MISC. PLASTICS	509	52	63	23	99	292	32	14	119
33 LEATHER TANNING & PRDTS.	17	1	1	1	4	12	1	1	4
34 FOOTWEAR, LEATHER PRDTS.	556	55	71	21	100	272	34	15	129
35 GLASS & GLASS PRDTS.	261	20	45	19	66	185	22	10	69
36 STONE & CLAY PRDTS.	347	31	51	20	79	220	24	11	86
37 PRIMARY IRON, STEEL MFR.	33	2	6	3	9	23	2	1	9
38 PRIMARY NONFERROUS MFR.	76	6	13	5	19	54	6	3	20

39 METAL CONTAINERS	16	1	3	1	4	12	1	1	4
40 FABRICATED METAL PRDTS.	300	23	51	22	76	213	25	11	79
41 SCREW MACH. PRDTS., ETC.	1272	95	219	101	358	906	94	50	329
42 OTHER FAB. METAL PRDTS.	-60	-4	-11	-4	-16	-43	-5	-2	-16
43 ENGINES & TURBINES	169	11	32	15	52	127	13	7	45
44 FARM MACH. & EQUIP.	506	37	89	38	134	359	42	19	134
45 CONSTRUC. MACH. & EQUIP.	3514	231	659	315	1083	2651	272	149	937
46 MATERIAL HANDLING MACH.	224	17	39	15	53	157	21	8	60
47 METALWORKING MACHINERY	397	26	74	35	122	298	31	17	106
48 SPECIAL MACH. & EQUIP.	120	10	18	7	27	76	9	4	30
49 GENERAL MACH. & EQUIP.	646	50	109	47	165	456	53	24	169
50 MACHINE SHOP PRDTS.	52	4	9	4	12	40	5	2	14
51 OFFICE, COMPUT. MACHINES	1155	86	200	84	280	876	113	41	316
52 SERVICE IND. MACHINES	132	9	23	10	36	93	11	5	35
53 ELECT. TRANSMISS. EQUIP.	122	9	22	10	36	89	9	5	32
54 HOUSEHOLD APPLIANCES	232	16	42	20	68	167	18	9	61
55 ELECTRIC LIGHTING EQUIP.	931	68	164	69	225	732	96	33	259
56 RADIO, TV, ETC., EQUIP.	103	8	17	8	27	71	7	4	26
57 ELECTRONIC COMPONENTS	9	1	2	1	3	7	1	0	3
58 MISC. ELECTRICAL MACH.	272	20	43	20	65	216	29	10	76
59 MOTOR VEHICLES, EQUIP.	7015	586	1103	455	1665	4726	549	240	1794
60 AIRCRAFT & PARTS	21	1	4	2	7	16	2	1	6
61 OTHER TRANSPORT. EQUIP.	251	17	47	22	77	189	19	11	67
62 PROFESS., SCIEN. INSTRU.	2341	171	406	168	605	1558	184	86	611
63 MEDICAL, PHOTO. EQUIP.	696	53	117	50	176	490	58	25	183
64 MISC. MANUFACTURING	3447	249	610	266	900	2600	314	130	935
65 TRANSPORT. & WAREHOUSING	16312	1257	2748	1126	3893	11749	1485	571	4366
66 COMMUNICA.-EXC. BRDCAST.	4851	402	768	314	1142	3287	389	165	1249
67 RADIO & TV BROADCASTING	0	0	0	0	0	0	0	0	0
68 ELEC.,GAS,WATER,SAN.SER.	9069	676	1579	662	2161	7137	939	322	2521
69 WHOLESALE & RETAIL TRADE	12595	1114	1843	741	3072	6916	655	425	2957
70 FINANCE & INSURANCE	3382	239	610	269	898	2622	318	129	927
71 REAL ESTATE & RENTAL	6550	472	1154	517	1830	4631	501	256	1712
72 HOTELS; PERSONAL SERV.	6559	577	928	258	1345	2293	263	194	1458
73 BUSINESS SERVICES	2019	155	337	134	496	1288	154	71	519
74 RESEARCH & DEVELOPMENT	0	0	0	0	0	0	0	0	0
75 AUTO. REPAIR & SERVICES	1829	172	254	100	400	1102	120	57	441
76 AMUSEMENTS	214	16	38	16	50	173	24	8	61
77 MED.,EDUC. SERVICES	2110	177	317	88	402	929	135	61	508
78 FEDERAL GOV'T ENTERPRISE	2074	156	353	149	541	1376	155	77	535
79 STATE & LOCAL GOV'T ENT.	0	0	0	0	0	0	0	0	0
80 IMPORTS	335	22	63	30	103	253	26	14	89
81 BUS.TRAVEL, ENT., GIFTS.	0	0	0	0	0	0	0	0	0
82 OFFICE SUPPLIES	0	0	0	0	0	0	0	0	0
83 SCRAP & USED GOODS	2141	136	409	195	668	1627	169	92	575
84 GOVERNMENT INDUSTRY	407961	31291	62710	26805	74636	271003	34658	14054	102777
85 REST OF WORLD INDUSTRY	0	0	0	0	0	0	0	0	0
86 HOUSEHOLD INDUSTRY	0	0	0	0	0	0	0	0	0
87 INVENTORY VALUATION ADJ.	0	0	0	0	0	0	0	0	0
88 STATE TOTAL	787125	54801	147896	53269	189322	572959	64081	28732	213670

*The data for this industry could not be made entirely consistent with the 1947 state output estimates. (See page 215.)

TABLE C.14

STATE ESTIMATES OF 1947
STATE AND LOCAL GOVERNMENT NET PURCHASES OF GOODS AND SERVICES
(THOUSANDS OF CURRENT DOLLARS)

INDUSTRY TITLE	46 WASHINGTON	47 WEST VIRGINIA	48 WISCONSIN	49 WYOMING	50 ALASKA	51 HAWAII	52 NO STATE ALLOCATION	53 NATIONAL TOTAL
1 LIVESTOCK & PRDTS.	175	81	318	25	0	0	0	12329
2 OTHER AGRICULTURE PRDTS.	196	101	425	38	0	0	0	15222
3 FORESTRY & FISHERIES	51	25	71	7	0	0	0	2812
4 AGRI.,FORES.,FISH. SERV.	-5	-3	-7	-1	0	0	0	-255
5 IRON, FERRO. ORES MINING	0	0	0	0	0	0	0	0
6 NONFERROUS ORES MINING	0	0	0	0	0	0	0	0
7 COAL MINING	1191	585	1944	185	0	0	0	74350
8 CRUDE PETRO.,NATURAL GAS	0	0	0	0	0	0	0	0
9 STONE & CLAY MINING	5	3	7	1	0	0	0	264
10 CHEM.&FERT. MIN. MINING	0	0	0	0	0	0	0	0
11 NEW CONSTRUCTION*	88376	28763	43719	18099	0	0	0	2539200
12 MAINT. & REPAIR CONSTR.	25120	12368	34243	4084	0	0	0	1260092
13 ORDNANCE & ACCESSORIES	13	5	21	1	0	0	0	891
14 FOOD & KINDRED PRDTS.	2666	1317	4729	423	0	0	0	179936
15 TOBACCO MANUFACTURES	0	0	0	0	0	0	0	0
16 FABRICS	44	20	78	6	0	0	0	3014
17 TEXTILE PRDTS.	10	5	21	2	0	0	0	756
18 APPAREL	575	271	1038	86	0	0	0	39593
19 MISC. TEXTILE PRDTS.	56	25	81	6	0	0	0	3380
20 LUMBER & WOOD PRDTS.	23	11	35	4	0	0	0	1299
21 WOODEN CONTAINERS	6	3	9	1	0	0	0	319
22 HOUSEHOLD FURNITURE	121	56	176	17	0	0	0	6784
23 OTHER FURNITURE	422	208	598	65	0	0	0	22748
24 PAPER & ALLIED PRDTS.	641	318	756	83	0	0	0	32136
25 PAPERBOARD CONTAINERS	303	149	420	51	0	0	0	15079
26 PRINTING & PUBLISHING	2986	1469	3864	438	0	0	0	151586
27 CHEMICALS,SELECT. PRDTS.	254	124	378	41	0	0	0	13941
28 PLASTICS & SYNTHETICS	0	0	0	0	0	0	0	0
29 DRUGS & COSMETICS	905	467	1785	164	0	0	0	65517
30 PAINT & ALLIED PRDTS.	23	11	34	4	0	0	0	1270
31 PETROLEUM, RELATED INDS.	1378	636	2038	192	0	0	0	78920
32 RUBBER, MISC. PLASTICS	132	57	204	15	0	0	0	8335
33 LEATHER TANNING & PRDTS.	5	3	7	1	0	0	0	279
34 FOOTWEAR, LEATHER PRDTS.	131	60	242	18	0	0	0	9405
35 GLASS & GLASS PRDTS.	80	39	111	12	0	0	0	4307
36 STONE & CLAY PRDTS.	97	44	144	13	0	0	0	5664
37 PRIMARY IRON, STEEL MFR.	10	5	14	2	0	0	0	524
38 PRIMARY NONFERROUS MFR.	23	11	32	3	0	0	0	1253

39 METAL CONTAINERS	5	2	7	1	0 0 0		272
40 FABRICATED METAL PRDTS.	92	45	128	14	0 0 0		4948
41 SCREW MACH. PRDTS., ETC.	388	186	548	61	0 0 0		20291
42 OTHER FAB. METAL PRDTS.	-19	-9	-26	-3	0 0 0		-1003
43 ENGINES & TURBINES	54	26	75	9	0 0 0		2679
44 FARM MACH. & EQUIP.	155	77	219	24	0 0 0		8311
45 CONSTRUC. MACH. & EQUIP.	1119	551	1549	188	0 0 0		55694
46 MATERIAL HANDLING MACH.	69	34	96	10	0 0 0		3788
47 METALWORKING MACHINERY	126	62	175	21	0 0 0		6309
48 SPECIAL MACH. & EQUIP.	34	16	51	5	0 0 0		1970
49 GENERAL MACH. & EQUIP.	197	95	274	29	0 0 0		10588
50 MACHINE SHOP PRDTS.	17	8	21	2	0 0 0		876
51 OFFICE, COMPUT. MACHINES	374	184	473	51	0 0 0		19386
52 SERVICE IND. MACHINES	40	20	58	7	0 0 0		2155
53 ELECT. TRANSMISS. EQUIP.	38	18	53	6	0 0 0		1944
54 HOUSEHOLD APPLIANCES	72	35	103	12	0 0 0		3710
55 ELECTRIC LIGHTING EQUIP	310	153	375	41	0 0 0		15689
56 RADIO, TV, ETC., EQUIP.	31	14	44	5	0 0 0		1645
57 ELECTRONIC COMPONENTS	3	1	4	1	0 0 0		152
58 MISC. ELECTRICAL MACH.	91	45	109	12	0 0 0		4588
59 MOTOR VEHICLES, EQUIP.	2062	975	2928	286	0 0 0		115375
60 AIRCRAFT & PARTS	7	3	9	1	0 0 0		336
61 OTHER TRANSPORT. EQUIP.	80	39	111	13	0 0 0		3981
62 PROFESS., SCIEN. INSTRU.	684	343	1046	114	0 0 0		38739
63 MEDICAL, PHOTO. EQUIP.	212	103	295	31	0 0 0		11463
64 MISC. MANUFACTURING	1107	545	1444	162	0 0 0		56902
65 TRANSPORT. & WAREHOUSING	5069	2484	6789	710	0 0 0		273057
66 COMMUNICA.,EXC. BRDCAST.	1434	682	2024	199	0 0 0		80139
67 RADIO & TV BROADCASTING	0	0	0	0	0 0 0		0
68 ELEC.,GAS,WATER,SAN.SER.	3021	1486	3623	393	0 0 0		152927
69 WHOLESALE & RETAIL TRADE	3167	1459	5655	522	0 0 0		202539
70 FINANCE & INSURANCE	1109	548	1408	161	0 0 0		55787
71 REAL ESTATE & RENTAL	1991	974	2863	323	0 0 0		105710
72 HOTELS; PERSONAL SERV.	1250	644	3343	291	0 0 0		111251
73 BUSINESS SERVICES	572	284	899	93	0 0 0		33563
74 RESEARCH & DEVELOPMENT	0	0	0	0	0 0 0		0
75 AUTO. REPAIR & SERVICES	493	221	760	65	0 0 0		29875
76 AMUSEMENTS	73	36	84	9	0 0 0		3652
77 MED.,EDUC. SERVICES	470	248	1027	92	0 0 0		36850
78 FEDERAL GOV'T ENTERPRISE	603	296	918	98	0 0 0		33968
79 STATE & LOCAL GOV'T ENT.	0	0	0	0	0 0 0		0
80 IMPORTS	107	53	148	18	0 0 0		5304
81 BUS.TRAVEL, ENT., GIFTS.	0	0	0	0	0 0 0		0
82 OFFICE SUPPLIES	0	0	0	0	0 0 0		0
83 SCRAP & USED GOODS	686	341	951	118	0 0 0		33995
84 GOVERNMENT INDUSTRY	123395	68857	166888	16100	0 0 0		6442000
85 REST OF WORLD INDUSTRY	0	0	0	0	0 0 0		0
86 HOUSEHOLD INDUSTRY	0	0	0	0	0 0 0		0
87 INVENTORY VALUATION ADJ.	0	0	0	0	0 0 0		0
88 STATE TOTAL	276801	129421	305203	44381	0 0 0		12542375

*The data for this industry could not be made entirely consistent with the 1947 state output estimates. (See page 215.)

TABLE C.15

STATE ESTIMATES OF 1958
STATE AND LOCAL GOVERNMENT NET PURCHASES OF GOODS AND SERVICES
(THOUSANDS OF CURRENT DOLLARS)

INDUSTRY TITLE	1 ALABAMA	2 ARIZONA	3 ARKANSAS	4 CALIFORNIA	5 COLORADO	6 CONNECTICUT	7 DELAWARE	8 DISTRICT OF COLUMBIA	9 FLORIDA
1 LIVESTOCK & PRDTS.	115	54	54	1286	99	193	25	95	277
2 OTHER AGRICULTURE PRDTS.	269	107	136	2681	224	459	55	246	697
3 FORESTRY & FISHERIES	3	2	2	31	3	5	1	1	6
4 AGRI.,FORES.,FISH. SERV.	-1028	-577	-459	-7014	-788	-1561	-159	-344	-2029
5 IRON, FERRO. ORES MINING	0	0	0	0	0	0	0	0	0
6 NONFERROUS ORES MINING	0	0	0	0	0	0	0	0	0
7 COAL MINING	691	370	340	6620	600	1045	144	402	1491
8 CRUDE PETRO.,NATURAL GAS	0	0	0	0	0	0	0	0	0
9 STONE & CLAY MINING	-177	-101	-80	-1250	-139	-265	-29	-59	-346
10 CHEM.&FERT. MIN. MINING	176	101	80	1244	138	263	29	58	345
11 NEW CONSTRUCTION	155346	107440	73208	1415656	144063	240372	50806	65543	352053
12 MAINT. & REPAIR CONSTR.	47980	28001	22180	355545	38634	70144	8250	15672	92562
13 ORDNANCE & ACCESSORIES	37	19	15	488	32	65	8	31	86
14 FOOD & KINDRED PRDTS.	2892	1448	1448	29431	2537	4510	626	2021	6609
15 TOBACCO MANUFACTURES		2	2	38	38	6	1		9
16 FABRICS	93	44	44	1010	80	156	19	74	223
17 TEXTILE PRDTS.	11	5	6	112	10	19	2	9	28
18 APPAREL	976	464	464	10278	830	1621	202	755	2319
19 MISC. TEXTILE PRDTS.	3	2	1	32	3	4	1	2	6
20 LUMBER & WOOD PRDTS.	7	4	3	54	5	10	1	1	14
21 WOODEN CONTAINERS	6	3	3	52	10	10		3	13
22 HOUSEHOLD FURNITURE	733	410	333	6531	605	1132	135	348	1508
23 OTHER FURNITURE	1653	966	793	13807	1399	2383	317	644	3245
24 PAPER & ALLIED PRDTS.	76	52	40	710	73	91	18	17	127
25 PAPERBOARD CONTAINERS	0	0	0	4	0	1	0	0	1
26 PRINTING & PUBLISHING	2313	1446	1125	19327	2013	3151	462	696	4255
27 CHEMICALS,SELECT. PRDTS.	3229	1786	1501	25832	2615	4890	573	1398	6598
28 PLASTICS & SYNTHETICS				0		0	0	0	0
29 DRUGS & COSMETICS	1852	844	952	18394	1602	2955	398	1456	4469
30 PAINT & ALLIED PRDTS.	1			5		1			1
31 PETROLEUM, RELATED INDS.	4772	2647	2158	43869	3951	7461	891	2412	9949
32 RUBBER, MISC. PLASTICS	819	439	359	9348	706	1364	169	563	1821
33 LEATHER TANNING & PRDTS.	17			0					0
34 FOOTWEAR, LEATHER PRDTS.	0	8	8	190	14	28	4	14	41
35 GLASS & GLASS PRDTS.				0					0
36 STONE & CLAY PRDTS.	46	25	21	441	38	71	9	24	95
37 PRIMARY IRON, STEEL MFR.	16	9	8	127	13	24	3	6	33
38 PRIMARY NONFERROUS MFR.	0	0	0	0	0	0	0	0	0

	C1	C2	C3	C4	C5	C6	C7	C8	C9
39 METAL CONTAINERS	0	0	0	0	0	0	0	0	0
40 FABRICATED METAL PRDTS.	0	0	0	0	0	0	0	0	0
41 SCREW MACH. PRDTS., ETC.	137	27	12	104	54	532	31	39	68
42 OTHER FAB. METAL PRDTS.	1164	226	119	841	517	5016	295	355	600
43 ENGINES & TURBINES	85	15	7	65	34	308	20	25	44
44 FARM MACH. & EQUIP.	434	84	42	318	187	1826	106	130	222
45 CONSTRUC. MACH. & EQUIP.	608	103	50	465	243	2196	141	177	311
46 MATERIAL HANDLING MACH.	1157	232	132	817	549	5511	309	371	606
47 METALWORKING MACHINERY	151	26	13	115	60	546	35	44	77
48 SPECIAL MACH. & EQUIP.	752	186	72	552	309	3428	170	203	362
49 GENERAL MACH. & EQUIP.	118	24	12	87	52	521	29	36	60
50 MACHINE SHOP PRDTS.	763	119	101	551	415	4166	225	296	440
51 OFFICE, COMPUT. MACHINES	2005	332	250	1446	1036	10274	570	733	1123
52 SERVICE IND. MACHINES	561	111	52	415	233	2247	133	161	282
53 ELECT. TRANSMISS. EQUIP.	141	26	12	107	56	527	32	40	71
54 HOUSEHOLD APPLIANCES	16	3	1	12	6	57	4	4	8
55 ELECTRIC LIGHTING EQUIP.	176	26	23	127	96	943	53	69	102
56 RADIO, TV, ETC., EQUIP.	1693	357	145	1291	670	6887	373	469	835
57 ELECTRONIC COMPONENTS	3	1	3	3	1	13	1	2	2
58 MISC. ELECTRICAL MACH.	708	99	97	508	396	3877	216	285	417
59 MOTOR VEHICLES, EQUIP.	10858	2426	1089	8018	4690	50344	2570	3183	5442
60 AIRCRAFT & PARTS	3	3	2	2	2	10	1	1	1
61 OTHER TRANSPORT. EQUIP.	1092	186	91	835	437	3948	253	318	558
62 PROFESS., SCIEN. INSTRU.	2271	500	209	1639	922	9133	534	613	1107
63 MEDICAL, PHOTO. EQUIP.	367	74	37	270	162	1635	90	112	188
64 MISC. MANUFACTURING	4343	734	478	3194	2065	20023	1153	1471	2353
65 TRANSPORT. & WAREHOUSING	9336	1783	1081	6730	4516	45900	2496	3123	4993
66 COMMUNICA.,EXC. BRDCAST.	4641	1024	479	3407	2045	21848	1121	1387	2346
67 RADIO & TV BROADCASTING	0	0	0	0	0	0	0	0	0
68 ELEC.,GAS,WATER,SAN.SER.	10434	1525	1414	7514	5779	57189	3143	4151	6099
69 WHOLESALE & RETAIL TRADE	5417	1592	352	4043	1680	19581	961	1017	2268
70 FINANCE & INSURANCE	4624	720	522	3411	2255	21528	1258	1627	2557
71 REAL ESTATE & RENTAL	6420	1264	559	4810	2583	24932	1481	1807	3205
72 HOTELS; PERSONAL SERV.	2615	1024	140	1760	623	8059	404	225	876
73 BUSINESS SERVICES	14383	3424	1323	10311	5756	59239	3311	3730	6861
74 RESEARCH & DEVELOPMENT	0	0	0	0	0	0	0	0	0
75 AUTO. REPAIR & SERVICES	2111	583	187	1575	812	9748	434	521	972
76 AMUSEMENTS	-899	-118	-133	-638	-533	-5242	-289	-384	-545
77 MED.,EDUC. SERVICES	7890	2788	656	5112	2612	30860	1593	1240	3067
78 FEDERAL GOV'T ENTERPRISE	1800	400	159	1320	713	7162	410	478	871
79 STATE & LOCAL GOV'T ENT.	175	30	14	134	70	630	41	51	89
80 IMPORTS	81	14	7	62	32	292	19	24	41
81 BUS.TRAVEL, ENT., GIFTS	0	0	0	0	0	0	0	0	0
82 OFFICE SUPPLIES	3465	770	317	2565	1408	14594	791	953	1698
83 SCRAP & USED GOODS	9905	1646	826	7538	3980	35358	2322	2901	5079
84 GOVERNMENT INDUSTRY	449009	91031	50259	323740	210620	2168828	116575	143990	235032
85 REST OF WORLD INDUSTRY	0	0	0	0	0	0	0	0	0
86 HOUSEHOLD INDUSTRY	0	0	0	0	0	0	0	0	0
87 INVENTORY VALUATION ADJ.	0	0	0	0	0	0	0	0	0
88 STATE TOTAL	1047519	207510	124168	745784	457510	4609353	248161	321995	513720

TABLE C.15

STATE ESTIMATES OF 1958
STATE AND LOCAL GOVERNMENT NET PURCHASES OF GOODS AND SERVICES
(THOUSANDS OF CURRENT DOLLARS)

INDUSTRY TITLE	10 GEORGIA	11 IDAHO	12 ILLINOIS	13 INDIANA	14 IOWA	15 KANSAS	16 KENTUCKY	17 LOUISIANA	18 MAINE
1 LIVESTOCK & PRDTS.	202	31	657	244	130	115	104	182	48
2 OTHER AGRICULTURE PRDTS.	524	78	1556	552	323	306	243	439	111
3 FORESTRY & FISHERIES	5	1	15	7	4	4	3	3	3
4 AGRI.,FORES.,FISH. SERV.	-993	-299	-3582	-1269	-1165	-1302	-780	-1374	-378
5 IRON, FERRO. ORES MINING	0	0	0	0	0	0	0	0	0
6 NONFERROUS ORES MINING	0	0	0	0	0	0	0	0	0
7 COAL MINING	1087	198	3392	1381	860	764	617	1056	261
8 CRUDE PETRO.,NATURAL GAS	0	0	0	0	0	0	0	0	0
9 STONE & CLAY MINING	-180	-52	-632	-235	-205	-221	-137	-240	-65
10 CHEM.&FERT. MIN. MINING	179	51	629	234	204	220	137	238	64
11 NEW CONSTRUCTION	196977	36307	762748	232585	187602	163330	136828	257621	44660
12 MAINT. & REPAIR CONSTR.	51695	13984	177073	69735	57229	58793	38337	65943	17285
13 ORDNANCE & ACCESSORIES	56	9	217	79	35	30	32	56	16
14 FOOD & KINDRED PRDTS.	5059	826	15460	6169	3602	3127	2649	4573	1124
15 TOBACCO MANUFACTURES	7	1	21	8	4	4	3	6	1
16 FABRICS	158	25	516	190	105	96	83	146	38
17 TEXTILE PRDTS.	22	3	64	24	14	13	11	19	5
18 APPAREL	1645	270	5320	1969	1117	1026	865	1525	398
19 MISC. TEXTILE PRDTS.	4	1	14	6	3	3	5	4	1
20 LUMBER & WOOD PRDTS.	8	2	28	10	8	8	5	9	2
21 WOODEN CONTAINERS	8	2	27		8	8	8	9	2
22 HOUSEHOLD FURNITURE	902	205	3163	1221	835	823	604	1045	279
23 OTHER FURNITURE	2110	480	6845	2863	2054	1931	1403	2378	596
24 PAPER & ALLIED PRDTS.	109	22	324	172	109	82	72	114	24
25 PAPERBOARD CONTAINERS	1	0	2	1	1				
26 PRINTING & PUBLISHING	2876	676	9233	4182	2986	2676	2000	3310	801
27 CHEMICALS,SELECT. PRDTS.	3912	932	13144	5017	3804	3862	2630	4569	1201
28 PLASTICS & SYNTHETICS	0	0	0	0	0	0	0	0	0
29 DRUGS & COSMETICS	3495	539	10273	3967	2340	2079	1707	2997	729
30 PAINT & ALLIED PRDTS.	1	0	2	1	1	1	1		
31 PETROLEUM, RELATED INDS.	6005	1325	21167	8046	5379	5269	3956	6847	1841
32 RUBBER, MISC. PLASTICS	1181	213	4316	1621	862	774	710	1227	338
33 LEATHER TANNING & PRDTS.	0	0	0	0	0	0	0	0	0
34 FOOTWEAR, LEATHER PRDTS.	30	4	97	36	19	16	15	26	7
35 GLASS & GLASS PRDTS.	0	0	0	0	0	0	0	0	0
36 STONE & CLAY PRDTS.	60	13	210	82	52	49	39	66	18
37 PRIMARY IRON, STEEL MFR.	19	5	64	24	19	20	13	23	6
38 PRIMARY NONFERROUS MFR.	0	0	0	0	0	0	0	0	0

	1	2	3	4	5	6	7	8	9
39 METAL CONTAINERS	0	0	0	0	0	0	0	0	0
40 FABRICATED METAL PRDTS.	0	0	0	0	0	0	0	0	0
41 SCREW MACH. PRDTS., ETC.	26	94	54	82	78	98	263	20	74
42 OTHER FAB. METAL PRDTS.	212	874	520	703	772	1091	2510	176	803
43 ENGINES & TURBINES	16	59	34	54	51	58	155	13	44
44 FARM MACH. & EQUIP.	80	318	188	261	276	381	909	65	281
45 CONSTRUC. MACH. & EQUIP.	113	421	241	389	360	412	1111	91	316
46 MATERIAL HANDLING MACH.	210	912	554	681	819	1257	2705	178	896
47 METALWORKING MACHINERY	28	104	60	96	89	103	277	22	79
48 SPECIAL MACH. & EQUIP.	137	533	312	396	429	669	1669	102	498
49 GENERAL MACH. & EQUIP.	22	87	51	69	75	106	253	17	77
50 MACHINE SHOP PRDTS.	146	656	412	472	613	970	1904	128	625
51 OFFICE, COMPUT. MACHINES	378	1666	1032	1238	1539	2364	4809	329	1573
52 SERVICE IND. MACHINES	103	400	233	338	343	454	1134	82	344
53 ELECT. TRANSMISS. EQUIP.	26	97	56	87	82	98	264	21	75
54 HOUSEHOLD APPLIANCES	3	11	6	10	9	11	29	2	8
55 ELECTRIC LIGHTING EQUIP.	34	152	96	112	144	223	434	30	144
56 RADIO, TV, ETC., EQUIP.	316	1159	666	973	937	1243	3355	235	932
57 ELECTRONIC COMPONENTS	1	2	1	2	2	2	6	1	2
58 MISC. ELECTRICAL MACH.	135	623	393	453	594	927	1774	123	593
59 MOTOR VEHICLES, EQUIP.	2013	7932	4696	5988	6593	10050	24120	1539	7221
60 AIRCRAFT & PARTS	1	1	1	1	2	2	5	0	1
61 OTHER TRANSPORT. EQUIP.	204	755	433	697	646	741	1996	162	567
62 PROFESS., SCIEN. INSTRU.	406	1609	936	1315	1364	1891	4719	323	1482
63 MEDICAL, PHOTO. EQUIP.	68	272	162	215	235	339	796	54	245
64 MISC. MANUFACTURING	815	3396	2056	2702	3062	4372	9578	688	3014
65 TRANSPORT. & WAREHOUSING	1734	7413	4524	5518	6632	10203	21879	1452	7039
66 COMMUNICA.,EXC. BRDCAST.	859	3441	2050	2573	2895	4456	10461	666	3180
67 RADIO & TV BROADCASTING	0	0	0	0	0	0	0	0	0
68 ELEC.,GAS,WATER,SAN.SER.	1998	9102	5737	6595	8613	13515	26120	1792	8654
69 WHOLESALE & RETAIL TRADE	957	3211	1720	2645	2203	3006	10306	620	2791
70 FINANCE & INSURANCE	874	3677	2239	2945	3363	4763	10217	750	3227
71 REAL ESTATE & RENTAL	1182	4476	2582	3867	3770	4815	12563	927	3687
72 HOTELS; PERSONAL SERV.	406	1395	700	1065	850	1334	5163	247	1630
73 BUSINESS SERVICES	2555	10108	5866	7990	8404	12163	30581	1988	9606
74 RESEARCH & DEVELOPMENT	388	1423	817	1019	1060	1736	4669	263	1310
75 AUTO. REPAIR & SERVICES	-173	-826	-529	-580	-802	-1289	-2368	-161	-808
76 AMUSEMENTS	1247	5079	2838	3480	3826	6625	17994	896	6212
77 MED.,EDUC. SERVICES	325	1249	720	1032	1037	1414	3665	252	1110
78 FEDERAL GOV'T ENTERPRISE	33	121	69	112	104	118	319	26	91
79 STATE & LOCAL GOV'T ENT.	15	56	32	52	48	55	148	12	42
80 IMPORTS									
81 BUS.TRAVEL, ENT., GIFTS.									
82 OFFICE SUPPLIES	635	2435	1415	1955	2007	2841	7235	484	2148
83 SCRAP & USED GOODS	1840	6884	3951	6394	5952	6762	18038	1488	5197
84 GOVERNMENT INDUSTRY	82889	349099	211457	259776	307257	473675	1041933	68045	332393
85 REST OF WORLD INDUSTRY	0	0	0	0	0	0	0	0	0
86 HOUSEHOLD INDUSTRY	0	0	0	0	0	0	0	0	0
87 INVENTORY VALUATION ADJ.	0	0	0	0	0	0	0	0	0
88 STATE TOTAL	172671	783298	451538	567679	644672	912976	2316112	140000	684567

TABLE C.15

STATE ESTIMATES OF 1958
STATE AND LOCAL GOVERNMENT NET PURCHASES OF GOODS AND SERVICES
(THOUSANDS OF CURRENT DOLLARS)

INDUSTRY TITLE	19 MARYLAND	20 MASSA-CHUSETTS	21 MICHIGAN	22 MINNESOTA	23 MISSISSIPPI	24 MISSOURI	25 MONTANA	26 NEBRASKA	27 NEVADA
1 LIVESTOCK & PRDTS.	210	505	603	217	68	205	34	65	26
2 OTHER AGRICULTURE PRDTS.	473	1232	1448	574	182	453	80	160	64
3 FORESTRY & FISHERIES	5	9	15			5	5	2	1
4 AGRI.,FORES.,FISH. SERV.	-1295	-2497	-2842	-1365	-588	-1244	-375	-740	-231
5 IRON, FERRO. ORES MINING	0	0	0	0	0	0	0	0	0
6 NONFERROUS ORES MINING	0	0	0	0	0	0	0	0	0
7 COAL MINING	1075	2326	3218	1282	427	1105	232	429	140
8 CRUDE PETRO.,NATURAL GAS	0	0	0	0	0	0	0	0	0
9 STONE & CLAY MINING	-225	-428	-520	-245	-102	-220	-65	-126	-39
10 CHEM.&FERT. MIN. MINING	224	426	518	244	102	219	64	125	38
11 NEW CONSTRUCTION	221496	254774	548070	277804	111589	245231	52357	104576	31402
12 MAINT. & REPAIR CONSTR.	61574	114876	152425	69639	27943	62123	17605	33579	10002
13 ORDNANCE & ACCESSORIES	75	172	188	55	17	72	10	20	9
14 FOOD & KINDRED PRDTS.	4792	11013	14806	5756	1835	4879	929	1729	599
15 TOBACCO MANUFACTURES	7	16	20	8	6	6	1	1	1
16 FABRICS	167	396	469	171	55	162	28	55	21
17 TEXTILE PRDTS.	19	48	61	25	8	19	4	7	3
18 APPAREL	1707	4059	4850	1807	587	1665	300	578	222
19 MISC. TEXTILE PRDTS.	5	10	13	5	2	9	1	2	1
20 LUMBER & WOOD PRDTS.	9	20	24	10	4	2	2	4	1
21 WOODEN CONTAINERS	9	19	23	10	4	9	4	4	1
22 HOUSEHOLD FURNITURE	1087	2222	2747	1101	411	1079	252	480	159
23 OTHER FURNITURE	2266	4351	6316	2699	988	2361	595	1102	326
24 PAPER & ALLIED PRDTS.	99	151	348	143	47	120	29	48	11
25 PAPERBOARD CONTAINERS	1	1	2	1	1	1	0	0	0
26 PRINTING & PUBLISHING	3039	5293	8830	3793	1378	3308	859	1545	419
27 CHEMICALS,SELECT. PRDTS.	4467	9067	11444	4971	1902	4437	1140	2191	694
28 PLASTICS & SYNTHETICS	0	0	0	0	0	0	0	0	0
29 DRUGS & COSMETICS	3103	7568	9880	3942	1242	3110	580	1106	397
30 PAINT & ALLIED PRDTS.	1	2	1	1	1	1	1	1	0
31 PETROLEUM, RELATED INDS.	7266	15079	18384	7206	2659	7180	1622	3086	1042
32 RUBBER, MISC. PLASTICS	1474	3250	3787	1271	424	1443	254	477	185
33 LEATHER TANNING & PRDTS.	0	76	89	32	10	30	5	9	4
34 FOOTWEAR, LEATHER PRDTS.	31	0	0	0	0	0	0	0	0
35 GLASS & GLASS PRDTS.	0	0	0	0	0	0	0	0	0
36 STONE & CLAY PRDTS.	71	149	186	71	25	71	15	29	10
37 PRIMARY IRON, STEEL MFR.	22	44	55	24	10	22	6	11	3
38 PRIMARY NONFERROUS MFR.	0	0	0	0	0	0	0	0	0

#	Industry	Col 1	Col 2	Col 3	Col 4	Col 5	Col 6	Col 7	Col 8	Col 9
39	METAL CONTAINERS	0	0	0	0	0	0	0	0	0
40	FABRICATED METAL PRDTS.	0	0	0	0	0	0	0	0	0
41	SCREW MACH. PRDTS., ETC.	15	47	24	91	39	96	219	183	93
42	OTHER FAB. METAL PRDTS.	113	398	218	865	368	1031	2393	1534	811
43	ENGINES & TURBINES	9	31	16	54	25	60	129	106	55
44	FARM MACH. & EQUIP.	44	148	80	314	133	362	839	575	301
45	CONSTRUC. MACH. & EQUIP.	68	221	114	387	179	430	914	752	395
46	MATERIAL HANDLING MACH.	104	387	220	938	379	1131	2722	1560	844
47	METALWORKING MACHINERY	17	55	28	96	44	107	229	188	98
48	SPECIAL MACH. & EQUIP.	75	230	124	563	209	596	1519	1145	554
49	GENERAL MACH. & EQUIP.	12	40	22	88	35	97	233	160	84
50	MACHINE SHOP PRDTS.	66	278	165	698	267	808	1991	956	595
51	OFFICE, COMPUT. MACHINES	179	719	419	1736	685	2034	4925	2534	1514
52	SERVICE IND. MACHINES	58	192	101	388	168	444	1014	745	381
53	ELECT. TRANSMISS. EQUIP.	16	50	26	92	41	99	219	181	93
54	HOUSEHOLD APPLIANCES	2	2	3	10	5	11	24	20	10
55	ELECTRIC LIGHTING EQUIP.	15	65	39	159	63	188	456	213	135
56	RADIO, TV, ETC., EQUIP.	185	565	293	1155	465	1177	2808	2372	1182
57	ELECTRONIC COMPONENTS	0	0	5	0	0	0	5	4	5
58	MISC. ELECTRICAL MACH.	60	265	159	655	257	778	1886	845	549
59	MOTOR VEHICLES, EQUIP.	1081	3493	1904	8322	3141	8864	22254	15765	8022
60	AIRCRAFT & PARTS	0	0	2	2	2	2	4	2	2
61	OTHER TRANSPORT. EQUIP.	122	397	204	696	322	771	1643	1352	709
62	PROFESS., SCIEN. INSTRU.	227	737	390	1576	677	1861	4316	3154	1545
63	MEDICAL, PHOTO. EQUIP.	36	124	68	276	276	310	743	499	263
64	MISC. MANUFACTURING	421	1559	871	3419	1411	3942	9257	5477	3124
65	TRANSPORT. & WAREHOUSING	859	3191	1821	7723	3029	8923	21785	12504	6957
66	COMMUNICA., EXC. BRDCAST.	454	1499	825	3618	1368	3914	9812	6694	3444
67	RADIO & TV BROADCASTING	0	0	0	0	0	0	0	0	0
68	ELEC., GAS, WATER, SAN. SER.	896	3867	2315	9623	3730	11293	27573	12703	8121
69	WHOLESALE & RETAIL TRADE	606	1501	710	3225	1254	3145	7910	8897	3675
70	FINANCE & INSURANCE	447	1702	957	3688	1535	4275	9960	5645	3330
71	REAL ESTATE & RENTAL	685	2202	1147	4302	1871	4781	10826	8534	4323
72	HOTELS; PERSONAL SERV.	267	540	228	1368	576	1673	4179	4892	1656
73	BUSINESS SERVICES	1421	4483	2376	10102	4194	11788	28083	20861	9947
74	RESEARCH & DEVELOPMENT	0	0	0	0	0	0	0	0	0
75	AUTO. REPAIR & SERVICES	219	604	316	1558	530	1493	4053	3461	1596
76	AMUSEMENTS	-72	-341	-210	-882	-339	-1059	-2595	-1057	-718
77	MED., EDUC. SERVICES	697	1801	916	5241	2121	6843	17171	13907	5367
78	FEDERAL GOV'T ENTERPRISE	186	584	305	1226	519	1391	3246	2530	1228
79	STATE & LOCAL GOV'T ENT.	19	64	33	111	52	123	262	216	113
80	IMPORTS	9	29	15	52	24	57	122	100	53
81	BUS. TRAVEL, ENT., GIFTS.	0	0	0	0	0	0	0	0	0
82	OFFICE SUPPLIES	357	1122	593	2456	988	2669	6431	4940	2440
83	SCRAP & USED GOODS	1097	3625	1867	6280	2963	7120	14969	12066	6371
84	GOVERNMENT INDUSTRY	41811	149951	84712	363989	142065	417080	1023566	617215	332986
85	REST OF WORLD INDUSTRY	0	0	0	0	0	0	0	0	0
86	HOUSEHOLD INDUSTRY	0	0	0	0	0	0	0	0	0
87	INVENTORY VALUATION ADJ.	0	0	0	0	0	0	0	0	0
88	STATE TOTAL	98394	336987	180983	784127	326741	891968	2033553	1203660	725503

TABLE C.15

STATE ESTIMATES OF 1958

STATE AND LOCAL GOVERNMENT NET PURCHASES OF GOODS AND SERVICES

(THOUSANDS OF CURRENT DOLLARS)

INDUSTRY TITLE	28 NEW HAMPSHIRE	29 NEW JERSEY	30 NEW MEXICO	31 NEW YORK	32 NORTH CAROLINA	33 NORTH DAKOTA	34 OHIO	35 OKLAHOMA	36 OREGON
1 LIVESTOCK & PRDTS.	38	461	49	1791	187	28	555	98	104
2 OTHER AGRICULTURE PRDTS.	100	932	116	4689	427	73	1313	225	218
3 FORESTRY & FISHERIES	1	9	2	33	5	1	14	3	3
4 AGRI.,FORES.,FISH. SERV.	-274	-2045	-413	-7887	-1088	-393	-3376	-870	-829
5 IRON, FERRO. ORES MINING	0	0	0	0	0	0	0	0	0
6 NONFERROUS ORES MINING	0	0	0	0	0	0	0	0	0
7 COAL MINING	207	2126	307	8578	1055	201	3031	642	625
8 CRUDE PETRO.,NATURAL GAS	-47	-363	-73	-1383	-197	-66	-597	-154	-146
9 STONE & CLAY MINING	47	361	72	1376	196	66	595	153	145
10 CHEM.&FERT. MIN. MINING									
11 NEW CONSTRUCTION	35405	243698	79657	1430791	173372	58612	622391	134266	126658
12 MAINT. & REPAIR CONSTR.	12585	102701	20190	382347	56866	17403	167792	43128	40905
13 ORDNANCE & ACCESSORIES	11	188	15	534	61	7	179	30	37
14 FOOD & KINDRED PRDTS.	928	9766	1294	41353	4673	781	13526	2660	2609
15 TOBACCO MANUFACTURES	1	13	2	62	6	1	18	3	3
16 FABRICS	31	360	39	1395	147	24	439	79	84
17 TEXTILE PRDTS.	4	37	5	186	18	3	55	10	10
18 APPAREL	320	3612	414	14437	1521	257	4544	835	864
19 MISC. TEXTILE PRDTS.	1	11	1	33	4	1	13	3	3
20 LUMBER & WOOD PRDTS.	2	17	3	67	8	2	25	6	6
21 WOODEN CONTAINERS	2	16	3	65	8	2	24	6	5
22 HOUSEHOLD FURNITURE	202	2125	305	7312	966	234	2853	643	650
23 OTHER FURNITURE	446	4107	725	15416	2238	548	6387	1552	1479
24 PAPER & ALLIED PRDTS.	18	192	38	617	125	23	318	85	79
25 PAPERBOARD CONTAINERS	0	1	0	2	0	2	2	2	2
26 PRINTING & PUBLISHING	583	5488	1046	19071	3215	767	8845	2284	2154
27 CHEMICALS,SELECT. PRDTS.	902	7925	1355	30899	4049	1109	12072	2849	2747
28 PLASTICS & SYNTHETICS	0	2	0	5	0	0	2	1	2
29 DRUGS & COSMETICS	639	6106	831	29293	3012	506	8894	1670	1593
30 PAINT & ALLIED PRDTS.	0	1	0	5	0	0	1	1	2
31 PETROLEUM, RELATED INDS.	1333	14535	1978	49507	6402	1483	18928	4159	4258
32 RUBBER, MISC. PLASTICS	239	3394	335	10458	1258	202	3687	697	783
33 LEATHER TANNING & PRDTS.	6	69	7	268	27	4	82	14	15
34 FOOTWEAR, LEATHER PRDTS.	0	0	0	0	0	0	0	15	0
35 GLASS & GLASS PRDTS.								0	
36 STONE & CLAY PRDTS.	13	148	19	493	64	13	187	40	42
37 PRIMARY IRON, STEEL MFR.	4	38	7	146	20	6	59	14	14
38 PRIMARY NONFERROUS MFR.	0	0	0	0	0	0	0	0	0

	C1	C2	C3	C4	C5	C6	C7	C8	C9
39 METAL CONTAINERS	0	0	0	0	0	0	0	0	0
40 FABRICATED METAL PRDTS.	0	0	0	0	0	0	0	0	0
41 SCREW MACH. PRDTS., ETC.	18	164	28	588	80	24	243	59	58
42 OTHER FAB. METAL PRDTS.	162	1451	270	5664	841	197	2361	580	543
43 ENGINES & TURBINES	12	90	18	342	49	16	147	38	36
44 FARM MACH. & EQUIP.	60	538	97	2044	298	74	851	208	198
45 CONSTRUC. MACH. & EQUIP.	82	637	127	2431	346	116	1049	270	257
46 MATERIAL HANDLING MACH.	162	1593	286	6049	940	185	2548	620	579
47 METALWORKING MACHINERY	20	159	32	609	86	29	261	67	63
48 SPECIAL MACH. & EQUIP.	102	1115	156	3942	520	109	1500	330	331
49 GENERAL MACH. & EQUIP.	16	158	27	560	83	20	235	57	55
50 MACHINE SHOP PRDTS.	105	1171	214	3739	712	130	1842	477	449
51 OFFICE, COMPUT. MACHINES	277	2895	537	9795	1755	343	4625	1187	1113
52 SERVICE IND. MACHINES	77	668	121	2590	362	97	1056	257	245
53 ELECT. TRANSMISS. EQUIP.	19	158	29	586	82	26	247	62	59
54 HOUSEHOLD APPLIANCES	2	17	3	66	9	3	27	7	6
55 ELECTRIC LIGHTING EQUIP.	24	259	50	848	164	31	423	111	104
56 RADIO, TV, ETC., EQUIP.	227	2197	340	7593	1017	284	3060	718	718
57 ELECTRONIC COMPONENTS	4	4	1	14	2	1	6	2	1
58 MISC. ELECTRICAL MACH.	98	1057	206	3409	678	125	1736	461	428
59 MOTOR VEHICLES, EQUIP.	1471	15893	2377	54473	7774	1667	22053	5086	5042
60 AIRCRAFT & PARTS	0	3	12	12	2	1	1	1	0
61 OTHER TRANSPORT. EQUIP.	148	1148	229	4369	621	209	1885	485	461
62 PROFESS., SCIEN. INSTRU.	315	2755	481	11347	1488	368	4340	1014	959
63 MEDICAL, PHOTO. EQUIP.	50	492	83	1769	263	61	741	179	172
64 MISC. MANUFACTURING	597	5707	1073	19985	3342	768	9152	2342	2207
65 TRANSPORT. & WAREHOUSING	1289	13418	2331	46988	7653	1519	20657	5091	4832
66 COMMUNICA., EXC. BRDCAST.	631	6826	1039	23512	3420	712	9605	2232	2196
67 RADIO & TV BROADCASTING	0	0	0	0	0	0	0	0	0
68 ELEC.,GAS,WATER,SAN.SER.	1444	15792	2994	50527	9902	1818	25448	6695	6255
69 WHOLESALE & RETAIL TRADE	728	7119	836	28180	2606	745	8749	1634	1752
70 FINANCE & INSURANCE	635	6019	1174	20734	3630	842	9856	2577	2415
71 REAL ESTATE & RENTAL	874	7524	1341	28652	3911	1125	11653	2834	2724
72 HOTELS; PERSONAL SERV.	370	3161	319	17408	1139	261	4094	547	569
73 BUSINESS SERVICES	1993	18380	2982	75158	9515	2202	27776	6252	5989
74 RESEARCH & DEVELOPMENT	0	0	0	0	0	0	0	0	0
75 AUTO. REPAIR & SERVICES	-281	3387	398	11308	1371	278	4074	829	881
76 AMUSEMENTS	-125	-1410	-277	-4446	-930	-158	-2333	-624	-577
77 MED.,EDUC. SERVICES	1137	10536	1360	54192	5050	817	15280	2659	2530
78 FEDERAL GOV'T ENTERPRISE	247	2213	369	8779	1129	292	3348	775	746
79 STATE & LOCAL GOV'T ENT.	24	183	37	697	99	33	301	78	74
80 IMPORTS	11	85	17	323	46	16	140	36	34
81 BUS.TRAVEL, ENT., GIFTS.	0	0	0	0	0	0	0	0	0
82 OFFICE SUPPLIES	471	4585	721	16860	2253	553	6599	1523	1495
83 SCRAP & USED GOODS	1348	10092	2094	39517	5653	1913	17116	4442	4183
84 GOVERNMENT INDUSTRY	61886	645538	108438	2290625	357116	71339	974965	235401	224930
85 REST OF WORLD INDUSTRY	0	0	0	0	0	0	0	0	0
86 HOUSEHOLD INDUSTRY	0	0	0	0	0	0	0	0	0
87 INVENTORY VALUATION ADJ.	0	0	0	0	0	0	0	0	0
88 STATE TOTAL	131035	1199805	241288	4893794	693724	171089	2070577	482730	460230

TABLE C.15

STATE ESTIMATES OF 1958
STATE AND LOCAL GOVERNMENT NET PURCHASES OF GOODS AND SERVICES
(THOUSANDS OF CURRENT DOLLARS)

INDUSTRY TITLE	37 PENNSYL-VANIA	38 RHODE ISLAND	39 SOUTH CAROLINA	40 SOUTH DAKOTA	41 TENNESSEE	42 TEXAS	43 UTAH	44 VERMONT	45 VIRGINIA
1 LIVESTOCK & PRDTS.	641	60	91	25	151	404	38	20	174
2 OTHER AGRICULTURE PRDTS.	1509	134	230	58	396	865	78	49	423
3 FORESTRY & FISHERIES	15	1	3	1	4	13	1	1	5
4 AGRI.,FORES.,FISH. SERV.	-3353	-292	-464	-389	-1284	-3256	-307	-181	-1294
5 IRON, FERRO. ORES MINING	0	0	0	0	0	0	0	0	0
6 NONFERROUS ORES MINING	0	0	0	0	0	0	0	0	0
7 COAL MINING	3333	279	539	193	888	2472	252	122	994
8 CRUDE PETRO.,NATURAL GAS	0	0	0	0	0	0	0	0	0
9 STONE & CLAY MINING	-598	-51	-87	-66	-220	-575	-56	-31	-225
10 CHEM.&FERT. MIN. MINING	595	50	86	66	219	572	55	31	224
11 NEW CONSTRUCTION	605352	44840	94265	52363	245329	677026	68920	25477	195509
12 MAINT. & REPAIR CONSTR.	169537	13964	26087	17565	58932	161332	16166	8417	61691
13 ORDNANCE & ACCESSORIES	212	22	25	25	42	140	12	6	54
14 FOOD & KINDRED PRDTS.	15213	1297	2442	717	3841	10314	1037	513	4330
15 TOBACCO MANUFACTURES	21	2	3	1	5	12	1	1	6
16 FABRICS	502	47	71	22	122	325	30	16	139
17 TEXTILE PRDTS.	63	5	10	3	16	38	4	2	18
18 APPAREL	5175	475	746	231	1292	3373	315	171	1454
19 MISC. TEXTILE PRDTS.	14	1	1	1	3	11	2	1	4
20 LUMBER & WOOD PRDTS.	27	2	4	2	8	22	2	1	9
21 WOODEN CONTAINERS	26	2	4	2	8	21	1	1	9
22 HOUSEHOLD FURNITURE	3049	273	434	234	894	2535	246	127	982
23 OTHER FURNITURE	6683	539	1095	554	2034	5852	608	290	2220
24 PAPER & ALLIED PRDTS.	332	22	67	25	85	314	38	13	103
25 PAPERBOARD CONTAINERS	2	0	0	0	1	2	0	0	1
26 PRINTING & PUBLISHING	9123	692	1599	805	2744	8547	931	404	3063
27 CHEMICALS,SELECT. PRDTS.	12614	1078	1892	1091	4066	10811	1058	568	4300
28 PLASTICS & SYNTHETICS	0	0	0	0	0	0	0	0	0
29 DRUGS & COSMETICS	10077	854	1638	433	2606	6342	623	334	2857
30 PAINT & ALLIED PRDTS.	2	0	0	0	1	2	0	0	1
31 PETROLEUM, RELATED INDS.	20415	1852	2859	1481	5820	16576	1598	824	6448
32 RUBBER, MISC. PLASTICS	4197	408	543	203	969	3003	281	138	1160
33 LEATHER TANNING & PRDTS.	0	0	0	0	0	0	0	0	0
34 FOOTWEAR, LEATHER PRDTS.	95	9	13	3	22	58	5	3	25
35 GLASS & GLASS PRDTS.	0	0	0	0	0	0	0	0	0
36 STONE & CLAY PRDTS.	204	18	29	14	55	162	16	8	62
37 PRIMARY IRON, STEEL MFR.	61	5	9	6	20	54	5	3	21
38 PRIMARY NONFERROUS MFR.	0	0	0	0	0	0	0	0	0

#	Industry								
39	METAL CONTAINERS	0	0	0	0	0	0	0	0	0
40	FABRICATED METAL PRDTS.	0	0	0	0	0	0	0	0	0
41	SCREW MACH. PRDTS., ETC.	250	22	35	24	84	227	22	12	88
42	OTHER FAB. METAL PRDTS.	2470	191	428	200	741	2159	231	106	814
43	ENGINES & TURBINES	148	13	21	16	54	141	14	8	55
44	FARM MACH. & EQUIP.	887	71	146	75	273	782	81	39	297
45	CONSTRUC. MACH. & EQUIP.	1050	89	153	116	386	1010	98	55	395
46	MATERIAL HANDLING MACH.	2708	201	497	192	738	2312	258	107	845
47	METALWORKING MACHINERY	262	22	38	29	96	250	24	14	98
48	SPECIAL MACH. & EQUIP.	1628	142	246	109	445	1297	130	63	501
49	GENERAL MACH. & EQUIP.	247	20	40	20	73	217	23	11	81
50	MACHINE SHOP PRDTS.	1937	137	375	144	498	1792	210	76	600
51	OFFICE, COMPUT. MACHINES	4854	349	919	370	1304	4438	509	196	1530
52	SERVICE IND. MACHINES	1096	90	173	97	352	966	98	50	375
53	ELECT. TRANSMISS. EQUIP.	251	22	36	26	88	233	23	12	91
54	HOUSEHOLD APPLIANCES	28	2	4	3	10	25	2	1	10
55	ELECTRIC LIGHTING EQUIP.	442	31	87	34	117	415	49	18	139
56	RADIO, TV, ETC., EQUIP.	3201	288	441	284	1021	2802	267	145	1091
57	ELECTRONIC COMPONENTS	6	1	2	2	2	6	1	1	2
58	MISC. ELECTRICAL MACH.	1813	123	362	139	472	1713	203	73	568
59	MOTOR VEHICLES, EQUIP.	23635	1994	3712	1705	6550	19806	2043	943	7409
60	AIRCRAFT & PARTS	5	1	1	1	5	5	2	2	2
61	OTHER TRANSPORT. EQUIP.	1887	160	274	208	693	1813	175	98	709
62	PROFESS., SCIEN. INSTRU.	4583	375	739	361	1410	3800	385	196	1512
63	MEDICAL, PHOTO. EQUIP.	781	63	129	62	228	681	72	33	254
64	MISC. MANUFACTURING	9493	717	1679	806	2795	8766	961	411	3141
65	TRANSPORT. & WAREHOUSING	21885	1653	3941	1602	5922	19203	2138	871	6851
66	COMMUNICA., EXC. BRDCAST.	10296	853	1662	733	2818	8646	906	407	3209
67	RADIO & TV BROADCASTING	0	0	0	0	0	0	0	0	0
68	ELEC., GAS, WATER, SAN. SER.	26647	1836	5253	2020	6898	24990	2948	1059	8308
69	WHOLESALE & RETAIL TRADE	9617	992	1033	669	3024	6718	513	396	3101
70	FINANCE & INSURANCE	10154	751	1832	891	3011	9604	1064	446	3392
71	REAL ESTATE & RENTAL	12030	1022	1801	1118	3994	10721	1053	562	4205
72	HOTELS; PERSONAL SERV.	4803	495	552	173	1411	2205	122	161	1385
73	BUSINESS SERVICES	29746	2481	4733	2137	8785	23683	2383	1212	9514
74	RESEARCH & DEVELOPMENT	0	0	0	0	0	0	0	0	0
75	AUTO. REPAIR & SERVICES	4509	425	604	275	1186	3408	321	167	1345
76	AMUSEMENTS	-2445	-160	-506	-179	-607	-2315	-281	-95	-749
77	MED., EDUC. SERVICES	17567	1521	2794	643	4527	10082	944	559	4882
78	FEDERAL GOV'T ENTERPRISE	3532	300	539	286	1104	2941	290	153	1176
79	STATE & LOCAL GOV'T ENT.	301	26	44	33	111	290	28	16	113
80	IMPORTS	140	12	20	15	51	134	13	7	53
81	BUS. TRAVEL, ENT., GIFTS.	0	0	0	0	0	0	0	0	0
82	OFFICE SUPPLIES	6999	601	1057	551	2103	5870	583	296	2287
83	SCRAP & USED GOODS	17073	1426	2535	1906	6332	16492	1609	895	6461
84	GOVERNMENT INDUSTRY	1037863	80255	182312	74384	281398	892415	97839	41009	323618
85	REST OF WORLD INDUSTRY	0	0	0	0	0	0	0	0	0
86	HOUSEHOLD INDUSTRY	0	0	0	0	0	0	0	0	0
87	INVENTORY VALUATION ADJ.	0	0	0	0	0	0	0	0	0
88	STATE TOTAL	2139516	166201	354977	167930	679569	1998109	210312	88116	684525

TABLE C.16

STATE ESTIMATES OF 1963

STATE AND LOCAL GOVERNMENT NET PURCHASES OF GOODS AND SERVICES

(THOUSANDS OF CURRENT DOLLARS)

INDUSTRY TITLE	1 ALABAMA	2 ARIZONA	3 ARKANSAS	4 CALIFORNIA	5 COLORADO	6 CONNECTICUT	7 DELAWARE	8 DISTRICT OF COLUMBIA	9 FLORIDA
1 LIVESTOCK & PRDTS.	139	88	68	1635	124	189	22	87	332
2 OTHER AGRICULTURE PRDTS.	966	636	472	11872	815	1417	126	640	2363
3 FORESTRY & FISHERIES	29	21	14	315	28	33	5	10	57
4 AGRI.,FORES.,FISH. SERV.	-379	-309	-181	-4710	-292	-561	-30	-153	-811
5 IRON, FERRO. ORES MINING	0	0	0	0	0	0	0	0	0
6 NONFERROUS ORES MINING	0	0	0	0	0	0	0	0	
7 COAL MINING	174	120	82	1897	165	204	32	68	359
8 CRUDE PETRO.,NATURAL GAS	0	0	0	0	0	0	0	0	0
9 STONE & CLAY MINING	-342	-276	-162	-4240	-265	-505	-28	-141	-732
10 CHEM.&FERT. MIN. MINING	272	220	129	3378	212	402	22	112	583
11 NEW CONSTRUCTION	200182	154038	127803	2374699	166855	249589	58193	116951	402066
12 MAINT. & REPAIR CONSTR.	40949	31509	19391	487383	34189	56236	4729	16581	86596
13 ORDNANCE & ACCESSORIES	21	15	9	317	21	40	8	24	60
14 FOOD & KINDRED PRDTS.	5403	3220	2669	64642	4762	7614	843	3888	13582
15 TOBACCO MANUFACTURES	9	7		1442	10	18	11	11	27
16 FABRICS	156	82	80	1744	135	200	25	107	393
17 TEXTILE PRDTS.	1	1	1	-4	0	-1	-2	-2	-1
18 APPAREL	806	392	417	9749	681	1185	121	734	2255
19 MISC. TEXTILE PRDTS.	90	53	46	1041	72	123	11	57	223
20 LUMBER & WOOD PRDTS.	39	23	20	435	36	49	7	23	92
21 WOODEN CONTAINERS	0	0	0	0	0	0	0	0	0
22 HOUSEHOLD FURNITURE	226	158	106	2423	219	255	43	80	452
23 OTHER FURNITURE	2568	1860	1199	27628	2463	2907	470	804	5016
24 PAPER & ALLIED PRDTS.	517	325	254	6052	457	699	80	320	1232
25 PAPERBOARD CONTAINERS	688	379	347	7570	616	851	117	426	1660
26 PRINTING & PUBLISHING	5568	4054	2605	60830	5252	6498	973	1850	11040
27 CHEMICALS,SELECT. PRDTS.	2305	1392	1157	27302	1919	3230	303	1532	5717
28 PLASTICS & SYNTHETICS	2	1		19	2	2	2	3	3
29 DRUGS & COSMETICS	4055	2103	2086	45483	3501	5249	637	2833	10283
30 PAINT & ALLIED PRDTS.	36	24	17	440	33	52	6	23	87
31 PETROLEUM, RELATED INDS.	3551	2479	1672	40701	3319	4529	612	1697	7686
32 RUBBER, MISC. PLASTICS	1096	625	546	13284	959	1584	170	863	2855
33 LEATHER TANNING & PRDTS.	9	6	0	131	0	0	2	0	0
34 FOOTWEAR, LEATHER PRDTS.			4		9	17		10	25
35 GLASS & GLASS PRDTS.	395	241	193	4320	370	474	73	208	890
36 STONE & CLAY PRDTS.	157	114	72	1700	159	177	33	55	308
37 PRIMARY IRON, STEEL MFR.	26	19	11	394	27	50	5	30	75
38 PRIMARY NONFERROUS MFR.	1	1	0	10	1	1	0	0	2

Industry									
39 METAL CONTAINERS	0	0	0	5	0	0	0	0	1
40 FABRICATED METAL PRDTS.	3	2	1	31	3	4	0	2	6
41 SCREW MACH. PRDTS., ETC.	148	106	68	1491	149	147	31	33	269
42 OTHER FAB. METAL PRDTS.	101	71	47	1087	99	114	20	37	203
43 ENGINES & TURBINES	0	0	0	0	0	0	0	0	0
44 FARM MACH. & EQUIP.	187	136	86	2074	179	224	34	70	376
45 CONSTRUC. MACH. & EQUIP.	379	307	180	4707	295	560	31	156	812
46 MATERIAL HANDLING MACH.	18	13	8	194	17	21	3	6	35
47 METALWORKING MACHINERY	275	205	128	3010	259	321	48	85	537
48 SPECIAL MACH. & EQUIP.	91	65	42	946	90	96	18	26	172
49 GENERAL MACH. & EQUIP.	132	101	60	1749	117	212	18	91	316
50 MACHINE SHOP PRDTS.	546	400	252	5744	541	588	108	147	1025
51 OFFICE, COMPUT. MACHINES	1385	1001	647	14941	1328	1576	254	446	2721
52 SERVICE IND. MACHINES	898	603	427	9605	862	1018	170	350	1849
53 ELECT. TRANSMISS. EQUIP.	710	549		8458	591	977	81	284	1497
54 HOUSEHOLD APPLIANCES	164	108	79	1831	152	202	28	79	360
55 ELECTRIC LIGHTING EQUIP.	662	464	313	7279	624	786	117	258	1364
56 RADIO, TV, ETC., EQUIP.	1315	740	663	15073	1144	1746	204	886	3266
57 ELECTRONIC COMPONENTS	63	45	29	686	63	72	13	23	125
58 MISC. ELECTRICAL MACH.	143	82	72	1713	122	204	21	106	367
59 MOTOR VEHICLES, EQUIP.	7318	5516	3423	89457	6378	10422	982	3696	16176
60 AIRCRAFT & PARTS	314	240	0	5	0	1	0	0	1
61 OTHER TRANSPORT. EQUIP.	1357	723	142	4305	282	529	45	243	782
62 PROFESS., SCIEN. INSTRU.	764	453	694	15189	1182	1742	216	915	3389
63 MEDICAL, PHOTO. EQUIP.	1272	949	379	8457	694	944	131	433	1778
64 MISC. MANUFACTURING	8148	5770	593	13928	1189	1488	214	387	2478
65 TRANSPORT. & WAREHOUSING	3914	2807	3856	92263	7470	10215	1328	3496	17246
66 COMMUNICA., EXC. BRDCAST.	215	156	1877	47179	3308	5518	491	2046	8858
67 RADIO & TV BROADCASTING	10630	7854	99	2221	219	222	45	54	398
68 ELEC.,GAS,WATER,SAN.SER.	866	259	4937	116678	10114	12452	1887	3479	20915
69 WHOLESALE & RETAIL TRADE	3147	2345	525	15371	259	2366	-95	1783	3907
70 FINANCE & INSURANCE	5485	4148	1494	36892	2696	4213	406	1321	6695
71 REAL ESTATE & RENTAL	1546	1057	2631	66317	4421	7792	561	2470	12012
72 HOTELS; PERSONAL SERV.	11040	8042	5263	132210	9422	3122	8	1568	4608
73 BUSINESS SERVICES						15345	1420	5444	24504
74 RESEARCH & DEVELOPMENT	1108	813	524	13671	944	1614	140	612	2529
75 AUTO. REPAIR & SERVICES	-690	-502	-317	-7124	-699	-713	-145	-171	-1274
76 AMUSEMENTS	7860	3523	4205	91752	6262	11133	1029	6870	22048
77 MED.,EDUC. SERVICES	2067	1386	1016	24677	1702	2907	248	1177	4857
78 FEDERAL GOV'T ENTERPRISE	253	176	119	2834	240	310	46	112	535
79 STATE & LOCAL GOV'T ENT.	33	26	15	401	25	48	3	13	70
80 IMPORTS	0	0	0	0	0	0	0	0	0
81 BUS.TRAVEL, ENT., GIFTS.	2799	1950	1349	33003	2407	3810	380	1436	6303
82 OFFICE SUPPLIES	54619	44736	27569	-31731	57220	-55140	13525	-105077	-35372
83 SCRAP & USED GOODS	365716	256154	171850	4122171	345825	452144	65091	162047	774464
84 GOVERNMENT INDUSTRY	0	0	0	0	0	0	0	0	0
85 REST OF WORLD INDUSTRY	0	0	0	0	0	0	0	0	0
86 HOUSEHOLD INDUSTRY	0	0	0	0	0	0	0	0	0
87 INVENTORY VALUATION ADJ.	0	0	0	0	0	0	0	0	0
88 STATE TOTAL	766712	557199	397598	8182378	695981	844155	156763	247163	1467980

TABLE C.16

STATE ESTIMATES OF 1963
STATE AND LOCAL GOVERNMENT NET PURCHASES OF GOODS AND SERVICES
(THOUSANDS OF CURRENT DOLLARS)

INDUSTRY TITLE	10 GEORGIA	11 IDAHO	12 ILLINOIS	13 INDIANA	14 IOWA	15 KANSAS	16 KENTUCKY	17 LOUISIANA	18 MAINE
1 LIVESTOCK & PRDTS.	200	42	694	267	168	137	110	188	50
2 OTHER AGRICULTURE PRDTS.	1385	322	4934	1726	1156	939	728	1269	384
3 FORESTRY & FISHERIES	33	8	-131	61	38	30	27	37	11
4 AGRI.,FORES.,FISH. SERV.	-429	-149	-1810	-603	-479	-384	-297	-421	-188
5 IRON, FERRO. ORES MINING	0	0	0	0	0	0	0	0	0
6 NONFERROUS ORES MINING	0	0	0	0	0	0	0	0	0
7 COAL MINING	214	48	798	360	224	180	154	224	62
8 CRUDE PETRO.,NATURAL GAS	0	0	0	0	0	0	0	0	0
9 STONE & CLAY MINING	-387	-133	-1634	-548	-429	-346	-269	-381	-168
10 CHEM.&FERT. MIN. MINING	309	106	1302	436	342	275	215	304	133
11 NEW CONSTRUCTION	282049	49199	681171	305493	195590	173490	332707	312059	62696
12 MAINT. & REPAIR CONSTR.	47771	14400	193126	72058	51858	41670	33558	48056	18200
13 ORDNANCE & ACCESSORIES	30	6	132	43	21	18	19	30	9
14 FOOD & KINDRED PRDTS.	8302	1639	27777	10243	6415	5229	4057	7521	1891
15 TOBACCO MANUFACTURES	13	3	59	19	10	8	9	14	4
16 FABRICS	258	45	773	299	189	154	109	224	47
17 TEXTILE PRDTS.	0	0	-3	2	2	1	1	1	0
18 APPAREL	1451	245	4335	1479	918	756	521	1207	250
19 MISC. TEXTILE PRDTS.	142	30	443	157	110	90	60	122	32
20 LUMBER & WOOD PRDTS.	59	11	190	79	49	39	31	55	12
21 WOODEN CONTAINERS	0	0	0	0	0	0	0	0	0
22 HOUSEHOLD FURNITURE	269	60	1020	479	293	235	206	290	78
23 OTHER FURNITURE	2937	711	11477	5361	3357	2683	2352	3213	933
24 PAPER & ALLIED PRDTS.	747	158	2570	984	629	510	401	697	186
25 PAPERBOARD CONTAINERS	1078	193	3340	1359	846	686	512	974	208
26 PRINTING & PUBLISHING	6416	1594	25128	11391	7239	5791	5023	6928	2077
27 CHEMICALS,SELECT. PRDTS.	3525	751	11583	4131	2777	2258	1641	3117	840
28 PLASTICS & SYNTHETICS	2	0	8	4	2	2	2	2	1
29 DRUGS & COSMETICS	6744	1185	20167	7721	4898	3987	2809	5842	1222
30 PAINT & ALLIED PRDTS.	50	11	185	70	44	36	30	48	14
31 PETROLEUM, RELATED INDS.	4465	1031	16984	7141	4453	3587	3088	4585	1324
32 RUBBER, MISC. PLASTICS	1760	333	5752	2062	1280	1047	797	1559	376
33 LEATHER TANNING & PRDTS.	0	0	0	0	0	0	0	0	0
34 FOOTWEAR, LEATHER PRDTS.	12	2	55	18	9	7	8	12	4
35 GLASS & GLASS PRDTS.	558	107	1875	811	494	399	324	541	126
36 STONE & CLAY PRDTS.	178	40	715	346	204	163	151	202	55
37 PRIMARY IRON, STEEL MFR.	37	8	165	53	26	22	24	38	11
38 PRIMARY NONFERROUS MFR.	1	0	4	2	1	1	1	1	0

#	Industry	C1	C2	C3	C4	C5	C6	C7	C8	C9
39	METAL CONTAINERS	0	0	0	0	0	0	1	0	0
40	FABRICATED METAL PRDTS.	1	4	2	3	3	6	14	1	4
41	SCREW MACH. PRDTS., ETC.	49	186	142	158	198	328	630	36	162
42	OTHER FAB. METAL PRDTS.	35	131	93	105	131	216	459	27	121
43	ENGINES & TURBINES	0	0	0	0	0	0	0	0	0
44	FARM MACH. & EQUIP.	70	235	171	192	240	387	860	52	216
45	CONSTRUC. MACH. & EQUIP.	186	423	298	383	477	608	1814	148	430
46	MATERIAL HANDLING MACH.	7	22	16	18	23	36	80	5	20
47	METALWORKING MACHINERY	105	338	250	287	359	562	1235	80	308
48	SPECIAL MACH. & EQUIP.	31	115	86	95	120	198	398	23	102
49	GENERAL MACH. & EQUIP.	61	165	113	126	153	240	703	45	164
50	MACHINE SHOP PRDTS.	193	683	520	575	721	1181	2395	143	599
51	OFFICE, COMPUT. MACHINES	502	1738	1266	1445	1807	2891	6212	383	1594
52	SERVICE IND. MACHINES	302	1173	793	928	1157	1887	4086	240	1126
53	ELECT. TRANSMISS. EQUIP.	317	830	582	723	900	1244	3344	251	824
54	HOUSEHOLD APPLIANCES	58	216	138	166	206	330	776	47	217
55	ELECTRIC LIGHTING EQUIP.	240	845	584	682	851	1355	3043	188	807
56	RADIO, TV, ETC., EQUIP.	429	1847	953	1292	1590	2497	6562	393	2075
57	ELECTRONIC COMPONENTS	22	81	60	65	81	138	289	16	72
58	MIS. ELECTRICAL MACH.	50	200	102	138	169	263	737	45	228
59	MOTOR VEHICLES, EQUIP.	3175	8944	6145	7291	9033	13390	35978	2456	8849
60	AIRCRAFT & PARTS	0	1	0	0	0	0	2	0	1
61	OTHER TRANSPORT. EQUIP.	146	401	269	292	357	573	1735	107	400
62	PROFESS., SCIEN. INSTRU.	415	1938	962	1340	1648	2602	6708	395	2209
63	MEDICAL, PHOTO. EQUIP.	246	1054	598	767	949	1521	3675	216	1126
64	MISC. MANUFACTURING	489	1552	1152	1328	1661	2572	5695	373	1421
65	TRANSPORT. & WAREHOUSING	3093	10312	7017	8312	10343	16097	38201	2436	10044
66	COMMUNICA.-EXC. BRDCAST.	1644	4860	3108	3903	4832	6995	19154	1331	5042
67	RADIO & TV BROADCASTING	73	272	209	228	286	480	935	53	235
68	ELEC.,GAS,WATER,SAN.SER.	4009	13169	9735	11053	13818	21888	48054	3027	12002
69	WHOLESALE & RETAIL TRADE	430	1385	-24	603	664	388	6491	500	2418
70	FINANCE & INSURANCE	1330	3794	2599	3202	3982	5727	14835	1058	3774
71	REAL ESTATE & RENTAL	2471	6465	4294	5534	6872	9278	26273	2000	6687
72	HOTELS; PERSONAL SERV.	825	1925	810	1373	1650	1779	9076	729	2538
73	BUSINESS SERVICES	4651	13594	8938	11068	13722	19939	53521	3725	13856
74	RESEARCH & DEVELOPMENT	0	0	0	0	0	0	0	0	0
75	AUTO. REPAIR & SERVICES	479	1370	895	1094	1353	1979	5520	380	1404
76	AMUSEMENTS	-235	-872	-670	-731	-918	-1534	-2997	-172	-751
77	MED.EDUC. SERVICES	2327	11771	4576	7482	9105	13792	41136	2481	14731
78	FEDERAL GOV'T ENTERPRISE	829	2640	1541	2052	2534	3626	10168	705	2876
79	STATE & LOCAL GOV'T ENT.	91	328	223	258	321	518	1189	71	315
80	IMPORTS	16	36	26	30	41	52	155	13	37
81	BUS.TRAVEL, ENT., GIFTS.	0	0	0	0	0	0	0	0	0
82	OFFICE SUPPLIES	1120	3536	2231	2805	3475	5134	13557	917	3667
83	SCRAP & USED GOODS	7283	44216	63982	84790	113400	149813	-12485	7803	8323
84	GOVERNMENT INDUSTRY	134153	471071	322963	372262	463028	746901	1723337	103913	451890
85	REST OF WORLD INDUSTRY	0	0	0	0	0	0	0	0	0
86	HOUSEHOLD INDUSTRY	0	0	0	0	0	0	0	0	0
87	INVENTORY VALUATION ADJ.	0	0	0	0	0	0	0	0	0
88	STATE TOTAL	262595	1015547	836855	777416	954072	1471378	3096999	208645	932337

TABLE C.16

STATE ESTIMATES OF 1963
STATE AND LOCAL GOVERNMENT NET PURCHASES OF GOODS AND SERVICES
(THOUSANDS OF CURRENT DOLLARS)

INDUSTRY TITLE	19 MARYLAND	20 MASSA-CHUSETTS	21 MICHIGAN	22 MINNESOTA	23 MISSISSIPPI	24 MISSOURI	25 MONTANA	26 NEBRASKA	27 NEVADA
1 LIVESTOCK & PRDTS.	213	436	612	247	106	198	38	73	28
2 OTHER AGRICULTURE PRDTS.	1448	3303	4260	1736	759	1374	258	597	212
3 FORESTRY & FISHERIES	39	65	115	50	22	43	9	17	17
4 AGRI.,FORES.,FISH. SERV.	-440	-1169	-1487	-693	-318	-528	-112	-346	-77
5 IRON,FERRO.ORES MINING	0	0	0	0	0	0	0	0	0
6 NONFERROUS ORES MINING	0	0	0	0	0	0	0	0	0
7 COAL MINING	240	417	710	304	132	249	53	95	26
8 CRUDE PETRO.,NATURAL GAS	0	0	0	0	0	0	0	0	0
9 STONE & CLAY MINING	-402	-1053	-1342	-622	-283	-480	-100	-307	-71
10 CHEM.&FERT. MIN. MINING	320	838	1069	495	225	382	80	244	56
11 NEW CONSTRUCTION	245763	369567	532572	212440	139996	266047	82553	109240	65000
12 MAINT. & REPAIR CONSTR.	50982	116601	162965	73450	32993	57866	12202	31869	7607
13 ORDNANCE & ACCESSORIES	47	94	98	34	11	46	6	11	0
14 FOOD & KINDRED PRDTS.	8645	18336	24676	9657	4166	7608	1406	2652	1153
15 TOBACCO MANUFACTURES	21	42	44	15	5	21	3	7	3
16 FABRICS	241	502	731	285	128	192	39	62	29
17 TEXTILE PRDTS.	-3	-4	1	2	2	-2	0	1	1
18 APPAREL	1392	3130	3988	1473	643	1049	183	305	191
19 MISC. TEXTILE PRDTS.	126	300	410	168	78	107	23	51	18
20 LUMBER & WOOD PRDTS.	59	114	176	70	31	52	11	17	7
21 WOODEN CONTAINERS	0	0	0	0	0	0	0	0	0
22 HOUSEHOLD FURNITURE	311	505	909	391	169	328	70	120	31
23 OTHER FURNITURE	3393	5609	10146	4456	1940	3713	810	1483	348
24 PAPER & ALLIED PRDTS.	779	1621	2282	923	402	721	141	276	102
25 PAPERBOARD CONTAINERS	1043	2059	3139	1241	552	873	179	281	120
26 PRINTING & PUBLISHING	7341	12733	22073	9701	4236	8038	1739	3342	796
27 CHEMICALS,SELECT. PRDTS.	3411	7772	10417	4203	1881	3012	592	1275	480
28 PLASTICS & SYNTHETICS	2	3	7	3	1	3	1	0	0
29 DRUGS & COSMETICS	6274	13229	19061	7411	3328	4964	999	1621	773
30 PAINT & ALLIED PRDTS.	57	117	159	64	27	55	10	21	8
31 PETROLEUM, RELATED INDS.	5137	9572	14734	6188	2648	5286	1058	2030	613
32 RUBBER, MISC. PLASTICS	1816	3916	5124	1964	843	1540	276	508	246
33 LEATHER TANNING & PRDTS.	0	0	0	0	0	0	0	0	0
34 FOOTWEAR, LEATHER PRDTS.	19	39	40	14	4	19	2	5	3
35 GLASS & GLASS PRDTS.	587	1066	1719	696	303	540	111	176	64
36 STONE & CLAY PRDTS.	224	337	624	266	111	243	50	81	21
37 PRIMARY IRON, STEEL MFR.	58	118	122	42	13	57	7	14	9
38 PRIMARY NONFERROUS MFR.	1	1	4	2	1	1	0	1	0

	1	2	3	4	5	6	7	8
39 METAL CONTAINERS	1	1	1	0	1	0	0	0
40 FABRICATED METAL PRDTS.	4	8	12	2	4	1	1	0
41 SCREW MACH. PRDTS., ETC.	191	262	571	110	212	48	76	15
42 OTHER FAB. METAL PRDTS.	141	227	408	75	149	31	52	14
43 ENGINES & TURBINES	259	441	744	137	281	0	0	0
44 FARM MACH. & EQUIP.	446	1169	1490	315	532	58	109	28
45 CONSTRUC. MACH. & EQUIP.	23	40	69	13	26	112	341	77
46 MATERIAL HANDLING MACH.	357	618	1078	209	400	6	11	3
47 METALWORKING MACHINERY	122	179	356	67	133	87	171	39
48 SPECIAL MACH. & EQUIP.	210	466	555	93	224	29	47	11
49 GENERAL MACH. & EQUIP.	721	1081	2120	403	805	38	96	33
50 MACHINE SHOP PRDTS.	1842	3058	5488	1045	2007	177	302	67
51 OFFICE, COMPUT. MACHINES	1249	2020	3693	681	1265	435	796	190
52 SERVICE IND. MACHINES	877	438	2817	573	1002	272	452	126
53 ELECT. TRANSMISS. EQUIP.	236	1601	693	126	231	212	559	132
54 HOUSEHOLD APPLIANCES	907	4260	2692	503	951	48	86	27
55 ELECTRIC LIGHTING EQUIP.	2021	139	6039	1056	1706	202	373	100
56 RADIO, TV, ETC., EQUIP.	91	501	251	44	98	337	599	257
57 ELECTRONIC COMPONENTS	226	22132	663	114	192	20	33	9
58 MISC. ELECTRICAL MACH.	10187		29894	5579	11097	36	71	31
59 MOTOR VEHICLES, EQUIP.	1	1	2	1	1	2163	5266	1478
60 AIRCRAFT & PARTS	532	1183	1346	211	561	0	0	0
61 OTHER TRANSPORT. EQUIP.	2082	4332	6312	1107	1685	90	224	85
62 PROFESS., SCIEN. INSTRU.	1136	2191	3388	602	1013	341	558	254
63 MEDICAL, PHOTO. EQUIP.	1630	2866	4969	974	1836	208	346	131
64 MISC. MANUFACTURING	11204	21285	33349	6241	11752	401	806	181
65 TRANSPORT. & WAREHOUSING	5359	12094	16351	3103	5572	2442	4917	1347
66 COMMUNICA., EXC. BRDCAST.	288	399	835	157	319	1115	2726	784
67 RADIO & TV BROADCASTING						71	111	24
68 ELEC.,GAS,WATER,SAN.SER.	14094	24105	41856	7991	15643	3355	6449	1525
69 WHOLESALE & RETAIL TRADE	1805	7296	5586	872	891	42	640	473
70 FINANCE & INSURANCE	4050	8801	12686	2506	4448	934	2269	568
71 REAL ESTATE & RENTAL	6848	16661	22228	4507	7573	1584	4346	1083
72 HOTELS; PERSONAL SERV.	2344	7919	7320	1343	2135	331	1430	534
73 BUSINESS SERVICES	14936	33093	45573	8708	15832	3196	7757	2150
74 RESEARCH & DEVELOPMENT	0	0	0	0	0	0	0	0
75 AUTO. REPAIR & SERVICES	1561	3526	4616	857	1649	318	791	234
76 AMUSEMENTS	-919	-1281	-2674	-504	-1022	-226	-360	-78
77 MED.,EDUC. SERVICES	12736	30239	39341	6745	8885	1689	2959	1765
78 FEDERAL GOV'T ENTERPRISE	2854	6644	8914	1689	2774	561	1354	419
79 STATE & LOCAL GOV'T ENT.	362	644	1043	189	373	76	139	41
80 IMPORTS	38	99	127	27	46	10	29	7
81 BUS.TRAVEL, ENT., GIFTS.	0	0	0	0	0	0	0	0
82 OFFICE SUPPLIES	3858	8374	11766	2219	3921	795	1822	534
83 SCRAP & USED GOODS	-40054	-247087	99875	63982	1561	25489	29651	-22368
84 GOVERNMENT INDUSTRY	522108	938873	1503707	272442	542031	110479	205477	59683
85 REST OF WORLD INDUSTRY	0	0	0	0	0	0	0	0
86 HOUSEHOLD INDUSTRY	0	0	0	0	0	0	0	0
87 INVENTORY VALUATION ADJ.	0	0	0	0	0	0	0	0
88 STATE TOTAL	928107	1493207	2748308	592265	1014408	260307	439700	129818

405

TABLE C.16

STATE ESTIMATES OF 1963
STATE AND LOCAL GOVERNMENT NET PURCHASES OF GOODS AND SERVICES
(THOUSANDS OF CURRENT DOLLARS)

INDUSTRY TITLE	28 NEW HAMPSHIRE	29 NEW JERSEY	30 NEW MEXICO	31 NEW YORK	32 NORTH CAROLINA	33 NORTH DAKOTA	34 OHIO	35 OKLAHOMA	36 OREGON
1 LIVESTOCK & PRDTS.	35	412	57	1771	211	40	574	130	135
2 OTHER AGRICULTURE PRDTS.	268	3044	331	13240	1425	296	4032	839	953
3 FORESTRY & FISHERIES	7	77	13	267	48	10	111	27	28
4 AGRI.,FORES.,FISH. SERV.	-120	-1193	-82	-4666	-561	-160	-1475	-262	-385
5 IRON, FERRO. ORES MINING	0	0	0	0	0	0	0	0	0
6 NONFERROUS ORES MINING	0	0	0	0	0	0	0	0	0
7 COAL MINING	40	458	80	1729	280	57	674	164	167
8 CRUDE PETRO.,NATURAL GAS									
9 STONE & CLAY MINING	-107	-1078	-77	-4192	-507	-142	-1332	-238	-347
10 CHEM.&FERT. MIN. MINING	85	859	62	3340	404	113	1061	190	276
11 NEW CONSTRUCTION	50918	291843	99144	1925142	228957	67222	613461	219054	165012
12 MAINT. & REPAIR CONSTR.	11645	122001	12449	470127	62487	15773	159285	31966	40754
13 ORDNANCE & ACCESSORIES	6	102	8	331	36	4	102	16	23
14 FOOD & KINDRED PRDTS.	1377	16364	2199	74332	7997	1438	22873	5165	5227
15 TOBACCO MANUFACTURES	3	45	4	148	16	2	46	7	11
16 FABRICS	37	404	70	2133	221	39	650	164	144
17 TEXTILE PRDTS.	0	-4	0	-5		1	-1	1	0
18 APPAREL	206	2422	333	12857	1109	171	3564	834	762
19 MISC. TEXTILE PRDTS.	24	242	32	1268	124	27	370	86	85
20 LUMBER & WOOD PRDTS.	9	103	18	479	59	11	160	40	37
21 WOODEN CONTAINERS	0	0	0	0	0	0	0	0	0
22 HOUSEHOLD FURNITURE	49	584	108	2103	370	74	866	216	216
23 OTHER FURNITURE	578	6642	1178	23365	4201	889	9738	2377	2466
24 PAPER & ALLIED PRDTS.	131	1506	209	6619	776	151	2129	485	499
25 PAPERBOARD CONTAINERS	158	1758	318	8744	1007	181	2818	720	637
26 PRINTING & PUBLISHING	1297	14734	2446	52704	9026	1944	21229	5056	5372
27 CHEMICALS,SELECT. PRDTS.	616	6671	843	32030	3290	674	9579	2152	2212
28 PLASTICS & SYNTHETICS	0	4	1	14	3	1	7	2	2
29 DRUGS & COSMETICS	968	10550	1792	56108	5720	1015	16938	4268	3747
30 PAINT & ALLIED PRDTS.	9	115	14	463	56	11	152	32	36
31 PETROLEUM, RELATED INDS.	858	10266	1520	38654	5671	1135	14139	3223	3467
32 RUBBER, MISC. PLASTICS	281	3384	446	15839	1599	273	4721	1062	1059
33 LEATHER TANNING & PRDTS.	0	0	0	0	0		0	0	0
34 FOOTWEAR, LEATHER PRDTS.	2	42	3	137	15		42	7	10
35 GLASS & GLASS PRDTS.	88	1030	188	4469	610	112	1583	399	371
36 STONE & CLAY PRDTS.	33	424	79	1371	267	51	605	149	152
37 PRIMARY IRON, STEEL MFR.	7	127	10	411	45	5	126	20	29
38 PRIMARY NONFERROUS MFR.	0	2	0	8	2	0	4	1	1

39 METAL CONTAINERS	0	1	0	5	0	0	1	0	0
40 FABRICATED METAL PRDTS.	1	8	1	33	4	1	11	3	3
41 SCREW MACH. PRDTS., ETC.	29	344	77	1130	249	51	544	145	139
42 OTHER FAB. METAL PRDTS.	22	264	49	940	166	33	389	97	97
43 ENGINES & TURBINES	0	0	0	0	0	0	0	0	0
44 FARM MACH. & EQUIP.	43	517	84	1791	307	63	721	169	182
45 CONSTRUC. MACH. & EQUIP.	119	1197	85	4655	563	158	1479	264	384
46 MATERIAL HANDLING MACH.	4	47	8	165	29	6	67	16	17
47 METALWORKING MACHINERY	65	731	119	2548	448	99	1043	245	266
48 SPECIAL MACH. & EQUIP.	19	225	46	755	152	30	341	87	86
49 GENERAL MACH. & EQUIP.	39	493	41	1753	210	43	560	98	138
50 MACHINE SHOP PRDTS.	116	1377	267	4521	914	189	2045	514	523
51 OFFICE, COMPUT. MACHINES	313	3602	635	12715	2264	476	5267	1283	1330
52 SERVICE IND. MACHINES	196	2283	432	8781	1441	284	3472	877	851
53 ELECT. TRANSMISS. EQUIP.	203	2117	213	8142	1082	276	2758	550	707
54 HOUSEHOLD APPLIANCES	39	446	73	1813	256	51	651	156	157
55 ELECTRIC LIGHTING EQUIP.	154	1768	296	6623	1063	220	2565	615	637
56 RADIO, TV, ETC., EQUIP.	323	3615	558	17768	1900	350	5475	1320	1239
57 ELECTRONIC COMPONENTS	13	172	31	562	106	20	243	59	61
58 MISC. ELECTRICAL MACH.	37	425	56	2053	206	38	608	138	138
59 MOTOR VEHICLES, EQUIP.	2035	23356	2429	87142	11423	2585	29401	5824	7370
60 AIRCRAFT & PARTS	0	1	0	6	1	0	2	0	0
61 OTHER TRANSPORT. EQUIP.	94	1250	97	4377	504	96	1370	229	334
62 PROFESS., SCIEN. INSTRU.	323	3536	602	18348	1936	348	5636	1417	1258
63 MEDICAL, PHOTO. EQUIP.	177	2002	349	9215	1149	214	3094	772	717
64 MISC. MANUFACTURING	302	3374	540	11848	2063	460	4810	1127	1232
65 TRANSPORT. & WAREHOUSING	1998	22798	3365	86965	12886	2739	31935	7308	7917
66 COMMUNICA., EXC. BRDCAST.	1092	11953	1284	48609	5905	1359	15738	3233	3879
67 RADIO & TV BROADCASTING	44	528	112	1685	366	73	803	208	205
68 ELEC.,GAS,WATER,SAN.SER.	2473	28570	4685	99010	17400	3730	40526	9559	10307
69 WHOLESALE & RETAIL TRADE	422	4260	-122	28779	585	126	4892	625	905
70 FINANCE & INSURANCE	858	9178	1060	35686	4834	1159	12289	2579	3104
71 REAL ESTATE & RENTAL	1615	16588	1530	67256	8153	2102	21582	4235	5463
72 HOTELS; PERSONAL SERV.	606	6318	85	30748	1901	519	7049	970	1634
73 BUSINESS SERVICES	3050	33470	3678	132961	15828	3893	44048	9082	10946
74 RESEARCH & DEVELOPMENT	0	0	0	0	0	0	0	0	0
75 AUTO. REPAIR & SERVICES	314	3562	354	13929	-1692	-383	4501	887	1114
76 AMUSEMENTS	-140	-1693	-356	-5405	-1171	-235	-2572	-666	-657
77 MED.,EDUC. SERVICES	2028	21254	3133	127938	10187	1739	34222	8400	7218
78 FEDERAL GOV'T ENTERPRISE	575	6095	683	27145	3009	686	8387	1787	2016
79 STATE & LOCAL GOV'T ENT.	59	704	114	2630	407	81	996	235	245
80 IMPORTS	10	102	7	396	48	13	126	23	33
81 BUS.TRAVEL, ENT., GIFTS.	0	0	0	0	0	0	0	0	0
82 OFFICE SUPPLIES	751	8228	996	34017	4232	944	11212	2414	2741
83 SCRAP & USED GOODS	520	-158656	44736	-653351	94674	37973	58781	75947	32772
84 GOVERNMENT INDUSTRY	86119	1029060	161598	3815952	588717	117936	1441503	335958	355264
85 REST OF WORLD INDUSTRY	0	0	0	0	0	0	0	0	0
86 HOUSEHOLD INDUSTRY	0	0	0	0	0	0	0	0	0
87 INVENTORY VALUATION ADJ.	0	0	0	0	0	0	0	0	0
88 STATE TOTAL	176564	1589411	357818	6843979	1134051	272729	2697400	757136	696126

TABLE C.16

STATE ESTIMATES OF 1963
STATE AND LOCAL GOVERNMENT NET PURCHASES OF GOODS AND SERVICES
(THOUSANDS OF CURRENT DOLLARS)

INDUSTRY TITLE	37 PENNSYL-VANIA	38 RHODE ISLAND	39 SOUTH CAROLINA	40 SOUTH DAKOTA	41 TENNESSEE	42 TEXAS	43 UTAH	44 VERMONT	45 VIRGINIA
1 LIVESTOCK & PRODTS.	599	45	96	35	172	482	50	22	183
2 OTHER AGRICULTURE PRDTS.	4187	332	639	265	1281	3349	290	170	1267
3 FORESTRY & FISHERIES	120	9	21		33	111	14	5	38
4 AGRI.,FORES.,FISH. SERV.	-1555	-135	-229	-153	-548	-1410	-106	-95	-483
5 IRON,FERRO.ORES MINING	0	0	0	0	0	0	0	0	0
6 NONFERROUS ORES MINING	0	0	0	0	0	0	0	0	0
7 COAL MINING	719	51	124	52	201	640	81	30	228
8 CRUDE PETRO.,NATURAL GAS	0	0	0	0	0	0	0	0	0
9 STONE & CLAY MINING	-1406	-122	-207	-136	-490	-1271	-97	-84	-436
10 CHEM.&FERT.MIN.MINING	1120	97	165	108	390	1013	77	68	348
11 NEW CONSTRUCTION	738954	71249	100389	73574	334072	738712	90691	39973	298553
12 MAINT. & REPAIR CONSTR.	168839	13714	26254	14935	54832	151863	14125	9106	52737
13 ORDNANCE & ACCESSORIES	116	12	14	4	26	90	9	3	34
14 FOOD & KINDRED PRDTS.	23583	1752	3740	1224	6803	18160	1762	780	7116
15 TOBACCO MANUFACTURES	52	6	6	2	12	41	1	1	15
16 FABRICS	647	41	111	31	192	478	49	19	196
17 TEXTILE PRDTS.	-3	-1	0	1	1	1	0	0	0
18 APPAREL	3541	248	564	126	1037	2414	199	88	1042
19 MISC. TEXTILE PRDTS.	365	25	61	23	121	278	23	14	111
20 LUMBER & WOOD PRDTS.	164	11	28	9	47	130	15	5	51
21 WOODEN CONTAINERS	0	0	0	0	0	0	0	0	0
22 HOUSEHOLD FURNITURE	932	65	162	68	253	844	112	39	297
23 OTHER FURNITURE	10511	742	1820	823	2926	9709	1258	470	3363
24 PAPER & ALLIED PRDTS.	2208	163	356	132	646	1774	181	82	675
25 PAPERBOARD CONTAINERS	2845	181	495	145	821	2193	244	88	873
26 PRINTING & PUBLISHING	22855	1647	3899	1805	6488	20982	2618	1042	7282
27 CHEMICALS,SELECT.PRDTS.	9704	705	1556	576	3022	7504	655	365	2937
28 PLASTICS & SYNTHETICS	7				2	132			
29 DRUGS & COSMETICS	16820	1067	2886	787	5002	12357	1238	493	5094
30 PAINT & ALLIED PRDTS.	161	13	25	10	46	132	13	6	49
31 PETROLEUM, RELATED INDS.	15151	1142	2472	1042	4238	13192	1538	621	4729
32 RUBBER, MISC. PLASTICS	4837	360	759	227	1390	3607	335	148	1447
33 LEATHER TANNING & PRDTS.	0	0	0	0	0	0	0	0	0
34 FOOTWEAR, LEATHER PRDTS.	48	5	6	2	11	37	4	1	14
35 GLASS & GLASS PRDTS.	1647	110	285	96	455	1358	166	56	512
36 STONE & CLAY PRDTS.	665	48	114	47	170	614	85	27	212
37 PRIMARY IRON, STEEL MFR.	145	15	18	5	33	112	11	4	42
38 PRIMARY NONFERROUS MFR.	4	0	1	0	1	4	1	0	1

#	Industry	C1	C2	C3	C4	C5	C6	C7	C8	C9
39	METAL CONTAINERS	1	0	0	0	0	1	0	0	0
40	FABRICATED METAL PRDTS.	12	1	2	1	3	10	1	25	4
41	SCREW MACH. PRDTS., ETC.	592	38	109	47	155	564	82	17	193
42	OTHER FAB. METAL PRDTS.	421	29	73	30	112	380	51	0	134
43	ENGINES & TURBINES	0	0	0	0	0	0	0	34	249
44	FARM MACH. & EQUIP.	784	58	131	59	215	714	90	94	485
45	CONSTRUC. MACH. & EQUIP.	1561	136	229	151	544	1412	108	3	23
46	MATERIAL HANDLING MACH.	73	5	12	6	21	67	8	53	360
47	METALWORKING MACHINERY	1128	82	192	92	321	1049	131	16	120
48	SPECIAL MACH. & EQUIP.	371	25	66	28	98	347	49	27	185
49	GENERAL MACH. & EQUIP.	614	57	85	42	176	519	46	98	720
50	MACHINE SHOP PRDTS.	2232	155	394	176	597	2105	291	252	1817
51	OFFICE, COMPUT. MACHINES	5683	402	982	440	1579	5232	676	146	1170
52	SERVICE IND. MACHINES	3691	250	647	255	1011	3265	425	159	913
53	ELECT. TRANSMISS. EQUIP.	2923	238	454	262	954	2636	244	27	214
54	HOUSEHOLD APPLIANCES	685	49	116	45	194	584	69	117	867
55	ELECTRIC LIGHTING EQUIP.	2742	196	466	201	772	2449	303	180	1681
56	RADIO, TV, ETC., EQUIP.	5534	377	922	287	1636	4213	421	11	85
57	ELECTRONIC COMPONENTS	268	19	46	19	68	245	34	20	185
58	MISC. ELECTRICAL MACH.	617	45	98	32	185	463	41	20	20
59	MOTOR VEHICLES, EQUIP.	31576	2641	4778	2453	9574	27669	2671	1514	9753
60	AIRCRAFT & PARTS	2	0	0	0	0	1	0	0	0
61	OTHER TRANSPORT. EQUIP.	1513	145	201	95	422	1257	109	63	453
62	PROFESS., SCIEN. INSTRU.	5629	360	966	275	1665	4206	432	170	1711
63	MEDICAL, PHOTO. EQUIP.	3176	211	546	180	909	2550	292	108	981
64	MISC. MANUFACTURING	5191	379	882	431	1499	4832	595	249	1659
65	TRANSPORT. & WAREHOUSING	34037	2531	5621	2520	9855	30047	3450	1494	10681
66	COMMUNICA., EXC. BRDCAST.	16544	1326	2558	1258	5186	14116	1296	780	5094
67	RADIO & TV BROADCASTING	880	59	68	68	228	835	121	37	285
68	ELEC., GAS, WATER, SAN. SER.	43921	3214	7443	3488	12332	40613	5107	2012	14004
69	WHOLESALE & RETAIL TRADE	4302	424	410	58	1842	1476	-478	112	1052
70	FINANCE & INSURANCE	13014	1025	2064	1085	4097	11582	1145	658	4066
71	REAL ESTATE & RENTAL	22610	1850	3463	1975	7560	19866	1673	1221	7005
72	HOTELS; PERSONAL SERV.	7037	692	834	476	2659	4943	-24	349	1994
73	BUSINESS SERVICES	46536	3729	7232	3626	14506	40290	3821	2231	14393
74	RESEARCH & DEVELOPMENT	0	0	0	0	0	0	0	0	0
75	AUTO. REPAIR & SERVICES	-4784	399	-718	360	1475	4091	371	225	1467
76	AMUSEMENTS	-2819	-190	-506	-218	-731	-2676	-386	-120	-914
77	MED., EDUC. SERVICES	32850	2076	5479	1214	10357	21551	1558	836	9674
78	FEDERAL GOV'T ENTERPRISE	8626	661	1358	615	2763	7071	613	385	2639
79	STATE & LOCAL GOV'T ENT.	1068	78	179	74	295	939	115	43	336
80	IMPORTS	133	12	20	13	47	120	9	8	42
81	BUS. TRAVEL, ENT., GIFTS.	0	0	0	0	0	0	0	0	0
82	OFFICE SUPPLIES	11742	905	1865	862	3619	9975	972	529	3627
83	SCRAP & USED GOODS	45256	-19766	47857	33292	30690	177902	54099	13525	39534
84	GOVERNMENT INDUSTRY	154803	114517	256792	108292	428972	1364170	164897	63761	485866
85	REST OF WORLD INDUSTRY	0	0	0	0	0	0	0	0	0
86	HOUSEHOLD INDUSTRY	0	0	0	0	0	0	0	0	0
87	INVENTORY VALUATION ADJ.	0	0	0	0	0	0	0	0	0
83	STATE TOTAL	2944154	213031	502574	260536	982145	2803188	361169	145017	1013334

TABLE C.16

STATE ESTIMATES OF 1963
STATE AND LOCAL GOVERNMENT NET PURCHASES OF GOODS AND SERVICES
(THOUSANDS OF CURRENT DOLLARS)

INDUSTRY TITLE	46 WASHINGTON	47 WEST VIRGINIA	48 WISCONSIN	49 WYOMING	50 ALASKA	51 HAWAII	52 NO STATE ALLOCATION	53 NATIONAL TOTAL
1 LIVESTOCK & PRDTS.	236	79	290	29	25	55	0	12249
2 OTHER AGRICULTURE PRDTS.	1725	563	2199	189	214	437	0	87634
3 FORESTRY & FISHERIES	48	17	54	-6	5	11	0	2338
4 AGRI.,FORES.,FISH. SERV.	-748	-245	-939	-63	-113	-221	0	-33303
5 IRON, FERRO. ORES MINING	0	0	0	0	0	0	0	0
6 NONFERROUS ORES MINING	0	0	0	0	0	0	0	0
7 COAL MINING	288	102	324	37	28	66	0	14204
8 CRUDE PETRO.,NATURAL GAS	0	0	0	0	0	0	0	0
9 STONE & CLAY MINING	-670	-219	-841	-57	-100	-198	0	-29999
10 CHEM.&FERT. MIN. MINING	533	175	670	45	79	157	0	23897
11 NEW CONSTRUCTION	303553	70996	303461	68879	75283	118899	0	15356000
12 MAINT. & REPAIR CONSTR.	76064	25553	92497	7395	10074	20911	0	3510180
13 ORDNANCE & ACCESSORIES	38	10	56	3	4	10	0	2230
14 FOOD & KINDRED PRDTS.	9143	3040	11500	1147	987	2091	0	487814
15 TOBACCO MANUFACTURES	17	4	25	2		4	0	1002
16 FABRICS	252	89	303	37	25	52	0	13611
17 TEXTILE PRDTS.	1	1					0	-17
18 APPAREL	1329	440	1734	184	146	279	0	75480
19 MISC. TEXTILE PRDTS.	157	55	193	20	20	37	0	7938
20 LUMBER & WOOD PRDTS.	64	23	74	9	5	13	0	3350
21 WOODEN CONTAINERS	0	0	0	0	0	0	0	0
22 HOUSEHOLD FURNITURE	369	132	406	48	31	83	0	18149
23 OTHER FURNITURE	4269	1531	4700	533	386	997	0	205312
24 PAPER & ALLIED PRDTS.	880	299	1078	109	95	206	0	45450
25 PAPERBOARD CONTAINERS	1102	394	1296	160	105	225	0	58844
26 PRINTING & PUBLISHING	9392	3334	10513	1138	906	2245	0	450210
27 CHEMICALS, SELECT. PRDTS.	4000	1352	5005	485	484	955	0	205895
28 PLASTICS & SYNTHETICS	3	1	3	0	1	1	0	137
29 DRUGS & COSMETICS	6555	2316	7932	950	671	1346	0	355084
30 PAINT & ALLIED PRDTS.	63	21	79	7	7	15	0	3255
31 PETROLEUM, RELATED INDS.	6026	2061	7099	720	597	1437	0	301171
32 RUBBER, MISC. PLASTICS	1848	608	2364	235	200	416	0	100623
33 LEATHER TANNING & PRDTS.							0	0
34 FOOTWEAR, LEATHER PRDTS.	16	4	23	1	2	4	0	923
35 GLASS & GLASS PRDTS.	634	226	728	89	56	134	0	33063
36 STONE & CLAY PRDTS.	254	90	278	33	19	57	0	12630
37 PRIMARY IRON, STEEL MFR.	47	12	70	4	5	12	0	2776
38 PRIMARY NONFERROUS MFR.	2	1	2	0	0	0	0	74

No.	Industry								
39	METAL CONTAINERS	0	0	1	0	0	0	0	21
40	FABRICATED METAL PRDTS.	5	2	5	1	1	1	0	240
41	SCREW MACH. PRDTS., ETC.	234	88	240	32	17	50	0	11243
42	OTHER FAB. METAL PRDTS.	164	59	181	22	14	37	0	8146
43	ENGINES & TURBINES	0	0	0	0	0	0	0	0
44	FARM MACH. & EQUIP.	314	109	355	38	30	75	0	15293
45	CONSTRUC. MACH. & EQUIP.	744	243	935	63	111	219	0	33307
46	MATERIAL HANDLING MACH.	30	11	34	4	3	7	0	1427
47	METALWORKING MACHINERY	467	166	523	56	46	114	0	22173
48	SPECIAL MACH. & EQUIP.	146	53	155	19	12	32	0	7088
49	GENERAL MACH. & EQUIP.	246	75	326	22	31	68	0	12399
50	MACHINE SHOP PRDTS.	889	323	951	115	71	202	0	42754
51	OFFICE, COMPUT. MACHINES	2302	824	2543	288	209	537	0	111051
52	SERVICE IND. MACHINES	1453	525	1608	195	124	319	0	72564
53	ELECT. TRANSMISS. EQUIP.	1323	445	1610	127	176	365	0	60841
54	HOUSEHOLD APPLIANCES	273	96	317	35	27	62	0	13761
55	ELECTRIC LIGHTING EQUIP.	1106	391	1252	138	105	258	0	54247
56	RADIO, TV, ETC., EQUIP.	2176	753	2657	294	230	475	0	115710
57	ELECTRONIC COMPONENTS	102	36	113	13	7	23	0	5091
58	MISC. ELECTRICAL MACH.	244	82	309	31	28	56	0	12986
59	MOTOR VEHICLES, EQUIP.	13382	4372	16620	1324	1657	3590	0	644465
60	AIRCRAFT & PARTS	1	0	1	0	0	0	0	33
61	OTHER TRANSPORT. EQUIP.	590	172	802	51	73	163	0	30389
62	PROFESS., SCIEN. INSTRU.	2197	777	2643	316	223	455	0	118191
63	MEDICAL, PHOTO. EQUIP.	1242	440	1452	172	119	265	0	64889
64	MISC. MANUFACTURING	2173	770	2434	255	218	533	0	102479
65	TRANSPORT. & WAREHOUSING	13962	4834	16283	1645	1456	3391	0	682209
66	COMMUNICA.,EXC. BROCAST.	7113	2362	8817	737	904	1875	0	344002
67	RADIO & TV BROADCASTING	343	126	358	46	25	75	0	16639
68	ELEC.,GAS,WATER,SAN.SER.	17963	6344	20129	2150	1716	4320	0	860167
69	WHOLESALE & RETAIL TRADE	1952	485	3451	146	452	587	0	114293
70	FINANCE & INSURANCE	5703	1934	6861	592	712	1512	0	268189
71	REAL ESTATE & RENTAL	10324	3439	12785	984	1436	2871	0	478069
72	HOTELS; PERSONAL SERV.	3303	946	4884	231	614	1025	0	163472
73	BUSINESS SERVICES	20031	6679	24623	2072	2512	5287	0	962185
74	RESEARCH & DEVELOPMENT	0	0	0	0	0	0	0	0
75	AUTO. REPAIR & SERVICES	2034	661	2561	201	259	546	0	98836
76	AMUSEMENTS	-1102	-406	-1151	-148	-80	-241	0	-53336
77	MED.,EDUC. SERVICES	12926	4460	16566	1874	1521	2661	0	722926
78	FEDERAL GOV'T ENTERPRISE	3714	1248	4619	408	477	952	0	182500
79	STATE & LOCAL GOV'T ENT.	423	147	486	52	39	98	0	21082
80	IMPORTS	64	21	79	5	9	19	0	2839
81	BUS.TRAVEL, ENT., GIFTS.	0	0	0	0	0	0	0	0
82	OFFICE SUPPLIES	4973	1679	6066	548	600	1266	0	242942
83	SCRAP & USED GOODS	61902	48378	-35372	18206	-4	5202	0	505615
84	GOVERNMENT INDUSTRY	614491	212761	711519	75013	59555	144459	0	30580640
85	REST OF WORLD INDUSTRY	0	0	0	0	0	0	0	0
86	HOUSEHOLD INDUSTRY	0	0	0	0	0	0	0	0
87	INVENTORY VALUATION ADJ.	0	0	0	0	0	0	0	0
88	STATE TOTAL	1239407	419971	1294808	190743	165982	334543	0	59082208

411

TABLE C.17

STATE ESTIMATES OF 1947
FEDERAL GOVERNMENT PURCHASES
(THOUSANDS OF CURRENT DOLLARS)

INDUSTRY TITLE	1 ALABAMA	2 ARIZONA	3 ARKANSAS	4 CALIFORNIA	5 COLORADO	6 CONNECTICUT	7 DELAWARE	8 DISTRICT OF COLUMBIA	9 FLORIDA
1 LIVESTOCK & PRDTS.	0	-588	0	-1768	-1521	0	0	0	0
2 OTHER AGRICULTURE PRDTS.	2013	770	917	16590	1747	773	129	7882	3572
3 FORESTRY & FISHERIES	-24	0	-14	-147	-1	-7	-13	0	-57
4 AGRI.,FORES.,FISH. SERV.	-554	-208	-221	-4700	-472	-221	-35	-2335	-1031
5 IRON,FERRO. ORES MINING	0	0	0	0	0	0	0	0	0
6 NONFERROUS ORES MINING	-4	-40	-184	0	-1968	0	0	0	0
7 COAL MINING	590	0	58	0	196	0	0	0	0
8 CRUDE PETRO.,NATURAL GAS	0	0	0	0	0	0	0	0	0
9 STONE & CLAY MINING	69	0	0	119	0	0	0	0	0
10 CHEM.&FERT. MIN. MINING	0	0	0	0	0	0	0	0	0
11 NEW CONSTRUCTION*	14548	12646	10160	95785	14375	10796	1388	5955	21622
12 MAINT. & REPAIR CONSTR.	6972	2615	2778	59101	5937	2778	436	29360	12964
13 ORDNANCE & ACCESSORIES	288	108	115	2439	245	115	18	1211	535
14 FOOD & KINDRED PRDTS.	4142	1553	1650	35108	3527	1650	259	17441	7701
15 TOBACCO MANUFACTURES	0	0	0	0	0	0	0	0	0
16 FABRICS	996	373	397	8440	848	397	62	4193	1851
17 TEXTILE PRDTS.	550	206	219	4661	468	219	34	2315	1022
18 APPAREL	399	150	159	3380	340	159	25	1679	742
19 MISC. TEXTILE PRDTS.	456	150	159	3382	340	159	25	1680	742
20 LUMBER & WOOD PRDTS.	737	46	336	826	34	28	10	3	179
21 WOODEN CONTAINERS	64	276	294	6245	627	294	46	3102	1370
22 HOUSEHOLD FURNITURE	651	24	26	543	55	26	4	270	119
23 OTHER FURNITURE	564	244	259	5516	554	259	41	2740	1210
24 PAPER & ALLIED PRDTS.		212	225	4784	481	225	35	2377	1049
25 PAPERBOARD CONTAINERS	140	53	56	1187	119	56	9	590	260
26 PRINTING & PUBLISHING	237	89	94	2008	202	94	15	997	440
27 CHEMICALS,SELECT. PRDTS.	387	145	154	3278	329	154	24	1628	719
28 PLASTICS & SYNTHETICS	33	12	13	276	28	13	2	137	61
29 DRUGS & COSMETICS	715	268	285	6061	609	285	45	3011	1329
30 PAINT & ALLIED PRDTS.	600	225	239	5084	511	239	37	2526	1115
31 PETROLEUM, RELATED INDS.	2886	1082	1150	24459	2457	1150	180	12151	5365
32 RUBBER, MISC. PLASTICS	364	136	145	3085	33	145	23	1532	677
33 LEATHER TANNING & PRDTS.	39	15	16	332	33	16	2	165	73
34 FOOTWEAR, LEATHER PRDTS.	466	175	185	3946	396	185	29	1960	866
35 GLASS & GLASS PRDTS.	26	10	11	224	23	11	2	111	49
36 STONE & CLAY PRDTS.	59	22	24	503	51	24	4	250	110
37 PRIMARY IRON, STEEL MFR.	254	95	101	2156	217	101	16	1071	473
38 PRIMARY NONFERROUS MFR.	894	335	356	7579	761	356	56	3765	1663

39	METAL CONTAINERS	5	2	2	45	5	2	0	22	10
40	FABRICATED METAL PRDTS.	145	54	58	1226	123	58	9	609	269
41	SCREW MACH. PRDTS., ETC.	34	13	13	286	29	13	2	142	63
42	OTHER FAB. METAL PRDTS.	189	71	75	1605	161	75	12	797	352
43	ENGINES & TURBINES	490	184	195	4153	417	195	31	2063	911
44	FARM MACH. & EQUIP.	48	18	19	408	41	19	3	202	89
45	CONSTRUC. MACH. & EQUIP.	209	78	83	1773	178	83	13	881	389
46	MATERIAL HANDLING MACH.	77	29	31	655	66	31	5	326	144
47	METALWORKING MACHINERY	123	46	49	1045	105	49	8	519	229
48	SPECIAL MACH. & EQUIP.	46	17	18	386	39	18	3	192	85
49	GENERAL MACH. & EQUIP.	270	101	108	2289	230	108	17	1137	502
50	MACHINE SHOP PRDTS.	80	30	32	674	68	32	5	335	148
51	OFFICE, COMPUT. MACHINES	47	17	17	395	40	19	3	196	87
52	SERVICE IND. MACHINES	94	35	38	798	80	38	6	397	175
53	ELECT. TRANSMISS. EQUIP.	1089	409	434	9235	928	434	68	4588	2026
54	HOUSEHOLD APPLIANCES	120	45	48	1019	102	48	8	506	224
55	ELECTRIC LIGHTING EQUIP.	307	115	122	2600	261	122	19	1291	570
56	RADIO, TV, ETC., EQUIP.	1064	399	424	9022	906	424	67	4482	1979
57	ELECTRONIC COMPONENTS	421	158	168	3571	359	168	26	1774	783
58	MISC. ELECTRICAL MACH.	368	138	147	3122	314	147	23	1551	685
59	MOTOR VEHICLES, EQUIP.	779	292	310	6605	664	310	49	3281	1449
60	AIRCRAFT & PARTS	5127	1958	2043	148531	4437	42627	431	21590	9643
61	OTHER TRANSPORT. EQUIP.	6612	2479	2634	56046	5630	2634	413	27842	12294
62	PROFESS., SCIEN. INSTRU.	790	296	315	6695	673	315	49	3326	1469
63	MEDICAL, PHOTO. EQUIP.	503	189	200	4263	428	200	31	2118	935
64	MISC. MANUFACTURING	788	296	314	6682	671	314	49	3320	1466
65	TRANSPORT. & WAREHOUSING	4624	1734	1842	39196	3938	1842	289	19472	8598
66	COMMUNICA., EXC. BRDCAST.	886	332	353	7510	754	353	55	3731	1647
67	RADIO & TV BROADCASTING	0	0	0	0	0	0	0	0	0
68	ELEC.,GAS,WATER,SAN.SER.	403	151	161	3415	343	161	25	1696	749
69	WHOLESALE & RETAIL TRADE	918	344	366	7784	782	366	57	3867	1707
70	FINANCE & INSURANCE	398	149	159	3374	339	159	25	1676	740
71	REAL ESTATE & RENTAL	1147	970	1200	13972	829	4322	406	847	1500
72	HOTELS; PERSONAL SERV.	1869	701	745	15847	1592	745	117	7872	3476
73	BUSINESS SERVICES	-1000	-375	-398	-8475	-851	-398	-62	-4210	-1859
74	RESEARCH & DEVELOPMENT	4803	2516	3842	43176	5481	1285	377	13630	8278
75	AUTO. REPAIR & SERVICES	95	309	74	508	321	47	12	179	85
76	AMUSEMENTS	44	22	32	1457	42	64	16	48	140
77	MED.,EDUC. SERVICES	9045	3410	3726	78547	7799	4428	648	37057	16630
78	FEDERAL GOV'T ENTERPRISE	439	164	175	3718	373	175	27	1847	815
79	STATE & LOCAL GOV'T ENT.	0	0	0	0	0	0	0	0	0
80	IMPORTS	7290	2734	2905	61794	6208	2905	456	30697	13555
81	BUS.TRAVEL, ENT., GIFTS.	0	0	0	0	0	0	0	0	0
82	OFFICE SUPPLIES	0	0	0	0	0	0	0	0	0
83	SCRAP & USED GOODS	-33829	-12686	-13479	-286751	-23807	-13479	-2114	-142450	-62900
84	GOVERNMENT INDUSTRY	120754	44049	47925	1005097	98733	45311	7974	495554	216275
85	REST OF WORLD INDUSTRY	-1033	-181	-493	-3730	-454	-645	-91	-795	-677
86	HOUSEHOLD INDUSTRY	0	0	0	0	0	0	0	0	0
87	INVENTORY VALUATION ADJ.	0	0	0	0	0	0	0	0	0
88	STATE TOTAL	176631	73013	77192	1560047	145234	116599	12474	661970	312522

*The data for this industry could not be made entirely consistent with the 1947 state output estimates. (See page 215.)

413

TABLE C.17

STATE ESTIMATES OF 1947
FEDERAL GOVERNMENT PURCHASES
(THOUSANDS OF CURRENT DOLLARS)

INDUSTRY TITLE	10 GEORGIA	11 IDAHO	12 ILLINOIS	13 INDIANA	14 IOWA	15 KANSAS	16 KENTUCKY	17 LOUISIANA	18 MAINE
1 LIVESTOCK & PRDTS.	0	-1412	-381	-314	-653	-328	-482	0	0
2 OTHER AGRICULTURE PRDTS.	2785	431	6568	1682	1405	1602	1901	1612	503
3 FORESTRY & FISHERIES	-8	-1	-4	-3	-2	-1	-12	-70	-46
4 AGRI.,FORES.,FISH. SERV.	-771	-91	-1676	-412	-230	-360	-511	-446	-134
5 IRON, FERRO. ORES MINING	0	0	0	0	0	0	0	0	0
6 NONFERROUS ORES MINING	-4	0	0	-80	0	0	0	0	0
7 COAL MINING	0	0	2103	788	45	85	2610	0	0
8 CRUDE PETRO.,NATURAL GAS	0	0	0	0	0	0	0	0	0
9 STONE & CLAY MINING	50	0	0	0	0	0	0	0	0
10 CHEM.&FERT. MIN. MINING	0	0	1	0	0	0	0	0	0
11 NEW CONSTRUCTION*	15334	5933	46854	14985	13587	16550	16694	13336	4726
12 MAINT. & REPAIR CONSTR.	9696	1144	21080	5175	2887	4521	6428	5610	1689
13 ORDNANCE & ACCESSORIES	400	47	870	214	119	187	265	232	70
14 FOOD & KINDRED PRDTS.	5760	680	12522	3074	1715	2686	3818	3333	1003
15 TOBACCO MANUFACTURES	0	0	0	0	0	0	0	0	0
16 FABRICS	1385	163	3010	739	412	646	918	801	241
17 TEXTILE PRDTS.	765	90	1662	408	228	357	507	442	133
18 APPAREL	555	65	1206	296	165	259	368	321	97
19 MISC. TEXTILE PRDTS.	555	65	1206	296	165	259	368	321	97
20 LUMBER & WOOD PRDTS.	418	159	236	171	90	17	142	348	126
21 WOODEN CONTAINERS	1025	121	2228	547	305	478	679	593	178
22 HOUSEHOLD FURNITURE	89	11	194	48	27	42	59	52	16
23 OTHER FURNITURE	905	107	1967	483	269	422	600	524	158
24 PAPER & ALLIED PRDTS.	785	93	1707	419	234	366	520	454	137
25 PAPERBOARD CONTAINERS	195	23	423	104	58	91	129	113	34
26 PRINTING & PUBLISHING	329	39	716	176	98	154	218	191	57
27 CHEMICALS,SELECT. PRDTS.	538	63	1169	287	160	251	356	311	94
28 PLASTICS & SYNTHETICS	45	5	98	24	13	21	30	26	8
29 DRUGS & COSMETICS	994	117	2162	531	296	464	659	575	173
30 PAINT & ALLIED PRDTS.	834	98	1813	445	248	389	553	483	145
31 PETROLEUM, RELATED INDS.	4013	473	8724	2142	1195	1871	2660	2322	699
32 RUBBER, MISC. PLASTICS	506	60	1100	270	151	236	335	293	88
33 LEATHER TANNING & PRDTS.	54	6	118	29	16	25	36	31	9
34 FOOTWEAR, LEATHER PRDTS.	647	76	1407	345	193	302	429	375	113
35 GLASS & GLASS PRDTS.	37	4	80	20	11	17	24	21	6
36 STONE & CLAY PRDTS.	82	10	179	44	25	38	55	48	14
37 PRIMARY IRON, STEEL MFR.	354	42	769	189	105	165	234	205	62
38 PRIMARY NONFERROUS MFR.	1243	147	2703	664	370	580	824	720	217

	7	1	16	4	2	3	5	4	1
39 METAL CONTAINERS	7	1	16	4	2	3	5	4	1
40 FABRICATED METAL PRDTS.	201	24	437	107	60	94	133	116	35
41 SCREW MACH. PRDTS., ETC.	47	6	102	25	14	22	31	27	8
42 OTHER FAB. METAL PRDTS.	263	31	572	141	78	123	175	152	46
43 ENGINES & TURBINES	681	80	1481	364	203	318	452	394	119
44 FARM MACH. & EQUIP.	67	8	145	36	20	31	44	39	12
45 CONSTRUC. MACH. & EQUIP.	291	34	632	155	87	136	193	168	51
46 MATERIAL HANDLING MACH.	108	13	234	57	32	50	71	62	19
47 METALWORKING MACHINERY	171	20	373	91	51	80	114	99	30
48 SPECIAL MACH. & EQUIP.	63	7	138	34	19	30	42	37	11
49 GENERAL MACH. & EQUIP.	376	44	816	200	112	175	249	217	65
50 MACHINE SHOP PRDTS.	111	13	241	59	33	52	73	64	19
51 OFFICE, COMPUT. MACHINES	65	8	141	35	19	30	43	37	11
52 SERVICE IND. MACHINES	131	15	285	70	39	61	87	76	23
53 ELECT. TRANSMISS. EQUIP.	1515	179	3294	809	451	706	1004	877	264
54 HOUSEHOLD APPLIANCES	167	20	364	89	50	78	111	97	29
55 ELECTRIC LIGHTING EQUIP.	427	50	927	228	127	199	283	247	74
56 RADIO, TV, ETC., EQUIP.	1480	175	3218	790	441	690	981	856	258
57 ELECTRONIC COMPONENTS	586	69	1274	313	174	273	388	339	102
58 MISC. ELECTRICAL MACH.	512	60	1114	273	153	239	340	296	89
59 MOTOR VEHICLES, EQUIP.	1084	128	2356	578	323	505	718	627	189
60 AIRCRAFT & PARTS	7131	841	18585	20632	4020	11289	4728	4125	1242
61 OTHER TRANSPORT. EQUIP.	9195	1085	19991	4907	2738	4287	6095	5321	1601
62 PROFESS., SCIEN. INSTRU.	1098	130	2388	586	327	512	728	636	191
63 MEDICAL, PHOTO. EQUIP.	699	83	1521	373	208	326	464	405	122
64 MISC. MANUFACTURING	1096	129	2383	585	326	511	727	634	191
65 TRANSPORT. & WAREHOUSING	6430	759	13980	3432	1915	2998	4263	3721	1120
66 COMMUNICA.-EXC. BRDCAST.	1232	145	2679	658	367	574	817	713	215
67 RADIO & TV BROADCASTING	0	0	0	0	0	0	0	0	0
68 ELEC.,GAS,WATER,SAN.SER.	560	66	1218	299	167	261	371	324	98
69 WHOLESALE & RETAIL TRADE	1277	151	2776	682	380	595	847	739	222
70 FINANCE & INSURANCE	554	65	1204	295	165	258	367	320	96
71 REAL ESTATE & RENTAL	3793	494	17430	3811	1341	1341	1394	2188	388
72 HOTELS; PERSONAL SERV.	2600	307	5652	1387	774	1212	1723	1504	453
73 BUSINESS SERVICES	-1390	-164	-3023	-742	-414	-648	-922	-805	-242
74 RESEARCH & DEVELOPMENT	4184	827	24264	2562	1603	2061	2665	4801	717
75 AUTO. REPAIR & SERVICES	135	163	297	58	71	71	132	85	25
76 AMUSEMENTS	57	16	377	99	62	42	56	61	18
77 MED.,EDUC. SERVICES	12610	1564	30729	7734	4437	6108	8474	7571	2334
78 FEDERAL GOV'T ENTERPRISE	610	72	1326	325	182	284	404	353	106
79 STATE & LOCAL GOV'T ENT.	0	0	0	0	0	0	0	0	0
80 IMPORTS	10138	1196	22041	5411	3018	4727	6720	5866	1766
81 BUS.TRAVEL, ENT., GIFTS.	0	0	0	0	0	0	0	0	0
82 OFFICE SUPPLIES	0	0	0	0	0	0	0	0	0
83 SCRAP & USED GOODS	-47043	-5550	-102279	-25107	-14001	-21936	-31186	-27222	-8193
84 GOVERNMENT INDUSTRY	159192	21983	354610	92001	47607	77585	105566	90540	33278
85 REST OF WORLD INDUSTRY	-794	-165	-3874	-1143	-887	-721	-784	-530	-344
86 HOUSEHOLD INDUSTRY	0	0	0	0	0	0	0	0	0
87 INVENTORY VALUATION ADJ.	0	0	0	0	0	0	0	0	0
88 STATE TOTAL	231309	33951	555247	157088	80594	128023	160602	139359	47570

*The data for this industry could not be made entirely consistent with the 1947 state output estimates. (See page 215.)

TABLE C.17

STATE ESTIMATES OF 1947
FEDERAL GOVERNMENT PURCHASES
(THOUSANDS OF CURRENT DOLLARS)

INDUSTRY TITLE	19 MARYLAND	20 MASSA-CHUSETTS	21 MICHIGAN	22 MINNESOTA	23 MISSISSIPPI	24 MISSOURI	25 MONTANA	26 NEBRASKA	27 NEVADA
1 LIVESTOCK & PRDTS.	0	0	-347	-501	0	-826	-2045	-244	-510
2 OTHER AGRICULTURE PRDTS.	4503	3292	2321	1544	1261	2499	540	1245	168
3 FORESTRY & FISHERIES	-22	-94	-24	-7	-16	-10	-3	-1	0
4 AGRI.,FORES.,FISH. SERV.	-1317	-966	-637	-342	-321	-689	-121	-243	-48
5 IRON. FERRO. ORES MINING	0	0	0	0	0	0	0	0	0
6 NONFERROUS ORES MINING	64	0	0	0	0	0	-6	0	0
7 COAL MINING	0	0	0	0	0	0	98	0	0
8 CRUDE PETRO.,NATURAL GAS	0	0	0	0	0	132	0	0	0
9 STONE & CLAY MINING	10	0	0	0	0	0	25	0	13
10 CHEM.&FERT. MIN. MINING	0	0	0	0	0	0	0	0	0
11 NEW CONSTRUCTION*	20958	17658	36463	16186	11630	16633	7538	11905	2850
12 MAINT. & REPAIR CONSTR.	16559	12147	8007	4303	4031	8661	1525	3050	599
13 ORDNANCE & ACCESSORIES	683	501	330	178	166	357	63	126	25
14 FOOD & KINDRED PRDTS.	9837	7216	4757	2556	2394	5145	906	1812	356
15 TOBACCO MANUFACTURES	0	0	0	0	0	0	0	0	0
16 FABRICS	2365	1735	1143	615	576	1237	218	436	86
17 TEXTILE PRDTS.	1306	958	631	339	318	683	120	241	47
18 APPAREL	947	695	458	246	231	495	87	174	34
19 MISC. TEXTILE PRDTS.	948	695	458	246	231	496	87	175	34
20 LUMBER & WOOD PRDTS.	51	91	251	119	382	100	89	5	13
21 WOODEN CONTAINERS	1750	1284	846	455	426	915	161	322	63
22 HOUSEHOLD FURNITURE	152	112	74	40	37	80	14	28	6
23 OTHER FURNITURE	1545	1134	747	402	376	808	142	285	56
24 PAPER & ALLIED PRDTS.	1341	983	648	348	326	701	123	247	49
25 PAPERBOARD CONTAINERS	333	244	161	86	81	174	31	61	12
26 PRINTING & PUBLISHING	562	413	272	146	137	294	52	104	20
27 CHEMICALS,SELECT. PRDTS.	918	674	444	239	224	480	85	169	33
28 PLASTICS & SYNTHETICS	77	57	37	20	19	40	7	14	3
29 DRUGS & COSMETICS	1698	1246	821	441	413	888	156	313	61
30 PAINT & ALLIED PRDTS.	1424	1045	689	370	347	745	131	262	52
31 PETROLEUM, RELATED INDS.	6853	5027	3314	1781	1668	3584	631	1262	248
32 RUBBER, MISC. PLASTICS	864	634	418	225	210	452	80	159	31
33 LEATHER TANNING & PRDTS.	93	68	45	24	23	49	9	17	3
34 FOOTWEAR, LEATHER PRDTS.	1106	811	535	287	269	578	102	204	40
35 GLASS & GLASS PRDTS.	63	46	30	16	15	33	6	12	2
36 STONE & CLAY PRDTS.	141	103	68	37	34	74	13	26	5
37 PRIMARY IRON, STEEL MFR.	604	443	292	157	147	316	56	111	22
38 PRIMARY NONFERROUS MFR.	2124	1558	1027	552	517	1111	196	391	77

#	Industry	(1)	(2)	(3)	(4)	(5)	(6)	(7)	(8)	(9)
39	METAL CONTAINERS	13	9	6	3	3	7	1	2	0
40	FABRICATED METAL PRDTS.	343	252	166	89	84	180	32	63	12
41	SCREW MACH. PRDTS., ETC.	80	59	39	21	20	42	7	15	3
42	OTHER FAB. METAL PRDTS.	450	330	217	117	109	235	41	83	16
43	ENGINES & TURBINES	1164	854	563	302	283	609	107	214	42
44	FARM MACH. & EQUIP.	114	84	55	30	28	60		21	4
45	CONSTRUC. MACH. & EQUIP.	497	364	240	129	121	260	46	92	18
46	MATERIAL HANDLING MACH.	184	135	89	48	45	96	17	34	7
47	METALWORKING MACHINERY	293	215	142	76	71	153	27	54	11
48	SPECIAL MACH. & EQUIP.	108	79	52	28	26	57	10	20	4
49	GENERAL MACH. & EQUIP.	641	470	310	167	156	335	59	118	23
50	MACHINE SHOP PRDTS.	189	139	91	49	46	99	17	35	7
51	OFFICE, COMPUT. MACHINES	111	81	53	29	27	58	10	20	4
52	SERVICE IND. MACHINES	224	164	108	58	54	117	21	41	8
53	ELECT. TRANSMISS. EQUIP.	2587	1898	1251	672	630	1353	238	477	94
54	HOUSEHOLD APPLIANCES	286	210	138	74	70	149	26	53	10
55	ELECTRIC LIGHTING EQUIP.	728	534	352	189	177	381	67	134	26
56	RADIO, TV, ETC., EQUIP.	2528	1854	1222	657	615	1322	233	466	91
57	ELECTRONIC COMPONENTS	1000	734	484	260	244	523	92	184	36
58	MISC. ELECTRICAL MACH.	875	642	423	227	213	458	81	161	32
59	MOTOR VEHICLES, EQUIP.	1851	1358	895	481	451	968	170	341	67
60	AIRCRAFT & PARTS	32090	17688	8692	4843	2964	8022	1124	2243	441
61	OTHER TRANSPORT. EQUIP.	15703	11519	7593	4081	3823	8213	1446	2893	568
62	PROFESS., SCIEN. INSTRU.	1876	1376	907	488	457	981	173	346	68
63	MEDICAL, PHOTO. EQUIP.	1195	876	578	310	291	625	110	220	43
64	MISC. MANUFACTURING	1872	1373	905	487	456	979	172	345	68
65	TRANSPORT. & WAREHOUSING	10982	8056	5310	2854	2673	5744	1012	2023	397
66	COMMUNICA.,EXC. BRDCAST.	2104	1543	1017	547	512	1100	194	388	76
67	RADIO & TV BROADCASTING	0	0	0	0	0	0	0	0	0
68	ELEC.,GAS,WATER,SAN.SER.	957	702	463	249	233	500	88	176	35
69	WHOLESALE & RETAIL TRADE	2181	1600	1055	567	531	1141	201	402	79
70	FINANCE & INSURANCE	945	694	457	246	230	494	87	174	34
71	REAL ESTATE & RENTAL	741	7004	1041	1993	688	4252	1058	2011	229
72	HOTELS; PERSONAL SERV.	4440	3257	2147	1154	1081	2322	409	818	161
73	BUSINESS SERVICES	-2375	-1742	-1148	-617	-578	-1242	-219	-437	-86
74	RESEARCH & DEVELOPMENT	11719	13885	11576	3270	1662	6543	1583	1267	1995
75	AUTO. REPAIR & SERVICES	81	125	150	121	89	214	258	106	78
76	AMUSEMENTS	90	195	205	78	23	114	14	33	51
77	MED.,EDUC. SERVICES	21267	17642	11996	6464	5233	12148	2064	4200	780
78	FEDERAL GOV'T ENTERPRISE	1042	764	504	271	254	545	96	192	38
79	STATE & LOCAL GOV'T ENT.	0	0	0	0	0	0	0	0	0
80	IMPORTS	17314	12700	8372	4499	4214	9055	1595	3189	626
81	BUS.TRAVEL, ENT., GIFTS.	0	0	0	0	0	0	0	0	0
82	OFFICE SUPPLIES	0	0	0	0	0	0	0	0	0
83	SCRAP & USED GOODS	-80343	-58936	-38850	-20879	-19557	-42022	-7400	-14800	-2907
84	GOVERNMENT INDUSTRY	275780	209984	141415	77872	72296	139398	26650	56375	10434
85	REST OF WORLD INDUSTRY	-577	-1982	-1788	-802	-427	-1685	-178	-527	-39
86	HOUSEHOLD INDUSTRY	0	0	0	0	0	0	0	0	0
87	INVENTORY VALUATION ADJ.	0	0	0	0	0	0	0	0	0
88	STATE TOTAL	411886	318594	233773	122908	105771	211138	42966	86933	18137

*The data for this industry could not be made entirely consistent with the 1947 state output estimates. (See page 215.)

TABLE C.17

STATE ESTIMATES OF 1947
FEDERAL GOVERNMENT PURCHASES
(THOUSANDS OF CURRENT DOLLARS)

INDUSTRY TITLE	28 NEW HAMPSHIRE	29 NEW JERSEY	30 NEW MEXICO	31 NEW YORK	32 NORTH CAROLINA	33 NORTH DAKOTA	34 OHIO	35 OKLAHOMA	36 OREGON
1 LIVESTOCK & PRDTS.	0	0	-1339	-120	0	-415	-952	-115	-826
2 OTHER AGRICULTURE PRDTS.	404	3817	757	9922	2832	605	4494	1788	1078
3 FORESTRY & FISHERIES	-5	-26	-1	-45	-15		-12	-5	-26
4 AGRI.,FORES.,FISH. SERV.	-117	-1113	-212	-2894	-754	-74	-1261	-477	-282
5 IRON, FERRO. ORES MINING	0	0	-40	0	0	0	0	0	0
6 NONFERROUS ORES MINING	0	0	45	0	0	0	0	0	0
7 COAL MINING	0	0	0	0	0	85	0	107	0
8 CRUDE PETRO.,NATURAL GAS	0	0	0	143	0	0	1163	0	0
9 STONE & CLAY MINING	0	0	0	0	88	0	0	0	0
10 CHEM.&FERT. MIN.* MINING	0	0	0	0	0	0	0	0	0
11 NEW CONSTRUCTION*	1632	19692	6364	111737	17903	5529	38407	19963	13950
12 MAINT. & REPAIR CONSTR.	1471	13999	2669	36386	9478	926	15851	5992	3541
13 ORDNANCE & ACCESSORIES	61	578	110	1501	391	38	654	247	146
14 FOOD & KINDRED PRDTS.	874	8316	1586	21615	5630	550	9416	3559	2103
15 TOBACCO MANUFACTURES	0	0	0	0	0	0	0	0	0
16 FABRICS	210	1999	381	5196	1353	132	2264	856	506
17 TEXTILE PRDTS.	116	1104	210	2870	747	73	1250	473	279
18 APPAREL	84	801	153	2082	542	53	907	343	203
19 MISC. TEXTILE PRDTS.	76	127	32	276	376	53	188	343	203
20 LUMBER & WOOD PRDTS.	155	1479	282	3845	1002	1	1675	48	1373
21 WOODEN CONTAINERS	14	129	25	334	87	98	146	633	374
22 HOUSEHOLD FURNITURE	137	1306	249	3396	885	9	1479	55	33
23 OTHER FURNITURE	119	1133	216	2946	767	86	1283	559	330
24 PAPER & ALLIED PRDTS.	30	281	54	731	190	75	318	485	287
25 PAPERBOARD CONTAINERS	50	476	91	1236	322	19	538	120	71
26 PRINTING & PUBLISHING	82	776	148	2018	526	31	879	204	120
27 CHEMICALS,SELECT. PRDTS.						51		332	196
28 PLASTICS & SYNTHETICS		65	12	170	44	4	74	28	17
29 DRUGS & COSMETICS	151	1436	274	3731	972	95	1626	614	363
30 PAINT & ALLIED PRDTS.	127	1204	230	3130	815	80	1364	515	305
31 PETROLEUM, RELATED INDS.	609	5794	1105	15059	3923	383	6560	2480	1465
32 RUBBER, MISC. PLASTICS	77	731	139	1899	495	48	827	313	185
33 LEATHER TANNING & PRDTS.	8	79	15	204	53	5	89	34	20
34 FOOTWEAR, LEATHER PRDTS.	98	935	178	2429	633	62	1058	400	236
35 GLASS & GLASS PRDTS.	6	53	10	138	36	4	60	23	13
36 STONE & CLAY PRDTS.	13	119	23	310	81	8	135	51	30
37 PRIMARY IRON, STEEL MFR.	54	511	97	1327	346	34	578	219	129
38 PRIMARY NONFERROUS MFR.	189	1795	342	4666	1215	119	2033	768	454

	1	2	3	4	5	6	7	8	9
39 METAL CONTAINERS	1	11	2	28	7	1	12	5	3
40 FABRICATED METAL PRDTS.	31	290	55	755	197	19	329	124	73
41 SCREW MACH. PRDTS., ETC.	7	68	13	176	46	4	77	29	17
42 OTHER FAB. METAL PRDTS.	40	380	72	988	257	25	430	163	96
43 ENGINES & TURBINES	103	984	188	2557	666	65	1114	421	249
44 FARM MACH. & EQUIP.	10	97	18	251	65	6	109	41	24
45 CONSTRUC. MACH. & EQUIP.	44	420	80	1092	284	28	476	180	106
46 MATERIAL HANDLING MACH.	16	155	30	404	105	10	176	66	39
47 METALWORKING MACHINERY	26	248	47	643	168	16	280	106	63
48 SPECIAL MACH. & EQUIP.	10	91	17	238	62	6	104	39	23
49 GENERAL MACH. & EQUIP.	57	542	103	1409	367	36	614	232	137
50 MACHINE SHOP PRDTS.	17	160	30	415	108	11	181	68	40
51 OFFICE, COMPUT. MACHINES	10	93	18	243	53		106	40	24
52 SERVICE IND. MACHINES	20	189	36	491	128	13	214	81	48
53 ELECT. TRANSMISS. EQUIP.	230	2187	417	5686	1481	145	2477	936	553
54 HOUSEHOLD APPLIANCES	25	241	46	628	163	16	273	103	61
55 ELECTRIC LIGHTING EQUIP.	65	616	117	1601	417	41	697	264	156
56 RADIO, TV, ETC., EQUIP.	225	2137	407	5555	1447	141	2420	915	540
57 ELECTRONIC COMPONENTS	89	846	161	2198	573	56	958	362	214
58 MISC. ELECTRICAL MACH.	78	740	141	1922	501	49	837	317	187
59 MOTOR VEHICLES, EQUIP.	164	1565	298	4067	1059	103	1772	670	396
60 AIRCRAFT & PARTS	1082	27373	1963	48778	6970	681	36606	4663	2603
61 OTHER TRANSPORT. EQUIP.	1395	13275	2531	34506	8988	878	15032	5682	3358
62 PROFESS., SCIEN. INSTRU.	167	1586	302	4122	1074	105	1796	679	401
63 MEDICAL, PHOTO. EQUIP.	106	1010	193	2625	684	67	1143	432	255
64 MISC. MANUFACTURING	166	1583	302	4114	1072	105	1792	677	400
65 TRANSPORT. & WAREHOUSING	975	9284	1770	24132	6286	614	10512	3974	2348
66 COMMUNICA., EXC. BRDCAST.	187	1779	339	4623	1204	118	2014	761	450
67 RADIO & TV BROADCASTING	0	0	0	0	0	0	0	0	0
68 ELEC.,GAS,WATER,SAN.SER.	85	809	154	2103	548	54	916	346	205
69 WHOLESALE & RETAIL TRADE	194	1844	352	4792	1248	122	2088	789	466
70 FINANCE & INSURANCE	84	799	152	2077	541	53	905	342	202
71 REAL ESTATE & RENTAL	688	2893	2311	29479	2964	741	11767	1094	4375
72 HOTELS; PERSONAL SERV.	394	3754	716	9756	2541	248	4250	1607	949
73 BUSINESS SERVICES	-211	-2007	-383	-5218	-1359	-133	-2273	-859	-508
74 RESEARCH & DEVELOPMENT	739	25189	1807	46619	4151	428	19872	2526	1483
75 AUTO. REPAIR & SERVICES	16	73	263	388	86	95	166	137	225
76 AMUSEMENTS	26	207	15	1018	60	12	256	50	46
77 MED.,EDUC. SERVICES	2030	19200	3402	54076	12345	1288	22496	7863	4949
78 FEDERAL GOV'T ENTERPRISE	93	881	168	2289	596	58	997	377	223
79 STATE & LOCAL GOV'T ENT.	0	0	0	0	0	0	0	0	0
80 IMPORTS	1538	14637	2791	38044	9910	968	16573	6265	3702
81 BUS.TRAVEL, ENT., GIFTS.	0	0	0	0	0	0	0	0	0
82 OFFICE SUPPLIES	0	0	0	0	0	0	0	0	0
83 SCRAP & USED GOODS	-7136	-67922	-12950	-176543	-45986	-4493	-76907	-29072	-17179
84 GOVERNMENT INDUSTRY	24006	215174	47063	620645	167332	16138	274212	103081	61363
85 REST OF WORLD INDUSTRY	-189	-1361	-156	-7344	-757	-249	-2428	-671	-436
86 HOUSEHOLD INDUSTRY	0	0	0	0	0	0	0	0	0
87 INVENTORY VALUATION ADJ.	0	0	0	0	0	0	0	0	0
88 STATE TOTAL	34512	350511	69762	1014743	240167	27463	449437	156859	99805

*The data for this industry could not be made entirely consistent with the 1947 state output estimates. (See page 215.)

TABLE C.17

STATE ESTIMATES OF 1947
FEDERAL GOVERNMENT PURCHASES
(THOUSANDS OF CURRENT DOLLARS)

INDUSTRY TITLE	37 PENNSYLVANIA	38 RHODE ISLAND	39 SOUTH CAROLINA	40 SOUTH DAKOTA	41 TENNESSEE	42 TEXAS	43 UTAH	44 VERMONT	45 VIRGINIA
1 LIVESTOCK & PRDTS.	-165	0	0	-798	-151	-6196	-1658	0	-143
2 OTHER AGRICULTURE PRDTS.	6225	1041	1874	650	2136	6900	971	175	8571
3 FORESTRY & FISHERIES	-18	-6	-6		-9	-19	0	-3	-55
4 AGRI.,FORES.,FISH. SERV.	-1802	-308	-515	-108	-589	-1841	-277	-48	-2504
5 IRON, FERRO. ORES MINING	0	0	0	0	0	0	0	0	0
6 NONFERROUS ORES MINING	0	0	0	0	0	0	-50	0	0
7 COAL MINING	6336	0	0	0	194	0	0	0	624
8 CRUDE PETRO.,NATURAL GAS	0	0	0	0	0	2	230	0	0
9 STONE & CLAY MINING	56	0	0	0	0	0	0	0	10
10 CHEM.&FERT. MIN. MINING*	0	0	0	0	0	140	0	74	0
11 NEW CONSTRUCTION*	49949	3427	15557	3993	24113	51278	4646	2290	19841
12 MAINT. & REPAIR CONSTR.	22660	3867	6482	1362	7408	23150	3486	599	31484
13 ORDNANCE & ACCESSORIES	935	160	267	56	306	955	144	25	1299
14 FOOD & KINDRED PRDTS.	13461	2297	3851	809	4401	13752	2071	356	18703
15 TOBACCO MANUFACTURES	0	0	0	0	0	0	0	0	0
16 FABRICS	3236	552		194	1058	3306	498	86	4496
17 TEXTILE PRDTS.	1787	305	926	107	584	1826	275	47	2483
18 APPAREL	1296	221	511	78	424	1324	199	34	1801
19 MISC. TEXTILE PRDTS.	1297	221	371	78	424	1325	199	34	1802
20 LUMBER & WOOD PRDTS.	213	7	288	14	210	412	368	72	3327
21 WOODEN CONTAINERS	2394	409	685	144	783	2446	9	63	0
22 HOUSEHOLD FURNITURE	208	36	60	13	68	213	32	6	289
23 OTHER FURNITURE	2115	361	605	127	691	2160	325	56	2938
24 PAPER & ALLIED PRDTS.	1834	313	525	110	600	1874	282	49	2549
25 PAPERBOARD CONTAINERS	455	78	130	27	149	465	70	12	632
26 PRINTING & PUBLISHING	770	131	220	46	252	786	118	20	1069
27 CHEMICALS,SELECT. PRDTS.	1257	214	359	76	411	1284	193	33	1746
28 PLASTICS & SYNTHETICS	106	18	30	6	35	108	16	3	147
29 DRUGS & COSMETICS	2324	397	665	140	760	2374	358	61	3229
30 PAINT & ALLIED PRDTS.	1949	333	558	117	637	1991	300	52	2708
31 PETROLEUM, RELATED INDS.	9378	1601	2683	564	3066	9581	1443	248	13030
32 RUBBER, MISC. PLASTICS	1183	202	338	71	387	1208	182	31	1643
33 LEATHER TANNING & PRDTS.	127	22	36	8	42	130	3	3	177
34 FOOTWEAR, LEATHER PRDTS.	1513	258	433	91	495	1546	233	40	2102
35 GLASS & GLASS PRDTS.	86	15	25	5	28	88	13	2	119
36 STONE & CLAY PRDTS.	193	33	55	12	63	197	30	5	268
37 PRIMARY IRON, STEEL MFR.	827	141	236	50	270	844	127	22	1148
38 PRIMARY NONFERROUS MFR.	2906	496	831	175	950	2969	447	77	4038

#	Industry									
39	METAL CONTAINERS	17	3	5	1	6	18	3	0	24
40	FABRICATED METAL PRDTS.	470	80	134	28	154	480	72	12	653
41	SCREW MACH. PRDTS., ETC.	110	19	31	7	36	112	17	3	152
42	OTHER FAB. METAL PRDTS.	615	105	176	37	201	629	95	16	855
43	ENGINES & TURBINES	1592	272	455	96	521	1627	245	42	2212
44	FARM MACH. & EQUIP.	156	27	45	9	51	160	24	4	217
45	CONSTRUC. MACH. & EQUIP.	680	116	194	41	222	695	105	18	945
46	MATERIAL HANDLING MACH.	251	43	72	15	82	257	39	7	349
47	METALWORKING MACHINERY	401	68	115	24	131	409	62	11	557
48	SPECIAL MACH. & EQUIP.	148	25	42	9	48	151	23	4	206
49	GENERAL MACH. & EQUIP.	878	150	251	53	287	897	135	23	1219
50	MACHINE SHOP PRDTS.	259	44	74	16	85	264	40	7	359
51	OFFICE, COMPUT. MACHINES	151	26	43	9	49	155	23	4	210
52	SERVICE IND. MACHINES	306	52	88	18	100	313	47	8	425
53	ELECT. TRANSMISS. EQUIP.	3541	604	1013	213	1158	3617	545	94	4920
54	HOUSEHOLD APPLIANCES	391	67	112	23	128	399	60	10	543
55	ELECTRIC LIGHTING EQUIP.	997	170	285	60	326	1018	153	26	1385
56	RADIO, TV, ETC., EQUIP.	3459	590	990	208	1131	3534	532	91	4806
57	ELECTRONIC COMPONENTS	1369	234	392	82	448	1399	211	36	1902
58	MISC. ELECTRICAL MACH.	1197	204	342	72	391	1223	184	32	1663
59	MOTOR VEHICLES, EQUIP.	2533	432	724	152	828	2587	390	67	3519
60	AIRCRAFT & PARTS	23118	2844	4767	1001	5486	33972	2563	441	29151
61	OTHER TRANSPORT. EQUIP.	21489	3668	6147	1291	7025	21954	3306	568	29857
62	PROFESS., SCIEN. INSTRU.	2567	438	734	154	839	2623	395	68	3567
63	MEDICAL, PHOTO. EQUIP.	1635	279	468	98	534	1670	251	43	2271
64	MISC. MANUFACTURING	2562	437	733	154	838	2618	394	68	3560
65	TRANSPORT. & WAREHOUSING	15028	2565	4299	903	4913	15353	2312	397	20880
66	COMMUNICA., EXC. BRDCAST.	2879	491	824	173	941	2942	443	76	4001
67	RADIO & TV BROADCASTING	0	0	0	0	0	0	0	0	0
68	ELEC.,GAS,WATER,SAN.SER.	1309	223	375	79	428	1338	201	35	1819
69	WHOLESALE & RETAIL TRADE	2984	509	854	179	976	3049	459	79	4146
70	FINANCE & INSURANCE	1294	221	370	78	423	1322	199	34	1798
71	REAL ESTATE & RENTAL	10497	406	1552	1076	4128	5733	176	617	7339
72	HOTELS; PERSONAL SERV.	6076	1037	1738	-365	1986	6207	935	161	8442
73	BUSINESS SERVICES	-3249	-555	-930	-195	-1062	-3320	-500	-86	-4515
74	RESEARCH & DEVELOPMENT	24663	3331	2833	750	4978	13719	3105	315	13720
75	AUTO. REPAIR & SERVICES	199	18	183	98	489	378	99	20	111
76	AMUSEMENTS	322	47	25	14	58	180	22	8	71
77	MED.,EDUC. SERVICES	32623	5089	8285	1832	9857	30151	4478	885	39466
78	FEDERAL GOV'T ENTERPRISE	1425	243	408	86	466	1456	219	38	1980
79	STATE & LOCAL GOV'T ENT.	0	0	0	0	0	0	0	0	0
80	IMPORTS	23692	4044	6777	1424	7746	24205	3645	626	32919
81	BUS.TRAVEL, ENT., GIFTS.	0	0	0	0	0	0	0	0	0
82	OFFICE SUPPLIES	0	0	0	0	0	0	0	0	0
83	SCRAP & USED GOODS	-109943	-18764	-31450	-6607	-35943	-112322	-16914	-2907	-152758
84	GOVERNMENT INDUSTRY	41188	68658	108965	24112	103881	397291	61150	10804	543741
85	REST OF WORLD INDUSTRY	-2872	-243	-389	-271	-1705	-1890	-189	-168	-856
86	HOUSEHOLD INDUSTRY	0	0	0	0	0	0	0	0	0
87	INVENTORY VALUATION ADJ.	0	0	0	0	0	0	0	0	0
88	STATE TOTAL	624093	95160	161602	36182	173855	595148	85053	17163	741672

*The data for this industry could not be made entirely consistent with the 1947 state output estimates. (See page 215.)

TABLE C.17

STATE ESTIMATES OF 1947
FEDERAL GOVERNMENT PURCHASES
(THOUSANDS OF CURRENT DOLLARS)

INDUSTRY TITLE	46 WASHINGTON	47 WEST VIRGINIA	48 WISCONSIN	49 WYOMING	50 ALASKA	51 HAWAII	52 NO STATE ALLOCATION	53 NATIONAL TOTAL
1 LIVESTOCK & PRDTS.	-406	-160	-196	-2451	0	0	0	-28012
2 OTHER AGRICULTURE PRDTS.	4257	562	1153	305	0	0	0	130772
3 FORESTRY & FISHERIES	-63	-12	-14	0	0	0	0	-931
4 AGRI.,FORES.,FISH. SERV.	-1204	-160	-303	-82	0	0	0	-36015
5 IRON, FERRO. ORES MINING	0	0	0	0	0	0	0	0
6 NONFERROUS ORES MINING	0	0	0	0	0	0	0	-2377
7 COAL MINING	34	5463	0	249	0	0	0	21302
8 CRUDE PETRO.NATURAL GAS	0	0	0	0	0	0	0	0
9 STONE & CLAY MINING	3	0	0	0	0	0	0	801
10 CHEM.&FERT. MIN. MINING	0	0	0	0	0	0	0	2
11 NEW CONSTRUCTION*	41027	9221	14641	6746	0	0	0	959000
12 MAINT. & REPAIR CONSTR.	15143	2015	3813	1035	0	0	0	452868
13 ORDNANCE & ACCESSORIES	625	83	157	43	0	0	0	18687
14 FOOD & KINDRED PRDTS.	8995	1197	2265	615	0	0	0	269019
15 TOBACCO MANUFACTURES	0	0	0	0	0	0	0	0
16 FABRICS	2162	288	545	148	0	0	0	64672
17 TEXTILE PRDTS.	1194	159	301	82	0	0	0	35715
18 APPAREL	866	115	218	59	0	0	0	25903
19 MISC. TEXTILE PRDTS.	867	115	218	59	0	0	0	10193
20 LUMBER & WOOD PRDTS.	1114	93	248	18	0	0	0	47855
21 WOODEN CONTAINERS	1600	213	403	109	0	0	0	4163
22 HOUSEHOLD FURNITURE	139	19	35	10	0	0	0	42264
23 OTHER FURNITURE	1413	188	356	97	0	0	0	36661
24 PAPER & ALLIED PRDTS.	1226	163	309	84	0	0	0	9094
25 PAPERBOARD CONTAINERS	304	40	77	21	0	0	0	15383
26 PRINTING & PUBLISHING	514	68	130	35	0	0	0	25115
27 CHEMICALS,SELECT. PRDTS.	840	112	211	57	0	0	0	2114
28 PLASTICS & SYNTHETICS	71	9	18	5	0	0	0	
29 DRUGS & COSMETICS	1553	207	391	106	0	0	0	46442
30 PAINT & ALLIED PRDTS.	1303	173	328	89	0	0	0	38956
31 PETROLEUM, RELATED INDS.	6267	834	1578	428	0	0	0	187423
32 RUBBER, MISC. PLASTICS	790	105	199	54	0	0	0	23637
33 LEATHER TANNING & PRDTS.	85	11	21	6	0	0	0	2542
34 FOOTWEAR, LEATHER PRDTS.	1011	135	255	69	0	0	0	30236
35 GLASS & GLASS PRDTS.	57	8	14	4	0	0	0	1717
36 STONE & CLAY PRDTS.	129	17	32	9	0	0	0	3853
37 PRIMARY IRON, STEEL MFR.	552	74	139	38	0	0	0	16520
38 PRIMARY NONFERROUS MFR.	1942	258	489	133	0	0	0	58078

#	Industry								
39	METAL CONTAINERS	12	2	3	1	0	0	0	345
40	FABRICATED METAL PRDTS.	314	42	79	21	0	0	0	9392
41	SCREW MACH. PRDTS., ETC.	73	10	18	5	0	0	0	2192
42	OTHER FAB. METAL PRDTS.	411	55	104	28	0	0	0	12298
43	ENGINES & TURBINES	1064	142	268	73	0	0	0	31822
44	FARM MACH. & EQUIP.	104	14	26	7	0	0	0	3123
45	CONSTRUC. MACH. & EQUIP.	454	60	114	31	0	0	0	13587
46	MATERIAL HANDLING MACH.	168	22	42	11	0	0	0	5022
47	METALWORKING MACHINERY	268	36	67	18	0	0	0	8007
48	SPECIAL MACH. & EQUIP.	99	13	25	7	0	0	0	2959
49	GENERAL MACH. & EQUIP.	586	78	148	40	0	0	0	17540
50	MACHINE SHOP PRDTS.	173	23	44	12	0	0	0	5168
51	OFFICE, COMPUT. MACHINES	101	13	25	7	0	0	0	3023
52	SERVICE IND. MACHINES	205	27	51	14	0	0	0	6116
53	ELECT. TRANSMISS. EQUIP.	2366	315	596	162	0	0	0	70763
54	HOUSEHOLD APPLIANCES	261	35	66	18	0	0	0	7812
55	ELECTRIC LIGHTING EQUIP.	666	89	168	46	0	0	0	19921
56	RADIO, TV, ETC., EQUIP.	2312	308	582	158	0	0	0	69132
57	ELECTRONIC COMPONENTS	915	122	230	63	0	0	0	27360
58	MISC. ELECTRICAL MACH.	800	106	201	55	0	0	0	23924
59	MOTOR VEHICLES, EQUIP.	1692	225	426	116	0	0	0	50615
60	AIRCRAFT & PARTS	20983	1517	3868	796	0	0	0	642309
61	OTHER TRANSPORT. EQUIP.	14360	1911	3616	981	0	0	0	429462
62	PROFESS., SCIEN. INSTRU.	1716	228	432	117	0	0	0	51305
63	MEDICAL, PHOTO. EQUIP.	1092	145	275	75	0	0	0	32669
64	MISC. MANUFACTURING	1712	228	431	117	0	0	0	51205
65	TRANSPORT. & WAREHOUSING	10043	1337	2529	686	0	0	0	300345
66	COMMUNICA., EXC. BRDCAST.	1924	256	484	132	0	0	0	57544
67	RADIO & TV BROADCASTING	0	0	0	0	0	0	0	0
68	ELEC.,GAS,WATER,SAN.SER.	875	116	220	60	0	0	0	26168
69	WHOLESALE & RETAIL TRADE	1994	265	502	136	0	0	0	59643
70	FINANCE & INSURANCE	865	115	218	59	0	0	0	25856
71	REAL ESTATE & RENTAL	4746	2311	4710	423	0	0	0	176412
72	HOTELS; PERSONAL SERV.	4060	540	1022	277	0	0	0	121426
73	BUSINESS SERVICES	-2172	-289	-547	-148	0	0	0	-64942
74	RESEARCH & DEVELOPMENT	10271	868	2834	490	0	0	0	365260
75	AUTO. REPAIR & SERVICES	631	62	101	159	0	0	0	7888
76	AMUSEMENTS	74	45	81	8	0	0	0	6100
77	MED.,EDUC. SERVICES	19675	2944	5922	1336	0	0	0	614835
78	FEDERAL GOV'T ENTERPRISE	953	127	240	65	0	0	0	28486
79	STATE & LOCAL GOV'T ENT.	0	0	0	0	0	0	0	0
80	IMPORTS	15833	2107	3987	1082	0	0	0	473503
81	BUS. TRAVEL, ENT., GIFTS.	0	0	0	0	0	0	0	0
82	OFFICE SUPPLIES	0	0	0	0	0	0	0	0
83	SCRAP & USED GOODS	-73472	-9779	-18500	-5021	0	0	0	-2197267
84	GOVERNMENT INDUSTRY	272739	41486	67563	17195	0	0	0	9288000
85	REST OF WORLD INDUSTRY	-896	-437	-1060	-87	0	0	0	-50000
86	HOUSEHOLD INDUSTRY	0	0	0	0	0	0	0	0
87	INVENTORY VALUATION ADJ.	0	0	0	0	0	0	1556000	0
88	STATE TOTAL	415460	69456	110244	28009	0	0	1556000	13375897

*The data for this industry could not be made entirely consistent with the 1947 state output estimates. (See page 215.)

TABLE C.18

STATE ESTIMATES OF 1958
FEDERAL GOVERNMENT PURCHASES
(THOUSANDS OF CURRENT DOLLARS)

INDUSTRY TITLE	1 ALABAMA	2 ARIZONA	3 ARKANSAS	4 CALIFORNIA	5 COLORADO	6 CONNECTICUT	7 DELAWARE	8 DISTRICT OF COLUMBIA	9 FLORIDA
1 LIVESTOCK & PRDTS.	16	-569	12	-256	-563	5	4	0	9
2 OTHER AGRICULTURE PRDTS.	16851	10175	8972	81240	16645	10513	1702	133092	19174
3 FORESTRY & FISHERIES	-3576	-361	-2384	-19429	-134	-180	-1017	0	-6542
4 AGRI.,FORES.,FISH. SERV.	1049	507	292	5848	777	215	142	2059	1446
5 IRON, FERRO. ORES MINING	0	0	0	0	0	0	0	0	0
6 NONFERROUS ORES MINING	6358	21507	7488	2988	9729	1360	0	0	0
7 COAL MINING	0	0	0	0	0	0	0	0	0
8 CRUDE PETRO.,NATURAL GAS	0	0	0	426	0	0	0	0	0
9 STONE & CLAY MINING	0	972	0	1892	0	0	0	0	0
10 CHEM.&FERT. MIN. MINING	0	0	0	0	0	0	0	0	0
11 NEW CONSTRUCTION	53293	80490	42122	372048	38317	42293	8850	18463	97111
12 MAINT. & REPAIR CONSTR.	25257	12193	7010	140827	18686	5129	3414	48912	34834
13 ORDNANCE & ACCESSORIES	15329	31589	1331	533673	25195	88311	883	575	23647
14 FOOD & KINDRED PRDTS.	492	140	132	11604	630	52	108	26	1858
15 TOBACCO MANUFACTURES	0	0	0	0	0	0	0	0	0
16 FABRICS	56	0	4	122	8	23	3	65	10
17 TEXTILE PRDTS.	51	0	0	74	0	21	3	0	1
18 APPAREL	2279	36	31	326	59	142	9	465	71
19 MISC. TEXTILE PRDTS.	446	38	33	845	322	5046	2675	496	491
20 LUMBER & WOOD PRDTS.	-147	-34	-133	-699	-25	-15	-5	-1	-89
21 WOODEN CONTAINERS	41	4	3	93	29	4	1	47	40
22 HOUSEHOLD FURNITURE	640	295	149	3653	445	82	90	561	910
23 OTHER FURNITURE	610	294	168	3401	450	122	82	1159	841
24 PAPER & ALLIED PRDTS.	1776	832	440	10061	1262	273	247	2195	2500
25 PAPERBOARD CONTAINERS	115	56	33	635	86	25	15	250	157
26 PRINTING & PUBLISHING	2318	1077	556	13183	1630	326	325	2444	3280
27 CHEMICALS,SELECT. PRDTS.	30891	788	530	9333	1557	889	11507	1220	30059
28 PLASTICS & SYNTHETICS	166	5	4	-1564	8	100	157	62	336
29 DRUGS & COSMETICS	367	214	172	6999	406	1978	196	2649	505
30 PAINT & ALLIED PRDTS.	79	34	14	464	50	3	12	-38	116
31 PETROLEUM, RELATED INDS.	3115	571	1392	134533	6360	1045	7929	2272	5154
32 RUBBER, MISC. PLASTICS	715	10	0	1986	192	1891	271	9	78
33 LEATHER TANNING & PRDTS.	0	0	0	0	0	0	0	0	0
34 FOOTWEAR, LEATHER PRDTS.	17	10	2262	131	17	47	2	161	19
35 GLASS & GLASS PRDTS.	4	0	4	328	8	5	0	0	6
36 STONE & CLAY PRDTS.	61	3	3	1565	5	68	1	83	6
37 PRIMARY IRON, STEEL MFR.	1508	35	30	1959	132	481	63	415	70
38 PRIMARY NONFERROUS MFR.	2856	627	738	8929	74	15176	81	63	427

#	Sector	C1	C2	C3	C4	C5	C6	C7	C8	C9
39	METAL CONTAINERS	4	0	0	-376	1600	0	268	0	36
40	FABRICATED METAL PRDTS.	-277	-1195	0	-439	76	-84	52	-12	297
41	SCREW MACH. PRDTS., ETC.	532	86	96	6591	148	1652	98	1124	234
42	OTHER FAB. METAL PRDTS.	692	86	183	10915	239	3120	125	1003	397
43	ENGINES & TURBINES	59	1460	31	4816	58	54894	6	4558	545
44	FARM MACH. & EQUIP.	-129	-78	-37	-784	-89	-9	-22	-51	-232
45	CONSTRUC. MACH. & EQUIP.	93	31	18	1190	265	139	30	214	305
46	MATERIAL HANDLING MACH.	1699	114	627	6563	2855	11415	51	56	540
47	METALWORKING MACHINERY	224	154	27	12254	256	10472	185	419	1123
48	SPECIAL MACH. & EQUIP.	81	6	8	3198	84	1758	41	131	353
49	GENERAL MACH. & EQUIP.	69	5	31	8289	20	9591	3	55	23
50	MACHINE SHOP PRDTS.	80	3	0	4899	124	2635	27	12	526
51	OFFICE, COMPUT. MACHINES	118	544	63	5242	68	1089	16804	476	1739
52	SERVICE IND. MACHINES	63	124	105	4252	41	1658	16	2203	61
53	ELECT. TRANSMISS. EQUIP.	302	25	9	14343	842	4125	6	126	482
54	HOUSEHOLD APPLIANCES	37	9	-8	5539	39	299	56	113	-248
55	ELECTRIC LIGHTING EQUIP.	504	-18	260	2455	-44	3059	14	-630	1
56	RADIO, TV, ETC., EQUIP.	25	1614	4	115195	58	12881	36	227	2988
57	ELECTRONIC COMPONENTS	1508	382	31	31012	41	4788	0	139	1072
58	MISC. ELECTRICAL MACH.	58	46	0	2495	131	527	0	466	698
59	MOTOR VEHICLES, EQUIP.	2604	154	231	13916	757	945	4514	1729	745
60	AIRCRAFT & PARTS	55421	42484	-1	940954	3226	684964	4162	-638	36031
61	OTHER TRANSPORT. EQUIP.	3712	171	113	43089	116	91003	457	18124	3896
62	PROFESS., SCIEN. INSTRU.	249	515	483	31380	473	27680	308	1761	411
63	MEDICAL, PHOTO. EQUIP.	862	250	0	12749	256	2089	1884	1028	1078
64	MISC. MANUFACTURING	682	218	66	4389	459	809	125	1353	354
65	TRANSPORT. & WAREHOUSING	23895	14222	9208	163785	19508	22033	4770	59516	40029
66	COMMUNICA.,EXC. BRDCAST.	4281	1984	1015	24381	2999	583	602	4239	6068
67	RADIO & TV BROADCASTING	0	0	0	0	0	0	0	0	0
68	ELEC.,GAS,WATER,SAN.SER.	8783	4079	2098	49980	6167	1222	1233	9054	12436
69	WHOLESALE & RETAIL TRADE	9515	6917	4172	76273	8065	13501	2106	9420	20732
70	FINANCE & INSURANCE	5	3	86	86	15	15	3	15	14
71	REAL ESTATE & RENTAL	1489	762	638	9620	1053	1691	190	4905	2419
72	HOTELS; PERSONAL SERV.	6059	2848	1520	34261	4325	963	841	7944	8509
73	BUSINESS SERVICES	12562	5798	2927	71698	8749	1627	1773	11234	17855
74	RESEARCH & DEVELOPMENT	51764	6938	2587	1367269	24903	54855	73818	30068	58324
75	AUTO. REPAIR & SERVICES	1756	1065	767	11171	1362	1901	217	5427	2796
76	AMUSEMENTS	88	70	70	3231	267	133	57	151	577
77	MED.,EDUC. SERVICES	974	612	314	19260	1620	1807	236	2140	1723
78	FEDERAL GOV'T ENTERPRISE	1370	648	352	7722	986	231	189	1987	1916
79	STATE & LOCAL GOV'T ENT.	2590	1264	746	14361	1943	571	346	5660	3546
80	IMPORTS	66092	31258	15979	372561	47570	11167	9116	96073	92448
81	BUS.TRAVEL, ENT., GIFTS.	0	0	0	0	0	0	0	0	0
82	OFFICE SUPPLIES	1170	706	623	5640	1156	730	118	9239	1331
83	SCRAP & USED GOODS	-650	523	1582	-8840	1234	2778	-324	39960	-2565
84	GOVERNMENT INDUSTRY	401048	192210	103363	2244895	293845	76573	54599	707771	555922
85	REST OF WORLD INDUSTRY	-5887	-1709	-2456	-27118	-3208	-4187	-603	-6401	-7501
86	HOUSEHOLD INDUSTRY	0	0	0	0	0	0	0	0	0
87	INVENTORY VALUATION ADJ.	0	0	0	0	0	0	0	0	0
88	STATE TOTAL	819213	478949	225229	7052332	557011	1295121	216289	1250092	1086557

TABLE C.18

STATE ESTIMATES OF 1958
FEDERAL GOVERNMENT PURCHASES
(THOUSANDS OF CURRENT DOLLARS)

INDUSTRY TITLE	10 GEORGIA	11 IDAHO	12 ILLINOIS	13 INDIANA	14 IOWA	15 KANSAS	16 KENTUCKY	17 LOUISIANA	18 MAINE
1 LIVESTOCK & PRDTS.	22	-434	62	39	100	27	19	10	5
2 OTHER AGRICULTURE PRDTS.	19398	4859	59101	18022	13342	13240	13010	14751	4927
3 FORESTRY & FISHERIES	-6171	-1066	-565	-350	-208	-22	-823	-5623	-3968
4 AGRI.,FORES.,FISH. SERV.	1673	125	1640	447	165	723	932	560	262
5 IRON, FERRO. ORES MINING	0	11510	0	0	0	0	0	0	19
6 NONFERROUS ORES MINING	38	0	1341	0	0	306	766	8312	0
7 COAL MINING	0	0	0	0	0	0	0	0	0
8 CRUDE PETRO.,NATURAL GAS	0	0	0	0	0	0	0	0	0
9 STONE & CLAY MINING	0	0	0	0	0	0	0	0	0
10 CHEM.&FERT. MIN. MINING	0	23465	5670	0	0	0	0	0	0
11 NEW CONSTRUCTION	70536	3001	137214	59064	61771	66691	67148	86746	15013
12 MAINT. & REPAIR CONSTR.	40318	252	39263	10696	3892	17383	22438	13436	6311
13 ORDNANCE & ACCESSORIES	3731	425	65480	103970	21929	9127	627	17430	5896
14 FOOD & KINDRED PRDTS.	713	0	3884	655	718	490	483	1156	43
15 TOBACCO MANUFACTURES	0	2	0	0	0	0	0	0	0
16 FABRICS	372	0	99	9	7	106	165	7	2
17 TEXTILE PRDTS.	181	17	80	37	0	0	1	5	0
18 APPAREL	986	18	323	335	57	63	140	783	17
19 MISC. TEXTILE PRDTS.	72	-132	1243	67	50	49	573	1235	61
20 LUMBER & WOOD PRDTS.	-168	2	-115	-120	-49	-9	-61	-116	-94
21 WOODEN CONTAINERS	7	57	21	6	38	5	5	155	2
22 HOUSEHOLD FURNITURE	1072	72	772	197	26	429	582	301	155
23 OTHER FURNITURE	975	176	941	256	92	419	542	323	152
24 PAPER & ALLIED PRDTS.	2928	14	2353	617	141	1202	1602	873	435
25 PAPERBOARD CONTAINERS	181	217	187	52	21	79	101	63	29
26 PRINTING & PUBLISHING	3853	2414	2933	760	138	1562	2099	1115	565
27 CHEMICALS,SELECT. PRDTS.	25705	2	49618	19930	1248	3259	34928	6033	66
28 PLASTICS & SYNTHETICS	82	138	2	56	124	6	347	243	0
29 DRUGS & COSMETICS	1119	94	12044	7894	712	1433	497	409	0
30 PAINT & ALLIED PRDTS.	140	4	60	13	-8	51	74	31	18
31 PETROLEUM, RELATED INDS.	1686	91	15598	14888	2461	15414	8973	104452	1833
32 RUBBER, MISC. PLASTICS	258	0	11525	9680	211	96	56	7	75
33 LEATHER TANNING & PRDTS.	0	0	0	0	0	0	0	0	0
34 FOOTWEAR, LEATHER PRDTS.	20	5	1181	67	165	13	13	15	5
35 GLASS & GLASS PRDTS.	6	0	137	76	0	2	6	7	0
36 STONE & CLAY PRDTS.	6	2	75	190	4	4	37	5	17
37 PRIMARY IRON, STEEL MFR.	101	15	14222	17989	118	52	338	77	17
38 PRIMARY NONFERROUS MFR.	295	224	51993	34743	1036	177	565	1307	75

#	Industry	C1	C2	C3	C4	C5	C6	C7	C8	C9
39	METAL CONTAINERS	878	0	1190	123	0	2	6	26	35
40	FABRICATED METAL PRDTS.	-10	1	664	500	205	134	-29	126	-10
41	SCREW MACH. PRDTS., ETC.	459	43	15339	4583	182	126	376	141	42
42	OTHER FAB. METAL PRDTS.	228	39	17824	5273	534	229	896	241	101
43	ENGINES & TURBINES	68	17	6377	15629	949	46	45	77	17
44	FARM MACH. & EQUIP.	-187	5	2857	447	1866	96	99	-51	-42
45	CONSTRUC. MACH. & EQUIP.	703	8	28663	589	1055	142	663	50	21
46	MATERIAL HANDLING MACH.	94	1	31494	1133	74	242	297	5	65
47	METALWORKING MACHINERY	4364	32	15639	4899	586	1028	429	117	15
48	SPECIAL MACH. & EQUIP.	1608	8	1515	802	49	350	71	41	5
49	GENERAL MACH. & EQUIP.	35	11	33044	18248	43	74	335	22	14
50	MACHINE SHOP PRDTS.	2400	6	1921	1245	18	522	117	43	0
51	OFFICE, COMPUT. MACHINES	89	17	1124	192	403	48	815	264	18
52	SERVICE IND. MACHINES	185	11	5626	1394	872	1857	340	53	87
53	ELECT. TRANSMISS. EQUIP.	2270	4	14984	9076	176	38	949	21	4
54	HOUSEHOLD APPLIANCES	26	-4	4811	8566	6399	87	264	39	-55
55	ELECTRIC LIGHTING EQUIP.	96	-23	-99	-27	-36	-43	39	100	222
56	RADIO, TV, ETC., EQUIP.	64	-7	247996	70687	10107	52	-68	19	72
57	ELECTRONIC COMPONENTS	129	0	14508	9070	1609	386	100	61	25
58	MISC. ELECTRICAL MACH.	608	17	6208	15397	302	402	19	302	69
59	MOTOR VEHICLES, EQUIP.	5197	81	12310	38468	728	1768	61	919	66
60	AIRCRAFT & PARTS	373929	-45	84529	160258	10180	307058	634	4681	8717
61	OTHER TRANSPORT. EQUIP.	889	46	5150	936	371	133	508	250	146
62	PROFESS., SCIEN. INSTRU.	1121	203	43983	5180	846	223	328	146	0
63	MEDICAL, PHOTO. EQUIP.	247	1	10364	357	216	23	59	71	112
64	MISC. MANUFACTURING	318	51	1817	562	159	184	214	146	6127
65	TRANSPORT. & WAREHOUSING	35039	4955	67587	28295	11966	22640	21313	33070	1041
66	COMMUNICA., EXC. BRDCAST.	7136	393	5328	1374	226	2880	3882	2044	2138
67	RADIO & TV BROADCASTING	0	0	0	0	0	0	0	0	0
68	ELEC., GAS, WATER, SAN. SER.	14615	817	11048	2857	503	5915	7958	4214	2138
69	WHOLESALE & RETAIL TRADE	14209	2390	31796	14065	6227	10478	8602	15404	2535
70	FINANCE & INSURANCE	18	1	31	11	10	10	8	8	8
71	REAL ESTATE & RENTAL	2665	459	7515	1982	986	1109	963	1893	426
72	HOTELS; PERSONAL SERV.	9954	612	8178	2155	528	4108	5456	3005	1487
73	BUSINESS SERVICES	21030	1120	15239	3901	535	8432	11415	5928	3045
74	RESEARCH & DEVELOPMENT	8479	2384	599007	16725	7771	6008	7684	20514	12200
75	AUTO. REPAIR & SERVICES	3036	679	836C	2239	1157	1279	1140	2152	494
76	AMUSEMENTS	181	30	1026	237	135	103	152	198	224
77	MED., EDUC. SERVICES	1166	123	7375	1894	1138	765	719	1054	338
78	FEDERAL GOV'T ENTERPRISE	2236	144	1912	508	140	932	1230	690	652
79	STATE & LOCAL GOV'T ENT.	4087	326	4238	1167	468	1793	2289	338	16286
80	IMPORTS	107889	6944	92290	24530	6771	44968	59938	33321	342
81	BUS. TRAVEL, ENT., GIFTS.	1347	337	4103	1251	926	919	903	1024	132
82	OFFICE SUPPLIES	-4115	1095	12491	4191	4309	227	-1381	2029	99715
83	SCRAP & USED GOODS	645351	45686	606891	162370	54434	274904	357630	209381	-1856
84	GOVERNMENT INDUSTRY	-5668	-975	-20667	-6051	-4250	-4236	-4397	-3610	0
85	REST OF WORLD INDUSTRY	0	0	0	0	0	0	0	0	0
86	HOUSEHOLD INDUSTRY	0	0	0	0	0	0	0	0	0
87	INVENTORY VALUATION ADJ.	0	0	0	0	0	0	0	0	0
88	STATE TOTAL	1434597	113496	2546102	937574	240166	830817	669522	595539	187140

427

TABLE C.18

STATE ESTIMATES OF 1958
FEDERAL GOVERNMENT PURCHASES
(THOUSANDS OF CURRENT DOLLARS)

INDUSTRY TITLE	19 MARYLAND	20 MASSA-CHUSETTS	21 MICHIGAN	22 MINNESOTA	23 MISSISSIPPI	24 MISSOURI	25 MONTANA	26 NEBRASKA	27 NEVADA
1 LIVESTOCK & PRDTS.	9	5	20	53	13	36	-391	-25	-172
2 OTHER AGRICULTURE PRDTS.	19165	30621	28019	19297	9497	31112	6322	9741	2409
3 FORESTRY & FISHERIES	-2316	-6568	-1421	-890	-3147	-737	-501	-19	-17
4 AGRI.,FORES.,FISH. SERV.	1457	1190	593	279	491	943	158	364	167
5 IRON, FERRO. ORES MINING	0	0	0	0	0	0	10380	0	0
6 NONFERROUS ORES MINING	0	0	0	0	0	11433	0	0	7412
7 COAL MINING	0	0	0	0	0	0	0	0	0
8 CRUDE PETRO.,NATURAL GAS	0	0	0	0	0	0	0	0	0
9 STONE & CLAY MINING	0	853	0	0	0	0	0	0	0
10 CHEM.&FERT. MIN. MINING	0	0	0	0	0	0	1708	0	244
11 NEW CONSTRUCTION	48506	83089	106393	47759	36571	81216	30681	37031	12422
12 MAINT. & REPAIR CONSTR.	35091	28565	14155	6630	11799	22596	3791	8729	4020
13 ORDNANCE & ACCESSORIES	41843	76546	173318	97386	2312	93867	0	173	631
14 FOOD & KINDRED PRDTS.	958	4580	1020	1330	440	998	78	589	111
15 TOBACCO MANUFACTURES	0	0	0	0	0	0	0	0	0
16 FABRICS	14	344	97	170	6	182	3	5	1
17 TEXTILE PRDTS.	1	1211	65	97	9	87	0	34	0
18 APPAREL	191	1546	101	65	45	766	22	36	8
19 MISC. TEXTILE PRDTS.	71	2060	15817	247	1599	387	24	-9	9
20 LUMBER & WOOD PRDTS.	-43	-47	-101	-88	-145	-52	-80	-8	-8
21 WOODEN CONTAINERS	7	11	10	23	3	11	2	3	1
22 HOUSEHOLD FURNITURE	917	645	233	68	288	464	70	195	104
23 OTHER FURNITURE	848	687	338	157	284	542	91	210	97
24 PAPER & ALLIED PRDTS.	2520	1865	765	282	810	1390	220	565	286
25 PAPERBOARD CONTAINERS	158	133	69	34	54	107	18	41	374
26 PRINTING & PUBLISHING	3307	2386	921	306	1050	1747	271	721	958
27 CHEMICALS,SELECT. PRDTS.	22462	1565	43975	3228	12198	9416	1091	745	56
28 PLASTICS & SYNTHETICS	-53	299	295	29	8	18	3	5	13
29 DRUGS & COSMETICS	2313	2445	7035	1945	458	3110	121	385	151
30 PAINT & ALLIED PRDTS.	118	67	-7	-7	34	40	5	20	0
31 PETROLEUM, RELATED INDS.	2635	4757	6024	3229	6110	5309	2367	578	4
32 RUBBER, MISC. PLASTICS	1375	3860	10583	58	128	101	101	0	0
33 LEATHER TANNING & PRDTS.	0	0	0	0	0	0	0	10	0
34 FOOTWEAR, LEATHER PRDTS.	192	2391	28	55	10	2281	6	0	2
35 GLASS & GLASS PRDTS.	21	12	29	22	9	16	0	0	0
36 STONE & CLAY PRDTS.	6	46	9	123	3	10	2	225	1
37 PRIMARY IRON, STEEL MFR.	1099	873	11555	161	34	299	21	34	8
38 PRIMARY NONFERROUS MFR.	1888	5968	29458	168	91	1032	352	604	102

#	Industry	(1)	(2)	(3)	(4)	(5)	(6)	(7)	(8)	(9)
39	METAL CONTAINERS	902	86	988	23		90		0	
40	FABRICATED METAL PRDTS.	-353	42	612	164	0	24		0	
41	SCREW MACH. PRDTS., ETC.	698	1391	11179	293	1	441		90	
42	OTHER FAB. METAL PRDTS.	619	3186	13218	533	96	1019		117	0
43	ENGINES & TURBINES	67	4134	53681	776	193	429	0	34	3
44	FARM MACH. & EQUIP.	-235	-161	950	502	-33	156	24	-50	20
45	CONSTRUC. MACH. & EQUIP.	158	392	21621	308	139	559	53	15	24
46	MATERIAL HANDLING MACH.	263	2718	22568	1204	260	101	47	14	8
47	METALWORKING MACHINERY	1789	7936	24199	1576	61	4043	22	29	-29
48	SPECIAL MACH. & EQUIP.	237	1241	1811	269	25	1189	-16	7	56
49	GENERAL MACH. & EQUIP.	54	4750	22707	126	19	126	10	47	0
50	MACHINE SHOP PRDTS.	261	1403		374	18	1835	0	1	7
51	OFFICE, COMPUT. MACHINES	1675	2186	957	9226	34	118	19	0	2
52	SERVICE IND. MACHINES	1370	3121	4082	2831	27	2400	6	35	1
53	ELECT. TRANSMISS. EQUIP.	915	8806	5515	2019	112	6468	3	21	9
54	HOUSEHOLD APPLIANCES	1337	1150	-413	4380	1108	82	23	8	6
55	ELECTRIC LIGHTING EQUIP.	30	3093	-119	-6	814	1753	14	8	2
56	RADIO, TV, ETC., EQUIP.	45493	60636	10419	3522	137	1041	5	-47	-12
57	ELECTRONIC COMPONENTS	443	27838	3740	1665	158	508	-30	1480	254
58	MISC. ELECTRICAL MACH.	521	1091	6572	272	34	563	1	81	8
59	MOTOR VEHICLES, EQUIP.	2215	2000	102875	2251	739	12038	22	41	8
60	AIRCRAFT & PARTS	83668	138459	68712	11768	1905	774137	94	197	45
61	OTHER TRANSPORT. EQUIP.	8176	22891	12124	787	41196	700	-22	-49	339
62	PROFESS., SCIEN. INSTRU.	1245	26276	12910	5852	133	2118	39	82	15
63	MEDICAL, PHOTO. EQUIP.	791	5642	837	1362	-8	2137	87	168	31
64	MISC. MANUFACTURING	1194	1282	1768	602	99	484	22	22	13
65	TRANSPORT. & WAREHOUSING	30229	35905	41203	18608	11990	38654	27	53	54
66	COMMUNICA., EXC. BRDCAST.	6119	4375	1650	524	1934	3183	6038	9992	3758
67	RADIO & TV BROADCASTING	0	0	0	0	0	0	490	1322	692
68	ELEC.,GAS,WATER,SAN.SER.	12539	9018	3452	1128	3974	6588	1018	2726	1419
69	WHOLESALE & RETAIL TRADE	12140	15873	21897	9841	4625	18169	2744	4220	1689
70	FINANCE & INSURANCE	15	17	15	6	5	19	2	3	2
71	REAL ESTATE & RENTAL	2923	3281	3001	1389	672	2710	672	941	302
72	HOTELS; PERSONAL SERV.	8578	6416	2695	1030	2769	4815	766	1946	975
73	BUSINESS SERVICES	18007	12700	4619	1359	5656	9148	1391	3881	2035
74	RESEARCH & DEVELOPMENT	97133	188703	56648	73634	4457	47752	1512	6357	3673
75	AUTO. REPAIR & SERVICES	3289	3689	3414	1626	836	3075	905	1110	545
76	AMUSEMENTS	281	440	594	195	51	289	32	96	464
77	MED.,EDUC. SERVICES	3580	14646	4209	2205	363	2115	189	365	146
78	FEDERAL GOV'T ENTERPRISE	1931	1473	645	261	629	1119	180	448	220
79	STATE & LOCAL GOV'T ENT.	3572	3004	1571	775	1220	2420	413	920	410
80	IMPORTS	93178	71075	31139	12624	30359	54034	8715	21599	10605
81	BUS.TRAVEL, ENT., GIFTS.	1330	0	0	0	0	0	0	0	0
82	OFFICE SUPPLIES	-2645	2126	1945	1340	659	2160	439	676	167
83	SCRAP & USED GOODS		4009	7257	5932	363	5999	1458	1383	-215
84	GOVERNMENT INDUSTRY	560127	445648	212028	95082	185237	347796	57594	135927	64014
85	REST OF WORLD INDUSTRY	-4239	-10553	-9975	-6381	-2313	-9869	-1078	-2656	-520
86	HOUSEHOLD INDUSTRY	0	0	0	0	0	0	0	0	0
87	INVENTORY VALUATION ADJ.	0	0	0	0	0	0	0	0	0
88	STATE TOTAL	1186378	1395438	1245497	455991	382846	1623460	140755	254606	120664

TABLE C.18

STATE ESTIMATES OF 1958
FEDERAL GOVERNMENT PURCHASES
(THOUSANDS OF CURRENT DOLLARS)

INDUSTRY TITLE	28 NEW HAMPSHIRE	29 NEW JERSEY	30 NEW MEXICO	31 NEW YORK	32 NORTH CAROLINA	33 NORTH DAKOTA	34 OHIO	35 OKLAHOMA	36 OREGON
1 LIVESTOCK & PRDTS.	2	9	-311	29	20	13	34	18	-242
2 OTHER AGRICULTURE PRDTS.	2524	21605	10001	111910	16012	4702	43235	14011	13596
3 FORESTRY & FISHERIES	-340	-1585	-185	-2294	-5453	-31	-968	-294	-21376
4 AGRI.,FORES.,FISH. SERV.	281	1206	603	2449	1358	98	1263	947	253
5 IRON, FERRO. ORES MINING	0	0	0	0	0	0	0	0	0
6 NONFERROUS ORES MINING	19	96	3026	6607	2356	0	0	1226	7124
7 COAL MINING	0	0	0	0	0	0	0	0	0
8 CRUDE PETRO.,NATURAL GAS	0	0	0	0	0	426	0	0	0
9 STONE & CLAY MINING	0	0	0	0	0	0	0	0	0
10 CHEM.&FERT. MIN. MINING	0	1751	0	0	0	0	0	0	0
11 NEW CONSTRUCTION	14664	87626	40989	229736	41322	55390	165910	65405	77302
12 MAINT. & REPAIR CONSTR.	6785	29019	14516	58484	32711	2328	30261	22807	6038
13 ORDNANCE & ACCESSORIES	621	24319	20253	201685	50299	0	180104	1486	1022
14 FOOD & KINDRED PRDTS.	282	1266	42	4723	517	67	959	475	565
15 TOBACCO MANUFACTURES	0	0	0	0	0	0	0	0	0
16 FABRICS	18	835	5	34301	1066	2	597	8	10
17 TEXTILE PRDTS.	3	343	0	305	153	0	341	0	5
18 APPAREL	109	5667	35	3338	3106	16	232	2387	50
19 MISC. TEXTILE PRDTS.	9	13891	128	18874	10473	18	1371	52	51
20 LUMBER & WOOD PRDTS.	-45	-53	-17	-172	-193	0	-96	-16	-967
21 WOODEN CONTAINERS	1	1106	4	39	6	2	15	5	102
22 HOUSEHOLD FURNITURE	185	720	366	989	868	38	611	586	88
23 OTHER FURNITURE	164	700	350	1396	791	56	725	551	144
24 PAPER & ALLIED PRDTS.	502	2013	1017	3209	2372	125	1842	1619	306
25 PAPERBOARD CONTAINERS	30	132	66	286	147	11	144	103	30
26 PRINTING & PUBLISHING	663	2617	1326	3883	3120	150	2308	2118	359
27 CHEMICALS,SELECT. PRDTS.	40	41164	487	21753	12795	41	63468	691	648
28 PLASTICS & SYNTHETICS	2	456	5	130	350	2	333	6	8
29 DRUGS & COSMETICS	57	17898	191	30048	854	90	1815	365	293
30 PAINT & ALLIED PRDTS.	25	86	45	44	113	1	51	73	1
31 PETROLEUM, RELATED INDS.	177	18380	4327	37633	573	8255	21138	26199	235
32 RUBBER, MISC. PLASTICS	132	4432	0	4722	360	0	53173	104	26
33 LEATHER TANNING & PRDTS.	0	0	0	0	0	5	0	0	0
34 FOOTWEAR, LEATHER PRDTS.	4295	84	10	4727	201	0	168	14	14
35 GLASS & GLASS PRDTS.	1	81	0	153	7	1	229	23	2
36 STONE & CLAY PRDTS.	0	271	3	896	5	1	184	4	4
37 PRIMARY IRON, STEEL MFR.	51	1215	31	4221	70	15	28310	61	199
38 PRIMARY NONFERROUS MFR.	712	32541	31	30599	388	2	51628	389	1186

	A	B	C	D	E	F	G	H	I
39 METAL CONTAINERS		2791	0	1149	0		1374	706	14
40 FABRICATED METAL PRDTS.	0	-1946	19	217	124		738	214	80
41 SCREW MACH. PRDTS., ETC.	-13	4577	84	8126	296	0	13920	142	179
42 OTHER FAB. METAL PRDTS.	25	8234	77	10297	340	0	14526	332	500
43 ENGINES & TURBINES	75	32859	35	11340	1273	40	15269	92	47
44 FARM MACH. & EQUIP.	9	-174	-101	143	-186	35	430	-149	9
45 CONSTRUC. MACH. & EQUIP.	-53	1021	19	2425	53	16	6036	455	109
46 MATERIAL HANDLING MACH.	19	1023	0	1799	2881	-7	13301	303	1940
47 METALWORKING MACHINERY	0	4774	48	10086	164	7	31251	504	153
48 SPECIAL MACH. & EQUIP.	238	922	9	1617	132	0	4739	176	67
49 GENERAL MACH. & EQUIP.	74	10139	5	13697	17	22	46706	160	152
50 MACHINE SHOP PRDTS.	507	1104	5	1897	44	7	6936	253	53
51 OFFICE, COMPUT. MACHINES	90	6491	56	17864	107	2	2263	51	51
52 SERVICE IND. MACHINES	9	3287	22	6792	779	4	6138	968	40
53 ELECT. TRANSMISS. EQUIP.	1289	10485	13	21510	2679	17	25392	195	1410
54 HOUSEHOLD APPLIANCES	-8	3248	9	-10293	1057	10	31416	55	227
55 ELECTRIC LIGHTING EQUIP.	-6	1004	-48	1099	305	4	-55	-60	-43
56 RADIO, TV, ETC., EQUIP.	4158	294563	96	368189	22676	-23	20021	1508	450
57 ELECTRONIC COMPONENTS	2320	32991	237	37690	2274	7	6911	444	388
58 MISC. ELECTRICAL MACH.	9	3618	38	9724	1383	0	17507	96	221
59 MOTOR VEHICLES, EQUIP.	34	8429	147	12554	532	16	44253	1003	386
60 AIRCRAFT & PARTS	86	154269	122	673373	979	60	685234	28850	1426
61 OTHER TRANSPORT. EQUIP.	740	49749	62	79456	1139	-44	13286	170	4477
62 PROFESS., SCIEN. INSTRU.	184	89509	228	172547	1130	29	14980	546	512
63 MEDICAL, PHOTO. EQUIP.	40	7739	37	78586	273	62	3720	79	127
64 MISC. MANUFACTURING	83	2420	163	4341	327	41	2217	268	285
65 TRANSPORT. & WAREHOUSING	5158	42413	14277	117919	25203	6057	72010	24373	12111
66 COMMUNICA., EXC. BRDCAST.	1231	4828	2443	6973	5779	268	4200	3914	637
67 RADIO & TV BROADCASTING	0	0	0	0	0		0	0	0
68 ELEC.,GAS,WATER+SAN.SER.	2518	9914	5023	14566	11836	560	8698	8027	1342
69 WHOLESALE & RETAIL TRADE	2164	21866	6325	57222	9738	3165	38022	10601	5985
70 FINANCE & INSURANCE	3	23	6	51	12	1	30	9	3
71 REAL ESTATE & RENTAL	325	3169	1321	13484	1613	482	6059	1400	2117
72 HOTELS; PERSONAL SERV.	1703	6876	3470	11280	8066	440	6390	5516	1087
73 BUSINESS SERVICES	3636	14140	7179	19587	17027	748	12047	11500	1756
74 RESEARCH & DEVELOPMENT	12762	186387	108741	569268	5155	22316	109846	32917	5833
75 AUTO. REPAIR & SERVICES	370	3550	1682	14947	1877	590	6779	1644	2521
76 AMUSEMENTS	55	527	49	4488	164	22	756	120	106
77 MED.,EDUC. SERVICES	413	1981	945	15972	2035	128	4855	728	1410
78 FEDERAL GOV'T ENTERPRISE	381	1559	785	2689	1813	105	1489	1245	264
79 STATE & LOCAL GOV'T ENT.	683	2990	1491	6465	3318	259	3251	2331	680
80 IMPORTS	18393	75224	37886	129881	87446	5092	71864	60064	12759
81 BUS.TRAVEL, ENT.., GIFTS.	0	0	0	0	0		0	0	0
82 OFFICE SUPPLIES	175	1500	694	7769	1112	326	3001	973	944
83 SCRAP & USED GOODS	-996	175	-244	28403	-3226	1232	8677	-1081	3771
84 GOVERNMENT INDUSTRY	109119	459245	230285	878669	523403	34812	464699	362971	89306
85 REST OF WORLD INDUSTRY	-1014	-8434	-1468	-40664	-4943	-1223	-14907	-3722	-2894
86 HOUSEHOLD INDUSTRY	0	0	0	0	0				
37 INVENTORY VALUATION ADJ.	0	0	0	0	0	0	0	0	0
88 STATE TOTAL	198979	1870975	519621	4209895	914972	147511	2485660	702313	240074

TABLE C.18

STATE ESTIMATES OF 1958
FEDERAL GOVERNMENT PURCHASES
(THOUSANDS OF CURRENT DOLLARS)

INDUSTRY TITLE	37 PENNSYL-VANIA	38 RHODE ISLAND	39 SOUTH CAROLINA	40 SOUTH DAKOTA	41 TENNESSEE	42 TEXAS	43 UTAH	44 VERMONT	45 VIRGINIA
1 LIVESTOCK & PRDTS.	29	1	7	-21	17	50	-412	5	16
2 OTHER AGRICULTURE PRDTS.	54745	3214	6912	6208	25669	46328	7321	2650	19021
3 FORESTRY & FISHERIES	-869	-673	-3477	-74	-1378	-7148	-46	-369	-6830
4 AGRI.,FORES.,FISH. SERV.	1747	257	972	183	640	3605	373	51	2531
5 IRON, FERRO. ORES MINING	0	0	0	0	0	0	0	0	0
6 NONFERROUS ORES MINING	1915	0	0	498	8618	20492	13923	0	1379
7 COAL MINING	0	0	0	0	0	0	0	0	0
8 CRUDE PETRO.,NATURAL GAS	0	0	0	0	0	0	0	0	0
9 STONE & CLAY MINING	426	1876	0	0	0	2813	0	0	0
10 CHEM.&FERT. MIN. MINING	0	0	0	0	0	0	403	0	0
11 NEW CONSTRUCTION	133977	9696	35488	47481	39508	164969	40206	17988	55731
12 MAINT. & REPAIR CONSTR.	41870	6186	23446	4384	15296	86845	8976	1220	61059
13 ORDNANCE & ACCESSORIES	101560	2469	262	31	42336	55509	9152	7506	32330
14 FOOD & KINDRED PRDTS.	1442	13	820	11	266	2614	112	10	2320
15 TOBACCO MANUFACTURES	0	0	0	0	0	0	0	0	0
16 FABRICS	3706	630	3226	3	1759	31	4	2	1931
17 TEXTILE PRDTS.	1177	0	61	0	25	43	0	1	40
18 APPAREL	4089	11	124	22	6599	2651	26	25	1573
19 MISC. TEXTILE PRDTS.	9125	12	26	23	7383	567	27	10	1880
20 LUMBER & WOOD PRDTS.	-109	-3	-98	-9	-109	-138	-6	-28	-135
21 WOODEN CONTAINERS	41	16	2	2	2	52	3	1	7
22 HOUSEHOLD FURNITURE	879	163	653	89	283	2278	218	19	1693
23 OTHER FURNITURE	1005	149	568	105	366	2098	216	29	1478
24 PAPER & ALLIED PRDTS.	2612	446	1757	268	884	6251	615	63	4563
25 PAPERBOARD CONTAINERS	197	28	104	21	74	390	41	6	271
26 PRINTING & PUBLISHING	3297	586	2329	336	1089	8206	797	75	6046
27 CHEMICALS,SELECT. PRDTS.	15614	67	31199	113	74901	17487	1088	40	33690
28 PLASTICS & SYNTHETICS	183	1	150		800	715	3	3	1059
29 DRUGS & COSMETICS	16518	111	463	119	1362	1919	157	57	2289
30 PAINT & ALLIED PRDTS.	80	21	90		18	293	25		232
31 PETROLEUM, RELATED INDS.	16342	871	825	238	7843	194040	7240	207	3105
32 RUBBER, MISC. PLASTICS	4687	616	149		461	227	12	95	288
33 LEATHER TANNING & PRDTS.	0	0	0	0	0	0	0	0	0
34 FOOTWEAR, LEATHER PRDTS.	817	32	7	6	2597	194	7	126	39
35 GLASS & GLASS PRDTS.	222	0	13	0	21	57	0	2	6
36 STONE & CLAY PRDTS.	204	2	2	2	8	188	2	1	435
37 PRIMARY IRON, STEEL MFR.	22115	112	37	19	224	522	133	12	127
38 PRIMARY NONFERROUS MFR.	22991	4992	47	3	2950	3520	497	242	804

#	Industry									
39	METAL CONTAINERS	2170	0	0			1574			0
40	FABRICATED METAL PRDTS.	1279	0	43		129	450			-253
41	SCREW MACH. PRDTS., ETC.	10582	247	68		311	499	2	0	163
42	OTHER FAB. METAL PRDTS.	11614	383	72		818	1619	77	10	398
43	ENGINES & TURBINES	13937	11	24		89	226	65	23	125
44	FARM MACH. & EQUIP.	252	-46	-190	0	131	-545	61	50	-471
45	CONSTRUC. MACH. & EQUIP.	3745	9	11	54	123	761	25	9	74
46	MATERIAL HANDLING MACH.	18477	36	46	49	777	3916	-55	4	999
47	METALWORKING MACHINERY	9421	373	38	22	1969	3671	3456	9	195
48	SPECIAL MACH. & EQUIP.	473	139	61	-21	707	1298	2	1003	61
49	GENERAL MACH. & EQUIP.	12709	476	8	10	95	360	1910	246	16
50	MACHINE SHOP PRDTS.	318	210	12	0	1061	1900	713	59	54
51	OFFICE, COMPUT. MACHINES	3615	11	25	24	92	311	4	367	177
52	SERVICE IND. MACHINES	6882	7	22	8	186	687	1098	87	556
53	ELECT. TRANSMISS. EQUIP.	28522	22	10	3	1348	992	28	13	407
54	HOUSEHOLD APPLIANCES	-2117	10	737	22	3094	506	234	234	188
55	ELECTRIC LIGHTING EQUIP.	1303	3	-33	13	375	106	48	2	-81
56	RADIO, TV, ETC., EQUIP.	71111	-193	1300	5	6470	6659	6	128	7675
57	ELECTRONIC COMPONENTS	39104	34	839	-30	466	2743	-29	4	3899
58	MISC. ELECTRICAL MACH.	5223	117	24	17	332	601	11	547	246
59	MOTOR VEHICLES, EQUIP.	7792	179	124	82	1681	5570	356	83	1311
60	AIRCRAFT & PARTS	150448	55	1114	-58	892	623636	49	39	7033
61	OTHER TRANSPORT. EQUIP.	43393	910	1366	38	462	2247	2563	1636	132127
62	PROFESS., SCIEN. INSTRU.	85139	949	322	82	1455	4020	282	19	501
63	MEDICAL, PHOTO. EQUIP.	1568	2132	0	0	22	518	106	952	1114
64	MISC. MANUFACTURING	3664	25	83	24	311	1407	54	35	557
65	TRANSPORT. & WAREHOUSING	62080	118	16826	5812	22702	103713	197	20	41303
66	COMMUNICA., EXC. BRDCAST.	6015	4976	4326	611	1969	15188	10459	2427	11225
67	RADIO & TV BROADCASTING		1085	0	0	0	0			0
68	ELEC.,GAS,WATER,SAN.SER.	12437	2224	8845	1265	4095	31120	1468	133	22953
69	WHOLESALE & RETAIL TRADE	27823	1948	6333	2587	8106	43427	3016	279	14967
70	FINANCE & INSURANCE	25	2	2	2	210	42	4730	1211	1
71	REAL ESTATE & RENTAL	6260	515	851	526	1971	5006	4	1	3729
72	HOTELS; PERSONAL SERV.	9033	1518	5954	928	3086	21270	493	269	15466
73	BUSINESS SERVICES	17330	3196	12799	1753	5592	44706	2103	224	33198
74	RESEARCH & DEVELOPMENT	109962	6550	26211	7277	249954	120156	4291	368	656042
75	AUTO. REPAIR & SERVICES	6994	577	1037	671	2426	5833	3401	2093	4202
76	AMUSEMENTS	631	85	63	39	142	475	687	305	149
77	MED.,EDUC. SERVICES	6225	684	257	129	1100	3962	816	18	1316
78	FEDERAL GOV'T ENTERPRISE	2093	342	1329	216	727	4787	478	54	3455
79	STATE & LOCAL GOV'T ENT.	4466	629	2349	471	1668	8832	929	137	6123
80	IMPORTS	101047	16478	64129	10430	35112	230948	23066	2610	166681
81	BUS.TRAVEL, ENT., GIFTS.	3800	-223	0	0	1782	0	508	184	0
82	OFFICE SUPPLIES	9923	-534	480	431	5951	3216	316	722	1320
83	SCRAP & USED GOODS			-4185	1234		-6999			-10480
84	GOVERNMENT INDUSTRY	646457	98856	378284	67369	232271	1386963	141617	18118	984441
85	REST OF WORLD INDUSTRY	-18545	-1369	-2618	-1239	-9679	-14065	-1368	-835	-5945
86	HOUSEHOLD INDUSTRY	0		0	0	0	0			0
87	INVENTORY VALUATION ADJ.	0		0	0	0	0			0
88	STATE TOTAL	2007273	176078	635577	160957	833251	3292032	299810	64847	2336222

433

TABLE C.18

STATE ESTIMATES OF 1958
FEDERAL GOVERNMENT PURCHASES
(THOUSANDS OF CURRENT DOLLARS)

INDUSTRY TITLE	46 WASHINGTON	47 WEST VIRGINIA	48 WISCONSIN	49 WYOMING	50 ALASKA	51 HAWAII	52 NO STATE ALLOCATION	53 NATIONAL TOTAL
1 LIVESTOCK & PRDTS.	-52	3	48	-338	0	0	0	-3019
2 OTHER AGRICULTURE PRDTS.	19290	8490	16764	3555	0	0	0	1072960
3 FORESTRY & FISHERIES	-13700	-508	-1299	-67	0	0	0	-136999
4 AGRI.,FORES.,FISH. SERV.	1265	107	234	70	0	0	0	44997
5 IRON, FERRO. ORES MINING	0	0	0	0	0	0	0	0
6 NONFERROUS ORES MINING	18385	2394	651	0	0	0	0	191514
7 COAL MINING	0	0	0	0	0	0	0	0
8 CRUDE PETRO.,NATURAL GAS	0	0	0	0	0	0	0	0
9 STONE & CLAY MINING	0	0	0	0	0	0	0	9543
10 CHEM.&FERT. MIN. MINING	0	0	0	0	0	0	0	10776
11 NEW CONSTRUCTION	110797	48426	50426	30678	0	0	0	3388000
12 MAINT. & REPAIR CONSTR.	30453	2540	5560	1671	0	0	0	1080831
13 ORDNANCE & ACCESSORIES	6783	70750	26396	0	0	0	0	2269928
14 FOOD & KINDRED PRDTS.	748	31	1774	28	0	0	0	52798
15 TOBACCO MANUFACTURES	0	0	0	0	0	0	0	0
16 FABRICS	10	6	194	2	0	0	0	50233
17 TEXTILE PRDTS.	1	0	13	0	0	0	0	4345
18 APPAREL	70	165	335	12	0	0	0	39567
19 MISC. TEXTILE PRDTS.	72	1396	3901	13	0	0	0	103312
20 LUMBER & WOOD PRDTS.	-561	-37	-142	-8	0	0	0	-5527
21 WOODEN CONTAINERS	7	3	6	1	0	0	0	2004
22 HOUSEHOLD FURNITURE	778	18	53	26	0	0	0	25001
23 OTHER FURNITURE	735	60	131	40	0	0	0	26010
24 PAPER & ALLIED PRDTS.	2154	94	229	87	0	0	0	71644
25 PAPERBOARD CONTAINERS	138	13	29	8	0	0	0	5000
26 PRINTING & PUBLISHING	2816	95	245	104	0	0	0	92029
27 CHEMICALS,SELECT. PRDTS.	3507	90434	5160	38	0	0	0	740038
28 PLASTICS & SYNTHETICS	23	323	33	2	0	0	0	5470
29 DRUGS & COSMETICS	421	237	1582	68	0	0	0	132564
30 PAINT & ALLIED PRDTS.	97	-5	-7	1	0	0	0	2707
31 PETROLEUM, RELATED INDS.	7840	5633	269	5460	0	0	0	725757
32 RUBBER, MISC. PLASTICS	31	73	4852	0	0	0	0	117609
33 LEATHER TANNING & PRDTS.	0	0	0	0	0	0	0	0
34 FOOTWEAR, LEATHER PRDTS.	19	9	340	4	0	0	0	22840
35 GLASS & GLASS PRDTS.	24	82	1	0	0	0	0	1621
36 STONE & CLAY PRDTS.	6	3	64	1	0	0	0	4831
37 PRIMARY IRON, STEEL MFR.	252	703	3033	11	0	0	0	113179
38 PRIMARY NONFERROUS MFR.	8466	2094	7267	2	0	0	0	330400

#	Industry	(1)	(2)	(3)	(4)	(5)	(6)	(7)	(8)
39	METAL CONTAINERS	16	3	440	0	0	0	0	17001
40	FABRICATED METAL PRDTS.	-170	-77	342	0	0	0	0	1937
41	SCREW MACH. PRDTS., ETC.	457	365	5013	30	0	0	0	91419
42	OTHER FAB. METAL PRDTS.	552	477	2273	27	0	0	0	113890
43	ENGINES & TURBINES	4485	30	10366	12	0	0	0	239137
44	FARM MACH. & EQUIP.	-190	27	1668	-5	0	0	0	5212
45	CONSTRUC. MACH. & EQUIP.	121	42	4061	6	0	0	0	80009
46	MATERIAL HANDLING MACH.	1625	1959	2382	0	0	0	0	135919
47	METALWORKING MACHINERY	2737	2771	7120	22	0	0	0	171276
48	SPECIAL MACH. & EQUIP.	987	829	1508	7	0	0	0	29778
49	GENERAL MACH. & EQUIP.	392	11	16259	1	0	0	0	199523
50	MACHINE SHOP PRDTS.	1498	1284	2112	6	0	0	0	41402
51	OFFICE, COMPUT. MACHINES	88	30	101	456	0	0	0	75198
52	SERVICE IND. MACHINES	642	34	4752	8	0	0	0	64416
53	ELECT. TRANSMISS. EQUIP.	322	696	13964	3	0	0	0	181869
54	HOUSEHOLD APPLIANCES	284	66	-54024	3	0	0	0	21090
55	ELECTRIC LIGHTING EQUIP.	9	1601	-68	-17	0	0	0	17342
56	RADIO, TV, ETC., EQUIP.	448	49	4977	5	0	0	0	1396909
57	ELECTRONIC COMPONENTS	129	425	1547	0	0	0	0	234404
58	MISC. ELECTRICAL MACH.	150	39	14239	12	0	0	0	9092
59	MOTOR VEHICLES, EQUIP.	620	274	11202	47	0	0	0	306363
60	AIRCRAFT & PARTS	375084	671	7784	90	0	0	0	6499132
61	OTHER TRANSPORT. EQUIP.	46787	365	9810	22	0	0	0	655097
62	PROFESS., SCIEN. INSTRU.	1252	231	8719	46	0	0	0	549020
63	MEDICAL, PHOTO. EQUIP.	69	26	234	0	0	0	0	136627
64	MISC. MANUFACTURING	515	381	581	14	0	0	0	35598
65	TRANSPORT. & WAREHOUSING	31083	11365	18331	4157	0	0	0	1439090
66	COMMUNICA., EXC. BRDCAST.	5203	156	416	185	0	0	0	169003
67	RADIO & TV BROADCASTING	0	0	0	0	0	0	0	0
68	ELEC.,GAS,WATER,SAN.SER.	10672	345	900	388	0	0	0	348002
69	WHOLESALE & RETAIL TRADE	13358	5133	10138	2094	0	0	0	644600
70	FINANCE & INSURANCE	16	4	5	1	0	0	0	621
71	REAL ESTATE & RENTAL	2486	941	2049	278	0	0	0	112000
72	HOTELS; PERSONAL SERV.	7344	353	841	309	0	0	0	246000
73	BUSINESS SERVICES	15280	377	1064	513	0	0	0	491701
74	RESEARCH & DEVELOPMENT	34060	33905	33101	4893	0	0	0	5176997
75	AUTO. REPAIR & SERVICES	3050	1068	2304	395	0	0	0	128996
76	AMUSEMENTS	198	104	204	18	0	0	0	17681
77	MED.,EDUC. SERVICES	1674	311	0	90	0	0	0	115993
78	FEDERAL GOV'T ENTERPRISE	1659	93	215	74	0	0	0	56289
79	STATE & LOCAL GOV'T ENT.	3117	304	654	187	0	0	0	113101
80	IMPORTS	80018	4487	10402	3597	0	0	0	2716543
81	BUS.TRAVEL, ENT., GIFTS.					0	0	0	0
82	OFFICE SUPPLIES	1339	589	1164	247	0	0	0	74484
83	SCRAP & USED GOODS	-1205	2723	5213	958	0	0	0	116565
84	GOVERNMENT INDUSTRY	484272	35666	79335	24855	0	0	3030000	19950992
85	REST OF WORLD INDUSTRY	-5483	-2312	-5329	-579	0	0	0	-306999
86	HOUSEHOLD INDUSTRY	0	0	0	0	0	0	0	0
87	INVENTORY VALUATION ADJ.	0	0	0	0	0	0	0	0
88	STATE TOTAL	1327924	341854	371612	84924	0	0	3030000	53593696

TABLE C.19

STATE ESTIMATES OF 1963
FEDERAL GOVERNMENT PURCHASES
(THOUSANDS OF CURRENT DOLLARS)

INDUSTRY TITLE	1 ALABAMA	2 ARIZONA	3 ARKANSAS	4 CALIFORNIA	5 COLORADO	6 CONNECTICUT	7 DELAWARE	8 DISTRICT OF COLUMBIA	9 FLORIDA
1 LIVESTOCK & PRDTS.	95	51	48	389	87	35	12	433	92
2 OTHER AGRICULTURE PRDTS.	-304	-7419	-297	-36714	-2604	-477	51	-320	-15620
3 FORESTRY & FISHERIES	-4129	-492	-2897	-20256	-149	-399	-327	5	-8022
4 AGRI.,FORES.,FISH.SERV.	371	176	121	2326	330	55	60	316	583
5 IRON,FERRO.ORES MINING	0	511	44	44	4744	0	0	0	0
6 NONFERROUS ORES MINING	14759	41560	-1265	2263	56785	0	0	0	0
7 COAL MINING	1300	0	0	0	317	0	0	0	0
8 CRUDE PETRO.,NATURAL GAS	0	0	0	0	0	0	0	0	0
9 STONE & CLAY MINING	74	-449	115	-474	3	46	46	0	178
10 CHEM.&FERT.MIN.MINING	0	0	0	0	0	0	0	0	0
11 NEW CONSTRUCTION	111695	65898	71489	515812	75737	55753	8684	8726	190624
12 MAINT.& REPAIR CONSTR.	30316	15054	10472	168024	25726	7258	4156	80530	42257
13 ORDNANCE & ACCESSORIES	61929	38812	7741	1439286	27836	181371	3108	78019	105781
14 FOOD & KINDRED PRDTS.	5429	2836	2961	49312	4529	1224	715	2492	11771
15 TOBACCO MANUFACTURES	0	0	0	0	0	0	0	0	0
16 FABRICS	65	4	2	79	4	23	6	41	8
17 TEXTILE PRDTS.	143	36	25	350	50	29	5	435	66
18 APPAREL	3316	265	187	1913	368	332	40	3215	487
19 MISC. TEXTILE PRDTS.	362	66	47	821	256	3209	1691	805	386
20 LUMBER & WOOD PRDTS.	138	68	47	774	117	32	19	347	194
21 WOODEN CONTAINERS	93	2	1	176	60	1	0	19	86
22 HOUSEHOLD FURNITURE	355	180	125	1849	294	99	44	1226	466
23 OTHER FURNITURE	891	460	322	4378	725	283	102	3748	1105
24 PAPER & ALLIED PRDTS.	995	509	355	5041	818	297	120	3805	1271
25 PAPERBOARD CONTAINERS	228	110	77	1355	198	44	35	383	340
26 PRINTING & PUBLISHING	2714	1167	796	20823	2627	-81	572	-7151	5195
27 CHEMICALS,SELECT. PRDTS.	56407	9329	989	19835	13581	3013	9774	9666	43539
28 PLASTICS & SYNTHETICS	732	1	1	4840	4	632	1225	9	898
29 DRUGS & COSMETICS	723	397	275	4668	569	952	105	4778	767
30 PAINT & ALLIED PRDTS.	53	26	18	324	45	13	7	140	77
31 PETROLEUM, RELATED INDS.	3714	1019	1599	153208	6379	1322	7120	8239	5555
32 RUBBER, MISC. PLASTICS	245	108	74	7351	177	4053	2956	1283	1074
33 LEATHER TANNING & PRDTS.	11	5	4	69	10	2	1	22	17
34 FOOTWEAR, LEATHER PRDTS.	13	7	357	58	10	12	2	88	13
35 GLASS & GLASS PRDTS.	92	50	77	3561	162	42	8	611	93
36 STONE & CLAY PRDTS.	220	-15	-24	6805	-20	267	-4	183	-54
37 PRIMARY IRON, STEEL MFR.	76	23	22	3624	174	2906	68	236	75
38 PRIMARY NONFERROUS MFR.	-1562	-686	-266	-2906	-1156	4882	-114	-10153	-1404

#	Industry									
39	METAL CONTAINERS	9	0	0	413	453	3	72	5	71
40	FABRICATED METAL PRDTS.	2317	4912	51	7906	194	1009	17	973	345
41	SCREW MACH. PRDTS., ETC.	106	109	204	5046	231	864	123	703	275
42	OTHER FAB. METAL PRDTS.	242	192	269	6409	533	1036	60	1501	418
43	ENGINES & TURBINES	452	1400	174	4235	351	44885	37	6343	831
44	FARM MACH. & EQUIP.	199	92	61	1157	157	34	30	260	285
45	CONSTRUC. MACH. & EQUIP.	203	83	50	2002	391	207	44	767	474
46	MATERIAL HANDLING MACH.	908	118	343	4293	1442	5413	34	794	374
47	METALWORKING MACHINERY	489	198	145	10849	447	4388	73	2512	1196
48	SPECIAL MACH. & EQUIP.	175	83	58	1745	138	585	28	1003	257
49	GENERAL MACH. & EQUIP.	484	230	294	30046	698	20435	35	1983	580
50	MACHINE SHOP PRDTS.	103	4	9	7002	137	3046	31	161	628
51	OFFICE, COMPUT. MACHINES	2519	5469	1009	37866	1778	5454	75670	14966	10530
52	SERVICE IND. MACHINES	75	60	90	3179	47	1253	8	1887	69
53	ELECT. TRANSMISS. EQUIP.	1261	660	617	47777	7489	9338	70	5449	1421
54	HOUSEHOLD APPLIANCES	33	18	13	355	25	379	5	219	51
55	ELECTRIC LIGHTING EQUIP.	10	23	29	2002	115	349	42	73	69
56	RADIO, TV, ETC., EQUIP.	7879	33982	16976	1016517	6741	53926	606	48756	90984
57	ELECTRONIC COMPONENTS	804	11008	275	104593	790	14364	233	4917	5519
58	MISC. ELECTRICAL MACH.	395	214	94	12904	1373	2170	351	1619	1845
59	MOTOR VEHICLES, EQUIP.	12390	534	1012	14219	3191	2669	14955	6547	3376
60	AIRCRAFT & PARTS	136108	56900	2874	1259839	27025	754769	5204	48701	65560
61	OTHER TRANSPORT. EQUIP.	8271	1701	1167	92083	2156	136813	899	44692	8576
62	PROFESS., SCIEN. INSTRU.	1784	5961	1802	52287	3987	28979	718	11777	3436
63	MEDICAL, PHOTO. EQUIP.	1775	765	375	17642	930	1971	1830	7418	1926
64	MISC. MANUFACTURING	151	43	43	1263	96	206	26	203	67
65	TRANSPORT. & WAREHOUSING	19948	6169	5362	182185	15886	25106	11473	11254	18728
66	COMMUNICA.,EXC. BRDCAST.	7439	3581	2482	44811	6514	1329	1143	10870	11244
67	RADIO & TV BROADCASTING	0	0	0	0	0	0	0	0	0
68	ELEC.,GAS,WATER,SAN.SER.	6004	2688	1845	42620	5619	256	1146	-7267	10651
69	WHOLESALE & RETAIL TRADE	15421	7824	5457	80153	12788	4364	1930	54175	20196
70	FINANCE & INSURANCE	37112	0	0	0	0	0	0	0	0
71	REAL ESTATE & RENTAL	2630	1169	812	7847	2695	1639	227	9968	4431
72	HOTELS; PERSONAL SERV.	7797	3832	2662	44485	6688	1706	1112	17559	11178
73	BUSINESS SERVICES	28199	16896	7477	243739	25854	16543	4736	69290	56358
74	RESEARCH & DEVELOPMENT	0	0	0	0	0	0	0	0	0
75	AUTO. REPAIR & SERVICES	530	385	226	2747	374	98	67	279	867
76	AMUSEMENTS	1494	2687	431		941	772	320	443	3403
77	MED.,EDUC. SERVICES	22700	12609	10712	212114	21890	18133	2770	33582	41853
78	FEDERAL GOV'T ENTERPRISE	2487	1209	839	14598	2156	493	370	4584	3665
79	STATE & LOCAL GOV'T ENT.	4041	2189	1539	16569	3102	1705	353	25221	4209
80	IMPORTS	41959	31349	22255	315377	53857	12875	10615	116366	92074
81	BUS.TRAVEL, ENT., GIFTS.	0	0	0	0	0	0	0	0	0
82	OFFICE SUPPLIES	2060	5389	1005	29619	2896	987	145	8419	11486
83	SCRAP & USED GOODS	-1384	-480	-316	-14282	-1545	504	-418	12745	-3543
84	GOVERNMENT INDUSTRY	475170	232934	161767	2729596	408613	101624	68450	1023687	685776
85	REST OF WORLD INDUSTRY	-13029	-7123	-5011	-51377	-9887	-5753	-1066	-86376	-13072
86	HOUSEHOLD INDUSTRY	0	0	0	0	0	0	0	0	0
87	INVENTORY VALUATION ADJ.	0	0	0	0	0	0	0	0	0
88	STATE TOTAL	1131277	617734	341133	9024687	833159	1544152	244861	1711203	1546564

437

TABLE C.19

STATE ESTIMATES OF 1963
FEDERAL GOVERNMENT PURCHASES
(THOUSANDS OF CURRENT DOLLARS)

	INDUSTRY TITLE	10 GEORGIA	11 IDAHO	12 ILLINOIS	13 INDIANA	14 IOWA	15 KANSAS	16 KENTUCKY	17 LOUISIANA	18 MAINE
1	LIVESTOCK & PRDTS.	110	30	252	100	168	94	70	-57	24
2	OTHER AGRICULTURE PRDTS.	-477	-1320	-753	-335	-82	-11	20	-196	1443
3	FORESTRY & FISHERIES	-6473	-1132	-543	-354	-153	-24	-849	-9232	-5298
4	AGRI.,FORES.,FISH. SERV.	815	43	480	133	14	270	387	255	102
5	IRON, FERRO. ORES MINING			0	0	0	0	0	0	0
6	NONFERROUS ORES MINING	0	12159	9957	-258	0	8410	164	0	0
7	COAL MINING	0	0	2822	792	0	0	4784	0	0
8	CRUDE PETRO.,NATURAL GAS	0	0	0	0	64	0	0	40	0
9	STONE & CLAY MINING	341	11	258	173	0	89	173	0	17
10	CHEM.&FERT. MIN. MINING	0	0	263		-71	0	62	62	0
11	NEW CONSTRUCTION	61966	46140	141174	41257	33414	82010	97116	48372	5666
12	MAINT. & REPAIR CONSTR.	55028	4620	51455	14705	5986	20133	27196	20250	7705
13	ORDNANCE & ACCESSORIES	19347	3872	167375	275225	56575	27778	8250	66632	16788
14	FOOD & KINDRED PRDTS.	8379	8137	14605	6030	7683	3303	3395	4740	4158
15	TOBACCO MANUFACTURES		0	0		4	0		0	0
16	FABRICS	312	1	63	0	36	67	108	4	2
17	TEXTILE PRDTS.	64	15	259	133	278	35	38	41	14
18	APPAREL	1618	111	1364	710	67	276	388	1238	101
19	MISC. TEXTILE PRDTS.	118	28	958	93	25	64	400	820	52
20	LUMBER & WOOD PRDTS.	255	20	230	65	88	92	125	93	35
21	WOODEN CONTAINERS	3	1	7	2	96	1	2	381	1
22	HOUSEHOLD FURNITURE	582	60	665	192	299	226	295	233	87
23	OTHER FURNITURE	1323	163	1819	528	300	544	687	580	210
24	PAPER & ALLIED PRDTS.	1558	174	1946	564	95	620	798	652	239
25	PAPERBOARD CONTAINERS	461	31	337	95	-742	160	222	155	61
26	PRINTING & PUBLISHING	7973	136	1408	314	5966	2295	3591	1971	854
27	CHEMICALS,SELECT. PRDTS.	29458	28049	56162	18599	525	9921	63642	5460	382
28	PLASTICS & SYNTHETICS	379	0	815	267	14	115	1457	1191	0
29	DRUGS & COSMETICS	968	164	5585	3028	2696	756	492	487	150
30	PAINT & ALLIED PRDTS.	100	8	135	31	345	36	57	35	13
31	PETROLEUM,RELATED INDS.	2400	294	15405	13427	1	13475	8420	92957	1820
32	RUBBER, MISC. PLASTICS	2636	44	13482	11256	31	314	507	122	326
33	LEATHER TANNING & PRDTS.	23	1	17	5	51	8	11	8	3
34	FOOTWEAR, LEATHER PRDTS.	12	3	208	18	-32	7	8	8	3
35	GLASS & GLASS PRDTS.	91	21	491	289	312	49	54	59	19
36	STONE & CLAY PRDTS.	-36	-4	139	769	110	-36	128	-29	-9
37	PRIMARY IRON, STEEL MFR.	110	8	2939	3764		130	469	138	7
38	PRIMARY NONFERROUS MFR.	-1319	-318	3034	4360		-699	-365	-580	-294

#	Industry									
39	METAL CONTAINERS	10	49	4	6	0	68	636	1	271
40	FABRICATED METAL PRDTS.	65	105	1061	183	100	612	2425	98	814
41	SCREW MACH. PRDTS., ETC.	29	202	664	74	143	482	1619	24	599
42	OTHER FAB. METAL PRDTS.	60	266	1298	192	321	797	2484	60	355
43	ENGINES & TURBINES	94	283	261	238	456	11082	2829	104	439
44	FARM MACH. & EQUIP.	49	134	235	159	1345	164	736	28	407
45	CONSTRUC. MACH. & EQUIP.	41	99	886	190	79	750	36519	27	972
46	MATERIAL HANDLING MACH.	54	74	209	168	239	613	14963	27	141
47	METALWORKING MACHINERY	79	279	344	971	103	2152	4077	94	4189
48	SPECIAL MACH. & EQUIP.	32	107	112	179	1124	355	894	37	611
49	GENERAL MACH. & EQUIP.	131	308	4511	807	23	16731	21588	69	596
50	MACHINE SHOP PRDTS.	5	46	103	585	2838	1355	2128	11	2877
51	OFFICE, COMPUT. MACHINES	471	1423	2385	1197	157	2261	10769	518	152
52	SERVICE IND. MACHINES	71	214	169	1368	2425	909	4070	15	9008
53	ELECT. TRANSMISS. EQUIP.	221	550	3116	673	97	16785	29935	187	34
54	HOUSEHOLD APPLIANCES	7	21	213	17	14	188	1223	8	249
55	ELECTRIC LIGHTING EQUIP.	16	7	128	11		668	1647	2	7548
56	RADIO, TV, ETC., EQUIP.	2231	4581	7202	6360	64014	158486	355763	1675	1118
57	ELECTRONIC COMPONENTS	1169	1605	2808	1307	3552	4691	9501	201	1539
58	MISC. ELECTRICAL MACH.	171	188	543	944	1100	14898	5288	56	2489
59	MOTOR VEHICLES, EQUIP.	236	811	4024	1190	2548	152129	36078	223	376877
60	AIRCRAFT & PARTS	1625	23843	4667	306087	11432	177302	70984	2115	3920
61	OTHER TRANSPORT. EQUIP.	13559	8733	2273	1584	1995	3543	14553	677	3251
62	PROFESS., SCIEN. INSTRU.	458	1312	1125	1045	2379	4402	26376	407	1170
63	MEDICAL, PHOTO. EQUIP.	203	622	613	523	672	946	9151	223	58
64	MISC. MANUFACTURING	19	20	40	31	31	123	384	7	
65	TRANSPORT. & WAREHOUSING	5696	35976	22946	17081	5862	37140	59123	4905	34343
66	COMMUNICA.,EXC. BRDCAST.	1992	5067	7390	5245	678	2988	10646	961	15389
67	RADIO & TV BROADCASTING									0
68	ELEC.,GAS,WATER,SAN.SER.	1792	4266	7255	4784	-880	1291	5018	465	
69	WHOLESALE & RETAIL TRADE	3768	10155	12770	9788	4221	8403	29117	2606	
70	FINANCE & INSURANCE	0	0	0	0	0	0	0	0	15821
71	REAL ESTATE & RENTAL	730	3019	1412	1737	1477	2484	8085	747	25190
72	HOTELS; PERSONAL SERV.	2018	5243	7248	5286	1259	3562	12532	1127	4010
73	BUSINESS SERVICES	5535	25074	24580	19382	11135	22018	129162	4738	14821
74	RESEARCH & DEVELOPMENT	0	0	0	0		0	0	0	51419
75	AUTO. REPAIR & SERVICES	142	281	282	280	87	208	597	159	655
76	AMUSEMENTS	239	973	889	573	754	1223	5626	178	933
77	MED.,EDUC. SERVICES	3645	18765	13014	11500	14971	23917	64506	2913	25411
78	FEDERAL GOV'T ENTERPRISE	656	1684	2394	1721	311	1065	3770	340	4943
79	STATE & LOCAL GOV'T ENT.	862	2540	2459	2187	2088	2972	10087	897	4264
80	IMPORTS	19574	46797	65039	50524	9593	21044	89942	10590	122503
81	BUS.TRAVEL, ENT., GIFTS.	0	0	0	0	0	0	0	0	0
82	OFFICE SUPPLIES	-24	1166	1050	969	1514	1729	4337	443	2620
83	SCRAP & USED GOODS	-540	-1105	-2564	-1482	1188	475	1308	107	-5995
84	GOVERNMENT INDUSTRY	123513	320021	445470	323735	72593	213835	753361	67799	913080
85	REST OF WORLD INDUSTRY	-2718	-8134	-7519	-6877	-7179	-9934	-33646	-2988	-12671
86	HOUSEHOLD INDUSTRY	0	0	0	0	0	0	0	0	0
87	INVENTORY VALUATION ADJ.	0	0	0	0	0	0	0	0	0
88	STATE TOTAL	222666	754678	865410	943031	331921	1302891	2315152	207090	1826852

TABLE C.19

STATE ESTIMATES OF 1963
FEDERAL GOVERNMENT PURCHASES
(THOUSANDS OF CURRENT DOLLARS)

INDUSTRY TITLE	19 MARYLAND	20 MASSA-CHUSETTS	21 MICHIGAN	22 MINNESOTA	23 MISSISSIPPI	24 MISSOURI	25 MONTANA	26 NEBRASKA	27 NEVADA
1 LIVESTOCK & PRDTS.	82	102	109	128	51	143	37	88	14
2 OTHER AGRICULTURE PRDTS.	-355	-713	-3339	-161	-176	-101	41	63	-142
3 FORESTRY & FISHERIES	-2760	-8243	-1536	-1016	-4026	-884	-700	-22	-1
4 AGRI.,FORES.,FISH. SERV.	556	377	222	48	198	284	74	152	69
5 IRON, FERRO. ORES MINING	0	0	0	0	0	0	1234	0	0
6 NONFERROUS ORES MINING	654	0	3842	0	0	6677	-4252	0	4220
7 COAL MINING	64	0	0	0	32	253	0	0	0
8 CRUDE PETRO.,NATURAL GAS	0	0	0	32	0	0	0	0	0
9 STONE & CLAY MINING	125	67	-69	51	34	232	32	29	-271
10 CHEM.&FERT. MIN. MINING	0	0	0	0	0	0	10	0	8
11 NEW CONSTRUCTION	83824	66944	74316	27681	37162	87011	44446	57158	63137
12 MAINT. & REPAIR CONSTR.	39845	34023	23514	10824	14982	28486	7192	12292	5363
13 ORDNANCE & ACCESSORIES	64584	100959	323306	228639	10374	170534	3695	4983	3339
14 FOOD & KINDRED PRDTS.	4377	13038	6634	12387	3927	5661	2486	4838	634
15 TOBACCO MANUFACTURES	0	0	0	0	0	0	0	0	0
16 FABRICS	11	235	62	109	6	116	1	2	1
17 TEXTILE PRDTS.	59	2913	205	56	26	285	21	26	10
18 APPAREL	575	2452	565	416	196	1462	154	190	75
19 MISC. TEXTILE PRDTS.	110	1391	10041	214	1034	332	39	48	19
20 LUMBER & WOOD PRDTS.	183	153	106	47	69	128	33	56	24
21 WOODEN CONTAINERS	3	4	3	44	1	4	1	1	0
22 HOUSEHOLD FURNITURE	437	414	303	163	169	360	90	143	61
23 OTHER FURNITURE	1028	1082	826	492	408	972	239	356	150
24 PAPER & ALLIED PRDTS.	1187	1185	885	501	464	1048	259	399	169
25 PAPERBOARD CONTAINERS	323	242	155	54	117	192	50	93	42
26 PRINTING & PUBLISHING	5044	2190	698	-838	1669	1149	354	1149	563
27 CHEMICALS,SELECT. PRDTS.	24817	4535	42220	9609	28079	27560	2896	2998	9492
28 PLASTICS & SYNTHETICS	717	1412	745	92	29	26	0	1	0
29 DRUGS & COSMETICS	1327	1543	3029	1157	371	1776	227	352	115
30 PAINT & ALLIED PRDTS.	73	67	62	20	26	62	12	21	10
31 PETROLEUM, RELATED INDS.	3086	5389	6210	3600	5838	5800	2414	873	283
32 RUBBER, MISC. PLASTICS	6737	7816	11323	278	681	475	61	76	30
33 LEATHER TANNING & PRDTS.	16	13	3	3	6	10	3	5	2
34 FOOTWEAR, LEATHER PRDTS.	38	386	15	17	5	369	4	2	2
35 GLASS & GLASS PRDTS.	85	248	112	297	37	124	29	36	14
36 STONE & CLAY PRDTS.	-32	117	-78	494	-16	-50	-11	982	-10
37 PRIMARY IRON, STEEL MFR.	1008	2541	3229	476	-22	878	11	44	5
38 PRIMARY NONFERROUS MFR.	-188	105	2253	-1197	-580	-1367	-354	136	-212

Code	Industry	C1	C2	C3	C4	C5	C6	C7	C8	C9
39	METAL CONTAINERS	338	44	279	52	0	104	0	0	0
40	FABRICATED METAL PRDTS.	2292	1125	583	259	310	1797	42	51	22
41	SCREW MACH. PRDTS., ETC.	586	736	1350	360	426	406	34	53	16
42	OTHER FAB. METAL PRDTS.	539	1288	2140	469	383	924	80	128	35
43	ENGINES & TURBINES	409	1184	40444	564	182	714	143	177	70
44	FARM MACH. & EQUIP.	264	192	307	142	119	197	39	74	34
45	CONSTRUC. MACH. & EQUIP.	266	590	27826	435	208	813	36	45	86
46	MATERIAL HANDLING MACH.	227	1424	10612	653	169	196	37	52	18
47	METALWORKING MACHINERY	762	2770	4921	878	168	3298	120	148	58
48	SPECIAL MACH. & EQUIP.	225	674	747	211	70	543	48	59	23
49	GENERAL MACH. & EQUIP.	753	9290	14888	1665	328	1740	95	392	48
50	MACHINE SHOP PRDTS.	305	1620	2946	419	21	2099	7	9	3
51	OFFICE, COMPUT. MACHINES	9181	13913	8454	46360	911	3402	717	885	348
52	SERVICE IND. MACHINES	1017	2220	2642	2041	34	1612	19	23	10
53	ELECT. TRANSMISS. EQUIP.	3622	15613	11861	5198	848	9560	259	344	189
54	HOUSEHOLD APPLIANCES	35	61	696	94	24	148	10	13	5
55	ELECTRIC LIGHTING EQUIP.	48	422	184	80	107	390	3	4	4
56	RADIO, TV, ETC., EQUIP.	217566	397708	21897	44726	4262	52461	2319	30490	2452
57	ELECTRONIC COMPONENTS	3696	35768	2329	3698	805	1472	227	1369	111
58	MISC. ELECTRICAL MACH.	2186	3698	7065	933	235	1447		156	39
59	MOTOR VEHICLES, EQUIP.	3221	3968	192457	3467	1959	7359	381	776	210
60	AIRCRAFT & PARTS	59697	160471	82909	20009	3797	764694	2343	2888	1475
61	OTHER TRANSPORT. EQUIP.	14692	37714	21132	3424	63068	4534	893	1134	433
62	PROFESS.. SCIEN. INSTRU.	3396	37646	12084	4728	753	4340	1005	1786	273
63	MEDICAL, PHOTO. EQUIP.	1549	3740	1340	1328	381	3074	329	402	162
64	MISC. MANUFACTURING	268	285	405	129	21	86	1	1	10
65	TRANSPORT. & WAREHOUSING	31467	41117	41865	12238	10382	24379	3468	7184	2654
66	COMMUNICA.,EXC. BROCAST.	10692	7819	4899	1537	3879	6122	1585	3047	1367
67	RADIO & TV BROADCASTING	0	0	0	0	0	0	0		
68	ELEC.,GAS,WATER,SAN.SER.	10280	5355	2382	-778	3496	3375	954	2513	1196
69	WHOLESALE & RETAIL TRADE	18909	18093	13255	7168	7320	15780	3926	6208	2652
70	FINANCE & INSURANCE	0	0	0	0	0	0	0		
71	REAL ESTATE & RENTAL	5828	3799	5360	2045	1104	3831	942	1088	730
72	HOTELS; PERSONAL SERV.	10573	8563	5739	2387	3925	7019	1786	3172	1398
73	BUSINESS SERVICES	41436	53319	63100	25153	13658	42151	5112	8803	6094
74	RESEARCH & DEVELOPMENT	0	0	0	0	0	0	0		
75	AUTO. REPAIR & SERVICES	646	428	358	173	217	367	224	260	285
76	AMUSEMENTS	1676	2249	2889	1071	282	1503	158	545	3433
77	MED.,EDUC. SERVICES	35448	124268	47241	26098	9821	29923	3699	7138	1745
78	FEDERAL GOV'T ENTERPRISE	3477	2671	1731	634	1275	2140	549	1015	452
79	STATE & LOCAL GOV'T ENT.	3821	5399	4554	3267	1667	5211	1251	1590	632
80	IMPORTS	69212	57168	43053	18527	34967	52330	16772	28039	11704
81	BUS.TRAVEL, ENT., GIFTS.	0	0	0	0	0	0	0		
82	OFFICE SUPPLIES	1668	2423	3959	2357	1003	2134	666	907	329
83	SCRAP & USED GOODS	-3509	-575	535	1572	-1059	303	907	-616	-340
84	GOVERNMENT INDUSTRY	649061	519055	345184	139639	240263	423199	107898	193468	85442
85	REST OF WORLD INDUSTRY	-11799	-17706	-15177	-11167	-5259	-17296	-4138	-5108	-2007
86	HOUSEHOLD INDUSTRY	0	0	0	0	0	0	0	0	0
87	INVENTORY VALUATION ADJ.	0	0	0	0	0	0	0		
88	STATE TOTAL	1443667	1810595	1553900	668928	507745	1809887	214948	388285	211111

TABLE C.19

STATE ESTIMATES OF 1963
FEDERAL GOVERNMENT PURCHASES
(THOUSANDS OF CURRENT DOLLARS)

INDUSTRY TITLE	28 NEW HAMPSHIRE	29 NEW JERSEY	30 NEW MEXICO	31 NEW YORK	32 NORTH CAROLINA	33 NORTH DAKOTA	34 OHIO	35 OKLAHOMA	36 OREGON
1 LIVESTOCK & PRDTS.	13	87	48	355	84	30	178	82	56
2 OTHER AGRICULTURE PRDTS.	56	-3890	-639	-5341	-1355	410	-1825	-60	-1774
3 FORESTRY & FISHERIES	-479	-2386	-213	-3355	-5897	-7	-819	-228	-27638
4 AGRI.,FORES.,FISH. SERV.	119	438	211	587	632	78	372	401	57
5 IRON,FERRO. ORES MINING	0	0	1587	0	15	0	0	0	0
6 NONFERROUS ORES MINING	0	4166	-33311	2999	-419	0	-1383	9324	43457
7 COAL MINING	0	0	0	0	0	0	2216	0	0
8 CRUDE PETRO.,NATURAL GAS	0	0	0	0	0	0	0	0	0
9 STONE & CLAY MINING	8	124	-34	14	-370	-196	351	-85	112
10 CHEM.&FERT. MIN. MINING	0	0	0	0	0	0	0	0	0
11 NEW CONSTRUCTION	8350	55378	60785	193377	44447	26308	110780	105141	89989
12 MAINT. & REPAIR CONSTR.	7809	34808	16554	77263	42314	6263	39554	29200	9292
13 ORDNANCE & ACCESSORIES	2634	64279	29798	187232	31742	2288	467153	11914	9845
14 FOOD & KINDRED PRDTS.	1406	6609	1105	19585	6110	2710	8050	3221	3307
15 TOBACCO MANUFACTURES	0	0	0	0	876				0
16 FABRICS	18	542	3	21981	290	1	381	4	9
17 TEXTILE PRDTS.	8	776	33	822	4193	13	866	46	42
18 APPAREL	181	7637	241	5535	6648	95	1029	3342	311
19 MISC. TEXTILE PRDTS.	14	8832	117	12196	196	24	1001	86	78
20 LUMBER & WOOD PRDTS.	37	159	76	342	2	29	177	134	41
21 WOODEN CONTAINERS	0	2792	1	13		1	5		250
22 HOUSEHOLD FURNITURE	81	402	190	1055	446	73	510	323	133
23 OTHER FURNITURE	181	997	469	3007	1007	180	1391	769	390
24 PAPER & ALLIED PRDTS.	215	1120	528	3155	1190	202	1490	882	402
25 PAPERBOARD CONTAINERS	67	266	128	463	356	48	261	235	51
26 PRINTING & PUBLISHING	1202	3382	1660	-746	6231	597	1159	3541	-378
27 CHEMICALS,SELECT. PRDTS.	313	41418	2192	22753	16311	638	58417	1182	2032
28 PLASTICS & SYNTHETICS	111	2015	1	2115	1095		1986	7	32
29 DRUGS & COSMETICS	85	6678	355	12931	710	141	1662	540	473
30 PAINT & ALLIED PRDTS.	13	96	28	150	75	10	97	51	17
31 PETROLEUM,RELATED INDS.	267	16673	4288	36533	1170	7575	19980	23498	796
32 RUBBER, MISC. PLASTICS	528	9686	97	9300	2779	38	48423	160	221
33 LEATHER TANNING & PRDTS.	3	13	6	25	18	2	14	11	2
34 FOOTWEAR, LEATHER PRDTS.	672	24	6	780	38	2	44	9	8
35 GLASS & GLASS PRDTS.	11	108	46	1494	68	18	967	67	59
36 STONE & CLAY PRDTS.	-9	1114	-7	3781	-27	-5	611	-17	-14
37 PRIMARY IRON, STEEL MFR.	188	390	18	1448	48	7	6107	132	260
38 PRIMARY NONFERROUS MFR.	-65	2740	-753	-2225	-862	-301	3710	-886	-505

Industry									
39 METAL CONTAINERS	0	978	0	415	1		489	195	18
40 FABRICATED METAL PRDTS.	130	9971	57	4434	122	0	3841	216	262
41 SCREW MACH. PRDTS., ETC.	35	1149	53	2042	426	26	1475	200	141
42 OTHER FAB. METAL PRDTS.	57	1948	112	3182	474	32	2176	345	395
43 ENGINES & TURBINES	53	26648	224	6400	1304	52	11485	350	291
44 FARM MACH. & EQUIP.	55	217	102	384	308	89	329	195	43
45 CONSTRUC. MACH. & EQUIP.	31	1359	58	3358	116	39	7687	566	184
46 MATERIAL HANDLING MACH.	14	493	58	1344	1434	23	6371	224	984
47 METALWORKING MACHINERY	57	2092	188	4609	320	81	11968	639	296
48 SPECIAL MACH. & EQUIP.	54	496	76	1206	196	31	1741	155	130
49 GENERAL MACH. & EQUIP.	1368	12515	151	19026	402	59	31933	2087	541
50 MACHINE SHOP PRDTS.	7	1229	11	2103	49	9	8056	294	54
51 OFFICE, COMPUT. MACHINES	653	32432	1204	90249	1821	444	9367	1625	1450
52 SERVICE IND. MACHINES	12	2367	31	4722	615	12	4518	770	43
53 ELECT. TRANSMISS. EQUIP.	4010	17933	410	44730	8983	160	49032	1176	7034
54 HOUSEHOLD APPLIANCES	4	59	16	968	47	6	705	24	23
55 ELECTRIC LIGHTING EQUIP.	6	983	5	1308	188	2	1545	7	31
56 RADIO, TV, ETC., EQUIP.	25306	534698	5257	767654	106208	1436	88426	62235	5861
57 ELECTRONIC COMPONENTS	4659	23825	533	42434	7896	141	5038	1179	600
58 MISC. ELECTRICAL MACH.	76	6560	154	10810	3911	48	8092	288	1311
59 MOTOR VEHICLES, EQUIP.	115	3922	506	12215	1561	191	118807	4581	676
60 AIRCRAFT & PARTS	968	170656	3840	771044	9104	1428	714477	103068	7563
61 OTHER TRANSPORT. EQUIP.	1422	77162	1397	127181	3585	553	24967	2119	8433
62 PROFESS., SCIEN. INSTRU.	554	28307	1551	61864	3423	349	9669	1634	2302
63 MEDICAL, PHOTO. EQUIP.	116	6872	518	58917	956	192	5206	760	626
64 MISC. MANUFACTURING	16	578	30	936	68	5	481	52	57
65 TRANSPORT. & WAREHOUSING	5709	56619	6965	96154	28620	5048	61000	23742	3666
66 COMMUNICA.,EXC. BRDCAST.	2228	8706	4172	14215	11896	1559	8231	7740	1531
67 RADIO & TV BROADCASTING									
68 ELEC.,GAS,WATER,SAN.SER.	2360	7322	3566	2911	12328	1298	3981	7281	-115
69 WHOLESALE & RETAIL TRADE	3510	17463	8257	46352	19278	3153	22312	14001	5839
70 FINANCE & INSURANCE	0								
71 REAL ESTATE & RENTAL	373	5390	1753	15260	2078	682	7532	3490	8689
72 HOTELS; PERSONAL SERV.	2119	9011	4297	18190	11419	1619	9650	7714	2125
73 BUSINESS SERVICES	7031	56724	14641	305012	38765	4487	70605	29402	13550
74 RESEARCH & DEVELOPMENT									
75 AUTO. REPAIR & SERVICES	97	426	576	835	427	135	464	434	234
76 AMUSEMENTS	405	3172	283	27626	936	134	3861	603	599
77 MED.,EDUC. SERVICES	4957	25311	11486	153565	26032	2473	54778	15660	17183
78 FEDERAL GOV'T ENTERPRISE	711	2893	1383	5260	3815	519	2909	2526	592
79 STATE & LOCAL GOV'T ENT.	533	4373	2027	18031	3177	798	7677	2958	2459
80 IMPORTS	11701	64940	32579	112357	113440	15649	50389	53621	15222
81 BUS.TRAVEL, ENT., GIFTS.	0								
82 OFFICE SUPPLIES	241	4176	1134	9945	2787	344	4259	1223	2084
83 SCRAP & USED GOODS	-932	-1892	-959	5235	-4725	-327	919	-2393	959
84 GOVERNMENT INDUSTRY	130760	549977	262406	1083705	703798	98764	580375	473074	125542
85 REST OF WORLD INDUSTRY	-1542	-14005	-6473	-60832	-9381	-2562	-25589	-9208	-8354
86 HOUSEHOLD INDUSTRY	0	0	0	0	0	0	0	0	0
87 INVENTORY VALUATION ADJ.	0	0	0	0	0	0	0	0	0
88 STATE TOTAL	234075	2033524	450353	4506977	1278369	186476	2766148	1009879	362566

TABLE C.19

STATE ESTIMATES OF 1963
FEDERAL GOVERNMENT PURCHASES
(THOUSANDS OF CURRENT DOLLARS)

INDUSTRY TITLE	37 PENNSYLVANIA	38 RHODE ISLAND	39 SOUTH CAROLINA	40 SOUTH DAKOTA	41 TENNESSEE	42 TEXAS	43 UTAH	44 VERMONT	45 VIRGINIA
1 LIVESTOCK & PRDTS.	201	13	35	55	93	244	34	15	97
2 OTHER AGRICULTURE PRDTS.	-525	-26	-1040	-9	-342	-9844	-84	114	258
3 FORESTRY & FISHERIES	-1555	-820	-4084	-78	-1167	-7604	-65	-397	-6957
4 AGRI.,FORES.,FISH. SERV.	543	93	357	53	154	1522	159	3	1072
5 IRON,FERRO. ORES MINING	29	0	0	0	0	904	0	0	0
6 NONFERROUS ORES MINING	11360	0	0	0	7708	17265	24432	0	2202
7 COAL MINING	9410	0	0	0	349	0	571	0	2089
8 CRUDE PETRO.,NATURAL GAS									
9 STONE & CLAY MINING	403	4	45	34	198	1043	-484	169	215
10 CHEM.&FERT. MIN. MINING	0	0	0	0	0	0	27	12	0
11 NEW CONSTRUCTION	92788	8031	58221	61012	157772	195677	43223	3491	68409
12 MAINT. & REPAIR CONSTR.	52300	6670	23071	5665	18733	105815	12198	1209	68603
13 ORDNANCE & ACCESSORIES	226416	7812	4332	3320	112105	160817	51654	19537	88387
14 FOOD & KINDRED PRDTS.	9784	491	4215	3680	2729	15521	1933	330	10440
15 TOBACCO MANUFACTURES									
16 FABRICS	2395	405	2222	1	1138	25	2	1	1247
17 TEXTILE PRDTS.	2874	10	21	18	69	235	22	7	102
18 APPAREL	5984	73	266	135	8829	4209	165	71	2343
19 MISC. TEXTILE PRDTS.	5900	18	39	34	4721	508	41	13	1247
20 LUMBER & WOOD PRDTS.	235	31	108	25	83	489	56	5	319
21 WOODEN CONTAINERS	61	38	1	1	3	96	1	0	2
22 HOUSEHOLD FURNITURE	653	73	238	73	250	1140	138	19	703
23 OTHER FURNITURE	1736	172	523	199	704	2637	336	58	1535
24 PAPER & ALLIED PRDTS.	1884	199	627	212	743	3073	382	59	1845
25 PAPERBOARD CONTAINERS	362	54	199	37	116	872	95	6	593
26 PRINTING & PUBLISHING	2603	846	3670	174	80	14360	1317	-132	11131
27 CHEMICALS,SELECT. PRDTS.	17548	661	21662	482	146631	20584	4905	169	32031
28 PLASTICS & SYNTHETICS	3521	126	1365	200	3482	2982	0	24	4647
29 DRUGS & COSMETICS	7032	12	351	10	1061	1879	248	76	1306
30 PAINT & ALLIED PRDTS.	109		39		36	195	21	3	118
31 PETROLEUM, RELATED INDS.	15755	920	1020	471	7959	166536	6732	279	3583
32 RUBBER, MISC. PLASTICS	9626	1681	2014	54	1900	463	69	312	2908
33 LEATHER TANNING & PRDTS.	19	6	10	2	6	43	5	0	30
34 FOOTWEAR, LEATHER PRDTS.	148	14	4	4	415	50	31	20	14
35 GLASS & GLASS PRDTS.	1013	-6	31	26	102	709	-14	10	82
36 STONE & CLAY PRDTS.	707		-13	-7	-33	681	210	-8	1917
37 PRIMARY IRON, STEEL MFR.	6892	736	37	10	250	1561		34	141
38 PRIMARY NONFERROUS MFR.	-472	1472	-481	-426	-70	-1628	-444	-65	-1064

Code	Industry	1	2	3	4	5	6	7	8	9
39	METAL CONTAINERS	724	0	1	0	47	518	6	0	11
40	FABRICATED METAL PRDTS.	3096	20	140	37	191	1114	165	15	1812
41	SCREW MACH. PRDTS., ETC.	2485	152	159	30	749	931	87	18	139
42	OTHER FAB. METAL PRDTS.	2901	163	171	71	914	1710	118	18	520
43	ENGINES & TURBINES	4399	68	143	126	138	999	154	33	447
44	FARM MACH. & EQUIP.	363	44	166	29	219	734	78	4	497
45	CONSTRUC. MACH. & EQUIP.	4842	23	36	32	492	823	4535	13	158
46	MATERIAL HANDLING MACH.	8899	35	59	32	2064	2033	39	12	576
47	METALWORKING MACHINERY	1394	394	146	110	361	3645	1894	668	408
48	SPECIAL MACH. & EQUIP.	559	61	101	43	2190	690	252	85	149
49	GENERAL MACH. & EQUIP.	16438	608	554	110	1264	3806	365	72	715
50	MACHINE SHOP PRDTS.	289	255	13	9	2393	2160	1328	439	76
51	OFFICE, COMPUT. MACHINES	22317	341	901	630	152	5642	772	722	3071
52	SERVICE IND. MACHINES	5191	9	21	17	3671	408	186	10	416
53	ELECT. TRANSMISS. EQUIP.	49273	325	2393	227	184	3546	862	179	10089
54	HOUSEHOLD APPLIANCES	426	5	14	9	75	83	11	4	29
55	ELECTRIC LIGHTING EQUIP.	1197	120	3	12		70	18	18	22
56	RADIO, TV, ETC., EQUIP.	135975	6416	2768	2036	37014	116410	8108	777	56583
57	ELECTRONIC COMPONENTS	40075	2215	7200	268	2721	15251	1961	1620	16719
58	MISC. ELECTRICAL MACH.	8508	511	97	68	1331	1220	116	452	461
59	MOTOR VEHICLES, EQUIP.	13746	220	340	281	4706	12347	1718	115	3523
60	AIRCRAFT & PARTS	261918	2024	3464	2025	19393	610287	41418	14303	16882
61	OTHER TRANSPORT. EQUIP.	71169	1822	2885	784	3467	8933	1319	303	201589
62	PROFESS., SCIEN. INSTRU.	48198	3865	2210	494	2172	6501	993	955	2448
63	MEDICAL, PHOTO. EQUIP.	3269	170	310	272	1044	2387	381	137	1620
64	MISC. MANUFACTURING	850	-29	23	23	56	291	43	3	120
65	TRANSPORT. & WAREHOUSING	57881	4716	14099	2251	19175	106646	10083	1150	45990
66	COMMUNICA.·EXC·BRDCAST·	11547	1791	6655	1184	3608	28992	3133	148	19924
67	RADIO & TV BROADCASTING	0	0	0	0	0	0	0	0	
68	ELEC.,GAS,WATER,SAN.SER.	6996	1723	7163	584	1128	28855	2780	-149	21651
69	WHOLESALE & RETAIL TRADE	28516	3164	10260	3187	10998	49330	5997	836	30307
70	FINANCE & INSURANCE	0	0	0	0	0	0	0	0	0
71	REAL ESTATE & RENTAL	8523	1526	1104	633	2321	8003	958	292	4595
72	HOTELS; PERSONAL SERV.	12995	1770	6287	1384	4467	28288	3187	258	18740
73	BUSINESS SERVICES	84996	4803	20264	4014	22030	115556	11787	1519	59460
74	RESEARCH & DEVELOPMENT	0	0	0	0	0	0	0	0	0
75	AUTO. REPAIR & SERVICES	449	135	425	171	309	1395	313	28	959
76	AMUSEMENTS	3193	505	388	239	787	2612	383	197	885
77	MED.·EDUC. SERVICES	74451	6855	8502	2681	19969	67848	11442	1179	18619
78	FEDERAL GOV'T ENTERPRISE	3998	583	2119	418	1312	9369	1032	65	6331
79	STATE & LOCAL GOV'T ENT.	9070	638	1458	1090	4108	9177	1399	404	4113
80	IMPORTS	50604	9429	52492	11772	35760	238658	11306	2074	115403
81	BUS.TRAVEL,ENT., GIFTS.	0	0	0	0	0	0	0	0	0
82	OFFICE SUPPLIES	4052	311	1657	828	1795	9874	702	100	1782
83	SCRAP & USED GOODS	-11	-589	-2888	121	971	-10419	-815	220	-8837
84	GOVERNMENT INDUSTRY	785195	108668	388267	83270	267093	1739671	194931	14962	1158127
85	REST OF WORLD INDUSTRY	-29972	-1969	-4131	-3633	-13808	-27864	-4429	-1386	-11500
86	HOUSEHOLD INDUSTRY	0	0	0	0	0	0	0	0	0
87	INVENTORY VALUATION ADJ.	0	0	0	0	0	0	0	0	0
88	STATE TOTAL	2308719	193708	657545	193413	946315	3911586	469035	68348	2107223

TABLE C.19

STATE ESTIMATES OF 1963
FEDERAL GOVERNMENT PURCHASES
(THOUSANDS OF CURRENT DOLLARS)

INDUSTRY TITLE	46 WASHINGTON	47 WEST VIRGINIA	48 WISCONSIN	49 WYOMING	50 ALASKA	51 HAWAII	52 NO STATE ALLOCATION	53 NATIONAL TOTAL
1 LIVESTOCK & PRDTS.	80	30	113	20	22	18	0	4904
2 OTHER AGRICULTURE PRDTS.	2449	504	-1085	12	14	-137	0	-91818
3 FORESTRY & FISHERIES	-15644	-775	-1386	-77	-9857	-514	0	-171914
4 AGRI.,FORES.,FISH. SERV.	453	10	44	32	241	381	0	16829
5 IRON, FERRO. ORES MINING	0	0	0	0	0	0	0	9067
6 NONFERROUS ORES MINING	-1616	0	0	0	95	0	0	241859
7 COAL MINING	0	9819	0	95	0	0	0	35231
8 CRUDE PETRO., NATURAL GAS	0	0	0	66	0	0	0	0
9 STONE & CLAY MINING	75	76	86	0	0	0	0	2653
10 CHEM.&FERT. MIN. MINING	0	0	0	0	0	0	0	382
11 NEW CONSTRUCTION	215938	91608	30060	40649	34204	11166	0	4010000
12 MAINT. & REPAIR CONSTR.	33686	4146	8973	3244	16119	22723	0	1413604
13 ORDNANCE & ACCESSORIES	28709	209437	77511	1790	3131	1613	0	5299596
14 FOOD & KINDRED PRDTS.	5774	784	10391	900	689	1270	0	316714
15 TOBACCO MANUFACTURES	0	0	0	0	0	0	0	0
16 FABRICS	6	2	123	1	1	1	0	32728
17 TEXTILE PRDTS.	57	25	45	10	18	9	0	11793
18 APPAREL	421	353	674	75	130	67	0	68651
19 MISC. TEXTILE PRDTS.	105	906	2501	19	33	62	0	68614
20 LUMBER & WOOD PRDTS.	155	18	38	14	75	107	0	6424
21 WOODEN CONTAINERS	1	1	2	0	1	74	0	4334
22 HOUSEHOLD FURNITURE	377	65	133	42	169	221	0	16721
23 OTHER FURNITURE	904	205	399	112	382	455	0	42468
24 PAPER & ALLIED PRDTS.	1033	206	408	120	452	566	0	47152
25 PAPERBOARD CONTAINERS	267	18	46	22	136	206	0	10489
26 PRINTING & PUBLISHING	3894	-493	-606	121	2397	4242	0	116692
27 CHEMICALS,SELECT. PRDTS.	7116	95581	5715	579	738	368	0	1036006
28 PLASTICS & SYNTHETICS	118	2054	146	0	0	0	0	41859
29 DRUGS & COSMETICS	634	290	922	110	192	103	0	73391
30 PAINT & ALLIED PRDTS.	59	7	21	6	27	38	0	2723
31 PETROLEUM, RELATED INDS.	7551	5378	842	5030	4326	1400	0	711104
32 RUBBER, MISC. PLASTICS	266	266	3879	30	1990	27	0	170547
33 LEATHER TANNING & PRDTS.	14	1	2	1	7	10	0	531
34 FOOTWEAR, LEATHER PRDTS.	11	5	59	2	3	2	0	4027
35 GLASS & GLASS PRDTS.	322	44	63	14	25	13	0	12139
36 STONE & CLAY PRDTS.	-25	-17	232	-10	-3	4440	0	22914
37 PRIMARY IRON, STEEL MFR.	279	766	597	5	1760	-26	0	45197
38 PRIMARY NONFERROUS MFR.	1076	385	11	-236	1213	-212	0	-10932

446

The page contains a dense numeric data table (an input–output style matrix) with row labels numbered 39–88 and eight unlabeled numeric columns. The values below are transcribed column-by-column in reading order; blank cells indicate positions with no printed value.

#	Industry	1	2	3	4	5	6	7	8
39	METAL CONTAINERS	47	14	198	0	0	19	0	6569
40	FABRICATED METAL PRDTS.	1372	776	707	20	35	57	0	58294
41	SCREW MACH. PRDTS., ETC.	210	349	512	45	607	15	0	27505
42	OTHER FAB. METAL PRDTS.	383	379	448	43	628	39	0	39818
43	ENGINES & TURBINES	4003	170	2708	69	121	63	0	179087
44	FARM MACH. & EQUIP.	222	18	261	17	112	172	0	10548
45	CONSTRUC. MACH. & EQUIP.	214	74	5176	18	31	29	0	104960
46	MATERIAL HANDLING MACH.	850	973	1185	18	31	16	0	69630
47	METALWORKING MACHINERY	2609	2196	3681	68	101	52	0	85524
48	SPECIAL MACH. & EQUIP.	405	290	622	24	40	24	0	16893
49	GENERAL MACH. & EQUIP.	762	156	11686	46	712	43	0	236194
50	MACHINE SHOP PRDTS.	1722	1536	2498	11	6	3	0	49104
51	OFFICE, COMPUT. MACHINES	2125	849	1727	2341	505	313	0	447595
52	SERVICE IND. MACHINES	518	26	3462	9	16	8	0	46950
53	ELECT. TRANSMISS. EQUIP.	2406	2785	28480	176	648	116	0	423170
54	HOUSEHOLD APPLIANCES	33	13	2910	5	9	5	0	9584
55	ELECTRIC LIGHTING EQUIP.	94	684	104	2	54	4	0	13246
56	RADIO, TV, ETC., EQUIP.	14123	3133	42665	1123	2663	1028	0	4686011
57	ELECTRONIC COMPONENTS	1009	1706	1362	110	1484	99	0	398035
58	MISC. ELECTRICAL MACH.	446	92	3155	38	434	34	0	109742
59	MOTOR VEHICLES, EQUIP.	1047	501	8742	157	327	142	0	662905
60	AIRCRAFT & PARTS	328786	3330	10205	1239	2295	2364	0	7532276
61	OTHER TRANSPORT. EQUIP.	71005	1548	16569	432	753	403	0	1124019
62	PROFESS., SCIEN. INSTRU.	1582	1444	5504	538	475	246	0	404775
63	MEDICAL, PHOTO. EQUIP.	846	378	772	150	261	192	0	147412
64	MISC. MANUFACTURING	103	84	125	2809	10	34	0	7909
65	TRANSPORT. & WAREHOUSING	23719	15570	10632	691	10261	13622	0	1320064
66	COMMUNICA., EXC. BRDCAST.	8809	483	1330	0	4546	6943	0	340778
67	RADIO & TV BROADCASTING	0	0	-501	369	0	0	0	263996
68	ELEC.,GAS,WATER,SAN.SER.	8089	-576	5860	1806	4735	8070	0	728145
69	WHOLESALE & RETAIL TRADE	16328	2904	2224	0	7322	9527	0	37112
70	FINANCE & INSURANCE	0	0	1999	373	0	0	0	162331
71	REAL ESTATE & RENTAL	3133	958	20174	797	1445	650	0	361412
72	HOTELS; PERSONAL SERV.	8857	877	137	2301	4356	6329	0	1980518
73	BUSINESS SERVICES	34762	6887	1104	0	11652	19135	0	20890
74	RESEARCH & DEVELOPMENT	719	54	8734	112	395	439	0	107035
75	AUTO. REPAIR & SERVICES	1045	636	538	117	80	305	0	1415549
76	AMUSEMENTS	24975	7345	2618	2239	2539	6240	0	114582
77	MED.,EDUC. SERVICES	2887	218	15129	243	1457	2175	0	198405
78	FEDERAL GOV'T ENTERPRISE	3605	1424	2293	603	1187	802	0	2649502
79	STATE & LOCAL GOV'T ENT.	69087	6060	1202	6937	40922	49866	0	142508
80	IMPORTS	201	250	117237	292	446	476	0	-53258
81	BUS.TRAVEL, ENT., GIFTS.	-2542	799	-8936	46	-1827	-3562	0	24448592
82	OFFICE SUPPLIES	542565	50623	0	48028	268495	392822	0	-643102
83	SCRAP & USED GOODS	-11315	-4897	0	-2004	-3489	-1806	0	0
84	GOVERNMENT INDUSTRY	0	0		0	0	0	2456000	
85	REST OF WORLD INDUSTRY	0	0		0	0	0	0	
86	HOUSEHOLD INDUSTRY							0	
87	INVENTORY VALUATION ADJ.							0	
88	STATE TOTAL	1466390	534824	478197	125257	425710	566297	2456000	64115488

Bibliography[*]

1. American Gas Association, Inc. Department of Statistics. *Gas Facts, 1964.* New York: 1965.
2. American Gas Association, Inc. Department of Statistics. *Gas Facts, 1965.* New York: 1966.
3. Anderson, Carolyn W., and McMillan, Douglas W. "State Estimates of Gross Private Domestic Investment, 1947, 1958, 1963." EDA Report No. 11 (Harvard Economic Research Project), August 1968.
4. "Apartment Building Experience Exchange of Rental Income and Operating Expense Data: Based upon Data of 1963 Operations." A special issue of *Journal of Property Management,* n.d.
5. Association of Oil Pipelines. "Oil Pipeline Construction Costs." Confidential Study, n.d.
6. Berner, Richard B. "State Estimates of Net Purchases of Goods and Services by State and Local Governments, 1947, 1958, 1963." EDA Report No. 12 (Harvard Economic Research Project), August 1968.
7. Buechner, William R. "State Estimates of Exports from the United States, 1947, 1958, 1963." EDA Report No. 9 (Harvard Economic Research Project), August 1968.
8. Carlsson, Bo, and Grubb, Norton. "State Estimates of Federal Government Purchases, 1947, 1958, 1963." EDA Report No. 13 (Harvard Economic Research Project), August 1968.
9. Civil Aeronautics Board. *Quarterly Report of Air Carrier Financial Statistics.* GPO, 1959.
10. Council of Economic Advisers. *Economic Report of the President, 1966.* GPO, 1966.
11. Dixon, Orani, and Wells, John V. "State New Construction Technologies." EDA Report No. 20 (Harvard Economic Research Project), September 1970.
12. Evans, W. Duane, and Hoffenberg, Marvin. "The Interindustry Relations Study for 1947." *Review of Economics and Statistics* 34 (May 1952): 97–141.
13. [Jack] Faucett Associates, Inc. "Components of Private Construction by State, 1947, 1958, and 1963." Prepared for the Harvard Economic Research Project. Unpublished worksheets, 1968.
14. [Jack] Faucett Associates, Inc. "Development of a Matrix of Interindustry Transactions in Capital Goods in 1963." Appendix D. Prepared for the Bureau of Labor Statistics, U.S. Department of Labor. Unpublished, 1966.

*Material published by the U.S. Government Printing Office, Washington, D.C. 20402, is cited as: GPO, [date].

15. [Jack] Faucett Associates, Inc. *Input-Output Transactions by Transportation Mode, 1947 and 1958.* U.S. Department of Transportation. Springfield, Va.: Clearinghouse for Federal, Scientific and Technical Information, Report No. PB 178 677, April 1968.
16. [Jack] Faucett Associates, Inc. "1958 Federal Construction." Unpublished worksheets.
17. [Jack] Faucett Associates, Inc. "1963 Interregional Commodity Trade Flows." Prepared for the Office of Business Economics, U.S. Department of Commerce. Unpublished. November 1970; revised March 1971.
18. Federal Aviation Agency. *Statistical Handbook of Aviation, 1959.* GPO, 1959.
19. Federal Aviation Agency. Office of Management Services, Data Systems Division. *Statistical Study of U.S. Civil Aircraft as of January 1964.* GPO, 1964.
20. Federal Communications Commission. "Bell Telephone System Selected Earnings and Balance Sheet Data, 1962." Unpublished worksheets.
21. Federal Communications Commission. "Bell Telephone System Selected Earnings and Balance Sheet Data, 1963." Unpublished worksheets.
22. Federal Communications Commission. "Bell Telephone System Selected Earnings and Balance Sheet Data of Multi-State Companies by States, 1962." Unpublished worksheets.
23. Federal Communications Commission. "Bell Telephone System Selected Earnings and Balance Sheet Data of Multi-State Companies by States, 1963." Unpublished worksheets.
24. Federal Communications Commission. *Broadcast Financial Data for Networks and AM, FM, and Television Statistics, 1948.* GPO, 1948.
25. Federal Communications Commission. *Statistics of Communications Common Carriers, 1957.* GPO, 1959.
26. Federal Communications Commission. *Statistics of Communications Common Carriers, 1958.* GPO, 1960.
27. Federal Communications Commission. *Statistics of Communications Common Carriers, 1963.* GPO, 1965.
28. Federal Communications Commission. *Statistics of the Communications Industry in the United States, 1946.* GPO, 1948.
29. Federal Communications Commission. *Statistics of the Communications Industry in the United States, 1947.* GPO, 1949.
30. Federal Communications Commission. *Statistics of the Communications Industry in the United States, 1948.* GPO, 1950.
31. Federal Power Commission. *Statistics of Electric Utilities in the United States, 1947.* GPO, 1949.
32. Federal Power Commission. *Statistics of Electric Utilities in the United States, 1958.* GPO, 1960.
33. Federal Power Commission. *Statistics of Electric Utilities in the United States, Privately Owned 1962.* GPO, 1964.
34. Federal Power Commission. *Statistics of Electric Utilities in the United States, Privately Owned 1963.* GPO, 1965.

35. Federal Power Commission. *Statistics of Natural Gas Companies.* GPO, 1958.

36. Fox, Karl A. "Functional Economic Areas: A Strategic Concept for Promoting Civic Responsibility, Human Dignity, and Maximum Employment in the United States." Unpublished. Ames, Iowa: Department of Economics, Iowa State University, January 10, 1969.

37. General Services Administration. "Annual Motor Vehicle Report." GPO, 1958.

38. General Services Administration. "Annual Motor Vehicle Report." GPO, 1963.

39. General Services Administration. *Inventory Report on Real Property Leased to the United States Throughout the World, as of June 30, 1958.* GPO, 1959.

40. General Services Administration. *Inventory Report on Real Property Leased to the United States Throughout the World, as of June 30, 1963.* GPO, 1964.

41. General Services Administration. "Purchased Materials Delivered to the Stockpile Between 1 January and 30 June 1947 and Between 1 July and 31 December 1947." Unpublished worksheets.

42. General Services Administration. "Quantities and Costs of Domestic and Foreign Materials Purchased or Obligated with Public Law 520 Funds through December 31, 1958." Unpublished worksheets.

43. General Services Administration. "Schedule of Inventories, Commodities in Storage and in Transit as of December 31, 1957." Unpublished worksheets.

44. General Services Administration. "Schedule of Inventories, Commodities in Storage and in Transit as of December 31, 1958." Unpublished worksheets.

45. General Services Administration. *Statistical Supplement to the Stockpile Report to the Congress, July–December 1962.* GPO, 1963.

46. General Services Administration. *Statistical Supplement to the Stockpile Report to the Congress, July–December 1963.* GPO, 1964.

47. General Services Administration. "Surplus Materials Transferred to the Stockpile Between 1 January and 30 June 1947 and Between 1 July and 31 December 1947." Unpublished worksheets.

48. Green, H. Albert. " 'Q' Model: Personal Consumption Expenditures Submodel." Unpublished. U.S. Department of Agriculture, ESG Working Paper No. 4, March 1966.

49. Harvard Economic Research Project. "Capital Stock Matrix, 1947." Unpublished data.

50. Harvard Economic Research Project. "Capital Stock Matrix, 1958." Unpublished data.

51. Hochwald, Werner. "Conceptual Issues of Regional Income Estimation." *Regional Income.* (Studies in Income and Wealth, Volume Twenty-one by the Conference on Research in Income and Wealth). Princeton: Princeton University Press, 1957.9–34.

52. Interstate Commerce Commission. *Seventy-third Annual Report on Transport Statistics in the United States, 1959.* GPO, 1960.

53. Interstate Commerce Commission. Bureau of Economics. *Carload Waybill Statistics, 1962: State-to-State Distribution.* Statement SS-1. GPO, June 1965.

54. Interstate Commerce Commission. Bureau of Economics. *Carload Waybill Statistics, 1964: State-to-State Distribution.* Statement SS-1. GPO, August 1967.

55. Isard, Walter, and Karaska, Gerald J. *Unclassified Defense and Space Contracts: Awards by County, State and Metropolitan Area, United States, Fiscal Year 1964.* Philadelphia: World Friends Research Center, 1965.

— Jack Faucett Associates, Inc.: See entries 13 through 17.

56. Labovitz, I. M. *Federal Revenues and Expenditures in the Several States.* Washington, D.C.: Library of Congress, Legislative Reference Service, September 19, 1962.

57. Lamale, Helen Humes. *Study of Consumer Expenditures, Incomes and Savings: Methodology of the Survey of Consumer Expenditures in 1950.* Philadelphia: University of Pennsylvania, 1959.

58. Leven, Maurice. *Income in the Various States: Its Sources and Distribution, 1919, 1920, and 1921.* New York: National Bureau of Economic Research, 1925.

59. Linden, Fabian, ed. *Expenditure Patterns of the American Family.* New York: National Industrial Conference Board, 1965.

60. Miller, Etienne H. "Foreign Travel Boom Continued in 1963." *Survey of Current Business* 44, no. 6 (June 1964): 22–26.

61. Nathan, Robert R., and Martin, John L. *State Income Payments, 1929–1937.* U.S. Department of Commerce, May 1939.

62. National Bureau of Economic Research. *Input-Output Analysis: Technical Supplement.* Conference on Research in Income and Wealth. Princeton: Princeton University Press for National Bureau of Economic Research, 1954.

63. National Science Foundation. *Federal Funds for Science.* Vol. I, *Federal Funds for Scientific Research and Development at Nonprofit Institutions, 1950–51 and 1951–52.* GPO, n.d.

64. National Science Foundation. *Geographic Distribution of Federal Funds for Research and Development, Fiscal Year 1965.* GPO, 1967.

65. National Science Foundation. *Reviews of Data on Science Resources.* Vol. I, NSF 6. GPO, 1965.

66. Ono, Mitsuo. "A Graphic Technique for Projecting Family Income Size Distribution." *American Statistical Association Proceedings of the Social Statistics Section* (August 1969).

67. Polenske, Karen R., and Smith, James F. "Alignment of 1960 BLS Consumer Expenditure Categories with the 80-Order OBE Input-Output Industrial Classification." EDA Report No. 5 (Harvard Economic Research Project), February 1968.

68. Polenske, Karen R., and Whiston, Isabelle B. "Personal Consumption Expenditures, 1947, 1958, 1963." EDA Report No. 7 (Harvard Economic Research Project), August 1968.

69. Polenske, Karen R., and Whiston, Isabelle B. "State Estimates of Personal Consumption Expenditures, 1947, 1958, 1963, Scheme II." EDA Report

No. 14 (Harvard Economic Research Project), August 1968.

70. Rodgers, John M. *State Estimates of Outputs, Employment, and Payrolls.* Lexington: Lexington Books, D.C. Heath and Company, forthcoming.

71. Ruggles, Richard, and Ruggles, Nancy D. "Regional Breakdowns of National Economic Accounts." *Design of Regional Accounts* (by the Committee on Regional Accounts). Edited by Werner Hochwald. Baltimore: The Johns Hopkins Press, 1961. 121–142.

72. Sasscer, Frances P. "Expansion of Foreign Travel." *Survey of Current Business* 39, no. 6 (June 1959): 9–14.

73. Scheppach, Raymond C. *1970 and 1980 State Projections of the Gross National Product.* Lexington: Lexington Books, D.C. Heath and Company, forthcoming.

74. Simon, Nancy W. "Personal Consumption Expenditures in the 1958 Input-Output Study." *Survey of Current Business* 45, no. 10 (October 1965): 7–20.

75. Studenski, Paul. *The Income of Nations.* New York: New York University Press, 1958.

76. Taskier, Charlotte E. "Alignment of the 450-order (Input-Output) Industries, 1947, with the 1958 Interindustry Sales–Purchases Study Sectors." Unpublished. Prepared for the Harvard Economic Research Project, n.d.

77. Taylor, Lester D. "Combining the 1960-61 BLS Survey of Consumer Expenditures and OBE Time Series Data in Projecting Personal Consumption Expenditures." Unpublished. Prepared for U.S. Bureau of Labor Statistics, Interagency Growth Study, April 20, 1967.

78. Tontz, Robert L., and Angelidis, Alex D. "U.S. Agricultural Export Shares by Regions and States, Fiscal Year 1963–64." Reprinted from U.S. Department of Agriculture: *Foreign Agricultural Trade of the United States,* November–December 1964.

79. Tontz, Robert L., and Lemon, Isaac E. "U.S. Agricultural Export Shares by Regions and States, Fiscal Year 1965–66." Reprinted from U.S. Department of Agriculture: *Foreign Agricultural Trade of the United States,* November 1966.

80. U.S. Bureau of the Budget. Executive Office of the President. *Standard Industrial Classification Manual.* GPO, 1957.

81. U.S. Bureau of the Budget. Executive Office of the President. *Standard Industrial Classification Manual, 1967.* GPO, 1967.

82. U.S. Bureau of the Budget. Office of Statistical Standards. *Family Income Distribution Statistics Published by Federal Agencies.* Statistical Evaluation Report No. 5. GPO, 1964.

83. U.S. Bureau of the Census. *Census of Business, 1948.* Vol. I, *Retail Trade– General Statistics.* GPO, 1952.

84. U.S. Bureau of the Census. *Census of Business, 1948.* Vol. III, *Retail Trade– Area Statistics.* GPO, 1951.

85. U.S. Bureau of the Census. *Census of Business, 1948.* Vol. VI, *Service Trade– General Statistics.* GPO, 1952.

86. U.S. Bureau of the Census. *Census of Business, 1948.* Vol. VII, *Service Trade–Area Statistics.* GPO, 1951.

87. U.S. Bureau of the Census. *Census of Business, 1958*. Vol. I, *Retail Trade— Summary Statistics*. GPO, 1961.
88. U.S. Bureau of the Census. *Census of Business, 1958*. Vol. II, *Retail Trade— Area Statistics*. GPO, 1961.
89. U.S. Bureau of the Census. *Census of Business, 1958*. Vol. V, *Selected Services—Summary Statistics*. GPO, 1961.
90. U.S. Bureau of the Census. *Census of Business, 1958*. Vol. VI, *Selected Services—Area Statistics*. GPO, 1961.
91. U.S. Bureau of the Census. *Census of Business, 1963*. Vol. I, *Retail Trade— Summary Statistics*. GPO, 1966.
92. U.S. Bureau of the Census. *Census of Business, 1963*. Vol. II, *Retail Trade— Area Statistics*. GPO, 1966.
93. U.S. Bureau of the Census. *Census of Business, 1963*. Vol. VI, *Selected Services—Summary Statistics*. GPO, 1966.
94. U.S. Bureau of the Census. *Census of Business, 1963*. Vol. VII, *Selected Services—Area Statistics*. GPO, 1966.
95. U.S. Bureau of the Census. *Census of Governments, 1942. City Finances, 1942 (Population over 25,000)*. Vol. III, *Statistical Compendium*. GPO, 1944.
96. U.S. Bureau of the Census. *Census of Governments, 1942. County Finances, 1942 Compendium*. GPO, 1944.
97. U.S. Bureau of the Census. *Census of Governments, 1942. Finances of Townships and New England Towns, 1942*. GPO, 1944.
98. U.S. Bureau of the Census. *Census of Governments, 1942. State Finances, 1942*. Vol. III, *Statistical Compendium*. GPO, 1943.
99. U.S. Bureau of the Census. *Census of Governments, 1957*. Vol. III, no. 5, *Compendium of Government Finances*. GPO, 1959.
100. U.S. Bureau of the Census. *Census of Governments, 1962*. Vol. I, *Government Organization*. GPO, 1964.
101. U.S. Bureau of the Census. *Census of Governments, 1962*. Vol. IV, no. 4, *Compendium of Government Finances*. GPO, 1964.
102. U.S. Bureau of the Census. *Census of Housing, 1960*. Vol. I, *States and Small Areas*. GPO, 1963.
103. U.S. Bureau of the Census. *Census of Manufactures, 1947*. Vol. I, *General Summary*. GPO, 1950.
104. U.S. Bureau of the Census. *Census of Manufactures, 1947*. Vol. II, *Statistics by Industry*. GPO, 1949.
105. U.S. Bureau of the Census. *Census of Manufactures, 1958. Numerical List of Manufactured Products*. MC58-300. GPO, 1960.
106. U.S. Bureau of the Census. *Census of Manufactures, 1958*. Vol. I, *Summary Statistics*. GPO, 1961.
107. U.S. Bureau of the Census. *Census of Manufactures, 1958*. Vol. II, *Industry Statistics*. GPO, 1961.
108. U.S. Bureau of the Census. *Census of Manufactures, 1958*. Vol. III, *Area Statistics*. GPO, 1961.
109. U.S. Bureau of the Census. *Census of Manufactures, 1963*. Vol. I, *Summary and Subject Statistics*. GPO, 1966.

110. U.S. Bureau of the Census. *Census of Manufactures, 1963.* Vol. II, *Industry Statistics.* GPO, 1966.

111. U.S. Bureau of the Census. *Census of Manufactures, 1963.* Vol. III, *Area Statistics.* GPO, 1966.

112. U.S. Bureau of the Census. *Census of Mineral Industries, 1954.* GPO, 1957.

113. U.S. Bureau of the Census. *Census of Mineral Industries, 1958.* Vol. II. GPO, 1961.

114. U.S. Bureau of the Census. *Census of Mineral Industries, 1963.* Vol. II. GPO, 1967.

115. U.S. Bureau of the Census. *Compendium of State Government Finances in 1947* (State Finances, 1947, no. 2). GPO, 1948.

116. U.S. Bureau of the Census. *Compendium of State Government Finances in 1957* (State Finances, 1957, no. 2). GPO, 1958.

117. U.S. Bureau of the Census. *Compendium of State Government Finances in 1962* (State Finances, 1962, no. 2). GPO, 1963.

118. U.S. Bureau of the Census. *County Business Patterns, 1962.* GPO, 1963.

119. U.S. Bureau of the Census. *County Business Patterns, 1964.* GPO, 1965.

120. U.S. Bureau of the Census. *Current Population Reports.* Series P-25, no. 289. GPO, August 1964.

121. U.S. Bureau of the Census. *Export Tabulations.* EA-663 and EA-664. GPO, 1963.

122. U.S. Bureau of the Census. *Governmental Finances in the United States, 1942.* GPO, 1945.

123. U.S. Bureau of the Census. *Highlights of U.S. Exports and Imports.* Report FT-990. GPO, December 1967.

124. U.S. Bureau of the Census. *Revised Summary of State Government Finances, 1942–1950.* State and Local Government Studies, no. 32. GPO, 1953.

125. U.S. Bureau of the Census. *Shipments of Defense-Oriented Industries.* Special Report MC63(S)-2. (Also in *Census of Manufactures, 1963.* Vol. I, *Summary and Subject Statistics,* pp. SR2-1 to SR2-23.) GPO, 1966.

126. U.S. Bureau of the Census. "Shipments of Defense-Oriented Industries: 1965 (Final)." In *Current Industrial Reports* MA-175(65)-2. GPO, 1967.

127. U.S. Bureau of the Census. *Statistical Abstract of the United States, 1947.* GPO, 1947.

128. U.S. Bureau of the Census. *Statistical Abstract of the United States, 1948.* GPO, 1948.

129. U.S. Bureau of the Census. *Statistical Abstract of the United States, 1949.* GPO, 1949.

130. U.S. Bureau of the Census. *Statistical Abstract of the United States, 1950.* GPO, 1950.

131. U.S. Bureau of the Census. *Statistical Abstract of the United States, 1959.* GPO, 1959.

132. U.S. Bureau of the Census. *Statistical Abstract of the United States, 1960.* GPO, 1960.

133. U.S. Bureau of the Census. *Statistical Abstract of the United States, 1961.* GPO, 1961.

134. U.S. Bureau of the Census. *Statistical Abstract of the United States, 1962.* GPO, 1962.
135. U.S. Bureau of the Census. *Statistical Abstract of the United States, 1964.* GPO, 1964.
136. U.S. Bureau of the Census. *Statistical Abstract of the United States, 1965.* GPO, 1965.
137. U.S. Bureau of the Census. *Statistical Abstract of the United States, 1966.* GPO, 1966.
138. U.S. Bureau of the Census. *Statistical Abstract of the United States, 1967.* GPO, 1967.
139. U.S. Bureau of the Census. *Statistical Abstract of the United States, 1968.* GPO, 1968.
140. U.S. Bureau of the Census. "Survey of the Origin of Exports of Manufactured Products, 1960." In *Current Industrial Reports* M161(60)-1. GPO, May 4, 1962.
141. U.S. Bureau of the Census. "Survey of the Origin of Exports of Manufactured Products, 1963." In *Census of Manufactures, 1963.* Vol. I, Special Report No. 3. GPO, 1966.
142. U.S. Bureau of the Census. *U.S. Census of Population, 1960.* Vol. I, *Characteristics of the Population.* GPO, 1963.
143. U.S. Bureau of the Census. *U.S. Commodity Exports as Related to Output, 1958.* GPO, 1961.
144. U.S. Bureau of the Census. *U.S. Commodity Exports and Imports as Related to Output, 1958.* GPO, 1962.
145. U.S. Bureau of the Census. *U.S. Commodity Exports and Imports as Related to Output, 1962 and 1961.* GPO, 1964.
146. U.S. Bureau of the Census. *U.S. Commodity Exports and Imports as Related to Output, 1963 and 1962.* GPO, 1966.
147. U.S. Bureau of the Census. *U.S. Exports.* Report FT-410. GPO, December 1967.
148. U.S. Bureau of the Census. *U.S. Exports.* Report FT-610. GPO, 1967.
149. U.S. Congress. Joint Economic Committee. Subcommittee on Defense Procurement. *Background Material on Economic Aspects of Military Procurement and Supply.* GPO, 1960.
150. U.S. Congress. Joint Economic Committee. Subcommittee on Defense Procurement. *Background Material on Economic Aspects of Military Procurement and Supply.* GPO, 1964.
151. U.S. Department of Agriculture. *Agricultural Statistics, 1958.* GPO, 1959.
152. U.S. Department of Agriculture. *Agricultural Statistics, 1959.* GPO, 1960.
153. U.S. Department of Agriculture. *Agricultural Statistics, 1964.* GPO, 1964.
154. U.S. Department of Agriculture. *Agricultural Statistics, 1965.* GPO, 1965.
155. U.S. Department of Agriculture. Agricultural Marketing Service. *Livestock and Meat Statistics.* Statistical Bulletin No. 230. GPO, July 1958.
156. U.S. Department of Agriculture. Agricultural Marketing Service. "Net Change in Inventories in the Agricultural Sector, 1947, 1958, 1963." Unpublished worksheets prepared for *Farm Income Situation.*
157. U.S. Department of Agriculture. Agricultural Marketing Service. Agricultural

Research Service (and U.S. Department of Commerce. Bureau of the
Census). *Farmers' Expenditures in 1955 by Regions of Production and Farm
Living . . . with Tables of Off-Farm Income.* Statistical Bulletin No. 224,
April 1958.

158. U.S. Department of Agriculture. Economic Research Service. *Farm Income:
State Estimates, 1949–1965.* FIS-203 Supplement. August 1966.

159. U.S. Department of Agriculture. Production and Marketing Administration,
Commodity Credit Corporation. *Report of Financial Conditions and
Operations, 1947–48, 1958-59, 1963-64.* GPO. (This is a monthly publica-
tion. All of the monthly issues for each of the three years were used.)

160. U.S. Department of Commerce. Bureau of Foreign and Domestic Commerce.
Division of Economic Research. *National Income, 1929-32.* Report
submitted as Senate Doc. No. 124, 73rd Congress, 2nd Session. GPO, 1934.

161. U.S. Department of Commerce. Bureau of Public Roads. *Highway Statistics
1963.* GPO, 1965.

162. U.S. Department of Commerce. Office of Business Economics. "Federal
Government Defense and Non-Defense Purchases, 1958." Unpublished
worksheets.

163. U.S. Department of Commerce. Office of Business Economics. "Industry
Description Appendix 1 to Input-Output Study, 1958." Unpublished.
November 1964.

164. U.S. Department of Commerce. Office of Business Economics. "Input-
Output Structure of the U.S. Economy: 1963." *Survey of Current Business*
49, no. 11 (November 1969): 16–47.

165. U.S. Department of Commerce. Office of Business Economics. *Input-Output
Structure of the U.S. Economy: 1963.* Vol. 1, *Transactions Data for
Detailed Industries.* GPO, 1969.

166. U.S. Department of Commerce. Office of Business Economics. *National
Income, 1954 Edition.* GPO, 1954.

167. U.S. Department of Commerce. Office of Business Economics. "The
National Income and Product Accounts of the United States: Revised
Estimates, 1929-1964." *Survey of Current Business* 45, no. 8 (August 1965):
6–56.

168. U.S. Department of Commerce. Office of Business Economics. *The National
Income and Product Accounts of the United States, 1929–1965: Statistical
Tables.* GPO, 1966.

169. U.S. Department of Commerce. Office of Business Economics. "1947 Input-
Output Table." Unpublished.

170. U.S. Department of Commerce. Office of Business Economics. "1958
Detailed NIPCE Listing." Unpublished worksheets.

171. U.S. Department of Commerce. Office of Business Economics. "1963 Net
Purchase Allocation for Federal Government Defense Industry." Unpublished worksheets.

172. U.S. Department of Commerce. Office of Business Economics. "1963 Net
Purchase Allocation for Federal Government Non-Defense Industry.
Unpublished worksheets.

173. U.S. Department of Commerce. Office of Business Economics. "Personal

Income by States and Regions in 1963." *Survey of Current Business* 44, no. 8 (August 1964): 15–23.

174. U.S. Department of Commerce. Office of Business Economics. *Personal Income by States Since 1929.* GPO, 1956.

175. U.S. Department of Commerce. Office of Business Economics. "State and Local General Government Net Purchases by Function and Industrial Origin, 1958." Unpublished worksheets, March 23, 1965.

176. U.S. Department of Commerce. Office of Business Economics. "The Transactions Table of the 1958 Input-Output Study and Revised Direct and Total Requirements Data." *Survey of Current Business* 45, no. 9 (September 1965): 33–49.

177. U.S. Department of Commerce. Office of Business Economics. *U.S. Income and Output.* GPO, 1958.

178. U.S. Department of Defense. Office of the Secretary of Defense. *Five-Year Trends in Defense Procurement, 1958–1962.* Washington, D.C.: June 1963.

179. U.S. Department of Defense. Office of the Secretary of Defense. *Military Prime Contract Awards by Region and State, Fiscal Years 1962–1966.* January 18, 1967.

180. U.S. Department of Health, Education, and Welfare. Office of Education. *Federal Funds for Education, 1954–55 and 1955–56.* Bulletin 1956, no. 5. GPO, 1956.

181. U.S. Department of the Interior. *Estimated Use of Water in the U.S., 1965.* Geological Survey Circular 556. GPO, 1968.

182. U.S. Department of the Interior. Bureau of Commercial Fisheries. *Fishery Statistics of the United States, 1958.* GPO, 1960.

183. U.S. Department of the Interior. Bureau of Commercial Fisheries. *Fishery Statistics of the United States, 1963.* GPO, 1965.

184. U.S. Department of the Interior. Bureau of Mines. *Minerals Yearbook, 1947.* GPO, 1950.

185. U.S. Department of the Interior. Bureau of Mines. *Minerals Yearbook, 1958.* Vol. III (Area Reports). GPO, 1959.

186. U.S. Department of the Interior. Bureau of Mines. *Minerals Yearbook, 1963.* Vol. III (Area Reports: Domestic). GPO, 1964.

187. U.S. Department of the Interior. Bureau of Reclamation. *Report of the Commissioner, 1965: Statistical Appendix.* Vol. I, pt. III.

188. U.S. Department of the Interior. Fish & Wildlife Service. *Fishery Statistics of the United States, 1947.* GPO, 1950.

189. U.S. Department of Labor. Bureau of Labor Statistics. *Capital Flow Matrix, 1958.* GPO, 1968.

190. U.S. Department of Labor. Bureau of Labor Statistics. *Construction.* February 1948.

191. U.S. Department of Labor. Bureau of Labor Statistics. *Construction.* May 1948.

192. U.S. Department of Labor. Bureau of Labor Statistics. *Employment and Earnings Statistics, 1909–1968.* GPO, 1968.

193. U.S. Department of Labor. Bureau of Labor Statistics. "Estimated Defense Purchases for Calendar Year 1962." Unpublished worksheets, June 1965.

194. U.S. Department of Labor. Bureau of Labor Statistics. "Listing of the 1947 Input-Output Table, 450-Order." Unpublished.

195. U.S. Department of Labor. Bureau of Labor Statistics. "The 1947 Interindustry Relations Study: Industry Classification Manual." Unpublished. June 6, 1952; revised March 20, 1953.

196. U.S. Department of Labor. Bureau of Labor Statistics. "The 1947 Interindustry Relations Study: Industry Reports." Unpublished.

197. U.S. Department of Labor. Bureau of Labor Statistics. *Projections 1970: Interindustry Relationships, Potential Demand, Employment.* Bulletin No. 1536. GPO, 1966.

198. U.S. Department of Labor. Bureau of Labor Statistics. *Study of Consumer Expenditures, Incomes and Savings.* Philadelphia: University of Pennsylvania, 1956.

199. U.S. Department of Labor. Bureau of Labor Statistics. *Survey of Consumer Expenditures, 1960–61.* GPO, 1966.

About the Authors

Karen R. Polenske is a Research Associate at the Harvard Economic Research Project. She received her Bachelor of Arts degree in 1959 from Oregon State College in Home Economics and has subsequently earned her Masters degree from the Maxwell School, Syracuse University, in the joint program of Public Administration and Economics and her Ph.D. from Harvard University in Economics. After receiving her Ph.D. in 1966, she taught for four years in the Department of Economics at Harvard. In 1970-1971, she spent the year at the University of Cambridge as a Senior Visitor at the Faculty of Economics and a Member of High Table at King's College. She belongs to the American Economic Association and the Regional Science Association.

Other contributors to this volume worked with Dr. Polenske on the multiregional input-output project and were all staff members of the Harvard Economic Research Project when the research was done. Carolyn W. Anderson, Orani Dixon, Frans J. Kok, and Isabelle B. Whiston were full-time research assistants at the Project. The others worked on a part-time basis. William R. Buechner and Peter Dixon were graduate students and Richard Berner, Bo Carlsson, W. Norton Grubb, and James F. Smith undergraduates at Harvard University; Mary M. Shirley was a graduate student at the Fletcher School of Law & Diplomacy, Tufts University.